S0-BOE-549

INSIGHT GUIDES
AUSTRALIA

NEXT 92 km

APA PUBLICATIONS L

Part of the Langenscheidt Publishing Group

🎋 INSIGHT GUIDE
AUSTRALIA

Editorial

Project Editor
Astrid deRidder
Series Manager
Rachel Lawrence
Publishing Manager
Rachel Fox
Art Director
Steven Lawrence
Senior Picture Researcher
Tom Smyth

Distribution

UK & Ireland
Dorling Kindersley Ltd, a Penguin Group company
80 Strand, London WC2R 0RL, UK
customerservice@dk.com

United States
Ingram Publisher Services
One Ingram Blvd, PO Box 3006
La Vergne, TN 37086-1986
customer.service@ingrampublisher
services.com

Australia
Universal Publishers
PO Box 307
St Leonards, NSW 1590
sales@universalpublishers.com.au

Worldwide
**Apa Publications GmbH & Co.
Verlag KG (Singapore branch)**
7030 Ang Mo Kio Ave 5
08-65 Northstar @ AMK
Singapore 569880
apasin@singnet.com.sg

Printing

CTPS-China

©2011 Apa Publications UK Ltd
All Rights Reserved

First Edition 1992
Sixth Edition 2011
Reprinted 2012

ABOUT THIS BOOK

The first Insight Guide pioneered the use of creative full-colour photography in travel guides in 1970. Since then, we have expanded our range to cater for our readers' need not only for reliable information about their chosen destination but also for a real understanding of the culture and workings of that destination. Now, when the Internet can supply inexhaustible (but not always reliable) facts, our books marry text and pictures to provide those much more elusive qualities: knowledge and discernment. To achieve this, they rely heavily on the authority of locally based writers and photographers.

Insight Guide: Australia is structured to convey an understanding of the region and its people as well as to guide readers through its attractions.

How to use this book

This book is carefully structured to convey an understanding of Australia's people and culture, and guides readers through its ancient sites, modern resorts and intense capital.

The **Best of Australia** section at the front of the guide helps you to prioritise what you want to do.

◆ The **Features** section, indicated by a pink bar at the top of each page, is a series of illuminating essays that cover the natural and cultural history of the country, as well as daily life, nature and the arts.
◆ The main **Places** section, indicated by a blue bar at the top, is a complete guide to all the sights and areas worth visiting. Places of special interest are coordinated by number with the maps.
◆ The **Travel Tips** listings section, with a yellow bar at the top, provides

Tjuta. Hermione has been a journalist and editor in Perth since 2003 and has written for many WA publications such as News Limited's *The Sunday Times* as a news reporter and feature writer, as well as community newspapers throughout the metropolitan region.

Fran Severn researched the food and wine scene of Australia, and enjoyed tasting her way through Oz. She has written about a school for butlers in London, worked on a cattle ranch in New Mexico, ridden camels in Morocco, and has got lost in the backstreets of Jerusalem. A private pilot, she has flown across the US and Canada. She's written more than 200 articles for publications as varied as *Delta Sky* and *Western Horseman*, is a contributing writer to the online travel publication *Striped Pot*, and blogs for *Chesapeake Life Magazine*.

full information on transport, hotels, activities from culture to shopping to sports, an A–Z section of essential practical information, and a handy phrasebook with authentic Australian words and expressions. An easy-to-find contents list for Travel Tips is printed on the back flap, which also serves as a bookmark.

The contributors

This fully revised and updated edition was commissioned, managed and edited by **Astrid deRidder**.

Melbourne-based **Jerry Dennis** updated the majority of the book. Jerry has written for many Insight Guides and edited three titles, on New South Wales, Queensland and Tasmania.

Hermione Stott updated the Western Australia and Northern Territory chapters. She also wrote the Insight Feature on Uluru and Kata

Their contributions build on the work of the following Australia-based writers for previous editions: **Ute Junker** (history and culture chapters, Modern Australian Cuisine, New South Wales and Canberra); **Kerry McCarthy** (Sydney's beaches and shopping districts); **Tania Sincock** (Flora and Fauna, Sports, and parts of South Australia); **Victoria Kyriakopoulos** (Melbourne and Victoria); **Dorothy Stannard** (Western Australia); **Ron Banks** (Northern Territory).

Past contributors include **John Borthwick, Paul Phelan, Amanda Burdon, Victoria Kyriakopoulos, Amanda Gryst, Dennis Schulz, Victoria Laurie** and **Rick Eaves**.

Picture research was by **Steven Lawrence**. The book was indexed by **Helen Peters** and proofread by **Janet McCann**.

Map Legend

Symbol	Description
— — - -	International Boundary
— — — —	State Boundary
—•—	National Park/Reserve
— — — —	Ferry Route
✈ ✈	Airport: International/Regional
🚐	Bus Station
✉	Post Office
ℹ	Tourist Information
∴	Archaeological Site
✝ ✝ ✝	Church/Ruins
✝	Monastery
☾	Mosque
✡	Synagogue
∩	Cave
🯅	Statue/Monument
★	Place of Interest
⚑	Beach
🯅	Lighthouse
🏰	Castle (ruins)
❄	Viewpoint

The main places of interest in the Places section are coordinated by number with a full-colour map (eg ❶), and a symbol at the top of every right-hand page tells you where to find the map.

Contents

LEFT: plying the waves in a rowing competition.

Maps

Inside front cover:
a map of Australia.
Inside back cover:
a map of Sydney
City Centre.

THE BEST OF AUSTRALIA: TOP ATTRACTIONS

Discover Australia's unique attractions – exciting adventure activities, absorbing museums, vast empty landscapes, and indigenous culture... here, at a glance, are our top recommendations

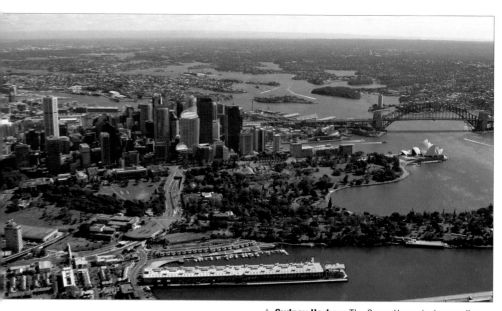

▽ **The Great Barrier Reef** More than 2,000km (1,240 miles) of mostly pristine coral gardens and rich aquatic life, the Reef rewards divers, snorkellers or those who simply gaze through glass-bottomed boats.

△ **Sydney Harbour** The Opera House is deservedly on everyone's list as a must-see attraction in Australia – it's on the Unesco World Heritage list, after all – and when you combine it with the iron bulk of Sydney Harbour Bridge, you have one of the great vistas of the world. *See page 107*

▽ **Uluru** Rising out of the parched red centre of the country, Uluru (Ayers Rock) is the dramatic touchstone of this ancient continent. It's a sacred site to its Aboriginal custodians, and worth travelling thousands of kilometres to see. *See page 282*

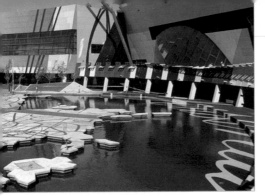

△ **Canberra's Museums and Galleries** Gathered around Lake Burleigh Griffin is what collectively amounts to the most impressive collection of educational and cultural showpieces in Australia. *See page 155*

△ **Australia's Wineries** In a nation rich in high-class, picturesque wineries, the Barossa, Clare and Coonawarra regions stand out as some of the finest. *See page 80*

◁ **Melbourne's Music Scene** A host of brilliant venues large and small helps to make this the finest music city in Australia. *See page 173*

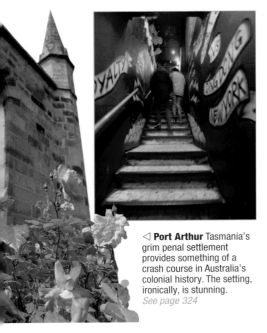

◁ **Port Arthur** Tasmania's grim penal settlement provides something of a crash course in Australia's colonial history. The setting, ironically, is stunning. *See page 324*

△ **Kakadu National Park** Of the numerous National Parks, this one is unmissable with its mixture of indigenous flora and fauna along with ancient Aboriginal culture. *See page 274*

▽ **Wildflowers in West Australia** Springtime, beginning in September, is when the countryside around Perth and southern West Australia is awash with technicolour blooms. *See page 312*

▷ **Boxing Day at the MCG** Up to 100,000 spectators and fans turn out to this world-famous Melbourne stadium for the beginning of a five-day test match, an epic even in the cricket world. Even if you don't follow the sport, go to the stadium for the party atmosphere. *See page 170*

THE BEST OF AUSTRALIA: EDITOR'S CHOICE

Our selection of the most awe-inspiring Australian scenery including perfect beaches, dramatic deserts and classic cityscapes; here are the best things to do on your visit Down Under

BEST ISLANDS

● **Fraser Island, Qld** There are endless beaches on this giant sand bar. *See page 233*

● **Kangaroo Island, SA** Seals, penguins, echidnas, kangaroos, emus and koalas all live here. *See page 215*

● **Lord Howe Island, NSW** This heavily forested isle has numerous walking trails, as well as diving and snorkelling facilities. *See page 136*

● **Magnetic Island, Qld** Just over the water from Townsville but a world away. *See page 237*

● **Maria Island, Tas** Maria Island is vehicle-free, so pack walking boots or hire a mountain bike at the ferry point. *See page 322*

● **Tiwi Islands, NT** Accessible only by boat or plane through organised tours, the islands are rich in Aboriginal culture. *See page 280*

BEST BEACHES

● **Bells Beach, Vic** This beach is famed worldwide for its spring surf contest. *See page 179*

● **Cable Beach, WA** A ride on a camel train along the beach at sunset is a great experience for kids. *See page 306*

● **Maslin's Beach, SA** The backdrop of sandstone cliffs makes this family-oriented beach one of the most beautiful in the state. *See page 207*

● **Noosa, Qld** As well as being an excellent surfing beach, Noosa benefits from a national park on one side and a shopping strip on the other. *See page 232*

● **Shark Bay, WA** A World Heritage Site, Shark Bay has marine wildlife galore. Hand feed dolphins at the bay's Monkey Mia. *See page 313*

● **Whitehaven, Whitsunday Island, Qld** As far as beaches go, Whitehaven is pretty unbeatable, and it's open for camping, too. *See page 255*

● **Wineglass Bay, Freycinet NP, Tas** This is a breathtaking sweep of white sands and azure sea. The best views are from Wineglass Bay lookout. *See page 323*

ABOVE: a shipwreck off the coast of Fraser Island.
LEFT: surf rescue members watch over the beach.

BEST FESTIVALS

● **Adelaide Fringe**
Rapidly expanding in size and popularity, the Adelaide Fringe festival attracts exhibitions and acts from around the world. *See page 202*
● **Henley on Todd Regatta, Alice Springs**
Waterless regatta held on the dry bed of the Todd River. Has to be seen to be believed. *See page 269*
● **Melbourne International Comedy Festival** The comedy festival takes over Melbourne for one month each year. *See page 167*

● **Music Festival, Barossa Valley**
Enjoy an evening of classical music combined with fantastic local wines. *See page 202*
● **Sydney's Gay and Lesbian Mardi Gras**
Enjoy the atmosphere at this hugely popular and flamboyant street parade. *See page 116*
● **Tasmania's Wooden Boat Festival**
This biennial event draws wooden-boat builders and lovers from across the globe. *See page 329*

ABOVE: Queen Victoria market. **BELOW LEFT:** Henley on Todd. **BOTTOM RIGHT:** Ballarat's Eureka moment.

BEST MARKETS

● **Adelaide's Central Market** A covered area packed with more than 200 shops, the main attraction is the wealth of local produce that SA is famed for. *See page 200*
● **Melbourne's Queen Victoria Market,**
A buzzing place where locals after fresh produce or deli specialities mix with tourists seeking souvenir clocks in the shape of Australia. *See page 172*

● **Sunday Bondi Markets** The Bondi Markets have helped establish more than a few of the most successful Sydney fashion designers. *See page 118*
● **Sydney Fish Market** The ultimate seafood experience, Sydney's Fish Market has fish auctions, market stalls, restaurants and even a cookery school. *See page 113*

BEST GALLERIES

● **Aboriginal rock art galleries at Kakadu, NT**
The rock art galleries, particularly at Nourlangie and Ubirr rocks, display some of the earliest paintings by man. *See page 275*
● **National Gallery of Australia, Canberra**
Repository of many of the finest artworks in the country. *See page 157*
● **National Gallery of Victoria, Melbourne**
The gallery has been split over two sites; one houses

national and one houses international works. *See page 170*
● **South Australian Museum, Adelaide**
Extensive Aboriginal and Pacific exhibits and a broad survey of regional natural history. *See page 203*

BEST COLONIAL TOWNS

● **Ballarat, Vic** An old gold-mining town. The Eureka Centre re-creates the day in 1854 when gold was discovered. *See page 183*
● **Broome, WA** The timber dwellings of Chinatown serve as a reminder of Broome's pearling days. *See page 305*
● **Hahndorf, SA** Pretty German town established in 1839 in the Adelaide Hills. *See page 207*
● **Richmond, Tas** One of the very best preserved

Georgian towns in all of Australia. *See page 321*
● **The Rocks, Sydney**
Site of the first European settlement, today The Rocks is virtually an open-air museum. *See page 110*

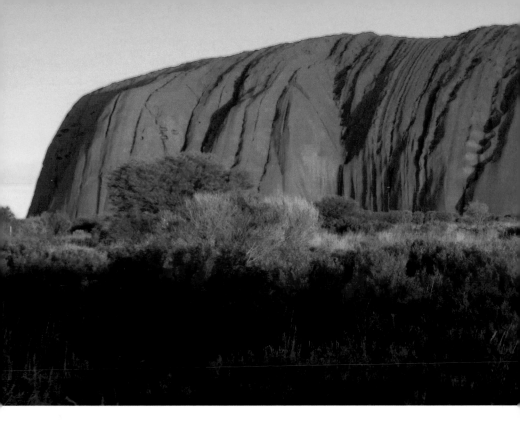

DOWN UNDER

You can call it the world's largest island, or the Earth's oldest continent. Either way, Australia is a place like no other

"**A**ustralia is like an open door with the blue beyond. You just walk out of the world and into Australia". – D.H. Lawrence (1922)

Australians like to think of their country as God's own – or God-zone in the vernacular. In recent years this philosophy has taken on a new resonance as a whole series of travails (of almost biblical proportions) has assailed the country. There has always been fire, but in February 2009 it took on a tragic dimension when bushfires destroyed a great part of the state of Victoria and took scores of lives. There have always been floods, but they attained a new scale when the fatal inundation in January 2011 affected 75 percent of Queensland. Even plagues of locusts have been sweeping the land. This might cause some to question the purpose of living at the far ends of the Earth, but for most Australians it provokes only a pause for thought to cherish their unique challenges.

This country of extremes is used to doing things the hard way. People have been inhabiting this daunting continent for around 50,000 years, and they know that for every down, there's an up-side to living in one of the most remarkable places on Earth. Try waking up to the bush dawn, as the kookaburras begin their maniacal laughs and the golden light pierces the gumtrees. That is one of the great outdoor experiences in Oz.

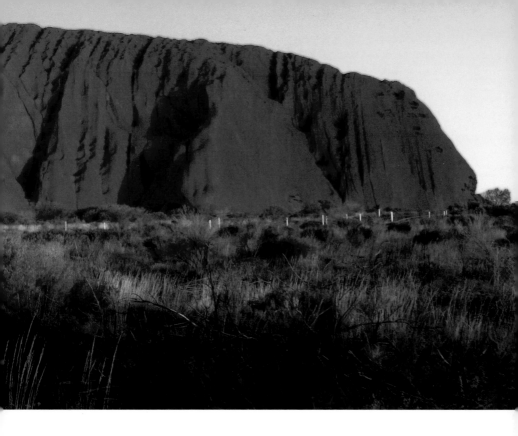

Even in Sydney, a dawn stroll along the harbour as the first ferries roll past the Opera House will convince you that this may well be the most gorgeous city on Earth.

Australia is a long way from anywhere else, which makes it a unique land with a people used to standing alone. The very differences that permeate the land, culture and history of Down Under have also given the place a singular strength and durability. Australians will most likely agree with Mark Twain that Australia is a rip-roaring good time, although it wasn't always so colourful. When the British colonists and convicts first arrived in the 1780s, they attempted to re-create the places and cultures of their homeland on the other side of the world, but the strangeness of the landscape, including the heat, rain (or endless droughts), expansive landscape and the otherness of it all meant that they could only ever be partially successful.

Today, Australians tend to be thankful for their distance from Europe and the United States, and embrace their (relative) proximity to Asia. The quirks of their homeland – the egg-laying mammals, the ghostly trees, the savage deserts, the spiders, even the menagerie of deadly snakes – have become a source of endless fascination. ❏

PRECEDING PAGES: two women enjoy the Brighton bathing boxes on the beach near Melbourne; the view from Q Deck in Surfer's Paradise, Queensland; Weano Gorge in the Karijini National Park, Western Australia. **ABOVE:** Uluru, also known as Ayer's Rock, towers above the flat lands of the Red Centre.

AN ANCIENT LANDSCAPE

Australia has been a continent for around 50 million years.
But the history of the land can be traced back much further,
to a time when the world was young

Australia's topography, so forbidding to the first European settlers in the late 19th century and so compelling to more recent arrivals, takes us back to the earliest history of our planet. Certain rocks have been dated back 3,500 million years, while large chunks of the landscape suggest continental movements dating back more than 1,000 million years.

Whereas much of Europe and the Americas have the landscapes of youth – snow-covered peaks, rushing waterfalls, geysers, active volcanoes, giant gorges and mountain lakes – Australia's blunted, stunted, arid lands speak of an age which must be treated with respect. It is a land in which even the animals and plants, developed in isolation, are strikingly different.

Forces of nature

The last great geological shifts in Australia took place some 230 million years ago, before the Permian period. It was then that the forces of nature convulsed the Earth's crust and created alpine ranges whose peaks extended above the snow line. Since then, modest convulsions on the eastern and western fringes have created low ranges (now known as tablelands), and volcanoes have occasionally erupted – but, generally speaking, Australia was already a sleeping giant when the rest of the world's landforms came into being. Barring unforeseen geological circumstances, it will also be the first continent to achieve equilibrium, a flattening of the land to the point where rivers cease to run, there is no further erosion, and landscape becomes moonscape.

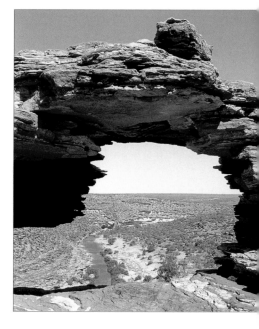

LEFT: a dry lake bed at sunrise.
RIGHT: Murchison Gorge, Kalbarri National Park.

Australia began to take shape 50 million years ago when it broke away from the great continent known as Gondwanaland. This landmass at one time incorporated Africa, South America and India. Australia broke free and drifted north, reshaping itself into a continent. The centre was rising from a shallow sea to unite what had been a series of islands. One of these islands, the Great Western Plateau, had been the only constant during much of this change, sometimes partly submerged but always the stable heart of the continent. Today that plateau spreads over almost half the continent, a dry and dramatic expanse of pristine beauty. It spreads from the west coast to beyond the West

Australian border, taking in the Kimberley and Hamersley ranges, the Great Sandy Desert, Gibson Desert and the Great Victoria Desert, and, although its topography has changed greatly, it houses the artefacts of ancient times.

A rock found near Marble Bar in the far northwest yielded the remains of organisms which lived 3,500 million years ago – the oldest form of life yet discovered. A dinosaur footprint is frozen in rock near Broome, and in the Kimberley, once a coral reef in a shallow sea, landlocked ocean fish have adapted to fresh water.

While much of the west is brown and featureless, every now and then something crops up

FLORA AND FAUNA

Australia's vegetation is dominated by the eucalyptus, the humble gumtree, which can be found in more than 500 different forms. It's hard to escape the smell, feel and sight of this tree, which is most often stunted, knotted and offers little shade.

Australian marsupials have developed in isolation in extraordinary ways, and into 120 different species – from the red kangaroo and the gliders that fly between trees, to tiny desert mice. The platypus and echidna are the world's only egg-laying mammals; the Queensland lungfish can breathe both above and under water. Australia has clear links to a time when the world was young.

to whet the appetite, perhaps because it is such a contrast with the surroundings. People will drive great distances to have a look at geological oddities. In the case of Wave Rock, 350km (220 miles) to the west of Perth, it's the edge of a granite outcrop, about 15 metres (50ft) high, that is curling over along a length a little over 100 metres (330ft), looking as if a giant wave had petrified mid-action. This distinctive shape derives from a process that commenced about 60 million years ago from a softening of some sections of the granite and subsequent water erosion, which eventually led to Wave Rock emerging from the ground.

Similarly, the magnificent Bungle Bungles on the southern edge of the Kimberley at the top of Western Australia are probably the most dramatic result of erosion in the country. This is a sandstone range that stretches 450km (280 miles) and occupies 640 sq km (247 sq miles) in the Purnululu National Park. The peculiar dome shapes of the peaks are dramatic enough, and when combined with the striping effect caused by alternating layers of orange and grey rock (according to the ferrous content), you have a heart-stopping site, unlike any other in the world. It was recognised as a World Heritage Site by Unesco in 1987.

Being so far from the main population centres, relatively few visitors or, indeed, Australians, ever get to see Bungle Bungles. Tourists are much more likely to find themselves at the country's more famous World Heritage-listed rock: Uluru. This, too, is sandstone, but just one monolithic form, the tip of a rocky equivalent of an iceberg, where the majority is hidden below the surface. The strength of Uluru lies in its homogeneity and in the absence of the flaws that have allowed the forces of erosion to eat away at the rocks that would once have surrounded it. The fact that it is surrounded by many kilometres of flat desert heightens the contrast.

The Lowlands

The central eastern lowlands, stretching south from the Gulf of Carpentaria and bounded by the Great Dividing Range to the east, form a sedimentary basin that has often been encroached upon by the sea. Although this is a catchment area of 1.5 million sq km (600,000 sq miles) for rivers running inland off the eastern range, much of the water is lost through evaporation or into the vast chain of salt lakes and clay pans.

The largest of the salt lakes, Lake Eyre, is also the lowest part of the continent at 15 metres (50ft) below sea level. For much of the time it is a lake in name only. Such was the rarity of its filling with water and the concomitant surge in birdlife after above-average rainfall in 2010 that numerous tour operators set up special sightseeing trips.

Much of the lowlands are so exceptionally harsh and inhospitable that it is difficult to imagine that beneath the surface lies the Great Artesian Basin, from which bores are tapped to provide water for livestock. The most ancient part of the basin area is the Flinders Ranges of

The Great Dividing Range dictates the climate of eastern Australia. The narrow strip between the range and the Pacific Ocean is where the rain falls and where the air stays relatively cool. Once you're across the range, everything drys out and becomes desert.

Mount Kosciuszko, at 2,230 metres (7,315ft), is the highest point in the Great Dividing Range, but equally majestic are the rainforests of the north and the moors of Tasmania.

The Glass House Mountains in southern Queensland were formed by volcanoes about 20 million years ago; they are formed from plugs of hardened magma piped up the centre

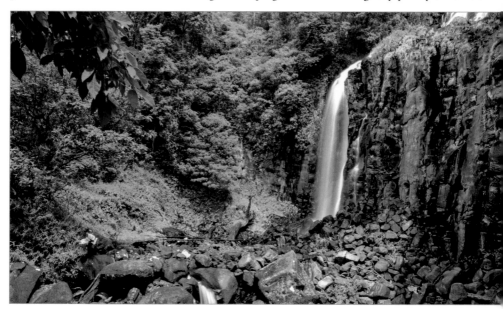

South Australia, in which there are rocks and remains dating back 1,000 million years.

The Highlands

Because of its immense age, Australia can no longer boast a true alpine range. The Great Dividing Range that runs parallel with the east coast for more than 2,000km (1,250 miles) is as diverse as any found on Earth, tropical at one end and subalpine at the other. It is a series of "fold mountains" where tectonic plates have collided and buckled.

ABOVE LEFT: wild flowers in the Hamersley Gorge, Pilbara. **ABOVE:** Mungalli Falls, near the town of Atherton in Queensland.

of peaks which have subsequently eroded away. The granite belt bridging the Queensland–New South Wales border and the Warrumbungle Mountains was born in similar circumstances.

Australia's last active volcano died only 6,000 years ago – just a few ticks on the geological clock. In Tasmania the effects of volcanic activity and two ice ages have created a distinctive wilderness. This can be seen in the Nut at Stanley, another of the nation's many geological oddities. This 150-metre (490ft) -high plug of volcanic rock was formed in similar fashion to the Glass House Mountains.

For a variation on the theme, make a trip out to the Undara Lava Tubes in outback Queensland, 130km (70 miles) west of the Atherton

Tablelands. In this case it is the absence of volcanic rock that is significant. When the long-extinct Undara volcano erupted around 190,000 years ago, streams of lava spread across the countryside and, as the surface of the rock cooled, the lava inside flowed on, leaving hollow tubs behind, up to 20 metres (65ft) in diameter. These were soon absorbed into the landscape and remained undiscovered until some of the tubes collapsed.

The Coast

The coastline of Australia is as spectacular and as varied as the centre. It ranges from the

El Niño events have caused recent mayhem, bringing increased rainfall over northern Australia and extended drought elsewhere. The latter has caused major anguish to river systems and has accentuated the danger of bushfires in those parts of the country already susceptible to them. There's little doubt that the devastating fires that hit Victoria in February 2009 were exacerbated by years of dry conditions.

Elsewhere, water is the problem. Tropical cyclones have regularly wrought havoc on the north and east coasts, most notably Cyclone Tracy that ripped into Darwin on Christmas Eve 1974, and Cyclone Yasi that just missed

limestone cliffs at the edge of the Nullarbor Plain to the jagged rock formations of Tasmania and western Victoria, from the mangrove swamps of the north to the spectacular beauty of the Great Barrier Reef – a lagoon which runs almost 2,000km (1,250 miles) down the Queensland coast and contains more than 2,000 coral reefs.

At risk

Australia manages to avoid the major fault lines that cause such trouble for its earthquake-plagued neighbours. It's pretty short of active volcanoes, too. Although there are plenty of other natural hazards to deal with, most are climate-related.

Cairns in 2011, but still brought lots of rain and winds. There have been several storms in tropical Queensland, including Cyclone Larry that hit the Innisfail and surroundings in 2006.

Further south, when droughts do break, they tend to do so with a vengeance. Rainfall at the end of 2010 and beginning of 2011 caused floods in southern Queensland that affected an area greater than France and Germany combined. Nothing happens by halves in Australia. Luckily, the Australian spirit is indomitable, and the local people work hard to recover quickly from events like these.   ❑

Above: the dramatic Tasmanian coast. **Right:** the Twelve Apostles as seen from the Great Ocean Road.

DECISIVE DATES

c.50,000 BC
The first Australians arrive, overland from New Guinea.

8000 BC
Returning boomerangs are used for hunting.

9th century
Seafarers from China possibly reach Australia's north coast.

1290s
Marco Polo's journal refers to a land south of Java, rich in gold and shells.

1606
Dutchman Willem Janszoon lands on the western side of Cape York Peninsula – the first verifiable European landing.

1642
Abel Tasman names the west coast of Tasmania Van Diemen's Land.

1688
English buccaneer William Dampier lands on the northwest coast.

1770
Captain Cook lands at Botany Bay, then sails northward, charting 4,000km (2,500 miles) of coast.

1773
The first picture of a kangaroo is seen in Britain.

1788
First Fleet arrives in Sydney Cove with a cargo of convicts.

1790
Second Fleet arrives.

1793
First free immigrants arrive.

1801–3
Matthew Flinders proves Australia is a single island by circumnavigation.

1813
Australia's own currency is established. The first crossing is made of the Blue Mountains.

1817
The name Australia is adopted (instead of New Holland).

1829
First settlers land at Fremantle, and found Perth two days later. Western Australia becomes a colony.

1830
All Aborigines in Tasmania are rounded up and herded into reserves.

1831
Publication of *Quintus Servinton*, the first Australian novel, by Henry Savery, a former convict.

1838
The Myall Creek Massacre: 28 Aborigines are butchered by white farmers.

1851
Gold discovered, first in NSW and then Victoria.

1854
Battle at the Eureka Stockade between state troopers and miners protesting against licence fees.

1855
Van Diemen's Land becomes Tasmania.

1859
European rabbits are introduced near Geelong; by 1868 they have eaten most of western Victoria's vegetation.

1860
First south–north crossing (Melbourne to Gulf of Carpentaria), by the Burke and Wills Expedition.

1861
The first Melbourne Cup horse race is watched by 4,000 people.

1868
The transportation of British convicts ends.

1880
Bushranger Ned Kelly is captured and hanged.

1883
Silver is discovered at Broken Hill, NSW.

1891
Delegates from the six colonies meet in Sydney to draft a constitution.

1893
Gold rush in Kalgoorlie, Western Australia.

1895
Banjo Paterson writes *Waltzing Matilda*.

1896
Athlete Edwin Flack represents Australia at the first modern Olympic Games.

1901
The six colonies join together to become a federation, the Commonwealth of Australia.

1914–18
330,000 Australians serve in World War I; 60,000 are killed, 165,000 wounded.

1915
Australian troops take a major part in the Gallipoli siege; more than 8,000 are killed.

1923
Chemist Cyril Callister creates Vegemite.

FAR LEFT: the First Fleet drops anchor in Sydney Cove. ABOVE LEFT: the first issue of the *Sydney Gazette* in 1803. ABOVE RIGHT: an Australian propaganda poster from World War I.

1928
Royal Flying Doctor Service is founded by Rev. John Flynn in Cloncurry, Queensland.

"We took the Hill. come and help us keep it!"

1932
Sydney Harbour Bridge opens.

1942
15,000 Australians are captured when Singapore falls to Japan. Japanese bomb Darwin.

1950
Immigration peaks at 150,000 new arrivals.

1954
Elizabeth II is the first reigning monarch to visit Australia.

1959
Danish architect Jørn Utzon wins the competition to design Sydney Opera House.

1967
Aborigines are finally granted Australian citizenship and the right to vote.

1973
Sydney Opera House is completed. Australian Patrick White wins Nobel Prize for Literature.

1974
The town of Darwin is flattened by Cyclone Tracy.

1985
Uluru, Kata Tjuta and the surrounding desert (now a National Park) are returned to Aboriginal control.

1986
The Australian film *Crocodile Dundee*, starring Paul Hogan, grosses $116 million in the United States.

1995
Australians protest strongly over French nuclear testing in the South Pacific.

1999
Australians vote against becoming a republic.

2000
Sydney hosts the Summer Olympic Games.

2002
A bombing in Bali kills 88 Australians.

2006
Melbourne hosts the Commonwealth Games.

2008
Kevin Rudd apologises to the Stolen Generation.

2009
Bushfires in Victoria claim 173 lives.

2010
Julia Gillard is the first woman elected as Prime Minister.

2011
Queensland is devastated by floods over 1 million sq km (386,000 sq miles).

DREAMTIME AND DISCOVERY

Living in harmony with the land, Australia's Aborigines developed a culture rich and complex in its customs, religions and lifestyles, which was abruptly interrupted by the arrival of the British in 1788

Long before the ancient civilisations in the Middle East, Europe and the Americas flourished, and more than 50,000 years before European, Asian or Middle Eastern navigators recorded visits to the shores of "the Great South Land", Australian Aborigines occupied this continent – its arid deserts and tropical rainforests, and especially its major river systems and coastal plains and mountains. Estimates by anthropologists put the population of Aborigines, prior to 1770, at more than 300,000.

The ancient traditions of these people are based on a close spiritual bond with every living thing and with the land as represented in rocks, rivers and other geographical features.

The dawn of creation

Dreamtime is the basis of all traditional Aboriginal thought and practice, informing their cultural, historical and ancestral heritage. Dreamtime was the dawn of all creation when the land, the rivers, the rain, the wind and all living things were generated. The individual exists within an eternal Dreaming, only attaining physical embodiment through a mother and briefly existing on Earth before returning to the Dreamtime continuum. The place of birth is key in relating an individual to a specific region or clan.

Tribal elders are responsible for maintaining the clan's group identity through its totemistic belief system. Each clan forms special bonds with a totem, usually an animal or a plant that acts as a protector and a symbol of group

---

LEFT: an early impression of an Aboriginal camp.
RIGHT: a cave painting of a turtle on Ubirr Rock at Kakadu in the Northern Territory.

HUNTERS AND GATHERERS

Aborigines lived in clans of 10 to 50 or more people. Their life in the harsh landscape of Australia was based on hunting by the men and fishing and gathering by the women. A good hunter knew intimately the habits of the creatures he stalked, was an expert tracker and understood the seasons and the winds.

Each tribe recognised the local landmarks and their links with the rich mythology of Dreamtime. Various geological aspects were sacred sites with their own personality and significance. The Aborigine considered himself, nature and the land inseparably bound and interdependent. In this state of unity, he (and she) achieved a balance with the environment.

identity. Through special ceremonies and other social and religious practices, the elders transmit their knowledge to younger generations.

Aborigines have always celebrated the adventures of their Dreamtime spirit heroes through paintings, songs and sacred dances. Rock paintings are of special significance, bearing the strongest psychological and ritual values. As Aboriginal language was not written, these paintings, along with the oration of legends by tribal leaders, were the main media for passing Dreamtime stories from one generation to the next.

The Aboriginal ceremony of celebrating with song and dance is called *corroboree*. For centuries the male dancers have been experts at mimicking the movements of animals; with these skills they reconstructed legends, heroic deeds or famous hunts. Bodies were elaborately painted, and songs were chanted to the accompaniment of music sticks and boomerangs clapped together.

Basic dance themes deal with hunting and food gathering, or sex and fertility; sometimes they take a humorous vein, but more often they deal seriously with the business of life. Some tribes use a long, hollow piece of wood which, when blown, emits a droning sound. This is the didgeridoo, whose sound is said to resemble the calling of the spirits.

EARLY EXPLORERS

The Greeks, the Hindus and Marco Polo had all speculated upon the location and nature of the "Great South Land". The Arabs, Chinese and the Malays had probably come and gone, as had the Portuguese. The Dutch came, looked and left, disappointed at not finding "uncommonly large profit".

At the end of the 17th century, the English explorer and privateer William Dampier was appalled by the bleak landscape of the northwestern coast, inhabited by "the miserablest people on earth".

The fertile east coast was missed by just a few kilometres by both the French explorer Louis Antoine de Bougainville and the Spaniard Luis Vaez de Torres.

Aborigines believe that a person's spirit does not die with their last breath, and that ceremonies are essential to ensure that the spirit leaves the body and becomes re-embodied elsewhere – in a rock, a tree, an animal, or perhaps another human form. This explains why such significance has been attached to the retrieval of cadavers or body parts from museums around the world, returning them to the country of their birth and performing the ceremonies to finally bring the spirit to peace.

Each person is the centre of an intricate web of relationships which give order to the entire

ABOVE: *Fishing*, portrayed by John Heaviside Clark.
RIGHT: Captain Cook, as depicted by Nathanial Dance.

world. Around two-and-a-half centuries ago, this delicate relationship with the land was thrown out of kilter with the arrival of the Europeans. Aboriginal culture had prepared the people for many things they might expect to face in life – except the coming of the white man.

The impact of Captain Cook

When James Cook, a 41-year-old Royal Navy lieutenant, dropped anchor in 1770 in an east-coast bay that so teemed with exotic new life forms he decided to call it Botany Bay, he verified by flag and map an idea that Europe had long suspected.

Cook had been sent by the Admiralty to Tahiti, at the request of the Royal Society, to observe a transit of the planet Venus. Among the company of 94 on his second-hand coal ship *Endeavour* were Daniel Carl Solander and Joseph Banks, two great botanists of the age.

After leaving Tahiti, Cook sailed southwest to New Zealand and spent six months charting both islands. He was then free to return to England by either the Cape or the Horn. Instead, he and his officers decided upon a route that would lead towards the unknown, the fabled South Land.

On 28 April 1770, *Endeavour* anchored in Botany Bay for one week. No naturalists before or since Solander and Banks have ever collected in such a short time so many new specimens of plant, bird and animal life. Meanwhile, the sailors ate their fill of seafoods, causing Cook at first to name the place Stingray Harbour Bay. He later changed it to Botany Bay because of Solander and Banks's discoveries.

A claim for the king

Sailing north, Cook sighted and named (but did not enter) Port Jackson, Sydney's great harbour-to-be. On 22 August, at Possession Island off the tip of Cape York, he hoisted the British colours and claimed the whole of the eastern side of the continent under "the name of New South Wales" for George III.

Upon reaching London in 1771, Cook reported to the Admiralty that he had found the east coast of New Holland, but not the Great South Land – if indeed such a place existed. During his voyage of 1772 to 1775, he destroyed the historical myth of the Great South Land by

---

CAPTAIN JAMES COOK

James Cook was stern and hot-tempered; physically, he was tall, dark and handsome. He was also, in the parlance of his time, a "tarpaulin", an officer who had prospered without the boost of an aristocratic birth.

Born in 1728, the son of a Yorkshire farm labourer, at age 18 he was apprenticed into the North Sea colliers. Enlisting in the Royal Navy in 1755, he distinguished himself as a navigator and a master, particularly on the St Lawrence River in Quebec, Canada, during the Seven Years' War with France.

A courageous and proud man, Cook was driven more by a sense of duty and personal excellence than by greed or God. All supplies of fresh food which his crew obtained he "caused to be equally divided among the whole company generally by weight, so the meanest person in the Ship had an equal share with myself [Cook] or anyone on board." As for the soul-snatching men of the cloth, he would never permit a parson to sail on any of his ships. Reflecting during his homeward journey upon the state of the Australian Aborigine, he took a remarkably enlightened view, writing the classic description of the noble savage: "In reality they are far more happier than we European; being wholly unacquainted with not only the superfluous but the necessary Conveniences so much sought after in Europe... the Earth and sea of their own accord furnishes them with all things necessary for life."

using the westerlies to circumnavigate the Antarctic. In 1779, he died at the hands of Polynesians in the Hawaiian islands.

The First Fleet

In May 1787, 11 small ships of the First Fleet under Captain (later Governor) Arthur Phillip sailed from Portsmouth. Eight months later, the 1,000 passengers and prisoners arrived at Botany Bay. Three-quarters of them were convicts, since Britain had been forced to find a new dumping ground for rebels, poachers, prostitutes and murderers after it lost the New World colonies in the American War of Independence. The auguries for Australia's future were not those of the Promised Land.

A quick survey showed two things: Cook's description of the place was far too generous; and two ships of the Comte de la Pérouse were also there, possibly shopping for a new continent on behalf of France's Louis XVI. Phillip hurriedly sailed 20km (12 miles) up the coast to Port Jackson and raised the flag for George III on 26 January 1788.

After 30 months of isolation, locked in by the natural prison of the alien bush and suffering from a lack of decent supplies, the settlement was down to half rations. When a ship finally

A TOUGH BEGINNING

Officers, marines, transportees, sheep, goats and cattle were disgorged in 1788 into a cove that is now overlooked by the Sydney Opera House.

The surgeon-general to the fleet rhapsodised that Port Jackson was "the finest and most extensive harbour in the Universe." It is said that even the convicts raised a cheer of joy. It is also noted that two Aborigines shouted "Warra! Warra!" (Go Away!); no one heeded. Thus the colony stumbled to life.

It was a rough beginning. The English authorities did not provision the expedition well; many of the tools were next to useless, and their crops failed to thrive in the unusually sandy soil.

appeared, to their despair, it was carrying not supplies but 222 elderly and ill female convicts. Fortunately, the supply ships of the Second Fleet were close behind.

The birth of Sydney

The tents at Sydney Cove were eventually replaced by brick and timber huts. Phillip tried to lay out a town along orderly lines, but conformity was not in the nature of its inhabitants. Short cuts soon became streets and, despite later attempts at order, the convenient jigsaw that resulted can still be observed today as the ground plan of Sydney's high-rise pile-up.

Sydney Town expanded west towards the fertile farming lands of Parramatta, but was still hemmed in by the impenetrable escarpment of the Blue Mountains. Explorers fanned out by land and sea to open new pastures and farms, and to establish even more isolated and savage prisons, such as Norfolk Island. This small piece of land in the Pacific originally figured in British strategy as a potential source for flax, needed to create sails. Unfortunately, the island became known as a hellhole of corporal punishment.

Conditions weren't that much better in Sydney. In 1804, prisoners at Castle Hill Reserve rose against the government. Some 200 convicts set out to capture Parramatta, then tried to seize the ships in Sydney Harbour. Troops swiftly quelled

and the demand for Bengal rum (which the Corps controlled) was so great that rum almost became the currency of the colony.

Captain Bligh fails again

Governor William Bligh (of *Bounty* fame) was despatched to clean up the Rum Corps' act, and to encourage free settlers to come to Sydney. However, the Corps, at the bidding of farmer and officer John Macarthur, pulled the second of the famous mutinies in Bligh's career, and in 1808 deposed him.

New South Wales and its penal settlements at Moreton Bay (now Brisbane), Norfolk Island

the rebellion at what became known as the Battle of Vinegar Hill. Nine of the ringleaders were hanged and another nine received between 200 and 500 lashes from the whip.

New South Wales was still costing London dearly (£1 million in the first 12 years), but it was turning a profit for its local landowners and the officers of the NSW Corps, otherwise known as "the Rum Corps". The Corps resisted the extortionate demands of trading-vessel masters, and developed its own monopolies. The colony had become such a vat of drunkenness,

LEFT: Sydney Cove soon after settlement.
ABOVE: a new barracks was built to house Australia's many convicts.

LACHLAN MACQUARIE

The initial brutality shown to convicts was tempered by the reforms of Governor Lachlan Macquarie (1810–21), by the hopes of some emancipists (freed convicts) that morality and dignity could prevail, and by a growing prosperity through trade. Macquarie, a paternalistic autocrat, stifled the Rum Corps' monopoly on the import of spirit, established the colony's own currency (1813) and first bank (1817), and encouraged the first crossing of the Blue Mountains (1813). His programme of public works and town planning (265 projects in 11 years) owes much to Francis Greenway, an emancipist transported to Sydney for forgery, who became the colony's leading architect.

and Van Diemen's Land (Tasmania) entered the 19th century with a reputation as "hell on Earth" – a reputation that the British hoped would serve as a deterrent to crime.

Forgers, unionists, and petty thieves caught for stealing bits of muslin or loaves of bread were thrown together in Australia, when death at the end of a noose would often have been more merciful. In attempting to escape, some inadvertently became the interior's first explorers. They fled into the bush; some believed that China lay beyond the Blue Mountains or that a colony of free men dwelt inland. On Norfolk Island, the only guaranteed method of escape

from the inhuman conditions was to commit murder in the hope of being hanged.

Transportation to Australia's penal settlements ceased by 1868. By then, 160,000 convicts had arrived; only 25,000 were women, a distortion which left its stamp on the harsh, frontier society for decades. These pioneers made few concessions to each other and none to the original inhabitants of the land.

No Man's Land

When the First Fleet arrived, no war was declared against the indigenous people. The British government simply declared the land *terra nullius* – literally, land belonging to nobody – based on the notion that the terri-

Edward John Eyre made an extraordinary journey in 1840, on foot, east to west along the coast of the Great Australian Bight. He began with an assistant, John Baxter, and three Aborigines. Some four-and-a-half months and 2,000km (1,250 miles) later, after an appalling journey mostly through desert, he and one Aborigine, a man named Wylie, walked into Albany on King George Sound. Baxter had been murdered by the other two, who then ran away.

There are many such explorers' tales of courage and folly, some still carved as messages on tree trunks, or buried beside dried-up billabongs.

In 1842, a 29-year-old Prussian draft dodger, Ludwig Leichhardt, landed in Sydney. He did not have good qualifications for an aspiring explorer: he could neither shoot nor see very well; he also had a poor sense of direction. He did, however, know how to spot potential benefactors.

By 1844, Leichhardt found sufficient backers for an ambitious northwesterly thrust across Queensland and into the Northern Territory. His ambition was to open up the land from Brisbane to Port Essington (Darwin), a distance of 4,800km (3,000 miles). With 10 companions, Aboriginal guides and a bullock team, he ran into innumerable difficulties, lost his provisions, and saw three of his men speared (one fatally) by natives.

Fourteen months after their departure, and long after being given up for dead, Leichhardt and his party staggered into Port Essington. Returning by sea to Sydney, these "men from the grave" were fêted as national heroes; the Prussian government even pardoned Leichhardt for his military desertion.

In April 1848, Leichhardt set out again, this time on a proposed transcontinental trek from Roma in southern Queensland to the Indian Ocean. His party of seven men and 77 beasts was never seen again, and their fate has become one of the great mysteries of the Australian bush. The first search parties could only report that the men probably went missing in western Queensland. The search continued for years, spurred on by finds of skeletons, relics and pack horses. Stories of a wild white man living among Queensland Aborigines in the 1860s suggested that one member, Adolf Classen, might have survived for some time.

Between 1852 and 1938, nine major searches were conducted for survivors or evidence of Leichhardt's party. But the desert has never relinquished the tale of their fate. The city of Sydney has, however, named one of its suburbs after him.

tory lacked human habitation and could therefore be obtained for free. The first settlers to arrive on Australia's remote shores could not understand the Aboriginal people's nomadic lifestyle or their profound connection to their tribal lands. It seemed that they came and went without reason across the sparse landscape.

European settlers occupied the land; Aboriginal resistance was met with savage reprisals. Those living in the vicinity of Port Jackson were the first to lose their lands, and, as settlement expanded, so began the cycle of attack and reprisal. Previously unknown European diseases brought death and misery to the Aboriginal

Domestic exploration

A continent of 7.7 million sq km (3 million sq miles), much of it searing desert or dense scrub, could not be explored easily. Before the crossing of the Blue Mountains in 1813, most significant exploration took place by sea. Two British sailors, Bass and Flinders, guessed correctly at the separation of Tasmania from the mainland. The French ships of Baudin in 1802, and later of Dumont d'Urville in 1826, scared the colonial authorities into establishing settlements in Tasmania and Western Australia respectively. Once the Great Dividing Range was penetrated in 1813, the drive for new lands, minerals and the glory of

people, while survivors were reduced to living in abject squalor around the periphery of the settlements. An ugly war of attrition prevailed, and massacres were exacted upon people who often had taken no part in any transgressions.

As the spread of settlement advanced, Aboriginal people ejected from their tribal lands were forced into territory belonging to their neighbours – adding internal conflict to an already difficult predicament. Either way, spears stood no chance against bullets.

LEFT: Matthew Flinders and George Bass charting the Bass Strait. **ABOVE:** John Wills, John King and Charles Grey set out on their ill-fated exploration of the interior in 1860. **ABOVE RIGHT:** farm life.

THE NEW SETTLERS

The transportation of convicts was phased out between 1840 and 1868. By 1860, the continent had been divided into five separate colonies, with each exhibiting (at times) more loyalty to Mother London than to any neighbouring siblings.

A major force within the colonies was the "squatocracy", the rich officers, emancipated convicts and free settlers who had followed the explorers into the fertile hinterlands. They had simply laid claim to or squatted upon enormous tracts of land, often 8,000 hectares (20,000 acres) or more. Like the merino sheep they introduced to their stations, the squatters both lived off and were the fat of the land.

being "first there" – wherever "there" happened to be – lured men and women on.

Early explorers believed that the westward-flowing rivers of the NSW interior led towards a vast inland sea. In 1830 Charles Sturt and his party set out on the Murrumbidgee River, following its current into the Lachlan and Murray rivers, finally reaching Lake Alexandrina near the South Australia coast. After travelling more than 1,000km (600 miles), they were within sight of the sea, but were unable to reach it. Instead, they had to row back against the current toward their starting point. Their 47 days' rowing, on meagre rations and against flood tides, left Sturt

In August 1860, Robert O'Hara Burke and W.J. Wills left Melbourne with a well-equipped team and a camel train (imported from Afghanistan). Their intention was to be the first party to cross the continent from coast to coast.

Burke was brash, inexperienced, supremely confident. Too impatient to wait for the supply camels to keep up, he took Wills and other team members, Grey and King, with him; from Innamincka on Cooper's Creek, he forged ahead in 60°C (140°F) heat. They reached the Gulf of Carpentaria in February 1861 and immediately began retracing their footsteps. Grey died along the way. The three emaciated

temporarily blind, but is one of the most heroic journeys in Australian exploration.

By 1836, the vast river systems were charted. Tasmania had been explored, and the genocide of its natives had begun. A decade later most of New South Wales, half of Queensland, and the southern and northern coasts had been thoroughly explored.

Heroes and villains

The 19th century is rich in tales of intrepid adventurers, some of whom were driven by the urge to explore unknown territory, but most were motivated by dreams of finding riches. One such tale of misadventures is now deeply ingrained in Australian folklore.

survivors finally reached their earlier camp at Innamincka where they had left another companion, William Brahe. But Brahe, who had waited four months for them, had departed only seven hours earlier. After rejecting the assistance of local Aborigines, Burke and Wills died in the Stony Desert. Only King, cared for by Aborigines, survived to tell the story. The Dig Tree is so called because when Brahe's party left camp, they left instructions carved into a tree that provisions were buried nearby. The tree still attracts tourists to this remote pocket of southwest Queensland. ❑

ABOVE: Burke and Wills arrive at the depot at Cooper's Creek. **RIGHT:** riding camels through the desert.

FROM GOLD RUSH TO WORLD WAR

After gold was discovered in the 1850s, a sudden influx of immigrants set out to make their fortune. A similar boom of outlaws set out to relieve them of it. Then, in 1901, the six quarrelling colonies became a nation

In 1851 Edward Hargraves, an Australian forty-niner (a fortune seeker of the 1849 California gold rush) returned home. He was certain, given the geological similarities he had observed between California and Australia, that gold must exist in New South Wales. Unbeknown to him, gold had been found 10 years earlier by a Rev. W.B. Clarke, but news of the discovery was suppressed. Upon seeing the gold, the Governor, Sir George Gipps, had said: "Put it away, Mr Clarke, or we shall all have our throats cut!"

The announcement on 15 May 1851 of "Gold Discovered!" near Bathurst, 170km (106 miles) west of Sydney, sent shock waves through the Australian colonies. The rush of prospectors to Bathurst was so great that the population of Victoria immediately nosedived. Melbourne employers offered a £200 reward for the discovery of gold near *their* city.

By July the prize had been claimed, and before the end of the year incredibly rich fields were in production in Victoria at Ballarat, Bendigo and Castlemaine. For the businessmen of Melbourne, the finds were a mixed blessing. While the prices of flour, blankets, bread, shovels and mining gear doubled and tripled, there was often no one to sell them. Melbourne and Geelong were almost emptied of able-bodied men.

The Roaring Days

The scene in the goldfields was one of frantic activity, where teams of four or six men worked a claim, digging, shovelling, washing and cradling from dawn to dusk. When the miners hit town, they careened around the streets on horseback or in cabs. At one Melbourne theatre, reported an eyewitness, the actors "were obliged to appear before the footlights to bear a pelting shower of nuggets – a substitute for bouquets – many over half an ounce, and several of which fell short of the mark into the orchestra."

Gold rushes flared like bushfire around the continent during the next two decades, and then sporadically for the rest of the century. The last great find was the Kalgoorlie-Coolgardie field in Western Australia in 1892–93. It was not only the shop assistants of Sydney and the sailors of Port Phillip who caught gold fever. In 1852 alone, 95,000 hopefuls from around the world flooded into New South Wales and Victoria.

ABOVE: *The Prospector* dreams of gold and riches in an 1889 painting by Julian Ashton. **RIGHT:** troopers storm the Eureka Stockade in 1854.

The Eureka Stockade

At Ballarat, near Melbourne, the early gold diggers smarted under the imposition, whether they struck gold or not, of a £1-a-month licence fee. Raids by thuggish police who enforced the licence fee *and* collected half the fine from defaulters added to their rancour.

In October 1854 a miner was kicked to death by a local publican, who (despite strong evidence against him) was cleared of the crime. Mass meetings attended by up to 5,000 miners railed against these injustices. The men demanded the granting of universal franchise and the abolition of licence fees. They formed the Ballarat Reform League and on 29 November made a bonfire of their mining licences.

The lieutenant-governor of Victoria, Sir Charles Hotham, sent in the "traps" (policemen) and troopers. Five hundred diggers built a stockade and swore to "fight to defend our rights and liberties". In the early hours of 3 December 1854, a force of 300 infantry, cavalry men and mounted police savagely attacked the sleeping stockade, whose defenders had dwindled to 150. Within 15 minutes it was all over. Six soldiers and 24 miners were dead.

Eventually an amnesty was proclaimed for the rebels, and the licence fee was abolished.

BUSHRANGERS AND REBELS

The gold rush created a new boom in bushranging, or highway robbery. Many an "old lag" (ex-convict), as well as poor settlers, saw that gold need not necessarily be dug from the ground. The proceeds from holding up a stagecoach or gold wagon could be good, and the work was a lot cleaner than digging. One Victorian gang in 1853 relieved the gold escort of 70,000 grams (more than 2,400 oz) of gold and £700 in cash; three gang members were sent to the gallows.

In the 1860s the most famous of the "Wild Colonial Boys" were the bushrangers Ben Hall, Frank Gardiner and John Gilbert. Well armed and superbly mounted – often on stolen racehorses – they pulled off audacious raids. In November 1864, Hall's gang of three, working the Sydney–Melbourne road, rounded up 60 travellers at once. Then came the prize for which they were waiting – the armed mail coach. While one bushranger covered the 60 captives, Hall and Gilbert shot the police guard and robbed the coach. Several of the captives came out of the bush, not to aid the police, but to watch the shoot-out.

From their first appearance, bushrangers were often sheltered by the rural poor, many of whom were descendants of political transportees. Their strong republican sentiments led them to regard some of the outlaws as rebels against the same enemy – the British, Protestant landlords and civil authorities.

While the incident is replete with tragedy and some farce, the Eureka Stockade and its flag continue to evoke the ideals of revolt against colonialism and bourgeois authority. As Mark Twain commented, Eureka was "the finest thing in Australian history… another instance of a victory won by a lost battle."

The Federation is born

In September 1900, Queen Victoria regally proclaimed that, on 1 January 1901, not only a new century but also a new nation would be born.

A federal government for the six Australian colonies was generally welcomed. Under the new Constitution the Queen remained head of state, retaining power over all foreign affairs. British parliamentary legislation could overrule any laws passed by the Commonwealth, and legal appeals ultimately were settled in London. Few Australians objected to this arrangement, for each of the six colonies felt more at ease in its dealings with the motherland than with the other colonies.

For her part, Britain did not let the new nation escape the interests of imperialism. She expected, and got, continuing support in her military involvements, and ample returns on her substantial investments in Australia.

THE KELLY GANG

Ned Kelly was born in 1854 and grew up among impoverished Irish farmers near Benalla, northern Victoria. He first ran foul of the law in 1877 when he shot a constable in the wrist. Teaming up with his brother Dan and two friends, Joe Byrne and Steve Hart, he fled to the bush and turned outlaw. The following year, in a shoot-out at Stringybark Creek, Ned killed three of a party of four police who were hunting him. From then on, the Kellys became part of Australian folklore.

Ned saw himself as a Robin Hood, a defender of the free against the oppressive British overlords. Instead of robbing coaches, his gang bailed-up whole towns, cutting the telegraph and robbing the bank before escaping.

The gang hid out in the Wombat Ranges, but in June 1880, on hearing that a train-load of police was on the way to arrest them, they captured the town of Glenrowan, Victoria, and held the townsfolk prisoner in the hotel.

A furious shoot-out erupted between the Kellys and the cops. Wounded, Ned donned his suit of home-made armour and attempted to escape. Instead, he stumbled into the police who at first thought they were seeing a ghostly apparition. Ned was shot down but not killed. The police torched the hotel and the other three members of the Kelly Gang died within, rather than surrender.

Four months later in Melbourne, Kelly was sentenced to death. He was hanged on 11 November 1880.

The quest for a capital

The new nation needed a capital. Sydney and Melbourne each wished it to be in its own state, and neither of the long-standing rivals would permit it in the other's. After considerable backbiting, a separate Australian Capital Territory was established at a point between the two cities, 320km (200 miles) from Sydney on the beautiful Monaro Tablelands. Some suggested naming the capital Shakespeare – hardly an appropriate choice considering the anti-intellectual cultural cringers who formed a vocal part of the Australian population. In 1913 the Aboriginal word "Canberra" was chosen instead.

gas and frozen winters, their losses were appalling – 23,000 dead in nine weeks in the First Battle of the Somme, 38,000 at Ypres, 10,000 at Bullecourt. The new nation was being cut down. Indeed, so was some of the old nation; more than 420 Aboriginal soldiers served in the war, largely from Tasmania's Bass Strait islands.

Many Australians were now questioning the sense of supporting Britain in what they saw as a "sordid trade war". But a deciding factor was the presence at Australia's helm of a feisty and dogged little man who was loved and loathed with equal passion: William Morris ("Billy") Hughes, or "the Little Digger".

The Great War

When Britain declared war on Germany on 4 August 1914, Australia, as a member of the British Empire, was automatically at war, too. The response by both Labor and Liberal parties was immediate. By the end of October the First Australian Infantry Force of 20,000 volunteers had been despatched to Europe via Egypt. Many were to die at Gallipoli (see page 40).

The Australian "Diggers" (soldiers) were deployed in France, on the Western Front, from April 1916. In the grisly attacks, through mustard

LEFT: *Bailed Up*, painted by Tom Roberts at the end of the 19th century. **ABOVE:** a photograph of Allied forces at Gallipoli in 1915.

THE CHINESE INFLUX

The vast majority of gold-diggers were British, but the Chinese were also numerous. In the five years from 1854, more than 40,000 flocked to the Victorian fields. The Chinese lived in their own communities, were diligent labourers, and produced only one Chinese bushranger, San Poo.

By 1887, Asian immigration was stifled. Australia inaugurated "the White Australia Policy" with federation and nationhood in 1901. The Immigration Act allowed an impossibly tough dictation test in any European language to be given to all non-European arrivals. It was not until 1966 that there was any genuine reversal of this race-based exclusion.

In 1916 Hughes pledged a supply of 16,500 Australian troops a month. Such a number could be raised only through conscription – previously, recruitment was voluntary. The proposal was defeated narrowly in a referendum, and Hughes was expelled from his own Labor Party. He set about forming a national coalition government and held a second referendum in December 1917. He was defeated but bounced back, winning a seat at the Versailles Peace Conference.

Of the 330,000 Australian troops who fought in the war, 226,000 (68.5 percent) were casualties, a greater percentage by far than suffered by any other Allied nation.

The Great Depression

Between 1929 and 1933 every government in Australia, both state and federal, was thrown out of office by an electorate deciding to "give the other mob a go – they couldn't be worse." But unfortunately they could do no better, for the Great Depression had arrived. Thirty percent of the country's breadwinners were on "Susso" (sustenance benefits). Wearing World War I surplus greatcoats, hundreds were tramping the Outback roads as "swagmen" looking for rural work.

Australia's economy was based heavily upon the export of wheat and wool, and upon continued borrowings from Britain. When world prices for primary products slumped by 50 percent, and when Britain withdrew £30 million from the Australian economy, the result was traumatic, especially for the poor.

Sir Otto Niemeyer of the Bank of England was despatched to scold Australians for living at an unsustainably high standard, to advise wage cuts and retrenchments, and to make sure that the interest was still paid on the loans.

World War II

When Britain again went to war against Germany in September 1939, Australia once more automatically entered the conflict. A Second Australian Infantry Force was raised and despatched to the Middle East.

In 1939 Australia's prime minister, the leader of the United Australia Party, was Robert Gordon Menzies, a clever, witty barrister and a deeply conservative Anglophile. He had earned the nickname "Pig-Iron Bob" by selling pig iron

THE DEATH TOLL OF GALLIPOLI

While Australia's troops trained in Egypt, Winston Churchill (then First Lord of the Admiralty in London) conceived a plan that was intended to relieve Turkish pressure on Russia's troops by forcing an entrance to the Black Sea. He wanted to capture the Dardanelles, and ordered the waiting Australian, New Zealand, French, British, Indian and Gurkha divisions to attack from the sea. The Turks, warned of British intentions, entrenched themselves in fortified positions along the ridges of the Gallipoli Peninsula. From these heights, their commanders (Mustafa Kemal and the German Liman von Sanders) were able to direct their fire upon the exposed beaches below without exposing their own troops to much risk.

From 25 April 1915, when they landed, until 20 December, when they withdrew, the British and Allied forces were pinned down to the near-vertical cliffs and narrow coves. There was both horrendous carnage and epic heroism. During the eight months of fighting at Gallipoli, 78,000 were wounded and 33,500 killed on the side of Britain and its allies. Of the dead, 8,587 were Anzacs (belonging to the Australian and New Zealand Army Corps). Almost as many French died at Gallipoli, and twice as many Britons, Indians and Nepalis fell. On the other side, 250,000 Turks died in battle. Nevertheless, out of this baptism by mud, shrapnel and gallantry arose Australia's first coherent sense of nationhood and identity.

to the re-arming Japanese, of whom Australia had become increasingly nervous.

While Australian air, land and sea forces fought in Britain, the Mediterranean, North Africa, Greece and the Middle East, Japan began to move south, first into French Indochina. Australian forces were sent to Malaya, the Dutch East Indies, Darwin and Rabaul (New Guinea) to try to stem the tide of the Japanese invasion forces.

In Canberra, Pig-Iron Bob was reviled for his Chamberlain-like prewar appeasement of the Axis powers. By October 1941 a Labor Government under John Curtin was in power.

of the continent. Australia faced the very real threat of invasion by Japanese troops.

The Australian war cabinet outraged Prime Minister Winston Churchill by diverting the 7th Australian Division from the defence of British Burma to the New Guinea and Pacific theatres. If it is true, as is commonly said, that the Australian nation was born at Gallipoli, it is no less true that with the fall of Singapore Australia finally came of age.

The tide turns

The tide began to turn against Japan in May 1942, when a combined fleet of American

A nation comes of age

The Japanese attack on the United States at Pearl Harbor confirmed Australia's great fear: to be isolated in an Asia at war. When Singapore fell on 15 February 1942, 15,000 of the 130,000 captured troops were Australian. The country was faced with the fact that a distant and beleaguered Britain could be of no real assistance against an imminent Japanese invasion.

Japanese planes bombed Darwin on 19 February and Broome on 3 March. Arms and food caches were established in the northern regions

LEFT: a World War I poster encourages South Australians to enlist. ABOVE: Sydney Harbour Bridge was completed in 1932.

and Australian forces checked the Japanese at the Battle of the Coral Sea. The US victory at Midway in June assured Allied control of the Pacific, but on New Guinea, Japanese foot soldiers were closing in on Australia's main base at Port Moresby. After months of guerrilla combat and hand-to-hand jungle fighting, the Australian troops finally pushed them back.

Of the 1 million Australian servicemen and women who enlisted, almost 10,000 died in Europe and more than 17,000 in the Pacific. Of those taken prisoner by the Japanese, 8,000 did not survive the Japanese camps. An Aboriginal complement of more than 3,000 bravely served in the forces, despite official discouragement early in the war. ❏

THE MODERN ERA

Over the past 60 years, Australia has witnessed a trebling of the population, industrial booms and economic slumps, rigid conservatism and progressive liberalism

Australian history since World War II has been an up-and-down saga – a rise to undreamed-of affluence in the 1950s and '60s when the wool prices boomed, followed by unexpected cracks in the great suburban dream. Today the image of the country as a conservative, Anglo-Saxon society somehow finding itself lost in Asia has been completely recast. But the road towards a cosmopolitan, liberal, middle-class Australia has been tortuous. For a small country – population-wise – of which it was said "nothing ever happens", there has been a succession of booms, recessions, political crises, wars, culture shocks and social changes.

The 1940s were the most difficult years in Australia's history, the long war against Japan emphasising the country's vulnerability. The war also shook up Australian society internally; many women served in the armed forces, or worked in factories or office jobs that had previously been reserved for men, and were reluctant to go back to the old inequality between the sexes.

Radical changes

In 1946, Australians voted an activist Labor government, led by Ben Chifley, into power with plans for an expanded social welfare programme. In quick succession, Chifley set up a government-owned airline, took initiatives in housing and education (the Australian National University was opened in Canberra), and ordered massive work projects such as the Snowy Mountains Scheme, which provided hydroelectric power for southeast Australia.

The most radical and revitalising change,

LEFT: sculpture at the National Gallery of Victoria.
RIGHT: migrants sail into Sydney Harbour in 1949.

however, occurred in immigration. The spectre of a Japanese invasion in World War II convinced Australians that the country's population must increase. Labor's immigration minister, Arthur Calwell, embarked upon one of the most spectacular migration programmes of the 20th century. Half of the assisted migrants were to be British, but the other half could come from anywhere – as long as they were white. More than 2 million migrants arrived between 1945 and 1965, helping Australia's population to leap from 7 to 11 million.

The nation still clung to its White Australia policy, and Calwell himself was a racist. (He made the infamous wisecrack, when asked whether he would permit Asian immigration, "Two Wongs don't make a white.") The policy was modified slowly in later years until it was formally abolished in 1973. So rapid has been the overturning of these anachronistic attitudes that at the present time one-third of all immigrants are Asian.

Into the modern world

Still, mainstream Australian culture changed slowly. In the 1950s, Australia remained a rigid society, one which had grown up in comparative isolation and was complacent and illiberal. It was still dominated by men, despite the post-

ians labelled "wowserism". Censorship was strict: James Joyce's *Ulysses* and D.H. Lawrence's *Lady Chatterley's Lover* were banned, and had to be smuggled into the country. The language was stamped with prejudices, many directed at migrants and refugees ("reffos").

Politically, the decade is referred to as the "Boring Fifties". A revived conservative party – known as the Liberal Party (although it was formally and ideologically unrelated to its British namesake and often far from liberal in its literal sense) – was led by the rabid Anglophile Robert Menzies. He proclaimed himself "British to his boot-straps" and was able to tap into the

war challenge from women: male rituals like sport, drinking and brawling predominated; homosexuals were persecuted as "poofters" and anyone with a beard or long hair was dubbed a "weirdo". Male values such as mateship were extolled, while "the missus" was expected to stay at home and look after the kids. It seemed, visually and ethically, a very working-class society, a land of boots and felt hats, of men in dank pubs calling each other "mate" or "sport".

The churches, especially the Roman Catholic Church, dominated morals; divorce was legal, but it was condemned and hard to obtain. Abortion remained illegal, the province of backstreet doctors. The nation was burdened with a suffocating puritanism which Austral-

growing Cold War hysteria, attacking the Labor Party for being riddled with Communists.

When rising unemployment threatened to turn the Liberals out of office, Menzies decided to plump for safe, middle-of-the-road policies that would disturb neither extreme of the electorate. The Labor Party split in 1955 on ideological lines and effectively kept itself out of power for another 17 years.

ABOVE LEFT: prime minister Ben Chifley with his 1948 Holden, Australia's first mass-produced car.
ABOVE: Queen Elizabeth II inspects Royal Australian naval personnel in Perth in 1962.
RIGHT: Barry Humphries as Edna Everage before she bestrode the international stage as a Dame.

"Development" became the national slogan; there were posters everywhere stressing peace, prosperity and progress, and even the arrival of rock'n'roll from the United States didn't seem to disturb the social equanimity. There were a few rebel groups, such as the bodgies (male) and widgies (female), who did such radical things as ride motorcycles and listen to Elvis, but it was hardly more than a milk-bar menace. Another nonconformist group was the Sydney "push", a group of freethinkers and libertarians who gathered at pubs and coffee shops and scorned the suburban coma ward which surrounded them. They wrote poetry and bawdy songs and, though mainly a male group, produced two remarkable women – Germaine Greer, author of *The Female Eunuch*, and the late Lillian Roxon, author of the first *Rock Encyclopedia*.

The affluent 1960s

Meanwhile, Australia had begun turning itself from a nation of primary industry (sheep, wheat and cattle) to one of manufacturing. Between 1940 and 1960 the number of factories doubled; fridges, washing machines, vacuum cleaners and cars became available to the great mass of the population for the first time.

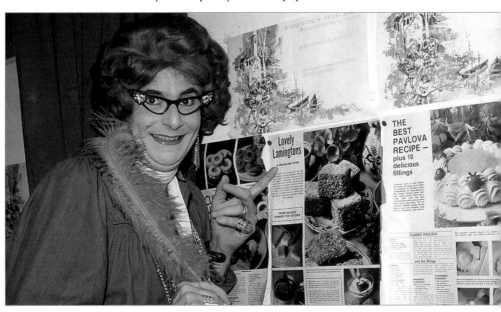

THE FLIGHT OF THE FREE SPIRITS

Every year from the late 1950s onward, thousands of young Australians left on their equivalent of the Grand Tour of London and other cities in Europe, seeking excitement and the sort of mind-broadening experience which was unavailable at home.

They could hardly be blamed. The newsreels of the time, seen now, are embarrassingly nationalistic, racist and sexist. The pubs closed at 6pm sharp each weekday, producing the infamous "six o'clock swill", when men crammed into bars and guzzled as much as they could between the end of work and closing time (women wouldn't have been allowed in even if they'd wanted to). Off-course betting was illegal, so SP (starting price) bookmakers flourished alongside sly-grog joints, where liquor could be bought after hours. There is another side to the story, too. During the prosperous 1950s Australia enjoyed the most even income distribution of any Western industrialised nation.

Well into the 1960s, the district of Earls Court in London became an Aussie ghetto; Rolf Harris, the entertainer, started his climb to fame by singing *Tie Me Kangaroo Down, Sport* at the Down Under Club; unique talents like Barry Humphries, Clive James and Robert Hughes all fled Australia. The nation's best artists and writers – Patrick White, Germaine Greer and Sidney Nolan among them – turned themselves into expatriates. At the time it seemed that little was happening back in Oz.

By the mid-1960s, Australians were enjoying (after the Americans) the highest standard of living in the world. They were also living in the most urbanised nation on Earth, with three-quarters of the population in cities – more than half of that on the eastern seaboard.

Links with the Old Country were weakened when Britain joined the European Economic Community; trade with the US and Japan grew to fill the gap. The 1951 ANZUS security treaty brought Australia and New Zealand securely within the USA's sphere.

In the meantime, the shape of Australian society was being entirely changed. In the

and abandoned its best egalitarian traditions to wallow in complacency. The Australian social ideal of communality was changing and with it, apparently, the Australian character.

A time of change

Cracks began to appear in the bland facade of Australian contentment. In 1962 Australia became involved in the Vietnam War; in the next 10 years she sent 49,000 conscripts, chosen by lottery, off to the jungles of Southeast Asia – where 499 were killed and 2,069 wounded. As in the United States, the anti-war movement breathed life into all forms of liberalisation,

early 1960s the number of white-collar workers exceeded, for the first time, the number of blue-collar workers, and then streaked far ahead. This booming group typically lived in comfortable suburban homes, owned cars and TVs, had bank accounts, and voted Liberal (Australian for "Conservative"). Australia, regarded for so long as a working man's paradise, had transformed itself (almost unnoticed) into one of the most middle-class nations in the world.

But, amid the prosperity, many were dejected over the fate of Australia and the consequences of its new-found wealth. Donald Horne wrote a book called, with heavy irony, *The Lucky Country* – a land that had squandered its opportunities

pushing Australia into an era of crisis and questioning *(see box opposite)*.

When the Labor Party, led by Gough Whitlam, finally won office in 1972 under the slogan "It's Time", it seemed to many that a clean break with the past had occurred and a promising new, progressive era was about to begin.

Labor moved quickly to abolish military conscription, to end Australia's involvement in Vietnam, to recognise China and to begin the long process of reconstructing the social welfare

ABOVE: feminist Germaine Greer offers some biting criticism of contemporary dolls.
RIGHT: Gough Whitlam listens to the governor-general's edict dismissing his government in 1975.

system. Everything appeared to happen at once, with plans under way for a universal health-care system, increased support for the arts (resulting in a spate of Australian films), and the formal end of White Australia.

But Whitlam didn't reckon on the economic and social impacts of big government spending. He managed to win another election in 1974 but was confronted with a sudden and unexpected world recession provoked by an oil price hike. Australians suddenly faced growing inflation and unemployment, and the government was beset by a series of damaging scandals.

Political crisis

Labor was hobbled in its programme by a conservative majority vote in the Senate. In 1975 the Liberal-National Country Party opposition, led by Malcolm Fraser, used this power to deny the government its money supply. Whitlam refused to resign, and the nation was thrust into a grave political and constitutional crisis. This was resolved in a controversial manner: the governor-general, Sir John Kerr, as the Queen's representative in Australia, dismissed Whitlam and called another election. It was an act that many considered illegal – in spirit, if not in the letter of the Constitution. Fraser won the subsequent election, consolidated his power and swore he would take politics off the front page.

Change is the constant

In 1983 a new Labor era began when Australians voted in a government led by Bob Hawke, an ex-union leader, ex-Rhodes scholar and ex-world champion beer drinker (2½ pints in 11

seconds). Hawke later wrote that this feat did most for his political career in a country "with a strong beer culture". The Labor Party became more right-wing, economically liberal and in closer touch with the increasingly powerful white-collar unions and business.

For the next 13 years, Labor ruled with little challenge (with Paul Keating taking over the prime ministership in 1991). Consensus became the catchword, with the government brokering historic accords between business and unions, promising unprecedented industrial peace, and finally introducing a national health-care system for all, Medicare.

THE SPIRIT OF THE 1960S

Student power, the women's movement, black power and sexual liberation groups began challenging the conservative consensus. The rigid censorship of books and films was slowly dismantled, allowing Australians the opportunity to pore over previously forbidden classics of literature such as *Lolita* and *Portnoy's Complaint*.

Aborigines had been allowed to vote in federal elections in 1967, but a "freedom bus" drove through Queensland and New South Wales in protest against the deep-rooted, systematic discrimination against black people. At the same time, it was found that 10 percent of Australians were living in chronic poverty; they included Aborigines, single parents, and the sick, handicapped and jobless.

At the same time, migrants began transforming the staid British social customs of their host country. At an obvious level there was the introduction of delicatessens, continental European food, open-air cafés, new varieties of music and a hectic sort of cosmopolitanism hardly imaginable before World War II. More profoundly, the migrants also opened Australians up to new ideas and new ways of looking at the world that have gradually altered the national character.

Spurred on by the new spirit, a revived Labor Party argued for new policies on a grand scale, and was led by its most inspiring politician for years, the towering, bushy-browed, charismatic Gough Whitlam.

This new-look Labor government had to deal with an ever-sliding Australian economy, starting off with a series of devaluations of the Aussie dollar (the "Pacific peso", as it wryly became known). Under Keating, Labor presided over a push towards free-market policies, yet was able to maintain some degree of social justice by keeping Australia's welfare system intact.

Diplomatically and economically, Australia linked itself much more closely to Asia, while on the home front Asian immigration was stepped up, shifting the emphasis away from European immigration. Women were admitted to more positions of power, and Aboriginal land rights

about becoming a republic at last – an initiative driven by the news that Sydney would host the Olympic Games in 2000.

Despite the steady achievements of these years, Australian voters wearied of Labor and in 1996 voted in a Liberal-National coalition government, led by the determinedly conservative John Howard. In economic matters, Howard advocated a freer market and smaller government. Conservatism also held out in the 1999 referendum, in which Australia voted against becoming a republic and (by the narrowest of majorities) opted to keep the Queen as head of state.

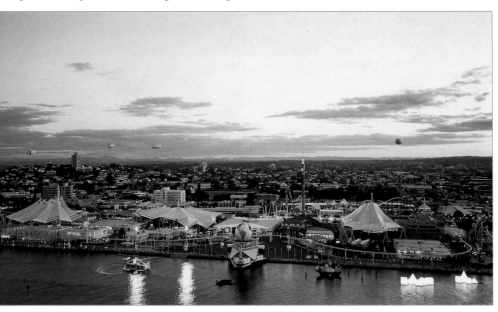

(control over their native homelands) was put on the national agenda. The celebration of the Bicentennial of British settlement in 1988 was a landmark of Australian self-confidence, but also a cause for some national soul-searching. In 1992, a High Court ruling, known as the Mabo case, finally abolished the historical fiction of *terra nullius* – the colonial doctrine that said Australia was uninhabited when the British colonists and convicts first arrived – and opened the way to Aboriginal land claims (*see Aborigines Today, page 67*).

The 1980s and 1990s saw a flowering of the Australian arts, with local film-makers and writers increasingly taking on an international profile. Australians also began talking seriously

Australia's economic outlook has improved steadily with the globalisation initiatives of successive recent governments, a booming resources industry and the often controversial privatisation of the transport, energy and communications monoliths. In recent years the Australian dollar has regained considerable ground against the US greenback, reaching parity in 2010. The country celebrated its newfound confidence in the euphoria of Sydney's staging of the 2000 Olympics. Dubbed the "best Games ever" by the IOC president, the Games were an unequivocal success, both as a mark of Australia's sporting prowess and as the ultimate high-profile evidence of Australia as an attractive travel destination.

There were clouds on the horizon, however. Howard championed a foreign policy more closely aligned with that of the United Kingdom and the United States. He then committed troops to the war in Iraq despite widespread public disquiet. A perceived connection of this presence to a recent spate of terrorist attacks across the Western world was reinforced by the 2002 Bali bombings, in which 202 people died, including 88 young Australians.

All change

John Howard went on to become Australia's second longest-serving prime minister after

The Labor Party, led by centre-left Kevin Rudd, took power, surfing a wave of expectation of change. In retrospect, these expectations may have been too high. Rudd was helming one of the few countries to escape largely undamaged in the global financial crisis, and while prudent financial management was to be expected, the aversion to reform was not. As the 2010 election loomed, the party's power brokers did the numbers and ousted Rudd as leader in favour of Julia Gillard. In a knife-edge result, and only with the help of a handful of independents, Julia Gillard became Australia's first female prime minister in September 2010. ❏

Robert Menzies. A buoyant economy and a disorganised Labor party helped keep him in office; however, an increasing disillusionment among the electorate, exacerbated by the government's treatment of refugees and its refusal to sign the Kyoto Agreement on climate change despite overwhelming evidence of global warming, finally saw Howard and his Liberal-National coalition ousted in 2007. Howard suffered the ultimate ignominy of losing his own seat after 11 years as prime minister.

LEFT: World Expo '88, held in Brisbane, had the theme "Leisure in the Age of Technology". ABOVE: a political banner raises racial awareness. ABOVE RIGHT: mosaic artwork on the banks of the Yarra River.

GOVERNMENT AND POLITICS

Australians are triple-governed – by local councils, and at the state and federal levels. Any time they're asked, most people state that politics is the least trustworthy of professions. There's a growing belief that a small nation of 20 million people can't produce enough talent to run three levels of government.

Judging by the acres of newsprint and airspace devoted to the topic, the nation is obsessed with politics, though no more than a few thousand people are members of political parties. Everyone votes in the national elections because they have to: federal law made it compulsory in 1924; unless you have a good excuse, you will receive a small fine for not voting.

THE URBAN AUSSIE

Most of the population live in cities and suburbs, and most of them on the coast. But that doesn't stop Australians dreaming of the wide-open Outback

According to myth, the "true Aussie" is a sun-bronzed stockman or jillaroo, riding the Outback range with a trusty sheepdog – which is like imagining all Americans to be tobacco-chewing cowboys, and Frenchmen going about in berets and striped shirts. Truth to tell, Australia is the most urbanised country on Earth, with 80 percent of the population living in cities (66 percent in the state capitals). The Great Australian Dream, still enjoyed by a huge portion of the population, is to live on your own plot of land, with a brick house with a red-tile roof, and host a barbie in the backyard.

Clinging to the coast

Most Australians now work in office jobs, and wouldn't recognise a trough of sheep dip if they fell in it. And although many still see the Outback as somehow embodying the most distinctive part of the country, relatively few have visited it, let alone considered living there. Even Patrick White, who set famous novels such as *Voss* in the furthest red-sand-and-spinifex deserts, never actually saw them (he got his images from his friend Sidney Nolan's paintings). White settled in Sydney's eastern suburbs, thousands of kilometres from the Red Centre.

The fact is that Australians have clung to the coast rather naturally, shrugging off the priggish, cramped and tight-lipped spirit of the first British settlers and openly embracing the more sensual and hedonistic spirit of their Mediterranean environment. At least in the 21st century, the coast – and specifically the beach – has a far

more powerful claim on Australian souls than the Outback. "How shall I put this delicately?" asks Sydney writer Robert Drewe. "Most Australians of the past three generations have had their first sexual experience on the coast. So is it surprising that for the rest of their lives the sexual and littoral experiences are entwined in their memories; that most Australians thereafter see the beach in a pleasurable light?" It is to the sea that Australians return at each crucial stage of their lives: as young kids, on honeymoon, as parents. It is to the sea that they were taken as children, and to the sea that they return in old age, to the endless retirement villages of the Queensland shores.

PRECEDING PAGES: Centre Place, Melbourne.
LEFT: ready for action on the beach at Surfers Paradise. **RIGHT:** King's Beach in Caloundra.

And how could it really be otherwise, in a country with such a climate and geography? It would take a serious effort of will not to lap up the perfect skies, the sea breeze, the glorious mounds of prawns and oysters, the bodies laid out on the sands and saturated in SPF 30+. Under the Antipodean sun, more austere national traits succumb to the easy-going, tolerant, obsessively casual Australian manner. It's no surprise to see a first-generation immigrant from Glasgow turn into a surfie overnight, or the daughters of black-shrouded Muslim women lolling bikini-clad in the outdoor beer garden of a pub.

funnel-web spiders, possums in the roof and snakes in the garden.

Despite the occasional natural menaces, relaxation is part of the territory in Australia. It takes something truly grim to rouse most people to anger – and there's always a swim, or a beer, or

> 66 *You must come here. The men are awful, like bits of cardboard, but the women are splendid.*
> Bruce Chatwin, writing to Paul Theroux 99

Leisure has become crucial to the Australian way of life – while working from 9 to 5 provides the means, it is at the weekends when Aussies truly come into their own, and few other places give people such opportunities to use their leisure well. Nature is close in Australia as nowhere else: in Sydney with its 70 metropolitan beaches, in Melbourne with one-third of its area devoted to parkland, or in Darwin where 4-metre (13ft) crocodiles are regularly fished from the harbour. Some visitors still arrive expecting kangaroos to hop across the tarmac. This may not be so, but even in the red-brick back blocks of suburbia a national park might begin at the end of the road, and residents may keep an eye out for

a crisp Chardonnay to calm them down. From railway workers to restaurant waiters, the most common response to questions these days is a breezy "No worries", "Too easy" or "Not a problem" – the latest incarnations of the 1950s slogan "She'll be right, mate". Politics is a matter to shake your head at ("The bastards are all the same" is the common refrain at election time). Economics, however, has become a matter of fascination, and taxi drivers and supermarket clerks can talk with authority on economic rationalism and exchange rates.

From convicts to democrats

Every country is shaped by its past, and few have had a stranger start than Australia's, as the dumping ground for Britain's petty criminals. As Robert Hughes remarked in *The Fatal Shore*, it's one of the great ironies of history that a land founded by felons should evolve into one of the world's most law-abiding societies. Few cities of equal size around the world are as safe, tidy and downright civil as Australia's.

Social commentators have tried to draw conclusions from the country's awkward origins: that the convict legacy instilled a disdain for authority, leading to its powerful union movement, or that it led to a blunt conformism, accepting serious curtailments of civil liberties for most of the 20th century. Hughes comes

As diverting as such theories are, the truth is that few modern Australians can really trace their lineages to convict times; most are the descendants of free English, Scottish and Irish settlers after the 1850s, or the wave of immigrants from the rest of the world a century later. Although the convict stain was once a matter of horror – an ignoble memory that any respectable society would excise, particularly from school books – the opposite is true in Australia today. Anyone who can dig up a convict ancestor now wears the fact as a badge of honour. In Sydney's Hyde Park Barracks Museum, schoolchildren eagerly type their

up with the formula "skeptical conformists": Australians like to think of themselves as rowdy rebels, talking big at the pub or behind authority's back, but obey with little question when it comes to the crunch. Other (more jaded) social commentators might say that Australia's beginnings as a penal colony have made it a corrupt place from day one. Many Australian officials, from police officers to immigration rubber-stampers, have a surprising arrogance; there is none more self-satisfied than the petty Aussie clerk who is able to say "No".

LEFT: urban kangaroos in Perth, made of bronze.
ABOVE: the beach is an active social scene where everyone in the community enjoys the sun.

RISING TENSIONS

In recent years events like the Bali bombs of 2002 and the wars in Iraq and Afghanistan have caused racial and religious tensions to shift. Where previously Aboriginal groups were the scapegoats for the ills of urban Australia, now the sizeable Arab communities are being targeted as troublemakers, despite living peacefully in Australian cities for decades. Tensions came to a head with the Lebanese in December 2005 and beach riots broke out in Sydney's eastern suburbs. The majority of the country was openly sickened by the riots; for a place that professes an idyllic paradise of sun and opportunity for all, it was a worrying development.

names into a computer bank to see if they too bear the felon's mark.

Sydneysiders, of course, are more likely to come up trumps in this game of ancestral rivalry, since theirs was the original convict settlement. Melbourne, being established by free settlers, has always seen itself as having a more respectable and cosmopolitan flavour.

There lies another of the great Australian stories: the antagonism between the two major redoubts of the urban Aussie: Sydney and Melbourne. Both have their distinctive character, both have world-leading attractions, and both are worth a lingering visit.

one another by an almost mystical bond. This image transmuted over the years from the miners of the gold rushes to the Outback drover and the ANZAC Diggers of Gallipoli.

The one obvious drawback of this stereotype was that it did not include women. The contribution of women on the frontier, in the arts, or in the factories during wars, tended to be brushed aside, so that by the 1950s Australia had earned a reputation as one of the most sexist societies in the developed world. The worst manifestation of the crass male spirit was known as the "Ocker Aussie" – the beer-swilling, pot-bellied, narrow-minded, gay-bashing, provincial

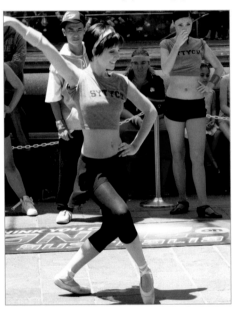

Colonial machismo

The traditional image of Australians as sturdy bush workers may have little to do with modern life, but it has been a robust stereotype. It's the local version of the great frontier myth that crops up in the United States, parts of South America and South Africa. By the 1890s, writers, poets and painters were suggesting that a distinctive national spirit had been forged in the great empty wilderness, and that this "New Man" was typified by a Kiplingesque mishmash of colonial values: naturally democratic, excelling at sports, blunt in his language, sardonic, self-reliant, independent, and not over-educated or burdened by musty traditions. Above all, an Aussie trusted his mates, who were bound to

THE RISE OF GAY CULTURE

Visitors hoping to find the "last refuge of unselfconscious masculinity" – as Ocker Aussies term it – may be disappointed. In recent times, gay culture has exploded in the country – especially in Sydney, which now has a higher concentration of gay residents than San Francisco.

At the first Gay Mardi Gras parade in 1978, police blockades were set up and 53 marchers were taken into custody. Today, the annual parade is the highest-attended event in the country, luring 300,000 to watch floats of fabulously attired folk having fun. In fact, Australia has turned into one of the most permissive and tolerant of societies.

redneck, who watched footie at the pub while the sheila stayed at home minding the kids. Barry Humphries satirised the type with Bazza MacKenzie, the simple-minded tourist who was always ready for a schooner and a chunder. Paul Hogan, as Crocodile Dundee, refined and introduced the persona to the world.

Like the long-ingrained racism, sexism abated with the general loosening-up of society in the 1970s. Aussie women have always been strong characters – perhaps even more blunt, independent and self-reliant than the men so loudly proclaimed themselves to be, out of sheer necessity – so in recent years they have easily taken

cranky if you sit in the back seat instead of up front (as a social equal would); and public officials, even prime ministers, are often known by their first names. The other side of the egalitarian coin is known as the "tall-poppy syndrome": a national resentment of high achievers and an inescapable urge to bring them down.

But is Australia a classless society? Patently not. There may be none of the rigid divisions of the British or the gross inequalities of the American system, but there are serious divisions of wealth and opportunity – and many believe that the gaps are increasing. According to pessimists, the great settler's dream of Australia as the

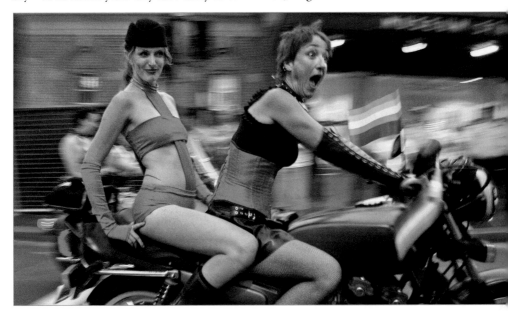

the lead in many fields. Still, as in other Western nations, women remain sadly under-represented in politics and top management positions.

Australian dreams

Perhaps the myth dearest to the Australian heart is that theirs is the most naturally democratic of societies – the frontier past, and distance from the Old World, have naturally levelled Aussies to equals.

Certainly the outward signs are there: waiters may still call you "mate"; taxi drivers can still get

FAR LEFT: a stop at the bar in Melbourne.
LEFT: street dancing in Perth.
ABOVE: Sydney's Gay and Lesbian Mardi Gras.

"millennial Eden" is being eroded. In a haphazard way, Australians have committed themselves to avoiding the errors of Europe and the US, and guaranteeing an unusual measure of social justice. But Australians are becoming increasingly materialistic, and less generous in their vision of society as a place where the weaker are protected. Australia's great narrative historian, Manning Clark, had a bleak vision of his compatriots before he died in the 1990s: "Mammon had infected the ancient continent of Australia," he intoned, in the manner of an Old Testament prophet. "The dreams of humanity had ended in an age of ruins."

Just don't try telling that to any Aussies on a sunny day. They'll already be at the beach. ❑

LIFE IN THE BUSH

The old stereotypes of rural Australia are disappearing
quickly, but there's still a distinct attitude of mind
among those who live "out there"

Ten-year droughts, dramatic floods, bush-fires whistling through the scrub – the same natural processes that allowed the Aborigines to eke out an existence from the land have made life unpredictable for most farmers. Yet despite constant threats of bankruptcy, few give up. They stick to the land, aided by their own brand of black humour and the solace of Saturday night at the pub.

Rural Australia – sometimes referred to as West of the Divide, The Bush, Back o'Bourke, Beyond the Black Stump or The Mulga – is, in some respects, an Antipodean myth. Most Australians rise each morning to spend another day at the factory or office, a far cry from the days when men tramped "the Wallaby Track" (the old sheep station shearing circuit), with belongings in a "swag" on the shoulder and a faithful blue-heeler cattle dog padding alongside.

Changing attitudes

The image of a roving jackaroo is a romantic one, and it wouldn't be out of place in the work of one of the country's literary folk heroes, Andrew Barton "Banjo" Paterson. His poem, *The Man From Snowy River*, is a tale of derring-do in the Victorian high country that still resonates with Australians and visitors today.

The other great turn-of-the-20th-century bush writer, author and poet Henry Lawson, had a more ambivalent and, arguably, grounded view of the bush. After a wretched childhood on the western New South Wales goldfields, Lawson kept returning to the bush to reinforce his dislike of it. He hated the unrelenting grey-green of the eucalyptus, the monotony and hopelessness (his word) of the countryside. Lawson railed against the heat on

the track to Hungerford, the "bloody flies", the thieving publicans, the greedy bosses, the arrogant squatters and the brutal police. He did, however, love the "bush battlers", the staunch early unionists and the great Outback tradition of mateship – male-bonding in the wild. These tough men often reciprocated his admiration, and many felt that Lawson, through his writing, was speaking for them.

Perhaps because of the residual influence of Lawson's writings, many visitors and even some urban Australians seem to believe that the Outback and its 170,000 farmers and graziers are stuck in an 1890s time warp. In fact, Aussie farmers are highly mechanised agribusiness people, mustering cattle by helicopter and trail bike, flying their own planes, and adept at using the internet to run their businesses. It's true, however, that workers on the stations put in long hours day in, day out, and often live in difficult conditions.

Another blind spot commonly found concerns the colour of cowboys. The best stockmen have always been black, although until the 1960s they were often paid half of what white workers received. As jackaroos, boundary riders, shearers and trackers, Aborigines have contributed skill and labour to Australia's rural prosperity, particularly in the Northern Territory and Western Australia. Furthermore, with the

Bush mischief

Many of the old clichés about laconic, resourceful, friendly country people still have a good deal of truth in them. And there's a helpfulness in the bush that is not always immediately apparent to the visitor, thanks to a little bush mischief on the side. Any enquiry for directions, for instance, can be met with a slow "buggered-if-I-know" reply, followed almost immediately with an entertaining series of precise directions. Australians would never deliberately misdirect visitors, for, in the Outback, misdirection may result in death, by either starvation or thirst.

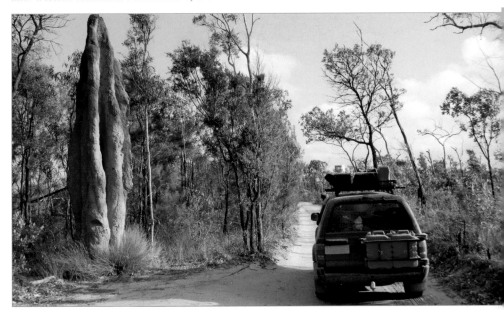

granting of land rights, Aborigines have taken over some of the cattle stations and found a degree of independence.

The country mentality

Despite all the changes of the past 100 years, it is still another world outside the Australian cities. But you don't need to trek all the way to the Outback to find a country mentality; it can be found in any small rural town where the architecture is at least semi-colonial and which services a broad rural area.

LEFT: jackaroos still manage the herds with the help of a horse and hound. **ABOVE:** driving in the Outback is best accomplished with a 4-wheel-drive vehicle.

Visitors from overseas wanting to "go bush" will find many specialised tourism operators catering for just that urge. Everything's available, from luxury air, bus and rail tours to motorised four-wheel-drive backpacker parties.

The Outback has resorts ranging from remote fishing camps to the accommodation conglomerates at Uluru (Ayers Rock) offering everything from camp sites to five-star luxury.

For extra authenticity it's worth seeking out one of the stations that accepts guests and gives them a flavour of what it's like to muster cattle or round up sheep in the sometimes inhospitable land of the Outback. The official tourism site for Queensland, for example, offers a range of options (www.queenslandholidays.com.au). ❏

A MULTICULTURAL SOCIETY

In the past 50 years the population has doubled and diversified. Immigrants have not always found it easy, but today's rich ethnic mix is seen as one of Australia's assets

When a survey in 1939 showed that the Australian population was comprised of 98 percent Anglo-Celtic stock, local newspapers proudly proclaimed that Australia was the most British country on Earth. In this monochromatic society, the only unusual accents were those of the new chums from corners of Ireland or the Scottish highlands. On the dinner table, foods were rarely more exotic than Yorkshire pudding, and Christmas was a time for huge Dickensian meals of roast beef or pork, no matter how brutally hot and tropical the weather.

All that changed after 1945, when Australia embarked on one of the most ambitious and successful immigration programmes of the modern era. The migrants were drawn first from the Mediterranean and Baltic countries of Europe; since the 1970s immigrants have come from around the world. Since the programme began after World War II, more than 6 million settlers from almost 200 countries have chosen to make Australia their home.

Immense diversity

Almost one-quarter of the population was born overseas; 15 percent speak a language other than English at home. In recent years, more than 40 percent of settler arrivals have come from Asia, with the British and Irish down to 14 percent. The humanitarian programme is gradually adding even more diversity to the population. In the 1990s, most of these arrivals came from the Balkans; lately African arrivals have topped the list.

LEFT: a baker makes his morning delivery in Perth.
RIGHT: Currumbin Wildlife Sanctuary, Queensland.

Just as the United States and Argentina were transformed by immigration in the 1890s, so the post-war influx has radically changed the structure and habits of Australian society. Take a seat on the Manly ferry or a Melbourne tram and you're as likely to be sitting next to the daughter of a builder from Athens as you are to a journalist from Naples or a car salesman from Thailand. There is a wonderful sense of cultural diversity to be had across Australia. Multiculturalism was first the guiding principle of Australia's immigration policy, but has become a cornerstone of Australian society in general. Aussies prize tolerance and respect for all cultures and races.

Although a multicultural society is a *fait accompli*, balancing the demands of such a heterogeneous population can be a delicate task. There have been missteps along the way, but since so many people have chosen Australia as their homeland, there is a strong motivation to work together and find solutions to ethnic or racial problems. Ethnic traditions and loyalties are respected and encouraged, but the first loyalty must be to the Australian legal and parliamentary system; multiple languages are promoted, but English is the official tongue of the country; coercive cultural practices, such as arranged marriages, are illegal.

and find work. Points are allocated for such categories as age, employability, English-language skill and so on, although concessions are sometimes made for immigrants willing to move to less popular states or far-distant country regions. Employability usually gets the highest weighting because of the greater contribution skilled migrants make to the economy.

The New Australians

When Australia became a nation in 1901, racial purity was top of the agenda; the notorious White Australia policy, instituted by the Immigration Restriction Bill, was one of the first

The closing door

Even as late as the 1970s, Australia welcomed almost anyone who applied as an immigrant. These days, more emphasis is laid on skills: of the 168,700 target set for 2010–11, 113,850 places were reserved for skilled migrants, with 54,550 places in the family category and 13,750 humanitarian places.

If the statistics are cold, the issue isn't. Immigration is still a major point of debate within Australian society; scarcely a week goes by without a politician, academic, or public personality adding to the discussion.

The immigration process can be laborious. Applicants are tested for their suitability to settle successfully, assimilate into the community

measures to be passed by the new parliament. It would govern migration for decades, and was not formally overturned until 1973.

Thus the first wave of non-British immigrants, brought over in the 1950s and 1960s, was drawn from Europe – mostly from Greece and Italy. Some 275,000 of these "New Australians" arrived in those years – although now, of course, they are Old Australians. Some 5 percent of the population is now of Italian descent, while Melbourne is often touted as the second-largest Greek city in the world.

The polyglot nation

Even during the 19th century, there had been some exceptions to Australia's monoculture. A large Chinese population came to Australia during the gold rushes of the 1850s (and survived the bitter resentment of Anglo miners, which occasionally erupted into violent attacks).

Several wine-growing valleys of South Australia, settled by Silesians in the 1840s, are still Teutonic in ethos. Remote Broome at the top of Western Australia was once full of Japanese pearlers. But these areas remained exceptions to the rule until the boom in different cultures that Australia received in the 1970s, once it truly opened its doors to the rest of the world, particularly to Asia. By the 1990s, one-third of all immigration was from Asian countries, and

remain undetected for years. When apprehended, they face the choice of rapid departure or mandatory deportation. The single biggest group of offenders in this category is British tourists overstaying their visas.

If media coverage is any indication, asylum-seekers – mainly Kurds from Iraq, Afghanis, or Sri Lankan Tamils – arriving by boat from the Indonesian archipelago are a major concern. The Howard government's Pacific Solution, whereby asylum-seekers are processed offshore, is still contentious and skirts the edge of the country's obligations under international law. Labor has followed the same policy since 2007.

the proportion has increased steadily. The new arrivals do not always find it easy to adapt, but their cultural influence is increasingly obvious in all regions of the country.

Other ways of settling

For those for whom all legal avenues have failed, or who are too desperate to go through the lengthy process, there is illegal immigration – often by arriving as a tourist and then overstaying the visa. It is estimated that there are 50,000 of people like this, many of whom

As a result of these waves of immigration, 2 million Australians speak a language other than English when they are at home. An ethnic radio and television broadcasting network – Special Broadcasting Service (SBS) – began in the 1980s to transmit in many languages (with television programmes subtitled in English), and SBS Television's evening news has the most wide-ranging foreign coverage of all the stations in Australia.

Overall, the Australian experience of immigration has been one of the most successful in history: the massive influx has been absorbed into society with remarkably little friction. Indeed, many optimists see this diversity as the key to the country's vitality. ❏

LEFT: giving away hugs in Melbourne. **ABOVE:** shopping at Subiaco Market in Perth. **ABOVE RIGHT:** Bhoj Indian Restaurant at the Docklands, Melbourne.

ABORIGINES TODAY

Captain Arthur Phillip reported that the first words the
Australian Aborigines said to his men in 1788 were
"Warra! Warra!" (Go away!). Given the subsequent cultural
attrition, their first reaction was remarkably prescient

Interest in the Aborigines is often piqued by
modern Aboriginal art. The symbolism
found within these paintings has helped
generate interest in learning about a culture
that is vastly different from any other.

In much of Aboriginal art, it all comes back
to the land. For Aboriginal groups, land rights
have always been a top priority. The land is a
crucial part of their being and their culture,
and the responsibility for protecting significant
sites is central to their spiritual life. Yet the Aborigines have been forced from their traditional
homes, and have seen sacred sites mined, built
on, flooded or destroyed.

There have been a few attempts at partial resti-
tution. The Northern Territory Land Rights Act
(passed in 1975) allowed Aborigines to make
claims to swathes of the Outback on the basis
of traditional ownership. The act also gave them
significant control over mining and other activities. Royalties from mining activities were dis-
tributed to various Aboriginal groups, and land
rights acts have been passed in various states in
an attempt to right the wrongs of history.

Growing resentment

There is a perception that Aboriginal dissent
did not surface until the 1960s and 1970s, but
in fact an Aboriginal rights association existed
in Sydney as early as 1924. The Melbourne-
based Australian Aborigines Advancement
League petitioned King George V for special
indigenous electorates in 1932. If colonial Australians believed (as many did) that Aboriginal

---

LEFT: a rock painting in Kakadu National Park.
RIGHT: traditional, highly structured *corroboree* dance
ceremonies still take place.

THE STOLEN GENERATION

If Aboriginal people have historically been hazy
about their rights, so too were the police and welfare
officers who forcibly removed up to 100,000 children from their parents between 1910 and 1970.
The idea was to assimilate mixed-blood Aboriginal
children into European society over one or two
generations. They were fostered into white homes
and forbidden to speak their own languages. Most
were given physically demanding or menial jobs,
many suffered abuse, and nearly all experienced
psychological damage. These sad children became
known as the Stolen Generation.

people owed them a debt of gratitude for having brought civilisation to *terra nullius*, they were disabused by the Aboriginal Progressive Association manifesto of 1938. Issued on the 150th anniversary of the landing of the First Fleet in Botany Bay, this document declared 26 January a day of mourning. "You took our land away from us by force," the manifesto said. "You have almost exterminated our people, but there are enough of us remaining to expose the humbug of your claim as white Australians to be a civilised, progressive, kindly and humane nation. By your cruelty and callousness towards the Aborigines you stand condemned in the eyes of the civilised world."

Political awareness grew steadily from the 1930s, culminating in the Freedom Rides of the mid-1960s, when activists rode in buses through Outback Queensland and New South Wales bringing their message to remote communities. Demonstrations resulted in violent clashes with police, pushing the Aboriginal plight on to the front pages and into middle-class homes.

Various lobby groups began to champion Aboriginal political rights. The first positive step came in 1949 when the Chifley government passed an act confirming that those who could vote in their states could vote for the Commonwealth. Aboriginal people in all states (except Queensland and Western Australia) had been entitled to vote

HOW ABORIGINES LOSE OUT

After more than 200 years of European settlement, Aboriginal Australians are the country's most disadvantaged group. Statistics show the sad results of the colonial experience: the average life expectancy for Aborigines is 10 years shorter than that for other Australians; they have three times the infant mortality rate and a far higher incidence of both communicable diseases, such as hepatitis B, and lifestyle diseases such as heart failure; an unemployment rate six times the national average; half the average income level; and a large proportion living in sub-standard housing or temporary shelters. Aborigines are also 16 times more likely to be imprisoned than other Australians.

in state elections since the 1850s; they didn't vote because no one told them they could.

By the early 1970s, this new-found political consciousness forced the government, led by Gough Whitlam, to develop a new policy of self-determination. This allowed Indigenous Australians to make decisions affecting their future, retain their cultural identity and values, and achieve greater economic and social equality.

The Department of Aboriginal Affairs was established in 1972, followed by the Aboriginal Development Commission (ADC) in 1980. The underlying concept was to bring economic independence to indigenous people by fostering business enterprises, but it didn't happen overnight. In 1988, while the rest of Australia celebrated 200 years of settlement at the Bicentennial, Aboriginal activists staged peaceful protest marches. White Australians were forced to admit that, for the Aborigines, the colonial invasion had been an unmitigated disaster.

Rights and wrongs

The public agenda changed in 1992, when the High Court of Australia overturned the legal fiction of *terra nullius*. The judges agreed that native title had always existed for land that had been continuously occupied by Aborigines; in 1993 the government set up a Native Title Tribunal to regulate claims. However, because 19th-century missionaries moved Aboriginal

Territory, which was introduced by the Howard government, has yet to prove its worth.

Perhaps the biggest step towards some type of reconciliation occurred on 13 February 2008 when, amidst a national outpouring of emotion, Prime Minister Kevin Rudd formally apologised to the Stolen Generation *(see page 65)*.

Success stories

Many Aborigines have successfully entered Australian society on their own terms. Neville Bonner became a senator of the Commonwealth Parliament and pastor Sir Doug Nichols was appointed Governor of South Australia. Oodgeroo Noonuccal (formerly Kath Walker)

peoples around, often splitting up clans by force, few Aboriginal groups could prove continuous occupation of their lands.

Aboriginal industry has been promoted by politicians, community activists and Aboriginal leaders. Most promising has been the creation of successful Aboriginal businesses, from shopping centres and cattle stations to craft shops.

The problems facing the Aborigines who live in remote communities – illiteracy, low wages, alcohol and drugs – resist simple solutions. A strong interventionist policy of cracking down on alcohol and delinquency in the Northern

LEFT: walking around Darwin. **ABOVE:** Geoffrey Gurrumul Yunupingu entertains the crowd.

was a prominent artist and author, while writers such as Herb Wharton and Evelyn Crawford are immensely popular.

Sport has seen several outstanding performers, including Evonne Goolagong-Cawley, who became a Wimbledon tennis champion, and athlete Cathy Freeman, who won a gold medal in the 2000 Olympics.

Music has always been central to Aboriginal culture and there has been a steady flow of acts who have crossed over into the commercial mainstream, from Jimmy Little in the 1960s to Yothu Yindi in the 1980s, on through Kev Carmody, Tiddas, Archie Roach and, the newest breakout phenomenon, Geoffrey Gurrumul Yunupingu. ❑

ABORIGINAL ART: PAST AND PRESENT

From Dreamtime to polymer paints, the artworks being created by modern Aborigines carry the symbolism of thousands of years of myth and tradition

It's contemporary yet traditional. It's today but it's timeless. Attaching a single label to modern Aboriginal art can be as difficult as establishing the meanings behind the symbols. But it does provide us with a unique cultural vision of Australia. The international explosion in Indigenous Australian art began in the early 1970s as a spark in Northern Territory, first in various groups in Arnhem Land and in the desert community of Papunya, west of Alice Springs. In Arnhem Land, missionaries encouraged tribal people to paint their designs, derived from traditional rock art and body decoration, on bark panels stripped from trees. Meanwhile in central Australia, teacher Geoffrey Bardon introduced polymer paints, producing an entirely new genre of art: the strongly symbolic dot style was born. Today the National Gallery in Canberra, all the state galleries, and many private galleries in all the major cities feature desert and Top End art.

Other Aboriginal communities have also earned distinguished reputations for their artisans: Tiwi islanders for their carving and distinctive painting; representations of WA's Kimberley region, as characterised by artists Rover Thomas and Paddy Carlton; and the blazing acrylics from Eubana Nampitjin of Balgo Hills. Works by the late Emily Kngwarreye put the central Australian community of Utopia on the map; her niece Kathleen Petyarre continues that tradition with her intricately detailed paintings, prints and batiks, which can be viewed at numerous galleries throughout Australia.

ABOVE: the Aboriginal Memorial, created by artists from Ramingini in the Northern Territory, is constructed of 200 hollow log bone coffins and can be seen in the National Gallery of Australia.

BELOW: a Tiwi Island man decorates a totem on Bathurst Island. With its strong patterns and use of colour, Tiwi art is recognised as being very attractive and highly collectable.

LEFT: *GiriGiri Le* (Bird of Paradise Man) can be found in the National Gallery of Australia, Canberra.

BUYING THE ART

In an industry with a turnover in the millions of dollars, the Aboriginal art market is rife with opportunists trying to rip off the buyers and/or the artists. As a buyer, you can take a few simple steps to avoid the common pitfalls. Prime amongst them is establishing the authenticity of the work. Ideally, buy direct from the artist or their community, an Aboriginal art and craft centre or a reputable dealer – look for membership of the Indigenous Art Trade Association or the Australian Commercial Galleries Association – and always ask for a certificate of authenticity and/or photographic provenance of the work. That way you can establish the title, the artist's name, community and language, the date of the work and the story behind it. After that, consider (with reference to the quality and price of other works by the artist) whether you are getting value for money. In recent years there have been several instances of exploitation of artists by unscrupulous traders, so enquire whether the dealer subscribes to an industry ethical code, such as the Australian Indigenous Art Code of Conduct.

LEFT: modern Aboriginal art is often created to evoke the culture of the Dreaming, without any strong connection to a particular Dreaming story or song.

RIGHT: a Jawun Shield from the late 19th century, its maker unknown, is now displayed in the National Gallery of Australia, Canberra.
BELOW: *Garth Eran and Evarth Eran* is a piece created by Thanakupi, one of the first Aboriginal artists to work in clay. Her art is a contemporary expression of her people's ancestral stories and laws, handed down through the generations.

THE ARTS

In music, drama, literature, film and the visual arts, Australia has absorbed influences from around the world and now has its own distinctive voice

There's good reason to believe that a fair number of visitors enjoy the opera or an orchestral concert whilst in Australia. This isn't to argue that Opera Australia is the best company in the world or that the Sydney Symphony has that something extra to get musical celibates across the line. Or perhaps it is, at least in the latter case, because what both these companies have is the Sydney Opera House as a home base. It's a Unesco World Heritage Site and dominates the harbour. It's the place all first-time visitors want to see, many going on the guided tour. The logical next step is to see a performance.

So what will you see? With both companies it will be work fit to grace any stage. The orchestra covers the standard classical repertoire but also has a strong record of commissioning contemporary Australian composers. Since 2009 Vladimir Ashkenazy has been Principal Conductor and artistic advisor. Before that he programmed a series of festivals of different composers, looking in depth at their canon. The latest, his two-year Mahler Odyssey, commenced in 2010.

Opera Australia splits its time between Sydney and Melbourne and tours with the odd production further afield. It programmes everything from high-profile and popular shows, such as Britten's *Midsummer Night's Dream* directed by Baz Luhrmann, through to chamber productions of challenging new Australian work. Queensland, Adelaide, West Australia and Victoria all have their own opera companies, while every state has its own orchestra.

Classical music is, of course, very much part of the Western tradition, Indeed, many of the pieces performed today predate the European discovery of Australia. When those first settlers arrived, almost all their cultural pleasures were transplanted from the mother country, much like their language, skills and crops. Indigenous Aboriginal culture, which dates back at least 50,000 years, was largely ignored.

The first stirrings of a specifically Australian cultural identity came in the 1890s and coincided with an upsurge in Australian nationalism. This was reflected initially in literature. It was the period when *The Bulletin* magazine's school of poets and short-story writers was

---

LEFT: "Symphony in the Sea" performed at Cottesloe Beach. **RIGHT:** the award-winning author Peter Carey.

founded, spearheaded by balladeers such as "Banjo" Paterson, who wrote *The Man From Snowy River* and *Waltzing Matilda*, and Henry Lawson, Australia's revered short-story writer. Their work celebrates the bush, mateship, Aussie nationalism and the triumph of the underdog, usually at the expense of the ruling Anglophile "bunyip aristocracy". Joseph Furphy wrote his novel *Such Is Life* at this time, capturing the world of rural dwellers in a style not dissimilar to Mark Twain's. Marcus Clarke's *For the Term of his Natural Life* was more of a potboiler, but did provide a gripping portrait of convict life in 1830s Van Diemen's Land (Tasmania).

Australian literature is born

Steele Rudd began his *On Our Selection* series in 1899, about life on poverty-stricken bush properties and featuring the characters Dad and Dave, who lived on for years in the wider world of radio and cinema. A little after Rudd, C.J. Dennis started celebrating city larrikins in his poems about *Ginger Mick and The Sentimental Bloke* (1915).

This creative leap was the start of a distinctive Australian literature, which continued strongly in the 20th century through the novels of Henry Handel Richardson, Miles Franklin, Christina Stead, Ruth Park and the towering,

THE SOAPS

Very little locally produced television finds its way beyond the shores of Australia, with the major exception of soap operas, which have consistently found an audience in the UK. *Home and Away* has been limping out of Sydney since 1987, but the one show from which so many impressionable viewers have drawn their image of suburban Australia is *Neighbours*. Such is the level of its following that an entire industry has evolved to serve the legions of fans who visit Melbourne. Various organised tours run to "Ramsay Street", and there's even a weekly *Neighbours*-themed pub quiz in a St Kilda hotel.

Nobel-prize-winning Patrick White. Today's high fliers include Peter Carey, Kate Grenville, Tim Winton and David Malouf. *(See the Further Reading list on pages 387–8.)* Australians are some of the most voracious book buyers in the world, and they flock to the many literary festivals in Australia.

Theatre

In theatre, Louis Esson began writing plays in a self-consciously Australian idiom in the 1890s, but it took a long time before any groundswell of home-grown drama could be detected. Ray Lawlor's *Summer of the Seventeenth Doll* (1955) was the first portrayal of clearly Australian characters to break out internationally and is still revived periodically. The 1970s saw an exponential expansion of Australian theatre as a wave of politically active writers filled the fringe theatres in the main cities. These writers inexorably moved into, and became, the mainstream. David Williamson is the best known of these and is still writing today. Of the next generation, Louis Nowra, Hannie Rayson and Joanna Murray Smith are consistently producing interesting work.

All the big cities have theatre companies, usually with a state-funded flagship accompanied by a range of smaller fringe enterprises. The Sydney Theatre Company is currently

The great anomaly of the Australian stage is the Bell Shakespeare Company. In 1990 John Bell effectively revived the role of the actor/manager, which had died out as a concept everywhere else, by setting up a company to tour Shakespeare around the country. It's still going and producing three shows a year.

Dance

Dance was one of the first disciplines in which colonial Australian culture began to reconnect with the country's indigenous population. Composer John Antill wrote *Corroboree*, a ballet suite, in 1946; it was performed as such in

run by actress Cate Blanchett and playwright Andrew Upson and offers a strong programme occasionally bolstered by some of Blanchett's Hollywood friends tempted by a spell on the boards in the Harbour City.

The large commercial theatres tend to be clogged up with clone musicals from Broadway or London's West End, with the odd home-grown production, such as *Priscilla Queen of the Desert*, going the other way.

LEFT: *The Ship That Never Was*, Tasmania's longest-running play, tells how convict shipwrights escaped in 1834 by hijacking a ship they had just built. ABOVE: actors in character for a stage production at the Belvoir Theatre in Surrey Hills.

1950, touring the country over the next decade. It combined Aboriginal and Western forms to great acclaim. Today the Bangarra Dance Company does the same thing; the company is directed and run by Aboriginal people. The company tours extensively in Australia and overseas, as does the Melbourne-based Australian Ballet, which presents both classical and contemporary repertoire. Cutting-edge smaller companies include Chunky Move, which leads the way in harnessing modern technology to complement its performers.

Images on canvas

A recognisable school of landscape painting in Australia emerged in the late 19th century, personified by Sir Arthur Streeton, Tom Roberts and the Heidelberg School (named after the Melbourne suburb, not the German town), which pioneered Australian impressionism. Today there is an art trail in the vicinity and, nearby, the Heide Museum of Modern Art. This property was, for a spell, the haunt of Albert Tucker, Joy Hester and probably Australia's best-known painter, Sidney Nolan. Nolan was one of a group of figurative painters working after World War II, identified as part of the Australian School. His series of paintings on Ned Kelly, the outlaw bushranger, became national icons.

In the early 1970s Sydney became the centre for an abstract expressionist movement which drew upon earlier painters such as Ian Fairweather and Godfrey Miller. Local artists were soon experimenting with hard edge, colour field and lyrical expressionist modes. A new breed of younger painters looked up to Brett Whiteley as the poster boy for artists living the rock'n'roll lifestyle.

In Melbourne, painter and printmaker Fred Williams established himself as the most important landscape artist of the post-war years with his haunting, semi-abstract depictions of the Outback.

Antipodean Rhythms

Australia has become as well known for its rock bands as its films; the pub music scene, especially in Melbourne and Sydney, is extraordinarily healthy. Performers such as Nick Cave, Wolfmother and the Temper Trap started off on the pub circuit and now enjoy international success. Others that made it big overseas include the Seekers, the BeeGees, AC/DC, Midnight Oil, inxs and Men at Work. The Aboriginal band Yothu Yindi, with didgeridoos and tribal dancers, is unmistakably Northern Territory. One of Australia's best-known exports (in Europe, at least) is Kylie Minogue, a former teenage soap star and now pop icon. At home the dance scene is pumping, and acts such as Pendulum have taken off overseas.

There are two unique musical fields in which Australians have twisted the popular American styles into something distinctly antipodean. Bush ballads may have died out, but American country and western music took off in the rural areas of Australia in the 1940s and 50s. Local singers adopted names like Tex Morton and Slim Dusty and began writing songs about outlaws, pubs, and the country myths of girlfriends past. Slim Dusty's *The Pub with No Beer* was a huge hit. More recently, Keith Urban has become a global star, while Kasey Chambers is the biggest name locally. Meanwhile, a hip-hop scene is blossoming with Adelaide's Hilltop Hoods and Sydney's Bliss 'n' Eso leading the charge.

Perhaps the best-known contemporary Australian artist is Tracey Moffatt, born in Brisbane in 1960. Her painterly films and photographic works have won international critical acclaim and been widely exhibited. She is symptomatic of a whole wave of artists working across various media who set out to challenge not just with the message, but also with the medium.

Brisbane's impressive new Gallery of Modern Art leads the way in this field, but Sydney's Museum of Contemporary Art and Melbourne's Australian Centre for Contemporary Art have consistently supported adventurous work. The multi-million-dollar Museum of Old and New

after, and, with a burst of dramatic talent and new government incentives, the film industry became Australia's biggest cultural export. The most celebrated films range from period pieces (Gillian Armstrong's 1979 version of the Miles Franklin classic, *My Brilliant Career*) to George Miller's 1996 talking pig, *Babe*; to Baz Luhrmann's dazzling dance comedy *Strictly Ballroom* (1992), and David Michôd's crime thriller *Animal Kingdom* (2010).

Australian actors Nicole Kidman, Cate Blanchett, Toni Collette, Geoffrey Rush, Eric Bana, Guy Pearce and Hugh Jackman have all become big names in Hollywood.

Art, just north of Hobart, opened with a bang at the beginning of 2011.

Pearls on film

Soldiers of the Cross (1899) is said to be the world's first feature film and, like the more famous *The Story of the Kelly Gang* (1906), was made in Australia. It took several more decades, however, for local cinema to find its voice; it wasn't until the 1970s that films emerged onto the world stage with the likes of *Mad Max* and *Picnic at Hanging Rock*. Progress was swift thereafter.

LEFT: Aboriginal band Yothu Yindi blends traditional instruments with rock music.
ABOVE: the heartbreaking film, *Rabbit-Proof Fence*.

Some actors and directors prefer to create work that reflects the realities of modern Australia. Since 2000, for instance, a spate of indigenous-themed films has been released, including *Rabbit-Proof Fence* (Philip Noyce's 2002 look at the Stolen Generation of Aboriginal Australians) and *The Tracker* whose director, Rolf de Heer, won international praise for *Ten Canoes*, the first Australian film to feature an entirely indigenous cast and to be spoken entirely in indigenous languages. *Samson and Delilah* (2008) portrayed the desperation of Aboriginal youth in central Australia; the film won the Caméra d'Or (Gold Camera Award) for best first feature film at the 2009 Cannes Film Festival. ❑

MODERN AUSTRALIAN CUISINE

It took a long time to happen, but food in Australia
is now distinguished for its quality, imagination
and a truly multinational diversity

Not so long ago, the term "Australian cuisine" conjured grisly images of meat pies, Vegemite sandwiches and sausage rolls. Not anymore; Australia is now a trendy paradise for foodies. Few places in the world have restaurants with such variety, quality and sheer inventiveness. From formal dining rooms to tiny beach-side cafés, menus explore the merging of Australia's bounty of native ingredients with international culinary traditions. Even the most basic corner diners, which once served up hamburgers and chips, now dish up focaccia with fresh King Island cheeses and exotic fruits.

In fact, Australia's culinary establishment may be the most adventurous in the world. Nearly every city has seen a swarm of "Mod Oz" restaurants with inventive chefs at the helm and an audience of willing epicures. This renaissance is due to two factors: the wealth of superlative Australian produce – including native foods – and the plethora of international cuisines brought to Australia by its immigrants. The mix of traditional flavours from around the world has inspired a flurry of innovation.

Slow start

The Australian palate, like the nation, is relatively young, and the current sophistication follows a bleak culinary history. The early settlers struggled to maintain their stolid British or Irish diets, subsisting on salted meats – either roasted, stewed or baked into pies. Various early recipes indicate that native animals were eaten but, apart from kangaroo (whose tails make a fine soup), were rarely appreciated. The unfamiliar harshness of the Australian bush bred tough bellies used to tinned beef and damper (the most basic bread of flour, water and a pinch of salt).

During the gold rush days of the 1850s, Chinese immigrants recognised the potential for cultivation and grew a great variety of herbs and vegetables. On some occasions, their industry saved white mining camps from starvation. Even the tiniest country town still has its Chinese restaurant, which for decades saved the citizens from complete culinary deprivation.

Even in the 1960s, the only things approaching an Australian cuisine were a couple of sweet confections – pavlova, a meringue pie shell filled with fruit and cream, and lamingtons, sponge cubes covered with chocolate and coconut. Of course, there was always Vegemite – the black, salty yeast spread that most Aussies were weaned on, though abhorred by most others.

Thanks to the climate, the "barbie" (barbecue) did become an Australian institution, but British roast dinners were turned out every Sunday; and on Christmas Day, in steaming hot summers, the hot roast turkey graced every table.

Culinary immigration

The massive migration from Mediterranean countries after World War II made the first real dent on Australia's palate. Italians in particular helped revolutionise cooking, introducing wary Aussies to the wonders of pasta, garlic and olive oil. Today, each capital city has its share of Italian restaurants serving authentic, well-priced

food: in Melbourne, Lygon Street is the heart of Little Italy; in Sydney, it's Norton Street in the Leichhardt neighbourhood.

This was only the beginning. The extension of immigration in the 1970s added myriad new cuisines. The great melting pot – or perhaps more appropriately, salad bowl – of Australian society meant that restaurants were suddenly opened by Lebanese, Turkish, Balkan, Hungarian and Spanish chefs. But the biggest impact by far has been made by the Asians. Restaurants featuring the cuisine of every country in the

ABOVE LEFT: freshly caught seafood in Perth.
ABOVE: the Richmond Hill Cafe & Larder.
ABOVE RIGHT: enjoying Chinese food.

Pacific Rim are found in rural villages almost as often as in major cities. Diners enjoy pristine teppanyaki Japanese dining rooms, and take-away lakhsa stalls. Singapore-style food courts have sprung up everywhere; even local supermarkets now stock Thai and Indian ingredients. Lemongrass, chilli, coriander and cardamom give new depth and flavour to many essentially European dishes.

Not that Australia has tossed off its British culinary heritage altogether. Your fish'n'chips might still come in folded newspaper, but inside is fresh-grilled barramundi instead of deep-fried cod. And although pies'n'peas are now thankfully low on the food chain, you can still get the Australian version at the occasional retro-chic diner.

Going local in the kitchen

The foundation of Australian cuisine is the quality and variety of its ingredients. Without them, all of the exotic spices and exciting recipes in the world would still result in dismal dining. Locally sourced produce, meats and fish are highly sought after. Aussies were slow to recognise the wealth of seafood in their waters, but now a range of fresh fish is on every menu. Small farms devote themselves to gourmet beef and poultry, while the quality of everyday vegetables rivals that grown on organic farms in

Europe or the United States. Far from pining for imports of French cheese, Greek olives or Italian wine, Australians produce their own, which are often rated superior to the imports.

Australia can be divided into regions that are known for particular produce: King Island cream, Sydney rock oysters, Bowen mangoes, Coffin Bay scallops, Tasmanian salmon, Illabo milk-fed lamb. Each state has its acknowledged specialities. Tropical Queensland produces a wealth of exotic fruits, like Bowen mangoes and papaya, succulent reef fish, mudcrabs and Moreton Bay Bugs (shellfish, not insects). From The Northern Territory come the white-fleshed

Towards a flavourful future

Established chefs who pioneered the Australian culinary adventure are being joined by a new generation of emerging talent which is eager to further explore gustatory possibilities. Wakuda Tatsuya, the acknowledged top chef in Australia, sees customers making reservations months in advance to dine at his self-named restaurant, Tetsuya's, in Sydney. But kitchens throughout Australia are being taken over by chefs in their 20s who are rated as highly as those far senior in both age and experience.

There is much flavour and excitement to be found in unpretentious neighbourhood res-

barramundi and Mangrove Jack, while in Darwin, sample buffalo burgers and crocodile steaks. New South Wales has Hunter Valley wines, Balmain Bugs and perfect Sydney rock oysters. Victoria produces some of the tenderest meats, such as Gippsland beef and Meredith lamb, Mallee squab and corn-fed chicken. Tasmania is one of the least-polluted corners of the globe, and has gained national attention for its salmon, trout, cheeses, oysters and raspberries. South Australia is home to the Barossa Valley wine industry, Coffin Bay scallops, olive oils, tuna and cultivated native foods. Finally, Western Australia has received rave reviews for its superb new wines from the southwest and for goat cheeses.

taurants, as well. Pub grub is as often spring rolls with satay dipping sauce and bruschetta with tomatoes, feta and basil as it is a meat pie or hamburger. Australians have a passion for pizza and will top a thin crust with everything from emu to pineapples to tandoori chicken. Local restaurants offer Moroccan-spiced chicken breast, chicken parmigiana, and lamb shank with red cabbage on the same menu. The wine and beer list at even the most humble restaurant will be more than adequate. Non-licensed establishments usually welcome BYO customers.   ❏

ABOVE: the Blue Duck restaurant overlooks the beach in Perth, Western Australia.

Bush Tucker Meets the Locavore Movement

As Australia's culinary consciousness matured, it looked inward to the foods native to its shores

The phrase "Bush Tucker" has become the buzz word for truly Australian ingredients, referring to edible flora and fauna found in the great storehouse of the Outback. Possum, quandong fruit, eels, bush tomatoes, emu and even witchetty grubs were common items on the Aborigine menu. The natives thrived off these foods for 50,000 years, but the arriving Europeans dismissed them as uncivilised.

When the restaurant scene exploded in Australia in the 1990s, many restaurants began to incorporate native elements into their elegant recipes. Chefs happily experimented with riberries, bunya nuts, wild rosellas and Kakadu plums. High-end restaurants featured main courses which used ingredients from the Outback in ways the Aborigines never imagined (and not just because they did not own Cuisinarts).

Much of that frenetic energy has simmered down. Modern Australian cuisine ("Mod Oz") has been tempered to mean appreciating and incorporating indigenous ingredients without ignoring the conventional pantry. There is still an obvious delight in using the more unusual ingredients in ways to satisfy the curious gourmand. Every major city has at least one restaurant with distinctive Bush Tucker courses. Along with standard offerings like lamb short loin with spinach soufflé, fine-dining menus will feature roasted emu wrapped in prosciutto and seared kangaroo rump with seasonal vegetables. Sweet potato mash is served alongside salads of warrigal and samphire greens. Wattle seed, pepper leaf and lemon myrtle join thyme and oregano as seasonings. Meanwhile, pubs serve deep-fried crocodile bites and pizza with kangaroo topping along with the expected meat pies or fish and chips.

The change in the concept of Bush Tucker reflects an evolution in the Australian attitude towards food. Culinary writers and food industry analysts see an increasing interest in nutrition

and in ways of using local ingredients and simple preparation techniques in cooking both at home and in restaurants. Those incorporate Australian ingredients, but that now often means foods from other cultures and traditions which have taken root in Oz.

The emphasis now is as much on how and where foods are grown as on what they are. "Grow and Buy Australian" is the new movement. Chefs and home cooks seek out locally sourced ingredients grown by sustainable methods. Consumers want to know that their produce was grown without pesticides and that their beef was grass-fed, their chickens free-range and their fish wild-caught. Farmers'

markets are springing up like mushrooms after a heavy rain in city centres as well as country towns. Increasingly, consumers want to meet the person who planted the lettuce, made the cheese or picked the fruit. Websites supply consumers with links to Australian raised, grown or produced food and drink that aren't available in local shops.

Chefs are responding to diners' interests for healthier menu items. "Hyper-local" is the new restaurant buzz-phrase for a chef who maintains his or her own garden for produce and herbs. Others have arrangements with farmers for regular purchases of fresh produce, cheeses and meats. For restaurants with their notoriously slim profit margin, buying locally is usually more economical. For their customers, it means fresher, healthier food. ❑

RIGHT: young crocodiles swim through the clear water in the Northern Territory.

AUSTRALIAN WINES

The Australian wine scene might be a late bloomer, but it has quickly earned the respect of the wine world's cognoscenti for the consistent quality delivered by the major labels and the mature treatment of varietals by the smaller producers

When Australian wines first appeared on the international scene, they were considered a novelty. But now, each of the six states and both territories boast vineyards and wineries. The great differences in climates and soils, often within a few kilometres of each other, create conditions for a range of wines as vast as the continent.

Although more than 140 varieties of grapes are cultivated Down Under, Europeans found no native grapes. Cuttings of plants from the Cape of Good Hope arrived with the First Fleet in 1788. By the 1850s, grapes were being grown in most Australian states. When the phylloxera epidemic (which decimated Europe's vineyards in the 1870s) spread to Australia, strict regulations and quarantine limited the damage. As a result, vines that were planted in Australia before the epidemic are some of the oldest in the world. That said, most of the nearly 2,500 wineries in Australia are less than 30 years old.

The most popular red grapes are Shiraz, Cabernet Sauvignon and Merlot. Chardonnay, Semillon and Riesling are the most popular whites. Once a mainstay of the industry, fortified wines – largely Muscats – still have a small but loyal following. "Stickies" is the name for golden sweet dessert wines made from grapes deliberately affected by Noble Rot, which concentrates their flavours and sweetness.

Australia is the sixth-largest producer of wine in the world and the fourth-largest exporter, selling to more than 100 countries and contributing A\$5.5 billion to the nation's economy. The largest export market by volume is the UK, which imports more than 270 million litres (67.5 million gallons) of Australian wine annually. The US and Canada are placed second and third. Coming up fast is China; an expanding economy has turned China into the fastest-growing wine market in the world and the fourth-largest export market for Australia.

Economic and climatic challenges

The Australian wine industry faces challenges from an oversupply of wine and grapes, the global economic downturn and a strong Australia dollar. There's also another obstacle not so easily dealt with: global warming. The continent is already at the edge of the sustainable grape-growing environment and most of Australia's 62 wine-growing regions are highly susceptible to climate change.

Australians thrive on challenges and, with the fate of one of their favourite luxuries and one of their most important exports at stake, this is one they take on with exceptional energy and enthusiasm. Wineries like Henschke in the Barossa and d'Arenberg in McClaren Vale, Tyrrell's in the Hunter Valley north of Sydney and Sandalford in West Australia draw on up to six generations of experience.

One advantage for Australian wine makers is the lack of regulations which define so much of European wine-making. This leaves them free to innovate with flexible wine-making practices. Growers lead the way in "canopy management",

Growers are buying property in the Snowy Mountains in southern New South Wales. With elevations of 2,200 metres (7,000ft), it's the highest land in Australia. As conditions throughout the rest of the grape-growing world deteriorate, the microclimate in the Snowys should develop as one of the best for grape cultivation. Growers think this will give them up to a century of compensation for predicted climate change.

Flying vintners

Since the harvest in Australia is six months earlier than in the northern hemisphere, wine

artificially controlling the heat and humidity of vineyards. Organic and sustainable viticulture and planting drought-resistant varieties are popular.

Mother Nature may be playing a role in climatic adaptation. Cleggert Wines in Langhorne Creek in South Australia has cultivated Australia's first indigenous grapes. Malian and Shalistan are both the result of natural genetic variations of Cabernet Sauvignon grapes, which were noticed and propagated by the wine maker. Whether this was a genetic accident or an evolutionary response to conditions is a matter of debate.

LEFT: Perth's well-known restaurant, Balthazar, has a great wine list. ABOVE: vineyards in the Barossa Valley are known for producing great red wines.

makers and grape growers can visit other wine regions internationally when those areas are busy with production. The passing on of proven techniques elsewhere to Australia's "flying wine makers" is evened out by the introduction of Australian ideas and innovations, particularly in France, Spain and Italy.

The 2009–10 harvest was 1.6 million tonnes, down 7.5 percent from the previous harvest. That still leaves an enormous inventory of existing vintages. Most of that consists of wines for which Australia is well known, particularly Shiraz, Cabernet and Chardonnay. However, those are wines which are produced equally well in many other places and create a marketing challenge for the Australian wine makers.

Expanding the market

To avoid becoming stereotyped as producers of a limited range of wines, Australians are exploring the potential of other grapes. They are planting European varieties like Barbera and Chenin Blanc, and some exotic varieties only a true oenophile would recognise, like Saperavi from Southern Russia and Spain's Doradillo, both of which are being cultivated in Victoria.

In the Granite Belt in Southeast Queensland, wine makers use the "Strange Bird Wine Trail" to market unfamiliar European varietals. The map points out wineries which bottle alterna-

tive varietal wines like Tempranillo, Malbec and Silvaner, which are rarely found on bottleshop shelves. While the immediate goal is to develop a domestic market for these wines, the long-range plan is to create wines fine enough to challenge their historic producers.

The grand tour

Wine tourism is a major industry, with each wine region uncorking new initiatives to attract visitors. Wine-lovers will have far more tasting rooms (also called cellar doors) to visit than the time or fortitude to do them justice.

South Australia produces more than half of the nation's wine, and focuses on Cabernet and Shiraz. This area was not affected by the phylloxera epidemic, and as a result, it has some of the oldest vines in the world. It's fitting then that the National Wine Centre of Australia is in Adelaide. The multimedia exhibits, demonstration vineyard and tasting room present an overview of the wine-making process and the delectable results. Nine distinct regions are within 90 minutes' drive of the Centre. Barossa Valley, Adelaide Hills and McLaren Vale are the most well known, but Langhorne Creek is considered a hidden gem. It is home to about 20 wineries, including Bleasdale, where the Potts family has been making wine since 1860, and Zontes Footsteps, where enthusiastic newcomers produced their first vintage in 2003.

Victoria boasts five diverse wine regions within an hour of Melbourne. Most of the wineries offer amenities beyond their liquid attractions. Cafés, spas, fine dining, luxury accommodation, even art galleries are part of the experience. The Yarra Valley has the oldest vineyards and there is a definite Mediterranean influence which reflects the approach by Italian wine makers who arrived in the 1860s. Meanwhile, the Geelong region along the Great Ocean Road in the southwest corner of Victoria takes advantage of climate and soil similar to Bordeaux and Burgundy.

New South Wales has the broadest range of climates in Australia, from the Alpine conditions of the Snowy Mountains to the coastal breezes of Shoalhaven Coast and the cool conditions of the Southern Highlands. With over 130 wineries, Hunter Valley, a two-hour drive north of Sydney, is the most established region, with a reputation for exquisite Semillon and Shiraz and acclaimed Chardonnay and Verdelho. Tourists can visit the Visitors' Information Centre in Pokolbin for maps, information and a chance to sample a few wines. It's also possible to sample many of the region's wines at the many tasting centres in and around Pokolbin. The Small Winemakers Centre, Boutique Wine Centre, Hermitage Road Cellars and the Hunter Valley Winegrowers are cellar doors showcasing smaller wineries which emphasise their individual approach to their art. South of Sydney, the Shoalhaven Coast is home to Coolangatta Estate, which was started in 1822. Nearby Kladis Estate is a relative newcomer, just 25 years old. Australian wine guru James Halliday ranks both as 5-star wineries.

The Australian Capital Region, while technically and politically independent, is physically within New South Wales. Clonakilla Estate at Murrumbateman routinely produces the finest-quality Shiraz-Viognier red blend (like Côte de Rotie) made in Australia.

For many years wine aficionados ignored Queensland's wines. The region produced well-respected wines until the 1930s when the domestic market turned to the southern states. Not until Ballandean Estate near Stanthorpe in the Granite Belt was established in 1961 did attention once again shift northward. Queensland wines are considered lighter, crisper and

The southwest corner of Western Australia is home to more than 170 wineries in 9 distinct regions. It is known for its Cabernet Sauvignon but it also has a reputation for Sauvignon Blanc and Zinfandel. With vines planted as early as 1829, viticulture in the Swan District which stretches from the east side of Perth northward pre-dates both Victoria and South Australia. The headliner region is Margaret River. Surrounded on three sides by the Indian and Great Southern Oceans, it has a distinctly Mediterranean climate and powerful Cabernet and Merlot. It also has the most well-developed and comprehensive tourism industry.

fruitier than varietals from other states. The most established region is the Granite Belt. Three hours west of Brisbane and the Gold Coast, it is 1,000 metres (3,000ft) above sea level and is the only area in Queensland with four distinct seasons. The crescent of higher ground from the Sunshine Coast Hinterlands to Brisbane's Scenic Rim and the Gold Coast Hinterland is home to several dozen new, small wineries. For a completely different experience, wineries near Cairns make wines from tropical fruits like mango, passionfruit and bush lime.

LEFT: a wine tasting at Chateau Tanunda.
ABOVE: wine casks are stacked and stored.

The island of Tasmania has a cool climate which lends itself to producing excellent sparkling wines. The sometimes fickle Pinot Noir enjoys the maritime influence and thrives here. Most of the 60 or so wineries are very small operations run by passionate vintners. The Jansz Vineyard with its connection to the French Champagne house Roederer is credited with bringing attention to Tasmania's sparkling potential. Wineries are clustered around Hobart on the Tasman Sea on the eastern side of the island and Launceston and the Tamar River to the west. On the east coast, Frogmore Creek is noted for its sustainable, organic viticulture techniques, while its wines have won awards for their compatibility with Asian cuisine. ❑

WHERE SPORT IS SUPREME

If you want to join the locals for a pint and a chat, you'll need to know how the local team is getting on

Arguably, sport was the language in which Australians first shouted: "Hey world, here we are!" Wherever people gather – in pubs, clubs, the workplace or around the barbecue – sport tends to be the major topic of conversation. They bet on it and brag about it, they eulogise or verbally flay its performers, analyse its conduct and speculate about its future. One thing they never do is tire of it.

The golden 1950s

The sports fixation reached its apogee in the 1950s, a period of Australian dominance in world swimming and tennis, plus its arrival as a force to reckon with in track and field, cycling, boxing, sculling and golf. The climax came in 1956: Australia dusted the United States 5–0 in the Davis Cup tennis final, while at the Melbourne Olympic Games, Aussie athletes won 35 medals – 13 gold, eight silver and 14 bronze – an astonishing number for the small population.

Australia has always punched above its weight at the Olympics, and continues to produce track and field stars. For many proud Aussies it all culminated in Cathy Freeman's gold-medal-winning run in the 400 metres at the Sydney Olympics in 2000.

The cricket mania

It's only in summer, when cricket grabs the public's imagination, that Australians are more or less united in their sporting focus. Spectator interest settles squarely on the national team in its Test Match encounters with the West Indies, India, Pakistan, New Zealand, South Africa and, most crucially, England.

A Test Match takes up to five days to complete; even then it frequently finishes in a draw. Yet the game is followed with religious zeal. Radios blare out the ball-by-ball commentary at the beach; pub discussions focus on the diving catch in the slips; and cricket is on TV, day in, day out. In the more than 100 years since Australia played its first Test series against England, nobody has been better at the game than a slightly built fellow by the name of Donald Bradman. "The Don" was to cricket what Pelé was to football or Babe Ruth was to baseball. *(See page 139.)*

A Test series is played over three to five matches, with the battlegrounds moving between Sydney, Melbourne, Adelaide, Brisbane and Perth. Ground capacities range from 30,000 to 100,000; lovers of the game say there are few greater sporting moments than to experience the opening "over" of an England v Australia Test before a capacity crowd. The Australian team was the top-ranking team for most of the 1990s and 2000s but has recently slipped in the rankings. Probably nothing hurt quite so much as the thrashing the England team handed out when they toured Australia in 2010.

If a five-day Test sounds too much to take in, consider watching a "limited-over" or one-day game. As the name implies, these are quick affairs that come and go in a heated rush and often wring participants and spectators dry with tension and drama. A standard one-day game gives each side 50 overs to bat and 50 to bowl,

lar football leagues in the world. It is estimated that each winter weekend in Melbourne, one person in 16 attends an Australian Football League (AFL) game; thousands more follow on TV. September's AFL grand final is one of the great sporting experiences.

The art of non-compromise

In Sydney and points north, footie of a different kind is the winter preoccupation. Rugby League started as a professional alternative to Rugby Union. It's played in a half-dozen provinces of a half-dozen countries, and to that degree qualifies as an international sport. League

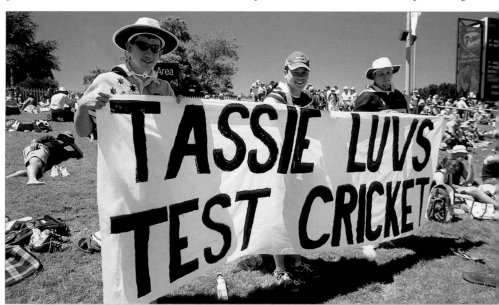

while the much newer T20 format gives each side 20 overs and usually lasts about 3 hours.

Aussie Rules footie

On the surface it seems incongruous that a country so fond of cricket, with all its esoteric customs and traditions, could have given birth to a game as apparently anarchic as Australian Rules football. The sport may be virtually unknown beyond Australia's shores, but in the southern states it's a passion, particularly in Melbourne: the city may have only 4 million inhabitants, yet Aussie Rules ranks among the most popu-

LEFT: a dedicated fan of the Sydney Roosters.
ABOVE: Tasmania makes a pitch for more big games.

attendances are nothing like as large as those of the AFL, but the Sydney clubs – such as St George, the Western Suburbs, Manly and Parramatta – keep their players fabulously well paid through the revenue from their slot machines

> The uncompromising style of defence in rugby prompted one American football coach to observe: "Our guys could never stand up to that sort of constant punishment."

and licensed clubs. In Brisbane and Sydney, the game found its roots in the working-class inner suburbs and, despite media overkill, hasn't significantly broadened its social base.

Rugby League is a physical rather than cerebral game. You don't have to play this game to feel how much it hurts. The game's appeal rests in its strong gladiatorial image and macho confrontations as pairs of teams slam into one another – although fans believe that a dazzling backline movement resulting in a try (touchdown) is one of the real joys in sporting life.

Two or three times a year in the State of Origin series, the New South Wales and Queensland teams engage in a brutal battle. The Aussie national side, known as the Kangaroos, regularly hops through tours of France and Great Britain unbeaten.

rule, three gifted Aboriginal athletes from Sydney's inner southern suburbs who all wound up wearing the gold shirts of the Australian team.

The world game

The history of soccer in Australia bears little comparison to other forms of football. The game first kicked off more than a century ago among British migrants, then more or less stagnated until post-World War II, with the arrival of migrants from Southern Europe. Now most clubs in the National Soccer competition – the A League – are dominated by players from the Italian, Greek, Croatian, Slavic, Maltese, Dutch

God's own game

According to its devotees, Rugby Union is "the game they play in heaven" – which is remarkable considering its relative popularity in New South Wales and Queensland, where angels are in short supply. If you enjoy rugby, watch the Wallabies (the national side) in action, especially if there's a spare ticket for a Bledisloe Cup match, which sees the Wallabies face up to the mighty All Blacks from New Zealand.

At club level, Rugby Union projects a social spirit often lacking in the professional codes. The game has a "silvertail" (upper-crust) image based partly on its strength in the universities and private schools. The "flying Ella brothers" of the 1970s were a contradiction to the class

and Macedonian communities. The national team, the Socceroos, continue to edge their way up the international ladder, and their success in the 2006 World Cup, consolidated by their performance in South Africa in 2010, has helped revive the sport's popularity at home.

Great individualists

The 1950s and '60s brought forth a rash of tennis talents, including Rod Laver, John Newcombe, Evonne Goolagong-Cawley and Pat Cash. Recent hopes, including Adelaide's Lleyton Hewitt, have not managed to reach the same heights consistently.

Australian golfers have generally kept their end up, and Greg Norman, "the Great White

Shark", was a phenomenon. Today Robert Allenby is the pick of the bunch.

But it has been those sports which pit the individual against the elements which have brought out the best in Australians. It's not surprising that swimming has been a top sport: kids are tossed into the pool almost as soon as they can walk. In the 1950s, Dawn Fraser became Australia's darling as much for her cheeky anti-establishment attitude as her victories. In the 1970s, Shane Gould followed in her wake, with a slew of Olympic medals. Australia's most recent swimming superstar is Ian Thorpe, who won three gold and two silver medals in the

Australian motor racing has produced Formula 1 world champions in Jack Brabham (three-times winner) and Alan Jones, while current driver Mark Webber is right up with the best of them. In motorcycle champs Wayne Gardner, Daryl Beattie, Michael Doohan and Casey Stoner, r. Yet the real local heroes of the track are the V8 touring car drivers. The class attracts heavy sponsorship for its championship series, the highlight of which is the Bathurst 1000 held in October, an endurance event that attracts an international field of drivers. The Formula 1 Grand Prix is held on Melbourne's Albert Park circuit in early March.

2000 Olympics, and in 2003 became the first swimmer ever to win three consecutive world titles in one event, the 400 metres freestyle. At the 2004 Olympics, "the Thorpedo" added four medals to his Olympic tally: two gold, one silver and one bronze.

Aussies have ruled the waves almost since surfing's inception as a competitive sport, with Mark Richards' four world titles marking him as one of the world's greatest-ever surfers. Names like Nat Young and Tom Carroll have permanent niches in a national surfing hall of fame.

A nation of punters

It is often said that Aussies would gamble on just about anything, but there's only one race that captures everyone's imagination and puts millions of dollars through the bookmakers and the agencies of the Totalizator Agency Board (TAB). That race is the Melbourne Cup.

At 3.30pm Melbourne time on the first Tuesday in November, the whole of Australia stops for the running of this classic horse race. The 3,200-metre (two-mile) event has become an international thoroughbred classic since it was first held at Melbourne's Flemington course in 1861. It's a public holiday in Victoria, and even the process of government is suspended so that the nation's decision-makers can watch the race. ❑

LEFT: Melbourne Demons vs Collingwood Magpies.
ABOVE: Mark Webber in the Red Bull Racing RB5 race car, Formula 1 testing at a race track in Spain.

Surf Culture

Introduced to Australia in 1912 by Duke Kahanamoku of Honolulu, surfing has become a way of life for many of Australia's coastal dwellers

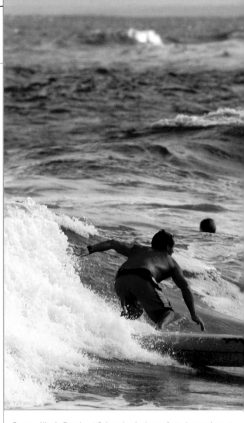

On a good day at Noosa Heads, Manly or countless other Australian beaches, thousands of surfers of all ages and on all kinds of equipment clog the line-ups. Surfing today is as mainstream as tennis, golf, cricket or football, and kids on the coast grow up riding every kind of surf craft imaginable. If you come across a Saturday-morning "nippers" (junior surf life-saving session), with kids who look as if they're barely out of nappies charging in and out of the waves, you would swear they're breeding a new, genetically modified amphibious race here.

The old surf clubs with their prime beach-front positions are still the social hubs of the Australian coast, where you can enjoy a cheap meal, a cold beer, or succumb to the dreaded "pokies" (fruit machines), all with unmatched ocean views. The old, framed black-and-white photos of past surf champions peer down, echoing earlier, simpler times. The worldwide boom of the surf industry means that professional surfers have the opportunity to set themselves up financially for life. Young surfers barely out of their teens drive luxury 4WD vehicles and buy mansions.

For a real surf experience, take a lesson, sit under a pandanus tree with a pie and a chocolate milk, go for another surf, then retreat to the surf club for a steak and a beer. Just see if you don't feel strangely good about the world again. Then go to bed, wake up and do it all over again.

LEFT: contemplating the waves on Main Beach, along the Gold Coast in Queensland.

ABOVE: King's Beach, at Caloundra, is the perfect place to learn to surf; the waves are typically small and the local people are friendly. Take your board up near the headland on the northern edge.

BELOW: the northern end of Bondi Beach has been rated a gentle 4 (with 10 as the most hazardous); the southern side is rated as a 7 due to a rather strong and consistent rip current.

A BRIEF HISTORY OF SURFING

Australian surfing as we know it began at Sydney's Freshwater Beach, when visiting Hawaiian champion Duke Kahanamoku *(right)* put on his historic display in 1914. However, there is some evidence of a surf culture among Indigenous Australians. The foundation meeting of the Greenmount Surf Club in 1908 paid tribute to a local Aboriginal man, named Churaki, for the many daring rescues he carried out in the surf prior to the club's formation.

Surf life-saving clubs were formed in the early 1900s to protect public safety, and quickly grew as social hubs for the emerging beach culture. Surfboards were built for ocean rescues and manned by teams of earnest paddlers, but proved poorly designed for rough ocean conditions.

Surf clubs remained unchallenged as the pinnacle of beach culture until the 1950s, when a group of Americans visited Australia to coincide with the 1956 Melbourne Olympics. Their surf-riding displays on revolutionary, short, light Malibu boards reverberated around the country. Freshly inspired surfers rejected the conservatism of the surf clubs for the freewheeling lifestyle of the wave-chasing surfie.

In the late 1960s and early 1970s, surfing's image reached an all-time low, associated as it was with laziness, drug use and antisocial behaviour. Beneath the hippy trappings, however, surfer rivalry was pushing the sport to greater heights. In the late 1970s, Australia's success in the first ever international competitions made the dream of pro-surfing a distinct possibility. Today, lucrative careers with million-dollar salaries and worldwide superstardom beckon the most successful surfers.

ᴀʙOVE: the mission of Surf Live Saving Australia (SLSA) is to provide ᵃsafe beach environment throughout Australia. They patrol beaches ᵃd educate the public about safety.

ᴙGHT: the SLSA has 153,000 members, of whom more than 43,800 ᴬtively patrol 400 Australian beaches. That makes it one of the ᴸgest volunteer organisations in the country.

ONE-OF-A-KIND WILDLIFE

Australia has been a separate island long enough
for evolution to take a unique path. The result
is a range of plants and animals that are
found nowhere else on Earth

Research findings are thin as to just how many people around the world actually believe that kangaroos are a regular sight on the city streets of Australia. It has become one of those stereotypical notions or urban legends, alongside the idea that most Aussie men are like Crocodile Dundee. Both ideas are popular, and yet both are almost entirely false. And yet, if you just wander down past the National War Memorial in Canberra, the nation's capital, at dusk, there's a very good chance that you'll find a mob of kangaroos grazing on the lawn.

In smaller towns and settlements, many of which appear to have only a toehold on the harsh antipodean landscape, the bush is often just over the back fence. The proximity of the wild means there's a fair likelihood of encountering a smattering of mammals, birds or reptiles that will surprise and delight a visitor from overseas. Even in the big cities, bereft of kangaroos as they may be, there will be possums to intrigue the tourist and frustrate the locals whose fruit they eat and whose eaves they burrow into.

Of the unique animals Down Under, possums, at least, have their counterparts in the Americas (the Virginia opossum); but the Australian kangaroo stands alone. There is nothing like it anywhere else in the world, and there's a reason for that. The sheer age of the Australian landmass and its isolation from other continents allowed its animals and plants to adapt to their unique environment and evolve independently of the rest of the world, unchallenged until the arrival of the European colonists and the onset of the technological age.

Eccentric mammals

For the perfect example of a uniquely evolved animal, take the Australian mammal. Warm-blooded and furred, mammals almost all give birth to live young and suckle them. There are three groups: placentals, marsupials and monotremes.

Elsewhere on Earth the placental group proliferates. However, very few examples of this group can be found among the native Australian fauna. The native dog, the dingo, is one, but was only introduced into Australia by Aboriginal immigrants within the past 20,000 years.

In Australia, marsupials are by far the most prominent group. Marsupials give birth to partially formed embryos which remain secure in a pouch until they are strong enough to survive independently. Most marsupials are herbivorous, but there are some that include insects, small reptiles or smaller mammals in their diets. The larger members of the carnivorous group include the Tasmanian devil and the Tasmanian tiger (thylacine). The latter, however, is now extinct (except in the minds of a few die-hard environmentalists who believe that a few lone individuals survive in the Tasmanian wilderness).

It is the herbivores that abound in the land Down Under, including the shy koala, which is not even remotely related to the bear family;

great was the slaughter that urgent steps were taken to save the koala in the 1920s. This laid-back marsupial is now a completely protected animal. The wombat is related to the koala, but instead of making its home up a tree and dining on gum leaves, it uses its powerful digging paws to make burrows under stumps, logs or in creek banks. It lives on roots, leaves and bark.

Monotremes are a unique and extraordinary group of animals. Rather than giving birth to live young, they lay eggs. However, they then suckle their young and display many other mammalian traits. The amphibious duck-billed platypus is a monotreme, as is the echidna (also

many varieties of possum, including the ringtail and the sugar glider; the wombat; and the macropods, or hopping marsupials, such as the kangaroo, wallaby and potoroo. Sadly for visitors just passing through, these species tend to be most active at dawn and dusk. Unfortunately, the typical Australian visitor is most likely to encounter these crepuscular creatures on the road, as a fleeting glimpse in the headlights of a vehicle.

The koala's habit of sleeping openly in the forks of gum (eucalyptus) trees made it an easy target for colonial hunters seeking koala fur. So

LEFT: a koala relaxes at Lone Pine Sanctuary in Brisbane. **ABOVE:** visitors can feed and pet the kangaroos at Lone Pine Sanctuary.

SAVING AUSTRALIA

Similar to movements in other parts of the world, a coordinated conservation movement emerged in Australia in the late 1970s, around the time of the nationwide campaign to protect Tasmania's Franklin River from being dammed.

The eco-movement gathered impetus during the 1980s, and is now well known. Environmental activists have managed to ensure many wild places are now safe for future generations to enjoy.

Notable victories include the protection of such landmark destinations as Fraser Island, Kakadu, the Daintree Rainforest, Tasmania's Southwest National Park and the Great Barrier Reef.

known as the spiny anteater). These two species are the only examples of living monotremes, although the fossil record suggests that monotremes were once widespread. A popular urban legend suggests that monotremes are a type of reptile; this has been thoroughly disproven by scientific study.

Snakes and lizards

Reptiles figure prominently in Aboriginal legend, particularly the venomous snakes such as the taipan, tiger snake, death adder and brown snake. Non-venomous species are also plentiful, as are lizards, which range from the tiniest of skinks to goannas more than 2 metres (6ft) long. Among the more exotic is the frill-necked lizard, which erects a frock of skin around its neck when confronted with danger. Don't confuse the frill-necked lizard with the bearded dragon, which has a mane of prickly spines. The blue-tongued lizard hunts snails and insects, often in city gardens. The eponymous blue tongue is often displayed as a bluff against danger.

Australia also has more than its share of frogs and toads, the most famous of which is the cane toad. Although it's not even a native, the cane toad has brought a whole lot of trouble *(see pages 94–5)*.

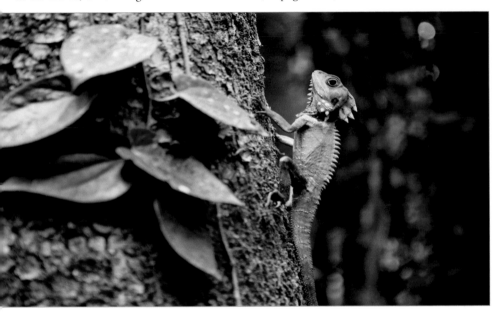

TREES OF LIFE

From a stroll through the leafy outer suburbs of Sydney to a bushwalk in the jarrah forests of Western Australia, you can easily expose your senses to the great Aussie bush. Just the range of eucalypts is immense, from a low, stunted, scrub-like bush to the great towering species of the highland woodlands. The mountain ash eucalyptus, found in the forests of Victoria and Tasmania, is the tallest flowering plant on Earth, growing to 70–90 metres (230–300ft) or more. Ghost gums appear silvery-white under the light of the moon, while rock-hard ironbarks are capable of blunting the toughest timber saws. Australia draws its national colours from the gold and green of the acacia, or wattle – it is hardy and usually one of the first species to rejuvenate after bushfires.

Most Australian trees have very hard timber. This made clearing the land an extremely arduous task for the early settlers, so when they encountered soft timber (such as cedar) they proceeded to fell it. In Tasmania, the Huon pine was found to be one of the best building timbers ever, and was especially prized by boat-builders. Western Australia's jarrah and the tough karri are also superb construction timbers. The jarrah forests are currently under threat from mining and foresters, and scientists are exploring ways to combat a disease called "die-back" that has affected the forests. A concerted effort to replant some of the tree life laid waste in the name of agricultural development is currently in process.

Sea life

Queensland's Great Barrier Reef is a wonderland blessed with numerous fish, shell and polyp species peculiar to Australian waters (*for more on the Reef's ecosystem, see pages 260–61*). But you don't have to go snorkelling in the Reef to sample the coastal wildlife; a scramble over any coastal rock platform will reveal shellfish, starfish, anemones, crabs and even the occasional octopus. Raising your eyes to the open sea may reward you with sightings of dolphins and whales. The latter follow migratory paths along the west, south and east coasts according to season. Sharks and lethal box jellyfish are the ones to avoid.

Eagles, hawks, crows and cuckoos of native origin all thrive, while the variety of habitats allows for many species of waterfowl. Some were hunted by the early settlers, and development has consumed many coastal habitats. Luckily, protective measures have saved many species from extinction.

Seeing is believing

If you don't have time to spend weeks in the bush spotting creatures in their natural environment, a suitable compromise is a visit to any of the larger nature reserves that exist on the fringes of the cities. Otherwise you can go to any of the

Airborne

Australia's early explorers were as intrigued by the birdlife they saw in the skies as they were by the kangaroos and koalas found on the ground. Flocks of raucous parrots and cockatoos can be found plundering the fruit trees. They include brilliantly plumed rosellas and lorikeets. The eccentric bowerbird builds a structure or bower to win the attention of a female. He adorns his court with brightly coloured trinkets (preferably blue) such as stones, glass or objects collected from gardens and houses.

city zoos, such as Sydney's Taronga Park or the Melbourne Zoo, or their rural offshoots – Western Plains Zoo in Dubbo or Healesville Sanctuary – and see most forms of local wildlife.

Plant life

From Queensland's steamy jungles to the delicate blossoms of New South Wales, there is no end to the variety of plant life. Like many animals, Australian flora has been affected by the introduction of foreign trees, grasses, shrubs and other plants. Some of these have flourished unchecked, completely altering the ecological balance. In the cities, the replanting of native trees has encouraged bird and insect life to return to these areas. (*For more on flowers see pages 312–13.*) ❑

LEFT: a Boyd forest dragon perches on a tree near Kuranda. **ABOVE:** Scuba diving near Cairns. **ABOVE RIGHT:** the rainbow lorikeet, pretty and precocious.

DANGEROUS WILDLIFE

Australia has many creatures that are hazardous to humans, but it's a two-way street. Humankind has been responsible for wiping out countless species, and we're only now realising the destruction we've caused

The second most famous interlopers onto the Australian mainland (after the First Fleet) were the cane toads. These giants were introduced in Queensland in 1935 to eradicate beetles that were attacking the key sugar-cane crop. The toads were unsuccessful in their official goal, and unfortunately they also wreaked havoc on local insect species. Even worse, the cane toad is toxic to anything that tries to eat it, giving it a privileged location on the food chain.

The cane toad is now spreading relentlessly across the country. Its story highlights the dangers of introduced species. Rabbits, foxes and cats have caused untold damage over the last 200 years, as have starlings and mynah birds. One stowaway starfish is estimated to have spawned 100 million descendants in Victoria's Port Phillip Bay.

The problem is that most introduced species thrive in an environment where they lack natural predators but enjoy a ready supply of food. Foxes and feral cats prey on small native mammals, rabbits destroy crops, wild pigs destroy vegetation around watercourses, and starlings, introduced to control caterpillars that were eating fruit crops in the Melbourne hinterland in 1857, began to feast on the fruit themselves.

ABOVE: when an adult cane toad is threatened, it secretes a milky-white fluid known as bufotoxin from glands behind the eye. This toxin is a Class 1 drug under Australian law; there have been human death due to the consumption or licking of cane toads.

BELOW: the starling is a threat to the native flora and fauna of Australia. WA has gone to great lengths to limit the bird's territory.

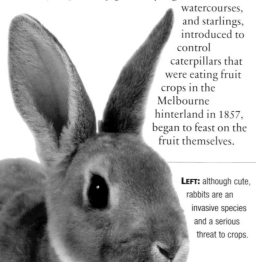

LEFT: although cute, rabbits are an invasive species and a serious threat to crops.

AUSTRALIA'S NATURAL-BORN KILLERS

Australia is a land where lethal killers abound…or crawl or slither or float or dive. Scorpions hide beneath rocks across the continent, great white sharks devour the occasional abalone diver off South Australia, saltwater crocodiles stalk fishermen (as do box jellyfish) in the Northern Territory, the venomous blue-ringed octopus waits on the reefs, and the funnel-web spider lurks in the gardens of suburban Sydney.

And as if that weren't enough, Australia possesses more species of venomous snakes than any other country on Earth. It is home to 40 snake species, and 12 of them, like the stunning copperhead, can inflict a fatal wound. The inland taipan, or fierce snake *(pictured below),* takes the prize as the world's deadliest snake: it is 50 times more venomous than the cobra. This rich reptilian diversity is not limited to the mainland: 32 known species of venomous sea snakes reside offshore.

However, dangerous liaisons between humans and these creatures are rare, with most sightings of killer animals confined to city zoos. In the wild, most animals prefer escape to confrontation with potentially lethal human beings.

BELOW: an inland taipan *(Oxyuranus microlepidotus),* the most venomous snake in the world, is almost never photographed due to its extremely shy nature.

OVE: in the past 100 years, bites from Sydney funnel-web spiders ve caused 13 deaths, and seven of those were children. Luckily, :e an antivenom was developed in 1981, there have been no ualties. If you are bitten by any large, black spider while in stralia, seek medical attention immediately.

PLACES

A detailed guide to the entire country, with main
sites cross-referenced by number to the maps

Australia has some fantastic cities: Sydney, with its glorious harbour
and the twin icons of the Opera House and the Harbour Bridge;
Melbourne, with its laneways, cosmopolitan café culture and plethora of sporting arenas; Brisbane, with its subtropical colonial architecture and burgeoning Southbank; Canberra, with its excess of museums
and galleries; Adelaide, with its churches and parks; Perth, with its river
and atmospheric old port; Hobart, with its colonial heart and mountain
backdrop; Darwin, with its frontier town flavour; even the Gold Coast
has its admirers for the sheer hubris of its high-rise development. And
don't forget, the large majority of the country's 22 million inhabitants
live in these cities.

Every country has cities, but no other country has a vast Outback with
Uluru at its parched red centre. Nowhere else has the Great Barrier Reef,
the Kimberley in northern West Australia, the pristine wilderness of Tasmania, or the Alpine splendour of the Great Dividing Range spreading
more than 2,000km (1,240 miles) down the eastern side of the country.

So make the most of the cities and enjoy the coast. The popular image
of Aussies as surf-loving beach dwellers is not without a grounding in
truth. There are, after all, thousands of kilometres of unspoilt beaches. But

many are the rewards for those who dig a little deeper. Australia's Aboriginal population thrived for 50,000 years without the need for cities, and they managed to spread across this whole Europe-sized continent, leaving tantalising fragments of rock art as their only record. You shouldn't limit your Australian experience to the well-trodden path.

So visit Sydney, but go to the Blue Mountains as well, or get right out to the isolated old mining town of Broken Hill. By all means visit Melbourne, but don't forget to go up into the high country and drive along the Great Ocean Road. See Brisbane and then consider stopping at the Reef, the islands and Daintree's tropical rainforest. From Canberra, head up to the Snowy Mountains. After Adelaide, visit the wine country of the Barossa or the underground desert dwellings of Coober Pedy. Perth has the Kimberley to the north and the ancient forests and picturesque wineries of Margaret River to the south. Hobart gives access to the wonders of Freycinet National Park or Cradle Mountain, and the remarkable Port Arthur Penal Settlement. Darwin, in the wild and monsoonal Top End, is the jumping-off point for Kakadu, with its rich Aboriginal culture, tropical wetlands and giant saltwater crocodiles.

And always, so far from all of these, but essential for anyone really wanting to taste the difference of this ancient land, is Uluru, the rock at the heart of the real Australia. ❏

PRECEDING PAGES: the surf rescue crew stands guard; Melbourne's Docklands; the beach at Palm Cove. **ABOVE:** P&O's *Oriana* is welcomed into Sydney Harbour.

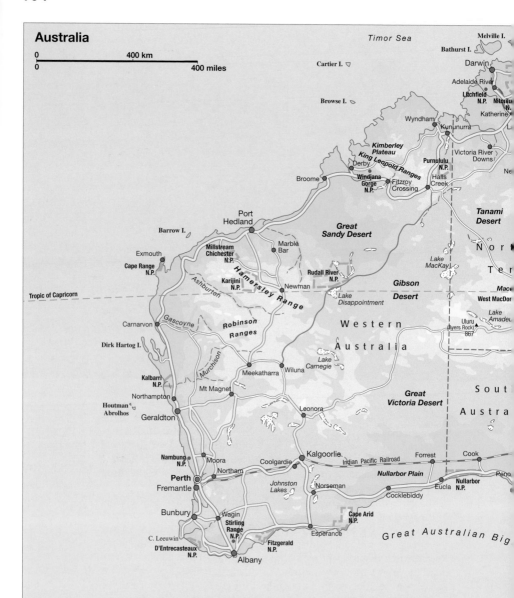

Australia

0   400 km

0   400 miles

Timor Sea

Melville I.

Bathurst I.

Cartier I.

Darwin

Adelaide River

Litchfield
N.P.   Nitmilu
N.

Browse I.

Katherine

Wyndham

Kununurra

*Kimberley
Plateau*

King Leopold Ranges

Victoria River
Downs

Purnululu
N.P.

Derby

Broome

Windjana
Gorge
N.P.

Fitzroy
Crossing

Halls
Creek

*Tanami
Desert*

N o r t

Barrow I.

Port
Hedland

Marble
Bar

*Great
Sandy Desert*

Lake
MacKay

T e r

Exmouth

Millstream
Chichester
N.P.

Mac

Cape Range
N.P.

Ashburton

Rudall River
N.P.

*Gibson
Desert*

West MacDor

Karijini
N.P.

Hamersley Range

Newman

Lake
Disappointment

Tropic of Capricorn

Carnarvon

Gascoyne

*Robinson
Ranges*

W e s t e r n

Lake
Amadeu

Uluru
(Ayers Rock)
867

Dirk Hartog I.

Murchison

A u s t r a l i a

Kalbarri
N.P.

Meekatharra

Wiluna

Lake
Carnegie

S o u t

Houtman
Abrolhos

Northampton

Mt Magnet

*Great
Victoria Desert*

A u s t r a

Geraldton

Leonora

Nambung
N.P.

Moora

Coolgardie

Kalgoorlie

Indian Pacific Railroad

Forrest

Cook

Northam

Nullarbor Plain

Peno

Perth

Nullarbor
N.P.

Fremantle

*Johnston
Lakes*

Norseman

Eucla

Cocklebiddy

Bunbury

Wagin

Cape Arid
N.P.

Stirling
Range
N.P.

Esperance

C. Leeuwin

D'Entrecasteaux
N.P.

Fitzgerald
N.P.

Great Australian Big

Albany

I N D I A N   O C E A N

Arafura Sea

C. Arnhem

Groote
Eylandt

*Gulf
of
Carpentaria*

Wellesley Is

Karumba

Burketown

Camooweal

Mount Isa

Cloncurry

Dajarra

Boulia

Winton

C. York

C. Greville

Weipa

Cape
York
Peninsula

Lakefield
N.P.

Cooktown

Laura

Cairns

Tully

Hinchinbrook I.

Townsville

Ayr

Mackay

Sarina

Mitchell

Gregory Range

Great Barrier Reef

*Coral
Sea*

Hughenden

Normanton

GREAT DIVIDING RANGE

Longreach

Barcaldine

Emerald

Rockhampton

Gladstone

Tropic of Capricorn

*Great Artesian
Basin*

*Simpson
Desert*

Birdsville

Yaraka

Queensland

Bundaberg

Fraser I.

Maryborough

Gympie

*PACIFIC
OCEAN*

L. Eyre
North

Cooper Creek

Quilpie

Charleville

Roma

Oodnadatta

Lake Eyre N.P.

L. Eyre
South

Marree

Gammon
Ranges
N.P.

Sturt N.P.

Cunnamulla

Toowoomba

Warwick

Murwillumbah

Brisbane

*Lake
Torrens*

Milparinka

Mutawintji
N.P.

Walgett

Moree

Glen
Innes

Lismore

Grafton

Leigh
Creek

*Lake
Frome*

Darling

Bourke

Armidale

Woomera

Flinders
Ranges
N.P.

Broken Hill

*New South
Wales*

Nyngan

Tamworth

Port Macquarie

Taree

Myall Lakes N.P.

*Lake
Gairdner*

Port
Augusta

Port Pirie

Kinchega
N.P.

Narromine

Dubbo

Wollemi
N.P.

Newcastle

Whyalla

*Eyre
Pen.*

Mungo
N.P.

Parkes

Bathurst

Sydney

Mildura

Wollongong

Port
Lincoln

*Yorke
Pen.*

Kingscote

Adelaide

Hay

Wagga Wagga

Kosciuszko
N.P.

Blue Mountains
N.P.

Canberra

A.C.T.

Cooma

Victor
Harbor

Wyperfeld
N.P.

Albury

Wodonga

Mt Kosciuszko
2230

Kangaroo I.

Coorong
N.P.

Victoria

Wangaratta

Snowy River
N.P.

C. Howe

Naracoorte

Grampians
N.P.

Bendigo

Croajingolong
N.P.

Mount Gambier

Ballarat

Melbourne

Morwell

Gippsland
Lakes N.P.

Portland

Geelong

Warrnambool

C. Otway

South East Cape

Bass Strait

King I.

*Furneaux
Group*

Marrawah

Burnie

*Tasman
Sea*

Devonport

Launceston

Queenstown

Tasmania

Hobart

South West
N.P.

South West Cape

Southport

Murray

SYDNEY

Map on page 108

The glittering harbour with its coat-hanger bridge, the pearly sails of the Opera House, the bronzed life-savers at Bondi Beach... most of the symbols that define Australia are located in Sydney

Sydney is where Australian indulgence finds its most spectacular backdrop, a city where leisure has been elevated to an art form. Yet Australia's largest metropolis, with four-and-a-half million people, can still baffle expectations. The natural beauty of the harbour and beaches often stands in stark relief to the man-made landscape: the narrow, traffic-clogged streets, the lacklustre architecture of its inner city, the endless orange-roofed expanse of its suburbia. However, if this is your first stop in Australia and the flight path of your aircraft takes you in a loop west of the city, with the Opera House and the Harbour Bridge cast in miniature against the harbour, chances are you'll be smitten.

A magnet for talent

To its critics – who mostly live in its traditional rival, Melbourne – Sydney is all glitz, obsessed with superficial show and appearance above substance. But none of this seems to matter to most Sydneysiders, and even less to visitors. The city continually lures many of the wealthiest, smartest and most artistically talented from the rest of Australia, and increasingly, the world, while real-estate values go through the roof. Everybody wants to live in "the capital of the Pacific Rim".

Yet few of the world's great cities have had such an unpromising start. On 26 January 1788, a fleet of 11 ships under the command of Captain Arthur Phillip landed a seasick gaggle of male convicts while the local Aborigines threw stones in a vain attempt to drive them away. The officers pitched their tents east of the freshwater Tank Stream at Sydney Cove, with the prisoners and their guards to the west (creating a social division that lasts to this day, with the wealthier suburbs of the east versus the have-nots of the west).

Main attractions
HARBOUR BRIDGE
OPERA HOUSE
BOTANIC GARDENS
SYDNEY TOWER
BONDI BEACH
BONDI MARKET
BLUE MOUNTAINS

LEFT: sailing Sydney Harbour.
RIGHT: the Opera House.

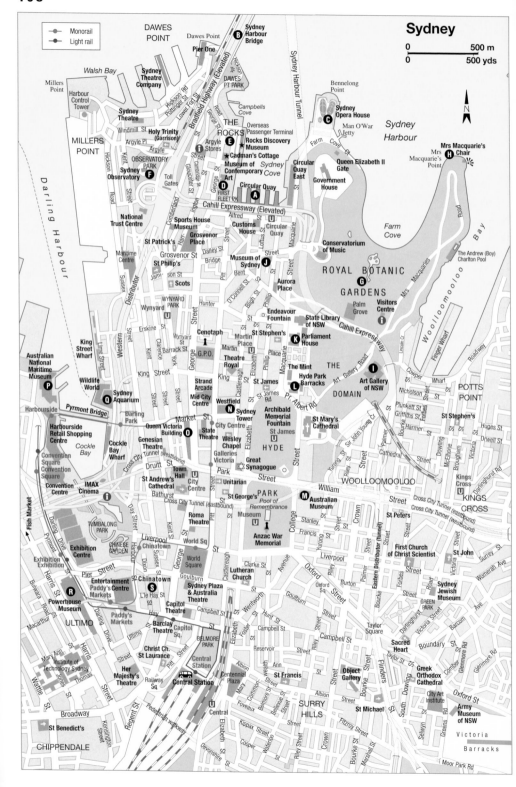

Sydney

Monorail
Light rail

0   500 m
0   500 yds

DAWES POINT
Dawes Point
Sydney Harbour Bridge **B**
Pier One

Walsh Bay
Sydney Theatre Company

Millers Point
Harbour Control Tower
Sydney Theatre
Windmill St   Holy Trinity (Garrison)
Argyle Pl
Argyle
St Patrick's

MILLERS POINT
OBSERVATORY PARK
Sydney Observatory **F**
Toll Gates

THE ROCKS
Argyle Stores **I**
Rocks Discovery Museum **E**
Cadman's Cottage
Museum of Contemporary Art **D**
Circular Quay **A**
FIRST FLEET PK

Campbells Cove
Overseas Passenger Terminal

Bennelong Point
Sydney Opera House **C**
Man O'War Jetty

Sydney Harbour

Mrs Macquarie's Chair **H**
Mrs Macquarie's Point

Circular Quay East
Queen Elizabeth II Gate
Government House

National Trust Centre
Sports House Museum
Grosvenor Place
St Philip's
Jamison St
Scots
St Patrick's

Customs House
Circular Quay
Museum of Sydney **J**
Aurora Place

Conservatorium of Music

ROYAL BOTANIC GARDENS **G**

Farm Cove

The Andrew (Boy) Charlton Pool

Wynyard Park
Cenotaph
Wynyard
G.P.O.
Theatre Royal
Strand Arcade
Mid City Centre
Westfield

Martin Place
St Stephen's **K**
Parliament House
The Mint
Hyde Park Barracks **L**
St James

Endeavour Fountain
State Library of NSW **i**

Art Gallery of NSW **I**

THE DOMAIN

POTTS POINT
St Stephen's

King Street Wharf
Australian National Maritime Museum **P**
Wildlife World
Sydney Aquarium **Q**
Pyrmont Bridge
Darling Park

Sydney Tower
City Centre
State Theatre
Archibald Memorial Fountain
St James
St Mary's Cathedral

WOOLLOOMOOLOO

Kings Cross
KINGS CROSS

Harbourside
Harbourside Retail Shopping Centre
Convention Square
Convention Centre
IMAX Cinema **i**

Cockle Bay
Cockle Bay Wharf
Genesian Theatre
Queen Victoria Building **O**
City Centre
Town Hall
St Andrew's Cathedral
Wesley Chapel
Galleries Victoria
Great Synagogue
Unitarian

HYDE PARK
Pool of Remembrance

Australian Museum **M**
St Peters

William Street

First Church of Christ Scientist
St John

Exhibition Centre
CHINESE GARDEN
TUMBALONG PARK
Chinatown
World Sq
World Square

St George's
Museum **U**
Roma Theatre

Lutheran Church
Anzac War Memorial

Liverpool
Oxford Street

Sydney Jewish Museum
GREEN PARK

Exhibition
Powerhouse Museum **R**
ULTIMO

Entertainment Centre
Paddy's Markets
Chinatown **S**
L'ile Hay St
Paddy's Markets

Sydney Plaza & Australia Theatre
Capitol Theatre
Barclay Theatre
Capitol Sq.
BELMORE PARK

Goulburn

Taylor Square

Sacred Heart
Greek Orthodox Cathedral
City Art Institute

Institute of Technology Sydney
Her Majesty's Theatre
Christ Ch. St Laurance
Central Station
Railway Sq
Central Station

Centennial Plaza
St Francis
Object Gallery
St Michael

Army Museum of NSW

SURRY HILLS

Victoria Barracks

Broadway
St Benedict's
CHIPPENDALE

Two weeks later, the women convicts disembarked, with a few children in tow (some of whom had been born during the 11-month voyage).

Today the site of these early landings is one of the most visited spots in Sydney: **Circular Quay** Ⓐ. This is the gateway to **Sydney Harbour** and the place where everyone should begin a visit. Ferries, Jetcats, water taxis and tour boats of every stripe plough in and out of its docks, taking passengers up and down the grand waterway of Port Jackson, described by Phillip as "the finest harbour in the world, where a thousand ship of the line may ride with the most perfect security." To get a feel for Sydney, hop on a ferry, take a seat outside and don't get off at all; all ferries eventually return home to the quay. There's a great view of Sydney's two familiar icons.

The Harbour Bridge

First to be constructed was the **Harbour Bridge** Ⓑ. The widest single-span bridge in the world, it was erected during the depths of the 1930s Depression as a symbol of hope in the future. It became dubbed the Coat Hanger, the Toast Rack and the Iron Lung (the latter for the number of people given work on its construction, which kept Sydney breathing). These days, despite dire predictions that rust is rotting it away from the inside, the bridge is still the major link between Sydney's northern and southern suburbs (there's also an underground tunnel).

The southeastern pylon on the Harbour Bridge is home to the **Pylon Lookout** museum (daily 10am–5pm; tel: 02-9240 1100; www.pylonlookout. com.au; charge), which leads up to a viewing platform with superb views of the harbour and city. Small-group guided climbs to the bridge's summit, each lasting 3½ hours, can be booked through BridgeClimb (daily; tel: 02-8274 7777; www.bridgeclimb. com). Unless you're seriously scared of heights, spend the cash and do the climb. You'll forget all about the deeply unattractive jumpsuits that are compulsory for safety once you see the priceless view from the top.

The Opera House

The second symbol began construction in 1959, and today is probably the most photographed site in Sydney. The **Opera House** Ⓒ (guided one-hour tours daily, every half-hour 9am–5pm; a two-hour backstage tour including breakfast is limited to eight visitors, daily at 7am; tel: 02-9250 7250; www. sydneyoperahouse.com; charge) is without a doubt one of the world's most spectacular buildings (or, as art critic Robert Hughes would have it, "the biggest environmental site-specific sculpture south of the Equator"). It was designed by Jørn Utzon, a Dane, after an international competition – although nobody at the time quite knew how it would be built. It was the first large-scale project to make extensive use of computer technology, but, even so, the construction was fraught with difficulties. Costs escalated. Utzon became caught up in the petty-minded moneygrubbing of Australian politics, and resigned in disgust in 1966. A state lottery raised

TIP

Take a ferry from Circular Quay to Cockatoo Island. It's a 20-minute journey out towards Parramatta and the reward is a Unesco World Heritage-listed jumble of 19th-century prison buildings and the remnants of a massive 20th-century shipyard. Take a picnic and wander at leisure.

BELOW: Sydney Harbour.

Ken Done (pronounced as in bone) is a popular local artist and designer who has a gallery in The Rocks exhibiting his paintings. A shop sells clothes, ceramics and other items featuring his work.

BELOW: Circular Quay and the city from the terrace of the Opera House.

the necessary cash, and by the time the completed building was opened by the Queen in 1973, it cost A$102 million – 15 times its initial budget. But few have ever complained about the price since. The Opera House became an immediate icon for Australia's new-found cultural independence.

Also overlooking the harbour, the Gothic Revival style is exemplified by **Government House** (guided tour only, every half-hour; Fri–Sun 10.30am–3pm; tel: 02-9931 5222; www.hht.net.au; free), formerly home to state governors and now open to the public. The ground-floor state rooms have some beautiful 19th- and 20th-century furniture and decoration.

Apart from the docking ferries, Circular Quay is a lively scene, packed with buskers, pedlars and office workers relaxing on their lunch breaks during the day, and busy with after-work drinkers and dining tourists at night. Just around the waterline lies the squat, yellow **Museum of Contemporary Art** ❶ (MCA; daily 10am–5pm; tel: 02-9245 2400; www.mca.com.au; free), whose outdoor café is the ulti-

mate lunch address on a sunny day. Those who might be inflamed by the idea of a video showing football star David Beckham asleep in a Madrid hotel room as a work of art might be tempted to keep their distance. But even if Sam Taylor Wood isn't your thing, the museum still won't disappoint: there's always a mix of fresh styles and new exhibitions to keep you interested.

The Rocks

Behind the MCA sits Sydney's most historic district, known as **The Rocks** ❷ after the sandstone bluffs from which the first convicts cut golden bricks for public buildings (take a look up the **Argyle Cut**, slicing straight through the cliffs – the pick marks are still easily identifiable). Almost immediately the area became the colony's main port, and warehouses grew up along the waterfront, backed by merchants' shops, offices, hotels, banks, bars and brothels that went along with the seafaring trade of the 19th century. But respectability always eluded The Rocks, and by the 1960s the area had long outlived its original mercantile function.

Today The Rocks is virtually an open-air museum, where you can absorb Australia's early history with a leisurely stroll – although the entire area is now unashamedly devoted to tourism. Avoid the markets on a Saturday unless you want to be stuck there for hours dodging the crowds. If you really want to visit, make it an evening excursion – you'll be spoilt for choice in overpriced but top-notch restaurants.

Sydney's oldest building

Next to the MCA is the tiny stone **Cadman's Cottage** (Tue–Sun 10am–4.30pm; free), built in 1816 and believed to be Sydney's oldest building, now housing a museum and an information centre. Only a small number of buildings remain from the first half of the 19th century. Many more date from the Victorian era, when cargoes

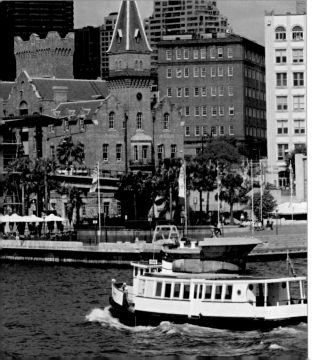

of wool, wheat and gold provided a rich source of income that allowed architectural flourishes of the period to blossom. The contrast between these ornate buildings and the simple, embellished stonework of the Georgian era is striking.

The Argyle Cut passes the **Argyle Centre** (a convict-era storehouse that is now a boutique shopping centre) and the **Garrison Church**, and eventually leads up a steep path to **Observatory Hill**. Although a fort was built on the hilltop in 1803 for officers in case of a convict uprising, the oldest building still standing is the Signal Station, which was erected in 1848. In 1855 the hill became the site for the **Sydney Observatory F** (daily 10am–5pm; tel: 02-9221 3485; www.sydneyobservatory.com.au; free), which began as a time-keeping device. Since 1982 the Observatory has been a museum of astronomy, with an imaginative **3-D Space Theatre** (daily, check times, bookings essential for night sessions; tel: 02-9221 3485; charge).

Today Observatory Hill is a lovely picnic spot with fine harbour views, making it a favourite viewing point for tourists and locals to watch the fireworks on New Year's Eve. Further towards Millers Point lies a network of narrow streets that have traditionally been home to wharf workers. The **Hero of Waterloo** and **Fortune of War** compete for the honour of being Sydney's oldest pub, with the **Palisade** one of the most atmospheric.

The Botanic Gardens

Following the waterline in the opposite direction from the quay leads you past the Opera House to the **Royal Botanic Gardens G** (daily sunrise–sunset; tel: 02-9231 8111; www.rbgsyd.nsw.gov.au; free) – a vast, voluptuous collection of antipodean flora, including some truly majestic Moreton Bay figs. Hidden amongst the sculpted lakes and exotic fronds is an excellent café-restaurant. If you decide to picnic on the lawns, be warned – the strutting, long-beaked ibis are notorious lunch burglars.

From **Mrs Macquarie's Point H** one gazes out at the tiny island of **Fort Denison**. This is also the site of the summer Open Air Cinema (one month every year; tel: 1300 366 649;

Bunting flutters on the old warehouses at The Rocks to celebrate Australia Day on 26 January.

BELOW: the Royal Botanic Gardens.

An installation at the Museum of Sydney symbolises links between Aboriginal and European cultures.

BELOW: the clock tower of the Sydney Central Railway.

www.stgeorgeopenair.com.au), where you can sip champagne and watch a recent film from a screen that seems to rise out of the harbour. You'd be hard-pressed to find a more beautiful backdrop to a cinema, but get in quick because tickets sell out fast.

Paths continue through the gardens to the **Art Gallery of New South Wales ❶** (Thur–Tue 10am–5pm, Wed 10am–9pm; tel: 02-9225 1744; www.art gallery.nsw.gov.au; free). This imposing edifice is crowned with the celestial names of Leonardo da Vinci, Michelangelo, Botticelli and the like, although not one of these artists is represented in the collection. What the gallery does contain is the country's finest grouping of Australian art, and the garden setting makes it perfect for an afternoon of browsing.

Sydney's **Central Business District** – the CBD, as many refer to it – is an oddly anonymous hodgepodge of glass skyscrapers and architectural styles from the past two centuries, all squeezed onto a street plan drawn up in Georgian times. It is best seen by strolling up Young Street from the

quay, past the 1846 classical revival **Customs House** (Mon–Fri 8am–midnight, Sat 10am–midnight, Sun 11am–5pm; tel: 02-9242 8551; www. cityofsydney.nsw.gov.au/customshouse; free) – now a cultural forum with an on-site lending library and rooftop restaurant – evoking Sydney's early days as a great imperial port.

Museum of Sydney

You then pass the **Museum of Sydney ❿** (daily 9.30am–5pm; tel: 02-9251 5988; www.hht.net.au; charge), which has entertaining sight-and-sound exhibits from the city's earliest days to today (*see pages 124–5*). Built on the site of the original Government House, remnants of the foundations (unearthed by accident in 1983) can now be seen inside the museum.

Cut over to Macquarie Street for a view of official Sydney: in quick succession come the **State Library** (Mon–Thur 9am–8pm, Fri 9am–5pm; Sat–Sun 10am–5pm; tel: 02-9273 1414; www. sl.nsw.gov.au; free) – which, although not the prettiest building in town, contains some of the most important archives of Australiana; **Parliament House ⓚ** (Mon–Fri 9am–5pm; tel: 02-9230 2111; www.parliament.nsw.gov.au; free) – the seat of the New South Wales state government; **Sydney Mint**; and **Hyde Park Barracks ⓛ**.

The barracks now houses one of Sydney's most popular museums (daily 9.30am–5pm; tel: 2-8239 2311; www. hht.net.au) charge). Designed in 1817 by convict architect Francis Greenway and completed in 1819, the building was first used to house hundreds of prisoners. Exhibits relating to the convict system include a re-creation of the prisoners' cramped canvas-hammock sleeping quarters.

At the end of Macquarie Street lies **Hyde Park**, with the powerful Art Deco **Anzac War Memorial**. To the east of the park on College Street stands the **Australian Museum ⓜ** (daily 9.30am–5pm; tel: 02-9320 6000; www.austmus.gov. au; charge), the oldest (1827) and one of the largest in the country. It is the foremost showcase of Australian natural history, and also includes an extensive Aboriginal section. Only a fraction of its collections is ever displayed, but the museum mounts ever-changing exhibitions designed to captivate visitors (and children in particular).

Sydney Tower

Cut back across Hyde Park towards Pitt and George streets, the two main arteries of the CBD, and where you'll find some very respectable shopping. The controversial needle of **Sydney Tower** is regarded as a phallic eyesore by many, but it has great views from the summit, plus the inevitable revolving restaurant – great for an after-hours cocktail.

Covering an entire city block is the **Queen Victoria Building** (Mon–Sat 9am–6pm; Thur until 9pm; Sun 11am–5pm; tel: 02-9264 9209; www. qvb.com.au; free). Built during the 1890s Depression as Sydney's main market, the arcade was lovingly restored in the 1980s as the city's leading collection of chic stores. The stained-glass windows, Byzantine arches and plaster ornamentaion have made the QVB, according to Pierre Cardin, "the most beautiful shopping centre in the world". Along with some chain stores and designer stores, you'll be able to feast on a few Australiana shops and the odd specialist boutique.

Darling Harbour

Slithering its way past the QVB is the controversial monorail, which, despite protests that it turns Sydney into a Disneyland, and promises by politicians that it will be torn down, shows no sign of slowing. This is the easiest way to get to **Darling Harbour**, largest of the city's modern developments. In the 1800s, this was the back door to Sydney, where most trading ships docked. It is now a touristy collection of shops and restaurants, with a **Maritime Museum** (daily 9.30am–5pm, Jan until 6pm; www.anmm.gov.au; free; *see pages 124–5*),

Aquarium (daily 9am–8pm; tel: 02-8251 7800; www.sydneyaquarium.com. au; charge), **Exhibition Centre** and **Chinese Garden** thrown in for good measure.

The Aquarium is the best place to see Australia's extraordinary aquatic life without getting wet – or eaten. As well as crocodiles and tanks full of multicoloured tropical fish, the Aquarium has transparent tunnels that take you underwater for a spectacular, fish-eye journey through various habitats teeming with sea creatures – the Great Barrier Reef, a seal sanctuary and the Open Oceanarium – where sharks, sea turtles and stingrays glide alongside.

After decades of trying to curb illegal gambling, the state government allowed a giant casino to be built, not far from the Maritime Museum in Pyrmont. **Star City Casino** (24 hours; tel: 02-9777 9000; www.starcity.com.au) brings a touch of Las Vegas to Sydney's waterfront.

Transfer to the Light Rail at the casino and get off two stops later at the **Fish Market** in Pyrmont (tel: 02-9004 1100; www.sydneyfishmarket.com.au). The ultimate seafood experience, Sydney's

Sydney Tower is often referred to by locals as Centrepoint Tower.

BELOW: sharks circle above at the Darling Harbour Aquarium.

Harbour-hopping

Sydney's green-and-yellow harbour ferries are perhaps one of the city's most pleasant form of public transport

Asurprising amount of the city can be seen by hopping from wharf to wharf. A five-minute ride directly opposite Circular Quay (the main ferry terminal) leads to the North Shore suburb of **Kirribilli**, where the prime minister and governor-general have official residences (and both are known to pop in to the legendary Kirribilli fish-and-chip shop for a meal beneath the bridge pylons).

On the other side of the bridge, **McMahons Point** is believed to have the best view in Sydney; running up to north Sydney, **Blues Point Road** has a string of much-favoured cafés. Only a bit longer is the ride to **Cremorne Point**, a dramatic promontory with a harbourside walk to Mosman (considered to be one of the best hikes in Sydney), where a ferry can be caught back to the quay.

Also accessible by ferry is **Taronga Park Zoo** (daily 9am–5pm; tel: 02-9969 2777; www.zoo. nsw.gov.au; charge). Surrounded by virgin bush, this must be one of the most beautiful zoo sites on Earth, with another heart-stopping panorama of the city (taronga is an Aboriginal word for "view across the water"). There are more than 5,000 animals in the collection, including all the local critters (this is your best chance to see a platypus, and many a snake that you would rather not encounter in the wild). In summer, classical, jazz and swing concerts are held in the zoo's gardens.

Around half of Sydney's beaches are within the harbour (nets are set up to keep the sharks at bay). One of the best, near the entrance to Middle Harbour, is **Balmoral**, which also has the famous Bathers's Pavilion restaurant on its shores. **Nielsen Park** at Vaucluse is a favoured picnic spot, while **Lady Jane** allows nude bathing. **Camp Cove**, on the southern side near the harbour entrance, permits topless bathing and is popular with families.

The most famous ferry ride of all is to **Manly**; it crosses through the open sea between the Heads, and on a rough day waves can dwarf the boats. The name was given by Captain Phillip in 1788 when he was struck by the "manly" bearing of the Aborigines he met there. In the 1930s, the isthmus became Australia's favourite holiday resort "seven miles from Sydney and a thousand miles from care." The family atmosphere has lingered. There is an 11km (8-mile) harbourside walk to the Spit from here (catch a bus back). On West Esplanade are **Manly Art Gallery and Museum** (Tue–Sun 10am–5pm; tel: 02-9976 1420; www.manlyaustralia.com.au; free), with a good selection of Australian paintings, and **Oceanworld** (daily 10am–5.30pm; tel: 02-8251 7877; www.oceanworld.com.au; charge) where visitors can watch sharks and stingrays being fed.

From Circular Quay a high-speed catamaran, the RiverCat, speeds down the river to **Parramatta** ("where the eels lie down" in the original tongue) – technically a city in its own right, although Sydneysiders persist in calling it a suburb. Parramatta still has several colonial buildings scattered around, including Old Government House (Tue–Fri 10am–4.30pm, Sat–Sun 10.30am–4pm; tel: 02-9635 8149; www.oldgovernmenthouse.com.au); an Explorer bus meets the RiverCat at the docks and transports passengers to the attractions.

Acting as a tourist attraction and famous Sydney icon, the harbour ferries transport more than 38,000 Sydneysiders into the city every day for work and they provide the quickest route to some seriously popular suburbs. ❑

LEFT: a harbour ferry approaches Circular Quay.

vast Fish Market mixes fish auctions, market stalls, restaurants and a seafood cooking school. Behind-the-scenes tours run on Mondays, Thursdays and Fridays (charge).

From here you can either take a stroll back to the monorail, or take the Light Rail back to Paddy's Markets, which leads to the **Powerhouse Museum** Ⓡ (daily 9.30am–5pm; tel: 02-9217 0111; www.powerhousemuseum.com; charge), a huge space devoted to science and technology, with lots of interactive displays *(see pages 124–5)*. From there, it is a short stroll back into Sydney's **Chinatown** Ⓢ, with its wall-to-wall Asian food.

Away from the centre

In many ways, it is the assortment of inner-city suburbs (as they are oddly called) that shows Sydney at its most genuine. In the late 19th century, row after row of terraced houses were thrown up as cheap accommodation for workers – usually with small gardens, tight porches and elaborate iron-lace decorations. In the early 20th century several families at a time would squeeze into these places, but as soon as they could, most moved out to the more spacious outer suburbs in search of the Aussie dream. But from the 1970s gentrification began apace.

In the inner west lies **Glebe** ❶, whose main thoroughfare, Glebe Point Road, is lined with boutiques and cafés – many catering to students from the nearby **University of Sydney**, a leafy haven which was built in a self-conscious Oxbridge style. Harbourside **Balmain** was once the raunchiest of working-class suburbs, with industrial dockworks and 41 pubs, one for every 366 residents. There are now 24 pubs, and the leafy ambience is decidedly more up-market. It can be reached by regular ferry from Circular Quay, and is an ideal spot for a Sunday stroll (the 19th-century waterfront residences are particularly impressive – they featured in Peter Carey's novel *Oscar and Lucinda*).

Kings Cross

The inner east is more of a mixed bag. In Victorian times, **Kings Cross** ❷ was an elegant, tree-lined suburb; in the 1920s and 1930s "The Cross" was Sydney's bohemian mecca, but the Vietnam War and the drug boom turned it into the city's sleazy red-light strip, albeit now on the decline. The recent addition of a horde of backpackers' hostels has hardly lifted the atmosphere.

Despite the grotty backdrop, The Cross also houses some of the city's most popular nightspots and best restaurants, not to mention a smattering of exclusive members-only (unless you're a gorgeous blonde, model or musician) bars, such as the infamous Hugo's on Bayswater Road. Don't be too wary of the area. It is worth exploring, although safer in a group, and some of the nightspots are pulsating pits of all-night dancing and cocktails.

While it's not a place to be at night, **William Street** is replacing the Paddington Street end of Oxford Street as the designer boutique capital of Sydney, with stylishly designed shop fronts popping up every month. Either side

BELOW: the less salubrious side of Kings Cross.

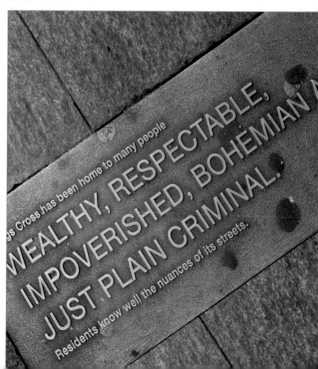

WEALTHY, RESPECTABLE, IMPOVERISHED, BOHEMIAN, JUST PLAIN CRIMINAL. ...gs Cross has been home to many people. Residents know well the nuances of its streets.

TIP

There are a lot of galleries in Paddington's backstreets where you can browse through the works of local artists, sculptors and photographers. Some of the smallest streets, such as Stafford Lane and Union, Broughton and Duxford streets, are very attractive.

of Darlinghurst and William the streets are filled with pretty, well-maintained homes, and **Victoria Street** houses more great eateries, fashionable bars and chic fashion stops.

Travel out into the eastern suburbs as far as Bondi Junction, and you'll find a sprawling shopping centre. **Oxford Street** has become another crucial promenade. It begins in the suburb of Darlinghurst, where hip bars and cool attitudes coexist with the best haircuts and the smallest dogs in town.

It is also where Sydney's gay community reigns supreme, most majestically where Oxford Street meets Taylor Square. Gay-friendly clubs, bars and shops snuggle happily together here, and every February the area hosts the **Sydney Gay and Lesbian Mardi Gras** parade. Thousands of Sydneysiders line the street, peek over balconies and try and nab a spot on a roof terrace while the flamboyant floats, processions, dancers and acts sashay past. A million more watch the event on TV from the comfort of their living rooms. Considering that homosexuality was illegal in NSW until 1982, prejudices seem to have been swept aside and locals of all backgrounds come out to applaud the efforts of the carefully constructed party.

Paddington

As Oxford Street enters **Paddington** ❸, the change in atmosphere is quite palpable. For many years now "Paddo" has been the address to have for young Sydneysiders. The colonial-style housing is chic (although not cheap!) and the boutiques, bars and restaurants that line Oxford are a weekend opportunity for the well-heeled and even betterdressed to show off their trendy tastes. It is not unusual to see the Paddo elite rummaging around the **Paddington Bazaar**, Sydney's oldest market, held in the grounds of the Uniting Church on a Saturday (10am–4pm), dressed in head-to-toe labels, straight from the covers of *Vogue*. However, the fairly recent addition of Bondi Junction's huge shopping mall has hit Paddo hard. The Sydney faves of Sass & Bide, Scanlon & Theodore and Lisa Ho survive, but more and more owners of small businesses are paying their last

BELOW:
hanging out on
Campbell Parade.

month's rent and closing up shop as they struggle to compete with the convenience of Bondi Junction or meet the ludicrously high rent rates. But if you love to people-watch almost as much as you love shopping for shoes, you will appreciate the community feel of Oxford Street – and it beats being stuck in an air-conditioned mall when there is sunny Sydney weather to soak up.

As you reach the summit of Oxford, before it heads along the dual carriageway to Bondi, you hit **Centennial Park**. A favourite spot all year round for those wanting some greenery, whether you want to run, rollerblade, picnic, cycle, horseride or just relax in a café with a coffee in the company of some very yummy eastern suburbs mummies, you can do it here. Great allyear round, in midsummer the Centennial is also home to the Moonlight Cinema (www.moonlight.com.au), a delightful opportunity to watch new blockbusters and old classics while lounging on a comfy beanbag in the park. Take a picnic (there are some great delis on Oxford) and a bottle of wine and relax in the great outdoors.

It's an unmissable treat for a Sydney summer night.

Sydney's beaches

From Paddington, it's a short bus or taxi ride to any of the eastern beaches – of which the most famous is certainly **Bondi ❹** (pronounced *Bond-eye*). It was from this great arc of sand in the late 1880s that the first Sydney "cranks" braved the ocean – breaking an old law that forbade swimming during daylight hours as indecent. The breakthrough came in 1902, when Manly newspaper proprietor William Gocher defied the ban and invited arrest. A similar challenge to the ban came the following year from a Waverley clergyman and a respectable bank clerk, and crowds of Sydneysiders soon followed suit. In 1906, the world's first life-saving club was set up, and 20 years later, crowds of up to 100,000 people were reported at Bondi on summer days. With its wide golden sands, ragged sandstone headlands and reliably fine rollers, Bondi had become another potent Sydney icon. Its status was further enhanced during the 2000 Olympics when Bondi

Australia has more than 11,000 beaches; if you look hard enough, you'll find one all to yourself.

Many beach hotels offer swimming pools right next to the ocean, just in case you prefer your water sans salt and waves.

BELOW: children learn to surf and swim from a very young age.

played host to the beach volleyball competition.

The beach is at its best, not surprisingly, in summer. Activity kicks off at dawn, with the joggers on the promenade, bodybuilders by the shore and surfies catching a few waves before work. Sun-worshippers arrive early, closely followed by busloads of tourists. The Bondi Pavilion opens up, selling ice creams and souvenirs; picnickers arrive with their fish and chips; and the activity continues until well after dark, when lovers take over the sands.

Bondi is also a suburb. **Campbell Parade**, the main beachfront thoroughfare, is a motley string of 1930s-era storefronts that seems to resist all improvement ("one of the great disappointments of Sydney," according to the writer Jan Morris). In the mid-1990s, talk of a Bondi Renaissance began as the suburb leapt to new heights of fashionability, and strings of New Australian restaurants opened on the North Bondi end. But still, the parade hangs on to its raffish, sand-gritted personality – and most Sydneysiders really would have it no other way.

The Bondi markets

The **Sunday Bondi Markets**, held each week 10am–5pm in the grounds of the Bondi Beach Public School, have helped establish many successful Sydney designers, and young hopefuls set up stalls each week in hope of being discovered. As if to emphasise the link, the streets behind the busy tourist trap of the parade are now lined with the fashionistas' boutiques, and are a great place to bag an expensive one-off.

But despite its historic and iconic status, the face of Bondi is changing. Slightly further away from the city than is comfortable – especially in summer when the 40-minute bus ride can take twice that time thanks to the throngs of tourists – Bondi is being eclipsed by some of the other eastern suburbs beaches, which are just as beautiful (although all much smaller than Bondi), but don't attract the crowds. The easiest way to see them all in a day is to walk the coastal path. **Coogee** is your best option to start from in summer because it is quicker to get to from the city on a bus.

After a face-lift, Coogee (once known as a poor cousin to trendy Bondi) is coming into its own with great restaurants and bars popping up all the time. The beach itself is flanked by the historic Wylie's Baths, hedonism and although the waves are not for surfers, there's many a boogie boarder to be found at the weekend. Deep Blue is probably the most high-class Coogee eatery, but A Fish Called Coogee can't be beaten for quality.

Following the coast along, you'll see the small beach of **Gordon's Bay**, after which you will hit **Clovelly**. Including a saltwater swimming pool and one of the best kiosks on the strip (try their milkshakes), Clovelly is popular with families because generally it doesn't get the big waves and it is a favourite spot for snorkelling. The Clovelly Hotel pub is also well known for its fantastic lunch and dinner menu – best served on one of their two decks – and you can rest assured that if there is a big sports game on, it will get some airplay on one of their massive screens.

Continue on through the stunning Waverly Cemetery until you come to **Bronte**. As well as being home to Aussie director Baz Luhrmann (and the late Heath Ledger), Bronte attracts parties of people throughout summer thanks to a crowd of free gas barbecues and some killer surf.

Next up is **Tamarama** beach, before you turn the corner to find yourself at Bondi. The walk is best in summer when there is little wind and before the sun hits its peak but, just in case, there are plenty of cafés and kiosks along the way to sustain you. If you are here in November, do not miss Sculpture by the Sea, a free exhibition of contemporary sculpture, which starts at Bondi and runs all the way to Bronte.

Watsons Bay

North of Bondi, New South Head Road runs to **Watsons Bay**, whose pub has the finest outdoor beer garden in Sydney, with views across the bobbing yachts to the city skyline. Next door is Doyle's, Sydney's oldest and best-known fish restaurant. It is a stiff hike up to **South Head** at the mouth of Port Jackson, but well worth it.

The route back to the city goes through one of the most exclusive suburbs, **Vaucluse**. At its centre is a magnificent mansion, **Vaucluse House** (Fri–Sun 9.30am–4pm; www.hht.net.au; charge), built in 1827 for the statesman, poet and explorer William Charles Wentworth. The tearooms are charming, as are the garden picnic grounds. Swanky **Double Bay** is synonymous with Old Money, although there is also a large Central European contingent that has made the grade.

The Blue Mountains

Just 65km (40 miles) west of Sydney lie the **Blue Mountains**, the range that divides the populous, beach-fringed coastal plain from Australia's notoriously flat, harsh interior. It was an effective barrier to the colony's first explorers, whose efforts to conquer this section of the Great Dividing Range were thwarted by the rugged sandstone cliffs. The footsteps of the trio who (in 1813) successfully found the narrow

The original owner of Vaucluse House, William Charles Wentworth, was born in 1790. The son of a convict, he took part in the first successful inland exploration across the Blue Mountains and co-founded the colony's first independent newspaper, The Australian, in 1824.

BELOW:
an aerial view shows Sydney's suburban sprawl.

Royal National Park

Only 32km (20 miles) from Sydney, the **Royal National Park** (daily sunrise–8.30pm; tel: 02-9542 0648; charge) was established in 1879 and is the world's second-oldest national park – after Yellowstone in the United States.

The Royal packs incredible natural diversity into a relatively small area. Offering riverside picnics, great surf beaches, clifftop heathland walks, rainforest cycle tracks and much more, the park also has more than 60 camping sites.

A daily entrance fee is charged, although if you're going to be spending a lot of time visiting the national parks, an annual pass is more economical.

There is a strict code of care when it comes to conserving the natural beauty of the parks, so read up on the rules and live by them while you're there.

TIP

If you visit the Blue Mountains at the end of September, take time to stop in Leura during the town's Garden Festival, when many of the beautiful private gardens open to the public (www.leura gardensfestival.com).

passes are now followed westwards by the main route out of Sydney, the **Great Western Highway**. Today those three pioneers – Blaxland, Wentworth and Lawson – are remembered in the names of towns along the highway as it winds up into the mountains. It was not until the 1920s that this "rude peculiar country" took off as a holiday destination for fashionable Sydneysiders. Small European-style guesthouses sprang up, catering to honeymooners and families escaping the summer heat. In 1932, a group of bushwalkers came across a farmer about to cut down a gorgeous blue gum forest in the Grose Valley. They begged him to stop, and in the end offered to buy the land. It was the beginning of a movement that has since protected almost 1 million hectares (2½ million acres) of Australia's most magnificent wilderness.

Despite the almost impenetrable barrier the Blue Mountains presented to early travellers, they are a sandstone plateau reaching a height of only 1,100 metres (3,600ft). Erosion has caused the stone fall away to form sheer cliff faces punctuated by picturesque waterfalls.

The **Blue Mountains National Park** (tel: 02-4787 8877; vehicle charges apply), totalling 247,000 hectares (950 sq miles), is well served by bushwalking tracks and picnic and camping spots. Small towns are riddled with fine restaurants, old-style cafés and antique stores catering to weekenders.

Leura

As you drive up from Sydney, first stop should be **Leura ❺**, a classic Blue Mountains hamlet; it's a tidy, picturesque railway town that makes an ideal lunch break. The region's main town, **Katoomba ❻**, is perched on the edge of the Jamison Valley, and shows off its natural wonders to the best advantage at **Echo Point**, which overlooks one of the state's most photogenic rock formations, the **Three Sisters**. Always busy with tourists, Echo Point has a well-equipped tourist information centre. A great place to take a breather before or after a hike, it might also be wise to take a picnic.

High on the list of breathtaking experiences is the **Scenic Railway** that winds down into a tree-clad gorge and

BELOW: Gardens of Stone National Park and Wolgan Valley.

is claimed to be the world's steepest railway. There are many footpaths for one-day walks in the area – an excellent choice is hiking down the Golden Stairs to the rock formations known as the **Ruined Castle**.

Katoomba has a giant cinema with a screen as tall as a six-storey building; its feature on the Blue Mountains, The Edge, is quite stunning.

Some 10 minutes' drive further west along the highway looms the **Hydro Majestic Hotel**, an Art Deco-style former casino that catered to high society in the 1920s and is now being restored. **Blackheath ❼** has some of the best guesthouses and restaurants, along with rewarding walks and the unmissable **Govett's Leap**, a spectacular lookout over the Grose Valley.

The village of **Mount Victoria** is the highest in the Blue Mountains. As in so many of the surrounding settlements, the preservation of historic buildings, especially along Station Street, makes this spot a pleasure to wander through, or bed down for the night in one of the beautiful cottages – priceless views guaranteed.

Jenolan Caves

As the road drops from the mountains down the steep Victoria Pass, it narrows to cross a convict-built bridge that was part of the first road through to the rich wool, wheat, cattle and sheep country to the west. A little way on, and 46km (29 miles) south of the highway, the magnificent Jenolan Caves incorporate a mighty series of underground limestone halls encrusted with stalactites and stalagmites. In the 1920s this was the premier honeymoon spot for young Australians, who regarded the arduous journey and difficult conditions as a badge of honour.

On the highway, 12km (7½ miles) past the Jenolan Caves turn-off, signposts point to a monument to the ingenuity used in solving one of the 19th century's greatest engineering problems at **Lithgow**. It is the railway line which originally conquered the steep descent out of the Blue Mountains, known as the **Zig-Zag Railway** – so named for its unique method of overcoming the almost sheer mountain side. The zigzag line was finished in 1869, but was abandoned in 1910 for a more modern

Leura's Everglades gardens (37 Everglades Avenue; daily 10am–5pm; tel: 02-4784 1938; www. everglades.org.au) integrate local and European trees and plants.

BELOW LEFT: the Skyway cable car crosses Jamison Valley. **BELOW:** Leura Post Office now houses a restaurant.

Map on pages 116–117

TIP

Almost every December the Domain hums with the only major music festival devoted solely to antipodean acts: Homebake. All the greats of the Australian and New Zealand music scene have headlined.

BELOW:
fishing in the Hawkesbury River.

descent. Dedicated train buffs have restored the line to give day excursions travelling back into railway history (daily 11am, 1pm and 3pm; tel: 02-6355 2955; www.zigzagrailway.com.au).

Picturesque colonial towns also cluster on the eastern edge of the Blue Mountains. Peppered with historic buildings, the atmosphere of these hidden settlements is truly unique. Acting like a kind of time capsule of Australian colonial history, the **Hawkesbury** area was established in 1794 when settlers arrived to farm their 12 hectares (30 acres). Many of the descendants from these pioneers still work and live in the district, giving it a truly rustic Aussie atmosphere.

There are countless bushwalking and camping opportunities in the town of **Windsor**, as well as the new Hawkesbury Regional Gallery (The Deerubbin Centre; Mon–Fri 10am–4pm, Sat–Sun 10am–3pm; tel: 02-4560 4441; free), but its main appeal is the atmospheric colonial architecture, the venerable Macquarie Arms Hotel and a lively Sunday street market. **Richmond** has a handful of fine Georgian

streetscapes and offers camping, canoeing and swimming.

Historic towns

Closer to Sydney, on the southwestern edge of the conurbation, lie several more historic towns. In 1805 John Macarthur was granted nearly 2,000 hectares (5,000 acres) to raise sheep in **Camden**, the beginning of the nation's wool industry. The Camden-Campbelltown-Picton region is still known as Macarthur Country, and **Camden Park House** (1835) is owned by descendants of John Macarthur; it is open to groups by appointment – tel: 02-4655 8466 – with an open day in the third week of September. Camden (pop. 8,000) is the centre of a dairy region focused on the Nepean River Valley.

Sixteen km (10 miles) southwest of Camden, tiny **Picton** also has numerous remnants of 19th-century settlement. Upper Menangle Street is listed by the National Trust as "representing a typical country town street" of 100 years ago. It is a fine base from which to explore the scenic surrounding region.

North of Sydney

An hour's drive north of Sydney lies one of New South Wales' most beautiful national parklands, **Ku-ring-gai Chase National Park ❽** (tel: 02-9472 8949; vehicle charge payable). Hundreds of Aboriginal carvings dot the cliffs here, which often give sweeping views of the countryside and Cowan Creek: the easiest to reach are on the **Basin Trail** off West Head Road. At the mouth of the Hawkesbury River is **Broken Bay ❾**, a favourite recreational area, where boaters and picnickers flock at weekends.

Palm Beach, home of the Aussie TV soap *Home and Away*, is one of Greater Sydney's smarter neighbourhoods, and its beach is rated highly by surfers. If you're short of time, you can visit this area by seaplane; these leave from Rose Bay in the city, landing in Pittwater. ❑

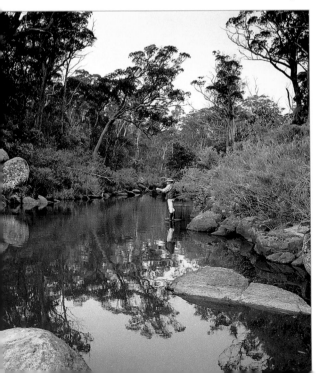

RESTAURANTS AND BARS

Restaurants

Prices for a three-course dinner per person with a half-bottle of house wine:
$ = under A$50
$$ = A$50–80
$$$ = A$80–120
$$$$ = over A$120

Across the Harbour Bridge

Aqua Dining
Corner Paul & Northcliff streets, Milsons Point
Tel: 02-9964 9998
www.aquadining.com.au
Open: L & D daily. $$$
With a blinder of a position by the Harbour Bridge, Aqua is ambitious modern cooking with a high success rate.

Milsons
17 Willoughby Street, Kirribilli
Tel: 02-9955 7075
www.milsonsrestaurant.com.au
Open: L Mon–Fri, D Mon–Sat. $$$
Up by the northern end of the bridge sits this reliable purveyor of modern Australian cooking.

Chinatown and Haymarket

The Eight
Level 3, Market City, 9–13 Hay Street, Haymarket
Tel: 02-9282 9988
www.theeightrestaurant.com.au
L & D daily. $
Sydney's biggest Chinese restaurant and dim sum venue. Go for brunch on Sunday. BYO.

Golden Century
393–399 Sussex Street, Haymarket
Tel: 02-9212 3901
www.goldencentury.com.au

L & D daily. $
Chinese-style seafood at its best, and with all the bustle of a Hong Kong dim sum restaurant.

Circular Quay to Bennelong Point

Aria
1 Macquarie Street, East Circular Quay
Tel: 02-9252 2555
www.ariarestaurant.com
Open: L Mon–Fri, D daily. $$$$
Contemporary cooking with a French influence scores a lot of points in this smart restaurant right on Circular Quay and with outstanding views.

Guillaume at Bennelong
Sydney Opera House, Bennelong Point
Tel: 02-9241 1999
www.guillaumeatbennelong.com.au
Open: L Thur–Fri, D Mon–Sat. $$$$
This award-winning restaurant offers modern French cuisine from Guillaume Brahimi. For food and setting it can't be beaten. Must book.

Downtown Sydney

Bilson's
Radisson Plaza Hotel, 27 O'Connell Street
Tel: 02-8214 0496
www.bilsons.com.au
Open: L Mon–Fri, D Tue–Sat. $$$$
The extravagant classic French-based cuisine from Tony Bilson is absolutely scrumptious and available in tasting menus at three price levels.

Botanic Gardens Restaurant
Royal Botanic Gardens,

Mrs Macquarie's Road
Tel: 02-9241 2419
Open: B Sat–Sun, L daily. $$
Another lovely setting, this time in the Botanic Gardens. Serves modern Australian dishes, but patience may be needed.

The Summit
Level 47, Australia Square, 264 George Street
Tel: 02-9247 9777
www.summitrestaurant.com.au
Open: L Mon–Fri, D daily. $$$
Revolving restaurant with amazing views, decorated in space-age style. You wouldn't notice if the food was poor, but it isn't.

Hyde Park to Surry Hills

Beppi's
21 Yurong Street (corner Stanley Street), East Sydney
Tel: 02-9360 4558
www.beppis.com.au

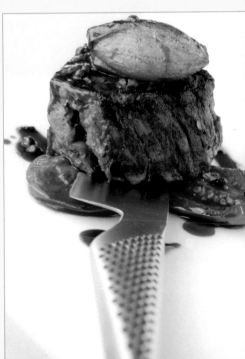

Open: L Mon–Fri, D Mon–Sat. $$$
This traditional restaurant, popular with the media, is the finest in Sydney's Little Italy. Opened in 1956 by Beppi Polese and family-run to this day.

Diethnes
336 Pitt Street, Hyde Park
Tel: 02-9267 8956
www.diethnes.com.au
Open: L & D Mon–Sat. $
One of Sydney's oldest Greek restaurants. Favourites like moussaka and lamb casserole, complemented by Greek coffee and baklava.

Longrain
85 Commonwealth Street, Surry Hills
Tel: 02-9280 2888
www.longrain.com
Open: L Thur–Fri, D daily. $$$

RIGHT: a steak dinner at The Summit.

Prices for a three-course dinner per person with a half-bottle of house wine:
$ = under A$50
$$ = A$50–80
$$$ = A$80–120
$$$$ = over A$120

Spacious 100-year-old warehouse with chic ambience and terrific fusion of Thai and Chinese.

Marque
4/5 355 Crown Street, Surry Hills
Tel: 02-9332 2225
www.marquerestaurant.com.au
Open: L Fri, D Mon–Sat. $$$
Elegant French cuisine from master chef Mark Best. For sophisticated food with imagination.

Machiavelli
123 Clarence Street
Tel: 02-9299 3748
www.machiavelli.com.au
Open: L & D Mon–Fri. $$$
Big, loud Italian restaurant. The massive antipasto dishes are the best.

The Malaya
39 Lime Street, King Street Wharf, Darling Harbour
Tel: 02-9279 1170
www.themalaya.com.au
Open: L Mon–Sat, D daily. $$$
Authentic Malaysian cuisine – reputedly the best laksa in town. Dine by the water.

529 Kent Street
Tel: 02-9267 2900
www.tetsuyas.com
Open: L Sat, D Tue–Sat. $$$$
Tetsuya Wakuda combines French and Japanese cooking techniques with the freshest of Australian ingredients to produce Sydney's most exciting food. Book way ahead.

The Wharf
Pier 4, Hickson Road, Walsh Bay
Tel: 02-9250 1761
www.wharfrestaurant.com.au
Open: L & D Mon–Sat. $$
Interestingly eclectic food in a casual industrial space propped out over the water.

Zaaffran
Level 2, Harbourside Shopping Centre, Darling Harbour
Tel: 02-9211 8900
www.zaaffran.com.au
Open: L & D daily. $$
Australia's only 5-star Indian restaurant. Traditional, home-style Indian cooking, presented with a contemporary flair.

Pyrmont
Flying Fish
Jones Bay Wharf, 19–21 Pirrama Road, Pyrmont
Tel: 02-9518 6677
www.flyingfish.com.au
Open: L Tue–Fri & Sun, D Mon–Sat. $$$
Old wharf building, offset by theatrical lighting. Fish prepared with flair.

Bel Mondo
Gloucester Walk (up Argyle Stairs from Argyle Street)
Tel: 02-9241 3700
www.belmondo.com.au
Open: D Tue–Sat. $$$
Watch the chef preside over the preparation of Italian-style food in an open kitchen on a raised dais.

est.
Establishment Hotel, 252 George Street
Tel: 02-9240 3000
www.merivale.com/establishment/est
Open: L Mon–Fri, D Mon–Sat. $$$$
Enjoy Peter Doyle's brilliantly accomplished modern cuisine in classy surroundings, with an adjoining sushi restaurant, cigar bar and an elegantly retro downstairs bar. Top marks.

Quay
Overseas Passenger Terminal, The Rocks
Tel: 02-9251 5600
www.quay.com.au
Open: L Tue–Fri, D daily. $$$$
Inspired cuisine with an unmistakable French influence puts Quay at the summit of local cuisine.

Sailors Thai
106 George Street
Tel: 02-9251 2466
www.sailorsthai.com.au
Open: L Mon–Fri, D Mon–Sat. $$$
Beautifully crafted Thai street food. There's a cheaper option in the downstairs canteen.

Yoshii
115 Harrington Street
Tel: 02-9247 2566
www.yoshii.com.au
Open: L Tue–Fri, D Mon–Sat. $$$$
Simplicity and experimentation are the key ingredients at this Japanese restaurant.

Original Balkan
217 Oxford Street Darlinghurst
Tel: 02-9331 7670
Open: L Fri–Sun, D daily. $$
Refreshed after a fire in 2010, the Balkan has some of the best and cheapest dishes in town, cooked the Croatian way. BYO.

Café Sel et Poivre
263 Victoria Street, Darlinghurst
Tel: 02-9361 6530
www.seletpoivre.com.au
Open: B, L & D daily. $
Good-value French cuisine, served with gusto. Opens daily at 7am for breakfast.

Hugos Bar Pizza
33 Bayswater Road, Kings Cross
Tel: 02-8116 8555
www.hugos.com.au
Open: D Tue–Sun. $$
If you've ever yearned for a super-cool hangout with high-class pizza, this is it.

Omerta
235 Victoria Street, Darlinghurst
Tel: 02-9360 1011
www.omerta.com.au
Open: D Tue–Sun. $$
Hard to keep quiet about such good sharing plates of Italian food.

LEFT: Chef Tetsuya Wakuda.

Glebe

Boathouse on Blackwattle Bay
End of Ferry Road, Glebe
Tel: 02-9518 9011
www.boathouse.net.au
Open: L Thur–Sun, D Tue–Sun. $$$
Some of Sydney's best seafood in a converted boathouse on the edge of the harbour.

Eastern suburbs

Claude's
10 Oxford Street, Woollahra
Tel: 02-9331 2325
www.claudes.com.au
Open: D Tue–Sat. $$$$
An up-market restaurant with discreet atmosphere, serving the best French food in Sydney with wonderful desserts. BYO.

Pier
594 New South Head Road, Rose Bay
Tel: 02-9327 6561
www.pierrestaurant.com.au
Open: L & D daily. $$$
Consistently voted Sydney's best seafood restaurant, this beautifully sleek outfit hovers over the harbour waters.

Northside

The Bathers' Pavilion
4 The Esplanade, Balmoral Beach
Tel: 02-9969 5050
www.batherspavilion.com.au
Open: L & D daily. $$$$
Long-established and still hitting the spot for that sophisticated beach-side occasion.

El Toro Loco
49–53 North Steyne, Manly
Tel: 02-9977 0999
www.eltoroloco.com.au
Open: B, L & D daily. $$
Tapas from TV chef Miguel Maestre in a boisterous waterfront barn.

Jonah's
69 Bynya Road, Palm Beach
Tel: 02-9974 5599
Open: B Sat–Sun, L & D daily.

$$$
Popular, long-established restaurant in a romantic setting with outdoor dining and water views. Not cheap, but good value.

Southside

Sean's Panaroma
270 Campbell Parade, Bondi Beach
Tel: 02-9365 4924
www.seanspanaroma.com.au
Open: L Fri–Sun, D Wed–Sat. $$$
An eccentric little place at the north end of Bondi Beach. The modern Australian menu keeps this local legend ahead of the arriviste pack. BYO.

Western suburbs

Pho Minh
42 Arthur Street, Cabramatta
Tel: 02-9726 5195
Open: B, L & D daily. $
One of the many Vietnamese noodle eateries in Cabramatta, basic but spacious, with very economical prices. Also has a seafood menu, and simple, no-fuss service.

Sahra by the River
2/76 Phillip Street, Parramatta
Tel: 02-9635 6615
www.sahrabytheriver.com.au
Open: L & D daily. $$
Classic Lebanese cooking that doesn't need belly dancing to draw the crowds, but it's there anyway at weekends.

Cafés, Bars and Pubs

Downtown Sydney

Hyde Park Barracks Café
Queen Square, Macquarie Street
Tel: 02-9222 1815
www.hyderparkbarrackscafe.com.au
Open: L daily. $$
Over the road from Hyde Park, this large café has a historic, colonial feel.

Modern Australian cuisine. Fully licensed.

Haymarket/Hyde Park

Civic Hotel
388 Pitt Street (corner Goulburn Street)
Tel: 02-8080 7000
www.civichotel.com.au
Open: L & D daily, bar till late. $$
The Civic's 1940s pub, with an attractive, retro style, hosts live music, club sessions and jazz.

Three Wise Monkeys
555 George Street (corner Liverpool Street)
Tel: 02-9283 5855
www.3wisemonkeys.com.au
Open: daily. $
A pub that attracts young locals as well as the fashion-conscious.

The Rocks

Hero of Waterloo
81 Lower Fort Street
Tel: 02-9252 4553
Open: daily. $
A truly historic Rocks pub and a local landmark. If you want to experience a true-blue Australian hotel,

this much-loved watering hole is a prime choice.

Suburbs

Bar Coluzzi
322 Victoria Street, Darlinghurst
Open: daily until late. $
A local landmark for coffee-lovers.

Piccolo Bar
6 Roslyn Street, Kings Cross
Open: daily till late. $
A tiny place in the thick of Kings Cross street activity, and something of an institution.

Royal Hotel
Five Ways, Paddington
www.royalhotel.com.au
Tel: 02-9331 2604
Open: L & D daily. $$
Situated in the pleasant, villagey Five Ways. Ornate Victorian architecture and affordable pub food.

Hotel Bondi
178 Campbell Parade, Bondi Beach
Tel: 02-9130 3271
Open: L & D daily until late. $
Loud, friendly, sun- and sea-soaked, despite its yuppification.

RIGHT: beach-front dining.

NEW SOUTH WALES

New South Wales's greatest asset is its diversity. From Sydney you can head north for tropical banana plantations, south for snowcapped mountains or west for the expanses of the Outback

There's a lot more to Australia's most populous state than its capital city. While Sydneysiders may have the harbour as their playground, elsewhere in the state you can unwind by hiking in the rainforest, diving at a coral reef, or just counting the cattle as they come in for the muster. Similarly, while Sydney may be enjoying a balmy day, there may be snow on the southern Alps and dust storms sweeping across the sunbaked towns in the western Outback, while monsoons flood the lush farming country of the northeast.

The Pacific Highway

For generations, the Pacific Highway has been Sydney's escape route to the sun. Generations of Sydneysiders have made the regular pilgrimage up the coast, fleeing the winter chill, the big-city hustle, or just the tedium of the everyday. Not so long ago, the road passed through country that was still largely undeveloped: after the outskirts of Sydney thinned out into nothingness, you were in a place where the bush and the breezes did most of the talking.

These days, the Pacific Highway has been transformed into a traffic-laden artery that cuts through expanding coastal towns and seafront subdivisions. However, motorists may still enjoy a flickering parade of gumtrees in the late afternoon light, along with occasional glimpses of the Pacific Ocean's white-lace hems (despite its name, the Pacific Highway is generally several kilometres from the coast).

At a pinch, you can make the drive to Queensland in 12 hours, but it's much better to take some time to explore the unpredictable patchwork of boutique wineries and old-fashioned milk bars, country pubs and fish'n'chips shops, fabled surf spots and vast tropical plantations. Three days is the bare minimum needed to sample at least some of the coast, but if you want to do some serious exploring, five days is recommended.

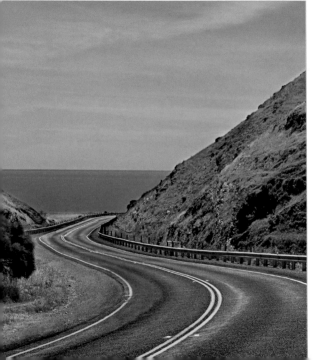

LEFT: the coastal road.

The trip north starts at Sydney Harbour Bridge. Northbound traffic soon throttles down into the four lanes of the Pacific Highway; at peak hours, this artery is clotted every few minutes at stop lights and suburban intersections, although at other times it flows freely. After negotiating past the cars of the well-heeled upper North Shore, you finally hit the beginning of the Newcastle Freeway at **Wahroonga**.

Where the highway crosses the **Hawkesbury River** at **Brooklyn**, a vista of ridges, valleys and arms of open water spreads east and west. This is a popular weekend playground for many Sydneysiders, who rent cabin cruisers and drift among the bays and inlets. Many companies offer cruises; a highlight is the River Boat Mail Run, the local post service departing from Brooklyn, which also carries passengers (www.hawkesburyriverferries.com.au).

Upstream lies **Wiseman's Ferry**, where former convict Solomon Wiseman opened the first ferry across the river in 1827. A free car ferry takes you to the rugged bush-clad sandstone cliffs of **Dharug National Park** (tel: 02-4320 4200). Walkers, cyclists and horse riders can travel a stretch of the Great North Road, literally carved out of the rock by convicts in the 1830s.

The commercial hub of this central coast region (a mixed bag of retirees, new industries and Sydney commuters) is a detour away at the not-terribly-alluring **Gosford**. But beyond the urban sprawl are the orchards and forests of the **Mangrove Mountain** area, plus a string of beautiful beaches to escape to. Nearby is the **Australian Reptile Park** (daily 9am–5pm; tel: 02-4340 1022; www.reptilepark.com.au; free).

At **Doyalson**, the Pacific Highway heads along a ridge between the ocean and **Lake Macquarie**. Frequently overlooked by tourists, the lake (particularly its western shore) is a fascinating relic of a past age, when working folk could afford water frontages. The mining village of **Wangi Wangi**, for many years the retreat of the artist Sir William Dobell, is a classic example of lake-shore charm.

Newcastle

The second-largest city in New South Wales, **Newcastle**, was long burdened with a reputation as an unsophisticated industrial hub. But when steel production stopped in 2000, the town worked hard to reinvent itself as a cultural centre. Helped by a lively waterfront development, beautifully preserved heritage buildings and a large student population to liven things up, it is developing as a destination in its own right. Newcastle also makes a great base to explore the region, with easy access to the boating and bushlands of Lake Macquarie to the south and expansive, wild Myall Lakes to the north, not to mention its own impressive surf beaches. As a bonus, there are the prosperous wineries of the lower **Hunter Valley ❶**, one of Australia's premier wine-growing districts.

Many of the area's hillsides were originally settled in the pursuit of coal. Coal mining is still a thriving local industry, along with aluminium smelters, giant

The redback spider is the most venomous in all of Australia. Luckily the antivenom is commerically available.

BELOW: milking a tiger snake.

New South Wales

open-cut mines and power stations, providing a surprising flipside to the area's famed wine industry. Turning off from Newcastle, you reach **Maitland**, a city rich in historic buildings. From there, the road leads through one winery after another, with most of them gathered around **Pokolbin**.

As the highway heads deeper into the valley, the pace of life slows down. **Singleton** is an appealing mixture of modern and old civic buildings and private homes.

The town of **Scone** (rhymes with *own*) is pretty but unremarkable save for its horsiness. This is the home of thoroughbred stud farms, horse shows and the sport of polo. Much of New England is squatter territory, where the sons and daughters of the landed gentry (or those aspiring to it) continue the traditions of Mother England: good riding skills, political conservatism and bad dress sense. Scone hosts several major polo tournaments, of course.

While the Hunter Valley is very pleasant to visit, its scenery is not that spectacular; in high summer, its low hills can become unbearably hot.

Many wine buffs now prefer to head an hour's drive further east to visit the lesser-known vineyards around **Mudgee**. The picturesque village of **Gulgong** makes an ideal base; it was the childhood home of the poet Henry Lawson, and has a centre devoted to him, as well as a pioneer museum.

Port Stephens

Back on the Pacific Highway, north of Newcastle the road crosses the Hunter River at Hexham and skirts the western shore of **Port Stephens**. Two-and-a-half times the size of Sydney Harbour and blessed with both calm swimming coves and ocean beaches perfect for surfing, Port Stephens is home to a number of popular resorts such as the sophisticated **Nelson Bay**, and quieter settlements such as **Tea Gardens** and **Hawks Nest**. The bay's most famous attraction is its large population of bottlenose dolphins. Between May and November it also offers whale-watching opportunities. The aquatic reserves at **Fly Point** and **Halifax Point** are popular with divers, and the surrounding bush offers ample walking trails.

The Hunter Valley region has more than 140 wineries to explore.

BELOW: Segenhoe Stud Farm, Scone.

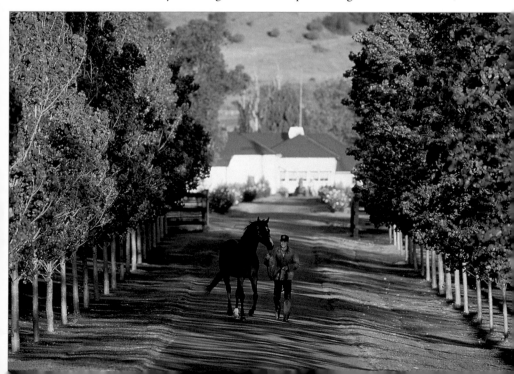

Whales and Dolphins

Watching a pod of dolphins splashing just beyond the breakers turns a day at the beach into something very special

The coast of New South Wales is one of the best places to see whales and dolphins in the wild. While dolphins frolic near the beach, the whales' winter migration takes them along the length of the state's coastline. Over the past few years, stray whales have spent several days in Sydney Harbour, to the delight of ferry passengers.

The most common whales are humpbacks, which travel north along the coast from about May, heading into the warm waters off the Queensland coast and returning south between September and November. Other species that are sighted less frequently include southern right whales, false killer whales, orcas, minke and, very occasionally, blue whales, the biggest creatures on the planet.

All the major holiday towns along the coast offer whale- and dolphin-watch cruises. Whale tours at Eden, deep on the state's south coast, have a fascinating edge to them, a little like visiting the scene of a crime with the criminal who did the deed. Until the 1930s, the town of Eden was a whaling station, and the various species of whales were all hunted in a gruesome alliance between killer whales and whaling boats. Paradoxically, Eden was one of the first towns in the state to develop a whale-watching industry, and its whaling history, the depth of knowledge that these operators bring to their task and their obvious affection for "their" whales make this more than just a wildlife tour.

A two-hour drive south of Sydney, Jervis Bay has a pod of resident dolphins, and the relatively placid waters of the bay make this a prime viewing spot for water-bound mammalian antics. To the north of Sydney, Port Stephens, Coffs Harbour and Byron Bay all offer their own whale- and dolphin-watching cruises.

Unlike the fast, acrobatic dolphins that never seem to idle for long, whales move slowly. On a whale-watch trip, the vessel will probably venture out into the open sea, where it will spend a good deal of time stopped and pitching in the waves while watching the whales. For anyone who suffers from motion sickness, this is not an ideal situation. If you start feeling queasy when you're out at sea, it's already too late to do much about it. If you are subject to seasickness, take medication well before you set foot on the boat.

An excursion is typically full of competitive anticipation, as children and adults alike vie to be the first to catch a glimpse of the quarry. However, once a whale sighting is made, vessels are not allowed to approach closer than 100 metres (330ft). Whales are curious creatures and they will often swim closer to a stationary vessel, but you can't count on a close-up look, and larger vessels with an upper deck will usually give you a better vantage point. The best place to stand is usually forward of the bridge.

Unfortunately, much of the action with whales and dolphins takes place below the water, and out of sight if you're standing on the deck of a boat. But if the vessel is properly equipped with the right equipment, you can tune in and listen to what's happening below. Whales and dolphins communicate via high-pitched squeaks and whistles. Whales, in particular, are known for their beautiful songs, and the humpback is one of the most vocal of all the whales. If your vessel has a hydrophone, an underwater microphone, you can listen to them talking over the public-address system. ❑

LEFT: the dusky dolphin is a different species from the more commonly seen Pacific white-sided dolphin.

Myall Lakes

About 40km (25 miles) north of Port Stephens you reach Bulahdelah, the gateway to the beautiful **Myall Lakes** ❷. Preserving these aquatic pearls as a National Park was an early victory for conservationists. Paperbarks, palms and other wetland vegetation crowd the shores, while the waterways are filled with bird life. Surrounding the chain of lakes is national parkland where nature-lovers may camp in the wild. The beaches at the tiny community of **Seal Rocks** are some of the most scenically exquisite along the whole NSW coast and benefit from different outlooks, so there's always one to suit the prevailing winds.

Seal Rocks has the first of a string of beaches at the northern end of the lakes leading to the holiday resort of **Forster**, the southernmost of the North Coast beach towns. Travelling north also entails crossing river after river, for the NSW coast is crenellated with the mouths of waterways which carry runoff from the Great Dividing Range. The further north you go, the more romantic the rivers become, their shores wilder, their bars and tides more spectacular.

Taree, about a two-hour drive from Newcastle, is a thriving market town in the dairy-rich **Manning Valley**. The beautiful Manning River runs through the middle of town and, if you follow it west to **Elands**, after an hour's drive you find yourself at **Ellenborough Falls**, one of the highest single-drop waterfalls in Australia.

The Manning and other valleys of the mid-North Coast are timber centres providing native woods and pine from vast forests which stretch westwards onto the New England Plateau. Here the highway winds through many kilometres of forest, and for a change of scene it is worth a detour along the well-made coast road from Kew to **Port Macquarie**. These are some of the prettiest beaches in the state, with rocky outcrops and golden sands. On the western side of the road there is yet another chain of ocean lakes, ideal for fishing and boating.

However, tourism has taken its toll on the landscape at Port Macquarie (a former penal settlement, founded in

To lessen the impact of walkers, national parks in New South Wales provide boardwalks over fragile terrain.

BELOW: relaxing in the bow net on a dolphin-watching expedition.

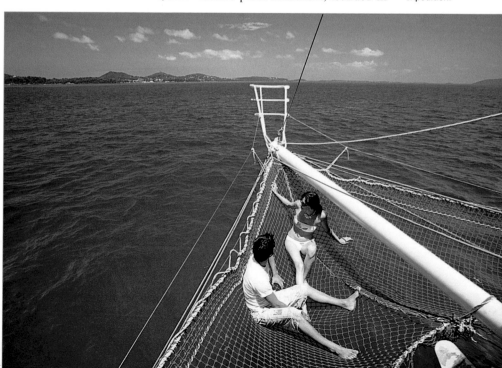

TIP

The views from the lookout tower at Cape Hawke in Booti Booti National Park (www. environment.nsw.gov. au/nationalparks) are spectacular. You can see south to the foot of Barrington Tops. The park has walking trails, a picnic area and camping facilities, but only Elizabeth Beach is patrolled by volunteer life-savers during the swimming season.

1821, and still full of historic sandstone buildings). Garish motels, retirement villages and timeshare resorts dot the headlands, and red-brick suburbia has taken over the flatlands to the west. But for all its superannuated qualities, there is still much to like about Port – good restaurants, top-quality accommodation and easy access to uncrowded beaches. **Wauchope**, a few kilometres up the Hastings River, is worth a visit for **Timbertown**, an award-winning replica of an old sawmilling village.

The highway again snakes inland and through the forests. It is worth making the 24km (15-mile) detour to take in the resort of **Crescent Head** – a pretty, peaceful town with fine surf and good golf. For a real escape, head south from Crescent on the old dirt coast road for 10km (6 miles) to a grassy headland and beach known as **Racecourse**. There's no sign, but a ranger will appear from nowhere after a day or two to collect a modest camping fee. Given the joys of an empty beach, uncrowded waves and occasional dolphin sightings, the minimal fee is a gift.

Nearby is the town of **South West Rocks**, perched on a picturesque headland, and the famous **Trial Bay Gaol**, which held convicts and, later, German war internees.

Continuing northwards, a distinctly tropical feel begins to permeate the air and, from **Macksville** on, banana plantations are a common sight and a good proportion of houses are built on stilts, Queensland-style, in order to catch the cooling breeze and keep things dry. Everywhere the dominant colour is a lush green, and the roadside signs tell you this is paradise. It isn't, but it's a step in the right direction. While you're filling the tank in Macksville, pop around to The Star pub, which sits right on the banks of the Nambucca River, as pretty and profane an ale house as you'll find anywhere.

Just south of Macksville, the small town of **Scotts Head** presents a long, clean beach and a caravan park.

Coffs Harbour

The timber port of **Coffs Harbour** ❸ is reputed to have Australia's best climate, and has developed into a major centre of North Coast tourism. Unfortunately, most motorists know Coffs only as the city of the Big Banana, another manifestation of Australia's bizarre tourist gigantism. Those with a taste for adventure can join whitewater professionals for a day of rafting action on the nearby **Nymboida River**.

Coffs is more or less the midway point between Sydney and Brisbane – around seven and six hours' driving distance, respectively. Travellers often plan to stay here overnight only, but end up staying a week. The town is alive with restaurants and pubs, particularly in the strip from the jetty to Park Beach. Parasailing, four-wheel-drive tours, the beach, golf and galleries fill the days.

Inland, the Bellingen Valley offers scenic pleasures quite different from the coast. Some parts of this valley, particularly the pebbled river banks, look more like parts of temperate Europe than east-coast Australia.

BELOW:
the beach at South West Rocks.

Bellingen

The beautiful village of **Bellingen** (which features dramatically in the climax of Peter Carey's novel *Oscar and Lucinda*) is, along with Nimbin to the north *(see page 135)*, the heart of alternative culture in NSW, although concessions have been made to capitalism since the real-estate boom hit and idyllic communal farms became worth millions. Bellingen retains a relaxed atmosphere and a strong alternative bent. Browse the local arts and crafts at the Old Butter Factory or the beautifully restored Hammond and Wheatley Emporium department store. If you're in the area in August or October you can take in the local jazz or global music festivals.

From Bellingen, take the Dorrigo Road to the small town of **Dorrigo**, a great base for exploring the **Dorrigo National Park** (tel: 02-6657 2309). The park is a fragment of the massive rainforest that covered the area until the 1920s, when loggers clear-felled in their search for Australian cedar, a timber so valuable it was known as red gold. From the Dorrigo Rainforest Centre (Mon–Fri 8.30am–4.30pm, Sat–Sun 9am–4.30pm; tel: 02-6657 2309; charge), you can take a number of walks, including the Skywalk, a wooden walkway stretched high over the forest canopy that is also open for nocturnal excursions.

The Pacific Highway swings inland yet again through the forests, this time emerging at **Grafton**, a lovely old town shaded with jacaranda trees (a wonderful sight in late October and early November) and situated on a bend of the Clarence River, 65km (40 miles) from its mouth. Grafton has some delightful 19th-century architecture enhanced by its wide, tree-lined streets. This is flood country, and the houses close to the river are tropical bungalows on stilts. Like several towns away from the coast, Grafton has been bypassed in the tourist boom, and prices for food and lodging are still reasonable.

North of Grafton, the highway follows the line of the Clarence River across flatlands to the coast, with rambling old houses peering out from behind fields of sugar cane. The village of **Maclean**, built on several hills

Dorrigo National Park is an area of exquisite natural beauty.

BELOW LEFT: a rainforest waterfall in Dorrigo. **BELOW:** a colourful local fair.

The strife of Byron: Coastal erosion is threatening several beach-front properties in Byron Bay and pitting homeowners against the local council. The building of protective sea walls is banned in favour of a "planned retreat" from those structures that tumble into the water.

a few kilometres upriver from Yamba, is quaint, quiet, and a great spot from which to view the workings of the Clarence with its fishermen and cane haulers. Fifteen minutes down a straight bitumen road is the resort of **Yamba**, once a sleepy hollow and now filled with shoddily built weekenders and more garish motels. But the pub on the headland and the beaches spread below are first-rate. Down the coast a few kilometres from Yamba, the village and famous surf point of **Angourie** is renowned for its rocky coastline and Blue Pools.

After a stretch of alternating river and cane scenery, the Pacific Highway clips the coast again at **Ballina**, the southernmost beach town in a string reaching to the Queensland border, collectively known as the Summerland Coast. Ballina, the scene of a minor gold rush in the 19th century, has now found more consistent treasure as a bustling tourist centre and fishing port.

The Highway now heads due north through magnificent rolling hills, but the alternative coastal route takes in some equally breathtaking coastal scenery, including the village of **Lennox Head**, ranked as one of the top 10 surfing spots in the world (the big waves come from May to July).

Byron Bay

The area's big tourist magnet is **Byron Bay ❹**, the easternmost town in Australia and a popular tourist destination.

In the 1960s, Byron was still a quiet rural community with an alternative bent. Today, its magnificent setting, with almost 30km (19 miles) of sandy beaches fringed by a fertile hinterland, has made it a mecca for the rich and the famous. Some, like global music star Jack Johnson, own property here; others ensconce themselves in the area's impressive array of luxury retreats.

The town is just as popular with the less well-off, who spend their time bodysurfing or relaxing in the sun, a laid-back lifestyle that has made the town a magnet for unemployed youth. In a classic case of biting the hand that feeds it, the local council has been battling to limit the number of visitors, but thus far without success.

Come to town on a crowded festival weekend and you may even sympathise with the council. Byron has a packed roster of festivals, devoted variously to blues, writers, films, jazz, and many more besides, during which times the town can get uncomfortably full.

However, the town's growth has not marred its natural beauty. While the beaches are a major attraction, the hinterland features a number of national parks and nature reserves, including **Tyagarah** and **Broken Head** nature reserves, **Arakwal National Park** (tel: 02-6620 9300) and **Cape Byron Headland**. Then of course there's the underwater world. Byron's most famous dive spot, the **Julian Rocks Aquatic Reserve**, is considered second only to the Great Barrier Reef on the east coast. This is where temperate waters and tropical waters meet, giving divers the oppor-

BELOW: surf school will teach you all the moves.

tunity to view an astonishing array of marine wildlife. A few gruesome incidents where divers have been taken by sharks has done little to lessen its popularity.

The best-known attraction in Byron's hinterland is **Nimbin**, Australia's original alternative community, the town where the 1973 Aquarius Festival launched Australia's hippy culture. While much of the town is still caught in a 1970s time warp, with luridly painted houses and shops and the scent of patchouli in the air, its drug community has moved on from marijuana to hard-core heroin. The overt drug peddling makes many visitors uncomfortable, and they tend not to linger.

A better option is to spend some time exploring the local area. The winding roads between Nimbin and Lismore, through undulating landscape covered in lush rainforest, offer some of the most scenic drives in the state. These pockets of rainforest, left untouched by the early settlers, were the focus of Australia's first anti-logging protest in the late 1970s.

Mount Warning

The rich soil in the area is a legacy of the giant, shield-shaped volcano that once covered the entire area. The remnant of its central vent is a 1,157-metre (3,780ft) peak called **Mount Warning** in English, **Wollumbin** (Cloud Catcher) in the local Bandjalung language. Its peak is the first spot in Australia to catch the rays of the rising sun, and offers dazzling views over the district. Also worth exploring are the **Border Ranges National Park** (tel: 02-6632 0000; vehicle entry fee) and the **Nightcap National Park** (tel: 02-6627 0200), including the 100-metre (328ft) -high Minyon Falls.

The border town of **Tweed Heads** has only recently emerged from the shadow of its flashier sister across the Queensland border, Coolangatta, but the tourist boom now proceeds apace. The end of one journey is the beginning of the next. As you cross the Tweed River, the North Coast of NSW falls behind, and what opens ahead is a very different beast: the Gold Coast of Queensland.

Patriotic statues at Tweed Heads.

BELOW:
the lighthouse at Cape Byron, the easternmost point of Australia.

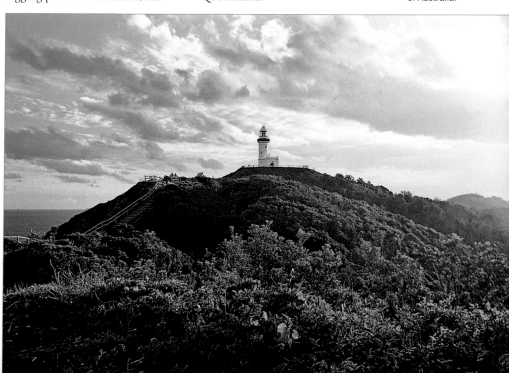

Two Pacific Gems

Norfolk Island and Lord Howe Island are lush green specks on the vastness of the Pacific Ocean

Two of Australia's tiniest tourist areas are also among the most attractive. Although Norfolk and Lord Howe are South Pacific islands, these are not atolls of palm trees and corals.

The sea life around the islands is quite phenomenal. In the surrounding waters, warm and cool currents collide, spawning a wealth of marine creatures including giant clams, sea turtles, clownfish, lionfish, tuna, butterfly fish and a wrasse known as the doubleheader, a species that is unique to the islands' waters. Its not surprising that diving is a major draw to the islands.

A rich and fascinating cultural heritage, relaxed lifestyle and rolling green pastures characterise **Norfolk Island**, 1,700km (1,050 miles) northeast of Sydney. No one lived here until a British penal settlement was established in 1788. The prison island became known for its harsh and cruel conditions.

The most bizarre event in Norfolk's history occurred after the British Government decided, in 1852, that the settlement was too expensive to maintain and evacuated all the inhabitants. At about the same time, on remote Pitcairn Island the descendants of the *Bounty* mutineers and the Polynesian women they took with them from Tahiti in 1789 (after dumping Captain William Bligh) were finding it difficult to grow enough food for their increasing population. So they were relocated to Norfolk Island in 1856, although a few later returned to Pitcairn.

Today there are fewer than 1,800 people on the 3,500-hectare (8,750-acre) island, but many of them share the same set of *Bounty* surnames. Indeed, so many Christians, Quintals, Youngs, McCoys, Adamses, Buffetts, Nobbses and Evanses crowd the telephone book that it's the only one in the world to publish subscribers' nicknames.

Norfolk is a self-governing territory within Australia. The tourist clutter of **Kingston** is the island's only town. Tax-free shopping here is very cheap, especially for fashionable wool and cashmere sweaters.

Down by the waterfront, the buildings of the early settlements are still in good condition – some are still used as government offices. The evening sound-and-light show along these buildings, which are remnants from a savage time, is well worth your while.

Norfolk Island doesn't promise a wild time. However, you feel close to history here, and there is enough to do to warrant several days' stay. Diving is a popular activity, and Fletcher Christian's descendant Karlene Christian, at the Bounty Dive Shop, offers daily diving groups.

Lord Howe Island

Much smaller than Norfolk Island, crescent-shaped **Lord Howe Island** is only 11km (7 miles) long and 2km (1¼ miles) wide, with a population of about 300. Visitors usually travel on bicycles.

This heavily forested and partially mountainous isle often has a cap of cloud on Mount Gower (875 metres/2,870ft), at the southern end. There are numerous walking trails, many birds and some unique vegetation. It is advisable to take a tour with a local guide, since it takes a resident expert to decipher the island's rich botany and bird life. ❑

New England

At **Murrurundi** the New England Highway climbs up, leaving the Hunter Valley to enter the Great Dividing Range, the vast upheaval which separates the coastal plains from the tablelands along the entire length of New South Wales. The town itself is set in a valley of the Liverpool Ranges, and seems constantly shrouded in mist.

The road winds into the ranges and onto the New England Plateau, eventually reaching the city of **Tamworth** ❺. This pretty town is the largest in the northwest with a thriving economy based on sheep and cattle. Tamworth's role as a commercial centre for outlying farms and ranches prompted a local radio announcer to establish a promotion on the cowboy theme. In the early 1970s he organised a country music festival and started calling Tamworth "the country music capital of Australia". At first, residents were wary of being stereotyped, but the annual festival is now the town's major draw, attracting thousands of fans every January. If you're in the area, it is worth a detour to Tamworth just to dine at Monty's (Armidale Road, tel: 02-6766 7000), one of Australia's best regional restaurants.

Not far from Tamworth, along a road that follows the bends of the Peel River, is the old gold-mining town of **Nundle**. Abandoned diggings and the ghostly town make it worth a detour. North of Tamworth, the New England Highway passes through spectacular country with rugged peaks and long plains dotted with quaint old mining towns. In **Uralla** you'll find the grave of the legendary bushranger Captain Thunderbolt, shot during a battle with police at nearby Kentucky Creek in 1870.

As its name suggests, the **New England Tableland** bears striking similarities, in both topography and climate, to the old country: England. Its altitude gives it frosty mornings nine months of the year, occasional snow and a year-round freshness.

Nowhere is this more evident than in the city of **Armidale** ❻, a scholarly town greened by parks and gardens, with two cathedrals and tree-lined streets. As well as the University of New England, Armidale has one other college and three boarding schools,

TIP

Follow Scenic Drive 19 for about 11km (7 miles) east out of Uralla, until you reach the privately owned village of Gostwyck. Beautiful little Gostwyck Chapel, set on the banks of a willow-edged stream, is covered with trailing vines that blaze red around April.

OPPOSITE: Lord Howe Island.
BELOW LEFT: a giant guitar.
BELOW: a perfect picnic spot.

establishing it as the major NSW seat of learning outside Sydney. The student population has given Armidale an air of youthfulness in contrast to its stately Victorian architecture.

The highway out of Armidale leads along a ridge to the watershed of the Great Dividing Range, 1,320 metres (4,330ft) above sea level, at **Guyra**, then on to the junction with the Gwydir Highway at **Glen Innes**, famous for its fine gemstones. Almost a third of the world's sapphires are mined in this area and, although most of the good spots are on commercial lease, you can search for sapphires, garnets, jasper, agate and numerous other stones at many places. The town itself features magnificent ornate buildings and is fringed by five lovely parks. The mist-shrouded **New England National Park** (tel: 02-6657 2309), east of Armidale, is beautiful.

Tenterfield ❼ is the next major town along the route, once chiefly famous as "the birthplace of Federation" (because Sir Henry Parkes first called for the Australian colonies to unite in a speech made in the School of Arts here in 1889), but now more

famous as the birthplace of Peter Allen's grandfather. The late, expatriate Aussie singer topped the charts in the early 1980s with a soppy eulogy to his grandfather called *Tenterfield Saddler*. For all that, it is a rather ordinary country town in which there is not a great deal except memories.

The Southern Highlands

The Hume Highway is the main road from Sydney to Melbourne, along the inland route. **Mount Gibraltar**, a denuded volcanic plug known locally as the Gib, rises above Mittagong and the surrounding terrain, marking the gateway to the Southern Highlands. Few people take the time to stop in Mittagong; they're heading either for the limestone Wombeyan Caves nearby, or the collection of picturesque country towns that have made the Southern Highlands a favourite weekend getaway for Sydneysiders.

The first town you'll come to is **Bowral**, 5km (3 miles) from **Mittagong**, which combines wide small-town streets with elegant big-city-style boutiques. A fashionable resort for well-to-do Sydneysiders in the 1880s, it is still favoured by a similar crowd today, which explains why the town has one of the most sophisticated dining scenes outside Sydney. Other attractions include the **Tulip Festival** in September–October and the **Bradman Museum** (daily 10am–5pm; tel: 02-4862 1247; www.bradman.org.au; charge) on St Jude Street, which details the career of Australia's most revered sportsman, cricketer Don Bradman, who died in 2001. The nearby **Mount Gibraltar Reserve** offers the chance to spot wombat and brush-tailed possum.

The gem of the Southern Highlands is **Berrima ❽**, a small village preserved just as it was in the first half of the 19th century. It is off the Hume Highway, about 8km (5 miles) west of Bowral, and most of it is protected by historic trusts. The township was established in 1831, and today many of its impressive old sandstone buildings have been converted to antique and craft galleries;

most of those with historical artefacts are open from 10am to 5pm daily. These include the Surveyor General Inn (1834), said to be the oldest continuously licensed pub in Australia; the Court House (1839), now the information centre and museum (daily 10am–4pm; tel: 02-4877 1505; www.berrima courthouse.org.au; free); the Gaol (1839), now a prison rehabilitation training centre; the Church of Holy Trinity (1849); and St Francis Xavier's Roman Catholic Church (1851).

Goulburn

The big country town of **Goulburn** is located 200km (120 miles) southwest of Sydney, about midway between the Southern Highlands and the national capital of Canberra. For most of its life Goulburn has been a staging post for travellers along the Hume Highway. In 1992 a bypass ended all that, and Goulburn today is a much more relaxed place without the trucks rumbling through. Its Georgian homes and two classical cathedrals belie its history as a centre of police action against the bushrangers who plagued

the surrounding roads in the 19th century. **Towrang Stockade**, 10km (6 miles) to the north, is sparse ruins today; outlaws like Ben Hall and Frank Gardiner gave this once-formidable penal settlement a wide berth.

Iron hitching posts still stand outside some of the graceful commercial buildings on the main street of **Yass**. Hamilton Hume, the explorer after whom the Hume Highway is named, spent the last 40 years of his life here; his **Cooma Cottage** can be inspected (Thur–Mon 10am–4pm; tel: 02-6226 1470; charge) and his tombstone can be visited in the local cemetery.

Gundagai, where the Hume crosses the Murrumbidgee River, has one of those quintessentially Australian names that songwriters find irresistible – it features in a number of tunes, from the classic *Road to Gundagai* to *When a Boy from Alabama meets a Girl from Gundagai*. The town has a colourful history – it was moved from its original site after one of Australia's worst flood disasters in 1852, when 89 people died – and was the favoured hunting ground for the bushranger Captain Moonlight,

Bowral holds an annual Tulip Festival.

BELOW: Donald Bradman's statue at the eponymous museum.

Sir Donald Bradman

Australia's finest cricketer and batsman, Donald George Bradman, affectionately known as "the Don", was born in Bowral in the Southern Highlands in 1908.

Bradman attracted attention at an early age, batting golf balls against a local water tank with only a thin strip of wood. He made his Test cricket debut in 1928, at the relatively young age of 20. Two years later, he scored a record 334 not out in a Test against England and, in a match against Queensland, the highest first-class innings ever achieved (452 not out) – a record he would continue to hold until 1959.

Bradman's international career spanned 20 years, during which he played in 52 Tests and captained the Australian team for more than a decade. His unequalled reputation stems from his unique batting average of 99.94 runs per innings – he made more than 35,000 runs throughout his career.

Sadly, in his final Test, he famously needed only a further four runs to reach an average of 100, but was dismissed for a duck (zero runs) on the second ball.

Bradman retired from the game in 1948 and continued to work as a stockbroker as well as serving as a selector for the Australian cricket team. He died in 2001 in Adelaide at the age of 92.

On an average day, you'll have to wait your turn for a photo opportunity by the cairn that marks the busy summit of Mount Kosciuszko. But there's a grassy knoll a little further down where you can sit on the granite rocks and enjoy the view.

who was tried at the courthouse in 1879. The town's most famous attraction is the statue of the dog on the tuckerbox, a statue that has retained Aussie icon status long after the poem that inspired it has been forgotten.

The Snowy Mountains

Some might argue that the Snowy Mountains don't really live up to their name. They're not particularly snowy, at least by international standards – the ski resorts at **Perisher Blue**, **Thredbo** and **Charlotte Pass** often rely on snow-making machines for backup during the short ski season. Nor are the peaks particularly impressive. Although it dominates the skyline, Australia's highest mountain, **Mount Kosciuszko** (pronounced *koz-ee-oss-ko*) is a not-quite-soaring 2,230 metres (7,315ft) high and can be conquered on a gentle hike. However, **Kosciuszko National Park ❾** (tel: 02-6450 5600; vehicle entry charge), the largest protected area in the state, is well worth a visit, with a number of beautiful walks, some of which can be accessed by the Thredbo ski lifts.

BELOW: snowboarding at Thredbo Resort.

Whether you're coming down the Monaro Highway from Canberra or along the Snowy Mountains Highway from the coast, the town of **Cooma**, at the intersection of the two highways, makes a good base and has a number of nice heritage buildings.

Some prefer to base themselves at **Jindabyne**, 60km (37 miles) west of Cooma on the shores of the lake of the same name. The original town of Jindabyne is buried under the lake – a picturesque history that made it the perfect setting for Ray Lawrence's acclaimed film, *Jindabyne*. Intrepid divers explore lake-bed remnants, including abandoned trucks and the few homesteads that weren't relocated before flooding.

The creation of Lake Jindabyne was part of the Snow River Hydroelectric Project, a 25-year, A$820-million scheme to provide energy for Sydney, Melbourne and the rest of southeastern Australia while diverting water to irrigate vast stretches of the Riverina district west of the mountains. Regarded as one of the great achievements of civil engineering, 100,000 people worked

Park Life

With more than 600 national parks or nature reserves in the state under the aegis of the NSW National Parks and Wildlife Service, you won't find it difficult to find a patch of accessible nature. At 44 of them you will have to pay a daily entry fee for your vehicle. Everywhere else you're free to come and go as you please. Where there is a fee, it's sometimes a matter of purchasing a "pay and display" ticket, so make sure you have plenty of coins on you. It is worthwhile calling the park office (telephone numbers provided in text) ahead of your visit to check whether there are current fire restrictions that could mean all or part of the park is shut. For full information on any or all of the parks, visit: www.environment.nsw.gov.au/NationalParks.

on the scheme, mainly immigrants from 30 different countries.

The timber town of **Tumut** on the Snowy Mountains Highway is known for its autumn colours and its May Festival of the Falling Leaves.

South of Tumut, the highway enters the national park and skirts the eastern shore of **Blowering Reservoir**, venue of numerous water-ski and speed-boat records including the fastest (510kph/317mph) and longest (1,673km/1,040 miles) runs.

Further on, the **Yarrangobilly Caves** (tel: 02-6454 9597) have become one of the Snowy Mountains' leading attractions. About 260 caves have been discovered in a 2.5 by 12km (1½ by 7½ mile) limestone belt around the 300-metre (1,000ft) -deep Yarrangobilly River valley. Few caverns anywhere can rival the variety and beauty of their calcite formations. Six caves are open to the public for inspection, five of them by guided tour only.

The road climbs rapidly into **Kiandra**, 90km (56 miles) from Tumut. Now a desolate road junction, it has two 19th-century claims to fame: it was the site of Australia's highest goldfield (1,414 metres/4,639ft), and the location of its first ski club. In fact, the 15,000 miners who lived in tents and shanties on these slopes around 1860 were holding competitive ski races before anyone in Europe. They strapped fence palings – "butter pads" – to their boots, to move around the surrounding countryside in the winter months.

Travellers proceeding towards Melbourne should turn west at the Kiandra junction. The road climbs to **Cabramurra**, the highest town (about 1,500 metres/4,900ft) in Australia. From this point, it's downhill 63km (39 miles) to the park's western gateway of **Khancoban**. From January to April, this road is a delightful trail through fields of wild flowers, forest stands of mountain ash and snow gum, a number of lovely blue lakes, and frequent herds of kangaroos.

The South Coast

NSW's South Coast remains less developed than its northern counterpart. The occasional boutique winery and eco-resort are more subtle, but amid its authentic mix of fishing ports and vacation towns, steel mills and cheese factories, primal forest and coal works, there's plenty to justify the journey. Those travelling **Highway One** (the Princes Highway) are at times only a short detour away from a windswept peninsular national park or an island whose best-known denizens are little penguins. Furthermore, because the highway south stays close to the coast, it is more scenic than the better-known Pacific Highway north from Sydney.

Departing the metropolis, the Princes Highway spectacularly skirts the rim of the **Illawarra Plateau** until descending suddenly to **Wollongong**, a major industrial city in an impressive natural setting. Some may argue that the smokestacks of the nation's largest steel works provide an unsightly backdrop to the otherwise pristine scene of surf and sandstone cliffs, but the heavy industry is the bread and butter for

A monument in Jindabyne to Sir Paul Edmund Strzelecki (1797–1873), the Polish explorer.

BELOW: Thredbo village before the snow arrives.

TIP

One of the finest vistas in Australia is to be had from Cambewarra Lookout in Morton National Park, just past the village of Kangaroo Valley, where a sweeping landscape of escarpment rainforest interspersed with tracts of dairy farmland greet the eye.

BELOW:
Kiama's Blowhole.

around 10 percent of Wollongong district's population of 285,000.

That population is spread along 48km (30 miles) of coastline from Stanwell Park in the north to Shellharbour in the south, but is mostly concentrated in the southern Wollongong and **Port Kembla** townships, which have a steel works, a copper smelter and an artificial harbour.

Back in 1797 explorer George Bass anchored in tiny **Kiama Bay** and remarked on a "tremendous noise" emanating from a rocky headland. Today, the **Blowhole** is the most popular attraction of the fishing and market town of **Kiama** ⑩. When seas are sufficiently high to force water geyser-like through a rock fissure, the spout can reach an amazing 60 metres (200ft) in height. Beware – visitors have been swept to their death off these rocks.

Kangaroo Valley

Southwards, a short distance of 20km (12 miles) west of **Berry** (the Town of Trees), is **Kangaroo Valley**, a lovely historic township set in an isolated vale among heavily forested slopes. Estab-

lished in 1829, today it is a favourite haunt of picnickers, bushwalkers and spring wild-flower lovers. The **Pioneer Museum Park** (tel: 02-4465 1306; www.kangaroovalleymuseum.com; charge) at Hampden Bridge contains a reconstructed 1880s dairy farm, a settler's hut and pioneering farm equipment. Kangaroo Valley is also the gateway to the magnificent **Morton National Park** (tel: 02-4887 7270; vehicle entry charge), which encompasses a large part of the Shoalhaven escarpment.

Nowra ⑪ is the hub of the Shoalhaven district, 162km (101 miles) south of Sydney. A regional farming centre and an increasingly popular focus of tourism, this river-bank city is 13km (8 miles) from the mouth of the Shoalhaven River. Regional attractions include HMAS *Albatross*, Australia's last naval air training station and host to the Fleet Air Arm Museum, which, as well as housing a fine collection of military treasures, offers views across the working base from its verandah (daily 10am–4pm; tel: 02-4424 1920; charge); **Greenwell Point**, where fresh oysters can be purchased from local

Hyams Beach

The best-known of all the Jervis Bay beaches is Hyams, on the southern shores of the bay, which has the whitest sand in the world (according to the *Guinness Book of Records*). The bay's sparkling waters, its underwater topography of arches, caves and rock stacks, and a marine population that includes groupers, wrasses, sharks, cuttlefish and sea dragons, also make this one of the state's finest dive sites.

Most of the dive sites are located on the seaward faces of the northern and southern headlands that guard the approaches to the bay. Shore diving is possible from Hyams Beach and Green Patch, but the best sites require a boat.

Dive operators in Huskisson can usually supply all the gear, as well as providing regular boat trips.

growers at the cooperative; and the **Nowra Raceways**, three separate modern tracks for horse racing, trotting and greyhounds. The horse-racing track is known as Archer Raceway after the home-bred winner of the first two Melbourne Cups (1861 and 1862). Archer's stall is maintained as a veritable shrine at Terrara House, now operating as a functions venue east of the town.

Jervis Bay

Surrounded on all sides but the southeast by 50km (30 miles) of headland and beaches, **Jervis Bay** (pronounced *Jar-vis*) is one of the South Coast's idyllic holiday spots. Once a port that rivalled Sydney Harbour (Port Jackson) as the colony's most important harbour, these days it's home to the Royal Australian Naval College, HMAS *Creswell*. Technically, this is part of Australian Capital Territory – co-opted under an act that stipulated the capital must have access to the sea – but that matters not a jot to tourists who are drawn here by the bay's blindingly white, tranquil beaches, the rugged cliff-side landscapes, and the heaths,

wetlands and forests that fringe the bay. Picnic in the **Booderee Botanic Gardens** (daily Oct–Apr 9am–5pm, May–Sept 9am–4pm, Dec, Jan holidays 8am–6pm; charge), Green Patch or Illuka beaches, or sign up for a bushtucker tour with the Wreck Bay Aboriginal Community. The clear waters and varied marine life, including soft corals, sponge gardens and giant cuttlefish, also make it a popular destination for scuba divers.

Ulladulla is a rapidly growing beach resort and fishing port which supplies much of Sydney's fresh fish daily, but hurry on through to allow time to visit Murramarang National Park and Pebbly Beach. At dawn and dusk you are almost certain to be joined by a mob of kangaroos bouncing around on the foreshore, charming food out of visitors and posing for photos.

Batemans Bay is a popular tourist, crayfishing and oystering centre at the mouth of the Clyde River. The wildlife refuge on the Tollgate Islands, just offshore, is frequented by penguins. At **Old Mogo Town**, east of the Princes Highway near Mogo, 12km (7½ miles)

The crenellated bridge leading to Kangaroo Valley.

BELOW: many people enjoy the water by boat.

The skeleton of killer whale Old Tom, who used to help whalers in their hunt, is now on display in Eden.

BELOW: one of the beaches at Narooma.

south of Batemans Bay, an old mine, a steam engine and a century-old stamper battery (ore crusher) attract modern-day fortune-seekers to this compact gold-rush theme park. Kids will love **Mogo Zoo** (daily 9am–5pm; tel: 02-4474 4930; www.mogozoo.com.au; charge), a privately owned zoo specialising in endangered animals including snow leopards, jaguars, Bengal and Sumatran tigers, and a pride of white lions.

Moruya ⑫, like Nowra to the north, is established several kilometres inland on the tidal waters of a river mouth. Its first home, Francis Flanagan's Shannon View (1828), is still occupied, and the Uniting Church (or Wesleyan, as it was known in the past) was built in 1864 of local granite. The 130-year-old granite quarry on the north side of the Moruya River once supported a town of its own. Among its notable clients has been Sydney Harbour Bridge.

As the Princes Highway winds through the hills into **Bodalla**, 38km (23 miles) south of Moruya, it's hard to miss the little town's **Big Cheese**. Some 4½ metres (15ft) high and equally wide, it was sculpted from metal in

early 1984 to bolster the community's image as a cheesemaking centre. The region's two largest cheese manufacturers produce almost 10,000 tonnes of fancy and cheddar cheese annually.

The waters off the Eurobodalla area, around the small coastal resort towns of **Narooma** and **Bermagui** – especially those around **Montague Island**, 8km (5 miles) off Narooma – yield record tuna, shark and kingfish catches. **Central Tilba**, 29km (18 miles) south-west of Narooma, is a beautifully preserved hamlet. Each of the village's two dozen wooden buildings, classified and protected by the National Trust, is as it was in the late 19th century. The ABC Cheese Factory is open (daily 9am–5pm; free) for cheese tasting, and ancient equipment is on display. Central Tilba was established in the 1870s when gold was discovered on Mount Dromedary. There are fine coastal views from the 825-metre (2,700ft) mountain top, reached by a walking track.

Bega

The lush dairy country continues around **Bega**, the far South Coast's biggest town, and famous for its eponymous cheese. There's probably a bylaw that forbids visitors to leave without sampling the local product: play it safe and take in a factory tour and cheese tasting at the Bega Cheese Heritage Centre (daily 9am–5pm; tel: 02-6491 7762; www.begacheese.com.au; free). Milking demonstrations on the revolving platform at the Brogo Valley Rotolactor Dairy, 23km (15 miles) north of Bega (Mon–Wed 2–5pm, daily during school holidays; free) are less corporate.

Merimbula and its sister town of **Pambula**, on the so-called Sapphire Coast, offer fine surfing, boating, fishing and oystering. Crucially, there is also a choice of unspoilt safe beaches, which makes this a prime summer destination for families, many of them from across the border in Victoria. **Eden**, the last sizeable town before you cross the Victoria state border, is located on **Twofold Bay**, once a thriving whaling port and now host to whale-watching tours. The **Eden Killer Whale Museum** (Mon–Sat 9.15am–3.45pm, Sun 11.15am–3.45pm; tel: 02-6496 2094; www.killer whalemuseum.com.au; charge) on Imlay Street recalls those 19th-century days.

During its whaling era, Eden had stiff competition as a port from **Boydtown** ⓭, established in 1842 by the banker-adventurer Ben Boyd on the south side of Twofold Bay. Boyd dreamed aloud that his settlement would one day become the capital of Australia. He established a steamship service to Sydney and erected many buildings, but in 1850 his empire collapsed. Boyd went bankrupt, fled Australia to the Solomon Islands, and was never heard from again.

All that remains of the grand scheme today are the **Seahorse Inn** – a magnificent building with stone walls a metre (3ft) thick, Gothic arches and hand-carved doors and windows – and **Boyd's Tower**, a 31-metre (102ft) sandstone lighthouse built in 1846 but never lit. The 8,950-hectare (22,110-acre) **Ben Boyd National Park** (tel: 02-6495 5000; vehicle entry charge) encompasses the coastal headlands north and south of Twofold Bay. Its highlights include stunning red sandstone cliffs, rich animal and bird life, and lovely wild flowers.

Western slopes and plains

The route due west from Sydney, along the Great Western Highway, passes through the Blue Mountains (*see pages 119–20*) and enters the vast grazing land beyond. **Bathurst** ⓮, Australia's oldest inland city, was a major pastoral centre even before the heady gold rush of the 1850s, although its elegant 19th-century buildings and its lively student population, courtesy of the local campus of Charles Sturt University (split between Bathurst and Wagga Wagga), give it a more sophisticated ambience than one might expect.

There's a packaged gold-rush experience at **Bathurst Goldfields** on the city's scenic **Mount Panorama**, where old-time diggings have been set up, and gold-panning demonstrations are given. A bit more authentic is

The discovery of a large nugget by a Mr Austin at Ophir in 1851 triggered Australia's first gold rush. More mayhem ensued when another discovery was made in Victoria six months later.

BELOW: Bathurst Courthouse is the home of the Bathurst Historical Museum.

TIP

Spring blossoms transform Cowra's Japanese Garden in early October, when it becomes the focus of *Sakura Matsuri*, the town's annual cherry blossom festival. The festival also features traditional Japanese foods, arts and crafts, kite flying, tea ceremonies, martial arts and *shakuhachi* flute recitals.

BELOW:
the Japanese
Garden at Cowra.

do-it-yourself panning at **Hill End** or **Sofala**, ghost towns north of Bathurst. Take a drive around the town and inner suburbs to see the civic buildings and grand mansions built from the profits of Australia's first gold rush.

In Bathurst, the scenic drive around Mount Panorama becomes a world-class motor-racing circuit for the 1,000km (600-mile) touring car and V8 race in October. Just over 50km (30 miles) west of Bathurst is the intensively photographed village of **Carcoar**, where more than 20 restored colonial buildings nestle in a picturesque little valley.

The highway runs through mainly sheep and wheat country to **Cowra**, a prosperous agricultural centre on the Lachlan River, which has a remarkable link with Japan. During World War II, Japanese prisoners of war interned in a camp there attempted a mass break-out during which nearly 231 of them were killed. The care local people gave to the graves of the prisoners so impressed the Japanese that they repaid them with the gift of a classical garden. The **Cowra Japanese Garden** (daily 8.30am–5pm; tel: 02-6341 2233; www.cowragarden.com.

au; charge) is a colourful oriental showpiece in the gold-brown central west of New South Wales.

Wagga Wagga

South of Cowra lies **Wagga Wagga**, shortened to Wagga (rhyming with *logger*) by just about everyone. Although it may seem like a sleepy country town, Australia's most populous inland city has several attractions, including the impressive Botanic Gardens, which have a walk-through aviary with over 300 bird species; the **Wagga Wagga Art Gallery** (Tue–Sat 10am–5pm, Sun noon–4pm; tel: 02-6926 9660; www.waggaartgallery.org; free) that houses the National Art Glass Collection; Charles Sturt University, which runs a prestigious wine course from its on-campus winery; and even a sandy river beach, on the banks of the Murrumbidgee close to the town's main street.

From either Cowra or Wagga the highway westwards becomes a basic two-lane blacktop, running fairly straight for 1,000km (600 miles) or so, until the approaches to Adelaide. Here you enter the true "sunburnt country", the "land of sweeping plains" of Dorothea Mackellar's famous poem. If you've yet to see any kangaroos, you'll probably spot them here – although they're likely to be caught in the glare of your headlights. Those cute warning signs have a serious purpose: 'roos are a dangerous hazard on these roads, particularly at night.

The harshness of the elements is burnt into the wild-west appearance of **West Wyalong ⑮**, 161km (100 miles) west of Cowra. Motorists should spurn the bypass and drive down the main street of the former gold-mining town. The quaint town of **Orange** is, predictably, a fruit-growing centre – but, not so predictably, the crops are apples and cherries (the town was named after the Duke of Orange). The extinct volcano **Mount Canobolas**, 14km (9 miles) southwest of Orange, has become a 1,500-hectare (600-acre) flora and fauna reserve with walking trails, picnic areas, waterfalls and a 360-degree view of the countryside from the summit.

Classic 2000 film comedy *The Dish* put **Parkes** on the map, or at least reminded us of a key episode in its history. The town, 93km (58 miles) west of Orange, is famous for its Observatory, housing a 64-metre (210ft) radio telescope which played a crucial cameo role in the 1969 moon landing. The Visitor Centre explains all (daily 8.30am–4.15pm; tel: 02-6861 1777; free).

The **Ophir Goldfields**, 27km (17 miles) northeast of Orange, were where Australia's first payable gold was discovered in 1851 and are now an official fossicking area. Banjo Paterson's birthplace is marked by a memorial 3km (2 miles) off the highway on the Ophir Road.

Dubbo

The Mitchell Highway runs through undulating terrain around **Wellington**. The **Wellington Caves**, 8km (5 miles) southwest of the town, have huge stalagmite formations in their limestone caverns. The last truly productive agricultural area is around the thriving

city of **Dubbo** ⓰, in the middle of the wheat belt, with large sheep and cattle properties and irrigated farms.

Dubbo's main attraction for tourists is the **Western Plains Zoo** (daily 9am–4pm; tel: 02-6881 1400; www. westernplainszoo.com.au; charge), which is an excellent wildlife park partnered with Sydney's Taronga Park Zoo. Animals are placed in settings as near as possible to their native conditions, and penned by moats rather than cages or fences. Australia has an inordinate number of jails as tourist attractions, and Dubbo is no exception: the **Old Dubbo Gaol** (daily 9am–5pm; tel: 02-6801 4460; www.olddubbogaol.com. au; charge), which was closed in 1966 after almost 80 years, has been restored (complete with gallows) and is open for self-guided inspection tours.

Narromine, 39km (24 miles) on from Dubbo and on the edge of the western plains, is a major citrus-growing area, and the local Citrus Packers Co-operative will let visitors have a look around. The terrain here provides thermal air lifts, making the area ideal for gliding. In the **Macquarie Valley Irrigation**

Taronga Park Zoo was officially opened in 1916.

BELOW:
the Wagga Wagga railway station.

Area, the town of **Trangie** is the centre of a large cotton-growing industry, and visits can be arranged to the nearby Auscott Cotton Farm. Harvesting and ginning take place from late April to June, the best time to visit.

The scenery starts to turn dry at **Nyngan** on the Bogan River, where the Barrier Highway begins. Here motorists should start keeping an eagle eye on the fuel gauge. There's only one fuel supply (at Hermidale) over the 128km (80 miles) to Cobar; only one stop (at Topar) between Wilcannia and Broken Hill; and few service stations from there to Yunta in South Australia.

Hay

It's a desolate drive on to **Hay** ⓱. Banjo Paterson's bitter poem *Hay, Hell and Booligal* was inspired by the almost treeless horizons and the sunparched tedium, broken only by the sight of an occasional emu, goanna or flock of budgerigars. The town, about halfway from Sydney to Adelaide, is a well-watered oasis on the banks of the Murrumbidgee River. For many years it was an important river crossing on the

stock route to Victoria; it also served as a major link in the legendary Cobb and Co. passenger coach network and is now the centre of an extensive horticultural and wool-producing area. An old Cobb and Co. coach, used until 1901, is on display at the coach-house, corner of Lachlan and Moppett streets, and Hay's Gaol Museum has a great array of pioneering memorabilia.

Balranald is another spot of green on the Murrumbidgee. Head north to visit the **Willandra Lakes World Heritage Site**, a 370,000-hectare (950,000-acre) system of Pleistocene lakes that contains evidence of Aboriginal habitation in Australia, stretching back 50,000 years. The dry lakes contain ancient hearths and middens, and the world's oldest cremation remains – a first sign of civilisation. The most accessible part of Willandra is **Mungo National Park** ⓲ (tel: 03-5021 8900; vehicle entry fee), about 150km (93 miles) north of Balranald. Its star attraction is the **Walls of China**, a geological phenomenon of 30-metre (100ft) -high walls of variegated sand running for 30km (19 miles).

A good base for visiting the park is the sleepy town of **Wentworth**, once one of the interior's most important towns. Its position at the confluence of the Murray and Darling rivers meant it controlled the river trade between NSW, Victoria and South Australia, until it was superseded by the coming of the railways. It is a pleasant enough base, although most of the so-called attractions, such as Old Wentworth Gaol and Pioneer World, can easily be skipped.

Broken Hill

Head north from Wentworth for 265km (165 miles) and you'll reach New South Wales' most remote outpost: **Broken Hill ⑲**. In this far corner, locals set their watches to South Australian time, half an hour behind. Although it belongs to NSW geographically and administratively, most of Broken Hill's trade and communication is conducted through Adelaide, which lies much nearer than faraway Sydney.

The city looms large in Australia's industrial history, with legendary unions eventually dominating the city by means of the Barrier Industrial Council. Its mineral wealth played the largest part in changing the nation from a strictly pastoral outpost to a more industrial base. With most of the streets named after minerals, it's impossible to ecape the town's mining past.

Delprat's Mine (tours Mon–Fri 10.30am, Sat 2pm; tel: 08-8088 1604; charge), BHP's original dig, is an almost black hill that dominates the city and gives the non-claustrophobic a chance to don a hard hat, lamp and boots for a guided tour. The route heads 120 metres (390ft) underground in pits that were started in the early, dangerous days of hand drilling. With former miners as guides, visitors will get a feel of the industry's terrible hardships. You can see reproductions of mine workings at **White's Mining Museum** (daily 9am–5pm; tel: 08-8087 2878; charge), off the Silverton Road.

But not everything in Broken Hill is related to the great black hill. This Outback town has become an unlikely font of the arts, renowned for several locally famous painters including the late Pro Hart, Jack Absalom and Hugh Schulz.

Cooling-off time in Bell's Milk Bar, Broken Hill.

BELOW: Broken Hill's redundant Junction Mine.

How The Hill Began

It all began in 1883 when a boundary rider and amateur geologist, Charles Rasp, stumbled across a lump of silver ore on a rocky outcrop he described as a "broken hill". From the claim that he and his syndicate pegged grew the nation's largest company, the Broken Hill Proprietary Co. Ltd.

Although it diversified widely and had completely moved out of Broken Hill by 1939, BHP is still spoken of with distaste in the city for its abrasive attitude to the workforce – the stuff of legend.

"The Hill" turned out to be the world's largest silver, lead and zinc lode, and, while other mining towns have tended to peter out over the years, this one is still going strong. It has yielded more than 147 million tonnes of ore from its 8km (5-mile) -long lode.

TIP

Visitors to Mutawintji who know what they're looking for can still find Aboriginal "barbecues" – small mounds where they would cook their meat and where the accumulation of hot animal fats bonded the soil into an erosion-resistant clump.

Among the 27 galleries in the city, **Pro Hart's** (Mon–Sat 9am–5pm, Sun 1.30–5pm; tel: 08-8087 2441; www.prohart.com.au; free) is the most quixotic. Besides a wide range of paintings by Hart himself, it also houses much of his private collection which includes works by Monet, Rembrandt, Dalí, Picasso, Dobell, Drysdale and Tom Roberts.

Broken Hill has also become a centre for one of Australia's unique institutions – the **Flying Doctor Service**, which transports medical care across the vast distances of the Outback by aircraft.

At night, head for the licensed social clubs to play the pokies (poker machines). The city's social life revolves around the Musicians, Sturt, Legion and Social Democratic clubs, which welcome visitors and have good facilities.

In red, rocky country it may be, but Broken Hill still has its beach resort at **Menindee Lake**, 110km (68 miles) away. This is the city's part-natural and part-artificial water-supply system, or at least it is when long-term drought hasn't dried it up. The lake and a system of other lakes and channels cater for boating and swimming; it combines with the adjacent **Kinchega National Park** (tel: 08-8080 3200; vehicle entry fee), home to many water birds.

The restored ghost town of **Silverton**, a mining centre 23km (14 miles) from Broken Hill, is not just an attraction for tourists; it's becoming a regular star in Outback film epics. With repainted shop and hotel signs, it has appeared in *A Town Like Alice*, *Mad Max II* and *Razorback*. Also in the Silverton area is the 100-year-old **Daydream Mine** (tours daily Easter–Nov 10am–3pm, Dec–Easter 10am, 11.30am; tel: 08-8088 5682; charge), where visitors can walk down into the old workings.

For the brave traveller with a bit more time, it's possible to drive right off the beaten track from Wilcannia to Broken Hill, with a detour through the opal fields. It's a rewarding diversion, but not one to be taken lightly because of its lack of sealed roads and limited fuel and water.

Mutawintji National Park

From Broken Hill, it's about 265km (165 miles) northeast to **Mutawintji National Park** (tel: 08-8080 3200), a surprising patch of greenness in the barren Bynguano Ranges. Strange and colourful rock formations surround ancient Aboriginal campsites, tools, engravings and paintings, which are explained in films shown at the visitor centre. Visitors must check in with the resident ranger on arrival. There are camping facilities, but no power. Ranger-guided tours are available during the cooler months.

White Cliffs, 297km (185 miles) from Broken Hill, is a lunar landscape of craters created by opal diggings, and where fossickers with permits can scrounge. Many residents live underground to escape the winds and extreme temperatures; some of them don't mind showing off the interiors of their white-walled subterranean settlements, which can be surprisingly luxurious. The best accommodation at White Cliffs is an underground motel or subterranean bed-and-breakfast.

BELOW: sunset over a lake in Kinchega National Park.

The historic buildings and wharf remnants at **Wilcannia** ⑳, 98km (61 miles) south of White Cliffs, are reminders of the days when its position on the Darling River made it a major inland port and earned it the title of Queen City of the West.

Take the highway from Wilcannia to Cobar, and about 40km (25 miles) before town, you'll find the turn-off to the **Mount Grenfell Aboriginal cave paintings** (tel: 02-6836 2692). Drive 30km (19 miles) along a good dirt road to the cave, a shallow overhanging rock shelter, for rare examples of the techniques of pigments applied by finger, in human, bird and animal outlines, and hand stencils.

Cobar

Cobar ㉑ typifies the resilience of the area's people as well as its hardy flora and fauna. From being a rip-roaring town of 10,000 people and 14 hotels not long after copper mining began there in the 1870s, its fortunes have fluctuated: 100 years later its population was under 4,000 and only one mine was operating; today the figures are 7,000 people and four mines. The Eleura lead, zinc and silver mine (which was opened in 1983) boosted the town's population and economy. The **Great Cobar Heritage Centre** (Mon–Fri 8.30am–5pm, Sat–Sun 9am–5pm; tel: 02-6836 2448; charge), in an old two-storey mining company office, gives a fascinating insight into the area and its people.

Cobar's Great Western Hotel is the epitome of country hotels with its massive first-floor verandah. Classification by the National Trust means that the exterior retains its original timberwork and iron lace but, on the inside, accommodation has been transformed into modern motel-style units.

North of Cobar, the Mitchell Highway meets the Darling River at the small and pleasant township of **Bourke** ㉒. Once an important port, Bourke has become immortalised in the colloquial expression, "out the back o'Bourke", signifying a place so remote that it is exceeded only by going "beyond the black stump". Take in the emptiness that surrounds Bourke, and you'll get a sense of what the Outback really means. ❑

Camels can cope well in the Outback's harsh conditions.

BELOW: where Mad Max drops in for a tinny.

RESTAURANTS AND BARS

Southeast NSW

Albury
The Commercial Club
618 Dean Street
Tel: 02-6057 2000
www.commclubalbury.com.au
Open: B, L & D daily. **$**
The Commercial Club is a massive social spot with a choice of eating options. À la carte Dining Room is the silver-service venue or there are the progressively cheaper Sevens Restaurant and Reflections Café.

Batemans Bay
On the Pier
Old Punt Road
Tel: 02-4472 6405
www.onthepier.com.au
Open: L daily, D Mon–Sat. Closed June–July. **$$**
Simple but stylish cooking in a building that sits right over the water.

Berry
Berry Wood-fired Sourdough Bakery
23 Prince Alfred Street
Tel: 02-4464 1617
www.sourdough.com.au
Open: B & L Wed–Sun. **$**
Items from the bakery are sensational and there's a fine deck. BYO.

Eden
Wheelhouse
253 Imlay Street
Tel: 02-6496 3392
Open: L & D daily (closed Mon May–Aug). **$$**
Down at the wharf, the Wheelhouse is set to grab the best of the local fish. It does so and then creates mouth-watering platters.

Jervis Bay
Seagrass Brasserie
13 Currambene Street, Huskisson
Tel: 02-4441 6124
www.seagrass.net.au
Open: L Sat–Sun, D daily. **$$**
Surf and turf produce equally at home in a nicely balanced menu with Asian tinges.
The Gunyah
Paperbark Camp,
571 Woollamia Road, Huskisson
Tel: 02-4441 7299
www.paperbarkcamp.com.au
Open: D daily. Closed July–Aug. **$$$**
Dinner plus B&B is a sensible choice at this eco-resort. Dinner in the elevated dining room is a successful mix of contemporary cooking with indigenous bush flavours. BYO.

Kiama
55 on Collins
Shop 1, 55 Collins Street
Tel: 02-4232 2811
Open: B & L daily, D Mon–Tue, Thur–Sat. **$$**
Effortlessly retaining the mantle of best restaurant in Kiama, 55 employs good local produce in innovative and satisfying combinations. Allow room for one of the fabulous desserts. BYO.

Narooma
Lynch's Restaurant
135 Wagonga Street
Tel: 02-4476 3022
Open: L & D daily. **$$**
Slightly old-fashioned feel to this small restaurant but the food is always interesting, sometimes inspired.

Thredbo
Credo
Riverside Cabins
Tel: 02-6457 6844
www.credo.com.au
Opening times dependent on snow and weather conditions. **$$**
This attractive chalet of timber and glass offers large helpings from a small but interesting menu. Beautiful outlook and sound cooking.

Wollongong
Diggies Beach Café
1 Cliff Road, North Beach, North Wollongong
Tel: 02-4226 2688
Open: B & L daily, D daily in summer. **$**
Find a spot in this lovely old listed building, grab a coffee and a well-crafted snack, and just hang out and watch the beach life.

Central NSW and Coast

Bathurst
Cobblestone Lane
2/173-9 George Street
Tel: 02-6331 2202
www.cobblestonelane.com.au
Open: L & D Tue–Sat. **$$**
Try some green mango and pawpaw salad with cuttlefish followed by local lamb fillet. Why wouldn't you when it's done this well?

Cowra
Neila
5 Kendal Street
Tel: 02-6341 2188

LEFT: freshly baked bread tempts the senses.

www.neila.com
Open: D Thur–Sat. **$$$**
A short menu of unclut-
tered dishes is devoted to
local produce. The results
are exquisite.

Nelson Bay
The Point
Sunset Boulevard,
Soldiers Point
Tel: 02-4984 7111
www.thepointrestaurant.com.au
Open: L & D Tue–Sun. **$$$**
There aren't many places
on the East Coast where
you can watch the sun setting over the water. This is
one, and it can be done
over some rather excellent
cooking, with an emphasis
on seafood. BYO.

Newcastle
Bacchus
141 King Street
Tel: 02-4927 1332
Open: L Thur–Fri, D Tue–Sat. **$$**
Nellie Melba sang here
when it was a theatre.
Now she'd be too busy
choosing from a terrific
wine list or munching on
the pitch-perfect cuisine.

Orange
Bistro Ceelo
179 Anson Street
Tel: 02-6361 1179
www.bistroceelo.com.au
Open: L Fri, D Wed–Sat. **$$$**
Fresh produce is crafted
with invention and
sophistication in this
newcomer that replaces
Selkirks in its old
Federation home.

Terrigal
Coastal
Shop 3, 5 Kurrawyba Avenue
Tel: 02-4385 3100
www.coastalbistro.com.au
Open: B, L & D daily. **$$**
Award-winning all-day
venue with strong
European leanings,
especially with the
evening tapas menu.

New England and North Coast

Armidale
Bistro on Cinders
14 Cinders Lane
Tel: 02-6772 4273
www.bistrooncinders.com
Open: B & L Mon–Sat, D Fri–
Sat. **$$**
Fine contemporary food
from a blackboard menu
in this relaxed haven.

Bangalow
Utopia
13 Byron Street
Tel: 02-6687 2088
Open: B & L daily. **$$**
A welcoming space where
ingredients are kept sim-
ple with a twist. BYO.

Byron Bay
dish
Corner of Jonson and Marvel
streets
Tel: 02-6685 7320
www.dishbyronbay.com.au
Open: D daily. **$$$**
Stylish but casual restau-
rant and raw bar with a
good wine selection.
Booking essential.

Nimbin
Rainbow Cafe
64A Cullen Street
Tel: 02-6689 1997
Open: B & L daily. **$**
Cooperative-run and
packed with vegetarian
offerings, although not
exclusively.

Tamworth
Cafe 2340
15b White Street
Tel: 02-6766 9466
Open: B & L daily. **$**
Fresh ingredients in
satisfying combinations.
Monty's
Quality Hotel Powerhouse,
Marius Street
Tel: 02-6766 7000
Open: D Tue–Sun. **$$**
Before relocating to Tam-
worth, chef Ben Davies
worked in Europe, win-

ning a Michelin star three
times.

Western Outback

Bourke
Port o' Bourke Hotel
33 Mitchell Street
Tel: 02-6872 2544
Open: L & D Mon–Sat. **$**
Good pub food in this
friendly old hotel.

Broken Hill
**Barrier Social &
Democratic Club**
218 Argent Street
Tel: 08-8088 4477
Open: B, L & D daily. **$**
The "Demo" is one of sev-
eral social clubs around
town and the competition
means that you can get
sizeable bistro meals very
cheaply.

Griffith
Clock
239-43 Banna Avenue
Tel: 02-6962 7111
Open: D Mon–Sat. **$$**
An open kitchen in the
heart of this former bank
pumps out high-class
dishes in a mod-Oz style.

Hay
Jolly Jumbuck Bistro
Riverina Hotel, 148 Lachlan
Street
Tel: 02-6993 4718
Open: L & D daily. **$$**
The Jolly Jumbuck is a
smart dining room of bare
brick and polished wood.
Classic bistro fare
explains its popularity.

Tibooburra
Tibooburra Hotel
Briscoe Street
Tel: 08-8091 3310
www.outbacknsw.com.au/
tibooburra.htm
Open: L & D daily. **$**
A friendly welcome and
huge meals to satisfy the
most demanding of itiner-
ant stockmen.

White Cliffs
**White Cliffs
Underground Motel**
Smith's Hill
Tel: 08-8091 6677
www.undergroundmotel.com.au
Open: D daily. **$**
Reasonable three-course
dinners; the bistro has a
more informal menu.

RIGHT: a dinner worth writing home about.

CANBERRA

The capital of Australia is a place conceived by accident, built by bureaucrats and located on a compromise. Considering all that, it's a remarkably pleasant place to visit

During one of his visits to Australia's national capital, the Duke of Edinburgh declared that **Canberra ㉓** (pop. 347,000) was "a city without a soul" – a royal snub the citizens of Canberra have never forgotten. In January 2003, raging bush fires spread into the city, destroying 530 homes and 30 farms, and killing four residents. The community spirit in the aftermath demonstrated that even if Canberra lacked soul, its residents still had hearts. But it is not a dearth of soul that troubles Canberra – the city is missing a sense of purpose. Like many administrative capitals, it is an artificial city, constructed not around any existing settlement, but simply out of thin Monaro air.

Intense rivalry

The reason Canberra was built at all can be traced to colonial jealousy: in 1901, at the time of the federation of the six Australian colonies, there was intense rivalry (which still exists) between Sydney and Melbourne over which was the chief city of Australia. After some wrangling, the founding fathers solved the problem by the compromise of inventing a new capital at an equally inconvenient distance from both. Thus a small and hitherto undistinguished valley in the southern tablelands of New South Wales was selected as the site.

Visitors often complain that they can never find the centre – even when they are actually standing in it. Canberra, the political, diplomatic and administrative capital of the Commonwealth, is simply not built as a commercial city, and so far it has stubbornly refused to look or act like one. In fact, what it looks most like, apart from a spread of pleasantly wooded suburbs, is a kind of semi-dignified Disneyland, complete with a **Captain Cook Memorial**

LEFT: the Carillon on the shore of Lake Burley Griffin. **RIGHT:** the Cook Memorial shows the routes taken by his various expeditions.

Free guided tours of Parliament House take about 45 minutes and include both Houses, the Great Hall and the roof.

Water Jet Ⓐ which flings water 140 metres (460ft) into the air. Visitors are either impressed or bemused by the city's uncluttered, circular road system that tends to lead the unwary around in circles. Of equal wonder is the absence of external TV antennae and the lack of front fences – both decreed aesthetically incompatible with Canberra's image.

Similarly, new homes are supplied with young native trees in order to promote the city's reputation as a leafy suburbia. In contrast to the absence of urban planning in other Australian cities, Canberra's character does impress. As a result, the capital is a city of showcase architecture. The main attractions are clustered in close proximity to **Lake Burley Griffin**, and a walk around the lake will provide great views of the city and parliaments.

Parliament House Ⓑ, which cost more than A$1 billion and is adorned with many art and craft works, was completed in 1988, just in time for the bicentennial celebrations. It is built into the side of Capital Hill on the lakeside, its roof grassed in order

to blend in, and extensive areas can be visited (daily 9am–5pm). When parliament is sitting, anyone can watch Australian parliamentary democracy in action from the Public Galleries. The livelier of the two chambers is the House of Representatives, and the best time to be there is Question Time. This is generally held at 2pm, for which you'll need to book by calling the Sergeant-at-Arms' office on 02-6277 4889 by 12.45pm on the day required.

Old Parliament House

Its predecessor, **Old Parliament House Ⓒ** on King George Terrace, now houses the **Museum of Australian Democracy** (daily 9am–5pm; tel: 02-6270 8222; www.moadoph.gov.au; charge) where a guided tour of the old chambers is combined with an insight into salient moments of political history.

When visitors step outside, they are confronted by contemporary politics. At the side of the glass-like pond at the front of the building sits the **Aboriginal Tent Embassy**, first set up here in the 1970s to focus attention on the Aboriginal land-rights campaign. It has been a permanent fixture since 1992. Depending on your point of view, it's either an icon or an eyesore; but it does serve to remind visitors of how many Aboriginal people feel that they do not share equally in the fruits of modern Australia.

National institutions

Also on the lake front, from west to east, are the **National Library** (Mon–Thur 9am–9pm, Fri–Sat 9am–5pm, Sun 1.30am–5pm, free guided tour 1.30pm last Sat of month; tel: 02-6262 1111; www.nla.gov.au; free), which has 4½ million books and whose displays include a model of Captain Cook's *Endeavour*; the **Questacon National Science and Technology Centre** (daily 9am–5pm; tel: 02-6270 2800; www.questacon.edu.au; charge), which has many enjoyable hands-on displays; the **National Portrait Gallery** (daily 10am–5pm; tel: 02-6102 7000; www.portrait.gov.au; free), the latest addition to the cultural precinct, opened in a brand-new building late in 2008 and presenting permanent and temporary exhibitions; the **High Court** (daily 9.45am–4.30pm; www.hcourt.gov.

au; free), grandiose enough to echo a Moghul palace; and the **National Gallery** (daily 10am–5pm; tel: 02-6240 6411; www.nga.gov.au; free), which has a fine collection of Aboriginal art and a Sculpture Garden.

On the Acton Peninsula is one of Canberra's more dramatic structures. The **National Museum of Australia** (daily 9am–5pm; tel: 02-6208 5000; www.nma.gov.au; free) houses an eclectic collection of artefacts. Highlights include the world's largest collection of Aboriginal bark paintings, convict clothing and leg irons, and a raft used by Vietnamese refugees who landed in Australia in the 1970s. Perhaps the oddest exhibit is the oversized heart of the racehorse Phar Lap, whose record-breaking achievements captured the country's imagination during the Great Depression until his premature death, apparently due to arsenic poisoning. Children have their own gallery, **KSpace FutureWorld**, at the National Museum. Here they can use touchscreen computers to design cities and vehicles, then watch their designs come to life on a 3D screen.

The National Gallery's Sculpture Garden is freely accessible from the path around Lake Burley Griffin.

BELOW: the National Museum of Australia.

Capital Insights

On the opposite shore from the National Library at Regatta Point, just by the bridge, is the **National Capital Exhibition** (daily Mon–Fri 9am–5pm, Sat–Sun 10am–4pm; tel: 02-6272 2902; www.nationalcapital.gov.au; free) – essential if you want to make sense of the layout of Canberra. The exhibition offers some curious sidelights to the shaping of the capital. According to the original plan, the surrounding hills were to be planted with flowering shrubs in different colours: Mount Ainslie in yellow, with plantings of wattle and broom, Black Mountain in pink and white with flowering fruit trees, and Red Hill – in red, of course. The plan was never implemented with any enthusiasm, although Red Hill does live up to its name, with its springtime flush of scarlet bottlebrush and *callistemon lanceolatus*.

Map on page 156

TIP

Every year during January and February, the National Botanic Gardens host a summer concert series on weekends at 6pm. Call the Gardens' visitor centre, tel: 02-6250 9540, for more information.

On Aspen Island, the **Carillon** tower, a 53-bell gift from Britain, plays musical selections to the residents at weekends.

North of the lake, the **Australian War Memorial Museum** (daily 10am–5pm; tel: 02-6243 4211; www.awm.gov.au; free) has a collection of relics, weapons, documents and photographs to match any of its kind in the world. The **Australian-American War Memorial** on Kings Avenue is known to local people as "Bugs Bunny" because the winged eagle that adorns its summit bears a mild resemblance to the famous rabbit.

West of the lake, the **National Zoo and Aquarium** on Lady Denman Drive (daily 10am–5pm; tel: 02-6287 8400; www.nationalzoo.com.au; charge) is worth a visit and includes a wildlife sanctuary.

In the midst of all the high-minded architectural efforts, Canberra retains considerable charm. It remains one of the few full-size cities in Australia where it's still possible to see kangaroos in the streets. For those who miss out on this spectacle, the nearby **Tidbinbilla Nature Reserve** offers a range of Australian flora and fauna.

National Botanic Gardens

Nature-lovers should also visit the **Australian National Botanic Gardens** (daily 8.30am–5pm; tel: 02-6250 9540; www.anbg.gov.au; free) at Black Mountain Reserve, which contains a huge range of Australian plants over 40 hectares (100 acres), the best of its kind in the country. The surrounding bush is one of the city's great attractions.

The city has acquired an impressive range of restaurants and several international-class hotels (such as the fabulous Art Deco Hyatt). Nightlife is improving, too: there are 300 cafés, restaurants and bars, a variety of cinemas and theatres, a casino, and some good music, ranging from classical to rock. When the Australian Parliament is in session you can watch the "pollies" go at each other hammer and tongs; it's the best free show in town.

Around Canberra

Canberra is a good jumping-off place for outdoor entertainment. There are easy day trips to old mining and farming towns such as **Captains Flat** and **Bungendore**.

A few hours' drive to the south are the **Snowy Mountains**, Australia's best ski area in winter and the setting for spectacular bushwalking in summer. About the same distance east is the **south coast** of New South Wales, with some of the prettiest beaches.

The **Deep Space Communications Complex** at Tidbinbilla (daily 9am–5pm; www.cdscc.nasa.gov; free) is active in the command, tracking and recording of a number of NASA space exploration projects, and is open to visitors.

Although the city is Australia's capital, it can seem surprisingly casual, with low-key security. The best times to visit are spring, when it's green and covered with blossom and wattle, and autumn, when the weather is balmy and the yellowing leaves of the deciduous trees are strikingly beautiful. ❑

BELOW: a memorial to air crew in the grounds of the war memorial.

RESTAURANTS AND BARS

Restaurants

Prices for a three-course dinner per person with a half-bottle of house wine:
$ = under A$50
$$ = A$50–80
$$$ = A$80–120
$$$$ = over A$120

City (Civic)

Courgette
54 Marcus Clarke Street
Tel: 02-6247 4042
Open: L Mon–Fri, D Mon–Sat. $$$
The murmur of voices suggests reverence for the food about to appear. Appropriate for some of the city's most imaginative modern cooking.

Mezzalira
Melbourne Building,
20 West Row
Tel: 02-6230 0025
www.mezzalira.com.au
Open: L Mon–Fri, D Mon–Sat. $$
Exquisite regional Italian cooking in the heart of the city. BYO.

Milk and Honey
Center Cinema Building, 29 Garema Place
Tel: 02-6247 7722
www.milkandhoney.net.au
Open: B & L daily, D Mon–Sat. $$
There's café eating or a more formal restaurant in the two dining areas of this bright modern enterprise with its ironic references to 1970s styling.

Tasuke
Sydney Building, 122 Alinga Street
Tel: 02-6257 9711
Open: L & D Tue–Sat. $
This tiny place looks like a sandwich bar but inside some of Canberra's finest and freshest Japanese food is lapped up by the cognoscenti. BYO.

Barton

Ottoman Cuisine
9 Broughton Street (corner Blackall Street)
Tel: 02-6273 6111
Open: L Tue–Fri, D Tue–Sat. $$
With a menu of superb Turkish delights, it may be prudent to put yourself in the hands of the chef and ask for one of the "banquets".

Dickson

Fekerte's
74/2 Cape Street, Dickson
Tel: 02-6262 5799
Open: L Thur–Fri, D Tue–Sat. $
Fekerte Tesfaye cooks up a range of wholesome meaty offerings as well as a comprehensive selection of excellent vegetarian options. BYO.

Parkes

The Ginger Room
Old Parliament House (enter by Queen Victoria Terrace)
Tel: 02-6273 4366
www.gingercatering.com.au
Open: D Tue–Sat. $$$
Elegant Pacific-rim eating in the refurbished former private dining room of Old Parliament House.

Kingston and Griffith

Artespresso
31 Giles Street, Kingston
Tel: 02-6295 8055
www.artespresso.com.au
Open: B & L daily, Sat–Sun, D Mon–Sat. $$
It's café meets bistro meets restaurant – but the modern Australian food is reliably good whatever you're after. BYO.

Manuka

Abell's Kopi Tiam
7 Furneaux Street
Tel: 02-6293 4199
Open: L & D Tue–Sun. $
A lot of Malaysian and other regional classics produced with aplomb in this busy but friendly restaurant. BYO.

Cafés, Pubs and Bars

City (Civic)

Blue Olive Café
56 Alinga Street
Tel: 02-6230 4600
Open: B & L Mon–Sat. $
In the lovely old Melbourne Building, loads of great snacks with an emphasis on home-baked bread and cakes. BYO.

Café Essen
Shop 5, 6 Garema Place
Tel: 02-6248 9300
Open: B, L & D daily. $
Primarily a coffee house, this old favourite does great breakfasts. BYO.

The Phoenix
23 East Row
Tel: 02-6162 1581
Open: L & D daily. $
A popular pub with a friendly and relaxed atmosphere. There's regular live music and local art.

Kingston

Silo Bakery
36 Giles Street
Tel: 02-6260 6060
www.silobakery.com.au
Open: B & L Mon–Sat. $
A popular and lively café is part of this excellent bakery. Some Mediterranean leanings.

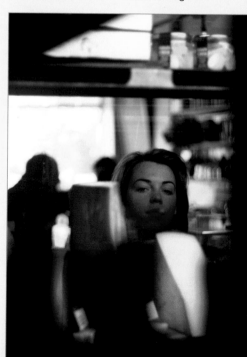

RIGHT: a dusky bar is perfect for an evening drink.

Maps on pages
164 and 178

MELBOURNE

The capital of Victoria is Australia's most
"European" city, a 21st-century metropolis
with an abundance of 19th-century charm
and a passion for culture and sport

That Melbourne continues to feature at or near the top of *The Economist*'s "most liveable city" table never surprises its residents, even if denizens of the harbour city across the border affect disbelief. Melbourne ❶ doesn't compete on brash big-ticket items like a beautiful harbour or amazing opera house, but simply and quietly gets on with being the sporting, cultural and dining capital of Australia. It's also a shopping magnet for many Australians, lured by boutiques known for their one-off designs. For visitors, that combination justifies an extended stay.

Newcomers will not find the most picturesque city. The Yarra River isn't the sparkling focal point that rivers are in some cities. Novelist Anthony Trollope considered the Yarra (or Yarra Yarra as it was) during a visit in 1871: "It seems to have but little to do with the city. But it is popular with rowers, and it waters the Botanical Gardens".

River development

Attitudes toward the Yarra River are changing, though slowly. There has been extensive work over the past few years, with the Southgate development, Federation Square and a massive rehabilitation programme at Docklands.

Trollope also complained that "there are no hills to produce scenery, or scenic effect. Though you go up and down the streets, the country around is flat – and for the most part uninteresting. I know no great town in the neighbourhood of which there is less to see in the way of landscape beauty." Well, say locals, if he'd looked up, he'd have seen the Dandenong Mountains. But Melbourne is more about hidden charms. It has copious parks and gardens to linger in, and leafy suburbs proliferate.

Main attractions
FEDERATION SQUARE
BLOCK ARCADE
THE LANEWAYS
OLD MELBOURNE GAOL
MELBOURNE MUSEUM
ROYAL BOTANIC GARDENS
NATIONAL GALLERY OF VICTORIA
ST KILDA

PRECEEDING PAGES: the Twelve Apostles.
LEFT: public art in Melbourne.
RIGHT: a sculpture decorates the Docklands.

Rowers on the Yarra River. Melbourne has a strong sporting history and hosted the 1956 Olympics and the Commonwealth Games in 2006.

Indeed, suburbs are intrinsic to an understanding of the city. One of Melbourne's most famous exports, Dame Edna Everage, may skewer them mercilessly but this city is the sum of its neighbourhoods. And when Edna was born out of Barry Humphries' appalled fascination with the monocultural suburbia he grew up in with its "politics of niceness", nobody could have anticipated that by 2006 the city he scorned would have so thoroughly embraced his creation as to approve the naming of a city laneway Dame Edna Place.

Power shifts

Melbourne now is not the city it was in the 1950s. At that time the majority of Australia's biggest companies were based in the Victorian capital and most overseas enterprises followed suit. Here was the seat of the Establishment where background and connections determined your entry to the corridors of power. There is still some residue of those times; stockbrokers, lawyers, bankers and company directors are more often than not the product of the city's elite grammar schools and colleges. Pitch up at the wrong barbecue and you'll still find men bragging about their private school and casually dropping the names of their more successful classmates.

But the balance of power between the rivals has shifted. Sydney now has the majority of major company headquarters and, with the exception of the mining companies and banks, the trend is in that direction. So Melbourne has had to reinvent itself.

Much of the impetus for this adjustment has come from changes in the population. Migration has always influenced the growth of the city, and the Anglo-Celtic dominance that lasted up to World War II has diminished with consecutive waves of migrants from Italy, Greece, the Balkans, Lebanon, Turkey, China, Vietnam and Eastern Europe. The genteel, refined European tastes of the past are still there, but they have been spiced by a more vibrant and outgoing approach to life.

The Melbourne that Ava Gardner

described in the 1960s, while shooting an adaptation of Nevil Shute's *On The Beach*, as the perfect place to make a film about the end of the world, is now a city of cool bars, radical architecture and sophisticated inhabitants.

Free men from the start

Unlike Sydney, Melbourne was not founded as a penal colony. Instead, early settlers were free men intent on building a new and prosperous life for themselves. In June 1835, John Batman, a land speculator from Tasmania, sailed his schooner into Port Phillip Bay, rowed up a broad river and declared: "This will be the place for a village." With a payment of goods including blankets, mirrors and axes, he persuaded the local Aborigines to "sell" him 600,000 acres (240,000 hectares) of prime land and drew up a document to legalise the purchase. This was later dismissed by the British Government, which accused Batman of trespassing on Crown Land.

A year later, the settlement beside the Yarra was named in honour of Lord Melbourne, Britain's prime minister. The first land sales took place soon after, and small properties at the centre of the settlement sold for £150. Two years later, the same properties were changing hands for £10,000.

It was the discovery of gold at nearby Ballarat in 1851 that propelled the sudden growth in population and prosperity which determined Melbourne's true character. This was also when its role as Australia's financial centre was established. The finds drew thousands of fortune-seekers from Europe, the USA and China; gold fever swept the country. But in time the alluvial gold ran out, and thousands of diggers left the goldfields to make Melbourne their home. The population more than quadrupled in 10 years, and the gold revenue financed new development in a rapidly expanding city determined to grow grand in style.

When Mark Twain visited on a lecture tour in 1895, he was entranced by what he saw: "It is a stately city architecturally as well as in magnitude. It

TIP

For marvellous city views and a peaceful drink in stylish surroundings right in the heart of the city, try Transit Lounge, the rooftop bar above the Transport Hotel in Federation Square.

LEFT: a familiar visual aspect of Melbourne – its graffiti.
BELOW: cast-iron details on Powlett Street.

SHOP

Melbourne is peppered with interesting little shops and boutiques. To get a real feel for the city you might consider taking a shopping tour around the less obvious streets and areas. Hidden Secrets Tours operates a number of "fashion walks" (tel: 03-9663 3358; www. hiddensecretstours.com).

BELOW: Melbourne's skyline.

has an elaborate system of cable-car service; it has museums, and colleges, and schools, and public gardens, and electricity, and gas, and libraries, and theatres, and mining centres and wool centres, and centres of the arts and sciences, and boards of trade, and ships, and railroads, and a harbor, and social clubs, and journalistic clubs and racing clubs, and a squatter club sumptuously housed and appointed, and as many churches and banks as can make a living. In a word, it is equipped with everything that goes to make the modern great city."

Ironically, by this time depression was setting in. Federation in 1901 saw the city take on the mantle of political capital until the move to Canberra in 1927. The Depression of the 1930s was followed by a spell of industrial growth and development, given extra impetus by post-war migration. When it hosted the 1956 Olympics, Melbourne was more than ready to take its place on the world stage. Substantial investment in the local equivalent of François Mitterrand's *grands projets* – particularly under Liberal

Premier Jeff Kennett in the 1990s – transformed the city and shifted its geographical axis.

Federation Square

The completion of **Federation Square** (tel: 03-9655 1900; www. fedsquare.com) in 2004 gave Melbourne its first popularly embraced public space. The ornately Victorian **Flinders Street Station** had been the city's signature building for years, and "under the clocks" was the traditional rendezvous point for a night out, a practice immortalised in a song of that name by seminal local band Weddings Parties Anything. But station steps are not necessarily the best place to loiter. Federation Square, on the other hand, has plenty of space, places to sit, cafés and bars, and is right opposite the station.

The design of Federation Square has its detractors, some of them vehement, but no one can deny its impact on the city. Built above unsightly railway yards, it serves to unite the Central Business District (CBD) with the Yarra. At its heart is a gently scalloped piazza paved with variegated sandstone, which inclines towards a small stage and a giant video screen. Concerts and public events attract large crowds and there always seems to be something going on.

The buildings behind, designed as "shards" sticking out of the ground, look as if they have been crazy-paved in a combination of glass, stone and zinc. The riches within include a branch of the National Gallery of Victoria – **The Ian Potter Centre** (daily 10am–6pm; tel: 03-8620 2222; www.ngv.vic.gov.au; free), which is one of those buildings that, inside, has an air of unpredictability. Walls are coming at you from all angles and there's no clue as to what may be around the next corner. Somehow it all works; the daylight comes in where it should and the art – all Australian – is displayed sympathetically. The **Australian Centre for the Moving Image**

has screenings, exhibitions, even video games; the programming is sometimes populist and always eclectic (daily 10am–6pm; cinema times as advertised; tel: 03-8663 2200; www. acmi.net.au; free except for some exhibitions and cinema). There is also the **Edge** performance space and a variety of bars, cafés and restaurants.

Behind Fed Square (as it quickly became known) is **Birrarung Marr**, an area of parkland on the river bank designed to acknowledge the original Aboriginal occupants of the land. Rock carvings and sculptural representations of shields and spears reflect the various tribes. Further on, the striking **Federation Bells** installation is worth seeing and hearing, and the passage of a bridge through to the Melbourne Cricket Ground ensures that plenty of people get to enjoy them.

Taking the tram

Melbourne's CBD is on an easily navigable grid and very walkable. Acting as backup is the **Circular Tram**, a free service that operates in a loop round the edge of the CBD. The tram system is one of Melbourne's great resources and, if you pick your route judiciously, a great way to discover the city.

St Paul's Cathedral , opposite Federation Square, was built between 1880 and 1891 to a design by William Butterfield, who never bothered to travel from England to see it. The stained glass and tiled floors are among the highlights.

On the other corner of Flinders and Swanston streets, **Young and Jackson's** pub is a Melbourne institution, renowned for the 19th-century nude portrait *Chloe* on the first floor, which was considered rather racy in its day.

Continue down Swanston Street to **Melbourne Town Hall** . Typical of the grand public buildings of the gold boom, it comes into its own during the International Comedy Festival every April when various performance spaces are carved out of its halls and meeting rooms and it takes on a real club atmosphere.

Collins Street crosses Swanston Street at this point and, were you to go uphill past the magnificent

The Windsor Hotel on Spring Street is a Victorian Heritage Hotel and dates from 1883.

BELOW: Federation Square.

Regent Theatre – pop into the foyer if it's open – you would come to what's known as the "Paris end", where a bunch of exclusive boutiques and designer stores tempts the wealthy tourists. To avoid that, go in the opposite direction.

Shopping arcades

Were you to continue walking a couple of blocks, you would be rewarded with the remarkable Gothic Revival facade of the **ANZ Bank Building** at the junction with Queen Street. But before that comes the **Block Arcade** **E** between Elizabeth and Swanston streets. In this Victorian marvel, thrill to the mosaic floors, etched glass roof, and the original shop fittings. The **Hopetoun Tearooms** has been purveying refreshment to refined shoppers for generations. Wind through to Little Collins Street and cross the road to **Royal Arcade**. You'll run the gamut of the slightly cartoonish statues of Gog and Magog, just behind you as you enter.

The far end opens into **Bourke Street Mall** **F**, the epicentre of old-style city shopping with the flagship department stores of the Myer and David Jones chains. At the Elizabeth Street end, the old **GPO** building has been successfully converted into a high-end shopping complex. The Myer store runs back across two blocks and has a bridge over to the bustling **Melbourne Central** retail hub which completely encloses the 1890 Shot Tower.

The Swanston Street entrance to Melbourne Central faces the imposing **State Library of Victoria** **G** (Mon–Thur 10am–9pm, Fri–Sun 10am–6pm; tel: 03-8664 7000; www.slv.vic.gov.au; free), which has had a rather large fortune spent on it in renovations. The **Reading Room** copies the famous one in London's British Museum.

The **QV Centre**, next to the library, is another shopping development, which attempts to emulate the feel of Melbourne's laneways in a more modern structure.

Following Latrobe Street beside the library and turning left on Russell Street, you'll find **Old Melbourne**

Gaol (daily 9.30am–5pm; tel: 03-8663 7228; www.oldmelbournegaol. com.au; charge). This is where Ned Kelly met his end. His death mask is on display along with some of his armour. The building is grimly atmospheric as it is, but extreme thrill-seekers can join a monthly overnight ghost hunt.

Return along Russell Street until you reach Little Bourke Street, Melbourne's **Chinatown**, a buzzing and colourful lane with several good eateries. Turn left on Spring Street and continue to the end where the **Carlton Gardens** across the road lead up to Australia's first World Heritage-listed structure, the **Royal Exhibition Building**. Access is normally only available for special events, but if you get a chance, nip in and have a look. It's a lovely spot.

Melbourne Museum

On the far side, that striking modern pavilion is the **Melbourne Museum** (daily 10am–5pm; tel: 131 102; www.museumvictoria.com.au; charge). The largest museum in the country, there is masses to see and it's all presented so alluringly that you can spend hours here without realising it.

The children's section is pitched just right, and other areas appeal to all ages, especially the Melbourne Story Gallery and the Bunjilaka Aboriginal Centre. There's an IMAX cinema too.

Victorian piles

Return to Spring Street and the state's seat of government at **Parliament of Victoria House** (tours Mon–Fri 9.30am, 10.30am, 11.30am, 1.30pm, 2.30pm, 3.45pm; tel: 03-9651 8911; www.parliament.vic.gov.au; free), another grandiose Victorian pile which still awaits the dome originally designed for it. Tours are available unless the houses are in session, in which case try for the public gallery.

The **Princess Theatre** opposite Parliament House is typical of its era, even down to the ghost story; ask for

details at the box office. Continue along Spring Street to another monolithic public building. This is the **Old Treasury** (Wed and Sun 10am–4pm; tel: 03-9651 2233; www.oldtreasury building.org.au; free). The permanent exhibits are linked to the history of the building and its role as Victoria's repository of gold. **Treasury Gardens**, alongside, simply crawls with possums after dark.

Walk through to **Fitzroy Gardens** where, under towering old trees, you will find **Cook's Cottage** (daily 9am–5pm; tel: 03-9419 4677; www. melbourne.vic.gov.au; charge). It's not hard to discover Australia if you were brought up there, you might think. But no, the whole thing was disassembled in Yorkshire, shipped round the world and rebuilt in Melbourne, making it the only 18th-century building in town. Elsewhere, look out for the model **Tudor Village**, sent as a gift from the people of Lambeth in London, grateful for Australian food parcels during World War II; and the **Fairies Tree**, a tree trunk carved with cute little figures.

The Old Melbourne Gaol also runs night tours four nights a week.

BELOW: a country locale for a weekend stroll.

The most famous plant in the Botanic Gardens is the "Separation Tree", an old river Eucalyptus around which a public party took place in 1851 to celebrate independence of Victoria from New South Wales.

BELOW:
the famous grounds of the MCG.

Across Wellington Parade, the Melbourne Cricket Ground, better known as the **MCG** , beckons to sports fans. Try to get in to see some kind of sporting action, but if not, there are tours (Gate 3; daily 10am–3pm if no event; tel: 03-9657 8879; www.mcg.org.au) of the 100,000-seat stadium. The new **National Sports Museum** (daily 10am–5pm; tel: 03-9657 8879; www.nsm.org.au; charge) is housed here and has interesting exhibits on cricket, racing, Aussie Rules and the Melbourne Olympics, all enhanced by the latest technology.

Return to Federation Square, turn left over the river, and go down St Kilda Road. Directly ahead of you is the grey stone **Shrine of Remembrance** (daily 10am–5pm; tel: 03-9661 8100; www.shrine.org.au; free). Built to commemorate the dead of World War I, it is aligned so that once a year at 11am on the 11 November – Remembrance Day – a beam of light shines on to the Stone of Remembrance and illuminates the word "love". A visitor centre nestles in the shadow of the main building.

Just across the way from the shrine is the Observatory Gate, one of the entry points to the **Royal Botanic Gardens** (daily 7.30am–sunset; tel: 03-9252 2300; www.rbg.vic.gov.au; free). Enthusiasts will enjoy the specialist areas, like the cactus garden or the cycad collection, but many simply wander through the beautifully tended grounds and drink in the tranquillity of the lakeside. There is also an excellent children's garden.

Arts precinct

Return to St Kilda Road and cross over to the bluestone bulk of the **National Gallery of Victoria** (Wed–Mon 10am–5pm; tel: 03-8620 2222; www.ngv.vic.gov.au; free). This is, in fact, **NGV International**, which houses the NGV's collection of work from overseas, as opposed to the Ian Potter Centre at Federation Square which specialises in Australian works. Stick your fingers in the water wall at the entrance, as generations have before you, and take your pick of the permanent exhibits or the visiting shows (for which a charge is usually

Sports Society

If Australians are sports mad, then Melbourne must be the asylum. It's not just the obsession with the sports themselves, but the determination to make every contest an event.

The first Tuesday of November is a public holiday, because that's when the Melbourne Cup is run. Each year the crowds at Flemington Racecourse seem bigger than the year before. In 2006, the record-breaking 129,000 crowd was not at Cup Day at all, but at the previous Saturday's Derby Day.

Boxing Day cricket invariably sells out at the MCG, but in 2010, for an exciting Ashes series where Australia was pitched against England, the first four days of the test match sold out in advance; that's 400,000 people if everyone turned up.

The Australian Rules Grand Final at the MCG in September is probably the biggest event of them all. Aussie Rules dominates Melbourne for seven months of every year. Every workplace and office has its own tipping competition, and everyone has to "barrack" for a team, irrespective of age, gender or interest. In this very Victorian sport (10 of the 17 teams are from the state), it came as a shock when the majority of the winners between 2000 and 2010 were from other states around Australia.

levied). Leonard Hall's stained-glass ceiling of the **Great Hall** accounts for all the people lying on their backs within, and beyond is the doorway to the **Sculpture Garden**.

Next door, distinguished by the huge mesh spire above it, is the **Arts Centre** ⓟ. This cultural powerhouse has three theatres presenting **Melbourne Theatre Company** productions and visiting opera, dance and drama companies. **Hamer Hall** is the city's formal concert venue, although currently undergoing a major renovation. If you carry on past the NGV and turn right, the striking building with the white geometric shapes all over it is the new MTC Theatre, and just beyond it, the equally new Melbourne Recital Centre.

At the river turn left along the South Bank where the promenade provides good views over the city, but not as good as those from the top of the **Eureka Tower** ⓠ and its Eureka Skydeck 88 (daily 10am–10pm; tel: 03-9693 8888; www.eurekaskydeck.com. au) which, all too predictably, is on the 88th floor.

You may want to cross over the river to visit the absorbing **Immigration Museum** (daily 10am–4.30pm; tel: 131 102; www.immigration.museum.vic. gov.au; charge), or **Melbourne Aquarium** (daily 9.30am–6pm, Jan 9.30am–9pm; tel: 03-9620 0999; www.melbourne aquarium.com.au; charge).

Crown Casino ⓡ (daily, 24 hours; tel: 03-9292 8888; www.crowncasino. com.au; free) on your left seems to go on forever; given the turnover on the tables and through the one-arm bandits, or "pokies" as they're known, the management probably hopes it will. Shops, restaurants, show venues and a cinema can be found inside.

Docklands

The architecturally stimulating **Melbourne Exhibition Centre**, or "Jeff's Shed" as the locals call it, since it was one of Premier Jeff Kennett's projects, comes next. On the river bank beyond is the distinctive outline of the historic ship, the *Polly Woodside*, docked in front of the new Convention Centre.

Stay on the path by the water round to **Docklands**, the latest area

BELOW: a statue in Docklands.
BELOW: the aquarium.

of Melbourne to be given an overhaul. You cross the river on the serpentine **Webb Bridge** and then follow the path through a sculpture garden that eventually leads to **Victoria Harbour,** with the **Etihad Stadium ⑤** on your right and glistening new developments of offices, apartments and restaurants on your left. The area is slowly finding its feet but it's worth wandering down for a look if only because it's unlike anything else in Melbourne.

It's time to hop on the Circle Tram clockwise to the junction of Latrobe and Queen streets. Walk north up Queen Street until reaching the extensive sheds of **Queen Victoria Market ❼** (Tue, Thur 6am–2pm, Fri 6am–5pm, Sat 6am–3pm, Sun 9am–4pm; tel: 03-9320 5822; www.qvm.com.au). It's a buzzing place where locals after fresh produce or deli specialities mix with tourists seeking souvenir clocks in the shape of Australia.

Little Italy

A short distance to the north, **Lygon Street** in Carlton, just 10 minutes by tram from the city centre, is sometimes known as **Little Italy.** It was this area that the waves of post-war Italian migrants adopted as their own, and at certain times of the year, such as when the Ferrari team is in town for the Grand Prix, streets are closed and the partying doesn't let up. Today Lygon Street is touristy, but a lively community of professional people and academics from adjacent Melbourne University keeps the place grounded. Coffee bars, bistros, trattorias, noisy pubs and pool rooms, as well as edgy fashion boutiques, contribute to a vibrant atmosphere.

Brunswick Street, a few blocks to the east, is hipper. In the evenings Melburnians drift here from around the city with bottles of wine tucked under their arms, looking for the latest BYO restaurant. They find cuisines from around the world, as well as Modern Australian. Wine bars, pubs with local bands and comedy nights, designer clothes stores, tiny retro fashion shops, gay and lesbian bookshops, artists' cafés of the type popular in the 1950s and '60s, full of earnest characters confused by daylight, all happily co-exist.

Melbourne Zoo in Parkville, west of Lygon Street, has been a favourite since it opened in 1862 (Elliott Avenue; daily 9am–5pm; tel: 03-9285 9300; www.zoo.org.au; charge). It has a comprehensive collection of indigenous animals, displayed in sympathetic surroundings, as well as species from further afield. Its elephant enclosure manages to re-create an Asian setting, and the food-court is themed to match.

St Kilda

St Kilda has always meant fun. Often sleazy, frequently illicit, but fun nonetheless. This bayside suburb is Melbourne's urban beach. There's no surf and few would brave a dip in the water, but the sand is clean and the beachfront on weekends is rather like Los Angeles' Venice Beach: rollerbladers and cyclists speed past, models preen themselves in the sun, and bodybuilders work out on

BELOW: Toto's Pizza House is popular with locals.

the grass. Fight for an outside table at a beach-front restaurant, or walk along the jetty for a distant view of the city skyline (there's a café at the end).

Roller coaster

Acland Street is famous for its cafés and cake shops. It displays the palate-delighting influences of Mittel Europe reflecting a strong Jewish presence, but other nationalities are crowding in. At the end of the street, **Luna Park**'s gap-toothed grin invites you to try the clattering roller coaster (Sept–Apr Fri 7–11pm, Sat 11am–11pm, Sun 11am–6pm, Jan–Feb Thur 7–11pm, May–Sept Sat–Sun 11am–6pm; tel: 03-9525 5033; www.lunapark.com.au; charge for rides).

The **Upper Esplanade** hosts a Sunday arts and crafts market, while in **Fitzroy Street** the restaurants take over the footpaths, Mediterranean-style, with their tables and umbrellas.

On the other side of the bay, over the Westgate Bridge (or take a ferry from Southgate), is **Williamstown**, a bayside village with plenty of cafés, restaurants and great views back to the city. On its outskirts lies one of Mel-bourne's best museums: **Scienceworks** (2 Booker Street, Spotswood; daily 10am–4.30pm; tel: 03-9392 4800; www.scienceworks.museum.vic.gov.au; charge), set in the grounds of an old pumping station. Its hands-on displays include House Secrets, which reveals what's really going on under the surface of a domestic environment.

Top market

North of St Kilda, **Prahran** has one of Melbourne's best markets (163 Commercial Road; Tue, Thur, Sat dawn–5pm, Fri dawn–6pm, Sun 10am–3pm; tel: 03-8290 8220; www.prahran market.com.au) and, in **Chapel Street**, a shopping strip that runs from op-shop (charity shop) to designer chic, with prices rising as you move north into South Yarra and affluent Toorak.

Como House (corner Williams Road and Lechlade Avenue, South Yarra; daily 10am–5pm, winter Wed, Sat–Sun; tel: 03-9827 2500; www.nattrust.com.au; charge) is a graceful colonial mansion built in 1847, set in grounds that demand that you go equipped with a picnic.   ❑

The Melbourne Exhibition Centre is also known as Jeff's Shed.

BELOW: a bridge over the Yarra River.

Music City

As well as having a throbbing local scene, Melbourne is a must-visit destination for international performers of all genres. It's partly down to the local audiences who love their music, know what they like, and are also pretty relaxed about trying something new. And it's a lot to do with the venues.

Every inner-city suburb seems to have two or three pubs or clubs where something will be happening most nights of the week. Old favourite the Esplanade Hotel – or "Espy" – in St Kilda will book hundreds of acts a year across its various bars. The Corner in Richmond, the Prince of Wales in St Kilda, the HiFi Bar in the city, and the Northcote Social Club in High Street, Northcote, present big-name overseas acts in intimate settings.

RESTAURANTS AND BARS

Restaurants

Prices for a three-course dinner per person with a half-bottle of house wine:
$ = under A$50
$$ = A$50–80
$$$ = A$80–120
$$$$ = over A$120

Central Melbourne

ezard
187 Flinders Lane
Tel: 03-9639 6811
www.ezard.com.au
Open: L Mon–Fri, D Mon–Sat. $$$$
Masterful cooking and huge flavours based on the cuisine of Southeast Asia have kept ezard at the summit.

Flower Drum
17 Market Lane
Tel: 03-9662 3655
www.flowerdrum.com

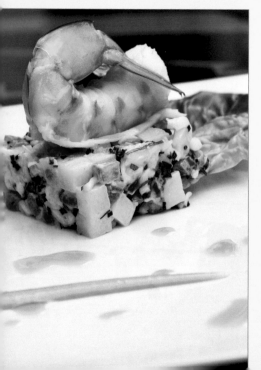

Open: L Mon–Sat, D daily. $$$
Once regarded as the pinnacle of Melbourne dining, this Cantonese eatery still offers fine food and expert service.

Grossi Florentino
80 Bourke Street
Tel: 03-9662 1811
www.grossiflorentino.com
Open: B, L & D Mon–Sat. $$$$
If it's florid surroundings and brilliant execution of Italian classics you're after, then this is the place.

MoVida
1 Hosier Lane
Tel: 03-9663 3038
www.movida.com.au
Open: L & D daily. $$
Booking essential at this popular and acclaimed Spanish joint that dishes up authentic tapas and sherry.

Pellegrini's Espresso Bar
66 Bourke Street
Tel: 03-9662 1885
Open: B, L & D Mon–Sat. $
An Italian café that channels the spirit and fun of the 1950s.

Taxi Dining Room
Transport Hotel, Federation Square
Tel: 03-9654 8808
www.transporthotel.com.au
Open: L & D daily. $$$
Occasion dining par excellence in this eyrie above Fed Square. A head-spinning list of wine and skilfully cooked European and Japanese food attract every celebrity in town.

Vue de Monde
Normanby Chambers,
430 Little Collins Street
Tel: 03-9691 3888
www.vuedemonde.com.au
Open: L Tue–Fri, D Tue–Sat. $$$$
Tables can be booked months ahead. The reward for those who get to sample the menu is sublime, adventurous modern cooking.

Docklands and South Bank

Bhoj Docklands
54 New Quay Promenade, Docklands
Tel: 03-9600 0884
www.bhoj.com
Open: L & D daily. $$
Melbourne's smartest Indian restaurant is also one of its best, with deftly cooked dishes from across the subcontinent.

Livebait
55b Newquay Promenade, Docklands
Tel: 03-9642 1500

www.livebait.com.au
Open: L & D daily. $$
Accomplished fish restaurant that makes the most of its waterside setting on the quay at Docklands.

Red Emperor
Southgate, South Bank
Tel: 03-9699 4170
www.redemperor.com.au
Open: L & D daily. $$
Southgate's ambitious and successful Chinese. Panoramic views of the city and the Yarra.

Rockpool Bar & Grill
Crown Complex, South Bank
Tel: 03-8648 1900
www.rockpool.com
Open: L Sun–Fri, D daily. $$$$
Melbourne's first exposure to the Neil Perry phenomenon is a subtle variation on his Sydney flagship with a meatier menu and flasher environment.

South Melbourne and Port Melbourne

Colonial Tramcar Restaurant
Departs corner Normanby Road & Clarendon Street, South Melbourne
Tel: 03-9696 4000
www.tramrestaurant.com.au
Open: L & D daily. $$$
The fun is in rattling around Melbourne for three hours in a historic tram while plates are ushered to your table.

The Graham
97 Graham Street,
Port Melbourne
Tel: 03-9676 2566
www.thegraham.com.au
Open: L & D daily. $$
A small menu is executed to perfection in this converted pub, with great friendliness and service.

LEFT: prawn is a popular dish, served in many ways.

The Court House
86–90 Errol Street,
North Melbourne
Tel: 03-9329 5394
www.thecourthouse.net.au
Open: L & D Mon–Sat. **$$**
A relaxed pub conversion that has quietly moved to the front ranks with its French-infused cuisine.

Cutler & Co
55–7 Gertrude Street, Fitzroy
Tel: 03-9419 4888
www.cutlerandco.com.au
Open: L Fri & Sun, D Tue–Sun. **$$$$**
This dazzling star on the scene sees chef Andrew McConnell hit new heights in adventurous contemporary cooking.

Matteo's
533 Brunswick Street,
Fitzroy North
Tel: 03-9481 1177
www.matteos.com.au
Open: D Sun–Fri. **$$$$**
A stylish neighbourhood restaurant that sets the bar high with its adventurous menu.

Shakahari
201–3 Faraday Street,
Carlton
Tel: 03-9347 3848
Open: L Mon–Sat, D daily. **$**
Legendary vegetarian establishment that serves its niche impressively and is imaginative enough to appease the unconverted.

Botanical
169 Domain Road,
South Yarra
Tel: 03-9820 7888
www.thebotanical.com.au
Open: B, L & D daily. **$$$**
Adventurous menu accomplished perfectly makes Botanical one of the reliables if you want to impress someone.

Jacques Reymond
78 Williams Road, Prahran
Tel: 03-9525 2178
www.jacquesraymond.com.au
Open: L Thur–Fri, D Tue–Sat. **$$$$**
Eight-course tasting menus take you on an incomparable journey through some of Melbourne's greatest French-infused cooking.

Café di Stasio
31 Fitzroy Street, St Kilda
Tel: 03-9525 3999
www.destasio.com.au
Open: L & D daily. **$$$**
This busy Italian has been thrilling St Kilda for years and shows no signs of losing its touch.

Circa the Prince
2 Acland Street, St Kilda
Tel: 03-9536 1122
www.circa.com.au
Open: B & D daily, L Fri & Sun. **$$$$**
A refurbished dining room and some of the most accomplished cooking in the city delight the most demanding of patrons.

Donovans
40 Jacka Boulevard, St Kilda
Tel: 03-9534 8221
www.donovanshouse.com.au
Open: L & D daily. **$$$**
A cross between a boat-house and a common room, Donovans comes up with splendid modern Australian cooking to match the peerless beach-side setting.

Mr Wolf
9–15 Inkerman Street,
St Kilda
Tel: 03-9534 0255
www.mrwolf.com.au
Open: L Tue–Fri, Sun, D Tue–Sun. **$**
Pizzas with a difference, and varied, child-friendly menu.

Stokehouse
30 Jacka Boulevard, St Kilda
Tel: 03-9525 5555
www.stokehouse.com.au
Open: L & D daily. **$$$**
Stokehouse will always attract people to its beachside location, but there's some seriously good Mediterranean cooking going on behind the scenes.

The Gin Palace
10 Russell Place
Tel: 03-9654 0533
www.ginpalace.com.au
Open: L & D daily. **$**
Plush decadence is the look behind the anonymous door in the city centre.

The Toff In Town
2nd Floor, Curtin House,
252 Swanston Street
Tel: 03-9638 8770
www.thetoffintown.com
Open: D daily. **$**
Turn left out of the lift and you get the Carriage Bar with its private booths, turn right and you enter an atmospheric live music venue. Both are recommended.

Melbourne Supper Club
161 Spring Street
Tel: 03-9654 6300
Open: D daily. **$**
Clubby, with deep sofas and discreet alcoves. A wonderfully refined place for a night on the town.

The Night Cat
141 Johnston Street, Fitzroy
Tel: 03-9417 0090
www.thenightcat.com.au
Open: Thur–Sun 9pm til late.
Live band venue featuring music for dancing to: funky soul, Cuban and salsa.

Dogs Bar
54 Acland Street, St Kilda
Tel: 03-8534 3020
www.dogsbar.com.au
Open: B, L & D daily. **$**
The ground floor of a lovely old dwelling oozes atmosphere and warmth. A local favourite in St Kilda.

RIGHT: Donovans restaurant.

VICTORIA

All the destinations in Victoria are within a day's drive of Melbourne – Alpine mountains, desert plains, pristine beaches, historic wineries, gold-mining villages and quaint spa towns

Around 5.5 million people live in Victoria, the smallest of the mainland states, which makes it heavily populated by Australian standards. Four million are in Melbourne though, so parts of Victoria can still feel pretty empty. Squashed down in the bottom right corner of the country, its northern border defined over hundreds of kilometres by the Murray River, Victoria is at its emptiest in the northwest where the Mallee, a semi-arid land of open plains, is given over to sheep, grain and national parks; and in the east, where the end of the Great Dividing Range curls round to peter out a few kilometres short of Melbourne. This high country of timber and cattle farming gets busier in winter as snow opens up the ski fields.

Victoria stuttered into life with the first permanent European settlement at Portland in 1834. Two years later pastoralists started crossing the Murray from the east and, with Melbourne growing, population increase was rapid. Aboriginal numbers, though, fell rapidly as introduced diseases and firearms took their toll.

In 1851 Victoria seceded from New South Wales. Within weeks gold was discovered and the new state's population and prosperity boomed. Indeed, the countryside is still littered with colonial mansions, and the towns with stately public buildings and hotels.

For being such a small state, Victoria manages to pack in a lot of attractions. The Great Ocean Road, the Goldfields and Wilson's Promontory are amongst the best known, but there are also coastal resorts, wineries, the inland ports of the Murray and some wonderful mountain scenery to explore. With good roads and comfortable distances to cover, Victoria is an easy state in which to lose yourself.

Main attractions
GEELONG
QUEENSCLIFF
THE GREAT OCEAN ROAD
PORT FAIRY
THE GRAMPIANS
THE GOLD TOWNS
THE MURRAY RIVER
THE DANDENONGS
BEECHWORTH
GIPPSLAND LAKES
WILSON'S PROM
THE MORNINGTON PENINSULA

LEFT: a stunning sunset.
RIGHT: playing in the waves at Torquay.

West of Melbourne

From Melbourne the Princes Freeway speeds through the plains along the western shore of **Port Phillip Bay**. For a glimpse of opulence, take the exit to **Werribee Park** (daily Nov–Apr 10am–6.30pm, May–Oct 10am–5.30pm; www.werribeepark.com.au; free). In a 60-room Italianate mansion built in 1877 by the pastoralist Chirnside family, visitors can sample a vivid display of flamboyant wealth. The extensive grounds are set off by a sculpture walk mostly made up of past winners of the Helen Lampriere Sculpture Prize. There are more fragrant pleasures to be found in the adjoining **Victoria State Rose Garden**.

Nearby, the **Werribee Open Range Zoo** (daily 9am–5pm; tel: 03-9731 9600; www.zoo.org.au; charge) re-creates African savannah with safari buses carrying you amongst the animals.

Geelong and the coast

As you drive on, the volcanic **You Yangs** dominate the skyline. Get closer to them by detouring to **Anakie**, home of **Fairy Park** (daily 10am–5pm; tel: 03-5284 1262; www.fairypark.com; charge), "Australia's first and oldest theme park", where dioramas from fairy tales unfold by the winding path to the top of a granite crag. It's very low-tech by today's standards, but kids love it and there's an excellent playgound, including the irresistible "do not touch this button".

Return to the highway and Victoria's second city. In its early days **Geelong** ❷ rivalled Melbourne as an outlet for Western District wool and later became an important manufacturing centre. After years of somnolence the city has shaken itself up – particularly by the waterfront, where quirky sculptures and a renovated pier are the focus.

A drive along the waterfront shows Geelong past and present – the old mansions, wool stores and piers, and the new industries, wharves and container terminal. Along the Barwon River are fine homes such as **Barwon Grange** (Fernleigh Street; Sun 1–4pm;

tel: 03-5221 3906; www.nattrust.com. au; charge), refurnished in the style of 1855, when it was built by a merchant shipowner.

For a whiff of nostalgia, take the Bellarine Highway out of Geelong and travel to **Queenscliff** ❸. This was "Queen of the Watering Places" in the 1880s when paddle steamers brought the fashionable to the handsome turreted hotels. There is still a haughty grandeur to the place. The Queenscliff fort (King Street; tours Sat–Sun and school holidays, 1pm, 3pm; tel: 03-5258 1488; charge), with red-brick walls and cannon, was built in the 19th century to defend Melbourne against a Russian invasion.

The road on to **Anglesea** meanders through seaside settlements, sleepy in winter and pulsing with life in summer. **Torquay** is the surf centre of Victoria, and **Bells Beach** is famed worldwide for its Easter surf contest. Beyond Anglesea, whose main claim to fame is the mob of kangaroos that live on the golf course, is the start of the **Great Ocean Road**, 200km (125 miles) of the state's most spectacular coastal scenery.

Beach bollards decorate the sands at Geelong near the town of Port Phillip Bay.

BELOW: bushwalking in Great Otway National Park.

Some of the Twelve Apostles.

BELOW: the Great Ocean Road leads past Apollo Bay.
BELOW RIGHT: an Inn Keeper in Flagstaff.

A favourite weekend spot from Melbourne is **Lorne** ❹, set on a picturesque bay with a bush backdrop and several restaurants and shops. The annual Pier-to-Pub Swim in January attracts entrants from across the nation.

In the **Great Otway National Park**, tracks wind through eucalyptus forest and fern gullies to waterfalls and lookouts. Walks vary from a gentle stroll along the St George's River to rock-hopping along to the Cora Lyn Cascades. A three-hour hike up to the **Erskine Falls** can be strenuous, while the less energetic can drive to a lookout.

Along the coast at **Kennett River**, a 6km (3½-mile) drive leads to the **Grey River Scenic Reserve**. It's a short walk (1.5km/1 mile round trip), one of the best in Victoria, up a fern gully amid towering blue gums.

For a panoramic view of the **Otway Ranges**, turn inland at **Skenes Creek** and drive up into the hills. After 15km (9 miles), turn left into the fern and mountain-ash forest along Turton's Track. When the country opens out again you are on a ridge. On the left, wooded spurs reach down to the sea;

on the right are the volcanic lakes and plains of the Western District.

From **Apollo Bay**, with its mixed artsy and fishing vibe, the Great Ocean Road leaves the coast to wind through the forest behind Cape Otway. Find the **Otway Fly** (daily 9am–5pm; tel: 03-5235 9200; www.otwayfly.com; charge), and enjoy a walk through the forest canopy on 600 metres (660 yards) of steel walkway, 25 metres (82 feet) above the ground. At **Cape Otway** a tour of the **Lighthouse** (daily 9am–5pm; tel: 03-5237 9240; www.lightstation.com; charge), which has watched over the hazardous entrance to the Bass Strait since 1848, is worthwhile. The setting is sublime.

The Twelve(ish) Apostles

Beyond Princetown lies the spectacular coastline of **Port Campbell National Park** ❺, where breakers have battered the soft limestone cliffs, creating grottoes and gorges, arches and sea sculptures rising from the surf. The road gives only occasional glimpses of the drama below, which includes the stark rock stacks of **The Twelve Apostles**

and the spray billowing through the fallen arch of **London Bridge**. It is an evolving landscape; as recently as September 2009 another of the stumps collapsed into the sea, leaving only a mound of rubble and just seven remaining Apostles. Stop at all the vantage points, follow the various trails at **Loch Ard Gorge**, and make the most of the new visitor centre.

Beyond Peterborough and the dramatic **Bay of Islands** lies **Warrnambool** ⑥, once a busy port and now a holiday centre. People flock here in winter to see the southern right whales off Logans Beach. Around the lighthouse is the **Flagstaff Hill Maritime Village**, a re-created 19th-century port with its chandlers, shipwrights and sailmakers (daily 9am–5pm; tel: 03-5559 4600; www.flagstaffhill.com; charge). The spectacular *Shipwrecked* sound-and-laser show runs nightly at dusk.- **Warrnambool Art Gallery** (Mon–Fri 10am–5pm, Sat–Sun noon–5pm; tel: 03-5559 4949; free) has a large collection of Australiana.

Beyond Warrnambool is **Tower Hill State Game Reserve**, a volcanic crater containing smaller cones where ducks nest, emus share your picnic and there's a good chance of seeing koalas. At dusk the 'roos come out as well.

Port Fairy

Along the coast is the fishing-village charm of **Port Fairy** ⑦, where brightly painted boats tie up at the jetty with their catches of crayfish and crab. Port Fairy was named by Captain James Wishart who brought his tiny cutter, the *Fairy*, into the Moyne River to find shelter during a sealing expedition in 1810. Sealers and, later, whalers built stone cottages which still nestle under the tall Norfolk Island pines shading the streets. You can drink at the **Caledonian Inn**, which opened in 1844 and has been in business ever since.

Griffiths Island, at the mouth of the river, was a whaling station, but is now a rookery for thousands of mutton birds that return in September from the north Pacific. The young hatch in January, and every evening until they leave in April you can watch the adult birds swoop in from the sea

The jetty at Port Fairy.

BELOW:
Loch Ard Gorge.

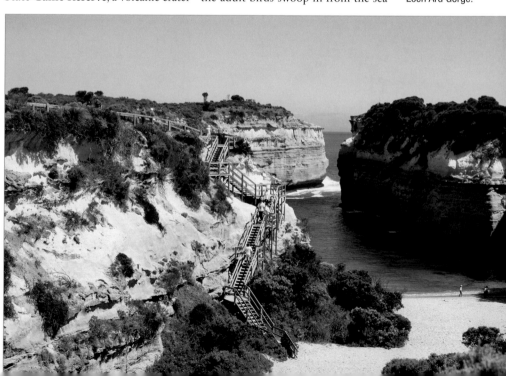

TIP

With the desert on one side and the sea on the other, Victoria is notorious for its changeable and unpredictable weather. Be prepared for cold winds, rain and searing heat all in the same day.

to feed their chicks, if you can see them – it can get very dark by the time they arrive and you simply hear a low whirring as they cruise past your head.

Portland ❽ – big wharves on a broad bay and solid 19th-century bluestone buildings – was a whaling station when Edward Henty arrived in 1834 and ploughed the first furrow in Victorian soil. Take the cliff walks at **Cape Nelson** and view the moonscape bluff of **Cape Bridgewater**, where wind and water have fashioned a petrified forest from scrub.

The coast road to South Australia skirts **Mount Richmond**, a sand-covered volcano ablaze with wild flowers in spring. It borders **Discovery Bay Coastal Park**, with its vast rolling sand dunes and stretches of unspoilt beach, and runs along the southern margin of **Lower Glenelg National Park ❾**, known for its gorge and delicate cave formations. You can drive or take a boat tour from **Nelson** up the gorge to the caves. The park is rich with 700 species of native plants, but most of it can be explored only by river or on rough, sandy tracks.

The Grampians

Pass through the wool town of **Hamilton** – see the **Big Wool Bales** – towards **Halls Gap**, where the ranges of the **Grampians National Park ❿** rise abruptly to dominate the surrounding plains. These craggy mountains are a series of rocky ranges thrown up by the folding of a sandstone mass into an uncommon cuesta formation – spectacular escarpments on the east side and gentle slopes to the west. Erosion has shaped bizarre rock sculptures, and waterfalls cascade over the sheer face.

Many scenic points are accessible by car, but there is wilderness aplenty for the more adventurous and walking tracks to suit all grades of hiker. You can drive past **Lake Bellfield**, where koalas feed in the manna gums, to the highest peak in the ranges, **Mount William** (1,367 metres/3,829ft). A 1.5km (1-mile) walk takes you to the summit. Return to Halls Gap via the Silverband Road to take in some of the highlights of the **Wonderland Range**.

On Mount Victory Road, short detours lead to **Reid Lookout**, high over the Victoria Valley, and home to

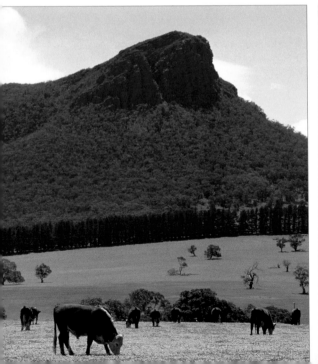

BELOW: cattle graze in the shadow of a mountain. **BELOW RIGHT:** climbing the Grampians.

kangaroos and emus. A 15-minute walk along the cliff top brings you to **The Balconies**, outcrops of sandstone that hang like giant jaws over the precipice.

As the road winds through the forest, stop at the viewpoint for the **McKenzie Falls** or take the walking track to the falls along the river, before going on to **Zumstein**. Walter Zumstein, a beekeeper and bush-lover who was a pioneer in this valley in the early 20th century, befriended the kangaroos, and each afternoon their descendants still leave the forest to be fed.

The Wimmera

The Western Highway travels through the heart of **The Wimmera**, the granary of Victoria. This sweep of golden wheat fields in an area the size of Wales stretches west to the South Australia border and north to the sand dunes and dry lake beds of **Wyperfeld National Park ⓫**. It is dotted with small townships, soaring silos, and populated by more sheep than people.

Horsham ⓬ is a small town, with the excellent **Horsham Regional Art Gallery** (Tue–Fri 10am–5pm, Sat–Sun 1–4.30pm; tel: 03-5362 2888; www. horshamartgallery.com.au; donation), and the **Botanic Gardens** are a nice contribution to the town.

Return east along the Western Highway towards **Ararat**. The town's first settler named a nearby peak Mount Ararat "for like the Ark, we rested there." Two French settlers, who saw that the soil and climate between Ararat and Stawell resembled that of France, planted the first vines in 1863, and wines, both red and sparkling white, have been produced at **Great Western** ever since. The road continues past forested hills to **Beaufort**, notable for its iron-lacework band rotunda topped with a clock tower.

The Eureka Stockade

Ballarat ⓭ is within an hour's drive of Melbourne, a far cry from the jolting day-long journey along potholed tracks that faced the miners bound for the gold-diggings in the 1850s.

On the southern side of the city, the **Eureka Centre** is being remodeled as the **Centre for Democracy at Eureka** (daily 9am–5pm; tel: 03-5320

Koalas are wild animals and should only be picked up or petted under the supervision of a trained professional.

BELOW: street performers entertain.

Aboriginal Art

More than 40 Aboriginal art sites have been found in caves and rock shelters in the Grampians. Some of the more accessible are in the **Victoria Range**, where you can see hand stencils in red ochre in the **Cave of Hands**, and a variety of paintings including animals, human figures and a kangaroo hunt in the **Glenisla Shelter**. Many of the geographical features of the region are woven into the Dreamtime legends, including the splitting of one of the Grampian ranges by Tchingal, a giant emu, to create **Roses Gap**. You can learn more about the area's traditional inhabitants at the **Brambuk Aboriginal Cultural Centre**, a striking building 2km (1¼ miles) south of Halls Gap (daily 9am–5pm; tel: 03-5361 4000; www.brambuk.com.au; free).

The clock tower in Bendigo peers out from what was once the post office; the building has now been renovated as a museum.

BELOW: panning for gold at Sovereign Hill, Ballarat.

5741; www.visitballarat.com; charge). At the site, a diorama brings to life the day in December 1854 when the name Eureka was etched into Australian history *(see page 37)*.

The rumbustious life of those times is re-created in the mocked-up gold-mining town of **Sovereign Hill** (daily 10am–5pm; tel: 03-5337 1100; www.sovereignhill.com.au; charge). In the main street, resembling Ballarat in the 1850s with its old-fashioned wooden shops, apothecary and confectioners, you can watch blacksmiths, tinsmiths and potters at work; sample a digger's lunch at the New York Bakery; or have a drink at the United States Hotel next to the Victoria Theatre where Lola Montez danced her famous and risqué spider dance. Take a ride on a Cobb & Co. coach and pan for gold in the creek. After a look around the Red Hill gully diggings, slake your thirst at the "lemonade" tent – the sly-grog shop where diggers celebrated their luck or drowned their sorrows. Then walk along the underground tunnel of the Quartz Mine, typical of the company mines where, in later years, the real

money was made. It is a ridiculously enjoyable day out and can be topped off with the *Blood on the Southern Cross* sound-and-light show that re-creates the drama of the Eureka Stockade.

Ballarat was born in the boom time, and its wide streets, verandahs and iron lace, towers and colonnades give it grace and distinction. **Ballarat Fine Art Gallery** (40 Lydiard Street; daily 9am–5pm; tel: 03-5320 5858; www.balgal.com; charge) is renowned for its Australian paintings, and the **Botanic Gardens** beside **Lake Wendouree** sport Italian statues and a blaze of begonias.

Gold towns

Other gold towns lurk to the north of Ballarat, where thousands of men dug their 12ft by 12ft (13.4 sq metres) claims with ant-like ardour. **Clunes**, the scene of the first gold strike on 1 July 1851, has an ornate town hall, and elegant banks and bluestone churches. **Daylesford**, a picturesque town on Wombat Hill, is known (along with its neighbour Hepburn Springs) as the spa centre of Australia. Nowadays, it's also known as a thriving weekend retreat for Melburnians, including a strong gay and lesbian contingent.

In **Castlemaine** the Greek temple-style market building and other fine edifices date from an era of promise never quite fulfilled. A short ride on one of the steam trains of the **Victorian Goldfields Railway** (Sun, Wed, some Sat; tel: 03-5470 6658; www.vgr.com.au) will take you to **Maldon**, the National Trust's first "notable town in Australia". Its gold-rush era streetscapes are terrific, as much for their tranquillity as their remarkable state of preservation.

In **Bendigo** ⑭, some of the richest quartz reefs in the world created a Victorian extravaganza. The scarlet **Joss House** is an interesting reminder of the thousands of Chinese who came to the "Big Gold Mountain", bringing with them temples, teahouses and festivals. The colourful Chinese dragon, Sun Loong, is 100 metres (328ft) long and the star of the Bendigo Easter Fair.

It is to be found in the **Golden Dragon Museum** (1–11 Bridge Street; daily 9.30am–5pm; www.goldendragonmuseum. org; charge). Elsewhere there are extravagant hotels, another good art gallery (42 View Street; daily 10am–5pm; tel: 03-5434 6088; www.bendigoartgallery.com. au; donation) and the **Central Deborah Goldmine** (76 Violet Street; daily 9.30am–5pm; tel: 03-5443 8255; www. central-deborah.com; charge) where you can take an underground tour.

The Murray

Echuca ⑮, 88km (55 miles) north of Bendigo, was an important port on the **Murray River** and its magnificent old timber wharf is now a major draw for visitors. You need a ticket to get in (daily 9am–5pm; tel: 03-5482 4248; www.portofechuca.org.au; charge) but it allows access to displays in two historic pubs and can be boosted to include a cruise on one of the historic paddle steamers. A cruise is *de rigueur* and allows you to relive the days when these mighty vessels, laden with cargo and passengers, made the river a busy thoroughfare, before the railways made

them obsolete. Think about renting a houseboat and making the river, lined with tall red gums, your home for a few days. Back on land, **Sharps Magic Movie House and Penny Arcade** (daily 9am–5pm; tel: 03-5482 2361; www.sharpsmoviehouse.com.au; charge), in the historic precinct behind the wharf, lets you relive the simple pleasures of pre-electronic entertainment.

The Murray Valley Highway loosely tracks the river as it heads northwest and rejoins it at **Swan Hill ⑯** where the principal pull is the **Pioneer Settlement** (daily 9.30am–4pm; tel: 03-5036 2410; www.pioneersettlement. com.au; charge), a collection of original historic buildings transplanted to this site to create a typical township of the 19th century. Time rushes by as you stroll in and out of shops and houses. You can cruise on a paddle steamer and, at dusk, take in a sound-and-light show.

It is another 196km (122 miles) to the city of **Mildura ⑰**. While many Australian centres claim the biggest of something, Mildura aims for the longest bar in the world – 91 metres (298ft)

In the last quarter of the 19th century, up to 30 steamboats were carrying gold-mining and other supplies along the Murray River. Then rail freight took over.

BELOW: paddle boats still ply the river.

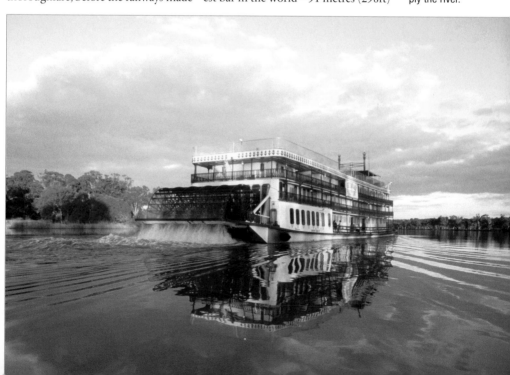

The Murray River supported many native fish such as the Murray cod and the silver perch. But the introduction of other species, particularly carp, destroyed aquatic plants and became a threat to the native fish, many of which have become threatened species.

BELOW: the wine barrels of Coldstream Hill Estate.

long, at the **Workingman's Club**; the largest fruit-juice factory; and the largest deckchair ever built (in front of a main-street motel).

Mildura is an exceptionally pleasant and friendly city, with its great climate and water pastimes of fishing, swimming and boating. The town, and the irrigation system that drew settlers to the area, were established by two American brothers, George and William Chaffey. William's imposing homestead, **Rio Vista** (199 Cureton Avenue; Wed–Mon 11am–4pm; tel: 03-5018 8330; www.milduraarts.net.au), can be seen at **Mildura Arts Centre** (currently closed for renovation). His other legacy is that, in US style, Mildura has streets with numbers rather than names.

The Murray River, of course, is the dominant attraction, and you can take to it and its series of locks with two-hour trips on the steam-driven *Melbourne* and dinner cruises on the *Rothbury* or *Mundoo*. There is also a wide range of houseboats for hire.

From here the Calder Highway runs back to Melbourne.

The Dandenongs

Approximately 50km (31 miles) east of Melbourne lie the **Dandenong Ranges** ⑱. Here, the mountain bluffs are riddled with both fern gullies and art galleries, while small towns like **Belgrave** and **Olinda** make lovely destinations for day trips, offering browsing opportunities in antique shops and cafés serving cream teas.

Attractions include the **William Ricketts Sanctuary** (daily 10am–4.30pm; tel: 131 963; www.parkweb.vic.gov.au; free), where romantically idealised Aboriginal spirit figures have been carved from wood by an elderly white sculptor and placed in a forest setting, and **Puffing Billy**, a narrow-gauge steam train that plies a 24km (15-mile) track from Belgrave to Gembrook (daily; tel: 03-9757 0700; www.puffingbilly.com.au).

The **National Rhododendron Gardens** at Olinda (daily 10am–5pm; tel: 03-8627 4699; www.parkweb.vic.gov.au; free) are at their spectacular best in October and November but are well worth a visit all year.

Directly north of the Dandenongs,

Black Saturday

On Saturday 7 February 2009, some of the worst bushfires on record roared through great swathes of Victoria and took the lives of 173 people. Years of drought, combined with a baking-hot summer, turned much of the country to tinder that was just waiting for the right spark.

As temperatures headed above 47°C (116°F), winds whipped up, some gusting over 120kph (75mph). Several dangerous, but to that point manageable, bushfires began to run out of control. Blazes jumped control lines and embers were blown hundreds of metres, setting off more spot fires which soon combined to create unstoppable fire fronts roaring across thousands of hectares. Houses, farmland and forests were razed and entire settlements were destroyed.

The Kilmore fire, as it became known, devastated Kinglake, Strathewen, Flowerdale and other townships to the north of Melbourne. When it combined with the Murrindindi blaze to the east, it virtually wiped out Marysville, where 34 people perished. Further east, in Gippsland, vast areas of forest were destroyed and much of Wilson's Promontory was affected. Over 1,200 homes were lost across the state and, as well as the human toll, wildlife was decimated and millions of hectares of forest and bushland were destroyed.

the **Yarra Valley** ⑲ now claims 55 wineries in its gently rolling countryside. Organised wine-tasting tours can be arranged or you can dip in to the odd cellar door as you pass through. One to look out for is **Yering Station** (38 Melba Highway; Mon–Fri 10am–5pm, Sat–Sun 10am–6pm; tel: 03-9730 0100; www.yering.com), Victoria's first vineyard but now a sparkling modern enterprise with a dramatic architect-designed centre and stunning views. Having the sumptuous **Chateau Yering** hotel with its excellent restaurants next door only adds to its appeal.

Yarra Glen is a relaxed centre to the area and a stop at the historic **Grand Hotel** is recommended. Take the road towards Healesville and pause at the **TarraWarra Museum of Art** (Tue–Sun 11am–5pm; tel: 03-5957 3100; www.twma.com.au; charge), which has changing exhibitions in its sleek, airy, award-winning space.

Only 61km (38 miles) from Melbourne is **Healesville** ⑳, best known for the **Healesville Sanctuary** (daily 9am–5pm; tel: 03-5957 2800; www.zoo.org.au; charge). This renowned open-air

zoo was established in 1934 to study and breed native fauna and has played a key role in helping to replenish Australia's endangered wildlife.

Travel north on the Maroondah Highway and after 24km (15 miles) turn off to **Marysville**. Once the base for Melbourne's closest ski field, the cross-country resort of **Lake Mountain**, it was razed by the Black Saturday bush fires *(see panel opposite)*. A winding road through **Yarra Ranges National Park** leads to the pretty village of **Warburton**.

For downhill skiing, return to the Maroondah Highway and work round to the northeast towards **Mansfield**, an important grazing and timber centre and the gateway to **Mount Buller** (1,808 metres/5,932ft), Victoria's largest ski resort. It lies just 3km (2 miles) from **Lake Eildon**, a 130-sq-km (50-sq-mile) body of water formed from the damming of five rivers to irrigate thousands of square kilometres of farmland. Today the lake is a paradise for waterskiers and fishermen angling for trout, perch and Murray cod.

The Puffing Billy makes its way through through the winding Dandenongs.

BELOW: the Ned Kelly statue at Glenrowan.

The Kelly Trial

Glenrowan Inn, 16km (10 miles) south-west of Wangaratta, was the site of Ned Kelly's last stand. Kelly's comrades were killed in a shoot-out with police as the inn burned to the ground, and Ned himself was brought to trial in Melbourne, subsequently to be hanged in the gaol there in November 1880.

Glenrowan has rather gone to town on its role in all this. **Kellyland** features computerised mannequins judderingly re-enacting the last stand at regular intervals throughout the day. Outside, a gigantic, technicolour Ned Kelly, in full armour and clutching his gun, looms over a block of tacky shops pushing Kelly kitsch. Many heinous crimes have been linked to Australia's most infamous bushranger, and there's no sign of it ending any time soon.

Kelly Country

Take the Midland Highway north and join the Hume Highway eastward. This is the heart of Kelly Country, the stamping grounds of the legendary Ned Kelly. Today, travellers on the Hume Highway through **Glenrowan** ㉑ can't miss his presence (*see panel, previous page*).

Benalla calls itself the "Rose City" after the thousands of bushes that bloom from October to April. These add colour to the unusual **Benalla Art Gallery** (Bridge Street; daily 10am–5pm; tel: 03-5762 3027; www.benallaartgallery.com; free) overlooking the Broken River.

Wangaratta ㉒ is a skilfully planned agricultural centre with a population of 17,000 on the Ovens River. Today it is noted for its wool mills, two interesting 19th-century churches, and the Wangaratta Jazz Festival which draws crowds every spring.

All towns here have one thing in common – a history linked to gold. In 1853, when gold was discovered in the valley of the Ovens River, dozens of prosperous mining settlements sprang into life almost overnight. By 1870, most of them had folded as the precious mineral became harder to find, but some of the towns survive as vital reminders of a thrilling history in a valley better known today for its wines.

Chiltern was originally established in the 1850s as Black Dog Creek. With its wide streets flanked by shops with Old West-style facades, the town has proved a popular film set. Today its main claim to fame is **Lake View Homestead** (Sun, Thur 1–4pm; tel: 03-5726 1317; www.nattrust.com.au; charge), the childhood home of novelist Ethel Richardson, who, as Henry Handel Richardson, wrote some of Australia's classic works, including *The Getting of Wisdom*.

Some 16km (10 miles) northwest of Chiltern is **Rutherglen**, centre of Australia's oldest vine-growing district and still the foremost producer of fortified wines.

On the border

Wodonga is the Victorian half of Australia's fastest-growing inland metropolis. Its big brother, **Albury**, across the

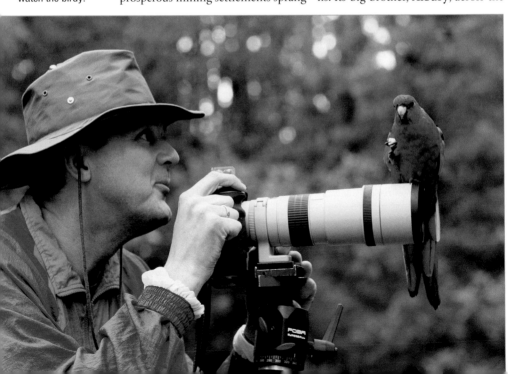

Murray River in New South Wales, gives the twin cities a combined population of more than 90,000. Hub of the Riverina district, which produces prodigious quantities of grain, fruit and livestock, Albury marks the site where the explorers Hume and Hovell discovered the Murray in 1824 after trekking south from Sydney.

The Murray Valley Highway passes through **Tallangatta**, at the eastern tip of **Lake Hume**. It is a new town, built in 1956 to replace the former community flooded by the damming of the Murray River. Traces of the old township – lines of trees, streets, even some buildings – eerily reappear at times of low water. The lake, four times the size of Sydney Harbour, is now a playground for swimmers, water skiers, anglers and birdwatchers.

Corryong ㉓, the last town before the border with New South Wales, features the **Man From Snowy River Folk Museum** (103 Hanson Street; Sept–May daily 10am–4pm; tel: 02-6076 2600; www.manfromsnowyriver museum.com; charge); its varied collection includes what has been enticingly described as "the most recognised snow-ski collection in Australia".

To the south is the village of **Nariel Creek**, where folk-music festivals are held on an old Aboriginal corroboree ground on New Year holidays and Victorian Labour Day weekend. Northwest of Corryong (access from Cudgewa) is **Burrowa Pine Mountain National Park** with rugged walks and views of the Snowy Mountains.

Beechworth

Return west, where the entire township of **Yackandandah** has been classified by the National Trust. Miners who came from California and the Klondike in the 1860s helped to give the place a lingering air of the American West. Today it is the centre of Victoria's largest strawberry industry.

Nestled in the midst of rolling hill country is northeast Victoria's best-preserved gold town, **Beechworth ㉔**.

No fewer than 32 of its buildings have been classified by the National Trust, including the towered **Post Office** (1867) with its Victorian stone construction, **Tanswell's Commercial Hotel** (1873) with its handsome facade and wrought-iron verandah, and the **Robert O Hara Burke Memorial Museum** (1856; daily 10am–5pm; tel: 03-5728 8067; charge), part of the historic precinct on Loch Street. This museum exhibits relics of the goldrush era – when 3 million ounces of gold were garnered in just 14 years. There is even a life-sized re-creation of a section of Beechworth's former main street. During its heyday the town had 61 hotels and a theatre which hosted international acts.

Mount Buffalo

South from Beechworth is a region of considerable natural beauty, the beginning of Victoria's high country. **Myrtleford** is the thriving centre of a walnut, tobacco and hop-growing region. **Mount Buffalo National Park ㉕**, a vast plateau at 1,370 metres (4,495ft), becomes a huge snowfield in winter, a

"The Man from Snowy River" started life in 1890 as a poem by bush poet Banjo Paterson. It became a silent film in 1920, and a popular modern version in 1982 spawned a sequel in 1988, a TV series in the 1990s and a stage musical. The poem was celebrated in the opening sequence of Sydney's Olympic Games.

BELOW: Tanswells Commercial Hotel.

A gazebo decorates the main street of Bairnsdale.

carpet of wild flowers in spring, and a popular spot for bushwalking in the summer and autumn.

Bright, a town of 5,000 famed for its autumn colours, is a short distance away. Oaks, maples and other hardwoods promote a serenity which belies its violent gold-rush days, including the notorious 1857 Buckland riots when white prospectors brutally ousted Chinese miners from their claims.

Mount Beauty is the gateway to the largest of the Alpine resorts at smart **Falls Creek** in **Alpine National Park**, where the après ski is as important as what happens on the slopes. Working south along the Great Alpine Road, **Mount Hotham** has downhill and cross-country runs, while **Dinner Plain** is an arresting 1980s resort.

Continue for 160km (100 miles) of attractive high-country motoring until the road joins the Princes Highway.

Bairnsdale

Bairnsdale, the commercial centre of **East Gippsland**, lies 285km (177 miles) east of Melbourne. A sheep, dairy and timber centre, it is best known for its fine **Botanic Gardens** and the "Sistine Chapel" murals in **St Mary's Catholic Church**. Nearby **Paynesville**, a boating resort, features the bizarre yet interesting **Church of St Peter**: a sailors' house of worship, it has a spire like a lighthouse, a pulpit shaped like the bow of a boat, and a sanctuary lighting fixture that was once a ship's riding lamp.

The Princes Highway eastwards runs all the way to Sydney but the only time it touches the coast in Victoria is at **Lakes Entrance** . This resort is situated at the narrow man-made inlet to the **Gippsland Lakes**, a long string of interconnected lagoons stretching west along the inner shore of the Bass Strait for some 80km (50 miles). They are separated from the sea only by a narrow band of dunes and hummocks called **Ninety Mile Beach**.

The normal population of Lakes Entrance increases by a factor of six in summer as holiday-makers pack the motels and caravan parks. Up-market accommodation is on offer at quiet **Metung**, a few kilometres to the west.

Fishing, boating and swimming are

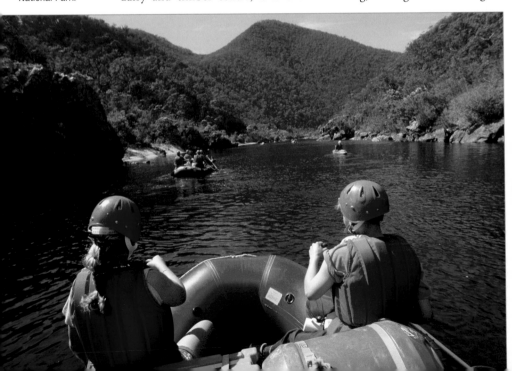

the main draws, while cruise boats offer regular sightseeing tours of the lakes. Sometimes called the Victorian Riviera, the area has consistent temperatures of about 20°C (68°F) in winter. The **Gippsland Lakes Coastal Park**, a reserve of dunes and heath along the lakes' seaward edge, and the **Lakes National Park**, a bird-filled woodland on a sandy peninsula between Lake Reeve and Lake Victoria, help protect natural features.

Snowy River National Park

Logging trucks seem to congregate at **Orbost**, a prosperous town of about 3,000 people near the banks of the lower Snowy River.

Snowy River National Park 28, in the mountains above, is popular with whitewater canoeists, who relish the challenge of riding the water through the deep gorges that contribute to the spectacular scenery of this often overlooked area. The Princes Highway then winds through its most remote stretch, 208km (129 miles) of mountains and rainforest, to reach the state border.

At Nowa Nowa, 22km (13 miles) from Lakes Entrance, a winding road will take you to **Buchan 29**. It hosts a rodeo over Easter, and a lumberjacks' contest in May, but its main attraction is its limestone caves, unquestionably the finest in Victoria. There are 350 here, but only three are open to the public, including the **Fairy Cave**, whose numerous honeycombed chambers are embedded with ancient marsupial bones (tours daily; tel: 03-5155 9264; www.parkweb.vic.gov.au; charge).

The southeast

At the hamlet of Genoa near the NSW border, a sealed side road turns south towards **Mallacoota**. This tiny resort town, much beloved by anglers and nature-lovers, is at the end of a 24km (15-mile) journey off the Princes Highway at Victoria's southeasternmost tip. It is surrounded by **Croajingolong National Park 30**, 86,000 hectares (212,500 acres) of rocky cliffs and open

beaches, rainforest, open woodland and health, stretching some 100km (60 miles) from the NSW border to Sydenham Inlet. Numerous nocturnal mammals (including possums and gliders) and many snakes – some venomous – make their homes in the park; hundreds of bird species include lyrebirds, oystercatchers, sea eagles and kingfishers. The pub at the charming village at **Gipsy Point** overlooks the inlet between Mallacoota and Genoa.

It's time for the long trek back towards Melbourne. The string of small cities along the Princes Highway from **Sale** comprises the **Latrobe Valley 31**, whose coal produces about 90 percent of the electricity for Melbourne and Victoria. The valley sits upon the world's largest deposit of brown coal, and open-cut mines and the steaming towers of power stations are everywhere.

Moe, the valley's largest and most modern city, is the site of **Old Gippstown** (daily 9am–5pm; tel: 03-5127 3082; www.gippslandheritagepark.com.au; charge), an 1850s theme park, where industrial and agricultural structures

In some of the limestone caves near Buchan (not those open to visitors) explorers have found tools and rock engravings dating back 17,000 years.

BELOW: speleothem formations in Royal Cave, Buchan.

The annual sand-castle competition on Rye beach in Mornington Peninsula draws a crowd every year.

BELOW: Sorrento Back Beach in Victoria.

and machinery have been transplanted to a garden setting. To see the real thing, and with a more dramatic backdrop, make your way to the tiny mountain community of **Walhalla** ㉜, where what was once Victoria's richest gold mine sits in a beautiful valley, now almost deserted.

Long Tunnel Extended Gold Mine is open for tours (daily; tel: 03-5165 6259; charge) and there's plenty more to keep you in this lovely spot.

Mount Baw Baw ㉝, the nearest downhill ski resort to Melbourne and a National Park, is a short distance to the northwest on the map, but to actually get there is a long and complicated drive down towards Moe and up again.

The Prom

The final swathe of goodies is to be found along the coast. **Wilson's Promontory** ㉞, a huge granite peninsula that represents mainland Australia's furthest thrust towards Antarctica, is the most popular national park in Victoria. The Prom, as it is affectionately called by regular visitors, features more than 80km (50 miles) of walking tracks

to long sandy beaches, forested mountain slopes, and heath and marshes packed with bird, animal and plant life. An estimated 100,000 people visit the park each year; access is managed carefully, but even the hot spots of **Tidal River**, **Squeaky Beach** and **Picnic Bay** rarely feel crowded. Just don't expect to find a camping spot in peak season without booking months ahead (tel: 131 963; www.parkweb.vic.gov.au).

The historic township of **Port Albert** to the east is worth a look for the **Port Albert Hotel** (1842) and the old timber jetty – at which eager 19th-century Chinese gold miners once disembarked. The **Gippsland Regional Maritime Museum** (daily Sept–May, June–Aug Sat–Sun, 10.30am–4pm; tel: 03-5183 2520; charge) is housed in the old Bank of Victoria.

Penguin Island

For many travellers, the most interesting stop in this final stretch to Melbourne is **Phillip Island** ㉟. It is connected to the mainland fishing community of **San Remo** by a bridge under which a flock of pelicans gathers daily for a feed. In an area of about 104 sq km (40 sq miles), there is a bewildering array of tourist attractions.

Phillip Island was the site of Australia's first motor-racing circuit (1928), and it still attracts crowds today when it hosts the Australian 500cc Motorcycle Grand Prix in October and the V8 touring car championship shortly afterwards. Among other attractions are koala and bird sanctuaries, scenic offshore rock formations, historic homesteads, pottery shops, and sports – from surfing, diving, sailing and fishing to golf, tennis, bowling and croquet. The relaxed north-coast summer resort town of **Cowes** is the tourist centre.

However, unquestionably the biggest regular attraction for Phillip Island visitors is the **Penguin Parade** *(see panel below)*. About 1.5km (1 mile) off the western tip of the island are the **Seal Rocks**, the breeding ground for Australia's largest colony of fur seals. Early December – the peak of the breeding season – is the best time to watch thousands of seals through coin-operated telescopes in the kiosk on the clifftop at Point Grant.

The Mornington Peninsula

The most popular weekend destination for Melburnians is the **Mornington Peninsula** ❸❻, which stretches down the eastern side of Port Phillip Bay. The Nepean Highway follows the bayside coast through a whole series of small resorts, all with beaches, some with bathing huts (although not as photogenic as the ones at **Sandringham**, closer to the city, that make it on to all the postcards). **Sorrento**, towards the tip of the peninsula, is the most attractive settlement and proudly offers a bayside beach as well as the more rigorous waters of the ocean. A ferry makes the short trip across the mouth of the bay to Queenscliff.

Further up on the eastern side of the peninsula sits **French Island** ❸❼. It used to be a prison farm and retains some of the old buildings. Most of the land is given over to a national park, with farming taking up the remainder, and it's one of the most peaceful places in the state, with hardly any cars. Visitors travel around by bike. Ferries to the island leave from Stony Point, or Cowes on Phillip Island. ❏

Just off the north coast of Phillip Island and accessed by a causeway, Churchill Island Heritage Farm has a very well-preserved homestead built in 1872 by Samual Amess, formerly Mayor of Melbourne (daily Apr–Sept 10am–4.30pm, Oct–Mar 10am–5.30pm; tel: 03-5956 7214; www.churchillisland. org.au; charge). A walk around the island is recommended too.

BELOW: a little penguin on Phillip Island.

Penguins on Parade

Every day at **Summerland Beach** on Phillip Island, hundreds of little penguins – we're not to call them fairy penguins any more – waddle from the waters of the Bass Strait to their protected burrows in the sand. Wings outstretched, they strut in small groups up a concrete ramp past throngs of curious human onlookers. This has developed into a serious, packaged tourist spectacle: there can be days when humans outnumber the penguins. In response to this there are now elite ticketing options, involving a "penguin sky box" or a small-group "more personalised intimate wildlife experience", which sees richer tourists led to a quiet beach by their own ranger. (Daily dusk; bookings 10am–5pm; tel: 03-5951 2800; www.penguins.org.au.)

RESTAURANTS AND BARS

Restaurants

Prices for a three-course dinner per person with a half-bottle of house wine:
$ = under A$50
$$ = A$50–80
$$$ = A$80–120
$$$$ = over A$120

Werribee

Joseph's
Mansion Hotel,
Werribee Park
Tel: 03-9731 4130
www.mansionhotel.com.au
Open: B, L & D daily. $$$
Imaginative and sound modern European cooking that adds significantly to the pleasure of the mansion's grand environs.

Geelong

Jack & Jill Restaurant
247 Moorabool Street

Tel: 03-5229 9935
www.jackandjillrestaurant.com.au
Open: L Mon–Fri, D Mon–Sat. $$
A left-field approach – mix small portions of three or four main courses rather than commit to just one – pays off in this fun-filled newcomer.

2 Faces
8 Malop Street
Tel: 03-5229 4546
Open: D Tue–Sat. $$
Seafood features in dishes such as bouillabaisse, but the preparation tends more towards the complex and offbeat. It's a small, intimate place.

Queenscliff

Point Lonsdale
Kelp Cafe
67 Point Lonsdale Road
Tel: 03-5258 4797
Open: B, L & D daily. $
Pared back modern decor reflects the cooking in this popular seaside café from breakfast through to dinner, when the seafood really shines.

Vue Grand Hotel
46 Hesse Street
Tel: 03-5258 1544
www.vuegrand.com.au
Open: B, L & D daily. $$$
It would be hard to find a more imposing setting than this. The cooking ventures to match it with bold colours and flavours.

Lorne

Ba Ba Lu
6a Mountjoy Parade
Tel: 03-5289 1808
www.babalubar.com.au
Open: B, L & D daily. $
A lively Spanish bar and restaurant where the tapas will fill a corner and the mains will fill a backpacker.

Port Fairy

Merrijig Inn
1 Campbell Street
Tel: 03-5568 2324
www.merrijiginn.com.au
Open: D Mon–Sat. $$$
Beautifully cooked contemporary Mediterranean food is teamed with an excellent wine list of old- and new-world labels to create one of the area's best dining experiences.

Dunkeld

Royal Mail Hotel
Corner Glenelg Highway and Parker Street
www.royalmail.com.au
Tel: 03-5577 2241
Open: D Tue–Sat. $$$
Not just the best restaurant in the Grampians, but one of the best in the state, with each day's 10-course tasting menu an adventure in itself. An acclaimed wine list completes the picture.

Ballarat

Phoenix Brewery
10 Camp Street
Tel: 03-5333 2686
www.ballarat.com/phoenix
Open: D Mon–Sat. $$
Running across three floors, including a cellar tapas bar, expect sharp contemporary cooking.

Daylesford

Lake House
King Street
Tel: 03-5348 3329
www.lakehouse.com.au
Open: B, L & D daily. $$$
There's theatre in the presentation and drama on the plate at this award-winning gourmand's delight. The insistence on the absolute best local produce goes a long way to explaining the quality.

Bendigo

The Bridge
49 Bridge Street
Tel: 03-5443 7811
www.thebridgebendigo.com.au
Open: L & D daily. $$
The beautiful modern dining room matches the food in this skilfully renovated landmark pub.

Echuca

Oscar W's
101 Murray Esplanade,
Echuca Wharf
Tel: 03-5482 5133
www.oscarws.com.au

LEFT: sampling wine in Sorrento Back Beach.

Open: L & D daily. **$$$**
At the top of the wharf with magnificent views of the paddle steamers chugging along the Murray below, Oscar W's scores on the food front too. Deceptively simple dishes feature idiosyncracies that denote a chef right at the top of his game. Kids get great, simple dishes.

Mildura
Stefano's
Mildura Grand Hotel,
Langtree Avenue
Tel: 03-5023 0511
www.stefanos.com.au
Open: D Tue–Sat. **$$$$**
A dining room of such renown that Melburnians make special trips out to enjoy it. You can see why. Each day's menu evolves according to the produce available so everything is fresh.

Yarra Valley
Eleonore's at Chateau Yering
42 Melba Highway, Yering
Tel: 03-9237 3333
www.chateauyering.com.au
Open: L Sat–Sun, D daily. **$$$**
This formal dining room makes eating an occasion, and the food deserves the reverence that that implies. The next-door café is a recommended alternative.

Healesville
Healesville Hotel
256 Maroondah Highway
Tel: 03-5962 4002
Open: L & D daily. **$$$**
Marvellously atmospheric dining room in this old hotel with great pub grub. Good wines, too.

Beechworth
Beechworth Bakery
27 Camp Street

Tel: 03-5728 1132
www.beechworthbakery.com
Open: B & L daily. **$**
People queue for the food at this local landmark. Its success has spawned a chain of six outlets across the state.
Provenance
86 Ford Street
Tel: 03-5728 1786
www.theprovenance.com.au
Open: L Sun, D Wed–Sun. **$$$**
The old Bank Restaurant has been stripped back, brought up to date and is now home to the region's most adventurous contemporary eatery.

Bright
Simone's
98 Gavan Street
Tel: 03-5755 2266
www.simonesrestaurant.com.au
Open: D Tue–Sat. **$$$**
Italian expertise applied to seasonal local produce to stunning effect.

Bairnsdale
The River Grill
2 Wood Street
Tel: 03-5153 1421
Open: L & D Mon–Sat. **$$$**
Lots of the best regional produce, including much from Bass Strait, served in a chic, contemporary setting.

Phillip Island
Harry's on the Esplanade
Upper Level, 17 The Esplanade, Cowes
Tel: 03-5952 6226
www.harrysrestaurant.com.au
Open: L & D Tue–Sun. **$$**
Loads of seafood on the menu in this laid-back bayside bistro, but carnivores are also well catered for.

Mornington Peninsula
Montalto
33 Shoreham Road,

Red Hill South
Tel: 03-5989 8412
www.montalto.com.au
Open: L daily, D Fri–Sat. **$$$**
The fabulous views from the glass and timber building, gardens full of sculpture, lovely picnic areas and dishes favouring local produce make this one of the Mornington Peninsula's best picks.
Salix
Willow Creek Vineyard,
166 Balnarring Road,
Merricks North
Tel: 03-5989 7448
www.willow-creek.com.au
Open: L daily, D Fri–Sat. **$$**
Excellent food to complement the local wines in this local favourite.

Bars
Benalla
North Eastern Hotel
1–3 Nunn Street
Tel: 03-5762 3252
www.northeasternhotel.com
Open: L Wed–Sun, D daily. **$**
Good-quality pub food in this attractive old hotel.

Maldon
Grand Hotel
26 High Street
Tel: 03-5475 2213
Open: L & D daily. **$**
Maldon offers unpretentious dining in a delightful historic pub from 1888. The menu covers the usual bases with local produce at compelling prices.

Metung
Metung Hotel
1 Kurnai Avenue
Tel: 03-5156 2206
www.metunghotel.com.au
Open: L & D daily. **$$**
On the water, this pub is well liked by both locals and visitors.

Portsea
Portsea Hotel
3746 Point Nepean Road
Tel: 03-5984 2213
www.portseahotel.com.au
Open: L & D daily. **$$**
The food at Portsea Hotel is reasonable pub fare, but having a beer on the lawn by the sea is not to be missed.

RIGHT: serving up a tasteful lunch.

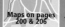

SOUTH AUSTRALIA

South Australia is renowned for food, wine and festivals. It is also blessed with a Mediterranean coastal climate, great beaches and awesome stretches of Outback

For a state that covers the gamut of Australian landscapes and culture, from the pastures of the coast, with its easy-going capital city, to the endless vineyards of the Barossa Valley, the barren beauty of the Coorong, the harsh grandeur of the Nullarbor Plain and the shifting colours of the Flinders Ranges, South Australia, is surprisingly neglected by visitors, whether from overseas or interstate. It's a puzzle. No other Australian state has such a high proportion of classic Outback desert and arable land. This vast hinterland has seen some strange sights, including the secretive rocket and defence system test site at Woomera.

Ancient landscapes

If you love the outdoors, then getting out in the timeless landscapes of the Outback is really something special. You could find yourself enjoying a desert sunset as you bathe in the warm springs at Dalhousie in the far north, sleeping undergound in subterranean Coober Pedy, or dealing with feelings of insignificance when you're the only person for kilometres on end. The vast landscapes of South Australia's Outback are steeped in Aboriginal history and culture and are pretty much untouched by the modern world. This is where you can experience the quintessential Australia that you may have seen in popular films such as *Rabbit-Proof Fence* or *The Adventures of Priscilla, Queen of the Desert*.

A big country town

Both visitors and locals often refer to **Adelaide ❶** as a big country town. Maybe it's the clean air, the friendly locals who smile at you on the street, the views of the green Adelaide Hills from the central business district (CBD), or maybe it's the space; the

Main attractions
ADELAIDE
THE BAROSSA VALLEY
THE FLINDERS RANGES
LAKE EYRE
COOBER PEDY
THE FLEURIEU PENINSULA
KANGAROO ISLAND
THE YORKE PENINSULA
THE NULLARBOR

PRECEDING PAGES: lavender fields.
LEFT: forest road on Kangaroo Island.
RIGHT: Adelaide's senior citizens gather.

TIP

The City Loop Bus (route 99C) is a convenient way to see the sights of Adelaide's CBD, and it's free. It operates daily at regular intervals both clockwise and anti-clockwise and takes in many of the city's attractions including the Central Market and North Terrace. Visit the Adelaide Metro InfoCentre (corner of King William and Currie streets) for timetables.

roads are wide, there are plenty of parks and the suburbs don't suffer from dense high-rise living. Combine this with a cheaper cost of living than the major cities on Australia's east coast, and you've got one very livable city.

Situated roughly one-third of the way from Sydney to Perth, this city of 1.2 million people is ideally placed to ignore the rest of the world – which, for most of its history, it did quite happily. Among Australians, Adelaide used to epitomise conservatism with a small 'c'. In the 1970s the city went through a cultural revival under the premiership of Don Dunstan, and for a while Adelaide led Australia on social and cultural reforms. While a legacy of world-class festivals and food and wine still remains, other parts of the Adelaide scene have not quite kept up.

Adelaide is a city that should be savoured slowly. It is possible to rock around the clock in Adelaide, if you know where to go, but it can be done better elsewhere (except at festival time, when no other Australian city can compare – *see page 202*). For

most of the year, to get the most out of Adelaide you should shift down a gear or two, move at a leisurely pace and meet the City of Churches on its own terms.

One's first impression of Adelaide is its sheer prettiness. This isn't an accident of nature. The city was laid out in a choice location according to the grand design of a British Army engineer, Colonel William Light, who founded the city in 1836. He came with a bevy of free settlers who had the express idea of founding a Utopia in the Antipodes. Sadly, Light – who was suffering from tuberculosis – was given a breakneck two-month deadline to choose a location and survey it. He managed the feat, choosing an inland site that was controversial at first, but his health collapsed; he had to retire, and died soon after.

The City of Light still follows the colonel's original design. From the air, the original city resembles a lopsided figure eight, with residential North Adelaide on one side of the Torrens River and the central business district on the other.

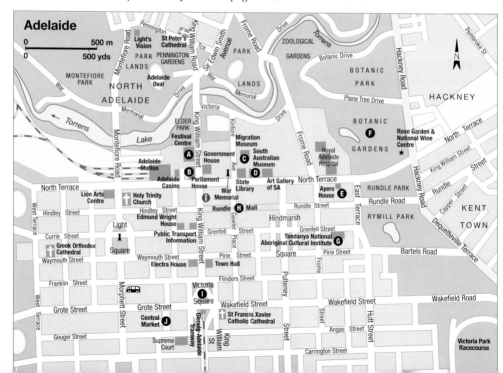

North Adelaide has some of Australia's grandest homes. It was intended as an exclusive enclave for the transplanted English gentry, who shipped out grand pianos and chandeliers from England to put in their colonial salons. Despite the prevailing local opinion that many were the "idiot sons" for whom there was no room in the old country, the gentry more or less thrived, in spite of itself, on the mineral and agricultural wealth of South Australia.

Also on the north side of the Torrens is historic **Adelaide Oval**, arguably the most beautiful cricket ground in all of Australia, and well worth a visit during the summer cricket season. At the northern end of the Oval stands the neo-Gothic **St Peter's Cathedral**, which has an ornate rose window above the door that depicts stories from South Australia.

South of the river, the central business district was designed for walking; it measures one imperial square mile and is surrounded by extensive parklands, studded with majestic gumtrees, which act as a scenic buffer between the city centre and the suburbs. This leafy moat means it is quite impossible to enter or leave the city without passing through restful greenery. The two halves are connected by King William Street, at 42 metres (138ft) wide, the broadest main street of any Australian capital city – one reason for the lack of traffic jams.

The main intersection in Adelaide is where North Terrace crosses King William Street. Most major attractions are within a few minutes' walk of this intersection.

The **Adelaide Festival Centre** (tel: 08-8216 8600; www.adelaidefestival centre.com.au) is the oldest multipurpose performing arts centre in Australia. Its four performance spaces host a variety of events and one-off shows including the nation's premier arts festival. Backstage tours run Tuesdays and Thursdays at 11am. The centre overlooks **Elder Park** by the River Torrens – once a rather unimpressive trickle, but dammed to form an artificial lake. Visitors can choose to take a two-person pedal boat out on the river or cruise to the zoo on board a Popeye

St Peter's Cathedral has several similar architectural features that are similar to Notre Dame Cathedral in Paris.

BELOW:
Adelaide's
Festival Centre.

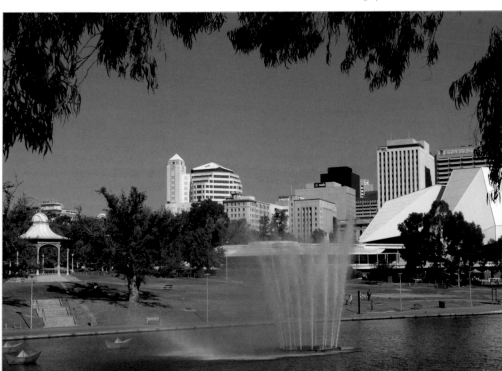

Festival Frenzy

Sydney, Melbourne and Perth all have their arts festivals, but none compares in size, prestige or sheer excitement to Adelaide's

The Adelaide Festival of Arts is held in March on even-numbered years and trades on the city's natural advantages. Few places in the world have such an extraordinary range of performance spaces, from the gleaming Festival Centre to the many outdoor amphitheatres and numerous intimate loft spaces. The weather is nigh perfect, with dry, hot days and clear, star-studded nights – and you can walk to every venue within about 15 minutes.

The festival actually operates on several levels. The official festival lures the high-profile international acts, and kicks off with free weekend concerts in Rundle Park, followed by firework displays. Tickets to the official shows are very reasonable compared with the prices charged in Sydney and Melbourne, and there is usually a string of free events.

At the same time, the Adelaide Fringe is for lesser-known performers and artists. It is second in size only to Edinburgh's annual shindig: literally thousands of acts arrive from all over Australia,

Europe and North America. Its popularity has seen it become an annual event. The chaotic, organic nature of the Fringe is what gives Adelaide its buzz. The focus tends to be around the bars and restaurants of Rundle Street East, where the festivities continue until dawn at the Fringe Club, while buskers and performers spread throughout the city.

With nearly 500 events in the programme, every spare corner of indoor space is devoted to some art exhibition, and every stretch outdoors to a site-specific installation. By any standards, it's a remarkable event.

At the same time as the Festival of Arts, Adelaide hosts Writers' Week, an event that lures the literary elite from around the globe. It is entirely free, with readings by famous authors and book launches held in the Pioneer Women's Memorial Gardens on King William Street, across from the Festival Centre.

Although nothing quite matches the festival for action, things are not too quiet in South Australia for the rest of the time. Every March, Adelaide hosts an enormous World Music Festival, known as Womadelaide, in Botanical Park. Tasting Australia is a huge biennial food and wine festival held in the city every odd-numbered year in October.

The Adelaide Festival of Ideas is a recent addition to the abundance of celebrations, and takes place every odd-numbered year during the winter. It attracts some of the world's leading writers and thinkers such as ex-prime ministers, journalists, political commentators and university professors. A typical festival could touch on such varied topics as the Middle East, globalisation, cloning, theology or even the existence of extraterrestrials.

The Barossa Valley hosts a music festival every October. Most of the concerts are classical in nature and held in Lutheran churches – although the accompanying indulgent meals and fine wines might well have appalled the region's founding fathers.

In early April in odd-numbered years, the Barossa Vintage Festival is a thanksgiving celebration for the region's grape harvest. The seven-day event, based in Tanunda, includes lavish tastings, grape picking and treading contests, and a vintage fair.

Between May and October most wine-producing areas hold food, wine and music festivals, the most notable being the Clare Valley Gourmet Weekend in May; McLaren Vale holds several, including the Sea and Vines festival in June. ❑

LEFT: exploring a temporary sculpture at the 2010 Adelaide Fringe Festival.

cruise boat, an Adelaide tradition that dates back to 1935; a 40km (25-mile) cycle and walking track also runs along the river.

Back on North Terrace is the monumental **Parliament House B**, completed in 1939, which is open to visitors (guided tours 10am and 2pm weekdays, when parliament is not sitting; free). Across the road is **Government House** (closed to visitors), the official residence of the governor of South Australia.

The eastern wing of **North Terrace** is the cultural heart of Adelaide with museums and galleries situated within easy walking distance of one another. Just behind the **State Library**, which houses a tribute to Australian cricket legend Sir Donald Bradman, the **Migration Museum C** (Mon–Fri 10am–5pm, Sat–Sun 1–5pm; tel: 08-8207 7580; www.history.sa.gov.au; free) is an excellent place to explore South Australia's cultural diversity.

The **University of Adelaide** could have been transplanted from Oxford, with its ivy-covered walls and dreaming spires. The **South Australian**

Museum D (daily 10am–5pm; tel: 08-8207 7500; www.samuseum.sa.gov.au; free) houses the world's largest collection of Aboriginal artefacts, as well as an extensive Pacific exhibit and a broad survey of regional natural history (the building can be identified by the huge whale skeletons displayed behind glass walls). The **Art Gallery of South Australia** (daily 10am–5pm; tel: 08-8207 7000; www.artgallery.sa.gov.au; free) has a renowned collection of 35,000 works. It displays a comprehensive collection of Australian art including landscapes by Sir Hans Heysen and Aboriginal Western Desert dot paintings, along with tasteful pieces by overseas artists.

North Terrace was once lined with houses like **Ayers House E**, the home of Sir Henry Ayers, who contrived to be premier of South Australia seven times – an Australian record – and after whom Ayers Rock (Uluru) was once named. The house is now a restaurant and living museum protected by the National Trust (Tue–Fri 10am–4pm, Sat–Sun 1–4pm; tel: 08-8223 1234; www.ayershousemuseum.org.au; charge). The elegant bluestone mansion

An invitation to dine in the South Australian Outback.

BELOW: the Art Gallery of South Australia.

The fountain outside Adelaide Arcade used to sit at the intersection of Rundle Mall and Gawler Place. When state Premier Don Dunstan opened the mall in 1976 the fountain flowed with champagne, much to the delight of 10,000 onlookers.

contains 40 rooms dating from 1846 to the 1870s, and the hand-painted ceilings and ornate chandeliers of the dining room and ballroom are particularly remarkable.

To the north of Ayers House lie the **Botanic Gardens** (daily; guided walks daily 10.30am; tel 08-8222 9311; free), 16 hectares (40 acres) of manicured lawns, trees, shrubs and lakes, with an impressive rose garden and some exceptional botanical buildings as well, from the old Palm House brought from Germany in 1875 to the extraordinary Bicentennial Conservatory of 1988.

South of Ayers House, in Grenfell Street, is the **Tandanya National Aboriginal Cultural Institute** (daily 10am–5pm; tel: 08-8224 3200; www.tandanya.com.au; free), the city's venue for theatre, dance, talks, demonstrations and constantly changing exhibitions of arts and crafts, representing all aspects of contemporary Aboriginal culture. The Institute has a shop selling native arts and crafts, and a café where visitors can try bush tucker.

The lively, busker-filled **Rundle Mall** was the country's first traffic-

BELOW: fresh blooms at the Adelaide Botanic Gardens.

free shopping mall, an idea of former state premier Don Dunstan, who in the 1960s turned Adelaide from a musty provincial centre into "the Athens of the South". He also originated the Festival Centre and introduced some of the most progressive state laws in Australia – laws to recognise Aboriginal land rights, decriminalise homosexuality and guarantee equal opportunity. Dunstan shocked staid old Adelaide, and much of Australia besides (on one occasion, he caused a media frenzy when he wore what were described as "pink hot-pants" to parliament).

In the centre of the city's square mile, King William Street opens out into **Victoria Square** , which is where you can catch the tram to the beach-side suburb of Glenelg. Just to the west is Adelaide's **Central Market** (Tue 7am–5.30pm, Thur 9am–5.30pm, Fri 7am–9pm, Sat 7am–3pm) – easily one of the most colourful in Australia. A giant covered area packed with more than 200 shops and stalls, it sells cheap fruit, vegetables, cheeses, meats, spices and

Vale of Cheers

It takes just over an hour to drive to the Barossa Valley, which lies 60km (35 miles) northeast of Adelaide. Along the way you will pass the actual Jacob's Creek, where the famous winery gets its name from, and then row after row of vines belonging to one of the more than 60 local wineries which produce more top-of-the-range wines than anywhere else in Australia, and include some of the most famous names in the business – **Peter Lehmann**, **Yalumba**, **Grant Burge**, **Penfolds** and **Wolf Blass**. Alongside these giants can be found numerous boutique producers who grow not for quantity, but to make the highest-quality wine possible from their venerable vines. Nearly all the wineries have tasting and salerooms, and many have barbecue and picnic areas as well as restaurants and cafés. Like a well-stocked cellar built up over many years, the wineries are spread the length of the Barossa Valley Way, which links most of the main towns in the region. Many Barossa wineries not only produce excellent vintages but also have magnificent grounds and buildings, like the palm groves at **Seppeltsfield**, picturesque **Chateau Yaldara**, and the two-storey historic blue-marble buildings at **Yalumba**. **Bethany Winery** has panoramic views of the valley, while **Rockford Wines** is one of the last bastions of traditional basket-press wine-making.

a variety of esoteric imported foods. But the main attraction is the wealth of local produce that South Australia is famed for, from Maggie Beer's pâtés and Adelaide Hills cheeses, to gourmet delights from the Barossa Valley and fresh local fish such as the delicately sweet King George whiting. There are plenty of tastings to be had as well. It's no wonder this is one of Adelaide's most popular attractions for both locals and visitors. There are also stalls selling books, crafts, jewellery and clothing, alongside cafés and cheap eateries.

The market encompasses Adelaide's **Chinatown**, which spills out into Gouger Street, one of the city's main restaurant strips. The others include O'Connell Street (North Adelaide), Rundle Street (East End) and Hindley Street (West End). Between them, they provide a fine choice of Chinese, Indian, Turkish, Italian, Malaysian, Japanese, Greek, African, Vietnamese, Russian, Lebanese, Thai and Australian eateries. Adelaide reputedly has more restaurants per capita than any other Australian city; it would be a shame not to visit as many as possible during your trip.

Hills and beaches

Cosmopolitan though it can be, Adelaide has never lost that country-town feeling. You can drive across the city in half an hour, and you can be in beautiful countryside in a fraction of the time it takes to leave the other major cities in Australia. Take any one of a dozen roads up into the **Adelaide Hills** and you can happily get lost in leafy, winding laneways. The hills are littered with small commuter suburbs such as **Blackwood**, **Aldgate** and **Crafers**, some of which are strikingly pretty. There are pubs with hilltop views and restaurants like Windy Point where you can dine overlooking the expanse of the city's twinkling lights.

Adelaide Hills offer something for most tastes, with bushwalks, markets, wineries, award-winning restaurants, wildlife parks and Birdwood's **National Motor Museum** (daily 10am–5pm; tel: 08-8568 4000; charge), which is the largest of its kind in Australia. You

Among the 400 vehicles in the National Motor Museum is an 1899 Shearer, built in Mannum, South Australia, and still running. Also on display is a Talbot which completed an epic 51-day journey from Darwin to Adelaide in 1908.

BELOW: the covered market in Adelaide is great for shopping regardless of the weather.

Nocturnal Walks

Warrawong Sanctuary (Tue–Sun from 9am; tel: 08-8370 9197; www. warrawong.com; charge), situated just 25 minutes outside of Adelaide in the Adelaide Hills, is a thriving home for more than 100 of Australia's native species of animals, including the mainland's only platypus population.

As most native mammals are active mainly at night, the Warrawong Sanctuary's guided nocturnal tour is an excellent way to get to know the local wildlife. The bilby, which has replaced the bunny as the local symbol for Easter, is one of the endangered marsupials that you will see on the tour. Nocturnal tours run for 90 minutes from sunset year-round, so call for precise times. There are also a number of self-guided walks available all year round from 9am–4pm.

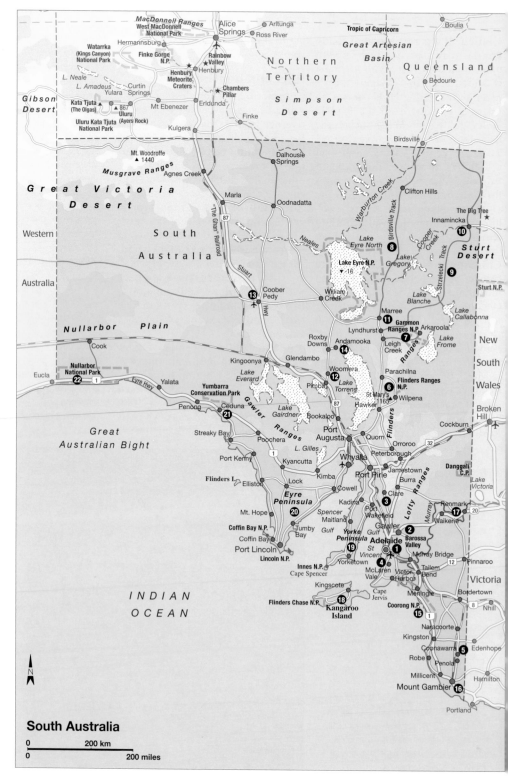

South Australia

0   200 km

0   200 miles

can easily spend a day lapping up the pretty German town of **Hahndorf** and its surroundings, a favourite weekend excursion for Adelaideans.

Another Adelaide ritual is to take the Glenelg tram from the city centre to the beach. The ride takes about 20 minutes and, while **Glenelg** has seen better times and now suffers from overdevelopment, the beach is wide, the sand is white and the site is wonderful.

If Glenelg is too crowded for your liking, Adelaide is blessed with a coastline border fringed by spacious, clean beaches that stretch for many kilometres. **Henley Beach** is a popular, more low-key option, and after a dip or a walk you can dine on some fish and chips at the grassy, beach-side square.

If you like to feel the warm sun all over your skin, drive down Main South Road (A13) for 20km (12 miles) until you see the turn-off on the right to **Maslin Beach.** It's an official nudist beach and its backdrop of sandstone cliffs makes it one of the most beautiful seaside settings in the state. Maslin is friendly and family-oriented,

but be warned: the gulf waters are fed by the Southern Ocean and the water can be brisk.

Valleys of vines

Adelaide sits amid the country's greatest wine regions, of which the **Barossa Valley 2** is easily the most famous. It was named in 1837 by Colonel William Light, Adelaide's far-sighted planner, because it reminded him of the countryside in Spain where he fought against Napoleon's army in the Battle of Barossa. The valley was settled in the 1840s by Germans seeking freedom to worship in the Lutheran Church. They brought the first vine cuttings with them, and, more than 150 years later, wine drinkers worldwide thank them for their forethought.

The Barossa is accessible either via the direct route from Adelaide through Gawler, or you can choose the scenic route via the Adelaide Hills which takes you through Cudlee Creek, onto Williamstown and then **Lyndoch**, which is the first major town in the valley. The enjoyable drive takes you past some of the city's reser-

The extreme wet weather in the spring of 2011 caused many Chardonnay grapes to ripen too quickly. Many vineyards were forced to watch their crops rot on the vine due to strict harvesting restrictions.

BELOW:
Chateau Tanunda.

Jacob's Creek, one of the world's most popular wine brands, is produced by Orlando Wines whose grapes were first planted by immigrants from Bavaria in 1847. In 1989 Orlando was bought by France's Pernod Ricard.

voirs. Just beyond Williamstown, stop at the **Whispering Wall**, which is not only an engineering feat but an acoustic phenomenon. The wall is curved in such a way that whisperings at one end can be clearly heard at the other which is 140 metres (460ft) away.

From Lyndoch in its forest setting, the Barossa Way continues on to **Tanunda**, the most distinctly German town in the region, which is renowned for its fine butchers and bakeries. Following the road to Nuriootpa, you can take a detour to the left down Samuel Road to visit **Maggie Beer's Farm Shop** (daily 10.30am–5pm; tel: 08-8562 4477; www.maggiebeer.com.au). Maggie is one of Australia's leading celebrity cooks and a Barossa icon – at her farm shop you can catch a daily cooking demonstration at 2pm or pick up some picnic supplies.

Back on the road it's not far to **Nuriootpa**, the commercial centre of the Barossa Valley. Keep following the road to Angaston, where the popular Barossa Farmer's Market takes place each Saturday morning.

Clare

Although the Barossa is the best-known wine-producing area in Australia, it is only one of five major wine regions within easy driving distance of Adelaide. **Clare** ❸ is the centre of the wine area of the Clare Valley/Watervale region about 130km (80 miles) north of Adelaide. Jesuit priests fleeing persecution in Silesia settled in the Clare Valley in 1848 and began making sacramental wines at Sevenhill Cellars. Today there are more than 20 wineries and 40 cellar doors in a 25km (15-mile) strip. The region is famed for its Rieslings, but you will also find some fine Shiraz and Cabernet Sauvignon. Many are boutique wineries whose labels are taking their place on some of the world's finest wine lists.

Some of the more renowned names in the business include Neil Paulett, Jeffrey Grosset, David O'Leary, Neil Pike and Mount Horrocks.

More than 60 cellar doors are dotted throughout **McLaren Vale** ❹, 42km (26 miles) south of Adelaide. Cartographers battle to fit all the vineyards on

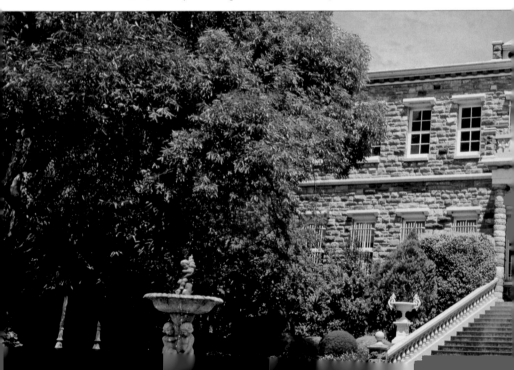

the map; they read like a wine-lover's roll of honour: Geoff Merrill, Hardy's Tintara and Wirra Wirra. This region is renowned for its reds, although there is plenty on offer to please lovers of white wine, including some fine Sauvignon Blanc and Viognier.

In the southeast of the state, on the way between Adelaide and Melbourne, the vineyards of the **Coonawarra ❺** area are justly famed for their reds. Vineyards at **Keppoch** and **Padthaway** are becoming equally well known. **Padthaway Estate Homestead**, now an exclusive hotel, is an imposing stone mansion in an oasis of green English-style gardens. The property was taken up as a sheep run in 1847, and the homestead was built in 1882. Today a number of vineyards spread over the acres where sheep once grazed.

The orchards of the **Riverland**, on the Murray River, produce nearly half of the state's wine grapes. The specialities of the region are brandies and fortified dessert wines. **Berri Estates** is the largest winery in the country, while smaller wineries include Bonneyview Wines at Barmera.

The most famous is **Banrock Station** near Kingston-on-Murray, which is well worth a visit. Their eco-friendly philosophy is reflected in the design of the visitor centre, which has information on how the winery helps to fund environmental programmes. The winery overlooks restored wetlands.

North from Adelaide

If you're not too keen on driving the vast distances of the Outback on your own, then you could choose to watch the scenery glide past you from the comfort of the **Ghan** *(see pages 267–8)*, one of the world's great rail journeys. It links Adelaide to the Red Centre, before continuing on to the tropical Top End. The Ghan gets its name from the Afghan camel traders who pioneered travel from Adelaide to the Red Centre.

The **Flinders Ranges** extend from near Port Pirie, where Mount Remarkable (975 metres/3,150ft) is the first major peak, to past Mount Painter in the desert and salt lakes to the north. At the top of the **Spencer Gulf**, the road turns away from the ocean and

TIP

Bundaleer Forest Weekend, held in March, is a music festival where artists perform outdoors in the forest. Hearing the Adelaide Symphony Orchestra while sitting on hay bales at sunset is a memorable experience. The forest is 10km (6 miles) south of Jamestown and about 2½ hours' drive from Adelaide. www.bundaleer festival.com.au.

BELOW:
Chateau Yaldara.

BELOW: Wilpena Pound in the Flinders Range.

heads into the arid heart of the continent. Here lies **Port Augusta** which, with Port Pirie and Whyalla, forms the basis of South Australia's industrial heart, known as the Iron Triangle. From Port Augusta, the road runs northeast through **Quorn**, then on to **Hawker**, the nearest township to the northern Flinders Ranges. You can travel between Port Augusta and Quorn on the steam locomotive of the historic **Pichi Richi Railway**, which operates on the oldest section of the Ghan track.

By a fortunate coincidence, the most spectacular feature of the Flinders Ranges is also the most accessible. **Wilpena Pound** at the southern end of the **Flinders Ranges National Park ❻** is a raised valley surrounded by quartzite hills. St Mary's Peak is the highest point in the ranges at 1,165 metres (3,758ft).

The only way into Wilpena Pound is on foot: there are a number of hikes that begin at the the visitor centre. By comparison with the thin, rocky soil and arid landscape outside, the pound floor is richly vegetated. In fact, Wilpena Pound attracts considerably more rainfall than neighbouring regions. Although the exterior walls of the pound are steep, the inside slopes are relatively gentle. The six-hour return hike up St Mary's Peak rewards you with breathtaking views. Although Wilpena Pound looks like a crater, it is the result of folding rocks, not the impact of a celestial object.

If Wilpena is your only destination in the Flinders, it is worth your while taking the time to detour north past the natural rock feature known as the Great Wall of China, then through **Parachilna Pass** to join the main Leigh Creek Road before heading south. Coming out of the pass, you emerge onto plains that typify central Australia; from here, as you look back, the open lip of Wilpena Pound clearly shows its strikingly symmetrical form.

The northern end of the Flinders Ranges more closely resembles the other mountains of central Australia than any other features in the south. The base for exploring the **Gammon Ranges National Park ❼** is

Arkaroola, a small settlement geared to the needs of tourists. Gorges and valleys filled with wild flowers and endless variations on the recurrent themes of rock, eucalyptus and folded hills prevail.

Desert tracks

The rugged wilderness and abundant wildlife of the northern Flinders can be easily explored by either foot or four-wheel-drive vehicle. There are several good vantage points where you can see the Flinders Ranges stretching south for many kilometres.

The roads north into the Outback – the **Birdsville Track ❽** or the **Strzelecki Track ❾** – are rough adventures, aiming towards the distant Queensland border. Not everyone likes the desert, but those who do will find the continual but almost imperceptible changes in scenery endlessly fascinating.

Along the Strzelecki Track, the last stop in South Australia is **Innamincka ❿**, a settlement with a population of fewer than 200 people where the only two buildings of note are the general store and the pub. Locals will be able to direct you to the Dig Tree *(see page 247)*, a few kilometres to the east on the border with Queensland, which marks the spot where a supply of food was left for starving members of the ill-fated transcontinental expedition, led by Burke and Wills. Camping by Coopers Creek after a few beers at the pub is now the embodiment of the Outback.

The Birdsville Track is deeply entrenched in the Australian psyche. It was developed as a route for driving cattle from western Queensland to Marree, SA, where they could be loaded onto railcars heading south. **Marree ⓫** itself was a trading depot for the Afghan camel drivers who opened up much of central Australia. The Oodnadatta Track northwest from Marree follows part of the original route that these Afghan traders took. The track skirts around the southern end of **Lake Eyre**, which is Australia's largest lake when there is water in it – it has filled to capacity only three times in the past 150 years, most recently in 2010.

TIP

You should not attempt the Strzelecki, Oodnadatta or Birdsville tracks without extensive Outback driving experience, a four-wheel-drive vehicle and a lot of preparation. The Strzelecki Track has no petrol, water or supply station for 500km (300 miles) between Lyndhurst and Innamincka.

BELOW:
Lake Eyre, South Australia.

At 15 metres (50ft) below sea level, Lake Eyre is the lowest part of the continent, a bowl that collects the monsoon rains of northern Australia.

The lake can be accessed at William Creek, whose pub bursts with character. Dalhousie Springs is an Outback oasis and is worth a 180km (112-mile) detour (one-way) off the track north of Oodnadatta.

Driving this far north into the Outback of South Australia you will eventually cross the **Dingo Fence**, which was completed in 1885 to keep dingoes to the north and out of the fertile sheep country of southeast Australia. It is the world's longest fence, stretching 5,320km (3,300 miles) from the Great Australian Bight in South Australia to southeast Queensland. It's questionable whether it has been successful – dingoes can still be found in the southern states – while it is thought feral animal populations in the south are booming due to lack of competition from native predators.

On the sealed Stuart Highway, which stretches 1,370km (850 miles) from Port Augusta to Alice Springs, the tiny settlement of **Pimba** marks the turn-off to **Woomera** ⑫, the rocket and research base that was only opened to the public in 1982. A visitor centre (daily Mar–Nov 9am–5pm, Dec–Feb 10am–2pm; free) has displays detailing the early days of rocketry. (Woomera is the Aboriginal term for spear launcher.) The Woomera Prohibited Area is adjacent to the town and spans 127,000 sq km (49,000 sq miles) – about the size of England. British nuclear tests took place at Maralinga, at the western reaches of the area, during the 1950s.

Coober Pedy

Coober Pedy ⑬, halfway to Northern Territory on the Stuart Highway, is the best-known town in Outback South Australia. This is the world's largest opal field (for white opals), where the relentlessly hot climate (sometimes soaring to 50°C/122°F or more) has forced the inhabitants to live underground in dugouts.

At first glance, the town looks like a hard-hit battlefield. The almost treeless terrain consists of hundreds of

BELOW:
an opal miner's dugout home at Coober Pedy.

mounds of upturned earth and abandoned mines where noodlers or fossickers have rummaged through the landscape in search of precious gems. If you should arrive during one of the area's regular dust storms, you could be excused for believing the apocalypse was nigh. But beneath the surface there are homes, shops, restaurants and even churches. There is an underground hotel, too, though suitable only for non-claustrophobics.

Visitors should note the beautiful natural patterns in the bare clay walls (and the lack of windows, compensated for by good air conditioning).

Unfortunately, the rapid increase in traffic aiming for the centre has rubbed off some of Coober Pedy's rough edges. For a more unique experience of an Outback opal town, venture off the beaten track to **Andamooka ⑭**, due north from Woomera, where fewer than 500 people dwell, but be aware that any rainfall can quickly leave you stranded. The striking ochre-coloured hills of the **Breakaways** lie 33km (20 miles) north of Coober Pedy. This arid landscape was an inland sea 70 million years ago.

Coorong and beyond

To the southeast of Adelaide, around the mouth of the Murray River, lies an indefinable maze of sandbanks and estuaries. This is the **Coorong National Park ⑮**, a haven for numerous species of waterfowl. The main features are the sand dunes of the **Younghusband Peninsula** that separate the shallow waters of the **Coorong** from the Southern Ocean, and the Coorong itself (*karangh* or *narrow neck* to the Aborigines), a long, thin neck of water stretching 120km (75 miles) from Lake Alexandrina and Lake Albert at the mouth of the Murray River to the saltpans and marshy ponds at the southern end.

If you lack a four-wheel-drive vehicle, it's a half-hour walk across the dunes to the ocean beach, an endless area of golden sand left mostly to the seagulls, oystercatchers, pelicans and only the occasional angler. A great number and variety of waterfowl feed on the water plants in the lagoons and drink at the freshwater soaks. For thousands of years Ngarrindjeri Aboriginal people lived here, netting fish in the lagoons, collecting cockles on the beach and fashioning reeds into rafts and baskets. You may come across their ancient shell middens in the sand dunes – you should not interfere with them in any way, out of respect for the Aboriginal culture.

To explore the Coorong fully, you need time, preferably a boat and, in the heat of summer near the drying salt flats, a strong nose. The spirit of the Coorong was well captured in the 1976 film *Storm Boy*.

South of the Coorong is a series of seaside holiday resorts, with this part of the coast renowned for its shellfish. At **Kingston** you can buy delicious fresh lobster at the jetty. In **Robe**, once an important port and retaining much of its early character, the Caledonian Inn, licensed in 1858, still caters to weary travellers.

Australia produces 97 per cent of the world's opal, from the common, milky opal to the rare and valuable black opal.

BELOW: a paddle-steamer on the Murray River.

TIP

There are several paddlewheel vessels (the *Proud Mary, Murray Princess* and *Murray River Queen*) running five- and six-day cruises along the river. Houseboats can be hired at Renmark, Loxton, Berri and Waikerie. More details: www.murrayriver.com.au.

A stone near the harbour commemorates the thousands of Chinese who disembarked here in the 1850s and tramped hundreds of kilometres through the bush to the Victorian gold diggings, to avoid the £10 arrival tax imposed at Victorian ports. Robe tends to be full in school holidays and overflows at Christmas and on New Year's Eve, but is a lovely, peaceful spot for the rest of the year.

Mount Gambier nestles on the side of a 5,000-year-old extinct volcano. Within its rim lie three craters, four lakes, and the mystery of why the largest, **Blue Lake**, turns from winter grey to brilliant azure from November through to March. Outside the city are the Tantanoola limestone caves.

Further north, the **Naracoorte Caves** (various tours; tel: 08-8762 2340; www.environment.sa.gov.au/parks; charge) contain not only beautiful limestone formations but also a fossil cave where the traces of many extinct animals are being unearthed. They include giant kangaroos, a wombat the size of a hippopotamus and a marsupial lion.

The Riverland

Renmark , northeast of Adelaide near the Victorian border, was the birthplace of the Murray River irrigation area in 1887. The drive along the **Sturt Highway** roughly follows the river through extensive orchards and vineyards supported by the Murray's waters. Half of South Australia's grapes and 90 percent of the state's stone fruit and citrus are grown in the Riverland. River transport is prominent here, too, with the paddleboat days remembered in the old steamer moored as a floating museum.

Barmera and nearby **Lake Bonney** are the recreational heart of the Riverland. Lake Bonney attracts a wide variety of watercraft: mainly windsurfers and sailing boats. In 1964, the pace increased considerably when Sir Donald Campbell used the lake for an attempt on the world water-speed record.

The air currents from the plains around **Waikerie** have made it one of the world's leading soaring centres. In summer, when sun-heated air rises in powerful thermals, gliders can be seen throughout the region. For flights, check with the Waikerie International Soaring Centre (tel: 08-8541 2644; www.waikeriegglidingclub.com.au). Waikerie's Aboriginal name means *many wings*, after the giant moth *wei kari*. It could easily refer to the abundant birdlife in the nearby Hart Lagoon.

Peninsulas and islands

The deeply indented coastline of South Australia has made a set of natural divisions, each with its own appeal. The **Fleurieu Peninsula**, south of Adelaide beyond McLaren Vale, is a popular holiday area for South Australians. **Victor Harbour** is the main resort – its hotels, motels and guesthouses are often full during school holidays. Among Victor's attractions are the little penguin colony on **Granite Island** (connected to the mainland by a causeway with a horse-drawn tram), an adventure park and winter whale-watching trips.

BELOW: the Remarkable Rocks are a granite formation in Flinders Chase National Park.

Cape Jervis, at the end of the peninsula, is the stepping-off point for **Kangaroo Island ⑱**. Until the end of the last ice age, 9,000 years ago, the island (Australia's third largest, after Tasmania and Melville) wasn't separated from the mainland. Even now, the finger of the Dudley Peninsula on the island appears to be reaching towards Cape Jervis. The island's main towns are **Kingscote**, **American River** and **Penneshaw**. Fishing, exploring the scenery and observing wildlife are the main activities for visitors. Seals, sea lions, penguins, echidnas, kangaroos, emus and koalas all live here in abundance. Nightly processions of penguins can be seen on the beaches around Kingscote and Penneshaw, and you can walk among one of Australia's largest colonies of sea lions at Seal Bay. At the large **Flinders Chase National Park**, the only enclosures are to keep the persistent wildlife away from picnickers.

From the gentle sandy beaches of the **Dudley Peninsula** to the pounding surf on the headland of **Cape du Couedic**, **Kangaroo Island** has a wide range of terrains. The lighthouse at the cape was built in 1906 as an essential navigation aid for coastal shipping. Near it lie two unusual features: **Remarkable Rocks**, a collection of granite boulders worn by the sea into fantastical shapes, some resembling animals and birds, others akin to Henry Moore sculptures; and **Admirals Arch**, a 20-metre (64ft) maw rimmed with fang-like blackened stalactites, framing a maelstrom of surging waves. These are primeval sites at odds with the placid nature of other parts of the island.

Yorke Peninsula

A loop of picturesque towns, **Yorke Peninsula ⑲** takes in the east-coast port of **Ardrossan** with its attractive water access and, down the coast, **Edithburgh** with its splendid clifftop views and its famous old pub, the Troubridge Hotel. The town's cemetery includes the graves of the 34 victims of the 1909 wreck of the *Clan Ranald*. The scenic route south to Yorketown is a magical drive offering great coastal views of offshore reefs popular with

Kangaroo Island is full of playful creatures, large and small.

BELOW: playful seals on the beach.

One transport firm made the Guinness Book of Records *in 1999 by hauling 45 trailers, weighing more than 600 tonnes, for 8km (5 miles) using one truck. In real life, few road trains haul more than six trailers in the Outback, and these will be transferred to individual trucks before they reach an urban destination.*

BELOW:
kangaroos in the
outback on Wilson's
Promontory.

local scuba divers. **Yorketown** is a small farming town surrounded by a series of salt lakes.

Towards the southwestern extremity of the peninsula is the great horseshoe-shaped sweep of **Pondalowie Bay**. Located in a national park, the bay is a fishing, diving and surfing paradise made even more appealing by its remoteness. A full seven hours' drive from Adelaide, it is a great place to camp and enjoy the beauty of the Southern Ocean coastline.

The ports of the Yorke Peninsula's west coast indicate its importance as a grain-growing area. It was from places such as **Port Victoria** that great windjammers left to race back to Britain and Europe with their cargoes of grain. Farming and fishing still play important parts in the peninsula's modest economy, but mineral wealth contributed a colourful chapter to the area's history. The discovery of copper at **Kadina** and **Moonta** led to the mass migration of Cornish miners and their families from southwest England. Along with the port town of **Wallaroo**, the two hamlets grew

as solid Cornish communities with strong Methodist influences, catering to about 30,000 people. The boom period has long passed, but the contribution of the Cornish Cousin Jacks and Cousin Jills, as they were known, remains an indelible part of the peninsula's heritage.

The long road west

Of all the great Australian highway routes, the 2,000km-plus (1,240-mile-plus) stretch from Adelaide to Perth is the one most frequently flaunted, with "We crossed the Nullarbor" stickers displayed on car and van windows. However, the road itself is no longer the challenge – rather it's the cost of fuel to propel a vehicle across several thousand kilometres of nothingness.

On the drive west towards Perth, the **Eyre Peninsula** ⑳ and the attractive township of Port Lincoln exert strong pressure to detour. Explorer John Eyre ploughed through the area in 1841 and, although burnt almost to a frazzle by the harshness of the hinterland, he was impressed by the spectacular coastline. The peninsula has its own historical charm in places like **Coffin Bay**, famous for its delicious oysters, and **Anxious Bay**. **Port Lincoln** itself has a large tuna-fishing fleet, cruises, and great white shark diving tours. Some of the shark scenes from the film *Jaws* were filmed here.

At **Point Labatt**, on the Flinders Highway, is the only seal colony on mainland Australia. If you would like to get a little closer, dolphin and sea-lion swimming tours depart from Baird Bay in the warmer months.

Ceduna ㉑ is the centre of a large pastoral industry, but surfers from both east and west coasts know it as a favoured stopping-off place in their pursuit of waves. It's blessed with golden beaches; Cactus is the break surfers speak of with the greatest reverence. But be warned, great white sharks prowl this coastline and shark attacks have occurred. The navigator Matthew Flinders named nearby

Denial Bay when he realised it was not the access to the elusive inland sea that was rumoured to exist in central Australia.

Inland from Ceduna is the 106,000-hectare (262,000-acre) tract of **Yumbarra Conservation Park**. Its sandy ridges and granite outcrops appear inhospitable, but the local wildlife (particularly emus and kangaroos) find it ideal. In winter the top of the bight is also a favourite spot for whale-watching. Head of Bight whale-watching centre (tel: 08-8625 6201; www.headofbight.com.au), 25km (15 miles) east of Nullarbor, offers a great opportunity to get out of the car and stretch your legs. Southern right whales are regularly seen from the spectacular cliffs here during the winter.

Ceduna is South Australia's most westerly town. From here to Norseman in Western Australia it is 1,232km (765 miles), and any other point shown on a map along the way is nothing more than a water storage base or a fuel station. That's what makes crossing the Nullarbor Plain such an intimidating prospect. There are no trees on the plain (nullarbor is Latin for *no tree*), as the limestone is unable to hold rain water.

Crossing the desert

The **Eyre Highway** hugs the coastline on its long route to Western Australia, passing through **Nullarbor National Park** ㉒ during the last stretch of South Australia. For the earlier pioneers, the coastal route was much harsher than the alternative of the interior. While vast stretches of the coastline are devoid of fresh water, limestone sinkholes in the plain might have provided ready supplies.

The desert is also traversed by the Trans-Australian railway, one of the world's great rail journeys, with one straight section that stretches 479km (298 miles), making it the world's longest. It is part of the Indian–Pacific passenger rail service that links Sydney to Perth (*see page 345*).

A lasting impression of the coastline of the **Great Australian Bight** is the sheer cliff formations that make the coastal strip near the Western Australian border so spectacular.   ❑

TIP

Overtaking a road train requires strong nerves, and you shouldn't even try on dirt roads. Courteous truckers will blink their right-turn indicator to show that the road ahead is clear.

BELOW: a road train stirs up the dust on the Eyre Highway.

RESTAURANTS AND BARS

Restaurants

Prices for a three-course dinner per person with a half-bottle of house wine:
$ = under A$50
$$ = A$50–80
$$$ = A$80–120
$$$$ = over A$120

Central City

Auge
22 Grote Street
Tel: 08-8410 9332
www.auge.com.au
Open: L Fri, D Mon–Sat. $$$
An award-winning Italian cuisine in a smart setting. Espresso, juices and antipasti are available all day from the impressive Sputini bar – it's the perfect spot for a break from all that shopping. They use local produce when possible.

Botanic Gardens Restaurant and Kiosk
Botanic Gardens,
North Terrace
Tel: 08-8223 3526
www.botanicgardenrestaurant.com.au
Open: B Sat–Sun, L Tue–Sun. $$$
On a fine day there's no better choice for lunch than the patio of this superb restaurant. Black swans bob on the lake by your table, while scents from the gardens add to the dreamlike setting. Wandering in the rose garden after lunch provides an ideal end to the meal.

Blake's
The Hyatt Regency
Tel: 08-8238 2381
Open: D Mon & Wed–Sat. $$$
Blakes has one of the country's most famous wine lists.

The Grange
Hilton Adelaide, 233 Victoria Square
Tel: 08-8217 2000
www.adelaide.hilton.com
Open: D Wed–Sat. $$$
Chef Cheong Liew has gained an international reputation as a pioneer of east-west fusion and he continues to win accolades at The Grange for his innovative and imaginative menus.

Red Ochre Restaurant
War Memorial Drive,
North Adelaide
Tel: 08-8211 8555
www.redochre.com.au
Open: L Mon–Fri, D Mon–Sat. $$
Specialising in bush tucker and native Australian produce, Red Ochre is the place to sample wallaby shanks or emu pâté. The Torrens Lake waterfront location gives you the best of both worlds, since they also have city views.

Rigoni's Bistro
27 Leigh Street
Tel: 08-8231 5160
www.rigonis.com.au
Open: B, L & D Mon–Fri. $$
An Italian brasserie which is a real scene for journalists, politicians and other hangers-on. Breakfast, lunch and dinner, served from 7am till late.

Universal Wine Bar
285 Rundle Street
Tel: 08-8232 5000
www.universalwinebar.com.au
Open: L & D daily. $$
Slick and stylish, the timber decor is backed by an impressive wine list and ever-changing menu.

The Oxford Hotel
101 O'Connell Street
Tel: 08-8267 2652
Open: L & D daily. $
A great bistro offering excellent service and outside dining.

Rundle Street East

The Austral Hotel
205 Rundle Street
Tel: 08-8223 4660
www.theaustral.com.au
Open: L & D daily. $
Modern Australian pub cuisine with stouts, ales and ciders all from South Australia.

Lemongrass Thai Bistro
289 Rundle St
Tel: 08-8223 6627
www.lemongrassthaibistro.com.au
Open: L Mon–Fri, D daily. $
An up-market Thai concern where kangaroo and crocodile fillet are served alongside other, more traditional, menu options.

Cibo Espresso
218 Rundle Street
Tel 08-8232 9199
www.ciboespresso.com.au
For rich Italian coffee and espresso as well as pastries, cakes and biscuits, look out for the red awning and umbrellas at Cibo Espresso. This place will give you the energy for the rest of your day.

Amalfi Pizzeria Ristorante
29 Frome Street
Tel: 08-8223 1948
Open: L Mon–Fri, D Mon–Sat. $
Amalfi's turns out authentic Italian dinner specials to its loyal supper crowd. Here you'll find a real cross section of Adelaide

LEFT: cool *gelato* is perfect for a hot afternoon.

nightlife, and the good-natured staff add to the appeal.

Chloe's Restaurant
36 College Road, Kent Town
Tel: 08-8362 2574
www.chloes.com.au
Open: L Mon–Fri, D Mon–Sat. $$$
Tradition and opulence in the surroundings are matched by adventure and accomplishment in the cooking. All of this, and a wine list to die for, makes Chloe's the perfect place for a night out.

Gaucho's
91 Gouger Street
Tel: 08-8231 2299
www.gauchos.com.au
Open: L Mon–Fri, D daily. $$$
Gaucho's is Australia's very first Argentinian restaurant. So that means really good steak, and lots of it.

Ying Chow
114 Gouger Street
Tel: 08-8211 7998
Open: D daily. $
One of the best-value restaurants in town and a favourite of many young Adelaidians, this busy, casual place serves first-rate regional Chinese dishes at low prices. BYO.

Paul's Restaurant
79 Gouger Street
Tel: 08-8231 9778
Open: L Mon–Fri, D daily. $
Simply prepared fish and chips. BYO.

Stanley's Fish Café
76 Gouger Street
Tel: 08-8410 0909.
Open: L Sun–Fri, D daily. $$$
King George whiting, garfish and tommy ruffs are some of the tastiest catches to look out for on the menu.

The Tap Inn
Kent Town Hotel,
76 Rundle Street, Kent Town
Tel: 08-8362 2116

www.tapinn.com.au
Open: L Wed–Sun, D daily. $$
A multimillion-dollar refurbishment has transformed this old local favourite into an outlandish venue complete with indoor golf-driving range. The golf theme continues into the Sand Bunker Beer Garden, where the schnitzels are so big they hang off the plate. Inside there's a more sober and tempting tapas menu.

Chianti Classico
160 Hutt Street
Tel: 08-8232 7955
www.chianticlassico.com.au
Open: B, L & D daily. $$
A popular, family-orientated restaurant offering pasta and other classic Italian dishes.

Good Life. Modern Organic Pizza
170 Hutt Street
Tel: 08-8223 2618
www.goodlifepizza.com
Open: L Mon–Fri, D daily. $
Pizzas made using locally sourced free-range and organic ingredients. Toppings are tasty and imaginative – free-range chicken with potatoes, garlic and rosemary, or smoked salmon with preserved lemons and caper mayonnaise, to pick two. Also in Glenelg and North Adelaide.

The Magill Estate Restaurant
78 Penfold Road
Tel: 08-8301 5551
www.penfolds.com.au
Open: L Fri, D Tue–Sat. $$$
About 8km (5 miles) from the city, the restaurant at Penfolds Magill Estate is highly recommended. Fine dining with views of vineyards and the city.

Splurge on a glass of Penfolds Grange Hermitage.

Star of Greece
The Esplanade
Tel: 08-8557 7420
Open: L Wed–Sun, D Sat (summer only). $$
Perched on the cliffs of Adelaide's southern beaches, Star of Greece is enhanced by a funky atmosphere and a menu that uses local ingredients. The name comes from a ship that ran aground off the coast. Limited openings outside summer period.

Bridgewater Mill
Mount Barker Road, Bridgewater
Tel: 08-8339 9200
www.bridgewatermill.com.au
Open: L Thur–Mon. $$$
Dine alfresco in the historic setting of this Adelaide Hills winery which is a regular award winner. The mill also houses the cellar door

and tastings for Petaluma wines.

Windy Point Restaurant
Windy Point Lookout, Belair Road, Belair
Tel: 08-8278 8255
www.windypoint.com.au
Open: D Mon–Sat. $$$
Located just above the lookout area at Windy Point, the restaurant has fantastic panoramic views over the city. Seasonal food and a wine list sourced mainly from SA.

Zorro's Charcoal Grill
60 Main Street, Hahndorf
Tel: 08-8388 1309
Open: L Thur–Mon. $$$
Hearty Serbian cooking with the emphasis on grilled meat. On Sundays, the roast is cooked on a huge spit.

The Lane Vineyard
Ravenswood Lane, Hahndorf
Tel: 08-8388 1250
www.thelane.com.au
Open: L daily. $$$
Succulent plates of local produce good enough to distract from the vineyard vistas.

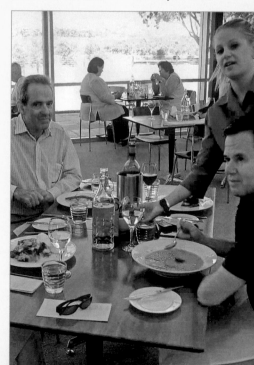

RIGHT: an afternoon snack is complete with wine.

Queensland

0   200 km
0   200 miles

Coral Sea

PACIFIC

OCEAN

Gulf of
Carpentaria

Badu I.   **Moa I.**
Torres Strait
Thursday I. ㉓ **Horn I.**
Prince of Wales I.   Cape York
Bamaga

Jardine River N.P.

Cape Grenville

Weipa

Iron Range N.P.

Cape

Coen   *Princess
Charlotte
Bay*   Cape Melville

York

Kowanyama   Lakefield
National Park

Peninsula

Mornington I.   Quinkan   Laura ㉒ ㉑   Cooktown
Wellesley Is   Reserve   Helenvale
Bentinck I.   Lakeland Downs
Daintree N.P.   Cape Tribulation ⑳
Chillagoe   ㉔   Mareeba   Mossman
Burketown   Karumba   Mt   Atherton ⑱   Cairns   ⑲
Boodjamulla   Surprise   Ravenshoe   Tully
N.P.   Normanton   Croydon ㉖   Georgetown   Undara ㉕   Mission Beach ⑰
Lawn Hill   Greenvale   Hinchinbrook I.
Gorge ㉗   Undara   Ingham
Riversleigh   Volcanic   Paluma Range N.P.   Magnetic I.
N.P.   Townsville ⑯
Camooweal   Charters   Ayr
Towers   Bowen
Lake   Airlie Beach ⑮
Moondarra   Cloncurry   Flinders Hwy   Proserpine   Whitsunday Group
Mount Isa ㉙   Julia Creek
㉘   Richmond   Hughenden   Mackay ⑭
McKinlay   Sarina
Dajarra   Kynuna   Matilda Hwy   Broad
Middleton   Sound
Winton   Muttaburra   Clermont   Yeppoon
Boulia ㉚   Great Keppel I.
Tropic of Capricorn   Rock- ⑬   Heron I.
Lark Quarry   Barcaldine   hampton
Dinosaur   ㉜   Emerald   Dingo
Trackways   Longreach   Capricorn Hwy   Gladstone
Bedourie   ㉛   Blackall   Biloela   1770
Carnarvon   Agnes Water
Windorah   Yaraka   National   Bundaberg ⑪
Park ⑫   Childers   Hervey Gt Sandy NP
Birdsville   **Queensland**   Carnarvon   Taroom   Bay ⑩ Fraser I.
㉟   Gorge   Maryborough ⑨
Augathella   Gympie ⑧
Charleville   Mitchell   Roma   Murgon   Noosa Heads
Quilpie   ㉝   Miles ㉞   Nanango   Maroochydore
South   Warrego   Caloundra
Hwy   Dalby   Sunshine Coast ⑦
Clifton Hills   **Darling**   Australia Zoo
Downs   Moonie   Caboolture
The Dig Tree   Toowoomba   Moreton I.
Innamincka   Thargomindah   St George   ⑤   Brisbane ①
Sturt   Cunnamulla   Bollon   Ipswich ③   Surfers ②
Australia   **Desert**   Dirranbandi   Warwick   Paradise
Goondiwindi   ④   *Gold Coast*
Hungerford   Wompah   Stanthorpe   ⑥ Lamington N.P.
Marree   Milparinka   Murwillumbah
Lyndhurst   Gammon   Wanaaring   Barringun   Moree   Lismore
Ranges   Goodooga   Tenterfield   Ballina
N.P.   **New South**   Bourke   Gwydir Hwy
Leigh   Lake   **Wales**   Brewarrina
Creek   Frome   Packsaddle   Walgett   Glen Innes   Grafton
Lake   Narrabri
Torrens   Mutawintji N.P.   Euriowie   Wilcannia   Coonamble   New England Range
Flinders   Cobar   Nyngan   Tamworth   Coffs Harbour
Ranges N.P.   Menindee   Coolabah   Gilgandra
Hawker   Broken   Barrier Hwy
Cockburn   Hill

QUEENSLAND

This is Australia's holiday state and the most visited destination after Sydney. Its major attractions include the magnificent beaches, the Great Barrier Reef and the unique rainforest

Queensland represents a sizeable chunk of Australia. At more than 2,000km (1,240 miles) from top to bottom and 1,450km (900 miles) at its widest point, its 1.73 million sq km (667,000 sq mile) area could happily contain an assortment of European countries or a few hefty American states. It is unsurprising then that within its confines can be found such a range of terrain: unsullied tropical rainforest, broad expanses of dusty cattle-grazing country – indistinguishable from desert at times – the ragged peaks of the Great Dividing Range, rolling hills and, to cap it all, some great beaches. Plus, tethered along the eastern shoreline, just beyond a scattering of achingly beautiful desert islands, is one of the world's natural wonders, the Great Barrier Reef.

Sun seekers

Queensland's proud claim to be the Sunshine State has been readily accepted not just by overseas visitors but also by other Australians who have been flocking to the state for their holidays for years. When winter arrives many dwellers in the cooler southern states hanker for a spot on one of the endless golden beaches on Queensland's vast coastline. And once they've tasted paradise it's a short step to opt for the sea change – the exchange of the perceived drab urban existence for the Technicolor joys of perpetual summer. Some move at once, others wait for retirement. Either way, a pattern of migration has long been established. However, it has accelerated to the point where more than 200 people a day are now resettling in the sun, although housing prices may slow that down.

Border crossing

Incomers can be found all along the coast, but the clearest concrete (in every

Main attractions

BRISBANE
GOLD COAST THEME PARKS
SUNSHINE COAST
FRASER ISLAND
CARNARVON GORGE
CHARTERS TOWERS
CAIRNS
THE DAINTREE
THE ATHERTON TABLELAND
CAPE YORK PENINSULA
LAWN HILL GORGE
MOUNT ISA
LONGREACH

PRECEDING PAGES: Hardy Reef.
RIGHT: the Eternal Flame of Remembrance burns for all fallen Anzac soldiers.

The Brisbane Botanic Gardens lie at the foot of Mount Coot-tha.

sense of the word) evidence is to be found in the developments to the north and south of Brisbane, on the Sunshine and Gold coasts. Queenslanders tend to take a laconic approach to the arrival of so many incomers from the southern states, seeing it as an affirmation of what they've always known about the superiority of life in the tropics.

Queensland is a gorgeous place, but sometimes great beauty comes with a price. Although the state was inundated with flood waters in the beginning of 2011, the tough Queenslander spirit has enabled the people to bounce back. Recovery has been swift for the most part, but it would be wise to check the details of your trip before traveling.

Brisbane

The state capital, **Brisbane ❶** (or *Brissie* as it's known to the locals), is Australia's third-largest city and has been transformed over the past few years. Close to half of the state's 4½ million people are to be found within its ambit, scattered over a series of low hills with the Brisbane River at its heart. Until quite recently there was much in the

claim that it was "the world's biggest country town", but visitors today will find an urbane and cosmopolitan city, where café culture has colonised the once musty streets.

Like Sydney and Hobart, this easygoing city emerged from nightmarish beginnings. A convict settlement was established at nearby Moreton Bay in September 1824, when the first party of prisoners – the hardest cases, convicted of further crimes since arriving in Australia – arrived from Sydney. Many of the convicts died, victims of the tyrannies of the guards, hunger, tropical disease and an indifference towards prolonging their own miserable lives.

The first convict establishment was at Redcliffe, but due to a shortage of water the penal settlement moved up-river to the site of today's city centre. It was named after Sir Thomas Brisbane (then Governor of New South Wales). The present government and shopping precincts overlie the original settlement.

Today's central business district (CBD), in an area cupped by the river, is a mixture of stately colonial buildings and eye-catching modern architecture, with greenery provided by the City Botanic Gardens at one end and Roma Street Parkland at the other.

The visitor information centre (Queen Street Mall between Albert and Edward streets; Mon–Thur 9am–5.30pm, Fri 9am–7pm, Sat 9am–5pm, Sun 9.30am–4.30pm; tel: 07-3006 6290; www.visitbrisbane.com.au) can help with the usual brochures.

One of the city's more prominent landmarks makes a good starting point, although **Brisbane City Hall** **Ⓐ**, an overbearing structure on King George Square, is undergoing extensive renovation. The hope is that it will reinvigorate King George Square, with its layered stone and concrete, broken up by entranceways to the transport hub underneath, which has struggled to become the great civic space its architects intended. The **Brisbane Museum**, which is normally located in the City Hall, has had to move round the corner into Ann Street where it hosts short-term locally themed exhibitions and work by contemporary artists (daily 10am–5pm; tel: 07-3403 8888; www.museumofbrisbane.com.au; free).

The historic centre

Anzac Square **Ⓑ** further up Ann Street is a place for reflection. A perpetual flame commemorating the city's war dead is aligned directly between the clock tower of the Central Railway Station and the **General Post Office**. The latter, with its Corinthian colonnades, can be accessed through tranquil Post Office Square. Follow the narrow lane flanking the building to Elizabeth Street and **St Stephen's Cathedral** **Ⓒ**. Within this precinct you will find the gracefully weathered Pugin's Chapel, also known as old St Stephen's Church, completed in 1850 to a design by celebrated Victorian (the era, not the state) Gothic architect Augustus Welby Pugin. Beside it reposes the more substantial cathedral that replaced it as Brisbane's seat of Catholicism in 1874.

Returning to the GPO and heading west, the shopping hub of **Queen Street Mall** stretches towards the river. The foyer of the former Regent Theatre is an unmissable paean to kitsch medievalism, which has survived virtually unchanged since 1929, although

Pictures of a flooded Brisbane flashed around the world in January 2011, but within months the city was back to normal, with the replacement of its washed-away riverside walkways the only major outstanding task.

BELOW LEFT:
Brisbane City Hall.
BELOW:
Mt Coot-tha
Botanic Gardens.

TIP

Eagle Street Pier is the departure point for paddlewheeler cruises on board the *Kookaburra River Queens I* and *II*. Lunch cruises depart Tue, Thur, Fri at noon and Sat or Sun at 12.30pm; dinner cruises Tue and Thur–Sun 7pm (tel: 07-3221 1300; www.kookaburra riverqueens.com).

for now it is only visible through glass doors at the back of a café occupying the old ticket office. Another slice of history remains in the refined Edwardian-style **Brisbane Arcade**, built in 1924 and now the city's oldest surviving shopping arcade.

Architectural historians acclaim the **Treasury Building** ⓓ as the finest example of Italian renaissance style in the country. Walk south along George Street to **The Mansions**, a group of 1890 terraced houses with handsome red-brick facades and pale sandstone arcading, now occupied by classy shops and restaurants.

Further down George Street is Queensland's **Parliament House** ⓔ (Mon–Fri 9am–4.15pm; tel: 07-3406 7562; www.parliament.qld.gov.au; free), begun in 1865. To the frustration of the architect, Charles Tiffin, who won a nationwide contest with his design on French renaissance lines, it took 24 years to see the work completed. There are conducted tours, or, when Parliament is sitting (usually May–Oct), a gallery pass enables you to sit in on debates which, given the abra-

sive nature of the state's politics, can be riveting. Another Tiffin design, **Old Government House**, is now part of Queensland University of Technology and can be found down the road.

Dropping away to the left is the inviting green expanse of the **City Botanic Gardens** ⓕ. Originally a vegetable garden for the penal settlement, its 20 hectares (50 acres) of formal lawns and flora now provides respite from the city's bustle for hordes of office workers, students and tourists. Highlights include an avenue of weeping willows planted over 150 years ago, and a boardwalk through mangroves growing on the river bank.

The river

Leaving the gardens at the north-eastern corner, pass the Former Naval Offices, follow the riverside pathway and take in the views. Eagle Street Pier is the starting point for various sight-seeing cruises. Then comes the acclaimed modernist construction that is Harry Seidler's **Riverside Centre** ⓖ. It houses some fine eateries. A short distance on lies the Customs House

BELOW: Brisbane's Treasure Casino.
BELOW RIGHT: the George Street mansions.

– now a function centre – opened in 1889 and crowned by a distinctive copper dome.

Looming ahead is Brisbane's most distinctive structure, the **Story Bridge Ⓗ** joining Kangaroo Point with the CBD. Tram tracks were removed in 1959 but otherwise it stands unchanged since its opening on 6 July 1940. At the time, it symbolised progress in an era of political and economic uncertainty, and even now, it radiates pride and permanence. Test its sturdiness and your fortitude by booking a bridge climb (tel: 07-3514 6900; www.storybridgeadventures.com.au).

Walking across the bridge is rewarded with fine views back across the city, but the easier way to **Kangaroo Point** is to hop on to one of the buzzing water ferries, the River Cat. Once across, there are plenty of adventure activities on offer at the old **Brisbane Naval Stores**, or you can just enjoy a pleasant stroll through the parkland where sculptures of varying degrees of accomplishment are lurking. Climb up the cliff steps for spectacular views and a glimpse of the historic **St Mary's Anglican Church**.

City-centre completists, however, will defer such delights and follow the road north behind the Riverside Centre, turn left up Wharf Street, and investigate **St John's Cathedral ⓘ** in Ann Street. This probably qualifies as Australia's newest Gothic cathedral; although work started in 1901, the final touches to the facade were only completed in 2009.

Just down Ann Street, **All Saints Church** (1862) is the oldest Anglican church in Brisbane. Cross into Wickham Terrace, nod in a knowing manner at Wickham Terrace Car Park, which won architect James Birrell awards for his innovative use of concrete, and amble along to the **Old Windmill Ⓙ**. Built in 1829 and one of only two convict buildings surviving from the first wave of construction, it is small and unprepossessing. A design flaw meant it never worked as a windmill, so to grind corn for the settlement convicts were put to work turning a treadmill. It

soon earned a soubriquet as the "tower of torture".

Continue along Wickham Terrace for 300 metres (330 yards) or so and take a path into **Roma Street Parkland Ⓚ**. Here the Roma Street railway shunting yards have been converted into a splendidly diverse area of waterfalls, lakes, misty crannies of tropical vegetation, and cultivated floral displays that attract their own ecosystem of insects and birds.

The nearby old residential area of **Spring Hill** is an attractive maze of early houses, some of them old Queenslanders – distinctive shady wooden homes built on stilts to maximise the circulation of cooling air. Worth seeking out are the Spring Hill Baths in Torrington Street, the first public baths in the state and sufficiently atmospheric to feature heavily in the film *Swimming Upstream*.

South Bank

Across the river to the west of the CBD is one of Brisbane's most vibrant areas, the rapidly evolving South Bank, with its impressive complex, the **Queens-**

The wry nickname "Brisvegas" is often applied to Brisbane. Rather than it being an allusion to the flurry of high rises in the CBD or sarcastic reference to the absence of any glijtzy nightlife, it apparently derives from an Elvis tribute CD released as recently as 1994.

BELOW: the storied Story Bridge.

Queensland Maritime Museum has a fine collection of vessels to investigate, including a Torres Strait pearling lugger and the Royal Australian Navy frigate, Diamantina. *The 1925 steam tug,* Forceful, *makes regular trips down the Brisbane River to Moreton Bay (tel: 07-3844 5361).*

BELOW: the wheel of Brisbane.

land Cultural Centre, and the sprawling pleasure gardens of South Bank Parklands. Cross over from the CBD by the Victoria Bridge and on the right can be found four key attractions. **The Queensland Museum**'s ❶ (daily 9.30am–5pm; tel: 07-3840 7555; www.southbank.qm.qld.gov.au; free) several million items include everything from Muttaburrasaurus, the most complete dinosaur skeleton found in Australia, to the tiny aeroplane Bert Hinkler flew from England to Australia in 1928. The museum also contains the **Dandiiri Maiwar Centre** devoted to Aboriginal and Torres Strait Islander cultures.

At the **Queensland Art Gallery** ⓜ (Mon–Fri 10am–5pm, Sat–Sun 9am–5pm; tel: 07-3840 7303; www.qag.qld.gov.au; free), core exhibitions are supplemented by touring art shows. A second gallery, the **Queensland Gallery of Modern Art** ⓝ (hours and details as above), or GoMA as it is known, opened in late 2006 and has quickly established an impressive presence with exhibitions of modern contemporary works in a sparkling purpose-built structure. Just behind it, a dramatic

new footbridge links the precinct with the CBD. This is one of two new river crossings in the city, the other being the new Go Between Bridge upstream, named, following a public vote, after Brisbane's quirkily perfect rock band, the Go-Betweens. (Somewhere in the process the bridge lost the hyphen.)

The **State Library** holds important historical archives. To the left after crossing Victoria Bridge is a fine **Performing Arts Centre** and behind it the Convention and Exhibition Centre. On the river bank is the Wheel of Brisbane (Mon–Thur 10am–10pm, Fri–Sat 9am–midnight, Sun 9am–10pm; tel: 07-3844 3464; www.thewheelofbrisbane.com.au; charge), a giant Ferris wheel offering superb views over the surrounding country.

Sands in the city

The site of the 1988 World Expo, **South Bank Parklands** ⓞ, has put many of the former Expo pavilions to innovative use. Attractions in the 16 hectares (40 acres) of riverside parkland include a diverse array of restaurants that take maximum advantage of the city's

Fortitude Valley

Many of Brisbane's suburbs will clamour for your attention, but none more brazenly than Fortitude Valley to the north of the CBD. Once Brisbane's premier commercial and retail hub – with some grand old buildings to match – it has been reborn as a cosmopolitan precinct of cool bars, funky eateries, pounding clubs, sweaty music venues and residential apartments. Street action radiates around the pavement cafés in **Brunswick Street Mall**, though new bars have begun surfacing in some of the surrounding blocks. Either way, the precinct pumps it up at weekends when the bohemian and fashionable let their well-coiffeured hair down.

Family (MacLachlan St) claims a 33,000-watt sound system and runs at weekends; the **Press Club** on Brunswick Street sees itself as cooler; on Ann Street **The Zoo** is the live band venue; and the **Wickham Hotel** is the gay HQ, although many other venues cater to the market.

Chinatown Mall in Duncan Street provides a range of Asian gastronomical possibilities including Thai, Malaysian, Korean and Japanese... but not so much Chinese. Excellent Chinese restaurants do operate within Chinatown but, in general, Chinese restaurateurs and shopkeepers have gravitated to Sunnybank, a well-to-do fringe suburb with a large expatriate Chinese community.

weather. Brisbane, once a culinary desert, now enjoys a reputation for chefs who take advantage of the state's natural resources: giant mud crabs, macadamia nuts, coral trout, oysters, mangoes and other delicacies.

South Bank even has a large swimming lagoon at Streets Beach, complete with imported sand.

Stick with the promenade by the river and at the end of the striking Goodwill Bridge, which takes pedestrian traffic across to the CBD, you will find the **Queensland Maritime Museum** ❶ (daily 9.30am–4.30pm; tel: 07-3844 5361; www.maritimemuseum.com.au; charge) with its collection of all things nautical, including a handful of vessels moored by the bank.

Urban Brisbane gives way quickly to rural. Just 8km (5 miles) west of the centre, the **Mount Coot-tha Botanic Gardens** consist of over 57 hectares (141 acres) of ponds and parkland, where thousands of plant species thrive. Further west, rainforest-cloaked mountains shelter the city and offer a generous choice of picnic spots, bush walks and wilderness areas, all within

half an hour's drive of the city centre.

To the east, downstream along the Brisbane River, you can reach the various beaches of **Moreton Bay** and the islands (some unpopulated) that make this a vast fishing and sailing paradise. Moreton Island features Mount Tempest, at 285 metres (935ft) the world's highest stabilised coastal dune.

The Gold Coast

South of Brisbane, the 32km (20-mile) stretch of coast from South Beach, just above Surfers Paradise, down to Coolangatta – which was pure bushland just two generations ago – is the fastest-growing tourist and residential area in Australia. The beaches, particularly **Burleigh Heads** set in a national park, are strikingly gorgeous, and from a heady apartment or hotel room on the umpteenth floor of a high-rise at **Surfers Paradise** ❷ the sight of sands stretching away to the north and south can be breathtaking. Down below, though, it's somewhat different. On the beach you can feel crowded in by towers thrown up with little evident architectural merit; height is the only

TIP

Descendants of the Kombumerri people, who once inhabited the area around Burleigh Heads, run various guided tours that explain the significance of rock formations and middens (Kalwun Paradise Dreaming; tel: 07-5578 3044; www.kalwun.com.au).

BELOW: enjoying the sun on the Gold Coast.

The ultimate blonde at Movie World.

BELOW: feeding the birds at Currumbin Wildlife Sanctuary.

yardstick, and the current leader is the Q1 building. Its claim to capture "the aura of modernity evident in world-famous buildings by architects such as Renzo Piano and Frank Lloyd Wright" seems to be the height of folly. Which, incidentally, is 323 metres (1,060ft).

Comparisons between Surfers Paradise and Ipanema, Miami and Cannes also seem wide of the mark. There's little sense of the style or class that such parallels might suggest. Stores are functional at best, tacky souvenir shops abound and patches of ground are purloined for haphazard collections of glorified fairground attractions, such as the Vomatron or the Sling Shot, both to be found on the corner of Gold Coast Highway and Cypress Avenue.

Night-time is when the place really comes alive, possibly because you can't see it so well. Party-goers take over the streets, casinos and restaurants and the clubs start buzzing. Unsurprisingly, the beaches can be pretty quiet in the morning; that's when families are out in force.

Away from Surfers, the super-rich are indulged at **South Beach** in the six-star (sic) resort, Palazzo Versace. Further south numbers of international visitors diminish and domestic tourists and hard-core surfies dominate.

Theme parks

The Gold Coast scores strong popularity points among the locals with its family-oriented theme parks. Performing dolphins and a dynamic water-ski show are the main pulls at **Sea World** (daily 10am–5.30pm; www.seaworld.com.au; charge); **Dreamworld**, a large amusement park with a reassuringly Australian atmosphere, combines laid-back fun with adrenaline-pumping rides as well as a section devoted completely to the Wiggles (daily 10am–5pm; tel: 07-5588 1111; www.dreamworld.com.au; charge); **Wet 'n' Wild** is a huge aquatic park with a mind-boggling variety of rides and adventures (daily May–Aug 10am–4pm, Sept–Apr 10am–5pm, 27 Dec–25 Jan until 9pm; www.wetnwild.com.au; charge). S

Surpassing them all as a tourist attraction is **Warner Brothers' Movie World**, where startling rides such as Superman Adventure and the Wild West Falls Adventure are augmented by stunt shows and special-effects displays (daily 10am–5.30pm; www.movieworld.com.au; charge). **Whitewaterworld**, the latest addition to the list, is a sister operation to Dreamworld and will make you soggy in ever-more imaginative ways (daily 10am–4pm; www.whitewaterworld.com.au; charge). Unfortunately none of these theme parks is cheap, but you can easily spend a day in each of them. The best plan is to arrive early and get the best value for your money.

Finally, the **Australian Outback Spectacular** packages up "a genuine Aussie Outback experience" which is, of course, nothing of the kind (Tue–Sun 7.30pm; www.outbackspectacular.com.au; charge).

For an antidote to excess, the **Currumbin Wildlife Sanctuary** (28 Tomewin Street, Currumbin; daily

8am–5pm; tel: 07-5534 1266; www. currumbin-sanctuary.org.au; charge) offers every variety of indigenous fauna, as well as the chance to act as a perch for flocks of lorikeets at feeding time.

The Darling Downs

Inland from Brisbane, the countryside is almost entirely ignored by tourists. Here, the tablelands give way to the Darling Downs, a vast area of beautiful, rolling plains and rich soil. **Ipswich ❸**, now an easy commute from Brisbane, is an old railway town whose history is well displayed at the Workshops Rail Museum (North Street; daily 9.30am–5pm; tel: 07-3432 5100; www.thework shops.qm.qld.gov.au; charge), but there are plenty of other interesting features on its heritage trail.

The pleasant city of **Warwick ❹** serves as a livestock industry hub. The second-oldest town in Queensland retains a good deal of historical character, much of it linked to prosperity deriving from the discovery of gold nearby. There are some beautiful buildings, but its most famous feature is the month-long Rose and Rodeo Festival, which attracts the country's best cowboys every October.

Hilly **Toowoomba ❺** is not just Queensland's largest inland conurbation but also a garden city of some note. Situated on the rim of the Great Dividing Range, with the Darling Downs laid out before it, Toowoomba is colourful all year but sensational when spring flowers bloom.

Lamington National Park ❻, in the McPherson Ranges directly behind the Gold Coast, is vast and offers some fabulous bushwalking through dramatic rainforest. Occupying part of the rim of an ancient volcano, Lamington has a wide range of ferns and hundreds of species of orchid.

The Sunshine Coast

North of Brisbane there are more of the contrasts between the sublime and the kitsch that characterise the Gold Coast, but with the Sunshine Coast the balance is very different. The beaches are just as glorious, but the resorts are less brash.

Follow the Bruce Highway out of Brisbane, and as the suburbs are left behind look out for the unique

BELOW:
the Ettamogah Pub
tilts in all directions.

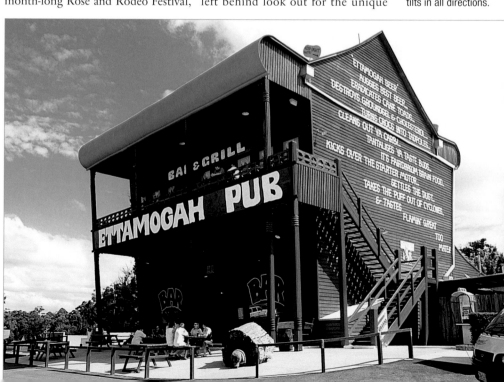

TIP

The sleek new Noosa
Visitor Information
Centre (Hastings Street,
Noosa Heads; tel: 07-
5430 5000) provides
information about
accommodation as well
as events like the Noosa
Long Weekend in June,
the Celebration of Food
and Wine in May and
Noosa Jazz Festival in
September.

BELOW: the
Glasshouse
Mountains.
BELOW RIGHT:
waiting for the
lunch boat to arrive.

geological formations of the **Glass House Mountains** looming up on your left, which dominate the landscape for several kilometres. Walks up them or drives between them are recommended. And it's the Glass House Mountains Road you'll want anyway for the **Australia Zoo** ❼ (daily 9am–5pm; tel: 07-5436 2000; www.australia zoo.com; charge), near Beerwah. The organisation has adjusted to life after "crocodile hunter" Steve Irwin by shifting the focus to his children Bindi and Robert, but otherwise continues virtually unchanged as both a tribute to Irwin and as a focus for the environmental work that he so assiduously promoted.

Back on the highway a cartoon Aussie boozer, the **Ettamogah Pub**, reacquaints us with the trashy, while **Aussie World** (daily 9am–5pm; tel: 07-5494 5444; www.aussieworld.com.au; charge), next door, is really a glorified fairground. Stay inland and take the Nambour Tourist Drive. Six kilometres (4 miles) south of Nambour, marvel at an enormous fibreglass fruit: The Big Pineapple. Buy local fruit, tour a pineapple farm, and learn about the pineapple industry in a theatrette inside the structure. This is but one of dozens of "Big Things" that litter eastern Australia, and, in its attention to detail, it's one of the less tacky. Really.

Coastal towns

All this can distract visitors from what is one of the most gorgeous stretches of Queensland's coastline. The action begins at **Caloundra**, where Bribie Island lies just across the Pumicestone Channel, but, more importantly, where the serious surf beaches begin. Caloundra is now a blossoming family resort. Further up, Mooloolaba is also seeing a spate of high-rise development. Beaches all along this stretch are gems. Try seeking out the unspoilt Marcoola Beach at Coolum, a relaxed and up-market settlement.

Many visitors stick with the Sunshine Highway all the way to **Noosa Heads** ❽. Noosa has been called the Cannes of Australia, a heady blend of beauty, sophistication and wealth. Nestling beside the tranquil waters of Laguna Bay, Noosa comes close to distilling the essence of the Australian Dream. Today Noosa is a collection of townships strung along the coast. The perfect waves that wrap around the points of Noosa's National Park rank among the world's finest, and surfers were the first to populate the area.

Publicity soon lured a different clique – the wealthy early retirees of Sydney, Melbourne and Adelaide. From the moment they saw Noosa Heads, these refugees from colder climes began buying up large tracts of the best land. Today, the village of Noosa is lined with glitzy restaurants and boutiques, although it can't seem to entirely shake off the raffish charm of old. Only a few metres from Hastings Street, Noosa's main business thoroughfare, swimmers still float lazily in a sea so clear you can see whiting and flathead scud across the bottom. Sheltering Noosa from the prevailing southeasterly winds is the headland, gateway to the 334-hectare (825-acre) Noosa National Park, an area of woodland and marshes on the south bank of the Noosa River.

Highway 1, the main coastal route from Brisbane to Cairns, stretches for 1,703km (1,058 miles), and, although it is being continually improved, don't think of it as a highway in the American or European sense; much of it is just a good-quality undivided two-lane road. Distances between coastal centres can be vast and, by comparison with more populated areas in the south of Australia, rural Queensland remains something of a diamond in the rough. Still, small diversions from the route north will reveal magnificent and uncrowded beaches, pristine rainforests, tropical islands, authentic country pubs, splendid fishing and diving, and the most mouth-watering local tucker.

Travelling north

Highway 1 runs through Gympie, a one-time gold-mining town which hosts a week-long Gold Rush Festival every October, then to atmospheric **Maryborough 9** which has a railway museum and some fine old Victorian buildings. From nearby Hervey Bay, a barge will carry you and your vehicle over to **Fraser Island 10** (see overleaf).

The Bundaberg Rum Distillery (Whittred Street; tel: 07-4131 2999) runs tours on the hour Mon–Fri 10am–3pm, Sat–Sun 10am–2pm.

BELOW:
all kinds of boards are welcome on the beach.

Fraser Island

Fraser is the world's largest sand island; its ecology is unlike any other – a fact that put it on the UN's World Heritage list in 1992

Instead of barren desert, which you might expect from a sand island, the entire interior is covered with a rich patchwork of forests whose muscular vegetation manages to survive on the nutrients in only the top 15cm (6 inches) of soil.

The island's landscape changes every few hundred metres, from classic Aussie scrub and reed-filled swamps surrounded by 60-metre (200ft) satinay trees, to expanses of lush rainforest, with plants so dense that they almost block out the sunlight. Amid the forests are some 40 freshwater lakes, including both perched (above sea level) and window lakes (at or below sea level). Some of them have water the colour of tea, while others are perfect blue with blinding white sands – **Lake Mackenzie**, for example, could be in the Caribbean.

This magnificent island has been reshaping itself over thousands of years. Enormous sand dunes creep like silent yellow glaciers, consuming entire forests then leaving them behind, petrified and ghostly. But plant life always revives; there are more independent dune systems on Fraser, showing sand and vegetation in different stages of interaction, than anywhere else on Earth.

The island won a permanent place in the Australian history books in the 1830s, when some shipwrecked British sailors were probably killed here by local Aborigines; the lone survivor, Eliza Fraser, spent many months living with local people before being "rescued" by an escaped convict. British settlers then used the island as a sort of natural prison camp for Aborigines. When fine wood was discovered soon after, the British herded the Aborigines off, killing many, it is said, by driving them into the sea.

For the past 30 years, Fraser Island has been at the centre of one of Australia's most vicious conservation disputes. In the 1970s came the battle to stop mining (the sands are rich in rutile and zircon); in the 1980s there was a long, and finally successful, campaign to ban logging on the island.

There are arguments about how to manage the booming number of annual visitors – from 10,000 in the early 1970s to 350,000 today. There can be few other World Heritage sites so readily available to the public, and the island's four ranger stations are kept busy managing the place in such a way that visitor pressures don't cause more damage.

Anglers head for **Waddy Point**, while nature-lovers seek out the soft sands of the deserted beaches (swimwear optional). The **Great Sandy National Park**, covering 840 sq km (325 sq miles), is a jigsaw of lakes, dunes, forest and beach.

For a small fee, anyone can bring a four-wheel-drive vehicle from the mainland, bounce along the island's trails, rip up and down **Seventy-Five Mile Beach** on the east coast and camp in designated areas. (Note that a four-wheel-drive is essential; tyre pressure should be reduced for beach travel, which should be attempted only at low tide. Count on getting bogged at least once during your visit.) There are plenty of organised tours for those daunted by off-road driving.

Non-tented sleeping options include Kingfisher Bay Resort, which is shrewdly conceived to repose so lightly amid scrub and natural lagoons as to be barely noticeable from the beach or from passing yachts. Even with 1,000 guests, it maintains an uncrowded sense of serenity and has become the accommodation of choice for affluent guests. ❑

BELOW: the beaches of Fraser Island are made up of sand that has been accumulating for 750,000 years.

Childers, on the highway to the north, is a National Trust-listed town surrounded by rolling hills covered in sugar cane. The town encapsulates the region's early architecture. A turn-off to Woodgate Beach and Woodgate National Park, about 40km (25 miles) down the side road, pays dividends.

The next major town north is **Bundaberg** ⓫ on the coast, 45km (28 miles) from Highway 1. For millions of Australians, Bundy is synonymous with rum. Here, in the heart of sugar country, is the distillery that put the town on the map. An inexpensive tour provides an insight into the production process, a visit to a museum and a taste of the product (Whittred Street; Mon–Fri 10am–3pm, Sat–Sun 10am–2pm; tel: 07-4131 2999; www.bundabergrum.com. au; charge). There is much else to see around town, including a selection of museums and a turtle hatchery. From Bundaberg, cruises and flights operate to **Lady Elliot Island**, 85km (53 miles) away, on the southern end of the Great Barrier Reef (see page 257).

The twin coastal resorts of **Agnes Water** and **Town of 1770** have become popular fishing and boating centres as well as being the departure point for visits to Eurimbula and Deepwater national parks with their pristine coastal landscapes.

Pass up the next detour, to the surprisingly attractive industrial centre of **Gladstone**, unless you happen to be interested in the world's largest aluminium plant (A\$355 million to construct) or you are one of the fortunate heading out by ferry or helicopter to Heron Island (see page 258).

Carnarvon Gorge

The Dawson Highway, heading west from Gladstone, is the route to one of Queensland's most outstanding national parks at **Carnarvon Gorge** ⓬. This 30km (16-mile) sandstone gorge has a profusion of palm trees, cycads, ferns and mosses as well as fine examples of Aboriginal rock paintings.

Rockhampton

Back on Highway 1, and north of the Tropic of Capricorn (marked by a roadside spire), **Rockhampton** ⓭ made headlines around the world when it

Rockhampton has stunningly well-preserved old hotels and warehouses down by the river. You can pick up heritage trail leaflets from the visitor centre in town.

BELOW:
Australia's colonial heritage is evident in the architecture.

The Gem Fields

Fortune hunters should head 270km (170 miles) inland from the town of Rockhampton to **Emerald**, a centre for the farming of cotton, citrus fruits, grapes and fodder crops. It is also a gateway to the famous central Queensland gem fields, where scores of latter-day pioneers fossick for precious stones. There's nothing fancy about the gem fields; in tents, caravans and tumble-down tin shacks the miners have traded traditional comforts for the freedom and excitement of their own frontier, their rewards being sapphire, topaz, amethyst and jasper. These are the largest sapphire-producing fields in the world, and some fossickers have struck it rich in their first week, but most haven't. Various fossicking parks give visitors a chance to try their hand.

Townsville has some impressive Art Deco buildings.

was the first city hit by the massive floods that inundated Queensland in January 2011. Normally it hums quietly as the commercial heart of central Queensland. A colourful former mayor, Rex Pilbeam, had a Brahman bull cast in concrete and erected at the northern entrance to the city (the Brahman is the breed favoured by cattlemen to the north), and a similar sculpture of a Hereford (the breed favoured in the south) at the southern end. When the beasts were made, Pilbeam – anticipating playfulness by locals – had several spare sets of testicles placed in storage. Hooligans struck the Brahman almost immediately. They were dumbfounded when workmen bolted on a replacement appendage the same day.

Rockhampton has a population of about 75,000, with modern pubs and office blocks interspersed among older buildings – and what buildings! The National Estate lists Quay Street in its entirety on its heritage register, and superb colonial homes are found in Agnes Street. Look out for the excellent collection of Australian art at **Rockhampton Art Gallery** (62

Victoria Parade; Tue–Fri 10am–4pm, Sat–Sun 11am–4pm; tel: 07-4936 8248; free), and the outstanding Botanic Gardens. Pick up a heritage guide from the visitor information centre in the old Customs House on Quay Street.

The starting point for **Mackay** ⓮, 333km (207 miles) to the north, is the large tourist information centre set in a replica of the Richmond Sugar Mill, the first in the area. Fanned by tropical breezes and surrounded by a rustling sea of sugar cane, Mackay is a pleasant city of wide streets and elegant old hotels. A stroll through the centre reveals an assortment of Victorian buildings interspersed with several displaying the sleek lines of 1930s Art Deco. North of the centre there are fine beaches and the new Marina Village.

Airlie Beach ⓯ and neighbouring **Shute Harbour**, 135km (84 miles) to the north, act as the gateway to the Whitsunday Islands *(see page 258).* There are fine eateries and accommodation from backpackers' hostels to four-star resorts. This is the place to find a berth on one of the many island-hopping yachts.

Townsville

Eyebrows used to be raised at the idea of visiting **Townsville** ⓰, but these days the state's second-biggest city is a relaxed and graceful place with plenty to attract the casual visitor. This is due in part to two destructive cyclones that ripped the foreshore apart in 1997 and 1998, prompting a A$29-million restoration along The Strand. The resultant 2.2km (1½-mile) stretch of white sand, swaying palms, water parks, play areas and casual restaurants redefined Townsville as a tropical resort city of considerable appeal. Townsville's residents congregate here to sunbathe, barbecue, browse and birdwatch.

Flinders Street, the main thoroughfare, has notable late 19th-century architecture, including many of the city's 58 National Trust-listed buildings. At its northern end the **Museum of Tropical Queensland** (daily 9.30am–5pm; tel: 07-4726 0600; www.mtq.qm.qld.gov.au; charge), its atrium dominated by a huge cross section of an 18th-century naval frigate, provides a good child-friendly introduction to the history, peoples and geology of the area.

Next door, **Reef HQ** (daily 9.30am–5pm; tel: 07-4750 0800; www.reefhq.com.au; charge) has a huge coral-reef aquarium as its centrepiece.

Overlooking everything is the craggy Castle Hill. In a typical display of civic pride, an early resident deduced that if Castle Hill were just a few metres higher, it could officially be called a mountain. He began carting soil up the hill and dumping it on top. The town never got its mountain, but the project became a kind of monument to obscure endeavour everywhere. Climb, or more likely drive, to the top for a different perspective of the city and look out to sea where **Magnetic Island** can be seen offshore.

It's only a 20-minute ferry ride from Townsville, but Magnetic Island feels worlds away. Hire a Mini Moke and hop from one bay to another, follow one of the many trails into the forest, or maybe stumble over an old wartime lookout post. There are plenty of places to stay at all budgets.

Townsville's relatively green hinterland strip is bordered by rocky mountain ranges that eventually give way to

The old British Leyland Mini Moke is enjoying a last hurrah on Magnetic Island. This distinctive vehicle of the 1960s doesn't go particularly fast but you're sitting so close to the ground, have so much wind blowing through your hair and are feeling so many bumps in the road through the rudimentary suspension that it feels as if you're hurtling along.

BELOW: Alma Bay on Magnetic Island.

Gold Towns

Head west from Townsville to gold country, and the vistas along the Flinders Highway rapidly turn from lush green to the parched semi-arid savannah of Australian myth. **Charters Towers**, 135km (84 miles) inland, owes its heyday to an Aboriginal boy who found gold in 1872 while on an expedition with prospector Hugh Mossman. A tiny town suddenly boomed. Of the splendid architecture that resulted, the restored Stock Exchange in the historic Royal Arcade is one of the city's 19th-century highlights. Gold is still produced locally, with companies reworking old sites. One is in **Ravenswood**, 38km (24 miles) south of the Flinders Highway, where among deserted shacks and derelict equipment two ancient pubs still function and there's a small museum.

Palm Cove has been designed around the 500-year-old Melaleuca trees that dot the town and beaches.

BELOW: a well-lit walkway along the water in Cairns.

the inland savannah. About 10km (6 miles) north of Ingham, as you reach the top of a steep hill, you are suddenly treated to one of the most breathtaking sights of the whole coastal trip. Be ready to stop and admire the view of **Hinch-inbrook Island** across the narrow man-grove-lined channel *(see page 255)*.

Gorges and beaches

From Cardwell northward the highway sticks pretty close to the coast, offering plenty of diversions to peaceful little spots for picnics, fishing and water sports. A trip up **Tully Gorge** offers dramatic scenery and the opportunity to take in some whitewater rafting.

Mission Beach ⑰, an 18km (11-mile) detour off the highway, is a relaxed, low-rise destination. The beach is perfect, the restaurants are good and there's always the option of a quick trip across to Dunk Island if you crave a spell on a westward-facing strand for a change.

This stretch of coastline bore the brunt of Cyclone Yasi in February 2011. Rebuilding was swift and even devas-tated Dunk and Bedarra islands were

expected to reopen within one year. Yasi followed Cyclone Larry of 2006, when the brunt of the damage was inflicted on **Innisfail**, 49km (30 miles) to the north. Even before that, locals' claims that this would be the next happening place in the region aroused some scepti-cism, but it's a nice enough town and its Art Deco architecture and Chinese temple are worth a look.

Gateway to paradise

And so on to **Cairns ⑱**, pulsat-ing visitor centre of tropical north Queensland. Until the 1980s, this was a sleepy provincial backwater wallow-ing in a swamp. Not terribly much had changed since it was founded just over a century before, on some not very picturesque mangrove flats, to service the gold and tin fields further inland. Then the tourism boom hit. There's still a core of old-style tropical charm in the languid pubs and distinctively Queensland-style porches, but today Cairns, with a population of 164,000, has a modern international airport, bustling shopping malls and a vast variety of restaurants. Almost any sporting activity – diving trips to the Reef, bungy jumping, whitewater rafting, tandem parachuting, hiking the Atherton Tableland – can be arranged.

The focus of Cairns remains the **Esplanade**. The waterfront is lined by high-rise hotels and backpacker accommodation, and there's always an array of picnicking locals beneath the Moreton Bay figs and palms. Its centrepiece is a huge landscaped swimming lagoon, classic red-and-yellow-garbed lifeguards in attendance, its lawns carpeted with minimally clad sunbathers. A leisure and shopping centre, the Pier is still struggling to impose itself, but weekend markets, and a marina for the region's marlin fishing fleet and pleasure boats, give verve to the waterfront.

The **Cairns Historical Museum** (corner Lake and Shields streets; Mon–Sat 10am–4pm; tel: 07-4051 5582; www.cairnsmuseum.org.au; charge) has exhibits on the more rough-and-ready past of the area, while the elegant **Regional Art Gallery** (corner Abbot and Shields streets; Mon–Sat 10am–5pm, Sun 1–5pm; tel: 07-4046 4800; www.cairnsregionalgallery.com.au; charge) has local artists' work on display as well as visiting exhibitions.

But the real attractions of Cairns lie beyond the town limits; either out to sea for the **Great Barrier Reef** (see page 256) or inland where the lush, cool plateau of the **Atherton Tableland** deserves extensive exploration. Like the rest of the region, it was opened up by prospectors in the 1870s. It is now a major dairy farm area, with a range of B&Bs and farm-stay accommodation with faintly chi-chi names (see panel on next page).

However, for many tourists there is only time for a day-trip package. This means taking the pleasant 64km (44-mile) return trip from Cairns to the village of **Kuranda**; one way by train, with vintage coaches climbing tortuously through spectacular scenery, tunnels and past impressive waterfalls; the other half of the journey by Skyrail, a cable car that almost brushes the rainforest tree tops. Consequently Kuranda is one big shopping opportunity, with a craft market (Wed–Fri and Sun), galleries, didgeridoo outlets and a host of restaurants and cafés. Beyond that, the station is charming and there's a butterfly sanctuary and aviary.

The far north

North of Cairns, the Cook Highway runs through one of the most classically gorgeous parts of Australia. Strings of uncrowded, palm-fringed beaches (including those of the beachside suburbs of Trinity, Kewarra and exclusive Palm Cove) look as Hawaii must have done before the developers arrived. Having said that, construction is moving apace and for Palm Cove in particular it's worth checking in advance on the likely impact that the latest building works may have on your holiday haven.

The Great Barrier Reef comes within 15km (9 miles) of the shoreline, and from various ports diving boats head out to the sand cays and coral reefs. One of the most popular starting

TIP

Drop in at the century-old Cairns Yacht Club to meet barnacled locals while washing down prawns with beer. Hemmed in on all sides by high-rises, the club has been assured that its two-storey weatherboard headquarters will remain unmolested by developers – for now. Its verandah is a fine place to sip a beer.

BELOW: diving at the Great Barrier Reef.

TIP

Heading north from Port Douglas, you pass cane farms and exotic fruit plantations to Miallo, famous as the place where actress Diane Cilento established her 500-seat Karnak Playhouse (tel: 07-4098 8111; www.karnak playhouse.com.au) with her late husband, the playwright Anthony Shaffer. It's worth a look just for the setting.

points lies some 80km (50 miles) north of Cairns. **Port Douglas** ⑲, like most of the coastal settlements, was founded after a gold rush in the 1870s, when the Gugu-Yalangi Aborigines were forced from their land. For a time it was more important than Cairns, but its popularity faded when the gold ran out. For the next century, Port Douglas boasted little more than two pubs and a pie shop. Today, the pubs and pie shop are still there, but they've been joined by glitzy new resorts like the Sheraton Mirage, which continues to attract world leaders and household names from the entertainment industry. There are also some fine restaurants and chic boutiques on Macrossan Street, and you can find nightly cane-toad races in one of the bars, but the palm-fringed village atmosphere that could still be enjoyed in the 1990s has long gone.

However, Four Mile Beach is among the region's most beautiful, while every morning dozens of boats head out from the marina for day trips on the Reef. Just offshore are the immensely popular Low Isles, and a string of excellent snorkelling

RIGHT: swimming at Mossman Gorge.

spots is only an hour away *(see page 261)*. Passages are available on everything from tiny yachts catering for only a dozen passengers right up to the massive Quicksilver catamarans that can shuttle hundreds of people at a time.

Rainforest

Returning to the highway, just north of the Port Douglas turn-off, is Mossman and the road to **Mossman Gorge**. A 3km (2-mile) walking circuit runs past mountain streams and lush, dripping foliage. Slightly further north, past rich sugar-cane country, the village of **Daintree** is the starting point for river trips. Just after dawn, the birdlife is extraordinary (parrots, ospreys, great white herons). Later in the day, you'll see saltwater crocodiles lounging in sunny bliss.

Cross the Daintree River by ferry (6am–midnight) and drive for 36km (23 miles) to **Cape Tribulation** ⑳. It's an incongruous name for one of Australia's most serene corners, but then Captain Cook was in a poor mood after his ship, the *Endeavour*, ran onto a

The Atherton Tableland

The hill country inland from Cairns offers respite from the tropical heat of the coast; with its sprinkling of attractive townships, inviting lakes, picturesque waterfalls and towering forests, it is deserving of proper investigation over a few days. With its elevation and associated rainfall, this fertile plateau at the northern end of the Great Dividing Range is prime dairy country. In the early days of colonial settlement, great areas of forest were cleared of valuable timber, leaving today's rolling pastureland.

It was the Chinese, originally drawn by tin and gold mining in the region, who led the way in agriculture, and evidence of their presence is manifest in **Atherton**, the main town in the area. The 1903 Hou Wang Temple (Herberton Road; Wed–Sun 11am–4pm; www.houwang.org.au) was the focal point of Chinatown.

Yungaburra, a few kilometres to the east, is dotted with heritage buildings and has a famed 500-year-old curtain fig tree, as well as being a good spot to see platypus – by the bridge. **Malanda** is worth a look, and **Millaa Millaa** is a pretty place to join a waterfalls circuit taking in four examples, with Millaa Millaa Falls being the highlight.

Millstream Falls are the widest in the country and can be found outside **Ravenshoe**, if you're not detained by the town's steam train.

reef in 1770. "This was where our troubles began," he noted in his log, and his subsequent naming of Mount Misery, Cape Sorrow and the like indicate a man who hadn't perked up.

Troubles returned in the early 1980s, when the Queensland government decided to push a road through the rainforest to improve access for tourists and remote Aboriginal communities. Hundreds of eco-activists descended on Cape Trib to throw themselves in front of the bulldozers. Ironically, this focused so much attention on the area that Cape Trib became a household name in Australia, and is now firmly on the tourist map. The road was eventually completed, but the outcry prompted a United Nations World Heritage listing for the Daintree area, which is now part of a national park.

Today, the isolated, otherworldly atmosphere of Cape Trib appears to have barely changed. There is a scattered community with a few grocery stores and, except for a couple of hours in the middle of the day, when tour buses arrive from Cairns, there are usually few people on the beaches. Meanwhile,

a cluster of new high-quality eco-lodges nestles in rainforest-covered hills. There are also coral reefs quite close to the shore, a very unusual phenomenon.

The contentious coastal road to Cooktown is now a reality – although barely. You need a four-wheel-drive vehicle to bounce through tunnels of virgin forest, plough across shallow rivers and up 45-degree inclines. Although you glimpse the sea rarely, the views and sense of isolation are worth it. The road is open all year with extreme caution – watch the tide at Bloomfield River unless you'd like to contribute to the crocodiles' diet. Otherwise, in a conventional vehicle, you can make the journey from Cairns on the inland Cape York Development Road, which was only fully sealed in 2006. Call in at the Lion's Den pub, just off the highway at Helenvale – it's one of the oldest in north Queensland, with the original wooden bar, piano and a vast array of pickled snakes.

Cooktown

At the end of the line is **Cooktown** ㉑, a place that has always had a Wild

Cooktown marks Captain Cook's enforced stay with a statue and a festival in June re-enacting his arrival in 1770.

BELOW: zip-lining above the trees.

The World's Oldest Rainforest

The rainforest is at least 100 million years old (compared with the Amazon's 10 million) and is a vital component of Queensland

All the Earth's rainforests are thought to have begun around present-day Melbourne some 120 million years ago, when Australia was a part of the great continent of Gondwanaland. When Oceania broke away, 50 million years ago, the drier land began to replace tropical conditions. The rainforests that once covered Australia retreated to less than 1 percent of the continent; logging has reduced that by more than half.

North Queensland's rainforest – now protected as part of the Wet Tropics World Heritage area and a patchwork of national parks – has the highest diversity of local endemic species in the world. Fully one-fifth of Australia's bird species, a quarter of its reptiles, a third of its marsupials, a third of its frogs and two-fifths of its plants are here in a tiny fraction of the Australian landmass.

Conservationists waged battles with the timber industry and the Queensland government throughout the 1980s. Ultimately, the eco-activists triumphed over the bulldozers; today most North Queenslanders accept the importance of the wet zones. With its capacity to attract visitors, it doesn't do the local economy any harm either.

As for the seething tangle of vines and ferns itself, the rainforest has always deployed a wide array of defences against intruders. First off, there's the taipan snake, whose bite is 300 times more toxic than a cobra's. Some other native snakes are nearly as dangerous. However, death by snakebite is rarer than death by lightning strike.

The local (non-venomous) python is hardly worth a mention, although the largest recorded scrub python, found in the Tully area, measured 8.5 metres (28ft) long. The saltwater crocodiles that lurk in the remoter rivers here only grow up to about 6 metres (20ft) – but that's still enough to grab the unwary by the legs and spoil their day with the death-roll they use to disable and eventually kill their victims.

If you see a tree goanna – a giant speckled lizard with enormous claws – don't startle it: it may confuse you with a tree, climb up your leg and disembowel you. (Why it would attack a tree in the first place isn't entirely clear.) A kick from a frightened cassowary – a 2-metre (6ft) -tall flightless bird with a bony crown – can tear open your ribcage so, if you meet one in the bush, give it plenty of room.

The barking or bird-eating spider, with a leg span up to 15cm (6 inches), may be found in areas bordering on rainforest and can deal you a nasty bite.

Dangerous plants

Even some plants are armed and dangerous. The heart-shaped leaves of the Gympie vine, for example, inject silica spines into any skin unlucky enough to brush it. It's "like a blow-torch being applied to your flesh", apparently.

The chances of encountering any of these horrors are minimal. Access for visitors is tightly controlled and any sightseeing is likely to be from defined paths or boardwalks, where the route is well marked.

You can take it a step further by visiting the **Daintree Discovery Centre** where the whole rainforest experience is packed into a fenced compound and enjoyed from either the raised boardwalk on the forest floor or an ariel walkway.   ❑

LEFT: be careful not to venture off the path when visiting the rainforests of Queensland.

West reputation as an isolated tropical refuge which you could escape to when nowhere else would have you. It is located on the mangrove estuary where Captain Cook spent seven weeks repairing the *Endeavour*. The local Gugu-Yalangi people were friendly, and it was the most significant contact between Aborigines and Europeans to that date. The time ashore gave Sir Joseph Banks the opportunity to make more detailed studies of local wildlife than he had been allowed at Botany Bay.

When an Irish prospector struck gold at Palmer River in 1873, Cooktown became one of Australia's busiest ports, with 94 pubs (many little more than shacks) and 35,000 miners working on the claims. There's a mural in the Middle Pub depicting those days when miners blew thousands of pounds' worth of gold dust in a single night, chased women such as the legendary Palmer Kate, passed out on drugged whisky and then woke up penniless in the swamps.

Cooktown still thrives on those memories, and it has maintained a languid charm. Poking between palm trees on the wide main street are many late 19th-century buildings, including the three surviving watering holes (to avoid confusion, known as the Top, Middle and Bottom pubs).

The **James Cook Historical Museum** (corner of Helen and Furneaux streets; daily 9.30am–4pm; tel: 07-4069 5386; charge) is one of the best in Australia and is located in the former convent of St Mary; exhibits include the original anchor of the *Endeavour*, retrieved from the Reef. The Cooktown cemetery, just north of town, is full of its own stories of the old pioneers.

The last frontier

Beyond Cooktown sprawls the **Cape York Peninsula**, a popular destination for four-wheel-drive expeditions in the dry season. The red-dust road runs from one lonely bush pub to the next, past ant hills, forests full of screaming cockatoos, and vast sandstone bluffs rich in Aboriginal rock art. It can take several days to get to Australia's northernmost point, the tip of Cape York, and it's essential that you travel with someone who has serious off-roading experience. It's best to go in convoy with at least one other vehicle.

The tiny township of **Laura** ㉒ at the southern tip of the Lakefield National Park (an expanse of marshland, lagoons, mangrove swamps and rainforest that is rich in flora and fauna) is one of the last accessible spots without a four-wheel-drive vehicle as long as you stay outside the park. It's worth the trip to see some fabulous Aboriginal rock art. Split Rock can be explored on your own, while other sites can be enjoyed in the company of Aboriginal guides booked through the Quinkan Regional Cultural Centre (tel: 07-4060 3457; www.quinkancc.com.au).

Heading north, the journey passes the bauxite-mining town of Weipa and the Jardine River Crossing (which has a ferry). Torres Strait is the end of the line, where there are campgrounds; 6km (4 miles) to the

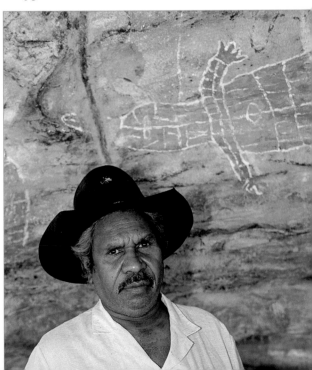

BELOW: a guide explains Aboriginal rock art at Laura.

Balancing Rock is not a trick of the eye, but rather a matter of physics.

BELOW: the wildlife can be as interesting as the geology.

northeast, at Punsand Bay, is the closest population to the continent's northernmost tip.

Boats run from Red Island Point (Bamaga) to Thursday Island, the administrative centre of the Torres Strait Islands, many of which were named by Captain Bligh when he passed through on an open longboat after the *Bounty* mutiny. From June to September, the ferry also operates from Punsand Bay. **Thursday Island ㉓** (pop. 3,500) was once one of the world's great pearling stations. Although there are no tourist traps or beaches of note, T.I. is a pleasant enough place to lay up after the rigours of the road. Its cosmopolitan mix of inhabitants is a carefree and friendly crowd who like to party. There are four old pubs, the more modern Jardine Motel, and a Japanese cemetery from pearling days.

A special way to take a close look at the far north Queensland coastline and the Torres Straits is a five-day return voyage from Cairns on the MV *Trinity Bay*, a working cargo ship supplying the remote Cape York communities all

the way up to Thursday Island. It's air-conditioned and comfortable, and dress and conversation are informal. (Tel: 07-4035 1234; www.seaswift.com.au).

The Queensland Outback

Most of Queensland's key destinations (and by far the majority of the population) are to be found on the coast, and yet much that is most fascinating about the place is to be found inland. It's impossible to get a real handle on the state until you've headed off into the Outback. There are countless ways to do it, but with the idea of describing a circuit (which needs a good parcel of time) let's look at a journey moving inland from Cairns. This is the starting point of the Savannah Way, which eventually winds up in Broome in northern Western Australia. The land is vast and there may be hundreds of kilometres between destinations, so keep a keen eye on the fuel gauge.

Chillagoe ㉔, 215km (134 miles) west of Cairns, is not actually on the Savannah Way but is worth a visit. It's a mining town with plenty of detritus from the industry to provide character. Limestone bluffs around the town add drama to the harsh terrain, while spectacular caves in the **Chillagoe-Mungana National Park** can be explored on your own or with guided tours. Book at the Hub (21–3 Queen Street; tel: 07-4094 7111; www.chillagoehub.com.au).

More subterranean wonders are to be found at the **Undara Lava Tubes ㉕** a few kilometres south of the Savannah Way, one of the best examples of lava-tube formation anywhere on the planet. These are created when lava follows the line of river beds, the lava surface cools but the molten material within flows out, leaving a tube behind. Some of the tubes are 15–20 metres (50–65ft) in diameter. Full resort accommodation is offered in beautifully restored vintage rail carriages relocated there for the purpose. (Various times; tel: 07-4097 1900; www. undara.com.au; charge.) It's also a Savannah Guide Station.

The Savannah Way continues on through **Georgetown** where there are a few significant buildings and the **Terrestrial Centre** in Low Street (Apr–Sept daily 8am–5pm, Oct–Mar Mon–Fri 8.30am–4.30pm; tel: 07-4062 1485; charge) which highlights the importance of minerals to the area. It's another 148km (92 miles) to **Croydon** ㉖, a friendly township with a well-preserved timber pub and an interesting historic precinct. From here there's an old railway service, the Gulflander, which runs through to **Normanton**, just a short distance from the **Gulf of Carpentaria**.

Towards the border with the Northern Territory, where the terrain is becoming drier and less hospitable, **Lawn Hill Gorge** ㉗ provides a green oasis and stakes a claim to be one of the most spectacularly beautiful locations in the state. Not many people get out this far, but, for those who do, there are kayaks to paddle down between sheer red sandstone cliffs, and easy hikes through the surrounding Boodjamulla National Park. A half-hour drive away is the World Heritage-listed Riversleigh Fossils site.

It's mines, all mines

Track south down dirt roads to **Mount Isa** ㉘ and discover the full significance of the finds at the **Riversleigh Fossil Display & Interpretive Centre** attached to the Outback at Isa complex (tel: 07-4749 1555; www.outbackatisa.com.au; charge). Mount Isa is a mining city truly in the middle of nowhere. A rich lode of lead, silver, copper and zinc was discovered here in 1923, and a tiny tent settlement rapidly developed into Australia's largest company town, dominated by the looming presence of the mine and its tailings. Working mine tours are no longer available, but you can take a two-hour underground tour of the ersatz Hard Times Mine, through the Outback at Isa operation.

The municipal boundaries of the Isa extend for 41,000 sq km (15,830 sq miles) – an area the size of Switzerland. Away from the mines, people relax at the artificial Lake Moondarra or socialise in any of the numerous licensed clubs, which welcome visitors. In August, Mount Isa hosts a three-day rodeo, the largest and richest in Australia.

TIP

For a scenic overview of Mount Isa, head for the **City Lookout** (a short drive off Hilary Street), preferably at dusk when the mine lights up. You can see the whole city sprawled out across a flat valley, backed by low hills, and all dominated by the mine.

BELOW: bareback riding in the Mount Isa rodeo.

The Flying Doctor Service was started in Cloncurry in 1928 by the Revd John Flynn to provide "a mantle of safety" over the Outback. Its first plane was supplied by the Queensland and Northern Territory Aerial Service (QANTAS).

The School of the Air, first established in Cloncurry, now operates from here, providing children on remote properties with direct radio and internet contact with a teacher. Its premises adjoin the Kalkadoon High School on Abel Smith Parade and can be toured (Abel Smith Parade; tours Mon–Fri 9am and 10am in term time; tel: 07-4744 8333; charge).

Cloncurry ㉙ is also a mining town, but in this case the main employer, the vast open-cut **Ernest Henry Mine**, is a bus ride away from the centre. Conducted tours are comprehensive and informative (tel: 07-4742 1361; charge). Among the attractions in town, John Flynn Place (corner Daintree and King streets; Mon–Fri 8.30am–4.30pm all year, Sat–Sun 9am–3pm May–Sept; tel: 07-4742 4125; charge) contains a museum devoted to the Royal Flying Doctor Service and its founder.

Waltzing in Winton

The Matilda Highway heads southeast through **McKinlay**, home of the pub used in the Crocodile Dundee films and now called the Walkabout Creek Hotel.

Some 241km (150 miles) further on sits **Winton ㉚**, a town full of character and home to the Waltzing Matilda Centre (50 Elderslie Street; Nov–Mar, Mon–Fri 9am–5pm, Sat–Sun 9am–3pm, Apr–Oct daily 9am–5pm; tel: 07-4657 1466; www.matildacentre.com. au; charge), which celebrates the song, its composer "Banjo" Paterson and all aspects of Outback life. This is also dinosaur country *(see panel below)*.

From Winton, the Matilda Highway continues to **Longreach ㉛** where two major attractions await. A local manufacturer helped develop the **Australian Stockman's Hall of Fame** (Landsborough Highway; daily 9am–5pm; tel: 07-4658 2166; www.outbackheritage.com. au; charge) as a fascinating tribute to the cattle drovers, shearers, jackaroos and entrepreneurs who opened up Australia to settlement.

Longreach was where Qantas set up its first operational base in 1922, and its original hangar, with the old sign still on it, has become part of the multimillion-dollar **Qantas Founders Outback Museum** (Landsborough Highway; daily 9am–5pm; tel: 07-4658

Dinosaur District

Detour south from Winton to **Lark Quarry Dinosaur Trackways** (tours at 10am, noon, 2pm; tel: 07-4657 1812; www.dinosaurtrackways.com.au; charge), where petrified footprints denote a dinosaur encounter millions of years ago.

The theme is maintained in two towns to the north: **Richmond** has Kronosaurus Korner (91–93 Goldring Street; daily 8.30am–4.45pm; tel: 07-4741 3429; www.kronosauruskorner.com.au; charge), a marine fossil museum, and **Hughenden** features the Flinders Discovery Centre (37 Gray Street; daily 9am–5pm; tel: 07-4741 1021; charge), with a replica of a dinosaur skeleton found locally. A concrete dinosaur in the middle of town presses the point home. Nearby is the majestic **Porcupine Gorge** with its 120-metre (400ft) -high walls.

3737; www.qfom.com.au; charge), which displays a retired Qantas Boeing 747 jumbo jet (still in flying condition), replicas of its early fleet of biplanes, and a comprehensive record of the national airline's growth.

Barcaldine ㉜ to the east is notable for a collection of vintage hotels and pubs, and as home to the Workers' Heritage Centre (Ash Street; Mon–Sat 9am–5pm, Sun 10am–4pm; tel: 07-4651 2422; www.australianworkersheritagecentre.com.au; charge), where a collection of historic structures house displays commemorating the role played by workers in the development of Australia.

The Matilda Highway continues south all the way to **Charleville** ㉝. The usual assortment of historic buildings is worth a look, but the points of difference are the **Cosmos Centre** (Qantas Drive; Apr–Oct daily 10am–5pm, Nov–Mar Mon–Sat 10am–4pm; tel: 07-4654 7771; www.cosmoscentre.com; charge), an observatory and museum which host astral viewing sessions; and the **Steiger Gun**, a bizarre device designed in 1902 to fire hot air into the sky in order to create rain.

Miles ahead

Heading east through **Roma** and then **Miles** ㉞, with its charming **Historical Village** (Murilla Street; daily 8am–5pm; tel: 07-4627 1492; www.mhv.org.au; charge), would eventually lead back to the east coast. But that would be to ignore two of Queensland's iconic sites. **The Dig Tree**, on the border with South Australia, is where the famous base camp of the Burke and Wills expedition just missed a rendezvous with the men who could have rescued them from starvation and death *(see page 211)*.

Finally, there is **Birdsville** ㉟. This isolated far western settlement has a population of 120, but each September it grows by five or six thousand for the Birdsville Races, when 300 light aircraft cram the airport, with their pilots camped under the wings. The 1884 Birdsville Hotel is a legendary watering hole. West of here are only the sand dunes of the Simpson Desert. A huge sandhill called **Big Red**, 36km (22 miles) to the west, marks the beginning of the famous Birdsville Track and is a popular spot for sunset parties. ❑

Café proprietor in Wyandra, 100km (60 miles) south of Charleville.

BELOW: the Australian Stockman's Hall of Fame.

RESTAURANTS AND BARS

Restaurants

Prices for a three-course dinner per person with a half-bottle of house wine:
$ = under A$50
$$ = A$50–80
$$$ = A$80–120
$$$$ = over A$120

Brisbane

E'cco
100 Boundary Street (corner Adelaide Street East)
Tel: 07-3831 8344
www.eccobistro.com
Open: L Tue–Fri, D Tue–Sat. $$$$
E'cco is one of Brisbane's most-awarded bistros. Chef Philip Johnson stresses simplicity. Essentially, his food relies on fresh ingredients and an unfussy preparation and presentation.

The Green Papaya
898 Stanley Street,
East Brisbane
Tel: 07-3891 5000
www.greenpapaya.com.au
Open: D Tue–Sun. $$
The Green Papaya is an interesting mix of classic and contemporary Balinese and Thai cuisine, created with local ingredients when possible. BYO.

Anise
697 Brunswick Street, New Farm.
Tel: 07-3358 1558
www.anise.com.au
Open: L Thur–Sat, D Mon–Sat. $$$
A bistro/wine bar, with the accent on French cooking, that only holds 21 diners. Anise provides some of the purest pleasures to be found in the city.

Gold Coast

Absynthe
Q1 complex,
9 Hamilton Avenue, Surfers Paradise
Tel: 07-5504 6466
www.absynthe.com.au
Open: L Mon–Fri, D Mon–Sat. $$$$
Celebrated French chef Meyjitte Boughenout lends a dash of Gallic élan to the 80-storey Q1 building. He is famous for juxtaposing the most unlikely of flavours to create taste sensations that are as beguiling as they are unexpected. His Golden Egg, for example, combines an egg mousse bisque with soya jelly and edible gold leaf.

The Broadbeach Tavern
Old Burleigh Road, corner of Charles Avenue, Broadbeach
Tel: 07-5538 4111
www.broadbeachtavern.com.au
Open: L & D daily. $
Good food from an extensive and surprisingly inexpensive menu. However, most people come here for the live entertainment, seven nights a week.

Ristorante Fellini
Marina Mirage, Seaworld Drive, Main Beach
Tel: 07-5531 0300
Open: L & D daily. $$$
Siblings Carlo Percuoco and Anna Cacace dish up superb Italian cuisine within their award-winning restaurant.

Noosa

Berardo's On The Beach
On the beach, Noosa
Tel: 07-5448 0888
www.berardos.com.au
Open: B, L & D daily. $$
A delightful location for some seriously well-constructed Noosa cuisine. The zucchini flower and saffron risotto is nicely offset by lemon thyme and goat's curd.

Yandina

Spirit House
20 Ninderry Road
Tel: 07-5446 8977
www.spirithouse.com.au
Open: D Mon–Sat. $$
It is well worth venturing into the hills above Noosa for the exquisite Thai food and idyllic waterside setting at Spirit House. There's also an acclaimed cooking school, if you enjoy the food so much you want to take it home.

Bundaberg

Spinnaker Bar and Bistro
1a Quay Street
Tel: 07-4152 8033
Open: L Tue–Fri, D Tue–Sat. $$
A Bundaberg institution and arguably the smartest restaurant in town. The emphasis at Spinnaker is on seafood dishes such as Moreton Bay bugs with lemon risotto.

Rockhampton

The Allenstown Hotel
8 Upper Dawson Road
Tel: 07-4922 1853
www.allenstownhotel.com.au
Open: L & D daily. $$
Pub food with a few gourmet subtleties thrown in for good measure. The restaurant was completely renovated in 2011.

LEFT: lunch at the Green Papaya.

Mackay
Church on Palmer Street

15a Palmer Street,
North Mackay
Tel: 07-4944 1466
Open: D Mon–Sat. **$$**
Street is a stylish restaurant specialising in steak and seafood. Serving Modern Australian dishes with a French influence.

Latitude 21
Clarion Hotel, Mackay Marina
Tel: 07-4955 9400
www.mackaymarinahotel.com.au
Open: B, L & D daily. **$$**
An intelligent blending of Asian, African and European food is served alfresco with views over the marina.

Townsville
C Bar Café
Gregory Street Headland,
The Strand
Tel: 07-4724 0333
www.cbar.com.au
Open: L & D daily. **$$**
Attractively situated on an artificial headland, right on the beach front, C Bar offers open-air dining with great sea views. With a café menu by day, and more up-market dining by night, C Bar will satisfy your cravings any time of day. There's a good menu for kids too.

Bistro One
30–34 Palmer Street
Tel: 07-4771 6333
Open: B, L & D daily. **$$**
Chic, modern, local fare with a Mediterranean influence.

Cairns
Ochre Restaurant
43 Shields Street
Tel: 07-4051 0100
www.ochrerestaurant.com.au
Open: L Mon–Fri, D daily.
$$$
Ochre is renowned for innovative handling of bush tucker and native species. Consider kangaroo terrine, crocodile wonton and emu pâté.

Palm Cove
Sebel Reef House Restaurant
99 Williams Esplanade
Tel: 07-4055 3633
www.reefhouse.com.au
Open: L & D daily. **$$$**
Renowned chef Philip Mitchell's fare exhibits deceptive simplicity. By day, he offers meze plates; by night, complex cosmopolitan feasts that satisfy all your senses.

Port Douglas
Flames of the Forest
Bus picks up diners from 6pm in Cairns, Palm Cove and Port Douglas.
Tel: 07-4099 5983
www.flamesoftheforest.com.au
Open: D Thur–Sat. **$$$**
Dine in the rainforest and listen to Aboriginal stories. Guests are picked up from town and transported to the Mowbray Valley where flames light a path to a clearing and candles flicker beside a stream. More candles illuminate tables, immaculately set. It's Lord of the Rings meets Alice in Wonderland – a magical experience and a story you'll love to tell back home.

Nautilus Restaurant
17 Murphy Street
Tel: 07-4099 5330
www.nautilus-restaurant.com.au
Open: D daily. **$$$**
Everybody in Port Douglas goes to the Nautilus at least once. All the celebrities have been – along with thousands of others who soak up the tropical ambience of a unique outdoor dining experience while enjoying the top-flight dinner menu.

Bars
Brisbane
Cru Wine Bar
22 James Street,
Fortitude Valley
Tel: 07-3252 2400
www.crubar.com
Open: B Sat–Sun, L & D daily. **$$**
Part bottle shop, part bar and part café, Cru serves great wine and tapas through most of the day.

Gold Coast
Charlie's 24-Hour Café, Restaurant & Bar
Cavill Avenue,
Surfers Paradise
Tel: 07-5538 5285
www.charlies24hours.com.au
Open: 24 hours a day. **$**
Everyone ends up here, it's said, while in Surfers Paradise. Well located and affordable, Charlie's hasn't closed its doors since 1976.

Cairns
Beethoven Café
105 Grafton Street
Tel: 07-4051 0292
Open: B & L daily. **$**
Bread of all descriptions with interesting fillings and, the clincher, spectacularly good cakes.

Croydon
Club Hotel
Corner Sircom and Brown streets
Tel: 07-4745 6184
Open: D daily. **$**
Standard Outback pub menu is enriched by wonderful old wooden building and friendly locals.

Mount Isa
Keane's Bar and Grill
Mount Isa Irish Club,
1 Nineteenth Avenue
Tel: 07-4743 2577
www.theirishclub.com.au
Open: B, L & D daily. **$$**
Mount Isa is flush with social and working social clubs (visitors welcome). The Irish is one of the biggest. The Tram Stop Coffee Shop offers an all-day breakfast and there's a lunch buffet in the Members' Bar.

RIGHT: prawns at C Bar Café.

THE RAINFOREST

Tropical or temperate, the rainforest is one of Queensland's defining characteristics, as well as a key tourist attraction

High rainfall – at least 2 metres (6½ft) – is a prerequisite for rainforest, and then it's generally a matter of latitude and proximity to the ocean which defines it as either tropical or temperate. The Australian state of Queensland is big enough to meet both of these requirements.

Rainforests are nature in *extremis*. Two-thirds of all the Earth's plant and animal species can be found within them, and in north Queensland the highest diversity of local endemic species in the world is present. It is the last bastion for many of these animals, while others are still being discovered, particularly in the upper regions under the canopy, an area only recently appreciated for the richness of its various flora and fauna.

It is estimated that the tropical rainforest stretching from just north of Cairns to Cape Tribulation and on to Cooktown is in the region of 110 million years old, and constitutes the last remnant of the forest that used to cover all of Australia and, before that, Gondwanaland. Now protected as an element of the Wet Tropics World Heritage Area, it is a key attraction for tourists. The economic rationale that has seen the destruction of forests elsewhere in Australia and round the world will probably now protect it.

ABOVE: the orange-thighed frog *(Litoria xanthomera)* is a tree frog native to a small area in tropical northern Queensland. The call of th frog is a long "aaa-rk", followed by a soft trill. They call after heavy monsoon rain, and often congregate around ponds, or at the edge o any standing body of water.

BELOW: when the platypus was first discovered in Australia, many European naturalists were convinced it must be an elaborate hoax. It is the only living member of its of its family *(Ornithorhynchidae)* and genus *(Ornithorhynchus)*, and is one of the few monotremes.

BELOW: there are more than 520 species of lizards found in Australia. The five main families of lizards are geckos, legless lizards, dragon lizards, monitor lizards (or Goannas), and skinks.

THE DAINTREE

Some of the most easily accessible rainforest, and therefore most visited, is in the Daintree National Park. There's a well-worn route from Cairns or Port Douglas up to Cape Tribulation, and every tour bus or expedition will stop at least once for a walk in the woods. In several places there are short boardwalk circuits from handy parking spots, and the way is marked by a series of interpretive boards. This makes it easy for the visitor to explore, and also helps in managing the forest by keeping tourists away from more pristine areas.

The complete packaged rainforest experience can be enjoyed at the Daintree Discovery Centre (daily 8.30am–5pm; tel: 07-4098 9171; www.daintree-rec.com.au; charge), a short distance north of the Daintree ferry. Boardwalks wend along the forest floor, and a steel walkway through the canopy allows an entirely different perspective on life as the birds see it. Audio guides are available and there are more of the ubiquitous interpretive boards. The cassowaries here seem used to visitors.

LEFT: the cassowary (*Casuarius casuarius*) is the third-largest flightless bird, after the ostrich and the emu. Its claws are particularly sharp, and cassowaries have been known to strike out at humans, although the legend that a human can be disembowelled with a single kick by the cassowary's strong legs has never been proven.

** GHT:** the red-necked pademelon *hylogale thetis)* is a small, rest-dwelling marsupial. The imal is very shy, and typically les in the forest during the day, ly emerging to look for food at ght. The pademelon was nearly nted to extinction by imported kes on the mainland, but can found throughout Tasmania.

ABOVE: to see the rainforest from a different perspective, take a zip-line tour that stops at several platforms perched among the tree tops.

THE GREAT BARRIER REEF AND THE ISLANDS

The Reef is not only Queensland's major attraction, it is one of the natural wonders of the world. It is both the largest coral reef on Earth and one of the most accessible, and also has a selection of stunning islands

BELOW: a fringing reef, Lady Elliot Island.

The world's largest coral reef consists of more than 2,500 separate, interconnected reefs, stretching more than 2,300km (1,430 miles) from just above the tip of the Cape York Peninsula in the north to just north of Bundaberg in the south.

In the nomination that saw the Reef given a World Heritage listing, one of the supporting arguments was that "Biologically, the Great Barrier Reef supports the most diverse ecosystem known to man. Its enormous diversity is thought to reflect the maturity of an ecosystem which has evolved over millions of years..." At the heart of that ecosystem is the polyp, a tiny animal consisting of little more than a mouth and surrounding tentacles to feed it – plus a limestone carapace into which it withdraws during the day. It is the skeletal remains of these creatures that form the basis of the reef. Individual polyps are linked by body tissue, thereby sharing the colony's food, but the main nutrient for a photosynthetic coral's food is algae cells within its tissue called zooxanthellae, which convert the sun's energy into nutrients.

Major threat

Over millions of years the reef has grown into the largest living entity in the world. This structure is fragile, however, and it only takes small environmental changes to disrupt its delicate balance. Coral bleaching is the major threat. If the water temperature rises by just a degree or two over a sustained period, the corals expel their zooxanthellae, lose their capacity for photosynthesis and become colourless. The process is not irreversible, but if the water does not cool within a month or so the coral will die.

Severe damage was caused by extended hot spells in 1997–8 and again in 2002, and most marine scientists believe that global warming not only exists but has a direct bearing on these incidents. The Australian Government finally signed the Kyoto Protocol in

December 2007 after the long-serving coalition government of John Howard was defeated at the ballot box.

There are other dangers, too. Human traffic can cause significant damage to coral, whether through chains and anchors from boats, or by snorkellers and divers who brush against polyps and damage or kill them. The Reef is also under pressure from the effects of poor water quality, which is often caused by soil and fertiliser runoff from the shore, and is not helped by the wash from cyclones. The Great Barrier Reef Marine Park was established in the 1970s to protect this magnificent resource; the Great Barrier Reef Marine Park Authority monitors the effects of tourism and fishing with research.

The islands

While only a few are literally coral islands, the 20 or so resort islands inside the Great Barrier Reef Marine Park offer many attractions. Lodging varies from five-star resorts to backpacker hostels and campsites. Some islands are dry, barren and windy; others are lush and covered with rainforest.

The South

Lady Elliot Island ❶ Dubbed an "Eco Island", this is a quiet and beautiful 42-hectare (103-acre) coral cay, with bungalow accommodation and some permanent tents. It is 80km (50 miles) from Bundaberg and reached by air. Its coral setting ensures easy access to good diving and snorkelling.

Lady Musgrave Island ❷ A tiny uninhabited cay available only for daytrippers or campers (with a National Parks permit). Access is by boat from Bundaberg. It offers diving and snorkelling within a brilliant blue lagoon.

Heron Island ❸ Only 1km (½ mile) long, this is the Reef's most famous coral cay and is number one for diving (along with Lizard at the northern fringe of the Reef). The Reef is certainly at its most accessible: where the beach ends, the coral begins, with its abundant marine life.

Great Keppel Island ❹ There are excellent white sandy beaches, long hiking trails, views of the mainland, and plenty of social activities. Great Keppel is not directly on the Reef; short cruises run out for divers. Access

Not all of the Reef's islands are made of coral. In fact, nearly all of the popular resort islands are continental in nature – the tips of offshore mountain ranges. The true coral cays of the real Reef are more numerous but tend to be smaller and more fragile.

BELOW:
a snorkeller
watches a
giant wrasse.

is by air from Rockhampton or by sea from Rosslyn Bay.

Brampton Island ❺ A mountainous island 32km (20 miles) from Mackay, Brampton has one resort set in a tropical garden. Sailing, water sports, beaches and rainforest walks are the attractions. Access is from Mackay and Shute Harbour but not for day-trippers.

The Whitsundays ❻

At the southern end of the archipelago, **Lindeman Island**'s resort is Australia's first Club Med, and beyond the buildings it has retained the beauty of its natural setting. There is tennis, swimming and fishing, and 20km (12 miles) of bushwalking trails through 500 hectares (1,230 acres) of national park. Access is from Mackay, Hamilton Island and Proserpine.

Three very different resorts co-exist on **Long Island**, and it is only a short boat trip from Shute Harbour. Long Island Resort is for all ages, and is particularly popular with the young. Peppers Palm Bay is ideal for a back-to-nature holiday with lovely beaches, clear water and coral, and solitude. The self-catering Paradise Bay Eco Resort provides waterside cabins.

The largest, most aggressively marketed Whitsunday resort on **Hamilton Island** has a high-rise hotel, a floating marina, an airstrip with direct flights to major cities and a full sports complex. With a pseudo-South Seas main street once described as "Daiquiri Disneyland", Hamilton Island is not the place for a quiet island sojourn.

The largest of the group, **Whitsunday Island** covers 109 sq km (42 sq miles) and has no resort, but does offer the fabulous Whitehaven Beach – a great option for campers (with permits).

A self-contained resort on a large, hilly island, **South Molle Island** is popular with families, and diving, swimming, sailing, golf, fishing and shopping are all offered. Travel is from Shute Harbour or Hamilton Island.

Daydream Island is a popular family resort with all the necessities for a good time at a reasonable all-inclusive tariff. Great beaches and a wide range of activities are just 15 minutes from Shute Harbour or Hamilton Island.

As the second-largest island in the Whitsundays, **Hook Island** provides budget camping and cabins as well as services for visiting yachts. There is an underwater observatory here and Aboriginal cave painting at Nara Inlet.

Hayman Island is an exclusive five-star resort set in a coral-trimmed lagoon, close to the outer Reef and a favourite with honeymooners. Access is from Hamilton Island, Proserpine, Shute Harbour and Townsville.

The Centre to the North

Magnetic Island ❼ is a large (5,000-hectare/12,400-acre) island and a national park; this pleasant, populated (2,300) haven is almost an outer suburb of mainland Townsville. There are plenty of walks in the rainforest, or up to the 500-metre (1,640ft) Mount Cook. Horseshoe Bay has a koala and wildlife park. Bikes, scooters and Mini Mokes can be rented.

Orpheus Island ❽ is in the Palm group northeast of Townsville and is very close to the outer Reef. An exclusive resort hidden among the trees has good accommodation and entertainment. Seaplane access from Townsville.

The washout from Queensland's massive floods at the beginning of 2011 is likely to have a major impact on the Great Barrier Reef, particularly off the coast of Southern Queensland, and its effects are likely to be felt for years.

OPPOSITE: a key venue for Hamilton Island's thriving wedding industry.
BELOW: diving and snorkelling are the islands' principal businesses.

Visiting the Reef

Every morning dozens of boats head out to various pre-selected sites. About an hour later, you'll be moored by the gorgeous coral

The easiest way to visit the Reef is not to stay on an offshore island but to take a day trip from **Cairns** or **Port Douglas**. You can also take Reef trips from **Cape Tribulation**. Trips from some of the island resorts or coastal towns further south, such as Townsville, tend to be less commercialised and sophisticated and, indeed, less frenetic.

Because the water is so shallow, snorkelling is perfectly satisfactory for seeing the marine life (in fact, many people prefer it to scuba diving; even so, most boats offer tanks for experienced divers and resort dives for people who have never dived before). Above the waves, the turquoise void might be broken only by a sand cay crowded with sea birds, but as soon as you poke your mask underwater, the world erupts. It's almost sensory overload: there are vast forests of staghorn coral, whose tips glow purple like electric Christmas-tree lights; brilliant blue clumps of mushroom coral; layers of pink plate coral; bulbous green brain coral.

Tropical fish with exotic names slip about as if showing off their fluorescent patterns: painted flute-mouth, long-finned batfish, crimson squirrelfish, hump-headed Maori wrasse, cornflower sergeant major.

A venomous killer

Thrown into the mix are scarlet starfish and black sea cucumbers. You definitely don't pick up the sleek conus textile shells – they shoot darts into anything that touches them, each with enough venom to kill 300 people. There are 21 darts in each shell and so, as one captain notes, "if they don't get you the first time, they'll get another try".

Almost all Reef trips follow a similar format. There's a morning dive or snorkel, followed by a buffet lunch; then, assuming you haven't eaten too much or had too much free beer, an afternoon dive. There should be a marine biologist on board to explain the Reef's ecology. Before you book, ask how many passengers the boat takes: they vary from several hundred on the Quicksilver fleet of catamarans to fewer than a dozen on smaller craft.

Regardless of your reason for visiting the Great Barrier Reef, weather will play an important part in your enjoyment of its scenic attractions. From late April through to October it's at its best, the clear skies and moderate breezes offering perfect conditions for coral viewing, diving, swimming, fishing and sunning. In November the first signs of the approaching "Wet" appear: variable winds, increasing cloud and showers. By January it rains at least once most days. And when the winds are up and the waters are stirred, visibility under the water diminishes. Furthermore, in rough seas excursion boats have fewer places to anchor and may be restricted to areas which have been over-visited and where, consequently, the coral has been damaged. Pick the time of your visit carefully.

In general, the further out the boat heads, the more pristine the diving (the Low Isles, for example, near Port Douglas, have suffered). But don't be conned by hype about the "Outer Reef"; although as the edge of the continental shelf it may be the "real" Reef, it looks exactly the same as other parts.

Even in the winter months, the water here is never cold, but it is worth paying a bit extra to hire a wet suit anyway; most people find it hard not to go on snorkelling for hours on end in this extraordinary environment. ❑

BELOW: an aerial view of Green Island, where a luxury resort will cater to your every need.

Hinchinbrook Island ❾ is accessible from Cardwell by boat. The jagged peaks, golden beaches and luxuriant rainforests of Hinchinbrook National Park can be fully explored by experienced hikers. The island's signature east-coast trail has limits on walker numbers so book in advance.

A small fragment of the Family Islands, **Bedarra Island ❿** has an exclusive resort set in rich rainforest with pure beaches and tranquil coves. Go via **Dunk Island ⓫**, where the recluse E.J. Banfield lived for 26 years at the turn of the 20th century, writing his *Confessions of a Beachcomber*. The island is a rainforested national park with a large resort nestled in one corner and a camping ground alongside it. Access is from Townsville, Cairns and Mission Beach.

Surrounded by coral reef, **Fitzroy Island ⓬** is a great place for diving and fishing. **Green Island ⓭** is a tiny coral cay just off Cairns with a good underwater observatory, but it's mostly for day-trippers. The most northerly island, **Lizard Island ⓮** is home to the marlin boats. Lizard allows access directly from the beach to the Reef and has stunning diving. Fly from Cairns.

The diving

With more than 2,000km (1,240 miles) of reef to choose from and numerous departure points, it is useful to have a grasp of the diving that awaits you.

Cod Hole, just off Lizard Island, is one of the best-known dive destinations because this one isn't just about coral gardens. You also get the chance to encounter potato cod, giant (up to 100kg/220lbs) man-sized fish that will nuzzle up to you in the hope of the food that most expeditions take along.

The **SS Yongala** passenger ship sank in 1911, but the wreck was only discovered 100km (60 miles) east of Townsville in 1958. The remains of the 110-metre (360ft) -long vessel are still intact and attract thousands of divers every year. Expeditions run from Townsville. **Wheeler Reef** is also accessed from Townsville and has a reputation for being one of the finest night dive sites, although with its range of coral, eels, sharks and countless other fish, it's good at any time of day.

Kayaks for hire on the islands.

BELOW LEFT:
Fitzroy Island.
BELOW:
Hinchinbrook Island.

Electric buggies are the popular way for tourists to get around Hamilton Island.

BELOW: a diver carefully navigates the coral reef.

Lady Elliot Island has several outstanding dive sites, including the **Blow Hole**, a cave dive accessible via two openings 25 metres (82ft) down on the eastern side of the Island. Lion fish and gnome fish are among the company likely to greet you. The **Anchor Bommies** nearby also has rays and the added interest of two coral-encrusted naval anchors sitting on the sea bed.

Agincourt Reef is the destination of the substantial Quicksilver operation. You can't miss their massive silver catamarans which transport visitors in their hundreds from pick-up points in Cairns, Palm Cove and Port Douglas out to their two-storey floating pontoon on the outer reef. Despite the numbers, the reef is well stocked with coral and associated marine life and ideal for beginners wanting a trial dive.

Heron Island has numerous attractions, including **Bommie**, one of the most famous dive sites on the reef. It is a nesting ground for green turtles between October and March. **Osprey Reef** is spectacular for its colony of white-tip reef sharks and some of the finest coral to be seen anywhere. Grey reef sharks, potato cod and dogtooth tuna are amongst the other inhabitants. Cairns and Port Douglas are the departure points.

Bait Reef is in the Whitsundays so boats run out of Airlie Beach to this wonderland of tropical marine life. Much of what interests is close to the surface, so snorkellers are well catered for along with novice divers who are comfortable up to 10 metres (32ft) down. **Hardy Reef**, also in the Whitsundays, is notable for a 70-metre (230ft) reef wall where numerous species of fish drift around both hard and soft coral.

Wolf Rock's four submerged volcanic peaks have swim-throughs and ledges along with a rich selection of subaquatic life. It's to be found on the Sunshine Coast off Double Island Point.

Ex-HMAS Brisbane, a former Royal Australian Navy destroyer, was scuttled off Mooloolaba on the Sunshine Coast as a wreck site. It's now 28 metres (92ft) down and experienced divers can look around parts of the ship's interior, helped by access holes. ❑

RESTAURANTS AND BARS

Restaurants

Prices for a three-course dinner per person with a half-bottle of house wine:
$ = under A$50
$$ = A$50–80
$$$ = A$80–120
$$$$ = over A$120

Airlie Beach
Capers Beach Bar and Grill
The Esplanade
Tel: 07-4964 1777
Open: B, L & D daily. **$$**
In prime position for the beach, Capers offers clean flavours in dishes good enough to distract from the views.
Fish D'vine
303 Shute Harbour Road
Tel: 07-4948 0088
www.fishdvine.com.au
Open: L & D daily. **$$**
Billed as a fish café and rum bar, there's a disappointing absence of the piratical here. But the fresh seafood more than makes up for that.
Shipwrecked Seafood Bar and Grill
Corner of Shute Harbour Road and The Esplanade
Tel: 07-4946 6713
www.shipwreckedbarandgrill.com.au
Open: L & D daily. **$$**
Perhaps start with Shipwrecked's ginger chilli bugs and move on to New Orleans blackened swordfish or look at any other combination of great fish. There are also steaks topped with prawns, lobster and calamari.
Whitsunday Sailing Club
Airlie Point

Tel: 07-4946 6138
www.whitsundaysailingclub.com.au
Open: L & D daily. **$**
You shouldn't be able to get food this cheaply in this setting, but the Whitsunday Sailing Club makes money on the gaming machines, so take advantage and dig in to the delicious eats.

Hamilton Island
Manta Ray Café
Marina Side, Front Street
Tel: 07-4946 8536
Open: L & D daily. **$$**
www.hamiltonisland.com.au/manta-ray-cafe
Everything from pizza and pasta to the finest seafood can be found in this laid-back venue where kids can eat for free.
Mariners Seafood Restaurant
Marina Village
Tel: 07-4946 8628
Open: D daily. **$$$**
The Coral Reef Platter is the ultimate choice at this haven for seafood-lovers. Enjoy your seafood with beautiful harbour views.
Romanos Restaurant
Marina Side, Front Street
Tel: 07-4946 8212
Open: D daily. **$$$**
www.hamiltonisland.com.au/romanos-restaurant
Some seriously high-quality Italian fare can be found at Romanos. Consider the scallops with caramelised carrot purée, crisp pancetta and watercress dressing.
Steakhouse Restaurant
Marina Side, Front Street
Tel: 07-4946 8019
Open: D daily. **$$**
www.hamiltonisland.com.au/steakhouse-restaurant
When all that fish begins

to pall, drop in at Steakhouse Restaurant for everything from the 250g Scotch fillet to the 450g T-bone.

Daydream Island
Mermaids Restaurant
Daydream Island Resort
Tel: 07-4948 8488
Open: L & D daily. **$**
www.daydreamisland.com
Mermaids offers café-style fare such as tropical open grilled sandwiches and salt and pepper calamari.

Dunk Island
Beachcomber
Dunk Island Resort
Tel: 07-4047 4740
www.dunk-island.com
Open: B & D daily. **$$$**
The island's main resort restaurant, Beachcomber specialises in tropical cuisine and buffets.

Magnetic Island
Banisters @ Arcadia
22 McCabe Crescent
Tel: 07-4778 5700
Open: L & D daily. **$$**
You're surrounded by water, so seafood makes sense and this is probably the best to be found on the island. BYO.
Barefoot Art Food Wine
5 Pacific Drive,
Horseshoe Bay
Tel: 07-4758 1170
Open: L & D Thur–Mon. **$$**
There's a bit of everything here. The wine list has more than 100 entries, and the food is Mod Oz with Asian touches.
Restaurant Le Paradis
Corner of Sooning Street and Mandalay Avenue, Nelly Bay
Tel: 07-4778 5044
www.fitzroyisland.com
Open: L & D daily. **$$$**

Resolutely French in approach – snails, cassoulet – and staking a claim for the top end of Magnetic Island dining.

Green Island
Emerald Restaurant
Green Island Resort
Tel: 07-4031 3300
Open: L & D daily. **$$$**
Emerald leaves no stone unturned in its effort to present fabulously luxurious cuisine. The service is flawless.

Great Keppel Island
Island Pizza
The Esplanade,
Fisherman's Beach
Tel: 07-4939 4699
www.gki.com.au/IslandP
Open: L & D daily. **$**
Relaxed environment with reliable pizzas, pastas and café staples. There's a bar as well. BYO.

Hayman Island
The Chef's Table
Hayman Island Resort
Tel: 07-4940 1838
www.hayman.com.au/dining/the-chefs-table
Open: D weekly. **$$$$**
At the Chef's Table, diners are treated to a six-course banquet with matching wines in the main kitchen, often hosted by Executive Chef, Glenn Bacon.

Fitzroy Island
Fitzroy Island Resort Restaurant
Fitzroy Island Resort
Tel: 07-4044 6700
www.fitzroyisland.com
Open: B, L & D daily. **$$**
A relaxed vibe with views of Welcome Bay, the Fitzroy Island Resort offers solid Australian cooking.

PROTECTING THE GREAT BARRIER REEF

The world's largest living entity is top of the list on many tourist itineraries, but its fragility means it's important to minimise visitor impact

The Great Barrier Reef may be the largest collection of living organisms on Earth, but it is also extremely fragile. Rising sea temperatures have added to the already considerable risk posed by tourism, pollution and natural enemies such as the crown-of-thorns starfish. Protecting the reef from its natural and mad-made enemies has become more important than ever, as we learn about the biodiversity under the waves. The reef's astonishingly complex and diverse ecosystem will disappear forever if precautions aren't taken immediately.

The appeal of the Great Barrier Reef to visitors is undeniable, and tourism is big business. But should you decide to visit the park, there are a number of things you can do to limit your environmental impact. Scuba diving is one of the main tourist draws to the reef, but it can take an average of 25 years for coral to recover from an accidental knock and scrape from an inexperienced diver. The main way to avoid causing damage to the reef is to take scuba lessons before you travel, and then to make sure you choose a recognised dive operator to take you to the site. Smaller groups of divers are also preferable as they are less likely to cause disturbance to the coral and its inhabitants.

If you fish, make sure you use the Marine Park Authority's zoning maps, which will let you know of any restrictions in the area. Be sure to return any unwanted or undersized fish to the water as quickly as possible. Use official campsites and take all litter, including fishing lines, with you when you leave.

ABOVE: clownfish live at the bottom of the sea in sheltered reefs or in shallow lagoons, usually in pairs. In the wild, they live in a symbiotic relationship with the sea anemone.

LEFT: a juvenile regal slipper lobster *(Arctides Regalis).*

ABOVE: a diver contemplates a sea fan, or gorgonian. A colony can be several metres high and across but only a few centimetres thick. There are more than 500 species of gorgonians in the ocean.

THE REEF'S GREATEST ENEMY?

For years, the worst threat to the Reef was thought to be the crown-of-thorns starfish *(above)*, an ugly creature that clamps on to coral and effectively spits its stomach out. Its digestive juices dissolve the polyps and leave great expanses of coral bleached and dead. The crown-of-thorns is poisonous to other fish and is almost indestructible: it can regenerate to full size from only a single leg and small piece of intestine.

With only a few around, it was easy to ignore its depradations on the reef, but in the early 1960s the pattern changed. Instead of a few crown-of-thorns starfish, suddenly there were millions. Green Island was the first to see the plague in 1962. From there it spread southwards, reaching the reefs around Bowen by 1988. Surveys between 1985 and 1988 established that about 31 percent of the reefs examined had been affected. Even after millions of dollars' worth of research, no one knows what caused the proliferation of the starfish. Furthermore, no economic way to get rid of the pest has presented itself.

Recently, however, marine biologists have decided to let the crown-of-thorns infestation run its destructive course. The latest wisdom posits that it is a natural, if poorly understood, part of the reef's life cycle and that the reef can return to pre-outbreak levels of coral in 10–15 years. Only time will tell if this scientific theory is correct.

ABOVE: a yellow crinoid *(phylum Echinodermata)* waves in the waters of the Great Barrier Reef. The name *crinoid* comes from the Greek word for *lily*, although this is an animal, not a plant.

RIGHT: six species of sea turtle call the Great Barrier Reef home, while there are two distinct genetic groups of the green sea turtle: one at the north end of the reef, and one at the south.

NORTHERN TERRITORY

Fewer than one in 100 Australians live in the vast Northern Territory, an untamed region with a climate, a landscape and a history all its own

The Northern Territory, or just "NT", is Australia in epic mode. Things here are larger than life – the sky, the distances, people's dreams and visions, the Earth itself. An area of 1.35 million sq km (521,240 sq miles) – more than double the size of France, yet inhabited by just 203,000 people – provides plenty of room to move.

The locals are a breed apart: tough, laconic, beholden to no one. Like the inhabitants of any inhospitable environment, they possess friendliness by the bucketful, a truly egalitarian spirit, and a wicked sense of humour.

Many urban Australians visiting NT's Outback feel as though they have entered a foreign land. They find a kind of detachment, a floating feeling of insubstantiality inspired by the uncomfortable knowledge that nothing human beings do here can ever touch the soul or the brute power of this ancient land.

Long distances

Despite its size, the Northern Territory fits neatly into a travel itinerary. There is the Red Centre – Alice Springs and the stunning hinterland in the Territory's south; various points along "The Track" (the Stuart Highway) heading north; and the Top End of Darwin, Kakadu and surroundings.

The distance between points of interest can be intimidating – roughly 1,600km (1,000 miles) from Alice to Darwin – but only by driving through NT do you get a true sense of its grand and ancient terrain.

Apart from the Top End, which is swamped by tropical monsoons from February to March each year, most of the Territory is an arid zone. Rainfall is minimal, averaging about 250 mm (9.8 inches) a year. But, when rain does come, it comes Outback-style: no half measures.

Main attractions
ALICE SPRINGS
ULURU–KATA TJUTA
  NATIONAL PARK
TENNANT CREEK
KAKADU NATIONAL PARK
DARWIN
TIWI ISLANDS

PRECEDING PAGES: Uluru at sunset.
LEFT: Simpson's Gap, near Alice Springs.
RIGHT: the Rim Walk in Kings Canyon.

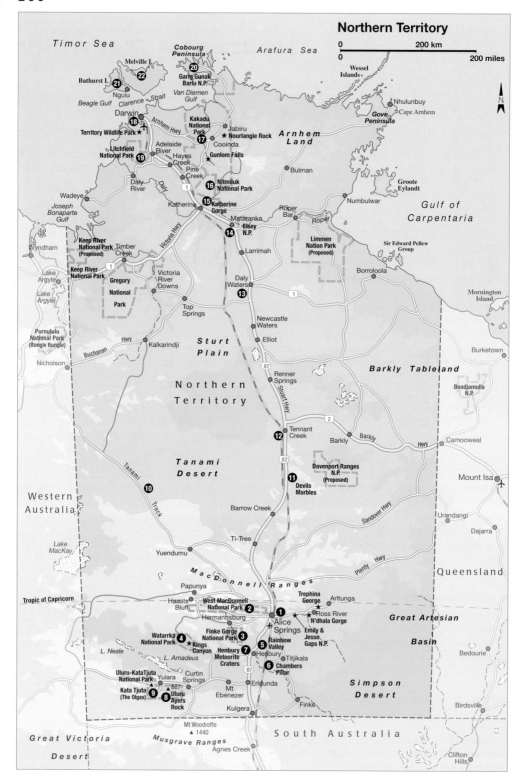

Northern Territory

0   200 km
0   200 miles

Timor Sea

Arafura Sea

Cobourg
Peninsula

Wessel
Islands

Melville I.

Bathurst I. ㉑ ㉒

Garig Gunak
Barlu N.P. ⑳

Nhulunbuy
Cape Arnhem

Nguiu
Beagle Gulf Clarence Strait

Van Diemen
Gulf

Gove
Peninsula

Darwin ⑱

Arnhem Hwy

Kakadu
National
Park

Jabiru

★ Nourlangie Rock

*Arnhem
Land*

Territory Wildlife Park ★

Adelaide
River

Cooinda

Litchfield
National Park ⑲

Hayes
Creek

Gunlom Falls

Pine
Creek

Bulman

Groote
Eylandt

Daly
River

Daly

Nitmiluk
National Park ⑯

Katherine

Katherine ⑮
Gorge

Numbulwar

*Gulf of
Carpentaria*

Wadeye

*Joseph
Bonaparte
Gulf*

Roper
Bar

Roper

Mataranka

Elsey ⑭
N.P.

Keep River
National Park
(Proposed)

Timber
Creek

Larrimah

Limmen
Nation Park
(Proposed)

Sir Edward Pellew
Group

Wyndham

Keep River
National Park

Victoria
River
Downs

Daly
Waters ⑬

Borroloola

*Mornington
Island*

*Lake
Argyle*

Gregory

*Lake
Argyle*

National

Park

Top
Springs

Newcastle
Waters

1

Burketown

Purnululu
National Park
(Bungle Bungle)

Hwy

Kalkarindji

*Sturt
Plain*

Elliot

Barkly Tableland

Nicholson

Buchanan

87

Renner
Springs

Boodjamulla
N.P.

**Northern
Territory**

Stuart Hwy

Mount Isa ✈

*Western
Australia*

*Tanami
Desert*

Tanami Track

⑩

2

Tennant ⑫
Creek

Barkly

Barkly

HWY

Camooweal

Davenport Ranges
N.P.
(Proposed)

87

⑪

Devils
Marbles

Sandover Hwy

Urandangi

*Lake
MacKay*

Barrow Creek

Ti-Tree

Dajarra

Yuendumu

Macdonnell Ranges

Plenty Hwy

Queensland

Tropic of Capricorn

Papunya

Haasts
Bluff

West MacDonnell
National Park ②

Trephina
George

Arltunga

Ross River
★ N'dhala Gorge

Great Artesian

Hermannsburg

Watarrka
National Park ④

Finke Gorge
National Park ③

① Alice
Springs

Emily &
Jesse
Gaps N.P.

Basin

L. Neale

Kings
Canyon

Henbury
Meteorite
Craters ⑦

Rainbow
Valley

Henbury

Titjikala

Bedourie

L. Amadeus

Uluru-KataTjuta
National Park

Yulara

Curtin
Springs

87

⑥

Chambers
Pillar

*Simpson
Desert*

Kata Tjuta ⑨
(The Olgas)

867

⑧ Uluru
Ayers
Rock

Mt
Ebenezer

Erldunda

Finke

Birdsville

Kulgera

Great Victoria

Mt Woodroffe
▲ 1440

Musgrave Ranges

South Australia

Desert

Agnes Creek

*Clifton
Hills*

The Red Centre

Australia's Red Centre is the heart of the country in more ways than one. For many visitors, Australia is primarily a nature trip, and it is here in central Australia that the continent's greatest natural feature stands – **Uluru**, or **Ayers Rock**. But just as two-thirds of the Rock's awesome mass lies hidden beneath the ground, so Uluru and the other main tourist sights represent the mere tip of the great iceberg that is the Outback.

Incidentally, the Red Centre isn't just a cute name. The sand and rock around here are red because of iron oxides found in the sandstone. The sun is red when it drops, and red scars mark the flow of mineral-rich, ultra-healthy water. Even some of the kangaroos are red.

Alice Springs

Alice Springs ❶ – or the Alice – is the natural base for exploring the Red Centre. It is a grid-pattern, sun-scorched town of squat, mostly modern buildings, which crouches in one of many gaps (or Outback oases) in the rugged **MacDonnell Ranges**. These hills – which turn an intense blue at sunset, as if lit internally – act like a wagon train, a protective ring that might just keep the expanse of the Outback at bay.

Alice has enjoyed a tourist boom, based on Uluru and Aboriginal art and culture. Its present population of 27,500, one-tenth of which is Aboriginal, represents the greatest demographic concentration for 1,500km (900 miles) in any direction.

By no means a picture-postcard town, Alice has strange powers of attraction: visitors find themselves drawn again and again to this incongruous outpost, and many who come here for short-term work wake up 10 years later and wonder what happened. It's not always easy to meet someone who was actually born in Alice.

Settlement began here in 1871 in the form of a repeater station on the Overland Telegraph Line, constructed beside the permanent freshwater springs. Lying 4km (2½ miles) north of the present township, the **Telegraph Station** (tours daily from 8am) and **Springs** form a popular tourist site. Then, as now, water dictated all human movement and settlement, and the line, running from Adelaide through Alice and up to Darwin, followed virtually the same route as the Track does now. The line linked the cities of Australia's south and southeast with the rest of the world, as it continued from Darwin through Indonesia to Singapore, Burma, British India and across Asia and Europe to colonial headquarters in London. Keeping the line open was a full-time job, and it is still possible to see some of the original telegraph posts, now disused, rising from the hard earth.

Alice developed slowly; in 1925, it had just 200 residents. Four years later, the coming of the Ghan – which at that time ran from Adelaide via Oodnadatta to Alice and is named after Afghan camel drivers who pioneered transport in these parts – saw things pick up, but the trip was fraught with hazards. In the mistaken belief that the Outback

Alice Springs gained fame through Neville Shute's 1950 novel A Town Like Alice, *filmed in 1956 with Peter Finch and in 1981 as a TV series with Bryan Brown. Its title echoes the longings of an Aussie prisoner of war in Malaya in World War II. Shute (1899–1960), a prolific London-born novelist, emigrated to Australia after the war.*

BELOW:
a telegraph station
in Alice Springs.

The Royal Flying Doctor service operates more than 50 aircraft and has around 500 full-time staff. It can make over 160 landings and deal with more than 600 patients each day, nearly 100 of whom will need an aerial evacuation.

BELOW: exhibits at the Northern Territory Aviation Museum.

never flooded, the track was routed across low-lying terrain; consequently, the train was often stranded, with additional supplies having to be parachuted in to the hapless passengers. A new, flood-proof route was completed in 1980, and the Ghan remains one of Australia's great rail journeys. In February 2004 Alice Springs ceased to be the end of the line, when the Alice–Darwin 1,420km (880-mile) extension was completed. The event fulfilled a century-old promise of a key economic and tourism link.

The Flying Doctor

In Alice, spend your first sunset on **Anzac Hill** to get the lie of the land. One of the town's most popular attractions is the **Royal Flying Doctor Service Visitors' Centre** (tours Mon–Sat 9am–4pm, Sun 1–4pm; free). The service, established in 1928 by the Rev. John Flynn – who now graces the A\$20 bill – provides essential medical treatment to many isolated communities and cattle stations the length and breadth of the Outback. Flynn's grave is 7km (4 miles)

west of Alice on Larapinta Drive – he is pinned down in perpetuity by one of the Devil's Marbles, poor chap.

Another popular spot is the **Alice Springs School of the Air** on Head Street, which services the educational needs of far-flung children. The school, unique in the world, conducts primary-level classes via radio, and the most notable of its 26 bases across the Outback is in Alice, covering an area of 1.3 million sq km (500,000 sq miles). It is the world's biggest classroom, and visitors can listen to lessons being taught there.

The **Alice Springs Desert Park**, situated just outside Alice at the base of the MacDonnell Ranges, is a must-see primer for anyone about to explore the desert. Its 35 hectares (86 acres) contain 320 arid-zone plant species and more than 400 desert-dwelling animals. The birds of prey nature theatre, where wild birds interact with park rangers in an astonishing way, is unforgettable.

The **Alice Springs Cultural Precinct** (10am–5pm; charge) on Larapinta Drive contains the Strehlow Research Centre, the Namatjira Gallery, the Museum of Central Australia, the Memorial Cemetery, the Central Australian Aviation Museum and the Araluen Centre, with four galleries.

The **Strehlow Research Centre** chronicles the life and work of Ted Strehlow, who was born at Hermannsburg, the Lutheran mission established in 1877. He became a patrol officer and researcher among the Arrernte people, winning their trust, and artefacts from his comprehensively documented collection that are not culturally sensitive are on display at the centre.

For non-aviators, the **Aviation Museum** is uninspiring; the cemetery is more interesting because the famous Aboriginal landscape painter, Albert Namatjira, and the legendary gold seeker Harold Lasseter (whose lives form a pretty comprehensive recent history of the region) are buried there, as are a number of Afghans, in a separate section at the back, facing Mecca.

If you find yourself in Alice in September, don't miss the **Henley-on-Todd Regatta**. This grandly named event is a boat race unlike any other. The "boats" are bottomless wrapa-

rounds, and teams of about eight runners inside each one race along the dry bed of the Todd River. Much merriment is had by all.

Around Alice

Alice's immediate surroundings offer numerous attractions. To the east, in the **Eastern MacDonnell Ranges**, **Emily Gap**, **Jesse Gap**, **Trephina Gorge**, **N'dhala Gorge** and the old gold town of **Arltunga** are interesting excursions.

Stretching west from Alice is the **West MacDonnell National Park ❷**, incorporating many of the gaps in the ranges. These include **Simpson's Gap**, accessible via an excellent cycle path from Alice; **Standley Chasm**, whose steep walls become alive with colour an hour either side of midday; **Serpentine Gorge**; the **Ochre Pits**, used by Aborigines for centuries; **Ormiston Gorge and Pound**, with some fine walking trails; **Glen Helen Gorge**, with a comfortable lodge nearby; and

The view from an aircraft provides a unique perspective on the arid land around Alice Springs.

LEFT: The Ghan takes 48 hours to travel from Adelaide to Darwin.
BELOW: the Henley-on-Todd Regatta.

TIP

Over 500kg (1,100lb) of metal have been found at the Henbury Meteorite Craters. Fragments of the meteorite can be seen at the Museum of Central Australia in Alice Springs (see page 269).

Redbank Gorge. A 223km (138-mile) walking track, the **Larapinta Trail**, constructed by local prisoners, connects many of the attractions of the MacDonnells. Guided treks along the whole track can be arranged in Alice.

To the south is **Finke Gorge National Park ❸**, featuring the picturesque Palm Valley, with its distinctive red cabbage palms, and the Finke River, whose watercourse is one of the oldest in the world at 350 million years in some areas. This park is accessed via Hermannsburg, by four-wheel-drive only.

Due west of here is one of Central Australia's star attractions – spectacular **Kings Canyon** and **Watarrka National Park ❹**. The 350-million-year-old canyon shelters a permanent rockpool, aptly named the Garden of Eden and visited during the magnificent four-hour **Canyon Rim Walk**. The nearby Kings Canyon Resort offers a range of accommodation. There is also accommodation 36km (22 miles) from the Canyon Rim Walk at Kings Creek station, which offers basic cabins and a camping ground.

The new **Mereenie Loop Road** is a dirt road that connects Watarrka National Park with Namatjira Drive and attractions like Glen Helen Gorge. The track skirts the desert's eastern edge and should not be tackled by a conventional vehicle without local advice. Beware of crossing camels.

Rainbow Valley

South of Alice lies **Pine Gap**, off-limits to visitors but notable as the largest US communications and surveillance base in the Asia-Pacific region. Most of the 400-odd Americans employed here live in Alice; they hold weekend barbecues and baseball games in town parks.

The Aboriginal rock carvings at **Ewaninga**, of undetermined age, remain cryptic and alluring. Kaleidoscopic **Rainbow Valley ❺** is a stunning rock formation (with primitive camping conditions), as is **Chambers Pillar ❻**, a solitary upstanding red ochre outcrop inscribed with the names and dates of early explorers, who used it as a convenient landmark.

The **Henbury Meteorite Craters ❼**, just off the highway, consist of 12 indentations, about 5,000 years old, the biggest of which (180 metres/590ft wide by 15 metres/49ft deep) was caused by four meteors, each the size of a 200-litre (44-gallon) drum. The craters have become occasional pools, sprouting plants and attracting a variety of animal life.

En route to Uluru is **Curtin Springs**, a sprawling cattle station established in 1930 to breed horses for the British Indian Army. The road-side pub is a bit of a showroom for weird and wonderful tourist paraphernalia.

Dominating the horizon is **Mount Conner**, a table-top monolith that many people initially mistake for Uluru. Conner, at 700 million years old, is 150 million years older than Uluru and Kata Tjuta and just 4 metres (13ft) lower than Uluru. The only way to visit Mount Conner is by helicopter or with Discovery Ecotours, both based in Yulara.

BELOW: walking around the rim of Kings Canyon.

Uluru

From here, the road leads to Australia's great Outback icon, **Uluru ➑** (**Ayers Rock**; charge for a three-day pass), whose surrounding Uluru-Kata Tjuta National Park was World Heritage-listed for its natural significance in 1987, and for its cultural significance in 1994. It was first sighted by a European in 1872 when explorer Ernest Giles noted a prominent hill in the distance. The following year, William Gosse discovered that the hill was in fact "one immense rock rising abruptly from the plain". After climbing it barefoot and soaking up its mystical aura, he enthused: "This rock appears more wonderful every time I look at it."

Uluru means "meeting place", and many Aboriginal Dreaming tracks or songlines intersect here. Spirituality is often grounded in common sense, and Uluru, with its permanent waterhole, abundant animal life, shelter and firewood, has been saving lives for millennia. The rock is sacred to the local Anangu people, who resumed ownership of the lands inside the national park in 1985, in a historic handover ceremony. The Anangu have a controlling interest on the park's board of management; the chairperson is Anangu, and the meetings are bilingual (Pitjantjatjara and English). No park policy or development occurs without consultation. The Anangu receive more than A$2 million in revenue under the terms of the handback, but there is a caveat: tourists are allowed to climb over the rock on a defined path, although their sacred places are still out of bounds.

Climbing Uluru is a major attraction for many visitors, but is considered by resident park rangers and rescue teams to be a dangerous activity. More than a dozen climbers have been killed, and every few days someone has to be rescued. The Anangu would prefer that no one climbed, but at the same time they respect tourists' urge to do so. In one local language, the word for the ubiquitous tiny black ant is *minga* – it

Uluru is the world's largest monolith. It stands 348 metres (1,142ft) tall and its circumference at the base is almost 9km (5½ miles); its elevation is 867m (2,844ft) above sea level.

BELOW: walking around Uluru.

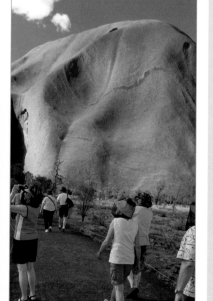

Titjikala

Many tourists want to experience life in remote Aboriginal communities. This is not always possible with the permit system for travel into the communities, but one community making a determined effort to forge close links with its visitors is **Titjikala**, 120km (75 miles) south of Alice Springs. Gunya-Titjikala arranges for visitors to stay at a tented campsite, joining Aboriginal families for witchetty grub hunts, picnics to scenic spots and kangaroo cooking in open pits.

The women will take you out into the bush for the witchetty grubs, digging around the roots of acacia trees with a crowbar to prise them from their burrows inside the roots. They will then quickly cook them in the ashes of a fire, and it is up to you to decide what they taste like. It's men's business to cook the kangaroo, burying the singed carcass upside down in a pit fire. The meat may be tasty but it comes out very rare.

Such activities provide an insight into Aboriginal life, with the activities run by the community itself – but it doesn't come cheap. An overnight stay in comfortable tent accommodation will cost A$1,300 per person. Promotional material suggests this is a luxury resort, but don't expect satin sheets and turned-down beds. It's comfortable enough if you're prepared to accept a certain rough-and-ready ambience. For bookings call 02-8347 1159 or see www.gunya.com.au.

The Yulara Resort has seven different tiers of accommodation, ranging from a camping ground to a luxury resort. Its water supply is drawn from underground rivers.

is also the word for tourist. This cutting-edge ecotourism is about as happy as this sort of cross-cultural marriage of convenience gets.

Recognising that the climb cannot be closed until more alternative activities are in place, the board of management opened a cultural centre in 1995 to mark the 10th anniversary of hand-back. An alternative to climbing is the 9.4km (5.8-mile) "base walk" around the rock, which is well marked. A self-guiding brochure is available from the cultural centre and numerous interpretive signs are displayed.

While more walks in the rock's vicinity are scheduled, **Kata Tjuta ❾** or **The Olgas** has a number of excellent trails, including the three-hour **Valley of the Winds** circuit. No climbing of Kata Tjuta (which means "many heads", referring to the 36 domes) is permitted and, just in case you get the urge to take home any souvenir rocks or sand, bear in mind that it is disrespectful to Aboriginal sentiments and that park

authorities receive, on average, two letters a week from visitors returning rocks they had taken, claiming that their luck has been bad ever since their stay in Uluru.

The 380,000-odd annual visitors to the national park are serviced by the award-winning **Yulara Resort**, which has been given a major refurbishment. There is a wide range of tours and activities available, and the sight of a sunset traffic jam has to be seen to be believed. Uluru, like the entire Red Centre, will humble you with its scale and overwhelm you with its beauty.

The first attempt at luxury tented accommodation on the edge of the Uluru-Kata Tjuta National Park burnt down when an official bush burn got out of control. **Longitude 131** is now back in business, with 15 air-conditioned tents *(see page 359)*.

Up the track

Anyone seeking the old-style Outback experience of endless long, hot, dirt roads may like to leave the highway 21km (13 miles) north of Alice Springs and head northwest along the **Tanami**

Track ❿ to rejoin civilisation 1,050km (660 miles) away at Halls Creek in the Kimberley. But, for most tastes, the 1,500km (930-mile) route along a good paved road to Darwin will suffice.

Heading north from Alice, one passes through the tiny community of **Barrow Creek**, before reaching the **Devil's Marbles Conservation Reserve** ⓫ (403km/250 miles from Alice), a series of granite boulders that litter either side of the highway for several kilometres. Some of the larger ones stand precariously balanced on tiny bases. It's thought they were once part of one solid block, broken and gradually rounded by wind and water erosion. The local Aboriginal people believe them to be the eggs of the rainbow serpent.

Tennant Creek

Tennant Creek ⓬ (504km/313 miles from Alice) is a gold town, although only one major mine is still in production. Gold was discovered in 1932 but the rush was short-lived and it seemed destined to become a ghost town, until the discovery of copper in the 1950s brought new prosperity. The town is 12km (7 miles) from the creek; the story goes that a cart carrying timber to build the first pub for the miners became bogged here. It was too much trouble to continue, so the hotel was erected on the spot. With a tree-lined double highway and a population of over 3,500, the town bears few signs of such a haphazard beginning.

To explore the remote **Barkly Tableland**, take the Barkly Highway east for 185km (115 miles), then turn north onto the Tablelands Highway and towards the remote township of **Borroloola** (pop. 600), just inland from the Gulf of Carpentaria and famous for its barramundi fishing. Like any journey that involves driving into the true Outback, this route requires ample preparation, including fuel, emergency rations and water. The last leg to Borroloola is on the Carpentaria Highway, an excellent sealed road.

North of Tennant Creek, the tiny township of **Renner Springs** marks a geographical and climatic end to the long, dry journey through the Red Centre: this is the southern extremity of the monsoon-affected plains of the Top End. But the changes between the desert and the plans are are slow and subtle. Termite mounds are fascinating features of this scrubby country. They are usually about 3 metres (11ft) high and point north–south, a position that allows termites the maximum benefit of both heat and shade. This orientation inevitably led to them being called "magnetic ant hills"; at first glance it does look as if they are built on compass bearings.

At **Elliott**, golfers can enjoy the far-out experience of playing nine holes on a desert course with well-kept greens.

Newcastle Waters is an historic stock-route junction town established as a telegraph station. In 1872 at **Frew's Ironside Ponds**, some 50km (31 miles) north of Newcastle Waters, the respective ends of the telegraph wire were joined to establish the overland communication link.

TIP

Visitors to Tennant Creek can tour the underground gold mine at Battery Hill Mining Centre, about 1.5km (1 mile) east of the town centre. There's an enormous ore crusher plus two museum buildings. Tel: 08-8962 3388. www.tennantcreektourism.com.au.

BELOW: a camel is an alternative means of transport.

The **Daly Waters Pub** 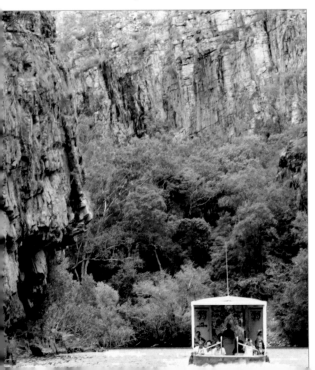 is worth a pause for a drink and rest. Built in the 1930s as a staging post for Qantas crew and passengers on multi-hop international flights, it is full of related memorabilia. **Mataranka** is a small town that was really put on the map only when an earlier rail track from Darwin was laid in 1928. Before that, it was part of the huge Elsey farming property (in 1916 Mataranka Station was established as an experimental sheep run, a project doomed to failure in this classic cattle country). Today, the surprise attraction is the **Mataranka Homestead Tourist Resort**, a 4-hectare (10-acre) section of tropical forest, including palms and paperbark trees adjoining the **Elsey National Park**. The nearby sparkling **Mataranka Thermal Pool**, with a water temperature of 34°C (93°F), is a real oasis amid the north's arid surrounds. Also adjacent to the tourist park is a replica of the Elsey Station homestead, made for the 1981 film *We of the Never Never*.

Katherine, 103km (63 miles) to the north, is the Top End's second most important town after Darwin. It has a population of 10,500 and a well-developed infrastructure of shops, camping grounds, hotels and motels. Since colonial days, Katherine has been an important telegraph station and cattle centre.

Katherine Gorge

To the east of the township, **Katherine Gorge** is one of the best-known features of the Territory. It's a massive stretch of sandstone cliffs rising to more than 100 metres (330ft) above the Katherine River, with 13 main canyons. The gorge is best explored by water. Tour boats operate mostly on the lower two canyons, but the more inquisitive traveller can explore the other 11 gorges upstream – by either hiring a canoe or swimming – for a total of 12km (7 miles) before the river widens out again. (The small crocodiles looking on are freshwater and don't attack humans, although they can be unnerving.) In recent years "saltie" crocs have been found; this has led to a ban on swimming.

The gorge system is part of the 1,800-sq-km (695-sq-mile) **Nitmiluk National Park**, which deserves at least a couple of days. There are also several walking trails in the park that follow the top of the escarpment, looking down into the gorge. Katherine is also home to a Savannah Guide Station. These eco-accredited specialist guides focus on heritage, culture, and the preservation of the natural environment.

From Katherine, the Victoria Highway strikes west towards the Kimberley region of Western Australia. Just before the WA border, there is a turnoff to **Keep River National Park**. Like the better-known formations across the border in the Purnululu National Park, Keep River features a series of fascinating banded sandstone towers that shelter a wide range of vegetation and animal life.

The richness of Kakadu

One of the brightest jewels in the whole array of Australian wilderness lies to

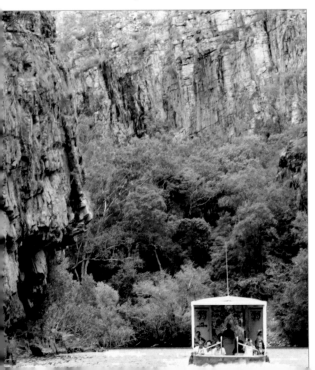

the north of Katherine, at **Kakadu National Park ⑰**. The park's prime accommodation and commercial centre is Jabiru, 250km (155 miles) southeast of Darwin. The richness of Kakadu defies description. Here, where the Arnhem Land escarpment meets the coastal floodplains, scenic splendour, ancient Aboriginal culture and paintings and an incredible array of flora and fauna come together in a brilliant, coherent whole.

The statistics of Kakadu – which is now on the World Heritage list – give some indication of what this area has to offer. The park covers 19,804 sq km (7,200 sq miles), with further extension likely. It is home to a quarter of all Australian freshwater fish, more than 1,000 plant species, 300 types of birds, 75 species of reptiles, many mammals and innumerable insects. Its world-famous galleries of Aboriginal art – particularly at Nourlangie and Ubirr rocks – give a significant insight into early man more than 20,000 years ago. In Kakadu the oldest evidence for the technology of edge-ground stone axes has been found.

Coming into Kakadu from the south, via the road from **Pine Creek**, one should detour into **Gunlom**, with its magical combination of waterfall and plunge pool. This oasis featured in the 1986 film *Crocodile Dundee* and is even more beautiful than its celluloid image.

Most visitors approach Kakadu along the sealed **Arnhem Highway** from Darwin. This road terminates at **Jabiru**, a service town for the Ranger Uranium Mine; the mine operates in an enclave surrounded by the national park and near to **Arnhem Land**, a great expanse of Aboriginal land that is closed to tourists. The juxtaposition of national park and uranium mine has provided ongoing controversy in Australian politics for years.

A good introduction to Kakadu is a boat tour on **Yellow Water**, at Cooinda, which offers the finest natural wildlife viewing anywhere in Australia. You are likely to see saltwater crocodiles, Jabiru storks, brolga cranes and a host of water birds, resident and migratory – but only during the dry season (May–Sept). During The Wet, when

It is possible that the earliest paintings at Ubirr Rock are up to 23,000 years old – which would make them the oldest artworks known anywhere on Earth.

BELOW: Kakadu National Park.

Rock paintings in Kakadu National Park.

BELOW: wetland in Kakadu National Park.

water is plentiful, the animals disperse across the region, and successful viewing is more haphazard.

Other easily accessible sights within the park are the paintings of **Ubirr Rock** and the towering faces of **Nourlangie Rock**. The splendid **Bowali Visitor Centre** has a permanent display setting out the features of the park. The **Marrawuddi Gallery** features displays of Aboriginal art, books, and gifts.

To see what makes Kakadu special, however, head out to one or more of the water holes nestled at the base of the escarpment.

The most popular conjunction of swimming hole and waterfall is **Jim Jim Falls**. The deep, cool pool and the nearby sandy beach are remarkably attractive and have the distinct benefit of being easy to visit, at least when the access road is open (June–Nov). Effort is well rewarded for those who decide to walk into nearby **Twin Falls**, where the two strands of water drop right onto the end of a palm-shaded beach. However, don't swim there because large and possibly hungry crocodiles have been known to move in. Both Jim

Jim and Twin Falls turn into seething maelstroms during wet-season flooding, at which time they are inaccessible to anyone without a helicopter. In the dry season, they are tranquil places of exquisite beauty, but you will need a four-wheel-drive vehicle.

The Adelaide River

On the Arnhem Highway to Darwin you cross the **Adelaide River**, and at that point you'll find the *Adelaide River Queen* (tel: 08-8988 8144), which can take you on a short (90-minute) river cruise to see the "jumping crocodiles", which leap almost clear of the water when offered a slice of steak, just as they do when catching birds and bats in midair. There are more croc cruises just down the river.

Darwin

Darwin ⑱, capital of the Northern Territory, was founded in 1869, after more than four decades of failed settlements in the north – abandoned one after another because of malaria outbreaks, cyclones, and supply failure due to the sheer distance from the other settlements. Named after the naturalist Charles Darwin, one of whose shipmates on the *Beagle* discovered the bay in 1839, it drifted on in a tropical stupor for decades, punctuated only by the discovery of gold at Pine Creek in 1870 and a minor revolution in 1919. Some 243 people were killed and another 300 injured in the first savage surprise Japanese bombing attack in February 1942, and Darwin suffered repeated raids over the following 18 months.

Asian influences

Today's Darwin has a pace that might – almost – be described as brisk, at least by Northern Territory standards. Once the neurotic front line of colonial Australia, the city's populace now reflects its proximity to Asia: the mix of some 50 cultures including Aborigines, Vietnamese, Filipinos, Malays, New Guineans, Pacific Islanders, Japanese and Indonesians – and Greeks and white Australians – provides a strong cosmopolitan flavour. That mix might have become more predominantly Asian had the Japanese advance in World War II not been stalled at New Guinea. When the Japanese bombed Darwin's port, there was mass panic, desertions, the evacuation of the civilian population, and the looting of homes by some of the army marshals who remained. The desperate dash for safety in the south became known derisively as the Adelaide River Stakes.

Discoveries of oil and gas in the Timor Sea have led to an influx of mining engineers, refinery workers and skilled tradesmen, feeding an economic boom. In turn, this has led to a housing boom, with apartment blocks proliferating and real estate prices rocketing. Many locals have cashed in on the housing boom, while doomsayers predict that the levels of economic and housing activity are not sustainable in the long term, and that the downturn will surely come. Meanwhile, the defence forces give another boost to the economy, with army, navy and airforce personnel spending at least two years in Darwin as part of their service.

Everywhere there is a spirit of optimism, although population mobility

TIP

As an alternative to walking, explore Darwin on the Tour Tub, an open-topped minibus that allows you to get on and off anywhere on its circular route. It can often be unbearably hot in the middle of the day. If exploring the city on foot, take your tour in the early morning or late afternoon.

BELOW:
stores in Darwin.

Cyclone Tracy

In four furious hours on Christmas Eve 1974, Cyclone Tracy swept in from the north and flattened the city. With gusts up to 280km (175 miles) an hour, the hurricane destroyed more than 5,000 homes – 80 percent of the city. The dead and missing totalled 66 in one of the most dramatic natural disasters in Australian history. With massive government funding, the city was rebuilt in the knowledge that the character and ambience of the old Darwin had been blown away forever.

Most of the old-style Darwin was levelled, to be replaced by a modern, more commercialised city. But of the over 30,000 residents evacuated in the nation's fastest-ever mass population shift, the majority returned. Today the city has 102,000 inhabitants.

The Darwin Government House is the residence of the Governor of the Northern Territory.

BELOW: shopping for sun cover.

remains an important factor. Many people leave the Territory on retirement to head south where health and aged care facilities are better.

The focal point of the city's defence was the **Old Navy Headquarters Ⓐ**. This simple stone building, dating from 1884, was a police station and courthouse. It and other historical buildings such as **Fannie Bay Gaol** (1883) and **Brown's Mart** (built in 1885, and the oldest in the city centre) contrast with Darwin's new cyclone-proof architecture, represented by the city's high-rise hotels, **Sky City Casino** and **Parliament House**.

Despite the changes, it is Darwin's natural charm and the relaxed Top End lifestyle that give the new city its appeal. The town is flanked by great expanses of golden sandy beaches and in the dry season – April to October – the vision of sand, clear blue skies and tropical flora makes Darwin immensely attractive.

For six months of the year **Darwin Harbour Ⓑ** becomes the playground of the area's boating populace. Many

people swim here, even though huge saltwater crocodiles are regularly pulled from the water. It may be more relaxing to swim at nearby **Mindil Beach** or **Vestey's** (named after the cattle company that once employed most Darwinians). Mindil Beach is the scene of a popular sunset market every Thursday evening (Apr–Oct 5–10pm). The Asian food stalls are marvellous.

Other markets are in **Parap** on Saturday morning (8am–2pm) and in **Rapid Creek** on Sunday (8am–2pm), **Nightcliff** markets Sunday (8am–2pm), and Mindil Beach Sunset markets run from May until October on Thursday and Sunday nights (5–10pm).

Fannie Bay

When the tides are right in early August at **Fannie Bay**, about 4km (2½ miles) from the city centre, Darwin conducts its famous **Beer Can Regatta**. Thousands of beer cans are used to build a fleet of wildly imaginative, semi-seaworthy craft. The whole city turns out to watch them race or wallow in the bay. This event is in keeping with Dar-

Darwin

0   1 km

0   1 mile

win's reputation as the world's beer-drinking capital.

In 1981 the ambitious **Museum and Art Gallery of the Northern Territory** (Mon–Fri 9am–5pm, Sat–Sun 10am–5pm; free) was opened. Its five galleries include one of the world's best collections of Aboriginal art and cultural artefacts, and archaeological finds from the Pacific region. Don't miss the fine collection of Aboriginal contemporary art, the Tiwi Pukumani burial poles and "Sweetheart", a stuffed saltwater crocodile 5 metres (17ft) long.

The **Fannie Bay Gaol Museum** (daily 10am–4.30pm; free) displays old cells and gallows from the prison's grim past.

Darwin's tropical nature makes a visit to the 34-hectare (84-acre) **Botanic Gardens** worthwhile, and fish-feeding at the **Aquascene** in Doctor's Gully Road, near the corner of Daly Street and the Esplanade, is lots of fun, especially with children. Fish can be hand-fed at high tide every day, at times advertised in the local paper.

Finally, the **Wharf Precinct** has undergone a major renovation: on any balmy afternoon, head out to the end of the pier, where dozens of restaurants have set up outdoor tables. It's the perfect place to drink in the tropical air, or drop a line to catch a passing Spanish mackerel. In 2010 the waterfront expanded to include a convention centre, high-rise apartments, offices, two major hotels and a wave pool for surfers. The total cost of the project was A$1 billion.

Exploring the Top End

About 60km (40 miles) south of Darwin on the Cox Peninsula Road, the **Territory Wildlife Park** provides a potted display of the Top End's varied bird, marine, and bush wildlife, and an aquarium representing an entire Top End river system, viewed from a shuttle train that potters around the 400-hectare (988-acre) property.

A two-hour drive to the southwest of Darwin is **Litchfield National Park** ⑲, 153 sq km (59 sq miles) of sandstone plateau with pockets of rainforest. It is one of the best areas in the Top End for bushwalking, but is even more

Frangipani provide a burst of colour in the landscape.

BELOW LEFT: an exhibit of snake life.
BELOW: termite mounds in the Northern Territory.

Map on page 266

TIP

However tempting the water might seem, it is unwise to swim off the coast of the Northern Territory between October and May. Box jellyfish, whose sting can be fatal, are usually present in significant numbers. Always observe the warning signs.

popular for its waterfalls and clear pools, which provide excellent swimming.

Darwin is the ideal base for exploring the remote, mangrove-filled north. Easily reached by light plane is the **Cobourg Peninsula** ⑳. Because it is on Aboriginal land, permission is required before visiting, but that can be arranged by tour operators. Cobourg was the site of one of the earliest attempts to establish a British base in northern Australia. Through a series of misadventures and bungles, Port Essington failed, but the bay in which it was built is a place of extravagant beauty in one of the most remote corners of the continent. **Seven Spirit Bay** here is perhaps the most out-of-the-way five-star resort in the world.

The Tiwi Islands

Splaying out to the north of Darwin like a giant ink blot, the two Tiwi Aboriginal islands, **Bathurst** ㉑ and **Melville** ㉒, are among Australia's most isolated outposts. Although the mainland is only 80km (50 miles)

away, dugout canoes rarely survived the journey, so the Tiwi culture and language developed separately from that of other Aboriginal groups. Early Dutch explorers met with hostility. When the British set up an outpost on Melville in 1824 it lasted less than five years, owing to Tiwi sieges and tropical disease. As a result, the Tiwis largely escaped the scorched-earth period of Australia's colonisation.

Control of their own affairs was returned to the Tiwis in the 1970s; most crucially, since they have never been moved, their land rights have never been disputed. This confident sense of possession may be why they are so outgoing; despite their once-fearsome reputation, they now bill their lands as the Friendly Islands.

Visiting the Tiwi Islanders requires a permit, organised by the Tiwi-owned tour company *(see box below)*. It's worth the journey: this remote coastline alternates between croc-infested mangrove swamps and blinding-white beaches where you can walk for many kilometres without seeing another person. ❑

BELOW: children of the Tiwi Islands.

BELOW: children of the Tiwi Islands.

Visiting the Tiwi Islands

The best time to visit is in late March or early April, during the Aussie Rules Tiwi Islands Football League Grand Final. On the same Sunday there is also the Tiwi Islands Annual Art Sale, where local jewellery, paintings, carvings, ceramics, weavings and fabrics are sold.

Visitors can only go on organised tours by boat or plane. The catamaran *Arafura Pearl* takes day-trippers to Nguiu on Bathurst Island for a visit to the art centre during the dry season. A charter plane allows visits to the three art centres on Bathurst and Melville Island (A$500 for a day trip). Call **Tiwi Art Network** on 08-8941 3593, or visit www.tiwiart.com.

Two-night plane charter visits to the islands are also available from **Aussie Adventure Tours** (tel: 08-8923 6523; www.aussieadventure.com.au).

RESTAURANTS AND BARS

Restaurants

Prices for a three-course dinner per person with a half-bottle of house wine:
$ = under A$50
$$ = A$50–80
$$$ = A$80–120
$$$$ = over A$120

Darwin

Char Restaurant
Admiralty House,
70 The Esplanade
Tel: 08-8981 4544
www.charrestaurant.com.au
Open: L Mon–Fri, D Mon–Sat. **$$$**
Char's reputation rests on their high-quality steaks. Located in the former navy HQ, this is alfresco dining among magnificent fig trees and frangipani.

Magic Wok
22 West Lane Arcade
Tel: 08-8981 3332
Open: L Mon–Fri, D Mon–Sat. **$**
Set-price menu cooked "turbo-wok" as you watch. You choose and load your plate from an extensive menu. This is an eclectic Chinese meal using a mix of Asian and Aussie ingredients; return for second or third helpings; bring your appetite.

Vietnam Saigon Star
60 Smith Street
Tel: 08-8981 1420
Open: L, Mon–Fri, D daily. **$**
Best Vietnamese nosh in the Territory; and cheap for such good-quality dishes. BYO and licensed.

Pee Wee's at the Point
Alec Fong Lim Drive,
East Point Reserve
Tel: 08-8981 6868
www.peewees.com.au
Open: D daily. **$$$**

Alfresco dining on the shores of Fannie Bay. Darwin's most up-market restaurant with prices and exotic menu to match. Essential to book.

Hanuman
93 Mitchell Street
Tel: 08-8941 3500
www.hanuman.com.au
Open: L Mon–Fri, D daily. **$$$**
Highly spiced, superbly presented Indian and Thai dishes renowned for consistent quality. It's the restaurant to which locals take their visitors to show off Darwin's culinary delights. Excellent, if pricey, wine list and imaginative menu with classy ambience.

Wisdom Bar and Café
48 Mitchell Street
Tel: 08-8941 4866
Open: B, L & D daily. **$**
Bright, breezy eatery in former dental surgery (hence the name) on the main tourist strip. Offers more than 50 beers from around the world, and if you drink them all (not necessarily on the same day) your name goes up on the Wall of Wisdom.

Victoria Hotel
27 Smith Street Mall
Tel: 08-8981 4011
Open: L & D daily. **$**
The oldest pub in town (built 1890). The Vic's historic sandstone walls have survived several cyclones. The Vic is a lively entertainment centre year-round with music, pub nosh and fun and games nightly during the dry season. It even has a mini-museum in the beer cellar.

Shenannigans
69 Mitchell Street
Tel: 08-8981 2100
www.shenannigans.com.au
Open: L & D daily. **$**
A rambling pub with a crowded beer menu and fair-quality food. The kind of pub that fills rapidly on Friday nights; music and dancing on Friday and Saturday.

Top End Hotel
Corner Mitchell and Daly streets
Tel: 08-8981 6511
Open: L & D daily. **$**
Overall the theme is sporty, with the food an adjunct to drinking.

Ducks Nuts Bar and Grill
76 Mitchell Street
Tel: 08-8942 2122
www.ducksnuts.com.au
Open: L & D daily. **$$**
Trendy eatery with good

coffee, a vodka bar and occasional live music. The sort of place to unwind after a hard day on the tourist trail.

Buzz Café
Cullen Bay
Tel: 08-8941 1141
Open: L & D daily. **$$**
Located over the water at the beautiful Cullen Bay marina, Buzz is one of the most popular eateries along a boardwalk of fine restaurants.

Alice Springs

Hanuman Restaurant
Crowne Plaza Hotel,
82 Barrett Drive
Tel: 08-8953 7188
Open: L, D Mon–Fri, D from 6pm Sat–Sun. **$$$**
Run by the owner of Hanuman's in Darwin, this is a fine dining experience in a desert setting.

RIGHT: massaman curry.

ULURU AND KATA TJUTA

Held sacred and owned by the Anangu Aboriginal people, natural rock formations Uluru and Kata Tjuta are two of the Northern Territory's largest and most iconic sites

In the southern part of the Northern Territory stands the colossal Uluru, a giant, sandstone rock which rises up 348 metres (1,160ft) above sea level from the flat desert floor. Also known by its colonial name, Ayers Rock, the title changed to Uluru when ownership was transferred back to the Anangu (the indigenous traditional owners) in 1985.

Uluru measures 5km (3¼miles) in length and 9.4km (5¾ miles) around. As each day passes the rock changes colour depending on the light and atmospheric conditions, and never remains the same hue. For the best experience, visit at sunrise. Watch from the new viewing area, Talinguru Nyakunytjaku (which means "look from the sand dunes"), to see the magical colours unfold.

Uluru is a sacred site for the Anangu. From a distance, Uluru looks smooth and featureless. But up close its face is weather-beaten, pitted with holes and gashes, ribs, valleys and caves. In the "Tjukurpa" or Creation Time (the traditional Anangu law that explains how the world was created) these features are related to the journeys and actions of ancestral beings across the landscape. It is hard to come away from Uluru without feeling enriched by its calm spirituality.

Climbing Uluru has become a controversial activity. The climbing path is about 1.6 km (1 mile) long and can be a treacherous and strenuous climb. Most of the over 35 deaths at Uluru were due to heart attack, so if you are not fit, do not attempt it. The climb up, across and down takes from two to three hours. However, being an Aboriginal sacred site, the owners ask you to respect their law and not to climb. The climbing route is a sacred path of spiritual significance that is only taken by a few Aboriginal men on special occasions.

LEFT: a chain handhold has been anchored on the rock to aid those who choose to climb Uluru; swift winds at the top of the rock can be dangerous.

ABOVE: the area that would later become the Uluru–Kata Tjuta National Park was separated from the Petermann Reserve in 1958; it was placed under the management of the Northern Territory Reserve Board and originally named the Ayers Rock–Mount Olga National Park

BELOW: Aboriginal pictograms, or rock art, can be seen in several caves near Uluru; these typically represent Dreamtime stories.

KATA TJUTA

Kata Tjuta, also known as Mount Olga (or colloquially as The Olgas), means "many heads" and is a group of more than 30 rounded red rock domes rising from the desert floor. The product of 550 million years of pressure from water and wind erosion, the natural phenomenon is under the protection of its Aboriginal owners in the Uluru–Katja Tjuta National Park and is inscribed on the World Heritage List.

Thirty kilometres (19 miles) west of Uluru, Kata Tjuta is a sacred Aboriginal men's place relating to knowledge that is considered powerful and dangerous. Most of this sacred knowledge has never been revealed to outsiders.

There are three walking trails: the Walpa Gorge, The Valley of the Winds and the Kata Tjuta dune viewing area. As you walk these peaceful trails, you may hear the sounds of birds such as Port Lincoln parrots and grey-headed honey-eaters piercing the silence.

ABOVE: the first dirt roads to the area now recognized as the Uluru-Kata Tjuta National Park were developed in 1948. The first tourists arrived by bus in the 1950s, but it wasn't until the early 1970s that the decision was made to remove all tourist accomodations to an area outside the park. By the year 2000 there were more than 400,000 annual visitors to the park, which is now jointly managed by the local Pitjantjatjara Aborigines and the National Parks and Wildlife Agency.

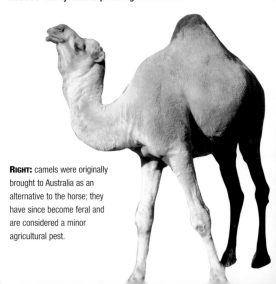

RIGHT: camels were originally brought to Australia as an alternative to the horse; they have since become feral and are considered a minor agricultural pest.

WESTERN AUSTRALIA

Two-thirds of the population of WA live in its attractive capital, Perth. The vast emptiness beyond includes barren desert, lush forests, rugged canyons and gold-mining towns

Western Australia is, quite simply, enormous. Covering more than 2½ million sq km (960,000 sq miles), it is much larger than the states of Alaska and Texas combined. In fact, if WA were a separate country, it would be the ninth largest in the world – and the emptiest. India is about the same size, with a population of 700 million, whereas the whole vast, dry expanse of Western Australia is inhabited by just 2 million people, three-quarters of whom live in Perth.

Being so far from the main Australian population centres on the east coast, WA conveys a feeling of utter isolation. **Perth** is the world's remotest state capital city, closer to Bali than it is to Sydney. Most of the state is parched and barren, but the north is lushly tropical and the southwest is temperate. In springtime, between September and November, many visitors travel from the eastern states just to see the profusion of wild flowers that turn the south into a riot of colour. Western Australia's vastness, small population and rugged scenery give this state a strong sense of being a new frontier, an impression which is heightened when you're only a few hours way from remote Outback scenery.

When planning a trip in WA, it's a good idea to keep an eye on the map scale and distances. It's all too easy to outline a weekend tour through an apparently tiny proportion of the state – only to add up the distances and find this would mean driving some 1,600km (1,000 miles). If you are based in Perth, with limited time to spare, consider joining an organised tour group or excursion. Several Perth tour operators run day, overnight and longer tours to WA's scenic highlights, such as the Margaret River region, Albany, Kalbarri National Park and the Pinnacles.

Main attractions
PERTH CITY
SWAN RIVER
HIS MAJESTY'S THEATRE
ROTTNEST ISLAND
THE PINNACLES
MONKEY MIA

PRECEEDING PAGES: the Perth skyline.
LEFT: swimming in Karajini National Park.
RIGHT: a Perth street performer.

Statue of James Stirling, the colony's first governor, outside the Town Hall.

The first arrivals

Western Australia was the arrival point for the first Australians. It is thought that, more than 50,000 years ago, the forebears of today's Australian Aborigines sailed across on bamboo rafts from what is now Indonesia, arriving in waves over many centuries. From the northwest, they gradually spread out to occupy the whole continent.

The first recorded European view of the west Australian coast occurred in 1616, when Dirk Hartog, a Dutch captain, sailed to what is now Dirk Hartog Island near Carnarvon. The first English explorer known to have visited Australia was William Dampier, who was on the *Cygnet* in 1688 when it was repaired at what is now Cygnet Bay in the Kimberley. He was unimpressed with what he saw, finding the land useless and the Aborigines the "miserablest people in the world".

In 1827, amid fears that the French might seize the coast, Captain James Stirling was despatched from Sydney to find a potential site for a western settlement. In 1829 the first colonists arrived to set up shop on a site he had spotted 16km (10 miles) upstream on the Swan River. Surrounded by black swans, a village of some 300 residents was founded and named Perth.

Inducing other colonists to head west was no easy matter. An acute labour shortage led to convicts being imported in 1850; by 1858, the population of Perth was still barely 3,000. But gold changed all that.

When news of the great finds of the 1890s at fields at Kalgoorlie to the east reached the outside world, Perth became the leaping-off point for one of the last great gold rushes. Still, many parts of the northeast were among the last to be settled in Australia, when some of the world's largest cattle stations were opened in the Kimberley. Throughout the 20th century, the discovery of mineral deposits throughout the state provided the main basis of its wealth – from uranium to gas and oil on the northwest shelf.

Perth

As in the gold-rush days, almost all visits to the wild west still start in **Perth** ❶, whose population now stands at

1.47 million. Set on the west coast, a high-tech counterweight to the older, heavily populated eastern cities, the city has become a symbol of Australian confidence.

Perth still lives in the shadow of the roaring 1980s, when it was the base of a posse of high-profile multimillionaires, exemplified by Alan Bond, who worked so closely with the Labor politicians of the time that the state was referred to as "WA Inc". But the powerful alliance collapsed in the wake of the 1987 Wall Street crash, when one tycoon after another was implicated in corrupt dealings, charged and jailed. Today, Perth is a chastened city, but remains well worth a visit.

The city takes full advantage of its setting on the serpentine Swan River. The dominant view is over **Perth City** where the **Swan River** widens into a broad bay about 1km (½ mile) across. On the edge of the business district, set high on an escarpment, is **Kings Park** Ⓐ, a 400-hectare (988-acre) reserve of botanical gardens and bushland offering panoramic views over the city and the river. Dominating the jetty on Riv-

erside Drive are the sail-shaped copper wings of the tower containing the **Swan Bells** (daily from 10am, closing times vary seasonally; charge to ascend the tower), a gift from the church of St Martin-in-the-Fields, Trafalgar Square, London, to mark Australia's bicentenary in 1988.

Successive mining booms since the 1970s have led large multinational and West Australia-based companies to build high-rise office blocks in Perth. Their presence has dramatically changed the city skyline, causing older residents to complain that the city has lost its intimate country-town feel. But the odd architectural gem can still be found. Tucked into the back of **Stirling Gardens** is **Old Court House** Ⓑ (1837), Perth's first brick building, which has a modest facade of Doric columns. On the whole, however, buildings predating the state's 1890s gold rush are rare. **Government House** Ⓒ (also in Stirling Gardens) stands as a true reflection of the beginning of the state. Constructed in the 1860s by convict labour, it placed a regal stamp of authority on the new settlement.

TIP

City-centre buses are free. The free service applies to all regular buses while they're in the central zone, as well as CATs (Central Area Transit), distinctive buses – red, blue or yellow, depending on the route – linking main tourist sights and running from early morning until early evening.

BELOW:
Perth's riverfront along Kings Park.

The Caller, *a sculpture by Gerhard Marks outside the Art Gallery of Western Australia.*

Some say the emerging Australian "larrikin" characteristic shows through in the upstairs windows, which are in the shape of a broad arrow – the motif on the uniforms of the convict builders.

Other early buildings include the **Deanery ⓓ**, on the corner of Pier Street, opposite Stirling Gardens, built by paroled convicts in 1859, and the Elizabethan-style **Cloisters** building **ⓔ**, at the western end of St George's Terrace, established in 1858 as the first public school for boys. The old **Town Hall ⓕ** (Hay Street Mall) was the last building in Perth to be built by convict labour (commenced in 1867). It has been the site of various entertainments as well as formal civic ceremonies and political meetings. It was a rallying point for conscription during both World Wars.

The city architecture of the 1890s gold rush includes **His Majesty's Theatre ⓖ**, also known as His Maj, at the west end of Hay Street. To discover more about the gold rush and its pivotal role in the city's development, visit the 1899 **Perth Mint** (eastern end of Hay Street; Mon–Fri 9am–5pm, Sat–Sun 9am–1pm; guided tour every 30 minutes; charge), among the world's oldest operating mints. Try picking up a block of gold worth A$250,000, minting your own medallion, or watch gold being smelted.

Two sections of town with contrasting histories are **London Court** and **East Murray Street Precinct**. London Court dates back to 1937, a monument to mock-Tudor kitsch whose curiosities include a clock tower at each end: one a replica of London's Big Ben, the other of the Gros Horloge in Rouen, France. East Murray Street is the genuine colonial item. It appears on the original town plans of 1838 and now stands lined by early 20th-century buildings.

On the northern side of the railway station, across the lovely **Horseshoe Bridge**, lies the **Perth Cultural Centre ⓗ**, comprising the **Art Gallery of Western Australia** (daily 10am–5pm; www.artgallery.wa.gov.au; free entrance and guided tours) and the Western Australian Museum. The art gallery displays more than 1,000 works of art, including one of the continent's best collections of Aboriginal art. One painting that is almost always included in a guided tour is *The Foundation of Perth* by George Pitt, depicting the wife of an early dignitary ceremoniously felling a tree to mark the city's founding. A copy of this painting was given to every WA school to mark the state's centenary celebrations in 1929.

The **Western Australian Museum** (daily 9.30am–5pm; www.museum.wa.gov.au; free) traces the history of the state from the formation of the Australian continent 120 million years ago to the present day. Don't miss the fascinating natural history section or the illuminating Katta Dijinoong Gallery devoted to Aboriginal history and culture.

In the museum's beautifully preserved **Old Gaol** (1856), life in the early days of the colony has been recreated in a collection of period interiors, including a 1917 pharmacy and an original court room. There is also a good little courtyard café here.

Just along from the Art Gallery of WA, and also forming part of the cultural centre, is the **Perth Institute of Contemporary Art** (gallery Fri 11am–9pm; Tue, Thur, Sun 11am–6pm; www.pica.org.au; free), which offers a lively programme of exhibitions, installations and events, as well as a great café-bar.

The cultural centre stands on the doorstep of **Northbridge ❶**, where Perth's ethnic diversity is displayed on a plate, as it were. You can walk past tanks of live mud crabs and crayfish, smell the sharp tang of lemongrass, chew on chickens' feet or dim sum at eight in the morning, or have a beer on the balcony of a pub, watching all the action on the streets below. Northbridge also has nightclubs and discos as lively as any in Sydney.

Another fruitful neighbourhood for restaurants and bars is **Subiaco**, a fashionable suburb on the western side of town (direct access on the Perth–Fremantle railway). Come here for brunch on Friday or Saturday and visit its funky weekend markets (**Station Street** and **Pavilion**), perhaps after a walk in nearby Kings Park.

Perth's seaside

Fremantle ❷, just 19km (12 miles) from Perth's city centre but deemed a city in its own right, was brushed up for the America's Cup race in 1987 and has since become one of Western Australia's most popular attractions. Unlike glittering Perth, the old port's colonial charms remain intact, including the **Round House** (which actually has 12 sides), WA's oldest public building (1830) and its first jail, built where Captain Fremantle landed to claim Western Australia for the Crown.

If you arrive by ferry, you will disembark at Victoria Quay, at the far end of which you will notice the sail-like roof of the excellent **Maritime Museum** (daily 9.30am–5pm; www.mm.wa.gov.au; charge), exploring all aspects of Fremantle's seafaring heritage from whaling and pearling to its role in World War II and as the place of disembarkation for thousands of post-war immigrants. The **Shipwreck Galleries** (same hours as the Maritime Museum, but free) on Cliff Street, is devoted to marine archaeology. It has relics from some of the many ships wrecked off

TIP

Fremantle is a 30-minute train ride from Perth railway station, and Transperth buses to Fremantle leave from St George's Terrace. But try to arrive by boat along the Swan if you can. The ferry from Barrack Street Jetty takes about an hour.

LEFT: leafy, laid-back Northbridge.
BELOW: the Round House.

WA's coast over the centuries, including original timber (partially reconstructed) and treasures from the Dutch ship *Batavia (see page 301)*.

Fremantle Prison (daily 10am–5pm; charge), a maximum security prison until 1991, offers a variety of tours including a torchlight tour. Ghost sightings are not guaranteed, but the tours include the gallows yard and hellish cell blocks built by convict labour in 1855.

One pleasure of Fremantle is to wander at random, soaking up the laid-back atmosphere and admiring the frilly ironwork of the gold-rush architecture. It has no shortage of restaurants and coffee shops (explore South Terrace, aka Cappuccino Strip), and plenty of interesting shops. On Fridays and weekends dip into the splendidly restored **Fremantle Markets** (corner of South Terrace and Henderson Street) for interesting crafts and souvenirs.

Perth's beaches

From Fremantle a string of soft sandy beaches stretches all the way to Hillary's Boat Harbour, 50km (30 miles)

north. Development, though continuous, is almost without exception low-rise and low-key, set well back from the shore. Each of the beaches has its fans. For surfing, head for **Scarborough** or **Trigg**; for a lively après-beach scene, choose **Indiana Cottesloe Beach** *(see page 310)*, which offers good food, cocktails and fabulous sunset views.

For family-friendly attractions, head for **Hillary's Boat Harbour**, where the AQWA (Aquarium of Western Australia; daily 10am–5pm; www.aqwa.com.au; charge) re-creates WA's five coastal environments. The highlight is the walk-through aquarium, representing the shipwreck coast where sharks, loggerhead turtles and stingrays glide smoothly overhead within centimetres of upturned faces. Other highlights include a touch pool, saltwater crocodiles of the far north coast and tropical fish of the coral coast.

Rottnest Island

Hillary's Boat Harbour is, along with Barrack Street Jetty in Perth and Fremantle, one of the springboards for **Rottnest Island ❸**, an idyllic getaway

Leighton and Port beaches are best for windsurfing.

BELOW: enjoying the sand and surf along the western shore.

Margaret River's Voyager Estate combines fine wines and 18th-century architecture inspired by Cape Town.

just 19km (13 miles) offshore. First settled as a natural prison for West Australian Aborigines, Rotto (as it is known locally) is now a favourite holiday spot. Private motor vehicles aren't allowed on the island, so visitors tend to wobble along on bicycles, which can be brought on the ferry or rented on the island.

Visitors can spend their time boating, golfing, playing tennis or just lazing on a quiet beach. In summer, divers come here to explore the world's southernmost coral reef. The island's pub, the Hotel Rottnest, originally served as the official residence of the Australian state governor; it now has live music on summer evenings. Facilities have recently been upgraded with a A$6.5 million makeover. Accommodation is limited to the Hotel Rottnest and Rottnest Lodge, and at peak times is allocated by public ballot, as demand is so high. If you want to stay overnight or longer, book well in advance.

The Swan Valley

If you have limited time during your stay in Perth, and can manage only one out-of-town trip, it is worth venturing into the **Swan Valley**. A major wine-producing area, it offers vineyard tours and elegant towns such as **Guildford ❹**, one of the earliest settlements in Western Australia, and is only 30 minutes by train or road from Perth's CBD. To follow the Swan Valley food and wine trail, a 32km (20-mile) loop linking some of the best vineyards and micro-breweries, as well as the Margaret River Chocolate Company, leave the town via the West Swan Road and return by the Great Northern Highway. Also along the route is **Caversham Wildlife Park**, the best place in the region for kangaroo-spotting for visitors too short of time to go bush. Caversham forms part of Whiteman Park (www.whitemanpark.com.au), packed with family attractions, including an excellent **Motor Museum** (daily 10am–4pm; charge).

The Southwest of WA

Head south of Perth for the region's top wineries and dense karri and jarrah forests, but be careful not to miss things along the way. The new Perth-to-Bunbury Highway is a direct and efficient way to get to Bunbury and

Getting to Rottnest Island

Rottnest's proximity to the mainland makes it an easy day trip by ferry from Perth. **Boat Torque Cruises** (tel: 08-9430 5844; www.boattorque.com.au) operates from Northport and the C Shed at Fremantle, and from the Barrack Street Jetty in Perth. **Hillary's Fast Ferries** (tel: 08-9246 1039; www.hillarysfastferries.com.au) run from Hillary's Boat Harbour, while **Oceanic Cruises** (tel: 08-9325 1181; www.oceancruises.com.au) set out from the B Shed at Fremantle, and Barrack Street Jetty in Perth.

It takes approximately 25 minutes to get to the island from Fremantle, around 45 minutes from Hillary's and 90 minutes from Perth. The cost of the ferry crossing includes the entrance charge to the island. The ferry crossing to Rottnest can get choppy. If you're prone to seasickness, or have children with you, take tablets beforehand.

The beauty of the island is perhaps best appreciated from the air, so you may want to consider taking the **Rottnest Air Taxi** (tel: 08-9292 5027; www.rottnest.de) instead of the ferry. You will also get there a lot quicker – taxis spend just 12 minutes in the air. Flights leave from Jandakot Airport in Perth for Rottnest Aerodrome at times arranged to suit you (cost is approximately A$80 return per person, based on three people sharing a four-seater aircraft).

Margaret River, but you'll have to take the old coast road if you don't want to miss the bits in between.

Immediately south of Fremantle the landscape is fairly industrial apart from **Rockingham** (47km/30 miles south of Perth), a springboard for Penguin Island, named after its colony of 1,100 penguins, and **Mandurah** (74km/40 miles from Perth), a fast-growing but nonetheless delightful town on the Peel Estuary. In high season the towns and campsites around Mandurah are busy with holidaymakers, but for the rest of the year they can be enjoyed in relative peace.

Further down the coast (140km/75 miles from Perth) is the dairy town of **Harvey**, dating back to 1890. The nearby **Yalgorup National Park** can be reached by the old coast road. It is a sanctuary for water birds and wildlife, though it is the colony of living, rock-like creatures known as thrombolites (the earliest-known life on Earth and very rare) that makes it special. The only access point is via the coast road, 25km (15 miles) south of Mandurah, indicated by a large brown sign for the Lake Clifton platform, an observation walkway built across the shallows containing the thrombolites.

The city of **Bunbury** ❺ (180km/110 miles south of Perth) is a busy port that owes its existence to Lt Henry St Pierre Bunbury, who travelled overland to the coast from Pinjarra in 1836. At **Koombana Beach**, just north of town, visitors can feed a community of bottlenose dolphins that visit the beach daily at the Dolphin Discovery Centre (daily 9am–3pm in winter, 8am–4pm in summer; charge).

Forests and vineyards

It was logging of the nearby forests that brought prosperity to the region; jarrah and blackbutt hardwoods abound here, and can be seen in much of the early architecture. Bunbury sits at the northern end of **Geographe Bay**, a large, sheltered waterway that has **Cape Naturaliste** as its northern spur.

From here a cape-to-cape hiking trail leads south to Cape Leeuwin, 135km (84 miles) away.

On the southern coast of the bay, the resort town of **Busselton** ❻ has a fine setting on the Vasse River. Its 2km (1¼-mile) jetty, the longest in the southern hemisphere, has an interpretive centre and a multimillion-dollar underwater observatory (daily Dec–Apr 8am–5pm, May–Sept 10am–4pm, Oct–Nov 9am–5pm; charge) that takes visitors 8 metres (26ft) below sea level for amazing views of fish and coral.

Margaret River ❼, 280km (173 miles) from Perth, is internationally famous for estate-grown and -bottled wines. Names like Leeuwin, Xanadu, Moss Wood, Devil's Lair, Howard Park and dozens more rival the world's best. This is crafted wine and a far cry from the mass production of Australia's eastern states. Margaret River's success sparked a Western Australian wine revolution that has encouraged quality production from Swan Valley down to the Great Southern region. Not only do many of these vineyards offer fantastic wine, but their restaurants repre-

A wedgetail eagle at the Eagle Heritage Raptor Centre, Margaret River.

BELOW: friendly face at the Dolphin Discovery Centre, Bunbury.

Drive carefully at dusk and at night, when wildlife is most active. If a kangaroo jumps in front of your car, don't swerve. Most fatal road accidents involving wildlife occur when drivers swerve, hit loose gravel on the side of the road and lose control.

BELOW: the Valley of the Giants Treetop Walk, Walpole.

sent better value for money than most establishments in Perth.

Surfing the big waves and swimming are two popular reasons locals visit the region. Yallingup, Injidup, Smiths Beach, Bunker Bay and Three Bears (only accessible by 4WD) are among the many surf breaks, but if you plan to tan, they are equally as inviting to lie on the sand and have a quick dip when the time comes to cool off.

Margaret River is also renowned for its cheese (www.mrdc.com.au), chocolate (www.chocolatefactory.com.au) and local microbrews. Check out the Duckstein (www.duckstein.com.au) for a cleansing ale.

Visits to spectacular caves such as **Mammoth, Lake** and **Jewel**, and browsing in arts and crafts shops, are alternatives to wine (and beer) sampling.

Cape Leeuwin ❽ marks the southwest extremity of Australia and the junction of the Indian and Southern oceans. This point marked the start of Matthew Flinders' odyssey when he set out to circumnavigate and chart the Australian coastline in 1790.

Inland lies **Pemberton**, surrounded

by three national parks – a region of giant karri and jarrah trees. Some of the trees are over 50 metres (160ft) tall – the world's tallest hardwoods. The adventurous can climb the **Gloucester Tree** to the fire tower, 60 metres (190ft) above the ground.

Travelling east along the coast road towards Denmark and Albany, stop at **Walpole** to view the ancient Tingle Forest from the Treetop Walk (daily 9am–4.15pm and 8am–5.15pm; wheelchair access; charge), a lofty ramp looping over the Valley of the Giants.

Further east is the **Stirling Range National Park ❾**, its conical hills and jagged peaks rising to 1,000 metres (3,300ft), presenting challenging walks. A seasonal centre for wild flowers, including native orchids, it receives Western Australia's only snowfall.

To the south, **Albany ❿** is where European settlement was first established in the western half of Australia. On Christmas Day 1826, Major Lockyer arrived from Sydney in the brig *Amity*, attracted by the splendid expanses of **King George Sound**, an enclosed waterway twice as large as Sydney Harbour.

Today tourists flock here from July to November to spot whales – an ironic attraction for a town that (until 1978) was the last operating whaling station in the southern hemisphere. A museum, **Whaleworld** (daily 9am–5pm, until 6pm in Jan; guided tours at 10am and 4pm; charge), tells the story.

Albany is also one of Australia's most picturesque towns, with a wonderful bay-side location and well-preserved 19th-century streetscapes. At nearby **Strawberry Hill** stands the state's oldest house, built in 1836 for the first government resident, Sir Richard Spencer. There is plenty of exploring to be done here. The **post office**, with its shingled tower, is the oldest in Western Australia, and the **Church of St John the Evangelist**, built in 1848, is the earliest house of worship in the state. Overlooking King George Sound is a memorial to the **Australian Light Horse** that served in Egypt, and Gallipoli in World War I. It was moved here from Port Said, Egypt, after the 1956 Suez War. Nearby Mount Adelaide, a military history precinct, looks down on the waters where the ANZAC Dardanelles invasion fleet assembled in 1914.

Perhaps the most spectacular park in the region is **Fitzgerald River National Park ⑪**, 185km (115 miles) northeast of Albany. It includes an impressive stretch of coastal landscape and also contains a group of mountains known as the **Barren Range**, with dramatic views of the Southern Ocean.

The easternmost town of **Esperance ⑫** is 750km (465 miles) from Perth. Local attractions include the salt-rich **Pink Lake** and the grave of Tommy Windich, an Aboriginal guide who accompanied explorer John Forrest on his two overland treks to Adelaide in 1870 and 1874.

Cape Le Grand and **Cape Arid** national parks offer superb beaches, an abundance of birdlife and some terrific campsites. Offshore lies a maze of beautiful islands called the **Recherche Archipelago**. On the road from

Albany to the capes, opportunities for camping, fishing and surfing present themselves at almost every turn.

The East

Around 200km (125 miles) north of Esperance is the crossroads town of **Norseman**, from where the Eyre Highway heads east across the vast Nullarbor Plain to eastern Australia, crossing the border into South Australia after 725km (450 miles). Alternatively, the route north heads to Kalgoorlie and the goldfields.

The goldfields

The birthplace of the West Australian goldfields was **Coolgardie ⑬**, 190km (118 miles) north of Norseman. In September 1892 it was the site of Australia's richest strike – producing 85kg (200lb) of gold in a single month. By 1900, it was a town of 15,000 people with a score of hotels, half a dozen banks, three breweries, two stock exchanges and seven newspapers. By 1905, however, the lode was running out. Today Coolgardie is an attractive, historic township with elegant buildings.

Emus are a fairly common sight in the road-side bush.

BELOW: the Super Pit at Kalgoorlie.

Kalgoorlie , 40km (25 miles) away, started off as Coolgardie's twin city, but it has survived as a thriving mining town of 29,000, the hub in a region full of boom and bust. When Irishman Paddy Hannan discovered gold here in 1893, it was soon realised that the wealth of the Kalgoorlie find far exceeded anything else ever found in Australia. Kalgoorlie's Golden Mile became the richest piece of real estate in the world.

However, water in the area was in short supply, so the celebrated engineer C.Y. O'Connor built a pipeline from Mundaring Weir near Perth, more than 500km (300 miles) away. Today, the area continues to yield 241 million grams (850,000 ounces) of gold per year.

Kalgoorlie's architecture retains much of its early charm, with the **Palace Hotel** being a fabulous example of Edwardian excess. The business district of Kalgoorlie is a leafy refuge from the moonscape of the mines; the continuing trade in beer, prostitution and minerals still reflects much of the town's earlier freebooting ways. For miners who gamble on

the Earth's riches every day, other (less legitimate) forms of gambling thrive – especially "two-up", a uniquely Australian game based on the toss of two pennies. When the Burswood Casino was about to open in Perth, the manager visited Kalgoorlie to see how Australia's most famous two-up school operated.

The main reason for visiting Kalgoorlie is to see the **Super Pit**, a working goldmine of awe-inspiring proportions. It runs tours on the third Sunday of every month, departing from the Super Pit shop in Kalgoorlie. Those whose visit does not coincide with the guided tours should head for the Super Pit lookout (daily 7am–9pm; free), just off the Goldfields Highway. It is best to come at night when the pit is lit up by high-voltage lights.

Many towns haven't fared as well as Kalgoorlie. Ghost towns such as **Gwalia** and **Kanowna** dot the area, while many outposts have seen their populations dwindle so much that they, too, will soon be deserted. In many of these centres stand the imposing relics of Australia's Wild West era.

BELOW: the Exchange Hotel, a pub in Kalgoorlie.

Wave Rock

The most famous inland attraction of the southwest is **Wave Rock** ⓕ, approximately 350km (250 miles) from Perth. This natural feature appears on almost every tourist brochure of Western Australia. The rock, a few kilometres east of **Hyden**, is at once exciting and disappointing to visit. From below, this 15-metre (50ft) -high lip of solid granite looks set to curl over and crush bystanders. But, taking a wider perspective, one sees that the wave is just one wall of a huge granite dome, underscored by erosion; and a walk along the top rather shatters the illusion.

While you are in the area of Wave Rock, you may like to take time to visit other interesting rock formations in the immediate area. **Hippo's Yawn** is a 20-minute walk away, and the **Humps** and the **Breakers** are also nearby. For details on how to get to these rocks, pop into the tourist office at the Wave Rock Wild Flower Shop and Visitor Centre (tel: 08-9880 5182).

Due west of the goldfields, farmers harvest the state's other golden bounty: wheat. **Merredin** is a busy town at the heart of one of the world's great grain belts. It was founded in 1891 around a water hole on the way to the goldfields, and has since become a research centre for improving the wheat yield of the area. Merredin's annual agricultural show is one of the most prestigious in the state. The town's tree-lined main street is best in November when the jacarandas bloom.

Situated on the Avon River, **Northam** is the central hub of the western wheat fields, and also the scene of a hell-for-leather river race each August, when hundreds of canoeists and power-boaters dash madly downstream in the Avon River Descent.

It wasn't until Robert Dale led an expedition over the Darling Range and into this 150km (90-mile) stretch of fertile valley that the early settlers could be certain that the west held land capable of sustaining livestock and crops. The valley's towns were settled soon after Perth. For an insight into the pioneering history, **York**, with its extravagantly designed town hall, **Toodyay** and **Mahogany Creek** are well worth exploring.

Traffic is scarce in rural areas. However, you are bound to encounter the massive "road trains" which can be several trailers long.

BELOW:
New Norcia's St Gertrude's College, adorned with Art Deco frescoes.

TIP

To discover more about Western Australia's history and heritage, visit the **Greenough Historical Hamlet** (daily 9am–5pm, museum 10am–4pm; charge includes a guided tour) on Brand Highway, a 20-minute drive south of Geraldton. Its collection of 19th-century colonial buildings, restored by the National Trust, includes a church and a schoolhouse.

North of Perth

The Perth to Darwin route is Australia's longest capital-to-capital haul. At 4,027km (2,502 miles), it is the most desolate trek.

A major attraction of taking the Great Northern Highway inland route rather than the coastal Brand Highway is **New Norcia** , 130km (80 miles) from Perth. The settlement was established by Benedictine monks in 1846 as an Aboriginal mission. The monastery is still operating, although many of the town's more impressive buildings are closed to the public. However, the Spanish architectural influence is interesting and the museum and art gallery (Aug–Oct 9.30am–5pm, Nov–July 10am–4.30pm; charge) provide fascinating insights into pioneer life. Guided tours of the settlement are available, or visitors can take a self-guided 2km (1½ mile) walk linking the major sites, including the Abbey Church, decorated with locally inspired sgraffito and an image of Our Lady of Good Counsel, said to have been held up to repel a bushfire in 1847. Be sure to come away with some of the delectable treats such as New Norcia nut cake and Dom Salvado Pan Chocolatti, produced by the monastery's bakery.

Heading up the coastal Brand Highway, the tiny town of **Gingin** – 82km (51 miles) north of Perth – is a good first stop. There are excellent fishing grounds off the coast, 48km (30 miles) to the west: estuaries such as the mouth of the Moore River at **Guilderton** are ideal for casting a line. Just to the south of Guilderton is the **Yanchep National Park** (vehicle charge), offering wetlands, woodlands, bushwalks, caves and an Aboriginal heritage trail.

Further north along the coast road is **Lancelin**, 127km (79 miles) north of Perth, protected by two large rock islands and surrounded by towering sand dunes. Gutsy winds off the Indian Ocean make it ideal for windsurfing and surfing. It attracts top international surfers, but also caters to novices keen to learn.

The Pinnacles

The only way of proceeding north of Lancelin is to follow the Brand Highway. Though considered the coastal route, it

The Pinnacles

Most organised tours north of Perth include a stop at the Pinnacles in Nambung National Park. These strange limestone formations are believed to have been shaped around 30,000 years ago by winter rain leaching into the sand dunes and turning the lower levels of the lime-rich sand into a soft limestone. Plants then grew upon the surface of the dunes, accelerating the leaching process and causing a hard cap to form around the roots of the plants. Wind erosion eventually removed the surrounding sand, leaving the hard rock exposed and moulding it into weird and wonderful shapes. The process continues to this day: submerged sections of the Pinnacles are thought to be at least as deep as the exposed sections are high.

BELOW: the Pinnacles.

is quite a distance inland, and you must turn off it in order to see the ocean.

Nambung National Park , 29km (18 miles) south of the coastal town of Cervantes and 245km (153 miles) from Perth, shouldn't be missed. The **Pinnacles Desert** within the park *(see opposite)* is a bizarre sight: a world of limestone spires all rising from smooth sand dunes. When Dutch explorers first saw the Pinnacles from their vessels, they thought they had found the ruins of a long-deserted city. In fact, they are entirely natural. A circular track leads around the spires (vehicle charge).

A short distance up the coast is **Jurien**, a lobster-fishing centre set on the shores of an attractive sheltered bay, framed by spectacular sand dunes. **Port Denison** (now referred to as Dongara-Denison), 170km (105 miles) further up the coast, has Australia's biggest rock lobster grounds; more than 400 fishing boats work the area.

Maritime Geraldton

From the Pinnacles, continue north along Brand Highway towards Geraldton. About 25km (13 miles) south of the city, look out for **Greenough Historical Hamlet** (daily 9am–5pm; charge including a guided tour), a collection of 19th-century colonial buildings, restored by the National Trust, that presents a vivid picture of life for the early settlers.

Geraldton , 425km (265 miles) north of Perth, supports a population of about 20,000 and is the administrative centre for West Australia's mid-coast region. It has a near-perfect climate, superb fishing conditions and fine sandy beaches that stretch north and south of Champion Bay. This stretch of coast saw many shipwrecks when early Dutch mariners heading for the East Indies were swept too far south.

The **Abrolhos Islands**, 64km (40 miles) offshore, have claimed many ships over the years, including the Dutch East Indiaman *Batavia*, which ran aground in 1629. Survivors waited behind while the captain and a few crew headed off for Java in an open boat. While the survivors were awaiting rescue, a mutiny broke out, driving loyal crewmen to a separate island. When the captain finally returned from

TIP

Skywest flies to Geraldton daily, departing from Perth domestic terminal. In Geraldton, hire a car from Avis, Budget or Hertz, which all have offices at the airport, and drive to Greenough and surrounding areas.

BELOW: Geraldton.

*The **Kalbarri Wild Flower Centre** (Ajana Road; July– Nov daily 9am–5pm; tel: 08-9937 1229) provides a nature trail or a guided walk through Kalbarri's Native Botanic Garden.*

BELOW: wildlife-spotting cruises leave from Monkey Mia.

his epic journey, many of the mutineers were hanged; two others were cast ashore to fend for themselves.

The Abrolhos sit on one of the finest reefs on the west coast, and divers can visit various wrecks. Many relics rescued from the deep are on view in the **Western Australian Museum** (daily 10am–4pm; entrance by donation) in Geraldton and at Fremantle's Shipwreck Gallery where the hull of the *Batavia* is on display.

For panoramic views of the area surrounding Geraldton, head for **Waverley Heights**. **Ellendale Bluffs** are notable for their sheer cliffs, at the base of which is a permanent water hole. Locals will advise you to visit **Chapman Valley**, at its most spectacular in spring (Sept–Nov) when the wild flowers are in bloom.

A century ago, **Northampton**, 48km (30 miles) north of Geraldton, was an important rural outpost. Recently it has been spruced up by residents to create an unusually pretty Outback town. Buildings such as **Chiverton House Museum** (Fri–Mon 10am–noon and 2–4pm; free) were built by

convict labour; the cemetery in the grounds of Gwalia Church records the passing of the convicts and free settlers who first came to the area.

About 20km (12 miles) away is **Horrock Beach**, with fine sand expanses and bays. When there is water in it, don't be surprised to see **Lake Hutt**, near Port Gregory, turn pink in the midday sun – a bizarre phenomenon caused by light refraction and naturally occurring beta carotene in the water.

Kalbarri National Park

Comprising 186,000 hectares (460,000 acres), **Kalbarri National Park** ⑲ (tel: 08-9937 1140) features a combination of stunning river gorges and towering sea cliffs. The park is set around the lower reaches of the Murchison River, which weaves its way to the Indian Ocean past the multi-hued sandstone formations of Red Bluff.

South of Carnarvon is the great system of peninsulas and inlets of **Hamelin Pool** and **Denham Sound**. These two huge expanses of water are protected in the northwest by **Dirk Hartog Island**. A pewter plate, nailed in

Exploring Kalbarri

To get the most out of Kalbarri National Park and the multitude of adventure activities on offer, especially when time is limited, you may want to sign up with a specialist tour operator.

• **Kalbarri Safari Tours**. For a quad bike tour, tel: 08-9937 1011.
• **Kalbarri Boat Hire**. For a canoe safari, tel: 08-9937 1245.
• **Kalbarri Abseil**. For rock climbing, tel: 08-9937 1618.
• **Kalbarri Sand-Boarding**. Like surfing, but on sand, tel: 1800 886 141.
• **Kalbarri Explorer Ocean Charters**. Deep sea fishing, tel: 08-9937 2027
• **Kalbarri Reefwalker Tours**. Coastal Cruises, tel: 08-9937 1356.
• **Kalbarri Aquarium** (daily 10am–4pm; tel: 08-9937 2027) provides a good overview of the local marine life.

Map on
page 292

1616 to a post on Cape Inscription by the Dutch explorer Hartog, marked the first known landing of Europeans on Australia's west coast. A replica of this plate is in the **Shark Bay Shire Office** (the original is in Amsterdam).

Dolphins at Monkey Mia

Despite its name, **Shark Bay** is one place where every visitor ventures into the water. That's because this is the site of **Monkey Mia ❷⓿**, perhaps one of Australia's most delightful tourist attractions. In the small bay near Denham township, wild dolphins come to shore to be fed and mingle with visitors. This came about when local fishermen started tossing fish scraps overboard to following dolphins – by 1964, they were coming in to be hand-fed. This unique interaction between humans and dolphins is still very delicate, so follow the rangers' instructions.

Monkey Mia is only the best-known corner of Shark Bay, which was declared a World Heritage area in 1991. Covering 2.3 million hectares (5.7 million acres), it comprises a series of cliff-lined peninsulas and islands with some 145 species of plants (28 endemic to the region, having developed in isolation). The extraordinary salinity of the southern parts of Shark Bay has allowed the growth of stromatolites at Hamelin Pool – giant masses of algae that are considered the oldest form of life on Earth (they probably first formed 3 billion years ago). Somewhat more exciting to observe are the many dugongs, humpback whales and green and loggerhead turtles that roam the splendid arc-shaped bays.

On Shark Bay's slender land prongs, scientists are reintroducing furry marsupials with quaint names like burrowing bettongs and western barred bandicoots. These native species, almost eaten to extinction by introduced foxes and cats, now live behind predator-proof fences.

The tropical north

Carnarvon ❷❶ is 1,000km (600 miles) north of Perth on the beautiful **Gascoyne River**. Sitting just below the Tropic of Capricorn, Carnarvon has warm winters and tropical summers that encourage vibrant tropical wildlife, and

A pair of pelicans at Monkey Mia.

BELOW:
dolphin- and
whale-watching
tours are popular
day excursions.

The Pilbara was the setting for Australia's longest strike, which lasted from May 1946 until August 1949. Aboriginal pastoral workers, claiming they were treated like slaves, demanded fair wages and better working conditions. Even after most of the demands were met, many did not return to the stations but pooled their meagre resources to set up cooperatives.

yield a huge banana crop and boatloads of prawns. The town was established in 1883, though Dutch explorer Willem de Vlamingh first landed nearby in 1697. Picturesque **Pelican Point** is good for swimming. **Miaboolya Beach** is worth a look, as is the **Bibbawarra artesian bore**, where water surface temperatures are 70°C (158°F).

Further north, a spectacular coastline unfolds, with blowholes, sheltered beaches and wild seascapes. The landlocked **Lake MacLeod** is famous for salt production. Inland, southwest of **Exmouth** is the **Cape Range National Park** ㉒, based along a rugged, dry limestone ridge. Boat trips through Yardie Creek Gorge are good, with predictable sightings of rock wallabies.

Offshore, **Ningaloo Reef** in its protected marine park stretches 260km (160 miles) from Amherst Point around North West Cape into the Exmouth Gulf. Western Australia's largest coral reef, with 250 species of coral and more than 500 fish types, Ningaloo is an unspoilt delight for divers. Coral outcrops can be reached just 20 metres (65ft) from the beach, though they extend 7km (12 miles) into the ocean. Dolphins, dugongs, manta rays, giant cod and sharks abound. Whale sharks visit the reef from March to June.

Coral Bay, 1,132km (703 miles) from Perth, is renowned for fishing and diving. Snorkelling tours go out from here or Exmouth.

The Pilbara

To the east of Exmouth lies the region called **The Pilbara**, focal point of the state's mineral wealth and one of the world's richest series of holes in the ground. Here, iron ore is king, and company towns seem to appear overnight amid the spinifex. Ore mined at such places as Tom Price and Mount Newman is freighted by rail systems to the coastline, where it is shipped off for national or overseas processing.

The northwest was first explored by the English pirate and explorer William Dampier in 1688 and 1699, so names based on *Buccaneer, Cygnet* and *Roebuck* (his vessels) litter the coast. The **Dampier Archipelago** includes **Barrow Island**, the centre for the North West Shelf oil and gas fields. Far from being an environmentally threatened area, it is classified as a wildlife sanctuary and has some unusual animal, bird and plant life.

Roebourne is the oldest town in the northwest, but in recent years its importance has waned because of the clout of the newly established mining towns. The ghost town of **Cossack** is a reminder of the one-time might of the local pearling industry (before it moved north to Broome and beyond), while a jaunt up the **Fortescue River** reveals the lush area around the Millstream, a bountiful supply of fresh water for many Pilbara towns. The **Millstream-Chichester National Park** is a fine outing for naturalists or hikers.

The magnificent **Karijini National Park** ㉓ (previously Hamersley Range National Park), with spectacular gorges and bluffs, can be reached from **Tom Price**. Karijini's visitor centre (daily, times vary seasonally; tel: 08-9189 8121)

BELOW: driving through the Outback in Pilbara.

is worth a look. Designed to withstand bushfires, the centre is shaped like a goanna (an animal sacred to the local Banyjima Aboriginal people) and contains information on the natural and cultural history of the area. Karratha, 40km (25 miles) from the port of Dampier, has been developed as the work base for the mighty Hamersley Iron concern.

For an indication of just how much ore might be coming out of the ground, take a look at the loading facilities at **Port Hedland ㉔**. This seaside town, which copes with more tonnage than any other port in Australia, is almost exclusively geared to handle the iron ore from the huge open-cut and strip mining centres of the Pilbara. Port Hedland is built on an island linked to the mainland by three long causeways. Visitors can view the loading from the wharves, where some of the world's largest ore carriers dock. The Port Hedland visitor centre offers daily tours of the BHP-Billiton Nelson Point and Port Authority workings, and half-day tours of Dampier Salt and BHP's Boodarie Iron.

Port Hedland has no shortage of drawbacks. Its tropical setting makes it prone to cyclones; its seas are considered unsafe for swimming, thanks to sharks and stonefish; and its industrial and mineral landscape might not be to everyone's liking. But the local fishing is excellent, there are nearby Aboriginal carvings, birdlife is abundant, and you can cool off in the town swimming pool or at Pretty Pool inlet.

To sample a real Western Australian Outback town, detour 193km (120 miles) southeast to **Marble Bar**. With a population of less than 400, it owes its existence to the discovery of gold in 1891 and 1931. The disused **Comet Gold Mine**, 10km (6 miles) south of town, has a museum and visitor centre.

Pearling centre

Coming from the south, along the vast monotony of the road between Port Hedland and Broome, the highway describes a gentle arc along a stretch of coastline known aptly as the **Eighty Mile Reach**.

During the 1920s, **Broome ㉕** was the capital of the world's pearling

The Outback town of Marble Bar is renowned as the hottest place in Australia. Daytime temperatures can regularly soar past 38°C (100°F), even in winter. In Dec–Jan, temperatures higher than 45°C (113°F) are common.

BELOW: hiking in Karijini National Park.

The church at Beagle Bay on the Dampier Peninsula has a unique mother-of-pearl altar.

industry, with more than 300 luggers (pearling vessels) competing for finds off the northwest coast of Australia. For the mostly Japanese divers, the real wealth lay in the mother-of-pearl shell, which was used in jewellery and for buttons; a pearl was an unexpected bonus. But it was a dangerous job, as the Japanese Cemetery testifies. Broome went into the doldrums when plastic buttons flooded the market after World War II. The recent development of cultured pearls has revitalised the industry (although the harvesting now occurs in remote aquatic farms), and several Broome jewellery shops, including one owned by the dominant pearling operator, Paspaley Pearls, sell fine pearls in a variety of settings. A stroll through the timber dwellings of Chinatown, with its multilingual street signs, provides an insight into what the town was like in the pearling days.

With a large Asian population, Broome has retained enough character to be one of Australia's most fascinating communities. Aboriginal culture thrives here, with an Aboriginal radio and TV station (Goolari, known as GTV), which broadcasts partly in local dialect. The town comes alive each August when fishermen, farmers, miners, drovers and tourists swell the population tenfold for the Shinju Matsuri – Festival of the Pearl.

Residents will point out such exotic attractions as the "Golden Staircase to the Moon", an optical illusion created when moonlight reflects on the ocean bed at low-water spring tides. At **Gantheaume Point**, when the tide is low, giant dinosaur tracks thought to be 130 million years old can be viewed.

The 22km (14-mile) **Cable Beach** was named after the underwater communication link between Broome and Java (and on to London), which was established in the 19th century. Today it is the core of Broome's tourist industry, with an up-market resort and crocodile farm complementing the glorious ocean beach. A ride on a camel train along the beach at sunset is a great experience.

Outback of the Outback

For Australians, the **Kimberley** region is the final frontier. About half the size of Texas but with only 26,000

The Dampier Peninsula

For those with a sense of adventure, a road trip from Broome to Cape Leveque traverses the whole Dampier Peninsula. Most people drive or fly straight through to Kooljaman Resort (www.kooljaman.com.au). But there are several Aboriginal communities who welcome visitors and offer accommodation and tours, and who are happy to share their knowledge about bush foods and medicines, traditional hunting and fishing techniques and their relationship with the land. Parts of the Cape Leveque Road are still unsealed, very sandy, and can be badly corrugated, so it is a good idea to hire a 4WD; the journey takes about two-and-a-half hours. Destinations include **Beagle Bay**. There is no accommodation but check out the famous Sacred Heart Church and its beautiful altar decorated with mother-of-pearl shell. **Middle Lagoon** (www.middlelagoon.com.au) offers great fishing, a lagoon safe for swimming, camping, beach shelters and self-contained log cabins. **Lombadina** (tel: 08-9192 4936) is another Aboriginal community further north. Their accommodation and tours are well established and their beach one of the most stunning. **One Arm Point** (tel: 08-9192 4932 and also known as Ardyaloon) is a few kilometres beyond Kooljaman. You can tour the aquaculture hatchery that is breeding juvenile trochus shells. When travelling across Aboriginal land, respect for the culture, privacy and people is paramount, so if you see a sign that says "no entry", abide by it.

inhabitants, encompassing ½-million-hectare (1.2-million-acre) cattle ranches and enormous Aboriginal tribal lands, it was first explored in the 1890s but has opened to travellers only over the past 20 years. The landscapes here are awe-inspiring, even by antipodean standards. The blood-red desert is sliced by lush, forest-filled gorges, where fresh-water crocodiles and stingrays swim; the coastline is torn by tropical fjords with tidal waterfalls that flow horizontally. Everything is on a gargantuan scale: vast meteor craters, petrified coral reefs and desert rivers that swell from 100 metres (330ft) wide in the dry season to 13km (8 miles) wide in the wet.

Generations of isolation have left the Kimberley region the most Aboriginal part of Australia, with some immense tracts of tribal land. Remote communities have their own language, newspapers and radio stations; Aboriginal guides work at the national parks and conduct tours of ancient cave paintings; and it has one of Australia's few Aboriginal-owned resorts (at Cape Leveque).

This independence was hard-won. White ranchers arrived here in the 1890s after the world's longest – and most gruelling – cattle drive across central Australia. Soon the Kimberley was the scene of a little-known Aboriginal uprising and of several massacres of indigenous peoples by settlers. Aboriginal bushrangers roamed the Kimberley, easily evading mounted police posses in the rugged terrain.

Derby ㉖, 216km (134 miles) along the highway northeast from Broome, is the administrative centre for the huge cattle-producing region of West Kimberley. Unlike bustling Broome, with a population of 10,000, Derby is a sleepy town where little seems to have changed over the decades. From here, sightseeing is mostly done by light plane: taking a flight from Derby over **King Sound** and the **Buccaneer Archipelago** ㉗ beyond will unfold one of the world's most spectacularly beautiful coastlines, a maze of islands, red cliffs and white beaches – uninhabited except for the mining communities of **Cockatoo Island** and **Koolan Islands**.

From Derby, you can either follow the main all-weather **Great Northern Highway** or turn off onto the

TIP

The only sensible time to visit the Kimberley, whose landscapes are hallucinatory even by antipodean standards, is Apr–Sept. At other times it is unbearably hot and humid, with a good chance of being isolated by flash floods.

BELOW:
sunset at
Cape Leveque.

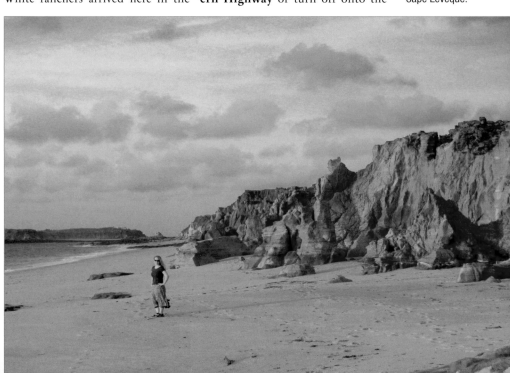

"Beef Road", which cuts through the heart of the Kimberley. Seven km (4¼ miles) outside Derby is a huge boab tree that is reputed to have been used as an overnight prison when transporting prisoners in colonial times. The boab (a close relation of the southern African baobab tree) is often known as the "bottle tree" and can have a circumference greater than its height – the girth frequently exceeds 10 metres (33ft).

Windjana Gorge National Park ㉘ (tel: 08-9191 1426), 145km (90 miles), to the east, is worth a visit for its eerie Windjana figures in Aboriginal rock paintings, and its huge flocks of spooky, screeching white cockatoos. **Tunnel Creek National Park** ㉙, 35km (22 miles) further on, allows you to walk through an underground stream course populated by bats. Only recently has this part of the Kimberley become accessible to people other than the toughest pioneers, cattlemen or prospectors. The roads are constantly being improved.

East of Derby, on the Fitzroy River near the township of Fitzroy Crossing,

is **Geikie Gorge** ㉚, 14km (9 miles) long, with limestone cliffs up to 30 metres (100ft) high. This is one of the most spectacular gorges in the northwest and a pleasant camping spot. Interesting tours conducted by Aboriginal rangers can be taken along the river, where freshwater crocodiles sunbake at the water's edge; down below, you can see sawfish and stingrays that have adapted to life in fresh water. On the eastern side lies **Fossil Downs**, a huge private cattle station (over 405,000 hectares/1 million acres), founded in 1886. It is the only Kimberley cattle station still owned by descendants of the original pioneers, the MacDonalds.

Regional centre

The Great Northern Highway cuts along the southern perimeter of the Kimberley before entering the new township of **Halls Creek** which, with its comfortable hotels and air-conditioned supermarkets, serves as a base for the regional pastoral industry. At Old Halls Creek, remnants of the 1884 gold rush can be seen. The rush made a few prospectors rich, but the harsh environment and shortage of water ruined a good many more.

South of Halls Creek, 130km (80 miles) away, is the meteorite crater at **Wolfe Creek** ❸, the second largest in the world – although it really comes into perspective when seen from the air.

The turn-off 110km (68 miles) north of Halls Creek leads to a 4WD track to one of the most astonishing natural features in the world: the **Bungle Bungle Range**. The Bungles cover some 640 sq km (247 sq miles) of the Ord River Valley with a labyrinth of orange and black (caused by the black lichen and orange silica) horizontally tiger-striped, domed mountains. Within the canyons and gorges of the **Purnululu National Park** ❷ are palm-filled grottoes, enormous caves and white-sand beaches. The rough track from the highway deters many, so a thriving industry has arisen in **Kununurra** to fly tourists over (and, more recently, into) the Bungle Bungles.

A true gem of the Kimberley lies to the north of Purnululu: **Argyle Diamond Mine** is the world's largest, extracting some 1,000kg (6.5 tons) of diamonds each year. The Argyle Diamond Pipe was discovered in 1979 and remains the only source of deep-pink diamonds. Air tours to the mine are available from Kununurra.

Wyndham ❸ is the most northerly port in Western Australia, a small scattered community that has changed little since the days of the gold rush. You can see large crocodiles lying on the mudflats below the Wyndham wharf. Cattle that miss their footing when being loaded onto ships provide an occasional meal.

The Ord River was dammed in 1971 to harness the monsoon runoff for irrigation; in recent years, this has opened up the East Kimberley to the cultivation of tropical crops. To the south, Lake Argyle in the **Carr Boyd Range** is the main reservoir (boat tours are available). The damming of the Ord River would have submerged **Argyle Downs Homestead**, home of one of the northwest's great pioneering families, the Duracks, so it was moved to a new location to escape the rising waters. It is now a museum about life for the early settlers of the Kimberley. ❏

The Kimberley is such an isolated region that the extraordinary "Bungles" were unknown to all but a few locals until 1983, when a photographer came upon them by chance.

BELOW:
a dry river bed in Bungle Bungle National Park.

RESTAURANTS AND BARS

Restaurants

Prices for a three-course dinner per person with a half-bottle of house wine:
$ = under A$50
$$ = A$50–80
$$$ = A$80–120
$$$$ = over A$120

Perth

Fraser's Restaurant
Fraser Avenue
Tel: 08-9481 7100
www.frasersrestaurant.com.au
Open: B, L & D daily. **$$$**
Top-quality local produce is used abundantly, from roast kangaroo loin with potato and celeriac crumble, beetroot and caramelised onion, to chargrilled WA rock lobster with spicy tomato sauce. The restaurant is situated in Kings Park.

Matilda Bay Restaurant
3 Hackett Drive, Crawley
Tel: 08-9423 5000
www.matbay.com.au
Open: B Sun, L & D daily. **$$$**
Situated on the banks of the Swan at Matilda Bay, this restaurant is popular for its beautiful views. The menu has rotisserie items, fresh crayfish, plus favourites such as char-grilled sirloin and rack of lamb.

C Restaurant Lounge
St Martin's Tower, level 33,
44 St George's Terrace
Tel: 08-9220 8333
www.crestaurant.com.au
Open: L & D, every day except Sat, D only, until late every night. **$$$$**
Located on the 33rd storey of one of the city's office buildings, this revolving restaurant offers superb views. The modern-Australian food is also excellent.

Jackson's
483 Beaufort Street,
Highgate
Tel: 08-9328 1177
www.jacksonsrestaurant.com.au
Open: D Mon–Sat. **$$$$**
One of Perth's top places to dine. Expect interesting combinations, such as apple risotto with grilled chorizo and scallops.

Lamont's
11 Brown Street
Tel: 08-9202 1566
www.lamonts.com.au
Open: B Sat and Sun, L Tue–Sun, D Wed–Sat. **$$$$**
Kate Lamont is one of Perth's best-loved foodies, and her riverside East Perth property has become a local institution. Showcases the best in local produce.

Indiana Cottesloe Beach
99 Marine Parade, Cottesloe
Tel: 08-9385 5005
www.indiana.com.au
Open: L & D daily. **$$$**
This majestic building sits perched above the sands at Cottesloe Beach. The style is colonial, but the food ranges from pasta to sushi. Get an ocean-side table and watch the sunset.

The Southwest

Albany Area

Maleeya's Thai Café
1376 Porongurup Road,
Porongurup
Tel: 08-9853 1123
Open: L & D Fri–Sun.
$$–$$$
One of the best dining options in the southwest. The food is fresh and fantastic. Many of the organic vegetables and herbs are grown in the gardens. Booking is essential.

Bunbury

Vat 2
2 Jetty Road, Bunbury
Tel: 08-9791 8833
www.vat2.com.au
Open: B, L & D daily. **$$$**
Located near the water in the Marlston Hill development, Vat 2 caters for those looking for a light snack (chicken salad with prosciutto, for example) or a more substantial meal (grilled meats and pastas).

Bunker Bay

Other Side of the Moon
Bunker Bay Road
Tel: 08-9756 9100
Open: B, L & D daily. **$$$$**
Located in the up-market Bunker Bay resort, with views over olive trees and the pool to the ocean. The food is Modern Australian and uses the best and freshest local produce, such as Pemberton marron and lamb. The desserts are divine.

Busselton and Vasse

The Old Post Office Tearooms
4 Queen Street, Busselton
Tel: 0458 224 661
Open: Tue–Sun 10am–4pm.
$$
Situated in a heritage building that was Busselton's old courthouse, jail and post office (now an arts precinct), this hidden gem serves home-made morning and afternoon

LEFT: lobster tail is perfectly paired with a crisp white.

tea, light lunches and high tea.

Bay Organics
63 Duchess Sreet, Busselton
Tel: 08-9751 1315
Open: B & L Mon–Sat. **$**
Bay Organics is a little cottage-like café selling delicious healthy food. The lentil burger is outstanding, as are the salads. The owners grow all the vegetables and herbs organically, and there is also a small organic grocery store inside. Worth a visit even if you're not into healthy food.

The Goose
Geographe Bay Road, Busselton
Tel: 08-9754 7700
www.thegoose.com.au
Open: B, L & D daily. **$$$**
Overlooking the ocean, right next to the Busselton Jetty, The Goose is a light and airy restaurant serving quality food. The modern menu changes regularly. Sample dishes include nasi goreng and seared tuna steaks. Gorgeous views whatever the weather.

Margaret River Region
Cape Lavender
Lot 4 Carter Road, Metricup
Tel: 08-9755 7552
www.capelavender.com.au
Open: L daily. **$$$**
The Cape Lavender restaurant has won several Gold Plate awards for its food. The menu includes items such as individual tarts filled with spinach, roast pumpkin, capsicum and feta topped with a rocket and olive salad, as well as more substantial meals. The farm also grows lavender, which is made into a variety of products, including lavender scones and lavender sparkling wine.

Lamont's
Gunyulgup Valley Drive, Yallingup

Tel: 08-9755 2434
www.lamonts.com.au
Open: B & L daily, D Sat.
$$$$
The elegant food at Lamont's is matched by the wonderful setting – perched over a lake in the middle of the bush. The menu includes sugar-cured Margaret River venison, black pepper shortbread and tapenade, and Pemberton marron, roasted baby potatoes, green veg, lime and chive *beurre blanc*.

Wino's
85 Bussell Highway, Margaret River
Tel: 08-9758 7155
Open: L Sat, Sun, D daily.
$$$
Located in the heart of Margaret River, Wino's is a chilled restaurant serving excellent food. The dark wood floors and the extensive tapas menu are European in character. There is an extensive wine selection, as you would expect.

Vasse Felix
Corner Caves and Harman's South roads, Yallingup
Tel: 08-9755 5425
www.vassefelix.com.au
Open: L daily. **$$$**
Vasse Felix is a top winery, and this is a top restaurant serving high-quality modern Australian food. The timber and stone building is a great place to sit and relax while you look out over the vineyards.

Walpole & Nornalup
Nornalup Teahouse Restaurant
South Coast Highway, Nornalup
Tel: 08-9840 1422
www.nornalupteahouse.com.au
Open: B, L & D Wed–Mon.
$$$
This beautifully converted cottage has an idyllic setting. The food is also

excellent. Call ahead because the opening times change from time to time, and booking on popular nights is highly recommended. Nornalup Teahouse is Perth's hidden treasure.

East

Kalgoorlie
Saltimbocca
90 Egan Sreet, Kalgoorlie
Tel: 08-9022 8028
Open: L Wed–Fri, D Mon–Sat. **$$$**
The house speciality here is the veal saltimbocca, in a creamy prosciutto, sage and white wine sauce. The restaurant is also known for its home-made pastas.

York
Imperial Hotel
83 Avon Terrace
Tel: 08-9641 1255
www.imperialhotelyork.com.au
Open: L, D Thur–Sun, B Sat–Sun. **$$$**
Dine in this beautifully restored 1800s pubs' which serves French cuisine such as smoked salmon served on home-made crumpets with beetroot relish and a horseradish chantilly, or order simple fish and chips from the bar.

The Ragged Robin
27 South Street, York
Tel: 08-9641 1266
www.raggedrobin.com.au
Open: L Sun, D Thur–Sat.
$$$
A relaxed and intimate fine-dining experience in a heritage-listed building. A typical dish is seared scallops on braised pork belly with pineapple and cauliflower purée.

North

Geraldton
Skeeta's Restaurant and Café
101 Foreshore Drive
Tel: 08-9964 1619
Open: B, L & D daily. **$$$**

Specialises in seafood, but they cater for non-fish eaters too, with pasta, steak and chicken dishes. The whiting fillets served with crispy gourmet potatoes and salad are a favourite, as is the seafood platter for two.

Kalbarri
Restaurant Upstairs
Porter Street, Kalbarri
Tel: 08-9937 1033
Open: B, L & D daily. **$**
The food and ambience are great, with a beautiful view of the river mouth and ocean. The interior is fresh and modern, with changing artworks from all around Australia.

Echo Beach
Porter Street, Kalbarri
Tel: 08-9937 1033
Open: B, L & D daily. **$**
The food and ambience are great, whether you want a simple coffee for a morning wake-up or a proper meal. The interior is fresh and modern.

Black Rock Café
80 Grey Street
Tel: 08-9937 1062
www.blackrockcafe.com.au
Open: B & L Tue–Sun, D Tue–Sat. **$$$**
The menu at Black Rock ranges from strawberry pancakes at breakfast to surf-and-turf dinners, potato rosti and salad. The view of the Murchison River as it meets the Indian Ocean is lovely.

The Grass Tree Café and Restaurant
94–96 Grey Street
Tel: 08-9937 2288
Open: B, L & D Thur–Tue.
$$$$
With its sweeping ocean views, the Grass Tree brings a touch of sophistication to this relaxed town. The food is part Asian and part European; the signature dish is shelled crayfish in creamy whisky sauce.

WILDFLOWERS OF WESTERN AUSTRALIA

In spring, the bush is ablaze with wild flowers, from bold and brilliant banksias to delicate ice daisies

Western Australia is known for its beautiful wild flowers. People travel from all around the country – and the world – to view the impressive display. The flowering is most spectacular during spring (August through to November), though at almost any time of year you will find some flowers brightening the olive- and sage-greens of the bush. Banksias, for example, often bloom in autumn or winter.

It might seem strange that such a dry landscape should produce so many wild flowers; there are various reasons for this success. For millions of years western Australia has avoided the sort of landmass upheaval that has caused species in other parts of the continent to die out. The flowers have also benefited from the lack of shade-casting trees and have enjoyed the protection of less engulfing plants and shrubs.

The state has some 10,000 species of wild flowers, 6,000 of which are native. Some areas are particularly well endowed: Kalbarri National Park, the karri forests around Pemberton, and the Stirling Ranges north of Albany. The southwest is known for its delicate flowers such as orchid, kangaroo paw and mountain bell.

Closer to Perth, John Forrest National Park is another rich area, or you could simply visit Kings Park Botanic Garden. We recommend you pack a picnic and a camera and take your time enjoying the rich palette of the blooms. The Western Australian Visitor Centre in Perth has maps to ensure you make the most of the wild-flower season.

ABOVE: a roadside display near Kalbarri in spring. If you have a speci interest in wild flowers it is worth taking an escorted wild-flower tour an option offered by most of the day-tour operators in Perth.

ABOVE: Albany bottlebrush. Bottlebrush is more commonly associated with the eastern states (it was one of the plants the naturalist Joseph Banks collected on Cook's voyage of 1770), but you will also find it in WA, especially in damp habitats.

BELOW: in spring, daisies of many types and colours carpet forest clearings, heathlands and fields.

GRASS TREES

Even if you are not in Western Australia during the wildflower season, the bush is a fascinating landscape with a rich biodiversity that is at last being championed by conservationists after well over a century of indiscriminate land clearance for agriculture.

Among the many types of eucalyptus (gumtrees), paper bark and banksias, the tree that perhaps stands out above all others is the grass tree *(Xanthorrhoea)*, with its distinctive fire-blackened trunk surmounted by a mop of spiky grass and spear-like flower shaft.

Grass trees are very slow-growing (about 1 metre/3ft every 100 years) but can live for hundreds of years, and their ability to survive in tough conditions has made them a symbol of the Australian Outback. Like many other bush plants, they have evolved to withstand bushfires; germination is actually assisted by fire. The distinctive flower shaft will often shoot up in the year following a bushfire, providing valuable food for wildlife in an otherwise charred, barren landscape. In contrast to the slow-growing trunk, the flowering stalk grows rapidly after germination, at a rate of 2–3cm (1 inch) a day.

The Grass trees are known as balga (black boys) to the Aborigines, who traditionally used a waterproof resin produced from the base of the plant to make glue. The shafts could also be used as spear heads, and the dried flower shafts could be rubbed together to create fire. The tender shoots could be eaten, and the nectar from the flowers of the plant was used to make a sweet drink. Today the Grass trees are prized by horticulturalists – plants saved from the developers' bulldozers can, with great skill and care, be transplanted and coaxed into life.

RIGHT: succulents, such as these in a forest near Karridale, also flourish in the south. Succulents survive in hot, arid areas. Their characteristic fleshy leaves, stems and roots store water and their compact shape reduces dehydration. The best-known type of succulent is the cactus, but there are many other forms.

LEFT: Banksias have large cone-shaped flowers comprising hundreds of tiny individual flowers. The temperate southwest corner of WA supports some 60 different species, many of which flower in winter. Banksias are named after Joseph Banks, Captain Cook's botanist, and were celebrated in the *Snugglepot and Cuddlepie* book and bushbaby drawings of the children's author and illustrator May Gibbs (1877–1969).

TASMANIA

Australia's smallest and remotest state is also the most temperate. It has no arid Outback, but there's an abundance of cool forests, rugged mountains, highland lakes, lush pasture and fruitful orchards

"How beautiful is the whole region, for form, and grouping, and opulence, and freshness of foliage, and variety of color, and grace and shapeliness of the hills, the capes, the promontories; and then, the splendor of the sunlight, the dim rich distances, the charm of the water-glimpses!" Such was the view of inveterate traveller Mark Twain, commenting on his voyage to Tasmania in the 1890s.

However, he then went on to point out the irony behind this observation: "And it was in this paradise that the yellow-liveried convicts were landed, and the Corps-bandits quartered, and the wanton slaughter of the kangaroo-chasing black innocents consummated on that autumn day in May, in the brutish old time. It was all out of keeping with the place, a sort of bringing of heaven and hell together."

This is the paradox of Tasmania, nowhere more so than at the Port Arthur Penal Settlement, the most popular of the state's myriad tourist attractions. It sits in a jaw-droppingly gorgeous setting: an amphitheatre of rolling green meadow leading down to the tranquil blue waters of Mason Cove, dotted with picturesque sandstone ruins glowing golden yellow in the watery sunlight. Even without the sun, there is something magisterial and uplifting about the setting. Yet this must be reconciled with its original role as a setting for a prison regime, which was considered by many to be the harshest in the British Empire.

Van Diemen's Land

That was in the days when the island was called Van Diemen's Land (after being so named by Abel Tasman in 1642) and when British colonists were establishing their second toehold on the Australian continent. It was a struggle to tame the inhospitable land

Main attractions
HOBART
RICHMOND
PORT ARTHUR
FREYCINET NATIONAL PARK
BAY OF FIRES
LAUNCESTON
THE TAMAR VALLEY
ROSS
BRUNY ISLAND
THE STYX VALLEY
QUEENSTOWN
STRAHAN
CRADLE MOUNTAIN
STANLEY
FLINDERS ISLAND

PRECEDING PAGES: a Tasmanian beach.
LEFT: the bridge at Richmond.
RIGHT: the blowhole at Bicheno.

The Salamanca Market is the perfect place to browse for used books.

BELOW: colourful squares.

and establish viable agriculture. Today there are still vast stretches of Tasmania that are only accessible by tough walking tracks. Even in populated regions, there is a sense of space. It's to be expected in an island the size of Ireland but with an eighth of the latter's 4 million people.

Tasmania's appeal resides in the range and beauty of its landscapes and natural features, from the lakes and mountains of the central highlands, culminating in the iconic Cradle Mountain, to the deserted beaches of the east coast where the aquamarine of the sea is offset by the vibrant orange lichen on the rocks. And if this isn't enough, try the islands in the Bass Strait where, such is the sparseness of the population, every motorist acknowledges every other.

Few venture to such far-flung outposts on their first visit, though. There are no international flights to Tasmania and just the odd cruise ship, so most visitors come via the mainland, either on the *Spirit of Tasmania* ferries from Melbourne to Devonport or by air into Hobart or Launceston.

Hobart

If you follow Twain's lead and make **Hobart ❶** your first port of call, you'll find a small, distinguished city nestling between the waters of the Derwent and the brooding bulk of Mount Wellington. These features have prevented the urban sprawl that affects many mainland cities, while a spell in the economic doldrums in the 1960s and 1970s meant that much of the old colonial architecture was spared from development. Today there are numerous well-preserved Georgian and Victorian buildings to give character and a nod back to old England.

Hobart's waterfront is a magnet. There are the classic views across to Mount Wellington and plenty of remnants of the thriving 19th-century port. At **Victoria Dock Ⓐ**, the beautifully restored **IXL Jam Factory** is on the site of the first wharf and now contains the remarkable, award-winning **Henry Jones Art Hotel**, and the University of Tasmania's **Centre for the Arts**.

Visit both, then wander across to the adjoining **Constitution Dock**. Consider fish and chips from one of the floating stalls, then head to **Salamanca Place** . This is the site of a pulsating Saturday-morning market, but even without that, the old stone warehouses are atmospheric and appealing. They house a lively arts centre as well as the usual selection of galleries, bars and cafés. Behind them is the pedestrianised **Salamanca Square**, a modern development that successfully latches on to the original buildings.

East along Salamanca Place, turn up Kelly's Steps to the eyrie of **Battery Point** , where a pristine collection of the city's earliest dwellings is to be found. At its centre is Arthur's Circus, doing a fine impression of a village green, while Hampden Road's range of eateries includes the peerless **Jackman & McRoss** bakery/café. The **Narryna Heritage Museum** (Tue–Fri and Mon in summer 10.30am–5pm, Sat–Sun 2–5pm, 12.30–5pm summer; tel: 03-6234 2791; charge) preserves a merchant's house in Victorian splendour.

Westwards along Salamanca Place brings you to the administrative centre of the state. The discreet sandstone-clad modernism of the **Supreme Court** on the left is balanced by the more conventional Victorian bulk of **Parliament House** on the right (tours when houses not sitting; Mon–Fri or daily 10am and 2pm; tel: 03-6233 2200; www.parliament.tas.gov.au; free).

Macquarie Street

A block further back, Macquarie Street has **St David's Cathedral** – the Georgian-style seat of the local Anglican bishop; the **Treasury Building** facing onto the formal gardens of Franklin Square; the **General Post Office**, built with the grandeur that characterises these buildings; the **Town Hall** ; the Art Deco sleekness of the **Mercury Newspaper Building**; and the **Tasmanian Museum and Art Gallery** (daily 10am–5pm; tel: 03-6211 4177; www.tmag.tas.gov.au; free).

The museum is a repository for colonial and contemporary art, local fauna, a collection of Chinese antiquities, and material illustrating early polar exploration. The **Maritime Museum of Tasmania** (daily 9am–5pm; tel: 03-6234 1427; www.maritimetas.org; charge) is small but worthwhile.

The Maritime Museum of Tasmania displays items from the seafaring history of Tasmania.

BELOW: Sir John Franklin's statue in Franklin Square.

An African figure made from beads at the Museum of Antiquities, part of Moorilla Estate Winery.

Another block back from the water, the main downtown shopping area centres on **Elizabeth Street Mall G**.

North, beyond the mass of the Royal Hobart Hospital, the old **Theatre Royal H** on Campbell Street is a blushing star. Its plush auditorium can usually be inspected if you employ a touch of charm at the box office, and it is well worth a look to appreciate the set-builder's art. The auditorium was completely rebuilt in 1984 after a fire.

A few blocks up Campbell Street the **Penitentiary Chapel and Criminal Courts I** (tours daily 10am, 11.30am, 1pm, 2.30pm; ghost tour 8.30pm; tel: 03-6231 0911; www.penitentiarychapel. com; charge) are all that remain of the original vast Hobart Gaol. Splendid tours are run by knowledgeable National Trust volunteers.

The Queens Domain

If you head northeast and can manage to cross some busy highways, **Queens Domain** has, since the early days, been a place of recreation, remembrance and, for the occupant of Government House, residence. The **Cenotaph J**

is flanked by a couple of interesting modern glass and stone pyramids that incorporate audio tributes to those lost in combat. The **Royal Botanical Gardens K** were established in 1828 and are faithful to the early vision of the founders by collecting every conceivable variety of flora.

North Hobart has a plethora of cosmopolitan bars, restaurants and entertainment venues. Further north still, **Runnymede** in New Town is an early 1830s homestead maintained by the National Trust (61 Bay Road, New Town; daily Aug–June 10am–4.30pm; tel: 03-6278 1269; charge) and worth a stop on the way to the **Moorilla Estate**. This winery not only claims one of Tasmania's leading restaurants but also houses arguably the most significant addition to Tasmania's cultural infrastructure in years: the **Museum of Old and New Art**. MONA (Main Road, Berriedale; daily 9am–4pm; tel: 03-6277 9900; www.mona.net.au; free) was built from scratch by entrepreneur David Walsh to house a wide-ranging and esoteric collection ranging from historical artefacts from the great civilisations through to challenging modern work, all loosely linked by the concept of sex and death as the driving forces of creativity. Its dramatic galleries opened at the beginning of 2011.

Kids can go wild in the suburb of Claremont, either at the eccentric **Alpenrail Swiss Model Village and Railway** (82 Abbotsfield Rd, West Claremont; daily 9.30am–4.30pm; tel: 03-6249 3748; charge), or at the **Cadbury Chocolate Factory** (Mon–Fri Sept–May 8am–4pm, June–Aug 9am–3pm; tel: 1800 627 367; charge). In the latter, the visitor-centre experience is a poor substitute for the now discontinued factory tours.

West of the city centre, Mount Wellington provides superb views of the city; make sure that you visit the **Cascade Brewery** (Cascade Road, South Hobart; daily, times vary; bookings essential; tel: 03-6224 1117; www.cascadebreweryco.com.au; charge). Relish the picturesque setting, a choice of tours, and the opportunity to drink your way through the sampling room. The brewery is also the starting point

for *Louisa's Walk*, a promenade through the **Female Factory** in which professional actors enact a gripping chapter in history (daily 2pm; booking essential; tel: 03-6238 4222; www.livehistory hobart.com.au; charge). You can visit the site on your own, too.

On the other side of the Derwent, the suburb of **Bellerive** fans out from **Kangaroo Bluff Battery**, an emplacement designed to guard the city from attack. The **Tasmanian Cricket Museum** (Tue–Thur, 10am–3pm, Fri 10am–noon; tel: 03-6282 0433) is located at **Bellerive Oval**, where state and international cricket is played in a village-green atmosphere.

Leaving Hobart via the **Tasman Bridge** is the first step towards the Tasman Peninsula, where so much colonial history was forged.

Richmond

The direct route goes across Sorell Causeway, but that would be to neglect the wonderful colonial township of **Richmond ❷**. It sits in the Coal River Valley, its convict-built stone bridge offset by the English village-style church

TIP

A joint venture between various agencies has seen the publication of a free booklet, *Great Short Walks*, which outlines 60 treks in some of the most beautiful areas in the state. There are information boards at the start of each route co-ordinated with the design of the booklet.

BELOW:
combining cricket and sunbathing.

Fishermen can often be seen unloading their catches at harbours all along the east coast.

on the hill beyond. This is the kind of setting that led Mark Twain to observe that "wherever the exiled Englishman can find in his new home resemblances to his old one, he is touched to the marrow of his being; the love that is in his heart inspires his imagination, and these allied forces transfigure those resemblances into authentic duplicates of the revered originals." Most of the town was built between 1824 and 1840, and it is the consistency in style that gives Richmond its charm. There's the obligatory gaol for this staging post on the Hobart to Port Arthur road, as well as a couple of churches. More recent attractions include a maze and the **Old Hobart Town Model Village** (21 Bridge Street; daily 9am–5pm; tel: 03-6260 2502; charge).

Pass through Sorell and pause, if you must, at the Colonial and Convict Collection (self-proclaimed as junk) at **Copping** before continuing to **Eaglehawk Neck**. This isthmus to the Tasman Peninsula is where the infamous Dog Line was set. A team of ferocious fidos was chained to a row of posts so that no convict could cross without

coming into range of at least one of them. See the fearsome statue.

There are gentler attractions nearby. The **Tesselated Pavement** suggests that nature has tiled the shoreline, while across the isthmus the **Tasman Arch** and **Devil's Kitchen** are popular stops on the bus tours to Port Arthur.

The **Tasmanian Devil Park** (daily 9am–5pm, later in summer; tel: 03-6250 3230; www.tasmaniandevilpark.com; charge) at Taranna is an optional stop before the main attraction: the **Port Arthur Penal Settlement ❸** (daily 8.30am–dusk; tel: 03-1800 659 101; www.portarthur.org.au; charge). *See page 324.*

Don't miss the **Coal Mines Historic Site.** Convicts provided the labour, and the ruins reveal grim evidence of their travails (daily 24 hours; free).

The East Coast

The Tasman Highway runs up the east coast, arriving first at the sleepy resort of **Orford.** Continue to Triabunna where ferries depart for **Maria Island ❹** (4 sailings daily, call for times; tel: 03-6234 2999; www.mariaislandferry.com.au). Originally a penal settlement, it

Tasmania

is now a national park and a haven for wildlife and walkers. No traffic is permitted unless you take a bicycle; the only accommodation is in unpowered bunkhouses in the settlement at **Darlington**. Natural wonders abound – **Fossil Cliffs** and the **Painted Cliffs** amongst them. Up the coast the old **Spiky Bridge** and pristine **Spiky Beach** are untrumpeted gems.

Swansea is a low-key resort with lovely views across Great Oyster Bay to the pink granite peaks of the Hazards on the **Freycinet Peninsula**, another of Tasmania's big tickets. It's quite a long drive to get there, but the rewards are worth it. First stop is **Coles Bay ❺**, the service and accommodation centre that happens to have some rather fabulous beaches. However, the main attraction is **Freycinet National Park ❻** (daily Nov–Apr 8am–5pm, May–Oct 9am–4pm; tel: 03-6256 7000; www.parks.tas.gov.au) and its headline act, **Wineglass Bay** (see panel below).

Bicheno, to the north, is a family resort with a pretty fishing boat shelter, the Gulch, and a big blowhole (picture on page 317). The **Douglas-Apsley**

National Park has a natural water hole and is a popular picnic spot.

The northeast

After a handful of other beach resorts, you wind round into **St Helens** on sheltered George's Bay. With a population around the 2,000 mark, it is the largest town on the east coast. It's a nice enough place, but better to follow the road out to **Binalong Bay** at the southern end of one of the world's great coastal stretches, the **Bay of Fires ❼**. It consists of 30km (19 miles) of some of the finest beach in the world and much of it is inaccessible by road. There are four-day guided walks which include a couple of nights at a stunning modern lodge, but otherwise you have to fend for yourself. Northern access is via the **Mount William National Park**, where the lighthouse at **Eddystone Point** marks the top of the bay.

The road inland from St Helens climbs steeply into tin country. A turn off to **Pyengana** reveals a cheese factory, the **Pub in the Paddock** where a pair of beer-drinking pigs dwell, and the less contrived appeal of

George's Bay has plenty of variety on offer for anglers. Estuary and bay fishing offers bream, salmon, flathead and trevally; deep-sea fishing adds trevalla, gemfish, blue grenadier and others; offshore reef options include stripey trumpeter, cod, perch and squid.

LEFT: the perfect shape of Wineglass Bay.

Freycinet National Park

There are few places in the world where the elements of landscape combine so winningly as at Freycinet National Park. The mix of mountains, forest, beaches and achingly blue sea, not to mention the abundant wildlife, is hard to match and impossible to beat. It's best just to surrender to it and allow as much time as possible to take it all in. And the best way to see it is to get out there and walk.

The most popular trek is the fairly stiff climb up to the saddle between two of the Hazards: Mount Amos and Mount Mayson. This houses the **Wineglass Bay** lookout. Even for regulars, the view down can take you by surprise; there's the faultless symmetry of the curve that gives the bay its name and, if you're lucky and the sun's out, the searing azure of the sea. For the first-time visitor, it is just breathtaking. It is not unusual to find groups of people settled on the benches or clumped on nearby rocks, gazing down in silence, lost in contemplation. (Or getting their breath back.) Some turn back now, while others scramble down to the beach, perhaps as part of a longer hike which could take in **Mount Graham** or **Mount Freycinet**, or to return via **Hazards Beach**. There are several shorter walks too, at **Cape Tourville**, **Sleepy Bay** or **Little Gravelly Beach**, for instance. Pick up a map at the visitor centre just inside the park.

The Gulag Peninsula

As the most fearsome prison of the Antipodes, Port Arthur's natural isolation made it the perfect site for the worst criminals

Port Arthur was designed from scratch to be the ultimate prison. Establishments in Hobart, Sarah Island and Maria Island predate it but all had their problems. The new place had to be secure and remote enough to make escape difficult, if not impossible, but it was also to employ the "enlightened" punishment regime favoured at the time.

In this setting, 110km (68 miles) from Hobart, security was not a problem; if the convicts escaped, the dog line at Eaglehawk Neck would stop them. The rumour that sharks patrolled the sea didn't exactly encourage a swim to freedom either.

With a population of prisoners, soldiers and settlers many Kilometres from anywhere, this was not just a prison but a penal settlement – and a settlement on an industrial scale. These convicts weren't basket-weaving but shipbuilding and timber felling; they were grappling with agriculture and animal husbandry. A thriving village grew up around the prison, with farms, shops and Australia's first railway system (pulled by convicts instead of mules). The population needed to be self-sufficient; for this to happen there had to be organisation and a firm grasp of logistics.

As tourists visit today, it could be argued that little has changed. Visitors have to be managed through the site, but it's all done with subtlety and style. On buying your ticket you are allocated a time for a boat cruise and another for the guided tour, ensuring that the constant flow of visitors is fed through as comfortably as possible. The quieter times are first thing in the morning before the bus tours arrive from Hobart, and mid-afternoon onwards when most of them have departed.

You are also given a playing card to use in the Lottery of Life exhibition that leads out to the main site. Each card corresponds to an inmate whose history you follow through the display. You may have been transported for stealing bread but worked your way through the system to win the prized ticket of leave. Or you may be a recidivist who meets a sticky end.

After this and the guided tour you can start exploring. The best-known building in Port Arthur is the long, squat sandstone **Penitentiary**, a former flour mill converted in 1848 into a 136-cell prison for the worst offenders, although they were allowed out during the day to work. Two bushfires in the late 1890s gutted this and other edifices.

Take a stroll up the path to the left to the **Commandant's House**, with an extraordinary view over the bay and the site. It was one of the few wooden houses to survive the flames.

The path from the bay runs past the ruined hospital to the **Separate Prison** – built in the 1850s on a radical concept of punishment being developed in Britain. Instead of physical pain, prisoners were subjected to total sensory deprivation: kept in tiny cells for 23 hours a day, they were not allowed to talk or interact with others. Not surprisingly, the treatment led to more derangement than rehabilitation; Port Arthur was used as a mental asylum in later years.

Harbour cruises run out around the **Isle of the Dead** and **Point Puer Boys' Prison**, and twice a day you can land on the former, which became the cemetery for the prison colony. A lone convict once lived on the island to dig the graves.

On the way back to the visitor centre, the shell of the Broad Arrow Café is part of a **Memorial Garden** to the victims of a gunman who massacred 35 people in and around the site in April 1996. Visitors should not broach the subject with staff. ❑

LEFT: many of the buildings were destroyed by bushfires which ravaged Port Arthur in 1897.

St Columba's Falls. Further inland, **Derby** has its gleaming **Tin Centre** (daily 9.30am–4.30pm; tel: 03-6354 1062; www.trailofthetindragon.com; charge) to provide a glimpse back to the days when the area's prosperity lay beneath the ground.

Scottsdale is notable for the architecturally adventurous **Forest EcoCentre** (daily 9am–5pm, 9am–3pm winter; tel: 03-6352 6466; free), where Forestry Tasmania uses the exhibition space to promote sustainable forestry. The road north runs to **Bridport** ❽ with its mix of holiday shacks and a tired resort playing host to fans of fishing and beaches. The acclaimed new **Barnbougle Dunes Golf Links** is a short distance out of town and is bringing in a new breed of pleasure seekers.

Purple people head to **Bridestowe Estate Lavender Farm** (daily Nov–Apr 9am–5pm, May–Oct 10am–4pm; tel: 03-6352 8182; free except Dec–Jan), a blanket of colour in December and January just before the crop is harvested. **Lilydale**, on the road winding down towards Launceston, has an attractive main street notable for historic **Barden-**

hagen's General Store, and the imaginative paint jobs that have been applied to the town's power poles.

Launceston

Tasmania's second city has undergone a revival in recent years due, to some extent, to the advent of cheaper air fares from the mainland and also to some shrewd investments in tourist infrastructure. Of particular note has been the development of the old railway workshops at Inveresk, especially the new site operated by the **Queen Victoria Museum and Art Gallery** (daily 10am–5pm; tel: 03-6323 3777; www.qvmag.tas.gov.au; free). This impressive complex combines art galleries with museum space marking the industrial history of the area. The Blacksmith Shop, complete with deafening soundscape, gives an impression of the labours of the past.

Launceston ❾ has more than its share of distinguished Victorian architecture on its undulating streets, and much pleasure comes from simply walking around the city centre. Indeed, Cameron Street, with its red-brick

Artist at work in the Blacksmith Shop of the Queen Victoria Museum and Art Gallery.

BELOW: Cameron Street, a typically well-preserved area of Launceston.

Cataract Gorge is one of Tasmania's premier attractions.

BELOW: vintage motorcycles at the National Automobile Museum of Tasmania.

terraces replete with filigree ironwork, must be one of the best-preserved streets of the era in Australia. It leads off **Civic Square**, which gathers up the grandiose **Town Hall**, the **Library** and the simple **Macquarie House**, a stone warehouse from 1830.

The main shopping area radiates out from **Brisbane Street Mall** and includes graceful **Quadrant Mall** and hapless modern construct, **Yorktown Square**. The **Old Umbrella Shop** (Mon–Fri 9am–5pm, Sat 9am–noon; free) in George Street has remained unchanged for the best part of a century and is now run by the National Trust.

To the east of the centre **City Park** is laid out Victorian style with original fountains, rotundas and a conservatory. A monkey enclosure contains macaques that have been exciting local children for years. Other highlights around the city include the original **Queen Victoria Museum**, reopened in 2011 after major renovations (daily 10am–5pm; tel: 03-6323 3777; www.qvmag.tas.gov.au; free), the **Design Centre of Tasmania** (Mon–Fri 9.30am–5.30pm, Sat–Sun 10am–2pm; tel: 03-6331 5506; www.

designcentre.com.au; charge), the **National Automobile Museum of Tasmania** (Sept–May 9am–5pm, June–Aug 10am–4pm; tel: 03-6334 8888; qwww.namt.com.au; charge) and **Boag's Brewery** (Mon–Fri 8.45am–4.30pm, Sat 10am–4pm; tour times vary; tel: 03-6332 6300; www.boags.com.au; free), where enthusiasts can take a tour and drink beer.

The river front has enjoyed a revival with **Seaport**'s hotel, restaurants and bars making the most of the setting, and a boardwalk eastwards runs past **Ritchies Mill**, home to **Stillwater**, one of several outstanding city eateries.

Few cities have such a remarkable phenomenon as **Cataract Gorge** within walking distance of the centre. Paths run along its steep walls – the southern one tough, the northern one easy. If walking is out, then pleasure boats sail part of the way up the South Esk River. Walkers can go all the way to the **Cliff Grounds** area where the gorge opens out into a basin, with gardens and a rotunda on one side, and grassy banks and an open-air swimming pool on the other. A chairlift and suspension bridge link the two sides.

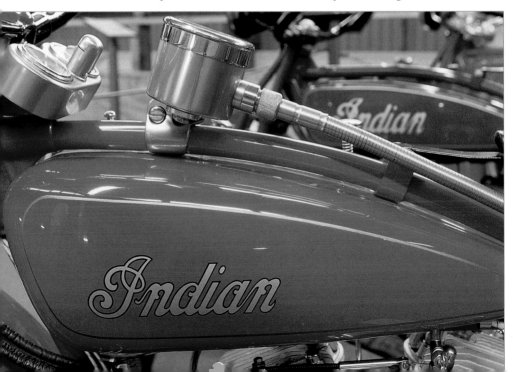

The Tamar Valley

Launceston's playground lies to the north in the **Tamar Valley**, an area best known for its vineyards. Although there is an officially sanctioned **Tamar Valley Wine Route**, with special signage (blue grapes on yellow), just as much fun can be had by following your nose.

Make a stop in **George Town** ⑩, where the first settlers on the Tamar pitched up. The **Watch House Museum** (Macquarie Street; Sept–May Mon–Fri 10am–4pm, Sat–Sun noon–2pm; June–Aug Mon–Fri 10am–3pm, Sat–Sun noon–2pm; donation) tells the story, and **The Grove** (25 Cimitiere Street; Sun–Fri 10.30am–4pm; tel: 03-6382 1336; charge) provides insight into prosperous colonial life.

Low Head at the mouth of the Tamar has the atmospheric **Pilot Station** where whitewashed houses, some for rent, are dotted around a green. There's a **Maritime Museum** (daily 10am–4pm or "late"; tel: 03-6382 1143; www.museum.lowhead.com; charge) and the chance to watch a pilot boat at work guiding vessels up the tricky river.

Batman Bridge is the only fixed crossing above Launceston. Turn right for **Beaconsfield** ⑪, a town which gained global notoriety when two miners were trapped in its gold mine in 2006. The impressive **Beaconsfield Mine and Heritage Centre** (daily 9.30am–4.30pm; tel: 03-6383 1473; charge) is housed in old mine buildings.

Beauty Point's attractions are on its wharf. **Seahorse World** (daily Sept–Apr 9.30am–3.30pm, May–Aug 10am–3pm; tours every half-hour; tel: 03-6383 4111; www.seahorseworld.com.au; charge) has seahorses, funnily enough. You can guess the main attraction at the neighbouring **Platypus House** (daily 9.30am–3.30pm; tel: 03-6383 4884; www.platypushouse.com.au; charge).

Detours from the road back to Launceston may include **Grindelwald**, a resort hotel for those yearning for a faux Swiss village, and **Tamar Island**, just north of the city, a wetlands reserve with an easily accessible boardwalk.

The Midland Highway

The Midland Highway runs down to Hobart and takes in some of the best of the colonial villages. **Longford** has numerous listed buildings, especially along Wellington Street, and **Brown's Big Store** has grand Victorian style. Close by are two country estates, both open to the public. **Woolmers Estate** has an exuberant mansion and extensive grounds containing a coach house, stables, cottages, and a working woolshed. Also at Woolmers is the **National Rose Garden** which will eventually feature over 500 varieties (daily 10am–4.30pm; regular guided tours of the house; www.woolmers.com.au; tel: 03-6391 2230; charge). **Brickendon Estate**'s **Historic Farming Village** has great character (Tue–Sun 9.30am–5pm; tel: 03-6391 1251; www.brickendon.com.au; charge).

Evandale ⑫, to the east of the highway, makes much of hosting the National Penny Farthing Championships each February, but there are numerous other pretexts for a visit: the two churches to St Andrew – one Anglican, the other, a more extravagant Uniting Church; the

A miner's cottage at the Grubb Shaft Museum in Beaconsfield.

BELOW: time stands still at the Grove in George Town for a home maid.

interior to **Brown's Village Store**; and the **Clarendon Arms**.

For a break from historic villages, follow the steep, winding C401 from Evandale up towards **Ben Lomond National Park** ⓭. Once you've negotiated the tortuous Jacob's Ladder, you arrive at the **Alpine Village**. In winter this is one of two snowfields in the state (the other is at Mount Field), and during the rest of the year there are some lovely Alpine walks.

Return to the Midland Highway for **Campbell Town**'s **Heritage Highway Museum** (Mon–Fri 10am–3pm; tel: 03-6381 1353; free). Elsewhere the theme is bricks: millions of them in the convict-built **Red Bridge**, and a few thousand set into the pavements on both sides of the highway as part of a project which will eventually see one brick for each of the 68,000 people transported to Van Diemen's Land.

Ross ⓮ is arguably the most unspoilt of all the historic towns. **Church Street** is unsurpassed in its Georgian structures and includes **Ross Village Bakery** from where, sticky cake in hand, you can relax. Continue down

to the stone **bridge** and follow the path behind the Uniting Church to the remains of the **Female Factory**.

Ross benefits from being bypassed by the highway, as does **Oatlands** ⓯, which has dozens of old sandstone buildings and the towering **Callington Mill** (daily 9am–4pm; free), but, lacking the shady elms that contribute so winningly to Ross's ambience, it attracts fewer visitors. Make the most of this and follow the town's walking trail in peace.

Kempton is the last town worth perusing, and then it's a straight run into Hobart, unless the Romanesque church of St Mark in **Pontville** interests you.

The Huon Valley

South from Hobart, the **Huon Valley** is an area that people don't necessarily see on their first visit to the island, but its gentle pleasures reward those who make the effort. For long draped with the orchards that gave the Apple Isle its name, the area is as likely to reveal vineyards or berries in its rolling meadows these days. In fact its providores and gourmet restaurants have made it something of a foodie's haunt.

Sticking to the coast road, check out the **Shot Tower** (daily 9am–6pm; tel: 03-6227 8885; charge) at **Taroona**, perhaps the exhibition in the foyer of the **Australian Antarctic Division HQ** (Mon–Fri 9am–5pm; tel: 03-6232 3516; free) outside Kingston, and the novel snorkel trail at **Tinderbox**, where you swim out and read a series of information boards on plates on the sea bed.

Kettering has a sparkling cove, but most people are there for the ferry to **Bruny Island** . It could be viewed as two islands joined by a narrow isthmus (The Neck) and locals refer to North Bruny and South Bruny. Either way, it's a lengthy 63km (39 miles) from top to bottom. **Adventure Bay** on the more rugged South Bruny is the main holiday centre, if you can call it that. Most activity involves walking or fishing, and maybe visiting **Cape Bruny Lighthouse** or **Fluted Cape**. A boat excursion stars seals, dolphins and any other aquatic life that turns up. **The Neck** has a penguin viewing point and a lookout reached by a steep flight of steps.

On the mainland, make your way to **Huonville**, the area's commercial centre, where visitor interest focuses on the river. There are easy walks or rigorous tests of your capacity to withstand intense G-forces on the **Huon Jet** boat.

Continuing south, **Franklin** is but a street along the river bank. However, the **Wooden Boat Centre** (daily 9.30am–5pm; tel: 03-6266 3586; www.woodenboatcentre.com; charge) is an interesting stop. For a small fee, you can follow the progress of students on an 18-month boatbuilding course. At the end of their studies they will have combined to build a complete vessel.

Into the woods

Geeveston is a timber town. The clues are easy to spot: the two huge trunks either side of the road as you drive in, the life-size carved wooden figures placed along the streets, and the **Forest and Heritage Centre** that doubles as the visitor centre in the middle of town. Geeveston is on the edge of a huge area of managed forest, and beyond that there's only the uninhabited wilderness of **Southwest National Park**, a World Heritage Area.

A carved statue in Geeveston, where the principal industry is timber.

BELOW: the beach on the Neck has protected areas for penguins and mutton birds.

The playground in Mount Field National Park has a wooden wombat.

BELOW: the Tahune Forest Airwalk.

The spectacular **Tahune Forest Air Walk** (daily Oct–Mar 9am–5pm, Apr–Sept 10am–4pm; tel: 03-6295 7170; charge), a 28km (17-mile) drive west, is a 600-metre (1,970ft) steel walkway high in the canopy, which gives a new perspective on life in the forest. Part of it is cantilevered out over the banks of the Huon River. Quieter, and just as alluring, is the **Hartz Mountains National Park**, where trails take a few minutes or several hours.

Pass through somnolent **Dover** and then turn inland to the **Hastings Caves and Thermal Springs** (daily Christmas–mid-Jan 9am–6pm, mid-Jan–Feb 9am–5pm, Mar–Sept 10am–4pm, Oct–Christmas 9am–5pm; tel: 03-6298 3209; charge). Bask in one and enjoy a guided tour of the other.

A dirt road leads to **Cockle Creek** ⑲, the most southerly point you can drive to in Australia. Consecutive settlements failed at whaling, logging and mining; now it just attracts tourists. Walkers can take on the multi-day **South Coast Track**. Many just walk the two hours each way to **South Cape Bay** and back.

And everyone else does the stroll to the bronze whale by the bay.

Wilderness

Visitors can penetrate furthest into the World Heritage Area along the Gordon River Road to Strathgordon.

Follow the course of the Derwent north from Hobart and dawdle for a while in **New Norfolk**, a town with a lumpen paper mill but also scenic stretches of hop gardens and their associated oast houses. The **Oast House** (daily 9am–6pm; tel: 03-6261 1322; charge) in Tynwald Park has a museum devoted to the industry. Elsewhere look out for a pair of sturdy old inns and, in **St Matthews**, traces of the oldest church in the state, buried beneath all the subsequent renovations.

It's just a few kilometres to the blissful tranquillity of the **Salmon Ponds Heritage Hatchery and Garden** (daily 9am–5pm; tel: 03-6261 5663; charge). Its history as a breeding ground of early introduced species is interesting, but the main pleasure is in just strolling in the glorious gardens.

Not far along the Gordon River Road, **Mount Field National Park** ⑳ can get busy with day-trippers from Hobart, so be prepared to share the boardwalks to the most accessible sights including **Russell Falls** and, above it, **Horseshoe Falls**. The **Tall Trees** trail provides a first taste of the giants of the forest, and another hour's walk brings **Lady Barron Falls** into range. Go deeper into the park for Alpine uplands and the snow fields.

Junee Cave, in Maydena, is the entrance to an extensive karst system. Just beyond the village, after a bridge, take a track on the right which winds round to the **Styx Valley** ㉑. At **Big Tree Reserve**, a boardwalk loop skirts through some of the highest trees in the country, all *Eucalyptus regnans* or swamp gum. There have been long battles by conservationists to save these and others like them from the loggers; the evidence is in scrawled rebuttals to the propaganda on the information boards erected by Forestry Tasmania.

Enjoy the long drive through wild mountain scenery to **Strathgordon**, perched at the end of **Lake Pedder**, and on for a final few kilometres to the engineering marvel of the **Gordon Dam** in all its grey concrete glory.

The Lyell Highway

As the Lyell Highway from New Norfolk climbs up to the Central Plateau, look for hydroelectric activity, with power stations and old workers' camps at **Tarraleah** and **Bronte Park**. Fishing fans should turn right down the Marlborough Highway for **Great Lake**. It has amazing trout and a remarkable collection of shack communities. Otherwise continue to **Derwent Bridge 22**.

This is where hikers finish the Overland Track at the visitor centre at the end of **Lake St Clair**. Casual visitors can embark on shorter walks, take a cruise up the lake, or combine the two by chugging to the far end and walking back. Make time to inspect **The Wall**, a long-term project by sculptor Greg Duncan to carve a 100-metre (328ft)-

long relief depicting the life and history of the Central Highlands (daily Sept–Apr 9am–5pm, May–Aug 9am–4pm; tel: 03-6289 1134; charge).

The drive continues past access points to the **Franklin River** for kayakers and whitewater rafters, until the landscape changes from lush green hills to bleak brown and grey. Gold, and then copper, was discovered here in the late 1800s. Trees were lopped to fuel the smelters, and sulphurous outpourings put paid to any remaining vegetation. The land is now entirely denuded. It's bleak but also strangely compelling.

In the midst of all this sits **Queenstown 23**, a rough-and-ready mining town, which now receives a daily influx of tourists who arrive on the steam-drawn (at least for the last few kilometres) **West Coast Wilderness Railway** from Strahan on the west coast. They may take in the old-fashioned **Galley Museum** (1 Driffield Street; tel: 03-6471 1483; Oct–Mar Mon–Fri 9.30am–6pm, Sat–Sun 12.30–6pm, Apr–Sept Mon–Fri 9.30am–5pm, Sat–Sun 12.30–5pm; charge), the **Miners Siding** public

The Miners Siding, a sculpture in Queenstown.

BELOW: the road spirals down from the mountains into Queenstown.

Cradle Mountain Lodge offers luxury accommodation on the edge of the National Park.

sculpture, or maybe just have a drink in the historic **Empire Hotel**.

Macquarie Harbour

Strahan ㉔ (pronounced *strawn*) began life as a timber town, thrived on the copper that passed through and always supported a small fishing fleet. Now, however, it's driven by tourism; this is down to its position on **Macquarie Harbour**.

It's almost obligatory for visitors to take a cruise (World Heritage Cruises daily 9am; tel: 03-6471 7174; or Gordon River Cruises, daily 8.30am; tel: 03-1800 628 288), which includes a swing through **Hell's Gates** at the mouth of the harbour, a look at a fish farm and then a tramp around the ruins on **Sarah Island**.

Probably the toughest penal establishment in the colony, Sarah Island was for the worst recidivists. From 1822 they were put to work fashioning ships from the local Huon pine and had to suffer appalling living conditions for the 11 years the establishment existed before all convicts were transferred to Port Arthur.

BELOW: Strahan harbour with one of the Gordon River excursion boats.

The cruise continues on to the **Gordon River** and a stop for a walk through the rainforest. Back at Strahan look into the visitor centre where, in a small theatre, the play *The Ship That Never Was* tells the story of Sarah Island (daily 5.30pm, plus Dec–Jan 8.30pm; tel: 03-6471 7700; charge).

The road north from Strahan passes the extensive **Henty Dunes**, which stretch for many kilometres behind Ocean Beach, and then turns inland to more mining towns. **Zeehan** is the most significant, having boomed in the 1900s on the back of silver. In those days the magnificent **Gaiety Theatre**, currently under restoration, could fill its 1,000 seats nightly with the biggest names of the era. The stimulating **West Coast Pioneers Museum** (Main Street; tel: 03-6471 6225; daily 9am–5pm; charge) has extensive displays on mining, minerals and local history.

Cradle Mountain

Continue through Rosebery and Tullah before making for Cradle Valley. The first sighting of **Cradle Mountain ㉕** looming up across Dove Lake must rate alongside the first view of the Opera House in Sydney in the chart of magical travel moments; you've got a pretty good idea what it should look like but are still blown away by the real thing. Drink it in, then it's a matter of picking your walk. Most choose the **Dove Lake** circuit, which takes up to two hours, but there are plenty of other options, all outlined on the maps available at the visitor centre.

Hardy hikers will tackle the 80km (50-mile) **Overland Track** (*see page 335*).

If the weather closes in – and it often does – look around Waldheim, the lodge occupied by Gustav Weindorfer, who first campaigned to designate the area a national park.

Continuing eastwards along the edge of the Great Western Tiers, there is hiking to be done in the vehicle-free **Walls of Jerusalem National Park**, but it is not to be undertaken lightly.

Detour north for **Sheffield**, which has put itself on the tourist map by commissioning murals to cover every available wall; and maybe have a look at the wilfully eccentric **Tazmazia** and the associated **Village of Lower Crackpot** (500 Staverton Road; daily Dec–Apr 10am–5pm, May–Nov 10am–4pm; tel: 03-6491 1934; www.tasmazia.com.au; charge), with its comical model houses.

Mole Creek Karst National Park is abundant with caves. Tours go into **Marakoopa Cave** (tel: 03-6363 5182; daily 10am–4pm; call for tour times; charge), which contains glow-worms, underground rivers and the superb Great Cathedral; and the smaller **King Solomon's Cave** (tel: 03-6363 5182; www.parks.tas.gov.au; daily 10am–4pm; call for tour times; charge).

Chudleigh has an acclaimed honey farm, and once you've stopped for your sweet tooth you'll be in to **Deloraine** ㉖. It's a pretty town on the banks of the Meander River, and a rewarding way of exploring it is to follow the trail of sculptures that winds along the main street and down by the river banks.

The north

The Bass Highway snakes its way north, but detour to **Latrobe** for its Victorian high street, and the **Australian Axeman's Hall of Fame** (daily 9am–5pm; tel: 03-6426 2099; charge), where proprietor and legend, David Foster, may be on hand to explain wood-chopping.

Devonport ㉗ is the home port for the *Spirit of Tasmania* ferries that traverse the Bass Strait. The centre need not detain you, but there is a good **Maritime Museum** (Tue–Sun Oct–Mar 10am–4.30pm, Apr–Sept 10am–4pm; tel: 03-6424 7100; charge) near the foreshore, and on Mersey Bluff, the **Tiagarra Aboriginal Culture Centre and Museum** (Mon–Sat 9am–5pm; tel: 03-6424 8250; charge). Besides historical artefacts, Tiagarra has a collection of 10,000-year-old rock art.

The Bass Highway continues along the north coast to **Ulverstone**, a comfortable family destination with nice parks, and a smattering of Victoriana.

Industry hits you with a thud at **Burnie**, where the shell of a massive paper mill and the state's biggest container port dominate. The **Pioneer**

As something of a labour of love, a team of volunteers spent several years restoring Queenstown's Paragon Theatre. This Art Deco classic was built in 1932 and reopened as a 60-seat luxury cinema in 2009. Unpolished, in-house-produced films tell the story of the restoration.

BELOW: a crystal-clear lake sparkles in the summer sun.

Cape Wickham lighthouse on King Island.

BELOW:
Patriarch Inlet, Flinders Island.

Village Museum (Mon–Fri 10am–3pm; tel: 03-6430 5746; charge), with its reconstituted 1900 street scene, is impressive, as are some of the works in the **Burnie Regional Art Gallery** (Mon–Fri 10am–4.30pm, Sat–Sun 1.30–4.30pm; tel: 03-6430 5875; free). And a short ride inland to **Fern Glade** provides a good chance of spotting platypus in the wild.

Wynyard has discreet appeal and **Table Cape** demands a visit in spring when the tulip farm is in full flower, but the lighthouse and the views from it are worth a look at any time.

Possibly the finest bay is at **Boat Harbour Beach**, and its lovely relaxed atmosphere has remained despite the arrival of more and more beach houses and summer visitors.

Visitor favourite **Stanley** ㉘ is dominated by the Nut, a huge plug of volcanic rock at the end of a spit. You can walk or take the chairlift to the top if you don't mind the wind. Down below, Alexander Terrace has well-kept cottages, one of which was the original home of Joe Lyons, the first Tasmanian prime minister.

The Van Diemen's Land Company (VDL) was crucial to Stanley. The old company store can be found near the wharf, while the clifftop-situated **Highfield** (Sept–May daily, June–Aug Mon–Fri 9.30am–4.30pm; tel: 03-6458 1100; charge) was company HQ.

An incarnation of VDL still manages the **Woolnorth** estate that covers the state's northwestern tip. The only way to visit is on a tour (daily if enough interest; tel: 03-6452 1493; charge) taking in a wind farm placed to take full advantage of the Roaring Forties, and dramatic **Cape Grim**.

The Bass Strait Islands

King Island ㉙ is best known for cheese from **King Island Dairy**; there's a shop to visit but no tours, so try **Currie**, the main town (if a handful of streets warrants the term), with its quaint harbour where giant crabs and crayfish are landed. There's a small museum, too, just below the lighthouse (Lighthouse Street; tel: 03-6462 1698; daily 2–4pm; charge).

Ships have often come to grief here, but **Cape Wickham Lighthouse**, on the northern tip, has played its part in keeping the numbers down. At **Yellow Rock Beach**, wreckage from a paddle steamer can still be seen in the surf.

In the south there's the intriguing **Calcified Forest**, while the **Kelp Industries** centre explains why tons of the stuff is hanging out to dry.

King Island is relatively flat and windswept, whereas **Flinders Island** ㉚ has some serious hills, culminating in **Mount Strzelecki**. The southern corner also has the immaculate sands of **Trousers Point** and **Fotheringate Beach**. The main town is **Whitemark**, but the important **Furneaux Museum** (daily 1–5pm summer, Sat–Sun 1–5pm winter; tel: 03-6359 8434 to confirm opening; charge) is up at **Emita**. Many of the exhibits stem from the time of the forced exile of Tasmania's Aboriginal population in 1838, and the chapel at nearby **Wybalenna** is on the site of their settlement. ❏

The Overland Track

Tasmania's most famous hiking trail threads its way through the fabulous landscapes between Cradle Mountain and Lake St Clair

First blazed in the 1830s by surveyors, gold prospectors and fur-trappers, the Overland Track is Australia's most famous walk – a six-day traverse of Tasmania's central plateau through an ancient glacial landscape. About 9,000 hikers undertake the 65km (40-mile) journey from Cradle Mountain to Lake St Clair each year, carrying all their equipment and supplies both in and out.

The hike is not easy, but the rewards are spectacular and accessible to anybody reasonably fit and well prepared. For most local bushwalkers (and an increasing number are travelling here from overseas) completing the track is a rite of passage, an unforgettable expedition among stunted buttongrass moorlands, craggy snow-capped peaks, myrtle and sassafras forests, and crystalline cold-water tarns. Such is its popularity that a new online booking system and a A$150 high-season (1 Nov–30 Apr) charge on top of park entry fees was introduced in 2005, restricting numbers to 60 hikers per day. All hikers are required to start at Cradle Valley in the National Park's north, and finish at Cynthia Bay on Lake St Clair. This one-way traffic eases the congestion on the route and ensures that every hiker experiences the best of the Overland Track.

Huts line the trail – seven on the main track; distances between each vary from 6.5km (4 miles) to 11km (7 miles) – although carrying a tent is essential in this World Heritage Area, with exposed escarpments subject to bitter weather. Hikers need equipment for all four seasons, regardless of when they are travelling – from sunglasses, sunblock and shirt collars, to thermals, waterproofs and a woollen beanie. Warm socks, gaiters and a good sleeping bag are a must. A hiking fuel stove, medical kit and 1:100,000 map are essential. Thongs (flip-flops) are suggested for foot relief around the huts after a long day in heavy boots.

What to carry is a delicate balance between distance, time and weight. Most walkers spend five nights on the trail. It's essential to pack light, to pick each item of clothing carefully and take only what's necessary. Be sure to carry enough food and water for an extra day in case of unexpected delays. A tip for hiking dinners is to add fresh ingredients to basic carbohydrate (pasta, rice or couscous) dishes, such as a squeeze of lemon juice. Salt, pepper, curry powders and chilli are ideal – experienced trekkers often say that food cannot be flavoured spicy enough after a long walk through a cold and unforgiving climate.

One of the walk's highlights (apart from a side-trip up Mount Ossa, at 1,617 metres/5,305ft the island's highest peak) is the camaraderie to be found around the huts each night. Everybody on the walk is considered equal – regardless of age, nationality or occupation – since all share in the rigours and delights of the hike. It's an experience so detached from the daily trivialities of the world outside.

For bookings, see www.overlandtrack.com.au, tel: 6233 6047 or visit the Cradle Mountain and Lake St Clair National Park visitor centres. See also www.parks.tas.gov.au for details on accommodation, transport and park entry fees. Contact Tasmanian Travel Centres for information on tour operators that offer private guided trips. ❏

RIGHT: a pile of driftwood is prepared for a fire on the Overland Track of Tasmania.

RESTAURANTS AND BARS

Restaurants

Prices for a three-course dinner per person with a half-bottle of house wine:
$ = under A$50
$$ = A$50–80
$$$ = A$80–120
$$$$ = over A$120

Hobart

Jackman & McRoss
59 Hampden Road,
Battery Point
Tel: 03-6223 3186
Open B & L daily. $
Jackman & McRoss is one of the most popular meet-and-greet venues in Hobart, both for locals and visitors alike. They are also the source of some of the best bread and best pastries around. The coffee is pretty good, too.

Lebrina
155 New Town Rd
Tel: 03-6228 7775
Open: D Tue–Sat. $$$
Lebrina Restaurant arguably lays claim to the title of best restaurant in the entire state of Tasmania. The European-inspired food is cooked with skill and precision and the service is always gracious.

M4
Elizabeth St Pier
Tel: 03-6224 4428
www.marqueiv.com
Open: L & D daily. $$$
The rebranded Marque IV has clean, contemporary lines and is one of Hobart's most comfortable dining rooms. Great food and a beautiful waterfront location make this a good choice for your big night out.

Piccolo
323a Elizabeth St,
North Hobart
Tel: 03-6234 4844
Open: L & D Tue–Sun. $$$
Piccolo is a welcome addition to the North Hobart dining scene. You can just drop in for a glass of wine or work your way through a three-course meal of Italian-inspired dishes.

Republic Bar and Café
299 Elizabeth Street,
North Hobart
Tel: 03-6234 6954
www.republicbar.com
Open: L & D daily. $$
Music, poetry, politics and beer are the priorities at the Republic. They do an excellent steak marinated in Jack Daniels.

Smolt
2 Salamanca Square
Tel: 03-6224 2554
www.smolt.com.au
Open: L & D daily. $$
Smolt has quickly become the darling of the Hobart foodie scene. Simple food cooked well is the hallmark experience here. The daily loaves of house-baked ciabatta are legendary, and the Spanish-inspired small plates very popular. It's a great place for morning coffee, too.

The Source
Moorilla Estate,
655 Main Road, Berriedale
Tel: 03-6277 9900
www.moorilla.com.au
Open: L daily, D Tue–Sat. $$$
This relatively new first-floor winery dining room is one of Hobart's most spectacular. Chef Philippe Leban has honed the Source's menu to a thing of beauty that matches the new MONA gallery next door.

Huon Valley

Peppermint Bay
3435 Channel Highway,
Woodbridge
Tel: 03-6267 4088
www.peppermintbay.com.au
Open: L daily, D Sat. $$$
One of Australia's best regional restaurants, Peppermint Bay also has one of the most beautiful aspects. Chef David Moyle maintains an impressive array of local suppliers, and creates distinctive, seasonal dishes.

Tasman Peninsula

Felons
Port Arthur Historic Site
Tel: 1800 659 101
www.portarthur.org.au
Open: D daily. $$
Felons is located within the historic site's visitor centre, so it's the perfect location if you've spent the day looking at the sights but are hungry for a good meal. Dinner can be a bit frenzied if you sit down just prior to the start of the popular ghost tour. Book later in the evening for a more leisurely dining experience.

Ross

Ross Bakery Inn
15 Church St, Ross
Tel: 03-6381 5246
Open: L daily. $
Ross Bakery Inn offers delectable home-made pies, breads and pastries which are cooked in a wood-fired oven to sheer perfection.

LEFT: enjoying a pint.

Swansea

Kate's Berry Farm
Addison St, Swansea
(3km/2 miles south)
Tel: 03-6257 8428
Open: L daily. **$**
Most tourists take the time to stop here, even if berries are out of season. The berry ice creams, Devonshire teas, breathtaking views and friendly welcome explain the popularity. In season, there are fresh berries available, too.

Coles Bay

Oyster Catcher
6 Garnet Avenue
Tel: 03-6257 0033
Open: L & D daily (summer to Easter) **$$**
The Oyster Catcher is just a wonderful place. It may be small, cramped, and with only a few tables, but the views of the Freycinet granite mountains are unforgettable. The food is soulful and the coffee pretty good, too.

St Helens

Blue Shed
Marina Parade
Tel: 03-6376 1170
Open: L & D daily. **$$**
A reincarnation of the former Captains Catch, with floor-to-ceiling windows providing expansive views of Georges Bay. Fresh oysters and local fish are the best bets here.

Launceston

Me Wah
39–41 Invermay Road, Invermay
Tel: 03-6331 1308
www.mewah.com.au
Open: L Tue–Sun, D daily. **$$**
Arguably the best Chinese food in the city, if not the whole state. Dumplings, abalone and duck are recommended.

Mud Bar and Restaurant
28 Seaport Boulevard
Tel: 03-6334 5066
Open L & D daily. **$$**
www.mudbar.com.au
One of the most satisfying dining experiences in town, everyone loves Mud's delicious Italian-inspired dishes. Add knowledgeable service, a relaxed mood and a waterside location for a winning combination.

Stillwater
Ritchies Mill, Paterson Street
Tel: 03-6331 4153
www.stillwater.net.au
Open: B & L daily, D Mon–Sat. **$$$**
The contemporary Australian dishes are beautifully balanced and always exciting – highly recommended for food-lovers. The degustation menu, matched with wine choices, is a great way to immerse yourself in it.

Tamar Valley

Strathlynn
95 Rosevears Drive, Rosevears
(3km/2 miles south)
Tel: 03-6330 2388
Open: L daily. **$$$**
A bucolic vineyard setting and a delicate distillation of the best local produce make for a sublime experience.

Elizabeth Town

Christmas Hills Raspberry Farm Café
Bass Highway
Tel: 03-6362 2186
www.raspberryfarmcafe.com
Open: B & L daily. **$**
An incredibly popular venue as tourists and locals flock to the location for dishes based on the berries grown here, including raspberry ice creams and chocolate-dipped raspberries.

Cradle Mountain

Highland Restaurant
Cradle Mountain Lodge, Cradle Mountain-Lake St Clair National Park
Tel: 03-6492 1303
www.cradlemountainlodge.com.au
Open: D daily. **$$**
With a wide-ranging menu, this is the best place to dine in the Cradle Mountain area.

Strahan

Risby Cove
The Esplanade, Strahan
Tel: 03-6471 7572
www.risby.com.au
Open: B, L & D daily. **$$**
A pleasant dining room right on the stunning harbour looking out at the port of Strahan. You can drop in for breakfast, for coffee or for a full evening meal.

Franklin Manor
The Esplanade, Strahan
Tel: 03-6471 7311
www.franklinmanor.com.au
Open: D daily. **$$$**
This venue sources its produce locally whenever possible, and the ocean trout from Macquarie Harbour is always a good option.

Stanley

The Old Cable Station
West Beach Road
Tel: 03-6458 1312
www.oldcablestation.com.au
Open: D daily. **$$**
Part of the Old Cable Station B&B, this restaurant is a little out of town, but it's worth the trip. A favoured feature is the wood-fired oven used for both pizza and lobster. Bookings are essential.

Burnie

Muddled
104 Wilson St, Burnie
Tel: 03-6431 9393
www.muddled.com.au
Open: D Tue–Sat. **$$**
The name might be confusing, but the food is better than most offerings in Burnie. They open their oysters to order, and if you order the simpler dishes, the food is fine.

RIGHT: a not-so-light snack.

FREYCINET NATIONAL PARK

Wineglass Bay is the headline attraction, but there is plenty more to see. Keen walkers could easily spend a few days here

The Freycinet Peninsula is one of the most beautiful places in the world. The combination of mountains, forest, beaches and blisteringly blue sea, not to mention the abundant wildlife, is hard to match and impossible to beat. It's best to surrender to it and allow as much time as possible to take it all in. Pitch a tent just back from the beach and get close to nature (but not too close; secure food from inquisitive wallabies and wombats). Alternatively, follow the path to luxury and book into the Freycinet Lodge, inside the park boundary, for a couple of nights of hedonism. Settle on the balcony of your cabin and watch the scurrying animals in the undergrowth below.

In summer there is good swimming to be had, while anglers are spoilt for choice. Above all, though, this is a place for walking. The Wineglass Bay Track is a must, whether it's just a climb up to the saddle for the view, or perhaps as part of a longer trek which could take in Mount Graham or Mount Freycinet. People with mobility problems or young children can still take on the shorter walks, some with views of Wineglass Bay. Another option is to join one of the boat trips around the peninsula which embark from Coles Bay.

ABOVE: the waters around the Freycinet Peninsula are rich in marine life, as well as being stunningly beautiful.

BELOW: the bright orange deposits on boulders along the shoreline in Freycinet and all along the east coast are in fact a type of rock lichen. They are a complex mixture of fungi and algae which extract nutrients from the rocks they're attached to.

LEFT: the Cape Tourville walk, which affords partial views of Wineglass Bay, is an easy 20-minute stroll around the lighthouse. While you walk, keep your eyes and ears open for unusual birds. Freycinet's avian visitors include yellow-tailed black cockatoos, and the rare white-bellied sea eagle.

VISITOR FACILITIES

The visitor centre is just a few hundred metres inside the park on the right-hand side. This is where park permits can be purchased and maps and guides picked up. Even those who have already paid their park fees should find a stop rewarding as there are displays about many aspects of the park's history and geology, as well as useful pointers towards the weather and the state of the various walks.

One of the walks starts immediately behind the visitor centre. The Great Oyster Bay walk is a 5-minute amble down to Richardson's Beach where the cormorants play, and the Hazards loom above.

The Centre is also the place to register for the campsites, which need to be booked in advance at all times. Indeed some, such as those at Honeymoon Bay (open only at Easter and in the summer) are so popular that a ballot system is used to allocate spaces. There are powered sites for caravans and RVs, and unpowered for tents. Electric barbecue facilities are provided at various points as all campfires are banned, although portable fuel stoves are allowed.

ABOVE: nothing beats that first view of Wineglass Bay which comes as a generous reward for the steep climb up to the saddle between Mount Amos and Mount Mason.
RIGHT: it can take 20 minutes to walk to the end of Wineglass Bay, and then the choice must be made whether to return via the saddle or Hazards Beach.

LEFT: a ranger from the Parks and Wildlife Service promotes the campaign to keep foxes out of Tasmania and increase awareness of the devastating consequences for indigenous animal and bird life if this predator were to gain a toehold in the state. Several species, already wiped out on the Australian mainland, would be endangered, including quolls and bandicoots.

✧ INSIGHT GUIDE   TRAVEL TIPS

AUSTRALIA

T RANSPORT

GETTING THERE
AND GETTING AROUND

By Air

Almost all foreign visitors travel to Australia by air. Brisbane, Cairns, Melbourne and Sydney are the major tourism gateways, with daily flights arriving from Asia, Europe and North America. Less frequent flights also arrive directly in Adelaide, Darwin, Cairns and Perth. More than 40 international airlines currently fly to and from Australia (see Major Airlines list).

Getting to Australia can be expensive. Fares vary widely, so seek advice from a knowledgeable travel agent before buying a ticket. A departure tax is included in the cost of your international ticket, so it no longer has to be paid at the airport when you leave.

There may be price advantages in pre-booking your domestic travel along with your flight to Australia, and since the launch of budget carriers Virgin Blue, Jetstar and Tiger Airways (see Domestic Flights), competition has lowered domestic fares

Flying Times

Sydney–Melbourne, 1 hr
Sydney–Perth, 4 hrs 50 mins
Melbourne–Adelaide, 1 hr 20 mins
Melbourne–Canberra, 1 hr
Brisbane–Sydney, 1 hr 25 mins
Brisbane–Melbourne, 2 hrs 20 mins
Adelaide–Alice Springs, 2 hrs
Perth–Adelaide, 3 hrs
Canberra–Sydney, 50 mins

considerably. The early birds often secure the best deals. Special pre-booked packages tend to incorporate inexpensive hotel and car rental rates.

Qantas usually offers good deals to Australia (it also operates Qantas Vacations). Tickets can be booked by calling 800-348 8145 (in the US), 800-348 8137 (in Canada), or 020-8222 9199 (in the UK).

Major Airlines Flying to Australia

Air Canada
Tel: 1300-655 767
www.aircanada.com
Air China
Tel: 02-9232 7277
www.airchina.com.cn
Air New Zealand
Tel: 132-476
www.airnewzealand.com
British Airways
Tel: 1300-767 177
www.britishairways.com
Cathay Pacific Airways
Tel: 131-747
www.cathaypacific.com
Emirates Airlines
Tel: 1300-303 777
www.emirates.com
Gulf Air
Tel: 1300-366 337
www.gulfairco.com
Japan Airlines (JAL)
Sydney based, tel: 02-9272 1111
www.jal.co.jp.en
Malaysia Airlines
Tel: 132-627
www.malaysiaairlines.com
Qantas
Tel: 131-313
www.qantas.com.au
Singapore Airlines
Tel: 131-011
www.singaporeair.com
South African Airways

Sydney based, tel: 1300-435 972
www.flysaa.com
Thai Airways International
Tel: 1300-651 960
www.thaiair.com
United Airlines
Tel: 131-777
www.united.com
Virgin Atlantic
Tel: 1300-727 340
www.virgin-atlantic.com

By Air

Australia's national domestic airline is **Qantas,** with competition on most routes, since the demise of Ansett in 2001, from **Virgin Blue** (tel: 136-789, www.virginblue.com.au). Qantas launched its own budget domestic airline, **Jetstar** (tel: 131-538, www.jetstar.com), and was then joined by **Tiger Airways** (tel: 03-9335 3033, www.tigerairways. com) on selected routes. Each of these airlines operates regular scheduled flights between all capital cities and regional centres throughout Australia. Both Jetstar and Pacific Blue (a subsidiary of Virgin Blue) operate from Australian cities to a number of Asian and Pacific destinations. **Qantas** (tel: 131-313, www.qantas.com.au) also operates regular scheduled flights between all capital cities and regional centres throughout Australia.

Although many domestic flights are often fully booked, cheap flights are regularly to be found by booking in advance. All the airlines offer cheaper deals for the first few seats with the rate increasing as the aircraft fills up. Conditions can be onerous, however, with checked baggage bringing additional fees on some ticket bands (all on Tiger), strict adherence to weight limits with hefty penalty rates for transgressors, and reduced flexibility to change flights with the lower fare bands. Some of the best deals are to be had if you are prepared to fly at off-peak times or book via the Internet. Some airlines add a fee for payment by credit cards.

Some of the best deals include both air travel and accommodation outside the main holiday seasons – check with airlines for special offers.

Each state is serviced by regional airlines such as QantasLink, providing access to remote destinations.

From the Airport

Sydney

Situated approximately 8km (5 miles) from the Central Business District (CBD), Sydney Airport is best reached by car, taxi or train. Just 10 minutes to the domestic terminals and 12 minutes to the international, trains run from Central Station up to eight times an hour on weekdays, and four times an hour on weekends. The only bus to the airport from the city is the No. 400, which runs from Bondi Junction and takes 40 minutes. For exact times and information visit www.airportlink.com.au, or tel: 131-500.

Canberra

Canberra airport is 7km (4 miles) from the city centre. An Airliner Shuttle bus charges A$9 each way; other bus companies run regular services into town too. The taxi fare is about A$25.

Melbourne

Melbourne's Tullamarine airport is

22km (14 miles) from the city centre. A taxi costs about A$50–60; for about half that price, the Skybus departs every half-hour. Avalon Airport is 55km (34 miles) from the city on the road to Geelong. Bus transfers are available to Southern Cross Station in the city.

Adelaide

The dual international/domestic airport, 8km (5 miles) from the city centre, has a Skylink shuttle bus, which runs about every 30 minutes, stopping at major hotels (tel: 08-8413 6196; www.skylinkadelaide.com). Adelaide Metro runs buses through the city to the airport seven days a week from 4.50am to midnight. A taxi into the city centre costs about A$20.

Brisbane

The domestic and international airport terminals lie 16km (10 miles) from the city centre. At any time when flights are arriving or departing a combination of bus and fast rail transport options provides easy connections between Brisbane Airport, Brisbane city and the Gold Coast. The hub is the city coach/rail terminus, and the "Trans-info" service (tel: 131-230) or the information desks at the airport will help you identify the easiest and most convenient way to get from A to B.

Darwin

Darwin airport is 12km (7½ miles) from the CBD, and a taxi costs around A$35. An airport shuttle (tel: 08-8981 5066) costs about A$10.

Perth

Taxis from the domestic and international airports to Perth city

Bargains by Bus

If you plan extensive bus travel in Australia, several discount plans offer unlimited travel within various time frames. There are also set-duration and set-distance fares.

cost around A$30 and A$35 respectively and to Fremantle A$45. One shuttle bus meets all flights and runs to accommodation in the city, while another travels between Fremantle and the airport (pick-ups must be pre-arranged by phone, preferably the day before). For the Perth shuttle, tel: 08-9277 7958. One-way trips are A$20 for adults from the international terminal and A$15 from the domestic terminals. Bookings for the Fremantle service are on tel: 08-9335 1614.

Hobart

The Airporter Bus meets all flights into Hobart International Airport and drops off at hotels in the city centre and inner suburbs. Charges are A$15 for adults one way or A$25 return; children and concessions A$8. A taxi to the city centre will cost about A$40.

By Bus

Long-Distance Buses

Competition between the major bus companies means many bargains are available when travelling by bus. The biggest company, with the most services, is **Greyhound Australia** (tel: 131 499; www.greyhound.com.au).

The standard of buses is high, with most having reclining seats, seats for the disabled, videos, washrooms and air conditioning. Smoking is prohibited on all buses. Bus terminals are well equipped with toilets, showers and shops, and are generally very clean. However, you should be aware that distances are enormous in Australia, so think twice before hopping onto the Brisbane–Cairns leg, because it takes more than 24 hours.

Greyhound has various money-saving passes, including ones that are based on kilometres travelled.

There are many other bus companies in Australia, offering a variety of transport/hotel packages departing regularly from capital cities. Prices are per day inclusive of bus travel, accommodation and various day tours or driver commentary. Some of the more adventurous routes are taken by deluxe four-wheel-drive vehicles, incorporating camping, and are accompanied by a cook.

BELOW: a Queensland taxi cab waits for a fare.

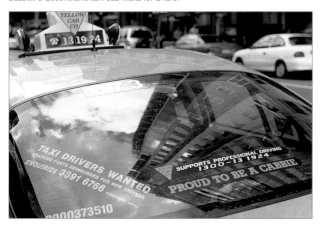

Sydney

Sydney has an extensive bus service with main termini at Circular Quay, Wynyard and Central Station. For all route information visit the Transport Infoline website: http://131500.com.au or tel: 131-500. At Circular Quay there is an information kiosk at the centre of the row of bus stops, on the opposite side of the street (Alfred St) from the ferry wharfs.

The easy-to-spot, red **Sydney Explorer** bus leaves every 18 minutes daily from Circular Quay and runs a continuous loop around 26 of the city's main tourist sites with running commentary. You can hop off as many times as you like or stay on for the full 100-minute journey.

The blue **Bondi Explorer** bus takes in 19 spots around the eastern suburbs. Departing from Circular Quay daily, this hop-on hop-off service covers a 30km (19-mile) route right up to Watsons Bay.

Canberra

In Canberra, ACTION bus services are adequate and modern, but you need to study a map and timetable together. It is possible to purchase daily and off-peak daily bus passes that allow unlimited rides on the buses. A red double-decker bus offers a 24-hour pass and you can get on and off as often as you like. Tel: 131-710; www.action.act.gov.au.

Melbourne

Called Metlink or the Met, Melbourne's public transport system is one of Australia's best. Trams form the basis of the system. There are about 750 trams venturing as far as 20km (12 miles) out of the city. Buses are the secondary form of public transport, often taking over when trams are out of service. Trains connect an underground city loop to the outer suburbs.

A good idea is to visit the Met Shop. Located at Melbourne Town Hall on the corner of Swanston and Little Collins streets in the city, it has a useful "Discover Melbourne" kit and provides all the information you could ever need. There is a wide choice of tickets that enable travel over various

Melbourne Transport

For telephone information on all public transport in Melbourne call the **Met Public Transport Information Centre**, tel: 131-638; open 6am–10pm daily or visit www.metlinkmelbourne.com.au.

Sydney Transport and Passes

The State Transit Authority operates the buses in Sydney, and **CityRail** the trains. Ferries are run by **Sydney Ferries**. For information on buses, trains and ferries from 6am–10pm daily, tel: 131-500. Or check www.131500.com.au, www.cityrail.info, www.sydneyferries.info or www.sydneybuses.info. The front of the White Pages phone book also has information on Sydney's transport.

The **Sydney Pass** is an all-inclusive sightseeing ticket that gives you unlimited travel on all ferries, buses and trains for 3, 5 or 7 days. Including harbour cruises, Explorer buses and return transfers on Airport Link trains, the pass also offers discounts on some major attractions. For more information visit www.sydneypass.info. Travel passes offer cheaper weekly rates and a **Travel 10** ticket gives a discount for 10 trips. Buy these passes from locations and stores displaying the transport symbol.

periods of time and throughout the various zones of the city (zone 1 is big enough to cover most visitors' purposes). There are daily and weekly options, and tickets for use on both trams and buses. A brochure from the Met Shop outlines the options and advises which are the best tickets for your plans. The new Myki smart travel card is available to non-residents and costs A$10 in return for automatically calculating the most cost-effective fares, but is probably not worth considering unless you are staying in the city for several days.

Adelaide

A free **Bee Line bus** follows the city shopping circuit from Victoria Square to the railway station along King William Street; it runs at 7.40am, 7.50am and 8am then every 5 minutes until 6pm daily except Friday when it continues every 10 minutes to 9.20pm. There are fewer buses on weekends so check timetables. The **City Loop** is another free bus; running every 15 minutes, it does a wider circuit of the city, stopping at or near most main sights. Detailed maps are available from Tourism South Australia; tel: 1300 655 276; www.adelaide.southaustralia.com.

All information regarding the Adelaide transport system is available from the Adelaide Metro InfoCentre on the corner of King William and Currie streets, tel: 08-8210 1000 or 1800-182 160; www.adelaidemetro.com.au.

Brisbane

For information on city buses in Brisbane, go to the underground bus station beneath the Myer Centre in the Queen Street Mall, open weekdays 8.30am–5pm, or the Transit Centre in Roma Street. Apart from the regular city buses, there are **Cityxpress** buses, which connect certain suburbs to the city, and **Rockets**, which are peak-hour

commuter services. Fares are based on a zone system and there are a number of special deals such as day or weekly passes. A free City Loop bus connects many of the key sites around the city centre.

Darwin and Alice Springs

Both Darwin and Alice Springs have town bus services that connect accommodation precincts with the CBD. **Darwinbus** (tel: 08-8924 7666) has tourcards that allow unlimited travel for one or seven days. **ASBUS** buses leave the interchange on Railway Terrace in Alice Springs, near the Coles supermarket. Comfortable, frequent and fast buses connect the three central attractions – Darwin, Alice Springs and Ayers Rock.

Greyhound Australia (tel: 131 499; www.greyhound.com.au) runs daily between Alice Springs and Yulara (Ayers Rock). It is 460km (286 miles) each way.

Perth

Perth has five bus routes with the Central Area Transit (CAT), four train lines including one to Fremantle, and ferries cross some sections of the Swan River. A Free Transit Zone (FTZ) covers buses, including the Central Area Transit (CAT) buses, in much of the city centre; for details ask at the Visitor Centre. The "**Perth Tram**" (actually a bus) operates a circuit of tourist attractions. Regular bus services have fares based on a zone system, with discount passes. For maps and on-the-spot information about all forms of public transport, a Transperth office is in the Plaza Arcade (off the Hay Street Mall), tel: 136-213; www.transperth.wa.gov.au.

High-speed ferries travel from Perth, Fremantle and Hillarys to Rottnest Island.

Tasmania

Metro Tasmania runs an extensive network of bus services in Hobart, and they are an easy way to reach sights that are more than a casual stroll from the town centre such as Hobart's beaches, the Taroona Shot Tower, the Cadbury Factory and Cascade Brewery. Buses run Mon–Thur 6.30am to 10.30pm and until midnight on Friday and Saturday. There is a limited service on Sunday and holidays.

By Train

A wide network of modern railways operates from coast to coast. The principal lines follow the east and south coasts, linking the cities of Cairns, Brisbane, Sydney, Melbourne, Adelaide and Alice Springs. The most comprehensive service is operated by **Countrylink**: reservations are required; tel: 132-232 (Australia-wide); www.countrylink.info.

The line between Sydney and Perth via Adelaide is the famous **Indian–Pacific** run (linking the Indian Ocean to the Pacific Ocean). On its 4,352km (2,700-mile) journey, taking 65 hours (three nights), the train crosses the treeless Nullarbor Plain, with the longest stretch of straight track in the world. Comforts include an observation lounge and bar. If money is no object you can travel in the historic Prince of Wales carriage, complete with wood panelling and cathedral glass doors.

Other popular scenic rail journeys run by Great Southern Railway (tel: 132-147 or 08-8213 4592; www.trainways.com.au) include the **Overland**, an overnight journey between Melbourne and Adelaide, and the **Ghan**, which runs from Adelaide to Darwin. The recently extended Ghan runs straight through the middle of the country, from Adelaide in South Australia through Alice Springs and on

to Darwin. The two-night, 3,000km (1,864-mile) trip can be broken in Katherine for short sightseeing tours by boat or helicopter, and Alice Springs for longer stopovers.

For travel in Western Australia it is possible to take a bus or train to the southern and southwest regions in the area bounded by Kalbarri, Meekathara, Kalgoorlie, Esperance, Albany and Augusta. For more details contact **Transwa**, tel: 08-9326 2600 or 1300-662 205, or visit www.transwa.wa.gov.au.

Tickets

The classes available are first, holiday and economy. First-class passengers have sleeping berths with showers in their cabin, a first-class restaurant and lounge. Other classes get aeroplane-style reclining seats and a buffet car.

A Rail Australia pass entitles international visitors to unlimited travel on **Countrylink**, **Queensland Rail** and **Great Southern Railway** services for a six-month period. Most states have their own passes as well.

The **Countrylink Backpacker Rail Pass** is only available to foreign passport holders and is valid for 14 days to six months of unlimited economy-class travel, plus some metropolitan train travel.

Sydney

Trains are the most time-efficient way to navigate Sydney. With a fairly frequent service, most of Sydney's main areas are covered, including the central "City Circle" stations – Central, Town Hall, Wynyard, Circular Quay, St James and Museum. Most do not run between midnight and 4.30am, when a **Nightrider** bus service takes over.

The **Airlink** trains run about every 10 minutes between the city and the

Brisbane Ferries

Brisbane ferries – City Cats – provide river crossings to Kangaroo Point, South Bank Parklands and along the river to other locations. They depart from Eagle Street Pier and Edward Street on the corner of the Botanic Gardens. They are fast, efficient and inexpensive.

domestic and international terminals, and the journey to Sydney's Central Station takes about 15 minutes.

Sydney's **monorail** glides from Central Station to the inner-west suburb of Lilyfield. Stops include Darling Harbour, Paddy's Markets, Star City Casino and the Sydney Fish Markets at Pyrmont.

Canberra

There are no train services in Canberra.

Melbourne

The city has an extensive train service, with all lines radiating out from the central Flinders Street Station. The Met Shop (Melbourne Town Hall, cnr Swanston and Little Collins streets; tel: 131-638) provides timetables and maps and sells tickets (also valid on city buses and trams). Apart from the underground city loop, stations are above ground. Train services on most lines depart every 15 or 20 minutes on weekdays, and every 20 to 30 minutes on weekends.

Adelaide

Train services are limited and are mostly used by locals to get out to far-flung suburbs. Generally speaking, you will need to rely on other forms of transport in Adelaide. One exception is the tram route linking Victoria Square in the city to the popular beach-side suburb of Glenelg, which tends to get quite busy in the summer months.

Brisbane

The electric **Citytrain** services are very efficient. They all pass through the city stations of Roma Street, Central and Brunswick on their way out to the suburbs. The Public Transport Information Centre is located in Central Station. There are tickets that enable unlimited travel in one day.

Darwin

There are no city trains serving Darwin.

Perth

Wellington Street is Perth's central station, with an underground terminal for the nearby Mandurah line.

Sydney Ferries and Cruises

Weather permitting, which it usually is, ferries are by far the most picturesque way of travelling around Sydney. Departing from the wharfs at Circular Quay, all tickets and timetables can be found at the Sydney ferries office.

The trip to Manly is the longest ferry run, covering 11km (7 miles) in 30 minutes. The alternative **Jetcat** service offers the same trip in half the time for slightly more money. There are currently temporary timetables in place for both services while the east side of Manly Wharf is redeveloped. Visit www.sydneyferries.info for exact times.

Ferries are a great way of getting to Taronga Zoo, Kirribilli and Watsons Bay, not to mention a good opportunity to see the harbour, bridge and Opera House from all angles.

The **Rivercat**, a high-speed catamaran, cruises all the way up the Parramatta River.

Harbour cruises are a great way to relax while seeing Sydney off dry land. Daily cruises start at 10.30am and depart from Wharf Four. With comfy seating and unlimited tea and biscuits, these STA cruises are less expensive than private options and the commentary provides an interesting addition to the scenic backdrop.

Transperth trains run south through Perth to Fremantle; north to Joondalup; and down the coast to Mandurah.

Hobart

Regular passenger rail services ceased in Tasmania in the 1980s, but there are a few tourist/heritage railways operating in the state. Visit www.puretasmania.con.au and www.donriver railway.au for more information.

By Sea

After arriving in Australia, a number of the international cruise lines continue around the coastline at a leisurely pace.

Day trips and cruises operate between the mainland and the Great Barrier Reef. Six-day cruises run from Cairns to Cape York. The coral-fringed Whitsunday Islands are one of the best cruising and yachting locations in Australia (rent yachts from operators at Airlie Beach – the motto is, if you can drive a car, you can sail a yacht). River cruises and houseboat rentals are available on major rivers such as the River Murray, or the Myall Lakes and the Murray River.

The only regular maritime services are the passenger and car ferries called *Spirit of Tasmania I and II*, operating between Melbourne and Devonport. The trip from Victoria can be rough and takes about 11 hours. Tel: 1800-634 906 (in Australia) or see www.spiritoftasmania.com.au.

Taxis

Sydney

All taxis are metered, so do not ride unless the meter is on. There is an initial hiring charge (called "flag fall"), then a set rate per kilometre thereafter. Between 10pm and 6am, this rate increases by 20 percent. A phone booking costs extra. There may be additional charges for road, bridge, ferry, tunnel and airport tolls. For information on taxis in NSW see the Taxi Council of NSW website, www.nswtaxi.org.au.
Premier Cabs: tel: 131-017
Taxis Combined: tel: 133-300
Legion Cabs: tel: 131-451
RSL Cabs: tel: 02-9581 1111
Silver Service: tel: 133-100.

In addition, there are companies that operate water taxis on the harbour. The price depends on the distance and time of day. **Water Taxis Combined:** tel: 02-9555 8888; **Yellow Water Taxis:** tel: 02-9299-0199.

Melbourne

Melbourne's transport system tends to curl up and go to sleep around midnight, after which taxis are the only form of transport available. **Melbourne City Taxis**, tel: 03-9335 3536; **Silver Top Taxis**, tel: 131 008.

Canberra

If you're waiting at a Canberra taxi rank with no taxis in sight, call **Canberra Cabs** on tel: 132-227 and they'll send one along. All taxis are metered. Between 9pm and 6am, the rate goes up. For more information, visit www.cancabs.com.au.

Adelaide

There are a number of taxi services available. **Adelaide Independent Taxi Service**, tel: 132-211; **Suburban Taxi**, tel: 131-008; **Yellow Cabs**, tel: 132-227.

Brisbane

The city's officially recognised sevices are **Yellow Cabs** (tel: 131-924) and **Black and White Cabs** (tel: 131-008). Both charge a booking fee, with a standard fixed flag fall weekdays 7am–7pm, and a standard rate per km. After-hours flag fall is higher.

Darwin

Darwin has three major taxi companies: **Darwin Radio Taxi**, tel: 131 008, **Arafura Shuttle**, tel: 08-8981 3300, and **Yellow Cab**, tel: 131 924.

Perth

Hail taxis on the street, find them at a rank, or phone **Black and White** on 08-9333 3333 or **Swan** on 13 13 30, for up to four passengers. Black and White also have maxicabs (up to 10 passengers) and a service for the disabled (tel: 136-294 for these). Rates are reasonable: a small flag fall charge followed by a rate per kilometre.

Hobart

Taxis can be hired in the street if their vacant sign is lit. All cabs use meters and tipping is not necessary. **Tasmanian Cabs**, tel: 131-008, will connect you to taxi companies in most of the major towns in Tasmania, including **City Cabs** in Hobart.

Motorcycles and Bicycles

Both are available for hire throughout Australia. Thoughtfully designed systems of bicycle paths provide good views or access to tourist sites – a pleasant, healthy and environmentally friendly alternative to the city bus tour.

Basic Motoring Rules

- Australians drive on the left.
- The law requires you to keep your seat belt fastened at all times, whether as driver or passenger.
- Overseas licences are valid throughout Australia.

Sydney

Bonza Bike Tours (www.bonzabiketours.com) offers 2–5-hour tours of the city from A$50, as well as bike hire. A range of mountain, hybrid and children's bikes, including dragsters, choppers and tandems, is for hire in **Sydney Olympic Park** (www.sydneyolympicpark.com.au). *Cycling Around Sydney* by Bruce Ashley is a useful guide available at **Bicycle NSW**'s offices at Level 5, 822 George St (tel: 02-9218 5400), or from book and bike shops.

Canberra

Cycling is perhaps the most pleasant choice for sightseeing in Canberra, as the terrain is flat and bike paths are extensive. Bicycles can be hired by the hour, by the day or by the week. If you intend hiring a bike, make sure to get a copy of the *Canberra Cycleways* map from the tourist office or bookshops.

Melbourne

Melbourne is fairly flat, which affords the cyclist a number of good long tracks. Bike paths lie along the Yarra River, the Maribyrnong and the Merri Creek. For general cycling information, contact **Bicycle Victoria** at Level 10, 446 Collins Street, tel: 03-8636 8888; www.bv.com.au. **Melbourne Bike Share** has docking stations around the city and, for a small fee, bikes are available for sightseeing. Helmets are compulsory, however, so go equipped or buy a cheap one from a local store.

Adelaide

Running alongside the Torrens River in Adelaide is the 35km (22-mile)-long Linear Park Bike and Walking Track, one of the best in Australia. You can hire bikes from **Linear Park Bike Hire**, tel: 08-8223 6271. You can also get free use of a bike for two hours within the city limits under a scheme run by **Bicycle SA** and **Adelaide City Council** called the City Bike Scheme. Once the two hours are up, an hourly rate applies. For more information see the Adelaide City Council website (www.adelaidecitycouncil.com) or contact the Cycling Information Centre at 46 Hurtle Square (tel: 08-8232 2644). Bikes can also be picked up from

Cannon Street Backpackers on Franklin Street, opposite the central bus station.

Brisbane

Brisbane City Council has built more than 500km (310 miles) of cycleways across the city. The riverside Bicentennial Bikeway, from the CBD along Coronation Drive to Toowong, is one of the most pleasant. Maps of popular cycleways can be found on the council's website www.brisbane.qld.gov.au.

Darwin

You can hire motorcycles along Mitchell Street. Try **Darwin Scooter Hire**, corner Peel and Mitchell streets. 50cc scooters are very popular for running out to the beaches around Darwin. Bicycles can be hired from some of the backpacker hotels, and some five-star hotels offer their guests cycle hire. There are plenty of cycle tracks; especially good is the one to East Point around Fannie Bay.

Perth

Cycle paths have been developed all around Perth, alongside the freeway and coast, into the hills and cross-country. The **Perth Bicycle Network** (www.dpi.wa.gov.au/cycling) is a useful source of information. Maps are available from bike shops, or the **Bicycle Transportation Alliance** (2 Delhi Street, West Perth, tel: 08-9420 7210). **All About Bikes**, on the corner of Riverside Drive and Plain Street, tel: 08-9221 2665, rents bikes, double bikes and quadcycles.

Hobart

Tasmania's longest-dedicated cycleway is the 15km (9-mile) Intercity Cycleway in Hobart. The bike club **Bicycle Tasmania** (www.biketas.org.au) has all the information you'll need.

By Car

Car Hire

By international standards, renting a car in Australia is expensive. The big three rental companies are **Avis**, **Hertz** and **Budget**, whose rates are just about identical. **Thrifty** and **Europcar** are also players in the market. The small outfits are usually much cheaper and offer special deals, but they may not offer all the services of the major companies – which can be useful. These include discounts for pre-booking overseas, and the ability to return the car to another city at no extra charge. Be aware that many rental cars have manual, rather than automatic, gears (the latter are pricier).

The big three have offices in almost every town, as well as at airports and rail terminals. They offer unlimited kilometre rates in the city, but when travelling in the Outback, rates are usually per kilometre. Compulsory third-party insurance is included in car rentals, but collision damage waiver is an add-on. More comprehensive insurance plans are available for an additional fee, or your travel insurance may cover them. Most companies have 25 as their minimum driver age, or will charge a premium for drivers aged between 21 and 25.

Since driving a conventional vehicle off sealed roads may invalidate your insurance, four-wheel drive (4WD) cars are expensive but worth considering for safe Outback touring. Camper vans are popular, especially in Tasmania; they aren't cheap, however, and it might work out more economical to rent a regular car and stay at budget hotels.

If you're getting around the Outback independently, you must constantly remind yourself that you're in frontier country. Do plenty of research and planning before you head off. Carrying adequate water, notifying people of your intentions, using reliable vehicles and protecting yourself from sunburn should be high on your list. Picking up hitchhikers is, in general, a bad idea.

Independent travellers should be aware that significant tracts of the Outback are designated as Aboriginal land, and a permit may be required to enter them.

Motoring Advice

If you do opt to explore Australia by car, keep in mind that distances are often huge and towns may be few and far between. Many visitors on short-term trips opt to fly between major cities.

The major highways linking capital cities are all sealed and of a good standard, but you don't have to go far to find yourself on dirt roads. In remote areas such as Cape York and the Kimberley, most 4WDs travel in pairs or teams, to assist one another when bogged.

The speed limit in a built-up area is 60kmph (37mph) and sometimes 50kmph (31mph) or 40kmph (25mph) in suburban residential areas; in the country it is usually 100kmph (62mph), unless otherwise signposted. Darwin has the most open roads in the country. Beyond city limits there is a maximum speed limit of 130kmph (81mph).

Drink driving is a major problem.

There is random breath testing for alcohol in most states. If you exceed .05 percent blood-alcohol level (ie more than three drinks), a hefty fine and loss of licence are automatic.

Fuel comes in super, unleaded, super-unleaded, LPG (gas) and diesel. It is becoming more expensive in remote country areas.

Each state has an Automobile Association that offers excellent maps and literature. For a small membership fee, they also provide a free, highly recommended, nationwide emergency breakdown service.

Automobile Associations

Sydney: National Roads and Motorists' Association (NRMA), 74–6 King Street, tel: 131-111; www. nrma.com.au

Melbourne: Royal Automobile Club of Victoria (RACV), corner Little Collins Street and New Chancery Lane; tel: 131-111; www.racv.com.au

Canberra: National Roads and Motorists Association (NRMA), Canberra Centre Shop CG5/6 Canberra Centre, City Walk, Civic, ACT 2600, tel: 131-111; www.nrma.com.au

Perth: Royal Automobile Club of Western Australia Inc. (RAC WA), 832 Wellington Street, West Perth, WA 6839, tel: 131-111; www.rac.com.au

Brisbane: Royal Automobile Club of Queensland (RACQ), GPO Building, 261 Queen Street, Brisbane 4000; tel: 131-111; www.racq.com.au

Adelaide: Royal Automobile Association of South Australia (RAA), 55 Hindmarsh Square, Adelaide, SA 5000, tel: 131-111; www. raa.net

Darwin: Automobile Association of the Northern Territory (AANT), 79–81 Smith Street, Darwin, NT 0800, tel: 131-111; www.aant.com.au

BELOW: you'll need a good map.

A CCOMMODATION

HOTELS, YOUTH HOSTELS, BED & BREAKFAST

Accommodation

Generally speaking, the standard of accommodation in Australia is high. In the capital cities and tourist areas you will find all the international hotel chains such as Hyatt and Sheraton as well as privately managed properties, including an increasing number of boutique hotels, offering a small number of individually styled rooms in often quirky and character-filled buildings. Serviced apartments are becoming more popular, especially in the cities, with Quest (www.quest.com.au) and the Oaks Group (www.theoaksgroup.com.au) the reliable leaders in the field.

While some destinations cater to well-heeled international visitors (such as Port Douglas, QLD), other regions have recognised the income generated by the young backpacker market and can provide an excellent choice of budget accommodation (for example, Darwin, NT). Log onto www.tntmagazine.com.au for information on Australia's youth hostels.

Sydney's hotels are significantly more expensive than anywhere else in Australia. Seasonal fluctuations in price often apply in heavily visited areas. One way to reduce the cost is to book accommodation online through one of the last-minute websites such as www.wotif.com or www.lastminute.com.au. Hotels from five-star down to three-star, self-contained cottages and bed and breakfasts throughout Australia use these websites to fill empty rooms, often at a significantly reduced rate, and it is now possible to book through these sites several days in advance.

Also check the hotel's own website for last-minute packages and special deals. Some hotel chains guarantee that the rate they offer on their website will be lower than could be found on any other booking website.

Farms and Homes

For a holiday with a difference, you can stay as a paying guest with Australian families in a private home or on a working farm.

B&Bs come and go, so the best source of current information is the **Bed and Breakfast and Farmstay Australia** (BBFA); visit www.australian bedandbreakfast.com.au covering more than 1,000 B&Bs and Farmstays. The Farmstays include everything from small dairy farms in the hills to vast grain farming and sheep- and cattle-grazing properties.

ACCOMMODATION LISTINGS

NEW SOUTH WALES

Sydney

Sydney has an almost overwhelming choice of hotels. The best method for making a decision, after budgetary considerations, is location. Most of the de-luxe hotels are located in the historic Rocks and city area. This has the major advantage of being right on Sydney Harbour, but there are other inner-city suburbs with harbour views. Potts Point, for example, has a wealth of accommodation, much of it moderately priced; it provides quick access to the city and has many fine restaurants and cafés.

Budget accommodation is mainly found in Kings Cross, the central business district, Bondi or Manly. Victoria Street in Kings Cross has a score of privately run hostels for backpackers; it's also the place to network with other travellers in arranging lifts, buying cheap flights, or buying a car for that extended road odyssey around Oz. A short trip from the city will take you to beautiful Bondi Beach. Glebe is also an attractive student neighbourhood with inexpensive hotel options. Manly is a beach suburb

with more of a family feel, with ferry transport to and from the city.

For details of the huge range of B&Bs on offer in Sydney, log onto www.australianbedandbreakfast.com.au.

CBD – Central Business District

Hilton Sydney
488 George Street
Tel: 02-9265 6045
Hilton Sydney is one of the most coveted hotels in the city. Central and super chic, it boasts the city's largest health centre, top-class restaurants and bars and stunning harbour views from the Executive Lounge. **$$$$**

Inter-Continental Sydney
Corner of Bridge and Phillip streets
Tel: 02-9253 9000
www.sydney.intercontinental.com
The grand historic Treasury building provides the introduction to a spectacular central skylit courtyard, with accommodation rising above. Many rooms with classic harbour views. Located in the Circular Quay area, within minutes of the Opera House and harbour. **$$$$**

The Observatory Hotel
89–113 Kent Street
Tel: 02-9256 2222
www.observatoryhotel.com.au
Discreet and elegant alternative to large hotels, tucked away behind Observatory Hill in The Rocks. Sydney's most sumptuous suites with antique-style furnishings, deep baths and excellent service. Facilities include a stunning star-ceilinged indoor pool and health spa, as well as an excellent restaurant. Popular with small groups of well-heeled business folk and romantic Sydneysiders. **$$$$**

Park Hyatt Sydney
7 Hickson Road, The Rocks
Tel: 02-9241 1234
www.sydney.park.hyatt.com
Rated as the most luxurious hotel in Sydney, where every attention is paid to personal service. Spacious, supremely comfortable rooms have privileged water-level views of the harbour and Opera House. Ideal location in The Rocks

area. **$$$$**
Quay West Suites Sydney
98 Gloucester Street, The Rocks
Tel: 02-9240 6000 or 1800-805 031
www.mirvachotels.com.au
Another of the modern towers that front Sydney Harbour, but this one has self-contained luxury apartments, as well as executive penthouses. There's also a Roman bath-style swimming pool. For a different view – looking back towards the Harbour Bridge from near the Opera House – Mirvac also owns a similar luxury apartment development called Quay Grand. **$$$$**

Shangri-La Hotel
176 Cumberland Street, The Rocks
Tel: 02-9250 6000 or 1800-801 080
Fax: 02-9250 6250
www.shangri-la.com
Quintessential harbour views from every room of this award-winning, 573-room modern tower hotel, one of several in The Rocks/Circular Quay area. **$$$$**

Sheraton on the Park
161 Elizabeth Street
Tel: 02-9286 6000
www.sheraton.com/sydney
Huge rooms with dramatic city and Hyde Park views. **$$$$**

Sir Stamford at Circular Quay
93 Macquarie Street
Tel: 02-9252 4600 or 1300-361 180
www.stamford.com.au
Classical French furnishings and beautiful paintings create a distinguished atmosphere. Located in the business district, this is a clubby place, popular with business people. The excellent restaurant is *the* place to close a deal. **$$$$**

The Waldorf Apartment Hotel
57 Liverpool Street
Tel: 02-9261 5355
www.warldorf.com.au
Glitzy tower containing one- and two-bedroom apartments with good views over the city centre and Darling Harbour. At the high end of this price range. **$$$**

Y Hotel Hyde Park
5–11 Wentworth Avenue

Tel: 1800-994 994
Tel: (overseas): +61 2-9264 2451
Fax: +61 2-9285 6288
Email: enquiry@yhotel.com.au
www.yhotel.com.au
Great inner-city location, with over 100 beds. Safe, clean and good facilities. Close to Oxford Street, over the road from Hyde Park. **$**

Inner Eastern Suburbs

Blue Sydney, A Taj Hotel
6 Cowper Wharf Road
Tel: 02-9331 9000
On the buzzing Wharf at Woolloomooloo, this boutique hotel has a choice of views from its many rooms, including the deluxe Ultra Loft. Blue's high standard of service and eclectic mix of heritage timber and modern minimalist interior will suit the younger, monied traveller who wants top-class restaurants and trendy bars on site. **$$$$**

Stamford Plaza Double Bay
22 Knox Street, Double Bay
Tel: 02-9362 4455
www.stamford.com.au
Fastidious interior decoration, with valuable original artworks. Each room has a carefully designed theme – there's even a Manhattan loft-style room. Double Bay is a wealthy suburb close to the city, known primarily for its fashionable shopping. **$$$$**

Kirketon Boutique Hotel
229 Darlinghurst Road, Darlinghurst 2010
Tel: 02-9332 2011 or 1800-332 920
www.kirketon.com.au
In the epicentre of hip Darlinghurst, ultra-modern, minimalist-style accommodation with restaurants and bars. **$$$**

Medina on Crown Executive
359 Crown Street, Surry Hills
Tel: 02-8302 1000 or 1300-633 462
www.medinaapartments.com.au
Surry Hills is an attractive and peaceful terrace-house suburb not far from the city centre, with a concentration of galleries, antiques shops

and restaurants. These are serviced apartments. **$$$**
Oaks Hyde Park Plaza
38 College Street, Sydney
Tel: 02-9331 6933 or 1800 222 442
www.theoaksgroup.com.au
Overlooking Hyde Park in the centre of the business district, large apartment-style rooms including full kitchen facilities. Functional design. **$$$**

Simpsons of Potts Point
8 Challis Avenue, Potts Point
Tel: 02-9356 2199
www.simpsonspottspoint.com.au
Beautifully restored historic house with authentic period decoration throughout. Potts Point is known for fashionable restaurants and cafés; easy access to the city by bus or train. **$$$**

The Grantham
1 Grantham Street, Potts Point
Tel: 02-9357 2377 or 1800 249 706
www.thegrantham.com.au
Many of these apartments have great views across the city skyline to the Botanic Gardens and Sydney Harbour. Functionally designed rooms with all the facilities you need. Good value for money. **$$**

Morgan's of Sydney
304 Victoria Street, Darlinghurst
Tel: 02-9360 7955
www.morganshotel.com.au
Fashionably located boutique hotel aimed at successful young business people, Morgan's is stylish and comfortable; the downstairs bar is the scene for beautiful people. Paid parking only. **$$**

Regents Court
18 Springfield Avenue, Potts Point
Tel: 02-9358 1533
www.regentscourt.com.au
The friendly management set up this designer hotel for a clientele of arts-orientated professionals. Nestled in a peaceful

PRICE CATEGORIES

Price categories are for a double room without breakfast:
$ = under A$80
$$ = A$80–130
$$$ = A$130–200
$$$$ = over A$200

backstreet of otherwise seedy Kings Cross, these huge sparse rooms of ultra-modern design lack views, but guests meet for drinks on the rooftop garden. **$$**

Sydney Marriott
36 College Street
Tel: 02-9361 8400
www.marriott.com
Facing Hyde Park, this 241-room hotel enjoys a fine reputation for the quality of its service. Amenities include rooftop pool and spa, and modern Australian cuisine in the Windows on the Park restaurant. **$$$$**

Albert & Victoria Court Hotel
122 Victoria Street, Potts Point
Tel: 02-9357 3200 or 1800-630 505
www.victoriacourt.com.au
Historic boutique hotel and B&B in elegant Victorian terraced house. Central, quiet location in the heart of Sydney's gastronomic precinct. **$$**

For backpackers, there is the **Jolly Swagman** hostel in Kings Cross, tel: 02-9358 6400; www.jollyswagman.com.au **$** and the **Sydney Central Backpackers** in the same street, tel: 02-9358 6600; www.sydneybackpackers.com.au **$**

Inner Western Suburbs
Australian Sunrise Lodge
485 King Street, Newtown
Tel: 02-9550 4999
www.australiansunriselodge.com
Newtown is a fairly bohemian student suburb, about 10 minutes' drive from the city, with great-value ethnic restaurants, pubs with live bands, and an interesting vibe. A modern hotel with sunny double, triple and family rooms. **$$**

Broadway University Motor Inn
25 Arundel Street, Glebe
Tel: 02-9660 5777
www.goldenchain.com.au
Located just opposite the University of Sydney, an area well known for its alternative lifestyle and a wide range of cafés. **$$**

Cremorne Point Manor

6 Cremorne Road, Cremorne Point
Tel: 02-9953 7899
www.cremornepointmanor.com.au
A ferry ride across the harbour connects the charming suburb of Cremorne Point to the city. This is a restored Federation mansion with excellent harbour views. **$$**

Eastern Suburbs
Coogee Bay Boutique Hotel
9 Vicar Street, Coogee
Tel: 02-9665 0000
www.coogeebayhotel.com.au
Heritage-style seaside pub, nicely renovated. Located opposite picturesque Coogee Beach with ocean views from the front rooms. Bus to city takes about 40 mins, taxi 15 mins. **$$$**

The Hotel Bondi
178 Campbell Parade, Bondi Beach
Tel: 02-9130 3271
www.hotelbondi.com.au
Bondi's landmark historic pub, right on the main street, has undergone a series of renovations and can now offer a moderate standard of accommodation, with five bars, café and entertainment. The pub is a bit raucous, so it is worth staying here only if you get a front room with ocean view; for these, you need to book well in advance. **$$**

Sinclairs of Bondi
11 Bennett Street, Bondi
Mobile: 0414-342 010
www.sinclairsbondi.com.au
500 metres/yards east of Bondi Junction. Cooking facilities. Also at Surry Hills. **$**

North Sydney
Harbourside Apartments
2A Henry Lawson Avenue, McMahons Point
Tel: 02-9963 4300
www.harboursideapartments.com.au
Terrific harbour views of the Opera House underneath the Sydney Harbour Bridge. Compact but comfortable – and the city ferry is right on the doorstep. **$$$**

Blue Mountains

Less than two hours' drive from Sydney, the Blue

Mountains are a popular getaway destination with a choice of accommodation in the main towns.
Blueberry Lodge and The Loft
Waterfall Road, Mount Wilson
Tel/fax: 02-4756 2022
www.bluemts.com.au/blueberry
Chalet in historic Blue Mountains village. **$$$$**

Echoes Boutique Hotel
3 Lilianfels Avenue, Katoomba
Tel: 02-4782 1966
www.echoeshotel.com.au
Modern luxury and old-fashioned atmosphere in this immaculately renovated boutique hotel with tremendous views. **$$$$**

Lilianfels Blue Mountains
Lilianfels Avenue, Katoomba
Tel: 02-4780 1200
www.lilianfels.com.au
Well-managed, tranquil resort located near most Blue Mountains attractions. Popular indoor pool/health club. Wonderful restaurant in early 20th-century guest-house makes for a special evening. **$$$$**

Rural NSW
Milton Park
Horderns Road, Bowral
Tel: 02-4861 1522
www.milton-park.com.au
One and a half hours' drive from Sydney, in the Southern Highlands, Milton Park is an elegant estate, offering horse riding, golf, tennis, bush walking and peaceful solitude. Fine cuisine using fresh seasonal produce. **$$$$**

North of Sydney

Casuarina Country Inn
Hermitage Road, Pokolbin, Hunter Valley
Tel: 02-4998 7888
Striking garden and vineyard views are provided from nine fantasy-themed suites. **$$$**

Grand Mercure Hunter Valley Gardens
Broke Road, Pokolbin
Tel: 02-4998 4000
www.hvg.com.au
A kind of garden theme park over 300 hectares (740 acres). There are three different places to stay

ranging from three- to four-star. **$$$**

Kim's Beach Hideaway
Charlton Avenue, on the beach, Toowoon Bay
Tel: 02-4332 1566
www.kims.com.au
Ninety minutes north of Sydney, Kim's has been a much-loved resort for generations. Now more luxurious than ever, it offers private beach houses, many facing directly onto the bay. And Kim's tradition of fresh hearty seafood dishes prevails. **$$$$**

Pips Beach Houses
14 Childe Street, Byron Bay
Tel/fax: 02-6685 5400
For romantic beach-front privacy, these are cabins hidden in the bush on the dunes of Belongil Beach. **$$$$**

Rae's on Watego's
8 Marine Parade, Watego's Beach, Byron Bay
Tel: 02-6685 5366
Near the Queensland border and designed after a 1920s Mediterranean villa with Indonesian-inspired interiors. Guests enjoy five-star cuisine in a terraced restaurant overlooking the beach. No children under 13. **$$$$**

Byron Bay Beach Resort
Beside The Beach, Bayshore Drive, Byron Bay
Tel: 02-6685 8000 or 1800-028 927
www.byronbaybeachresort.com.au
This resort offers 78 self-contained cabins set among native gardens of large beach-front property. **$$$**

Peppers Convent
Halls Road, Pokolbin, Hunter Valley
Tel: 02-4993 8999
www.peppers.com.au
Early 20th-century Roman Catholic convent with guest rooms and restaurant. **$$$$**

Peppers Guest House
Ekerts Road, Pokolbin, Hunter Valley
Tel: 02-4993 8999
www.peppers.com.au
The extensive gardens are ablaze in spring and autumn, but Peppers is perhaps most famous for its restaurant – Chez Pok. **$$$$**

AUSTRALIAN CAPITAL TERRITORY

Canberra

Because Canberra is so spread out, location is important. While some hotels are close to the shopping and business district, others are within walking distance of the National Gallery and Parliament House. Each outer suburb has its own shopping complex and restaurants.

Hyatt Hotel Canberra
Commonwealth Avenue, Yarralumla
Tel: 02-6270 1234
www.hyatt.com
A part of the city's history, the Hotel Canberra is an elegant example of Australian Art Deco design. Custom-designed 1920s carpets, period-outfitted staff and interior balconies complete the picture. Set on extensive landscaped gardens and located within the Parliamentary Triangle. **$$$$**

Canberra Rex Hotel
150 Northbourne Avenue, Braddon
Tel: 02-6248 5311
www.canberrarexhotel.com.au
Reliable four-star hotel, popular with business people. An easy walk from the central business district, with an indoor pool, sauna and gymnasium. **$$$**

Crowne Plaza Canberra
1 Binara Street, City
Tel: 02-6247 8999

www.crowneplaza.com.au
Centrally located next to Canberra Casino and Convention Centre, close to shopping, theatres, cinemas and restaurants, the Crowne Plaza has 24-hour room service, a health club and undercover parking. **$$$**

Olims Canberra Hotel
Corner of Limestone and Ainslie avenues, Braddon
Tel: 02-6243 0000
Freecall: 1800-475 337
www.olimshotel.com
Only about 1km (½ mile) from the city centre and very close to the war memorial, this Heritage-listed property has split-level apartments designed around a central courtyard. **$$**

Rydges Lakeside Canberra
London Circuit, Canberra City
Tel: 1800-026 169
www.rydges.com
Closer to the commercial centre of the city, rooms provide great views of the lake and surrounding mountains. There are several pleasant bars in which to unwind. **$$$**

Diplomat Boutique Hotel
Corner of Canberra Avenue and Hely Street, Griffith
Tel: 02-6295 2277
Freecall: 1800-026 367
www.diplomathotel.com.au
Canberra's boutique hotel offers honeymoon packages in a spa suite. Large rooms,

extensive facilities, 3km (2 miles) from city centre. **$$$$**

Forrest Hotel and Apartments
30 National Circuit, Forrest
Tel: 02-6295 3433
Freecall: 1800-676 372
www.forrestinn.com.au
Close to Parliament House and the National Gallery; in leafy surrounds. Some rooms have park views. **$$$**

Oxley Court Serviced Apartments
Corner of Oxley and Dawes streets, Kingston
Tel: 02-6295 6216
Freecall: 1800-623 960
www.oxleycourt.com.au
A good choice for families and small groups. Spacious fully self-contained apartments a short drive from the city centre. **$$$**

Hotel Heritage
203 Goyder Street, Narrabundah
Tel: 02-6295 2944
Freecall: 1800-029 346
www.domahotelscanberra.com.au
Hotel rooms and family apartments 12 minutes from the city centre and close to many tourist attractions. **$$**

Canberra City YHA Hostel
7 Akuna Street, Canberra City
Tel: 02-6248 9155
Freecall: 1800-300 488
www.yha.com.au
One of the best YHA hostels in Australia. Within walking distance of shops,

restaurants, nightclubs and the Jolimont Centre. Facilities include a rooftop barbecue area, an indoor pool, spa and sauna. Some double/twin and family rooms. **$**

Victor Lodge
29 Dawes Street, Kingston
Tel: 02-6295 7777
www.victorlodge.com.au
Friendly place, close to the railway station, 5 minutes' drive from Parliament House. Offers twins or bunk rooms with shared bathrooms. Breakfast included, and bicycles available to rent. **$**

Outside Canberra

Brindabella Station
Brindabella Valley Station, Brindabella
Tel: 02-6236 2121
www.brindabellastation.com.au
Historic homestead set in classic Australian bush, between two national parks. A superior country retreat, with five comfortable rooms. **$$$**

VICTORIA

Melbourne

Melbourne has a wide range of accommodation. There are a number of designer or boutique hotels with fashion-conscious interiors, as well as a range of

PRICE CATEGORIES

Price categories are for a double room without breakfast:
$ = under A$80
$$ = A$80–130
$$$ = A$130–200
$$$$ = over A$200

apartment-style accommodation, which often provides more space and facilities for the same price as a hotel. The seaside suburb of St Kilda offers moderate accommodation. The classified columns of Budget-priced hotels lie mainly at the Spencer Street end of the city, around the bus and train terminal, and the new blocks rising around the Docklands development are increasing apartment availability in that area.

Adelphi
187 Flinders Lane
Tel: 03-8080 8888
www.adelphi.com.au
An ultra-modern hotel in the heart of the city. Fabulous room-service choices. Spectacular views from the rooftop bar and the pool, which is cantilevered over the street and has sauna and steam rooms alongside. **$$$**

Albert Heights Serviced Apartments
83 Albert Street, East Melbourne
Tel: 03-9419 0955

Freecall: 1800-800 117
www.albertheights.com.au
Modern apartment units, all facing a central garden courtyard and spa pool. Functional but tasteful, the

units include all expected facilities. **$$**

Batmans Hill Hotel
623 Collins Street
Tel: 03-9614 6344
www.batmanshill.com.au
Old-fashioned and friendly style under an elegant, historic exterior. **$$$**

Crown Promenade Hotel
8 Whiteman Street, Southbank
Tel: 03-9292 6688
Freecall: 1800-776 612
www.crownpromenadehotel.com.au
This 39-floor hotel towers above the Yarra River and a vast casino and entertainment complex that includes cinemas, restaurants and live entertainment. **$$$$**

Downtowner on Lygon
66 Lygon Street, Carlton
Tel: 03-9663 5555
Freecall: 1800-800 130
www.downtowner.com.au
Carlton is the cosmopolitan location of this hotel near the university. Stylishly decorated rooms. Guests receive gold membership to the Melbourne City Baths. **$$$**

Georgian Court
21–5 George Street,
East Melbourne
Tel: 03-9419 6353
www.georgiancourt.com.au
Comfortable Bed & Breakfast situated on a tree-lined street, across from beautiful Fitzroy Gardens and just a short walk to the city centre. Thirty-one rooms; dinner available most nights. **$$**

Hotel Grand Chancellor
131 Lonsdale Street
Tel: 03-9656 4000
Freecall: 1800-753 379
www.ghihotels.com
Comfortable rooms, close to Melbourne Cricket Ground and shopping district. **$$**

Grand Hyatt Melbourne
123 Collins Street
Tel: 03-9657 1234/131 234
www.melbourne.grand.hyatt.com
Ostentatious display of brass and marble right down to the huge black-marble bathrooms. Popular for business conventions. **$$$$**

Hotel Como
630 Chapel Street, South Yarra
Tel: 03-9825 2222

Freecall: 1800-033 400
www.mirvachotels.com.au
The Como wins awards year after year for its attention to comfort and uniquely designed suites. In the fashionable South Yarra district, famous for its fine restaurants and boutiques. **$$$$**

Intercontinental Melbourne the Rialto
495 Collins Street
Tel: 03-9620 9111
Freecall: 1800-221 335
A stunning makeover has returned this 1891 classic of Venetian Gothic architecture to being one of the city's greats. **$$$$**

Jasper Hotel
489 Elizabeth Street
Tel: 03-8327 2777
Freecall: 1800-468 359
www.jasperhotel.com.au
Contemporary boutique accommodation located next to popular Queen Victoria Markets. **$$$**

The Langham
Southgate Avenue, Southbank
Tel: 03-8696 8888
www.melbourne.langhamhotels.com.au
Central to the Southgate Development, this high-rise promotes an aura of untrammelled luxury with the bonus of exceptional city views. Private prom-enade to the shopping district. **$$$$**

Manor House Apartments
36 Darling Street, South Yarra
Tel: 03-9867 1266
www.manorhouse.com
Well-furnished apartments in the exclusive restaurant and shopping district of South Yarra. **$$$**

Melbourne Metro YHA
78 Howard Street, North Melbourne
Tel: 03-9329 8599
www.yha.com.au
Huge property with fine facilities. Breakfast and dinner service. **$**

The Nunnery
116 Nicholson Street, Fitzroy
Tel: 03-9419 8637
Freecall: 1800-032 635
www. nunnery.com.au
Converted Victorian building close to the city, with comfortable heated rooms, good facilities and a friendly atmosphere. Some dormitory-style accom-

modation for A$30. **$**

Olembia Guest House
96 Barkly Street, St Kilda
Tel: 03-9537 1412
www.olembia.com.au
Cosy and friendly guesthouse with dorm rooms, singles and doubles. Very good facilities, heating, parking and a pleasant guest lounge. **$**

Pensione Hotel
16 Spencer Street
Tel: 03-9621 3333
Freecall: 1800-81616
www.pensione.com.au
A modern hotel with simple but good rooms. **$$**

Quest Carlton Clocktower Apartments
255 Drummond Street, Carlton
Tel: 03-9349 9700
Freecall: 1800-062 966
www.clocktower.com.au
Stylish apartments in the bustling Lygon Street area. **$$$**

The Sofitel
25 Collins Street
Tel: 03-9653 0000
www.sofitelmelbourne.com.au
Guest rooms start on the 36th floor and offer sweeping views across Melbourne and Port Phillip Bay. The fancy restaurant has returned and the bar and café at the top still welcome visitors who want the view without the room. **$$$$**

Vibe Hotel Carlton
441 Royal Parade, Parkville
Tel: 03-9380 9222
www.vibehotels.com.au
Bright, modern and ideal for the university and Melbourne's Little Italy. **$$$**

The Victoria Hotel
215 Little Collins Street
Tel: 03-9669 0000
Freecall: 1800-331 147
www.victoriahotel.com.au
Budget, standard and superior rooms offered in this good standard hotel. Within walking distance of the CBD. **$$**

The Westin
205 Collins Street
Tel: 03-9635 2222
www.westin.com.au
Facing City Square in Swanston Street, it's hard to get more central than this. Combine that with sleek interiors and fine service.

$$$$

The Windsor
103 Spring Street
Tel: 03-9633 6000
www.thewindsor.com.au
For the old wealth of Melbourne, there is no question about the Windsor's supremacy. This majestic National Trust building in the centre of Melbourne is one of the few in Australia originally built as a hotel. Intended in 1883 to provide the most luxurious accommodation in Melbourne, the Windsor in many respects still holds that title. Excellent service, combined with old-world interiors and a famous high tea at 3pm. **$$$$**

Outside Melbourne

Amaroo Caravan Park and YHA Hostel
Corner of Church and Osborne streets, Cowes
Tel: 03-5952 2548
www.amaroopark.com.au
In the main town of Phillip Island, this is the best budget accommodation by far. Friendly hostel and caravan park with evening meals, bicycles for hire and organised tours to the Penguin Parade and Wilsons Prom. **$**

Comfort Inn Shamrock
Corner of Pall Mall and Williamson streets, Bendigo
Tel: 03-5443 0333
www.hotelshamrock.com.au
Grandiose country hotel from the gold-mining period. Ornate roof structure and surrounding balconies. Rooms range from inexpensive traditional rooms to de-luxe suites. **$$$**

Cumberland Lorne
150 Mountjoy Parade, Lorne
Tel: 03-5289 4444
Freecall: 1800-037 010
www.cumberland.com.au
A memorable scenic drive down the Great Ocean Road, and you're in one of Victoria's favourite seaside playgrounds. The hotel offers a variety of suites with wonderful views and complimentary recreational activities, right in the heart of the friendly town. **$$$$**

Hotel Pension Grimus
224 Breathtaker Road,
Mount Buller
Tel: 03-5777 6396
www.pensiongrimus.com.au
A great hotel in Victoria's
premier ski-resort area.
Legendary skier hosts Hans
and Lotte Grimus (Hans has
a ski lift named after him)
run a friendly, great-value
lodge. All rooms have
double spa baths. Families
welcome; babysitting
available. **$$$**
Lake House

4 King Street, Daylesford
Tel: 03-5348 3329
www.lakehouse.com.au
Located in "Spa Country",
this is a luxurious retreat on
the shore of Lake
Daylesford with one of
Victoria's finest restaurants.
Everything from the pastries
to the preserves is made on
the premises. You can visit
local wineries, a sheep
station and Hanging Rock
(scene of the picnic in Peter
Weir's classic film). **$$$$**
Luxury Townhouses

1 Delany Avenue, Bright
Tel: 03-5750 1433
www.brightmotorinn.com.au
Part of the otherwise
undistinguished Bright
Motor Inn, these houses live
up to their name and throw
in the best location in town
right by the river. **$$$$**
Mt Ophir Estate
Stillards Lane, Rutherglen
Tel: 02-6032 8920
www.mount-ophir.com
Historic winery buildings,
plus two homesteads with
four bedrooms in each.

There is an emu and elk
farm, vineyards and forests,
as well as an organic
cropping farm. **$$**
**Southern Grampians
Cottages**
33–5 Victoria Valley Road, Dunkeld
Tel: 03-5577 2457
www.grampianscottages.com.au
Attractive log-style cabins,
self-contained with wood
fires, spas and kitchens, in
a bushland setting. Located
next to a national park full
of wildlife and nature walks.
$$

SOUTH AUSTRALIA

Adelaide
Adelaide has been
spaciously planned, so if
you need to be within
walking distance of the
Festival Centre, South
Australian Art Gallery, and
lively East End neighbour-
hood, make sure to stay in
the Central Business
District. However, North
Adelaide is just a short
distance across the Torrens
River and has a wealth of
historic B&Bs with views of
the Adelaide Hills. The
suburb of Glenelg is an
attractive beach-front
community with many
Mediterranean-style houses
and restful ocean views.
Budget accommodation in
central Adelaide is limited,
with hostels clustered
around the Central Bus
Station on Franklin Street –
a wider selection can be
found in the attractive
beach-side suburb of
Glenelg.

Central Adelaide (CBD)
Hyatt Regency Adelaide
North Terrace, Adelaide
Tel: 08-8231 1234
www.adelaide.regency.hyatt.com
Luxurious tower
accommodation and a
casino housed in an historic
railway station downstairs.
Best location in the centre
of town, right beside the
Adelaide Festival Centre.
Rooms provide excellent
views of the city. **$$$$**

Stamford Plaza Adelaide
150 North Terrace, Adelaide
Tel: 08-8461 1111
www.stamford.com.au
Adelaide's original five-star
hotel has been refurbished
and includes a delightful
terrace garden for
breakfasts and buffets. In
the centre of town with city
views. **$$$$**
Hilton Adelaide
233 Victoria Square
Tel: 08-8217 2000
www.adelaide.hilton.com
Located adjacent to the
Central Markets as well as
Gouger Street restaurants
with views over Victoria
Square. The Grange
restaurant, located
downstairs, is highly
acclaimed. **$$$$**
**Medina Grand Adelaide
Treasury**
2 Flinders Street
Tel: 08-8112 0000
Serviced one- and two-
bedroom apartments and
studios in the centre of town
on Victoria Square. Located
in the grand Heritage-listed
treasury building. **$$$$**
Grand Chifley Adelaide
208 South Terrace
Tel: 08-8223 2800 or 1300-650
464
www.hotel208.com
With views of the attractive
South Parklands directly
opposite, this four-star
property is 15 minutes' walk
to the city and close to the
business centres of
Parkside, Unley and
Wayville. **$$**

Mercure Grosvenor Hotel
125 North Terrace
Tel: 08-8407 8888
www.mercure.com.au
Opposite the Skycity
Adelaide, the casino in the
centre of town, this makes
an ideal base for walking to
all major attractions. **$$**
Adelaide Backpackers Inn
112 Carrington Street
Tel: 08-8223 6635
Freecall: 1800-247 725
www.adelaidebackpackersinn.net.au
Dormitories and annexe
with singles and twins. Free
hot apple pie and ice cream
every night. **$**
Adelaide Central YHA
135 Waymouth Street, Adelaide
Tel: 08-8414 3010
Freecall: 1800-222 942
www.yha.com.au
A modern YHA hostel with
good facilities; films every
night. Family rooms and
doubles/twins with private
bathrooms available. **$**

North Adelaide
**Freedom Adelaide
Meridien**
21–37 Melbourne Street,
North Adelaide
Tel: 08-8267 3033
Freecall: 1800-888 228
www.adelaidemeridien.com.au
Fashionable street in North
Adelaide, known for its
cafés, boutiques and
parklands. Modern terraced
structure comprises
standard and executive
suites. **$$**
**North Adelaide Heritage
Apartments & Cottages**

Various locations in North Adelaide
Tel/fax: 08-8272 1355
www.adelaideheritage.com
Manages many B&Bs in
Heritage-listed properties –
including manor houses, a
fire station and iron-lace
villas – in the historic
boulevards of North
Adelaide. **$$$**
Princes Lodge
73 Lefevre Terrace, North Adelaide
Tel: 08-8267 5566
www.princeslodge.com.au
Friendly management and
good location in North
Adelaide, within walking
distance of the city. Light
breakfast is served. **$$**

Glenelg (beach)
Stamford Grand
Moseley Square, Glenelg
Tel: 08-8376 1222
www.stamford.com.au
Beautiful views of the ocean

PRICE CATEGORIES
Price categories are for a
double room without
breakfast:
$ = under A$80
$$ = A$80–130
$$$ = A$130–200
$$$$ = over A$200

or the Adelaide Hills from this grand highrise resort in seaside Glenelg. Award-winning hotel provides extra-large rooms and touches of the Victorian era. **$$$$**

Glenelg Beach Hostel
1–7 Moseley Street, Glenelg
Tel: 08-8376 0007
www.glenelgbeachhostel.com.au
Everything from seven-bed dorms to family rooms – and no bunk beds. **$**.

Outside Adelaide
Adelaide Hills
Thorngrove Manor
2 Glenside Lane, Stirling
Tel: 08-8339 6748
www.slh.com
About 20 minutes by car from Adelaide, this is a Gothic fantasy complete with turrets and gables. Although it sounds tacky, the Manor offers five-star luxury with large private suites furnished with valuable antiques, and a fine restaurant. **$$$$**

Grand Mercure Mount Lofty House

74 Mt Lofty Summit Road, Crafers, Adelaide Hills
Tel: 08-8339 6777
www.mtloftyhouse.com.au
Historic country estate that is now a boutique hotel. Located in the Adelaide Hills with views of the Piccadilly Valley and only a 20-minute drive from the city. **$$$**

Barossa Valley
Collingrove Homestead
Eden Valley Road, Angaston
Tel: 08-8564 2061
www.collingrovehomestead.com.au
National Trust-listed homestead in the Barossa Ranges with extensive English-style gardens and antiques; ideal for a peaceful escape. **$$$**

Langmeil Cottages
89 Langmeil Road, Tanunda
Tel/fax: 08-8563 2987
www.langmeilcottages.com
Beautiful views from self-contained units, with the use of bicycles, barbecue and swimming pool. **$**

Kangaroo Island
Lighthouse Keeper's Cottage

Cape Borda, Kangaroo Island
Tel: 08-8559 7235
www.parks.sa.gov.au/flinderschase
Stay in one of the unique heritage cottages in Kangaroo Island's wilderness. Bookings handled by National Parks & Wildlife, South Australia, Flinders Chase National Park, Kangaroo Island. **$**
(Coonawarra (wine region)

Padthaway Estate Homestead
Riddoch Highway, Padthaway
Tel: 08-8765 5555
www.padthawayestate.com
Magnificent 19th-century mansion amid the Padthaway Estate vineyards, home of fine Australian champagne-style wines. Six rooms, cosy lounges with fireplaces and a relaxed friendly service. **$$$**

Outback
Arkaroola Wilderness Sanctuary
Arkaroola, northern Flinders Ranges via Port Augusta
Tel: 08-8648 4848
Freecall: 1800-676 042

www.arkaroola.com.au
A rugged Outback landscape 600km (373 miles) north of Adelaide, rich in native flora and fauna. **$$**

Desert Cave Hotel
Hutchison Street, Coober Pedy
Tel: 08-8672 5688
Freecall: 1800-088 521
www.desertcave.com.au
De-luxe underground hotel in Australia's most famous opal-mining Outback community 850km (528 miles) north of Adelaide. Most residents live below ground as an escape from the desert sun. Choose underground suites with their naked rock walls and impressive skylit foyer. **$$$$**

The Underground Motel
Catacomb Road, Coober Pedy
Tel: 08-8672 5324
Freecall: 1800-622 979
www.theundergroundmotel.com.au
A more economical choice in (or under) Coober Pedy, also with natural rock walls; friendly comfortable place with a guest kitchen for self-catered breakfasts. **$$**

QUEENSLAND

Queensland's coastline is a near-continuous strip of excellent beaches, with hundreds of holiday resorts. While Brisbane itself has no beaches, it is an excellent base or jumping-off point for exploring the south of Queensland. Cairns in the far north is the direct arrival point for visitors to the Great Barrier Reef and Cape York. An hour further north, the village of Port Douglas is smaller, more charming and more convenient (it also has the Four Mile Beach, while Cairns faces mudflats).

Camping
For an excellent guide to Queensland camping grounds, contact:
The Environmental Protection Agency, PO Box 155, Brisbane Albert Street, Queensland 4002.
Tel: 07-3227 8197

Fax: 07-3227 8749
Or vist them at www.epa.qld.gov.au. They publish a Queensland National Parks and Wildlife Service booklet entitled *Camping in Queensland*, detailing over 280 places to camp in national parks, state forests and water reserves. Bookings are recommended to avoid disappointment.

Brisbane
Acacia Inner City Inn
413 Upper Edward Street
Tel: 07-3832 1663
Friendly inner-city facility with a range of accommodation choices, and a sociable environment. Continental breakfast inclusive. **$$**
Brisbane City YHA Hostel
392 Upper Roma Street, Brisbane
Tel: 07-3236 4999
www.yha.com.au

There are excellent facilities in this backpacker-orientated youth hostel. Located in trendy Paddington, close to the city, the hostel has an inexpensive restaurant for breakfast and dinner. **$**
Base Backpackers
308 Edward Street
Tel: 07-3211 2433
Freecall: 1800-676 340 (reservations only)
www.palacebackpackers.com.au
Smack opposite Central Station and with everything you need, including the famous Down Under Bar. **$**
Oaks 212 Margaret
212 Margaret Street
Tel: 07-3012 8020
Freecall: 1800-036 990
www.theoaksgroup.com.au
Good-value well-appointed apartments. This is one of eight blocks dotted around the city run by the Oaks group. **$$$**

Conrad Treasury
William and George streets
Tel: 07-3306 8888
Freecall: 1800-506 889 (reservations only)
www.conradtreasury.com.au
The Treasury building – which houses Brisbane's casino – is one of the finest 19th-century structures in the city. Accommodation is in individually decorated suites, featuring many of the original furnishings. **$$$$**
Central Dockside Apartments

44 Ferry Street, Kangaroo Point
Tel: 07-3981 6644
www.centralgroup.com.au
Spacious self-contained apartments, each with a sweeping view from a private balcony. Across the river from the city but there's a ferry at the bottom of the garden. **$$$$**

Explorers Inn
63 Turbot Street
Tel: 07-3211 3488
Freecall: 1800-623 288
www.explorers.com.au
Budget-style accommodation in the Brisbane CBD, 150 metres/yards from the Queen Street Mall and a range of bars and restaurants. **$$**

The Marque Hotel Brisbane
103 George Street
Tel: 07-3221 6044
www.chifleyhotels.com
Refurbished 99-room hotel with a distinctive casual elegance. A 5-minute walk to the Southbank Parkland across the river. **$$$**

Mercure Brisbane
85–7 North Quay
Tel: 07-3237 2300
www.mercurebrisbane.com.au
Great location on the Brisbane River overlooking the Cultural Centre, Southbank Parkland, and more. Comfortable accommodation just a few minutes' walk from the Central Business District and casino. **$$$**

Il Mondo Boutique Hotel
25–35 Rotherham Street, Kangaroo Point
Tel: 07-3392 0111
A boutique hotel where every room is individually decorated. Close to Kangaroo Point. **$$$**

Quay West Suites Brisbane
132 Alice Street
Tel: 07-3853 6000
Freecall: 1800-672 726
(reservations only)
www.mirvachotels.com.au
One- and two-bedroom apartment accommodation in the city centre, overlooking the Botanic Gardens. All suites have balconies. **$$$$**

Quest on Story Bridge
85 Deakin Street, Kangaroo Point

Tel: 07-3249 8400
www.questonstorybridge.com.au
One-, two-, and three-bedroom apartments from this trusty chain in Kangaroo Point in a location handy for the Southbank, CBD, and the Gabba. **$$**

Spring Hill Terraces
260 Water Street, Spring Hill
Tel: 07-3854 1048
www.springhillterraces.com
Modern and comfortable self-contained apartments and budget rooms in a good location, about 5 minutes' drive from the city centre. **$$**

Stamford Plaza Hotel
By the Botanic Gardens (corner of Margaret and Edward streets)
Tel: 07-3221 1999
Freecall: 1300-301 391
(reservations only)
www.stamford.com.au
Brisbane's finest luxury hotel, located in the city centre beside the historic Botanic Gardens. Impressive oil paintings of early Queensland grace the lobby, which extends alongside a serene central courtyard, providing a haven from the inner city. Elegant rooms of generous country-style proportions overlook the winding Brisbane River. Try the excellent Siggi's at the Port Office restaurant for special occasions. **$$$$**

Watermark Hotel Brisbane
551 Wickham Terrace
Tel: 07-3831 3111
Freecall: 1800-777 702
(reservations only)
www.watermarkhotelbrisbane.com.au
Up-market hotel with European-style decor, located near Roma Street Parkland and Transit Centre. **$$$$**

Southern Queensland Outback

Talgai Homestead
Allora–Ellinthorp Road, Allora, Southern Darling Downs
Tel: 07-4666 3444
A small, friendly hotel with cottages in the grounds of a National Trust-listed homestead furnished with antiques. Total relaxation guaranteed. **$$$$**

Central Queensland Outback

Albert Park Motor Inn
Ilfracombe Road, Longreach
Tel: 07-4658 2411
Very comfortable with modern facilities, within walking distance of the Stockman's Hall of Fame and the Qantas Founders' Outback Museum. **$$**

Carnarvon Gorge Wilderness Lodge
Carnarvon Gorge, via Rolleston, Queensland
Tel: 07-4984 4503
Freecall: 1800-644 150
(reservations only)
www.carnarvon-gorge.com
Unique timber and canvas safari cabins have their own Outback charm, and make a good base for exploring the gorge with its ancient plant life and fossilised Aboriginal rock art. **$$$$**

Gold Coast

There are dozens of generic high-rises along this 35km (20-mile) stretch of sand, which includes Surfer's Paradise, but most people who come here have their hotel already organised through package tours. There are also many small motels for the independent traveller.

Broadwater Keys
125 Frank Street, Labrador
Tel: 07-5531 0839
www.broadwaterkeys.com.au
About 100 metres/yards from the Broadwater, self-contained units available on daily and weekly rates. **$$**
Motels such as **Sunset Court** in Surfers Paradise (tel: 07-5539 0266) are typical of the cheap Aussie vacation hangouts here – functional, often with a kitchen, and not far from the beach. **$$**

Palazzo Versace
94 Sea World Drive, Main Beach
Tel: 07-5509 8000
Freecall: 1800-098 000
www.palazzoversace.com
The world's first hotel designed by Versace is predictably over the top. **$$$$**

Sheraton Mirage Resort and Spa
Sea World Drive, Main Beach
Tel: 07-5591 1488
Freecall: 1800-073 535
(reservations only)
www.sheraton.com
Low-rise luxury resort with comprehensive health club facilities. Restaurants highly rated. **$$$$**

Sunshine Coast

Hyatt Regency Coolum Golf Resort & Spa
1 Warran Road, Coolum
Tel: 07-5446 1234
www.coolum.hyatt.com
About 90 minutes' drive north of Brisbane, a championship golf-course resort set in natural bushland with ocean beach front, and its own lifeguard on duty. **$$$$**

Noosa Blue Resort
16 Noosa Drive, Noosa
Tel: 07-5447 5699
Freecall: 1800-463 854
www.noosablue.com.au
A stylish boutique resort perched high on Noosa Hill, with sweeping views of Noosa's coastline and hinterland, and only 450 metres/yards from its Hastings Street social and shopping centre. Luxury self-contained suites with spas and fine attention to detail. **$$$$**

Fraser Island

Kingfisher Bay Resort and Village
North White Cliffs, Fraser Island
Tel: 07-4194 9300
Freecall: 1800-072 555
www.kingfisherbay.com
The only de-luxe property on this stunningly beautiful World Heritage-listed island. (Arrive by car ferry or catamaran from Urangan, approx 3½ hours' drive north of Brisbane.) For a fee

PRICE CATEGORIES

Price categories are for a double room without breakfast:
$ = under A$80
$$ = A$80–130
$$$ = A$130–200
$$$$ = over A$200

the resort provides tours to scenic sites, or you can rent a four-wheel drive. **$$$**

Lamington National Park

Binna Burra Mountain Lodge
Beechmont
Tel: 07-5533 3622
Freecall: 1300-246 622
www.binnaburralodge.com.au
An eco-accredited lodge in world-heritage area with over 160km (100 miles) of hiking tracks. Packages include rustic cabin accommodation, all country-style meals, abseiling, and flying fox, rainforest and bird-spotting walks. Camping sites and permanent safari tents also available. **$$$**

O'Reilly's Rainforest Guest House
Lamington National Park Road, Via Canungra
Tel: 07-5502 4911
Freecall: 1800-688 722
(reservations only)
www.oreillys.com.au
Friendly family-run guesthouse which has been providing accommodation, naturalist guide services, touring and special events in this beautiful world-heritage region for over 80 years. About 2 hours' drive southwest from Brisbane. **$$$**

Far North Queensland

Archipelago Studio Apartments
72 Macrossan Street, Port Douglas
Tel: 07-4099 5387
www.archipelago.com.au
Self-contained apartments right on Macrossan Street and only 50 metres/yards from Four Mile Beach. Proprietors Christel and Wolfgang are a goldmine of local knowledge. **$$$**

Gilligan's Backpackers Hotel & Resort
57–89 Grafton Street, Cairns
Tel: 07-4041 6566
Freecall: 1800-556 995
www.gilligansbackpackers.com.au
Only a few years old, this luxury backpackers offers rooms with air conditioning, en-suites and balconies. **$**

The Lakes Cairns Resort & Spa
2 Greenslopes Street, Cairns
Tel: 07-4053 9411
Freecall: 1800-666 614
www.thelakescairns.com.au
Adjoining the Botanical Gardens and close to the city action without complete immersion, a thoughtfully designed resort in natural surroundings. **$$$**

Port O'Call Lodge
Corner of Port Street and Craven Close, Port Douglas
Tel: 07-4099 5422
www.portocall.com.au
YHA associate. The best

option for budget accommodation, about 1km (½ mile) from the town. Four-share and private rooms, cooking facilities, bar and bistro, a pool, and courtesy bus to and from Cairns (Mon–Sat, conditions apply). **$$**

The Reef Retreat
10–14 Harpa Street, Palm Cove
Tel: 07-4059 1744
www.reefretreat.com.au
Good-value resort accommodation in Palm Cove, 20 minutes north of Cairns. Natural tropical setting, idyllic beach, bars and alfresco dining. **$$$**

Sebel Reef House & Spa
99 Williams Esplanade, Palm Cove
Tel: 07-4055 3633
www.reefhouse.com.au
Elegant tropical resort only 25 minutes north of Cairns on Palm Cove's golden beach. The design is refreshingly light and spacious. **$$$$**

Sheraton Mirage Port Douglas
Davidson Street, Port Douglas
Tel: 07-4099 5888
Freecall: 1800-818 831
(reservations only)
www.sheraton-mirage.com.au
The glitziest resort in the fast-developing town of Port Douglas. All the man-made five-star luxury you can imagine, including 2 hectares (5 acres) of swimmable blue lagoons and an 18-hole international-standard golf course. **$$$$**

Sofitel Reef Hotel Casino
35–41 Wharf Street, Cairns
Tel: 07-4030 8888
Freecall: 1800-808 883
www.reefcasino.com.au
This luxury development in Cairns includes a nightclub, rainforest conservatory, five restaurants and a casino. All suites have balconies and modern wood-grain furnishings in a vaguely tropical Queensland fashion. **$$$$**

Sovereign Resort Hotel
128 Charlotte Street, Cooktown
Tel: 07-4043 0500
www.sovereign-resort.com.au
A relaxed "plantation-style" resort hotel in the heart of Cooktown. Excellent balcony

restaurant, and the air conditioning is welcome at the end of a warm day. Airport courtesy pick-up by arrangement. **$$$**

Yungaburra Pub
6-8 Kehoe Place, Yungaburra
Tel: 07-4095 3515
www.yungaburrapub.com.au
A fine example of Federation-style architecture in the quiet village of Yungaburra and a comfortable base for exploring the rolling hills of the Atherton Tablelands. The rooms are simple but pleasantly decorated, there's good pub food and staff are friendly. **$$**

Far North Eco Resorts

For a more natural and unspoilt environment, the following resorts provide a glimpse of real North Queensland.

Cape Trib Beach House
Cape Tribulation Road (38km/24 miles from the ferry)
Tel: 07-4098 0030
www.capetribbeach.com.au
Dormitory and family cabins as close to the beach as the National Parks Authority will allow. Kitchen/laundry facilities, swimming pool and bistro/bar. **$$**

Cape Tribulation Exotic Fruit Farm B&B
Lot 5 Nicole Drive, Cape Tribulation
Tel: 07-4098 0057
www.capetrib.com.au
A fruit-tasting and farm tour in a permaculture orchard; will add another dimension to your rainforest experience. **$$$$**

Daintree Eco Lodge & Spa
20 Daintree Road, Daintree
Tel: 07-4098 6100
Freecall: 1800-808 010
www.daintree-ecolodge.com.au
Comfortable lodges set in the rainforest opposite the tropical Daintree River. Only 90 minutes north of Cairns on a sealed road – no ferry crossing. Multi-award-winner for its spa and eco-tourism incorporating indigenous culture. **$$$$**

The Elandra Mission Beach
Explorer Drive, Mission Beach

BELOW: luxury living at the Sheraton Mirage Port Douglas.

Tel: 07-4068 8154
www.elandraresorts.com
South of Cairns and high above historical Tam O'Shanter Point, surrounded by rainforest, with commanding views of Dunk and Bedarra islands. Spacious verandahs look out to sea and a short stroll leads to a private beach. **$$$$**

Kewarra Beach Resort
Kewarra Beach
Tel: 07-4057 6666
www.kewarra.com
Private, deluxe bungalows hidden in tropical beachfront property 20 minutes from Cairns. Quiet relaxation after busy day trips. Fine collection of Aboriginal and Torres Strait art and historical artefacts. **$$$$**

Peppers Bloomfield Lodge
PO Box 966, Cairns
Tel: 07-4035 9166
www.bloomfieldlodge.com
Remote and beautiful location abutting Cape Tribulation National Park. Private cabins hidden in the rainforest, overlooking the Coral Sea. Possible to continue by four-wheel drive to Cooktown and surrounds. Minimum four-night packages include all meals, flight transfers from Cairns and a guided rainforest walk and river cruise. **$$$$**

Red Mill House
11 Stewart Street, Daintree Village
Tel/fax: 07-4098 6233
www.redmillhouse.com.au
Excellent B&B in an old Queenslander house set in spacious gardens near the Daintree River. Caters especially to keen birdwatchers and nature-lovers. **$$$**

Silky Oaks Lodge and Healing Waters Spa
Finlayvale Road,
Mossman River Gorge
Tel: 07-4098 1666
Freecall: 1300-134 044
www.silkyoakslodge.com.au
Some 27km (17 miles) from Port Douglas, this rainforest hideaway lies on the edge of Mossman Gorge, which adjoins Daintree National Park. The treehouses and river houses have all the creature comforts you need, plus a spa, restaurant, and

rainforest excursions and canoe trips on the Mossman River. **$$$$**

Undara Lava Lodge
Mount Surprise
Tel: 07-4097 1411
www.undara.com.au
Accommodation is in quaint refurbished railway carriages on the edge of the Undara Volcanic National Park. Qualified guides conduct interpretive tours through ancient caverns. **$$**

Coconut Beach Resort
Cape Tribulation Road,
Cape Tribulation
Tel: 07-4098 0033
Hideaway accommodation nestled in the rainforest, and only minutes to the beach from its Cape Restaurant. A "canopy crane" is an innovative way to view the rainforest treetops from above, and the resort has its own boat for reef trips. **$$$$**

Cape York

Punsand Bay Camping Resort
Via Bamaga, Cape York
Tel: 07-4069 1722
www.punsand.com.au
This resort, which offers camping facilities and airconditioned cabins for Cape York's annual influx of four-wheel-drive adventurers as well as air travellers (via Bamaga or Horn Island), provides access to some of the most remote, historic and beautiful sites on the Cape York Peninsula – rainforest, streams, and endless unpopulated beaches. **$**

Great Barrier Reef & Whitsunday Islands

A number of the more up-market island resorts – Lizard, Bedarra, Dunk, Heron and Brampton – are accessed by sea, or (more commonly) by air, so remember to factor this in when costing your getaway. Bedarra Island and Dunk Island Resorts were closed for refurbishment until the end of 2011 after damage from Cyclone Yasi.

Bedarra Island Resort
Bedarra Island, via Mission Beach
Freecall: 1800-134 044
www.bedarraisland.com
Bedarra Island Resort has created a mystique surrounding its rich and famous guests. Privacy is the draw, since only 15 individual luxury villas are nestled in the beach-front foliage. Guests (no under-16s) are free to explore the island by motor dinghy and find their private beach to settle down on with their champagne-filled picnic hampers. **$$$$**

Brampton Island
Via Mackay
Tel: 07-4951 4499
Tel: 1300-134 044 (reservations)
www.brampton-island.com
Intimate resort on an island which is almost entirely on national parkland; you can take the mini-train to the daily fish feeding. Located 32km (20 miles) northeast of Mackay (a 20-minute flight or 50-minute launch trip). Activities include golf, catamaran sailing and other sports. Reef trips and seaplane flights additional. **$$$**

Daydream Island Resort and Spa
Whitsunday Islands, Shute Harbour
Tel: 07-4948 8488
Freecall: 1800-075 040
(reservations only)
www.daydream.net.au
Family-style resort on a smallish, pretty tropical island with a wide range of free activities including outdoor cinema. Day trips to Outer Reef and Whitehaven Beach. **$$$**

Dunk Island
Via Townsville
Tel: 07-4068 8199
Tel: 1300-134 044
www.dunk-island.com
Almost completely rainforested, Dunk is home to richly diverse native flora and fauna. It has walking trails, an Australian farm and game fishing, and is 45 minutes by ferry from Mission Beach. Good for families with a full range of activities, four levels of accommodation and childminding facility. **$$$**

Fitzroy Island Resort
Fitzroy Island, PO Box 2120, Cairns
Tel: 07-4051 9588
www.huntgroup.com.au
A continental or "high" island reached by catamaran from Cairns, Fitzroy features beach cabins with private facilities and beach bunkhouses with communal facilities. **$$$**

Great Keppel Island Resort
Via Rockhampton
Tel: 07-4939 2050
www.greatkeppelresort.com.au
Catering to couples and families, the resort is 25km (15 miles) of white sandy beach and provides land- and water-based activities, ranging from water-skiing and sailing to tandem skydiving. **$$$**

Great Keppel Island Holiday Village
Great Keppel Island
Tel: 07-4939 8655
Freecall: 1800-180 235
This Youth Hostel Association site offers camping, safari tents and on-site cabins. Book well ahead for this popular location. Snorkel gear for rent, bushwalks and other activities. Facilities include café and shop. **$$$**

Green Island Resort
PO Box 898, Cairns
Tel: 07-4031 3300
Freecall: 1800-673 366
www.greenislandresort.com.au
Forty-five minutes by fast catamaran from Cairns, Green Island Resort is a luxury eco-tourist development built on a coral cay. Also popular with large numbers of day visitors. **$$$$**

Hayman Island Resort
Great Barrier Reef,
North Queensland
Tel: 07-4940 1234
www.hayman.com.au
One of the Whitsunday Islands, located between

PRICE CATEGORIES

Price categories are for a double room without breakfast:
$ = under A$80
$$ = A$80–130
$$$ = A$130–200
$$$$ = over A$200

the coast and the Great Barrier Reef, Hayman Island is another total luxury resort. A modern, three-level complex overlooks a vast pool and the sea. Young children are welcome and a crèche and babysitting are available. Even so, it's a popular honeymoon venue. **$$$$**

Heron Island Resort
Via Gladstone
Tel: 07-4972 9055
Tel: 132-469 (reservations only)
www.heronisland.com
A coral cay located right on the Great Barrier Reef and one of the world's top dive sites, the island is a pristine national park, bird sanctuary and turtle rookery. Turtles come in the summer to lay their eggs, and tiny hatchlings emerge from December to April. Whales arrive in August and September. During the mating season hundreds of indigenous birds are joined by migrating species to nest and rear their young in the lush forest of pisonia trees. No televisions in the rooms.

High standard of tropical cuisine; fishing trips; guided walks; sunset wine and cheese cruises; overnight camping trips to uninhabited Wilson Island.

Hinchinbrook Island Wilderness Lodge and Resort
Tel: 07-4066 8270
www.hinchinbrookresort.com.au
Accommodation is in architect-designed tree houses linked by an aerial boardwalk. If you're scared of heights, take a beach cabin instead. **$$$$**

Island Leisure Resort
4 Kelly Street, Nelly Bay, Magnetic Island
Tel: 07-4778 5000
www.islandleisure.com.au
A short ferry ride from Townsville, a family-style resort comprising 17 self-contained units in a tropical village garden setting only 50 metres/yards from the beach. **$$$**

Lizard Island
Via Cairns
Tel: 07-4060 3999
Freecall: 1800-737 768
www.lizardisland.com.au

Thoroughly exclusive atmosphere on the most deluxe resort island of the Barrier Reef. The northernmost Reef island, Lizard's natural beauty includes excellent dive sites and idyllic calm waters with a colony of giant clams. Sophisticated cuisine and world-class game fishing. No facilities for children under six. **$$$$**

Long Island Resort
Tel: 07-4946 9400
www.clubcroc.com.au
Relaxed resort on its own bay with the emphasis on water sports and fun, but offers quiet woodland walks if you want to get away from it all. **$$$$**

Orpheus Island Resort
Private Mail Bag 15, Townsville Mail Centre
Tel: 07-4777 7377
www.orpheus.com.au
Designed as an intimate, secluded resort, with only 21 beach-front rooms available. Emphasis on couples and romantic picnics. Surrounded by national park on an island

11km (7 miles) long and 1.5km (1 mile) wide. **$$$$**

Pumpkin Island
South of North Keppel Island, PO Box 1151, Kenmore, Qld 4069
Tel: 07-4939 4413
www.pumpkinisland.com.au
Five large cabins are available; each accommodates five to six people and has both solar power and gas appliances. You'll need to bring your own food and linen. Transport to the island is by charter boat arranged when you book. **$$$**

Reef View Hotel
Hamiilton Island
Tel: 07-4946 9999
www.hamiltonisland.com.au
There is a range of room types on this self-contained island, all of which are expensive. Choose from the Beach Club, Reef View Hotel, Whitsunday Apartments and the Palm Bungalows and Terrace. Palm Terrace is the cheapest while the exclusive Beach Club is at the other end of the spectrum. **$$$$**

NORTHERN TERRITORY

Darwin

Darwin is spread over a large area, and although many hotels can be found in the city centre, a number of pleasant options are located a short drive away. Keep in mind that the rates are often significantly higher during the dry season of May–October.

Since Darwin is the starting point for so many adventure travel options, a good selection of accommodation for backpackers and the budget-conscious is on offer, much of it conveniently near the Transit Centre.

Crowne Plaza Darwin
32 Mitchell Street, Darwin
Tel: 08-8982 0000
Tel: 1300-363 300 (reservations)
www.crowneplaza.com.au
Centrally located high-rise, views of the harbour and

city. Spa and health club. **$$$$**

Skycity Darwin
Gilruth Avenue, Darwin
Tel: 08-8943 8888
Freecall: 1800-891 118
www.skycitydarwin.com.au
A beach-side casino hotel on 7 hectares (18 acres) adjoining a golf course and the Botanic Gardens. **$$$$**

Marrakai Luxury All Suites
93 Smith Street, Darwin
Tel: 08-8982 3711
www.marrakai.com.au
Located in the city area, this is a high-rise of balcony apartments close to the mall. Barbecue area. Ideal for families or groups. Secure underground car park. **$$$**

Novotel Atrium Darwin
100 The Esplanade, Darwin
Tel: 08-8941 0755
www.novotel.com.au
On the Esplanade in downtown Darwin, just a

short walk from the city centre, with its own indoor tropical rainforest. Spacious hotel rooms and two-bedroom suites. **$$$**

Parap Village Apartments
39–45 Parap Road, Parap
Tel: 08-8943 0500
Freecall: 1800-620 913
Five minutes' drive from the city centre and 10 from the airport, standard or de-luxe large apartments overlooking two swimming pools. **$$$$**

Mantra on the Esplanade
88 The Esplanade, Darwin
Tel: 08-8943 4333
Freecall: 1300-557 575
On the Esplanade overlooking Darwin Harbour, foreshores, tropical parklands and the city skyline. Apartment style or traditional hotel services. **$$$**

Botanic Gardens Apartments

17 Geranium Street, The Gardens, Darwin
Tel: 08-8946 0300
www.botanicgardensapts.com.au
High on a hill overlooking the Botanic Gardens and the Arafura Sea. **$$$$**

Travelodge Mirambeena Resort Darwin
64 Cavenagh Street, Darwin
Tel: 08-8946 0111
www.mirambeena.com.au
In the heart of the city, with lush tropical pool area. Treetops restaurant, poolside bar and café, mini-golf and gym. **$$$**

ABOVE: roomy Palm Bungalow, Hamilton Island, Queensland.

Palms City Resort
64 The Esplanade, Darwin
Tel: 08-8982 9200
Freecall: 1800-829 211
www.palmscityresort.com
Modern motel rooms or tropical-style villas with balcony barbecues. **$$$**

Steeles at Larrakeyah
4 Zealandia Crescent, Darwin
Tel: 08-8941 3636
Mobile: 0407-442 373
www.steeles-at-larrakeyah.com.au
Private, quiet B&B close to shops, Mindil Beach markets and Botanic Gardens. Hosts Janette and Roger are knowledgeable long-term Territorians. **$$**

Frogs Hollow Backpackers Lodge
27 Lindsay Street, Darwin
Tel: 08-8941 2600
Freecall: 1800-068 686
www.frogs-hollow.com.au
Popular spacious hostel in city, 10-minute walk to Transit Centre. Clean and friendly; off-season rates. **$**

Kakadu

Gagudju Crocodile Holiday Inn
1 Flinders Street, Jabiru (Kakadu)
Tel: 08-8979 9000
www.gagudju-crocodile.holidayinn.com
Shaped like a giant crocodile, with the swimming pool as its stomach, this is the only de-luxe hotel in the Kakadu National Park. **$$$**

Seven Spirit Bay Wilderness Lodge
Garig Gunak Barlu National Park, Arnhem Land
Tel: 08-8979 0281
www.sevenspiritbay.com
A 45-minute flight from Darwin transports you to the natural harmony of the tropics. Guests stay in freestanding, airy, hexagonal habitats, each with an open-air bathroom, set in a tropical garden. Located in Garig Gunak Barlu National Park in Aboriginal Arnhem Land, where entry is by permit only and extremely limited. Two-night packages start at A$1,300 for twin rooms. **$$$$**

Katherine

All Seasons Katherine
Cypress Street (off Stuart Highway), Katherine
Tel: 08-8972 1744
www.accorhotels.com.au
A 3-hour drive from Darwin brings you to this historic town and tours of the stunning Katherine Gorge. Two levels of accommodation. **$$**

Gagudju Lodge
Cooinda
Tel: 08-8979 0145
Freecall: 1800-500 401
www.gagudjulodgecooinda.com.au
Situated on the Yellow Water Billabong, 1km (½ mile) from the Warraadjan Cultural Centre. Provides both comfortable units and budget rooms. **$$$**

Alice Springs
Alice Springs is the service town for the Central Australian desert, and many striking attractions within a short driving distance make it worth considering as part of your itinerary. Uluru (Ayers Rock) is about six hours' scenic desert drive away; and the small village of Yulara caters for its visitors.

Crowne Plaza Alice Springs
82 Barrett Drive, Alice Springs
Tel: 08-8950 8000
www.ichotelsgroup.com
Low-rise luxury resort with spectacular views of the MacDonnell ranges. **$$$**

Lasseters Hotel Casino
93 Barrett Drive, Alice Springs
Tel: 08-8950 7777
www.lassetershotelcasino.com.au
Comfortable rooms in radiating wings up to three storeys high. Casino facilities and the glitz of gambling does not impinge on those who prefer to wander the spacious gounds with its pool. **$$$**

Alice Springs Resort
34 Stott Terrace, Alice Springs
Tel: 08-8951 4545 or 1300-134 044 (reservations)
www.alicespringsresort.com.au
Five minutes' walk to town, quality rooms, oasis-style pool area and à la carte restaurant. **$$$**

Desert Palms Resort
74 Barrett Drive, Alice Springs
Tel: 08-8952 5977
Freecall: 1800-678 037
www.desertpalms.com.au
One kilometre (½ mile) from town, great-value air-conditioned villas with private verandahs and lush tropical pool area. **$$**

Todd Tavern
1 Todd Mall, Alice Springs
Tel: 08-8952 1255
www.toddtavern.com.au
The only traditional pub left in Alice. Meals are served noon–9pm. **$**

Alice Springs YHA
Corner of Parsons Street and Leichhardt Terrace, Alice Springs
Tel: 08-8952 8855
www.yha.com.au
Built within the walls of a Heritage-classed outdoor movie theatre; close to shops, cafés and pubs. **$**

Uluru (Ayers Rock)

Longitude 131
Yulara
Tel: 1300-134 044 (reservations)
www.longitude131.com.au
A line of individual tents makes up the accommodation of this five-star eco-resort just 9km (5 miles) from Uluru. Guest numbers are restricted to 30 at a time. **$$$$**

Sails in the Desert Hotel (part of the Ayers Rock Resort)
Yulara Drive, Yulara
Tel: 08-8957 7888
Freecall: 1300-134 044 (reservations)
The premier hotel at Yulara, famous for its soaring white "sails" which shelter outdoor areas from the intense desert sun. **$$$**

Outback Pioneer Hotel and Lodge
Yulara Drive, Yulara
Tel: 08-8296 8010
Freecall: 1300-134 044 (reservations)
Ayers Rock location with both comfortable private rooms and dormitory-style accommodation. **$$**

Kings Canyon

Kings Canyon Resort
Luritja Road, Watarrka National Park
Tel: 08-8956 7442 or 1300-134 044 (reservations)
www.kingscanyonresort.com.au
Six kilometres (4 miles) from the spectacular canyon, providing all levels of accommodation. **$$$**

Kings Creek Station
via Lasseter Highway or Mereenie Loop Road from Alice Springs
Tel: 08-8956 7474
www.kingscreekstation.com.au
Basic cabins under canvas and camping ground on working farm wth camels. **$**

PRICE CATEGORIES

Price categories are for a double room without breakfast:
$ = under A$80
$$ = A$80–130
$$$ = A$130–200
$$$$ = over A$200

WESTERN AUSTRALIA

Perth

Aarons Hotel
70 Pier Street, 6000
Tel: 08-9325 2133
Toll free: 1800-998 133
Fax: 08-9221 2936
www.aaronsperth.com.au
Centrally placed, on free
CAT bus route around Perth.
Modern and comfortable
rooms, and a bright bar and
grill; good, friendly service.
$$

Bailey's Parkside Hotel-Motel
150 Bennet Street, 6004
Tel: 08-9220 9555
Toll free: 1800-199 477
www.baileysmotel.com.au
Homely hotel opposite park
within walking distance of
the centre or 5 minutes on
free city buses. Comfortable
units with air conditioning,
swimming pool and
barbecue. The restaurant
serves home-style cooking,
and the room tariff includes
continental breakfast. **$**

Bel Eyre Motel
285 Great Eastern Highway,
Belmont
Tel: 08-9277 2733
www.beleyremotel.com.au
Convenient location,
courtesy airport transfers
and swimming pool. **$$**

Broadwater Resort Apartments
137 Melville Parade, Como 6152
Tel: 08-9474 4216
Toll free: 1800-644 414
www.broadwaters.com.au
South of the river, minutes
away from shopping, Perth
Zoo and restaurants.
Heated swimming pool, spa
and tennis court, and
Australian cuisine
restaurant with alfresco
courtyard. Apartments have
full kitchen. **$$$**

Criterion Hotel Perth
560 Hay Street, 6000
Tel: 08-9325 5155
Toll free: 1800-245 155
Fax: 08-9325 4176
www.criterion-hotel-perth.com.au
Central, beautifully restored
Art Deco building in main
shopping area, with "British"
pub in basement. **$$**

Durham Lodge
165 Shepperton Road,

Victoria Park 6100
Tel: 08-9361 8000
Fax: 08-9361 8101
www.durhamlodge.com
South of the river, a short
drive/bus to the centre and
southern attractions: the
zoo and Burswood. Elegant
old home with baby grand
piano and comfortable
furnishings. Private guest
wing; spa bath or showers,
air conditioning, TV, DVD,
phone, bar and fridge. **$$**

Duxton
1 St George's Terrace, 6000
Tel: 08-9261 8000
Toll free: 1800-681 118
www.duxton.com
Beautifully renovated hotel
in a heritage building,
formerly Perth's old tax
office. Close to the Concert
Hall, State Governor's
Residence, Swan River and
shops. **$$$$**

Hotel Ibis Perth
334 Murray Street
Tel: 08-9322 2844
www.ibishotels.com.au
In the centre of Perth, with
popular restaurants and
bars. **$$**

Kings Perth Hotel
517 Hay Street
Tel: 08-9325 6555
www.kingshotel.com.au
Central location near the
Mall and Swan River; good
value. **$$**

Seasons of Perth
37 Pier Street
Tel: 08-9325 7655
Freecall: 1800-999 004
(reservations)
www.seasonsofperth.com.au
Boutique hotel featuring a
large swimming pool in a
spectacular courtyard.
Ideally located close to the
best shopping and the Swan
River. **$$**

Sheraton Perth
207 Adelaide Terrace
Tel: 08-9224 7777
www.sheraton.com/perth
De-luxe and centrally
located; all rooms have
breathtaking views of the
Swan River or the city
skyline. **$$$$**

The Witch's Hat
148 Palmerston Street
Tel: 08-9228 4228
Freecall: 1800-818 358

www.witchs-hat.com
Near the bus terminal and
Perth railway station. A
Victorian residence with
alfresco dining and internet
café. **$**

YMCA Jewell House
180 Goderich Street
Tel: 08-9325 8488
www.ymcajewellhouse.com
Large, with clean,
comfortable rooms. A
15-minute walk to the city,
or catch the free Transperth
Red CAT bus, which passes
outside. **$**

Fremantle and Perth Environs

The Loose Box
6825 Great Eastern Highway,
Mundaring
Tel: 08-9295 1787
www.loosebox.com
Located in the ranges 35km
(20 miles) east of Perth, six
private cottages are
available to guests of the
restaurant, acknowledged
as one of the finest in
Australia. **$$$$**

Rendezvous Observation City Hotel
The Esplanade, Scarborough Beach
Tel: 08-9245 1000
www.rendezvoushotels.com
Luxury hotel on the beach, a
rare example of a high-rise
building on the coast. Wide-
ranging facilities include
several restaurants and
bars, nightclub, pool, spa,
tennis courts and gym. **$$$**

Esplanade Hotel – Fremantle
Corner of Marine Terrace and Essex
Street, Fremantle
Tel: 08-9432 4000
www.esplanadehotelfremantle.com.au
Elegant gold rush-era
building with atrium, two
pools, three spas, fitness
centre, bar and two
restaurants. Most rooms
have private balconies with
views overlooking popular
parklands, tropical gardens
and pools. Across Marine
Terrace lawns is Fishing
Boat Harbour, with restaur-
ants and entertainment.
$$$$

Pier 21 Apartment Hotel
7–9 John Street, North Fremantle
Tel: 08-9336 2555

www.pier21.com.au
On the banks of the Swan,
with river views, fully
serviced one- and two-bed
air-conditioned apartments
with kitchen, TV, VCR and
DVD. Indoor and outdoor
pools overlooking the river
marina, two spas, tennis
and squash courts.
Barbecue area. **$$**

Ocean Beach Hotel
Corner of Eric Street and Marine
Parade, Cottesloe Beach
Tel: 08-9384 2555
www.obh.com.au
Overlooking the Indian
Ocean, refurbished, modern
and lively location with
seafront restaurant, café,
pizza-bar and two bars
heavily used by younger
clientele. **$$**

Flag Motor Lodge
129 Great Eastern Highway,
Rivervale
Tel: 08-9277 2766
Freecall: 1800-998 044
www.flagmotorlodge.com.au
Inexpensive units, some
with cooking facilities.
Restaurant and room
service; swimming pool, bus
to city. **$–$$**

Kilkelly's B&B
82 Marine Terrace, Fremantle,
6160
Tel: 08-9336 1744
Fax: 08-9336 1571
www.wt.com.au/~kilkelly
Renovated 1883 mariner's
cottage opposite Fishing
Boat Harbour. Stroll to
restaurants, markets and
shops. **$$**

Around Perth

Atrium Hotel
65 Ormsby Terrace, Mandurah,
6210
Tel: 08-9535 6633
Fax: 08-9581 4151
www.the-atrium.com.au
Within walking distance of
the beach, this hotel is

centred on an impressive atrium with a palm-fringed, heated indoor pool and spa, cocktail bar and restaurant (7am until late). One-, two- and three-bed apartments with full cooking facilities. There's another pool outdoors, plus sauna, tennis, and games room. **$$**
Hansons
60 Forest Road, Swan Valley, Henley Brook 6055
Tel: 08-9296 3366
Fax: 08-9296 3332
www.hansons.com.au
This is a cool and elegant hotel with a fine restaurant featuring local ingredients prepared in style. Close to the vineyards and microbreweries of the Swan Valley, and with lovely views over the surrounding countryside. With a swimming pool and access to the river. Six spa rooms and four en-suite rooms leading to either a balcony or courtyard. The tariff includes breakfast. **$$**

Margaret River/ Southwest

Cape Lodge
Caves Road, Yallingup
Tel: 08-9755 6311
www.capelodge.com.au
Stunningly beautiful and

tranquil country retreat between Yallingup and the Margaret River. This mansion within a plantation and gardens overlooks a private lake and features de-luxe suites and rooms, both in the homestead and in the new A$3-million development. **$$$$**
Chandlers Smiths Beach Villas
Smiths Beach Road, Yallingup 6282
Tel/fax: 08-9755 2062
www.chandlerssmithsbeach.com.au
On a hillside surrounded by national park, 15 comfortable villas, all with beach and ocean views. The villas are 4km (2½ miles) south of Yallingup and 5 minutes from Smiths Beach for swimming and surfing; two-bed villas have full kitchen facilities, TV and VCR. Laundry and barbecue on site. **$$**
The Grange on Farrelly
18 Farrelly Street, 6285
Tel: 08-9757 3177
Toll free: 1800-650 100
Fax: 08-9757 3076
www.grangeonfarrelly.com.au
Small, stylish motel set in gardens; short stroll to the main street, restaurants and shops. Some rooms have spas, some four-poster beds; all have ensuite, air conditioning, TV

and tea/coffee facilities. The restaurant is in a historic building serving Asian-influenced food. **$$**
Margaret River Holiday Cottages
Lot 2, Boodjioup Road, Margaret River
Tel/fax: 08-9757 2185
Home-style two-bedroom cottages in a tranquil park setting; fully equipped and ideal for families. There are bushland walks to see kangaroos and flora. **$$$**
Merribrook
Armstrong Road, off Cowaramup Bay Road, Cowaramup
Tel: 08-9755 5599
www.merribrook.com.au
Small and relaxing luxury resort comprising nine private chalets. Treatments such as aromatherapy massage and reflexology are complemented by superb food. Prides itself on providing an hospitable and eco-friendly experience. **$$$**
Wellington House B&B
Station Road, Walpole 6398
Tel: 08-9840 1103
www.wellingtonhouse.com.au
Set in 14 hectares (35 acres) of natural forest near the Valley of the Giants and Tree Top Walk. Has three large, well-furnished, en-suite rooms, and another

with a separate bathroom. There is a communal lounge with log fire, TV and VCR, and a sun deck with great views to the forest. **$$**

Broome/Kimberley

Cable Beach Club Resort
Cable Beach Road, Broome
Tel/fax: 08-9192 0400
www.cablebeachclub.com
Located on beautiful Cable Beach. De-luxe bungalows in the style of pearling-masters' houses reflect Broome's Asian heritage, with wide verandahs and lattice screens. There are lush tropical gardens, waterfalls and swimming pools. **$$$$**
El Questro
Gibb River Road, Kununurra
Tel: 08-9169 1777
www.elquestro.com.au
A vast cattle station in the Kimberley, on the edge of the Chamberlain Gorge, El Questro offers many classic Outback activities like barramundi fishing, night crocodile spotting and mustering the herds by helicopter. Offering a choice of stays, from inexpensive campsites to luxurious suites along with gourmet cuisine at the homestead. **$-$$$$**

TASMANIA

Hobart

Adelphi Court YHA
17 Stoke Street, Newtown
Tel: 03-6228 4829
www.yha.com.au
Hostel as well as guesthouse accommodation within easy range of the restaurant and entertainment strip of North Hobart. **$**
Old Woolstore Apartment

PRICE CATEGORIES

Price categories are for a double room without breakfast:
$ = under A$80
$$ = A$80–130
$$$ = A$130–200
$$$$ = over A$200

Hotel
1 Macquarie Street
Tel: 03-6235 5355
Freecall: 1800-814 676
Accomplished conversion of old commercial building handy for the waterfront. **$$$**
Graham Court Apartments
15 Pirie Street, New Town
Tel: 03-6278 1333
www.grahamcourt.com.au
Helpful and friendly management make this a favourite for families or groups happy to be north of the CBD. **$$**
Hotel Grand Chancellor
1 Davey Street, Hobart
Tel: 03-6235 4535
Freecall: 1800-625 138
This de-luxe hotel is

situated in the historic Docks area, within walking distance of popular restaurants. Panoramic river views. **$$$**
The Henry Jones Art Hotel
25 Hunter Street
Tel: 03-6210 7700
www.thehenryjones.com
Stunning conversion of the old jam factory on the waterfront. The art hotel concept is to have paintings by contemporary artists hung throughout the building, all for sale. Everything a top hotel should be. **$$$$**
Hobart Tower Motel
300 Park Street, Newtown
Tel: 03-6228 0166
www.hobarttower.com.au

One of the best-value options in Hobart. The rooms are spacious and provide a high standard of comfort and facilities. Family units available. **$$**
Lenna of Hobart
20 Runnymede Street, Battery Point
Tel: 03-6232 3900
Freecall: 1800-030 633
www.lenna.com.au

Award-winning colonial hotel ideally located in Battery Point, the historic headland above Salamanca Place which is the home of Hobart's trendy restaurants and cafés. **$$$$**

Quest Waterfront Serviced Apartments
3 Brooke Street
Tel: 03-6224 8630
www.questwaterfront.com.au
Spacious, immaculately finished apartments, in the heart of the waterfront action. **$$$**

Rydges Hobart
Corner of Argyle and Lewis streets, North Hobart
Tel: 03-6231 1588
Freecall: 1800-801 703
www.rydges.com
Grand historic hotel in leafy North Hobart, minutes from the city centre, offering luxury antique suites or contemporary decor. **$$$**

Theatre Royal Hotel
31 Campbell Street
Tel: 03-6234 6925
Idiosyncratic management style can test guests' initiative but good rooms in great location offer very good value. **$$**

Battery Point

There are many small, historic B&Bs in the Battery Point area. Although quite a few have succumbed to Ye Olde Twee and are decked out with throw-pillows and beaming hosts, the location is excellent.

Crelin Lodge
1 Crelin Street, Battery Point
Tel: 03-6223 1777
Fully self-contained one- and two-bedroom holiday apartments. **$$$**

Outside Hobart

Wherever you go in Tasmania, you're never far away from quality historic accommodation. In popular destinations, such as Launceston, Strahan, Stanley and the Tasman Peninsula, there are a number of beautiful cottages and a spattering of luxury lets in larger homes.

Tasman Peninsula

Stewart Bay Lodge
Arthur Highway, Port Arthur
Tel: 03-6250 2888
www.stewartsbaylodge.com
Award-winning natural-design log cabins all with log fires, overlooking Stewarts Bay; a short walk from the Port Arthur Historic Site. **$$$**

Strahan

Franklin Manor
The Esplanade, Strahan
Tel: 03-6471 7311
www.franklinmanor.com.au
Situated at the edge of Macquarie Harbour, including rooms within the historic mansion and in the old stables, within a short walk of Strahan harbour. **$$$$**

Piners Loft
89 The Esplanade, Strahan
Tel: 03-6471 7036
www.pinersloft.com.au
Amazing pole-house construction overlooking Macquarie Harbour. Features innovative design in timber using recycled huon pine, celery-top pine and other prized local timbers. This is a place where travelling groups of two to six people can experience luxury at a reasonable cost. **$$$$**

East Coast

Bicheno Backpackers Hostel
11 Morrison Street, Bicheno
Tel: 03-6375 1651
Recommended as the budget option. **$**

Bicheno Gaol House Cottages
81 Burgess Street, Bicheno
Tel: 03-375 1430
Stay in the old prison and be within walking distance of all the town's attractions. **$$$**

Edge of the Bay Resort
2308 Main Road, Coles Bay
Tel: 03-6257 0102
www.edgeofthebay.com.au
Perched right above the beach there is a mixture of sleek modern one-bedroom units with floor-to-ceiling views of the Hazards, or slightly older two-bedroom cabins where the design hasn't been honed quite so well. **$$$$**

Freycinet Lodge
Freycinet National Park, via Coles Bay
Tel: 03-6257 0101
www.freycinetlodge.com.au
Environmentally sensitive resort development in unspoilt coastal setting. Comfortable private bush cabins lead down to tiny beach areas. Restaurant and bar overlook Great Oyster Bay. Seasonal whale watching, diving with seals, hiking and special tour programmes available. **$$$$**

Piermont Retreat
Tasman Highway, Swansea
Tel: 03-6257 8131
www.piermont.com.au
Magnificent stone-built cottages overlooking their own beach. This is the place to recharge the batteries between trips to the pool and the tennis court. **$$$$**

The Midlands

Brickendon Historic and Farm Cottages
Woolmers Lane, near Longford
Tel: 03-6391 1251
www.brickendon.com.au
Have the old farm to yourself after the visitors have left and enjoy these superb wooden cottages. **$$$**

Colonial Cottages of Ross
12 Church Street, Ross
Tel: 03-6381 5354
www.rossaccommodation.com.au
A choice of four immaculately restored cottages sleeping between two and six. **$$$**

Quality Inn Prospect House
1384 Richmond Road, Richmond
Tel: 03-6260 2207
www.choicehotels.com.au
A sumptuous country house on the edge of town with one of the local destination restaurants on site. **$$$**

Oatlands Lodge Colonial Accommodation
92 High Street, Oatlands
Tel: 03-6254 1444
The most effusive welcome in the state at this well-run cosy B&B. **$$$**

Ross Bakery Inn
15 Church Street, Ross
Tel: 03-6381 5246
Plenty of treats from the

BELOW: Edge of the Bay Resort in Coles Bay.

bakery if you choose this historic B&B. **$$$**
Woolmers Estate
Woolmers Lane
near Longford
Tel: 03-6391 2230
www.woolmers.com.au
Live it up on the estate in these settlers' cottages. **$$$**

Derwent Valley

Giants' Table and Cottages
Junee Road, Maydena
Tel: 03-6288 2293
www.giantstable.com.au
Comfortable cabins with lake behind where you're virtually guaranteed to spot platypus. Well placed for the Styx Valley and Lake Pedder. **$$**
Old Colony Inn
21 Montagu Street, New Norfolk
Tel: 03-6261 2731
Old Colony is an attractive old pub now given over to a bed and breakfast. The mock-tudor half timbering extends inside. **$$**
Woodbridge on the Derwent
6 Bridge Street, New Norfolk
Tel: 03-6261 5566
Sheer luxury in this strikingly renovated place just by the bridge. **$$$$**

The North

Abbey's Cottages
1 Marshall Street, Stanley
Tel: 1800 222 397
A collection of cottages close to the centre of Stanley, all full of character and original features and offering very good value for money. **$$$**
Boat Harbour Beach House
12 Moore Street,
Boat Harbour Beach
Tel: 03-6445 0913
A house with everything you could possibly need, including a huge deck with views out to sea. Another house on the beach is rented out by the owners. **$$$**
Peppers Calstock
Lake Highway, Deloraine
Tel: 03-6362 2642
A Georgian mansion set in extensive gardens, Calstock offers elegant rooms,

exquisite French cuisine and no reason to leave. **$$$**
Devonport Historic Cottages
66 Wenvoe Street, Devonport
Tel: 03-6424 1560
Three refurbished two-bedroom cottages on offer. **$$$**
Furners Hotel
42 Reiby Street, Ulverstone
Tel: 03-6425 1488
Gloriously ornate exterior isn't quite matched by the rooms, but still a sound choice. **$$**
Mersey Bluff Caravan Park
Devonport
Tel: 03-6424 8655
Plenty of space for camping near the sea, and some cabins available too. **$**
Silver Ridge Retreat
46 Rysavy Road, Mount Roland, via Sheffield
Tel: 03-6491 1727
www.silverridgeretreat.com.au
Idyllic rural getaway featuring self-contained accommodation located right at the foot of breathtaking Mount Roland. There are great walks, especially to Roland summit. It is also only a 40-minute drive to Cradle Mountain. **$$$**
Tall Timbers Hotel Motel
3–15 Scotchtown Road, Smithton
Tel: 03-6452 2755
www.talltimbershotel.com.au
A symphony to timber indeed, this woody establishment has rooms in a range of styles and prices as well as a pool, bistro and bar. **$$**
The Waterfront Wynyard
1 Goldie Street, Wynyard
Tel: 03-6442 2351
A steady if unremarkable motel to be chosen for its location. **$$**

Central Highlands

Bronte Park Highland Village
Bronte Park, 6km (4 miles) north of the Lyell Highway (Lake Country)
Tel: 03-6289 1126
A half-hour's drive from Lake St Clair, this utterly peaceful holiday village features converted hydro-electric workers' huts, now a favourite with fishermen. Well-designed private

cottages and an inexpensive restaurant serving simple but excellent fish dinners. Access by Tasmanian Wilderness Transport from Launceston or Devonport. **$$**
Central Highlands Lodge
Haddens Bay, Miena
Tel: 03-6259 8179
Pleasant motel units behind the lodge. In the lodge there's an enticing bar and dining room where anglers can eat their catch and enthral slow-footed tourists with tales of how they caught it. **$$$**
Cradle Mountain
Cradle Mountain Lodge
Cradle Mountain
Tel: 03-6492 1303
Freecall: 1800-737 678
www.cradlemountainlodge.com.au
Wilderness retreat with secluded cabins and Alpine spa at the entrance to the Cradle Mountain–Lake St Clair National Park. There are over 20 walking tracks and the chance to breathe what Australian scientists claim is some of the purest air in the world. **$$$**

Bass Strait Islands

Furneaux Tavern
11 Franklin Parade, Lady Barron, Flinders Island
Tel: 03-6359 3521
Excellent cabins up the hill behind this welcoming modern pub. **$$**
Interstate Hotel
Patrick Street, Whitemark, Flinders Island
Tel: 03-6359 2114
Standard but comfortable rooms that put you at the heart of the action, if that's the word for this placid island. **$$**
King Island Holiday Village
Grassy, King Island
Tel: 03-6461 1177
Fly from Wynyard or Melbourne; hire cars are available. This clean, green Bass Strait island is well worth holidaying in. It produces Australia's finest beef and cheese and is the shipwreck capital of the Antipodes, with more than 60 wrecks in the past 200 years. An ex-mining town, Grassy has a population of

around 50. Look out over gorgeous empty beaches and experience three coasts within an hour's drive. **$$**

Launceston

Penny Royal Leisure Inn
147 Paterson Street, Launceston
Tel: 03-6331 6699
Freecall: 1800-060 954
Historic watermill-turned-hotel with rooms or self-contained apartments, restaurant and tavern. Five minutes to Cataract Gorge. **$$$**
Peppers Seaport Hotel
28 Seaport Boulevard, Launceston
Tel: 03-6345 3333
Chic modern development with a range of trendy bars and restaurants on the boardwalk below. **$$$$**
The Sebel
St John Street, Launceston
Tel: 03-6333 7555
It's got a lot of rooms for a boutique hotel, but they are all executed with such taste and intelligence that you can almost justify paying the prices being asked. **$$$$**

Tamar Valley

Pilot Station
399 Low Head Road
Tel: 03-6382 1143
Simple cottages but a terrific atmospheric place to stay within the museum precinct. **$$**
Comfort Inn The Pier
5 Elizabeth Street, George Town
Tel: 03-6382 1300
www.choicehotels.com.au
Pleasant rooms and apartments overlooking the river and well served by the pub's accomplished bistro. **$$$**
Quality Hotel Aspect Tamar Valley Resort
7 Waldhorn Drive, Grindelwald
Tel: 03-6330 0400
High-class accommodation in nutty Swiss-themed resort. **$$$$**

A CTIVITIES

FESTIVALS, THE ARTS, NIGHTLIFE, SHOPPING, SPORT AND CHILDREN'S ACTIVITIES

FESTIVALS

The peak months for the arts in general are March, during the **Adelaide Fringe Festival**, and October for the **Melbourne International Festival of the Arts**, the **Fringe Festival** and the **Writers Festival**.

A list of some of the annual events held in Australia follows. Dates may vary, so refer to the Australian Tourist Commission's very comprehensive calendar booklet of current dates.

January

Australia-wide
Australia Day (26 Jan). There are parades, concerts and fireworks around the country, including concerts at Sydney's Darling Harbour and fireworks along Melbourne's Yarra River.
Hobart
Hobart Summer Festival, and *MONA FoMA (early Jan)*
Melbourne
The *Australian Open* is a world-class Grand Slam partner to the French Open, the US Open and Wimbledon.
Tamworth (NSW)
Country Music Festival.
Sydney, Melbourne, Gold Coast, Adelaide and Perth
Big Day Out (late Jan–early Feb). One-day outdoor rock music festival.

February

Canberra
Royal Canberra Show. Typical agricultural show: animals, crafts, wood chopping, fireworks, etc.

Hobart
Australian Wooden Boat Festival. One of the world's leading maritime festivals. Held biennially (2011, 2013)
Hobart Cup Carnival. Tasmania's premier horse-racing event.
Royal Hobart Regatta.
Launceston
Festivale Music. Arts, food and wine festival held over a weekend.
Melbourne
Melbourne Fashion Festival. Designers and retailers in a stylish array of parades and special events.
Perth
Perth International Arts Festival. Three weeks of arts and multicultural activities.
Rottnest Channel Swim. Swimmers attempt the 20km (12 miles) between Cottesloe Beach and Rottnest Island.
Sydney
Sydney Gay and Lesbian Mardi Gras (throughout Feb). The parade on the last Saturday evening is the world's biggest gay and lesbian Mardi Gras.

February/March

Adelaide (SA)
The city comes alive during the Adelaide Festival, held every two years (2012, 2014, etc.) in February and March. Street theatre is everywhere, spontaneous and usually funny, with nonstop partying. The festival includes a mainstream schedule of international performances in the Festival Centre, plus the ever-popular Fringe Festival which is now a yearly event – three weeks of stand-up comedy, alternative theatre and visual arts. Similar in concept and quality to the Edinburgh Fringe Festival, the Adelaide Fringe draws comedians and other acts from around the English-

speaking world and it is well worth making a trip to Adelaide.

At the same time, Writer's Week brings important scribblers from around the world and a huge audience of adoring listeners to hear them read and discuss their work. There is also a Visual Arts Festival, a showcase of cutting-edge artworks, which can take place in any form – even in the homes of artists. During the festival, there are extra information booths in Rundle Mall and a number of free publications which give listings and information about the daily events.

Adelaide Fringe (held annually). New theatre, comedy, visual arts and music. The cutting-edge counterpart to the *Adelaide Festival of Arts (see The Arts, page 367).*

March

Adelaide (SA)
Adelaide Cup. South Australia's premier horse-racing event.
Womadelaide. World and roots music festival held annually.
Clipsal 500. Motor-sports festival.
Ballarat (Vic)
The Ballarat Begonia Festival. World-famous begonia display and 10 days of festival activities.
Brisbane (Qld)
Ideas Festival. Four days of focus on ideas, innovation and invention.
Canberra (ACT)
Celebrate Canberra. A 10-day celebration of the nation's capital with fireworks and hot-air ballooning.
Rally of Canberra. Biggest car rally event on the eastern coast.
Gold Coast (Qld)
Australian Surf Lifesaving Championships.

Margaret River (wa)
Salomon Masters. Annual all comers surfing event.
Melbourne (Vic)
March is usually the best time of year in Melbourne, packed with events taking a punt on the good weather. *Moomba*, one of Australia's largest outdoor festivals, is held in the first two weeks of March. Over 200 activities include the world's best water-skiers on the Yarra, the bizarre birdman contest for amateur aviators, and games, music and rides in the Alexandra Gardens.

Also look out for the *Melbourne Food and Wine Festival* and the start of the *Melbourne International Comedy Festival*.
Australian Grand Prix. Four-day round of the FIA Formula 1 World Championship.
Australian International Airshow. Australia's biggest aviation and aerospace event, held biennially (2011, 2013).

March/April

Bendigo (Vic)
Awakening of the Dragon Festival (date is variable). The world's longest Chinese imperial dragon parades through the streets every Easter Monday.
Broome (WA)
Broome Arts and Music Festival. The remote pearling community comes alive with Aboriginal art shows, artists' markets and more.
Byron Bay
East Coast International Blues and Roots Festival. Massive music gathering over Easter attracts world-famous groups and solo stars.
Margaret River (WA)
Margaret River Pro. Draws top surfers from around the world.
Newcastle (NSW)
Surfest. An annual surfing event with surf film competition included.
Port Fairy (Vic)
Folk Festival (Labour Day weekend).

April

Australia-wide
Anzac Day (25 April). Australia's day to commemorate all who fought in wars. Marked by parades by former soldiers and dawn ceremonies.
Canberra (ACT)
Celebrate Canberra Balloon Fiesta. See dozens of hot-air balloons take to the skies from the forecourt of Old Parliament House.
National Folk Festivals (Easter weekend). Gathers fiddlers and folk musicians from all over Australia.

ABOVE: His Majesty's Theatre on Hay Street, Perth.

Fremantle (WA)
Fremantle Street Arts Festival. Celebrating the art of busking.
Melbourne (Vic)
Melbourne International Comedy Festival. One of the world's best.
Melbourne International Flower and Garden Show. Australia's premier horticultural show.
Sydney (NSW)
Royal Easter Show. Agricultural show and amusement park extravaganza.
Tasmania (Tas)
Targa Tasmania. Major car-racing event covering Tasmania's scenic coastline and mountain passes.
10 days on the Island (held every other odd year).

May

Alice Springs (NT)
Bangtail Muster. A day of Outback fun including a parade in honour of all cattlemen from Central Australia.
V8 Supercar Championships.
Barossa Valley (SA)
Riverland Balloon Regatta. Beautiful visions of dawn and late-afternoon skies dotted with colourful balloons.
Paniyiri. Australia's largest Greek festival.
Clare Valley (SA)
Clare Gourmet Weekend. Wineries join with prominent restaurants for the complete gourmet experience.
Sydney (NSW)
Sydney Writers Festival. Australian and international authors convene.

June

Alice Springs (NT)
Beanie Festival. Quirky event with special classes to make "beanies"

(close-fitting woollen caps).
Finke Desert 200km Race. Cars, bikes and buggies race along the dry river bed from Alice to Finke, stop overnight and race back. Spectators camp along the river bank.
Alpine resorts
Opening weekend. The Queen's birthday weekend is the signal for the opening of the ski season – snow or no snow!
Barmera (SA)
Riverland Country Music Festival. Country music of all varieties in over 20 venues.
Barunga (NT)
Barunga Festival. Aboriginal people gather for four days of dancing, athletics, arts and crafts. Advisable to bring a tent.
Geelong (Vic)
National Celtic Folk Festival. Celebration of Scottish, Welsh, Irish and Cornish heritage with theatre, music, crafts, sports and food.
Laura (Qld)
Dance and Cultural Festival. Biennial Aboriginal event at a dedicated site 15km (9 miles) from Laura.
McLaren Vale (SA)
McLaren Vale Sea and Vines Festival. The McLaren Vale wineries present food and wine to visitors.
Mildura (Vic)
Mildura International Balloon Fiesta. Incorporating the Ballooning World Cup and National Championships.
Sydney (NSW)
Sydney International Film Festival. A month-long festival.

July

Australia-wide
NAIDOC Week. Celebrates the history,

culture and achievements of Aboriginal and Torres Strait Islander people.

Alice Springs (NT)
Lions Camel Cup. Camels are brought from all over Australia to compete. A day of fun, with fireworks.

Brisbane (Qld)
Brisbane Festival. The arts shindig held every two years (even numbers).

Darwin (NT)
Darwin Cup Festival. Cup Day is accompanied by loads of live music. *Beer Can Regatta (date is variable).* Traditional Darwin water race, where competing vessels must be constructed entirely of beer cans.

Melbourne (Vic)
Melbourne International Film Festival.

Stroud (NSW)
Stroud International Brick and Rolling Pin Throwing Contest. Four towns called Stroud (also in England, Canada and the USA) simultaneously hold this bizarre contest.

August

Adelaide River (NT)
Adelaide River Show Rodeo, Campdraft and Gymkhana. Activities range from a bush dance to a country music talent quest. Big money prizes.

Alice Springs (NT)
Alice Springs Rodeo. Bareback bull riding, steer wrestling and calf roping from the Northern Territory's best. *Henley on Todd Regatta.* Waterless regatta held on the dry bed of the Todd River. The "Sea Battle" is fought with flour bombs and water cannons between four-wheel-drive "boats".

Barossa Valley (SA)
Barossa Classic Gourmet Weekend (August). Wineries combine with restaurants to provide samples of gourmet fare.

Brisbane (Qld)
Ekka. City-meets-country show.

Darwin (NT)
The *Darwin Festival* celebrates the end of the tropical dry season with entertainment, arts and cultural events in parks and venues around Darwin. The festival strongly reflects the Asian-Pacific and Aboriginal communities of Darwin.

It overlaps with the *Darwin Fringe Festival*, which showcases local visual and performing arts.
Darwin Festival. Eighteen days of dance, cabaret, outdoor concerts, film, visual arts and comedy.

Geraldton (WA)
Sunshine Surfmaster. Big prizes.

Hervey Bay (Qld)
Hervey Bay Whale Festival. Marks the opening of the whale season.

Melbourne (Vic)
Melbourne Writers Festival. Australian and foreign writers discuss their works.

Mount Buller (Vic)
World Aerials. The international aerial ski championships.

Mount Isa (Qld)
Mount Isa Rotary Rodeo. Australia's biggest rodeo, held since 1959.

Noosa (Qld)
Noosa Jazz Fest. Live jazz including the famous "Woods" Picnic Concert.

Gove Peninsula (Arnhem Land; NT)
Garma Festival is a celebration of the Yolngu culture of East Arnhem Land, with a different theme each year. It is part-conference, part-festival, part-education seminar. Delegates live in a tent city for up to five days. A unique experience on a coastal scarp 30km (18 miles) from the mining town of Nhulunbuy.

Toowoomba (Qld)
Australian Heritage Festival.

Jondaryan Woolshed hosts a week of historic rural Australian activities featuring bullock teams, steam engines and hand shearing.

September

Adelaide (SA)
Royal Adelaide Show. Adelaide's major agricultural show.

Bathurst (NSW)
Bathurst 1000 Touring Car Motor Race. Popular Mount Panorama event.

Birdsville (Qld)
Birdsville Races. Horse races in aid of the Royal Flying Doctor Service.

Brisbane (Qld)
River Festival. A 10-day event celebrating Brisbane's waterways. *Brisbane Writers Festival.*

Broome (WA)
Shinju Matsuri Festival of the Pearl. A 10-day festival honouring Broome's Asian heritage. Pearl jewellery, Chinese feasts and more.

Canberra (ACT)
Floriade. Australia's largest spring floral festival.

Perth (WA)
Perth Royal Show. Perth's major agricultural event.
Western Australia Wildflower Festival. Huge range of unique Australian wild flowers at their best at Kings Park.

Sydney (NSW)
Festival of the Winds. The sky above Bondi Beach is filled with kites. *Sydney Marathon.*

October

Alice Springs (NT)
Masters Games. Veteran athletes compete in many sports.

Gold Coast (Qld)
V8 races. Three days of car racing.

Melbourne (Vic)
Antipodes Festival. Australia's largest ethnic celebration and reputedly the biggest Greek festival in the world. *Melbourne International Festival of the Arts & Melbourne Fringe Festival.*

Noosa (Qld)
Noosa Triathlon Multi-sport Festival. See them run, swim, cycle and play golf and volleyball.

Phillip Island (Vic)
The Australian Motorcycle Grand Prix.

Wynyard (Tas)
Tulip Festival.

November

Australia-wide
Melbourne Cup Day. Australia's premier horse-racing event is celebrated throughout the country.

Below: most Aussie nightlife revolves around the pub.

On the first Tuesday in November the whole of Australia stops for the running of this famous race at the Flemington Racecourse. It's accompanied by a huge carnival in Melbourne where the locals don their finest and most outrageous hats to attend.

Fremantle (WA)
Festival of Fremantle. Exhibitions, concerts, and a huge street carnival.
Perth (WA)
Awesome Festival. Entertainment and workshops for the under-25s.
Wangaratta (Vic)
Festival of Jazz.

December

Eltham (Vic)
Montsalvat National Poets, Spoken Word and Vision Festival. Poetry performed in beautiful grounds.
Hobart (Tas)
Summer Festival, including Taste of Tasmania Festival (late Dec–early Jan). Food and entertainment add up to a nonstop party on the docks.
Sydney–Hobart
Sydney to Hobart Yacht Race. Famous blue-water yacht race has its dramatic Boxing Day start in Sydney Harbour.

THE ARTS

Theatre

Sydney
The **Sydney Opera House** is a focal point of fine performances, including concerts, opera, ballet, theatre and films, but it isn't the only venue. Among the larger performance venues are the Capitol Theatre, the State Theatre and the Theatre Royal.

The Sydney Theatre Company has a harbourside home in the Wharf Theatre – a renovated old wharf in the Rocks – and presents an extensive schedule of productions here and at the newer Sydney Theatre across the road. The Sydney Dance Company occasionally performs at both venues, and **Bangarra Dance Theatre** combines modern and traditional Aboriginal dance at various venues around the city. The **Seymour Centre** stages a variety of unusual shows, and **Company B** at the **Belvoir Street Theatre** has a history of experimentation. There are also three drama spaces at the Opera House. Smaller venues include the **Darlinghurst Theatre** and **Stables Theatre** in Kings Cross, the **New Theatre** in Newtown, the **Footbridge**

Theatre at Sydney University and the stunning **Ensemble Theatre** at Milsons Point.

The best guide to entertainment in Sydney is in the *Sydney Morning Herald's* Metro section every Friday.

Canberra
The **Canberra Theatre Centre** on Civic Square (tel: 02-6243 5711; www. canberratheatre.org.au) contains a theatre, playhouse and gallery, and presents everything from Shakespeare to rock music. **Tilley's Devine Café Gallery**, corner of Brigalow and Wattle streets, Lyneham (tel: 02-6247 7753; www. tilleys.com.au), is one of Canberra's more bohemian venues, featuring musicians, storytellers, poetry readings and art exhibitions. It was originally set up as a centre for women, but is now open to all.

Consult the *Fly* section in the Thursday edition of the *Canberra Times* for what's on. Also the free monthly magazine *BMA* lists bands and other events.

Melbourne
Melbourne is noted for its high-quality live performances of comedy, theatre and music. There are always theatre productions at the city's major arts venue, the **Arts Centre**, which has three theatres. The **Melbourne Theatre Company** presents both there and at its new purpose-built venue round the corner behind the NGV. Major commercial theatres include the grand **Princess Theatre**, 163 Spring Street; **Her Majesty's**, 219 Exhibition Street; the **Comedy Theatre**, 240 Exhibition Street; and the spectacularly refurbished 2,000-seat **Regent Theatre**, 191 Collins Street. Smaller-scale but more adventurous work can be found at the **Malthouse**, 113 Sturt Street, Southbank; **Red Stitch**, 2 Chapel Street, St Kilda; and **La Mama**, 205 Faraday Street, Carlton.

The best listings for Melbourne's lively arts scene can be found in the Entertainment Guide in every Friday issue of *The Age* newspaper, or the free weekly street press, *Inpress* and *Beat*.

Adelaide
The home of performing arts is the **Adelaide Festival Centre** (www.adelaide festivalcentre.com.au). The centre has regular performances of theatre, dance and concerts and is the main venue for the Adelaide International Festival of Arts (www.adelaidefestival.com. au). The State Theatre Company of South Australia appears regularly at the Festival Centre. **The Bakehouse**

Theatre on Angas Street is a more intimate venue where smaller theatre troupes perform. While they regularly tour the country and overseas, Australian Dance Theatre is based in Adelaide and can be seen at the Adelaide Festival Centre or **Her Majesty's Theatre** on Grote Street. The free magazine *Adelaide Review* lists theatres and galleries.

Brisbane
Brisbane's main theatre company is the Queensland Theatre Company, based at the **Performing Arts Complex**. The Brisbane **Powerhouse** also offers regular performances and exhibitions, and downtown you'll find a plethora of new acts.

Darwin
Darwin's multicultural arts festival runs for three weeks in August. The focus is on indigenous artists with dance, music and an open-air festival club each night. A fringe festival takes place in June. Local plays are performed at **Brown's Mart**, a historic sandstone building on Smith Street. Folk music can be heard on weekends at **Happy Yess (ok) Club** on Bennett Street in the city.

Perth
Perth has a vibrant cultural life and is the proud home of Australia's longest-running arts event, the Perth International Arts Festival, which takes place in February and March (www.perthfestival.com.au).

Outstanding drama is regularly presented by the **Black Swan Theatre Company**, **Perth Theatre Company** and **Deckchair Theatre**.

Children's events, such as the international arts festival, the Awesome Festival in November–December, include contributions by **Barking Gecko Theatre** and **Spare Parts Puppet Theatre**. Given Perth's Mediterranean climate, outdoor concerts and performances are popular in the summer months.

Perth's multitude of theatres and concert venues offer year-round entertainment. The **Perth Concert Hall** is the performance home for the West Australian Symphony Orchestra; **His Majesty's Theatre** houses the West Australian Ballet and Opera companies, and the **Playhouse** is the base for the Perth Theatre Company and the Black Swan Theatre Company. Other venues offering plays, musicals and cabarets are the **Burswood Casino's Theatre**, the Art Deco-style **Regal Theatre** and the **Subiaco Theatre Centre**.

Hobart

The **Playhouse Theatre** (tel: 03-6234 1536) is an amateur company presenting a mix of old favourites and modern performances. The **Theatre Royal** (tel: 03-6233 2299) is Australia's oldest working theatre with walls of convict-carved stone.

Comedy

Sydney

The **Sydney Comedy Store** at the Entertainment Quarter hosts some of the world's and Australia's top comics from Tue to Sat. Other local bars have popular comedy nights, including **The East Village**, **Palmer Street** and **Fringe Bar** on Oxford Street.

Canberra

Canberra Irish Club holds a comedy competition called Green Faces (www. irishclub.com.au). **The Canberra Theatre Centre**, **Street Theatre** and **Royal Theatre Canberra** host touring comedians and travelling comedy roadshows. Check out the entertainment section of www.outin canberra.com.au.

Melbourne

The Last Laugh was the birthplace of Melbourne's reputation as comedy capital and it is still going strong. It is situated in the **Athaenum Theatre** at 188 Collins Street. The **Melbourne International Comedy Festival** offers three weeks of the best comedy in Australia (see Festivals, page 365). The festival website, www.comedy festival.com.au, is also a good source of information..

BELOW: spoilt for choice.

Adelaide

March is the best time for comedy when venues all over the city burst with shows by comics who flock from around the world to perform in the **Adelaide Fringe** festival.

The Rhino Room on Frome Street hosts home-grown and international comics each Wednesday and Friday night. The Adelaide casino **Sky City** has also started to host comedy nights on Thursdays, while **PJ O'Briens** on East Terrace has a regular comedy night on Tuesdays.

Brisbane

The **Dockside Comedy Bar** (www. docksidecomedybar.com.au), by the river, at the bottom of the Dockside Hotel building on Ferry Street, hosts some of Australia's comics Wed–Sat nights. The **Sit Down Comedy Club**, at 186 Given Terrace in the Paddington area, is an established comedy venue; details of events can be found on www. standup.com.au.

Darwin

There are no regular comedy clubs in Darwin, but the **Darwin Entertainment Centre** and **Brown's Mart** occasionally put on events.

Perth

Perth's comedy scene centres around the **Comedy Lounge**, Thursday nights at the Hyde Park Hotel (corner Bulwer and Fitzgerald streets, North Perth; tel: 08-9328 6166; www.comedy lounge.com.au).

Hobart

Comedy in Hobart can be found in three venues hosting events, if somewhat sporadically. The **New Sydney Hotel** is the most consistent. The focal point is the **Hobart Comedy Festival**, which runs each January. It claims to be "the world's smallest cultural event".

Cinema

Sydney

For foreign films, art films and generally good films, go to the **Chauvel** in Paddington, **Cinema Paris** in the Entertainment Quarter and the **Dendy** at Opera Quays or Newtown. The more commercial films are shown at multi-cinema complexes on George Street in the city and Bondi Junction. The majestic old **State Theatre** in the city is the site of the annual Sydney Film Festival.

Every June, art cinemas in Sydney showcase the best films selected from recent film festivals around the world.

Canberra

There are cinema complexes around the Civic Square area. The eight-screen **Dendy Electric Shadows** (tel: 02-6247 5060; www.electricshadows.com. au) complex in the new Canberra Centre on Bunda Street shows art-house and foreign-language films. The **National Film and Sound Archives** screens a broad variety of films (www. nfsa.afc.gov.au).

Melbourne

Quality art and independent films are shown at the fabulous original Art Deco **Astor Cinema** in St Kilda and the **Kino** in Collins Street, **Cinema Nova** in Carlton and the **Australian Centre for the Moving Image (ACMI)** in Federation Square. In the summer there are outdoor screenings in the **Royal Botanic Gardens**, and there's even a rooftop cinema on one of the office blocks in the CBD.

Adelaide

Art films are shown at the **Nova** and the **Palace**, both in Rundle Street; also at the **Trak** in Toorak Gardens, the **Mercury**, and at the Art Deco **Capri** cinema in Goodwood.

Brisbane

Greater Union within the Myer Centre on Queen Street Mall has mainstream fare. Brisbane has a good range of summer outdoor cinemas, including the **Sunset Cinema** at the City Botanic Gardens and the **Moonlight Cinema** (www.moonlight.com.au) at Brisbane Powerhouse in New Farm Park. Check www.ourbrisbane.com for comprehensive film listings.

Darwin

Outdoor cinema is popular in the dry season at the **Deckchair Cinema** (that's what you sit in), Jervois Road off Kitchener Drive near the Wharf Precinct; mainly arthouse films rotated through a weekly programme. Tel: 08-8981 0700. Multiplexes showing first-release mainstream films are located in **Mitchell Street** in Darwin city and at **Casuarina Square** shopping centre complex 8km (5 miles) from the city (bus route 4).

Perth

Two major chains, **Greater Union** and **Hoyts**, carry big-distribution films, but Perth is full of small, independent cinemas. Buy the West Australian newspaper for programme details. The **Astor** at 659 Beaufort Street, Mount Lawley, is an Art Deco building showing modern and classic films. The **Somerville Auditorium** at the

Above: another glorious day at the cricket at Bellerive Oval, Hobart.

University of WA, Nedlands, is the main venue for Perth Festival Films, which takes place in February.

Hobart

The independent **State Cinema** (tel: 03-6234 6318; www.statecinema.com.au) is well known and well loved for its eclectic programming – it screens anything from surf films to world cinema and the latest Australian releases. Other venues include **Eastlands Village Cinemas** (tel: 03-6245 1033) and **Hobart Village Cinemas** (tel: 03-6234 7288).

Music

Sydney

Whatever your taste in music, it can be satisfied in Sydney. The Sydney Symphony Orchestra, under Vladimir Ashkenazy, appears regularly with leading Australian and international conductors at the **Opera House**.

To listen to jazz, try the **Basement**, 29 Reiby Place, or **Vanguard** at 42 King Street in Newtown.

The band scene is nearly always in pubs, which are scattered throughout the city and suburbs; almost every little place will have live music on Friday and Saturday nights. In general, the best rock pubs are in Surry Hills, Newtown and Annandale: try the **Hopetoun** in Surry Hills. Other good bets are the **Metro Theatre** in the city centre and **The Gaelic Club** in Surry Hills. Better-known and international rock acts tend to play the **Enmore** or **Hordern Pavilion**.

Canberra

Canberra's only professional music group, the Canberra Symphony

Orchestra, performs half a dozen times a year. Most of the concerts take place at **Llewellyn Hall**, but the popular Proms concert, held every February, takes place in the grounds of the governor-general's residence, **Government House**.

Popular jazz nights are held at the **Hippo Bar** at Garema Place on Wednesday nights, and the last Sunday of every month at the **Kamberra Wine Company Cellar Door** in Lyneham.

The student community of the ANU (Australian National University) has live bands perform at the **ANU Union Bar** during term; big-name touring bands and DJs play at the **Refectory**.

Melbourne

The Melbourne Symphony Orchestra performs at a variety of locations from March to October.

Much of Melbourne's rock and jazz scene is found in its thriving pub venues. Listen to the gig guide on the FM stations 3RRR, 3MMM and 3PBS. The **Esplanade Hotel** (Espy) and the **Prince of Wales Bandroom**, both in St Kilda, have been a good rock bet for years, as have the **Corner Hotel** in Richmond, the **Hi-Fi Bar** in the city and the **Evelyn Hotel** in Brunswick Street. The **Northcote Social Club** and the **East Brunswick Club** keep the flag flying a little further from the city centre. A popular jazz venue is **Bennetts Lane** in the city. Cover charges vary widely depending on what night of the week and what band is playing. Shows are free on some nights, but generally cost from around A$15.

The best listings for Melbourne's music scene can be found in the Entertainment Guide (EG) in every

Friday issue of The Age, or the free weekly street press, Inpress and Beat.

Adelaide

Check the Gig Guide in Thursday's edition of the Advertiser newspaper, or the free publication Rip It Up, for what's on in Adelaide. The free Adelaide Review also lists musical events.

The Adelaide Symphony Orchestra regularly performs at the **Grainger Studio**, a refurbished Art Deco building in the heart of Adelaide's West End. There are also regular gigs and concerts at the **Festival Centre** including the popular Adelaide Cabaret Festival each June. There is a healthy live pub scene in Adelaide and some notable venues include the **Grace Emily** on Waymouth Street for local bands and **The Royal Oak** in North Adelaide for jazz. There are also a number of pubs on and around the east end of Rundle Street that regularly host live music.

Brisbane

Brisbane has a lively pop and rock scene; **The Zoo** and **The Rev** in Fortitude Valley are popular venues, as is the new **Hi-Fi Bar**, sister venue to the one in Melbourne.

For classical music, the home of the prestigious Queensland Orchestra is the 1800-seat **QPAC Concert Hall**, one of Australia's most spectacular concert venues, situated on the corner of Grey and Melbourne streets. For jazz, the **Brisbane Jazz Club**, on the river at 1 Annie Street, Kangaroo Point, is ever popular.

Darwin

Darwin Symphony Orchestra gives concerts at the **Darwin**

TRANSPORT

ACCOMMODATION

ACTIVITIES

A – Z

LANGUAGE

Entertainment Centre on a regular basis. Visiting artists perform at the **Botanical Gardens** in the dry season, and in the grounds of the Skycity casino near Mindil Beach. There are free concerts on the **Esplanade** during the Festival of Darwin.

Perth

Perth Concert Hall at 5 St George's Terrace (tel: 08-9231 9900), home to the Western Australia Symphony Orchestra, is the hub of the city's classical music scene. The prestigious Conservatorium at WAAPA (**West Australian Academy of Performing Arts**) attracts a wealth of jazz musicians. JAZZWA (www.jazzwa.com) has a complete rundown of current events.

Hobart

The responsibillity for providing Tasmania with its classics falls to the Tasmanian Symphony Orchestra. The TSO, established in 1948, performs most of its concerts at **Federation Concert Hall** (tel: 1800 001 190) in Hobart or, when in Launceston, at the **Princess Theatre**.

Big names in pop, rock and comedy tend to play at the **Derwent Entertainment Centre** in Hobart's northern suburbs. Elsewhere there are numerous pubs with live music; the **Republic Bar and Café** in north Hobart probably has the best range of local and visiting artists. Other pubs with good live music are **Knopwood's Retreat**, **Irish Murphy's** and **Bar Celona**, all in Salamanca Place. Check the local press for details.

NIGHTLIFE

Sydney

In some of the Sydney clubs and rock pubs you will be uncomfortable if you are over 30; in others if you are under 30. Dress codes vary, from up-to-the-minute designer fashion only to "neat casual". Sloppy or dirty clothing will often keep you out on the street. If you are one of those who look eternally young, you must have ID to prove that you're over 18 (the minimum legal drinking age). For up-to-date listings, consult the weekly *Drum Media*, Friday's *Sydney Morning Herald Metro* entertainment supplement, or check out www.sydney.citysearch.com.au.

Canberra

Because of Canberra's liberal licensing laws, quite a few bars are open 24 hours a day. The **Canberra Casino** at Glebe Park (21 Binara Street) is open from noon to 6am daily. **ICBM** (50 Northbourne Ave) is probably the busiest club.

Melbourne

Melbourne offers a huge choice of nightclubs and wine bars offering cheap gigs. Just stroll along Brunswick Street, Fitzroy, and take your pick. St Kilda still buzzes as it has for years, while newer hubs for an action-packed night out include Sydney Road, Brunswick, and High Street, Northcote – both to the north of the city centre.

Laneways in the CBD provide a mixed bag of bars, clubs and live music venues. Many of these places are to be found behind anonymous doorways and attract punters through a mixture of word of mouth and discreet advertising. Most of the nightclubs in the "West End" King Street strip now exist as table-dancing and men's clubs.

Check out *The Age* for listings of gay and lesbian venues.

Adelaide

The grand old railway station on North Terrace now houses a **casino**, for those inclined. The "sin centre" of Adelaide is Hindley Street, although few will be shocked by it. Interspersed with excellent restaurants you'll find strip clubs, bars, porno bookshops and the usual persons of the night. The west end of Hindley Street, between Morphett Street and West Terrace, has a cleaner vibe and some good bars, pubs and nightclubs.

Brisbane

The busy late-night spots in Brisbane are the Riverside Centre, Elizabeth Street, Petrie Terrace and Fortitude Valley. New eating places are constantly cropping up in New Farm.

Pick up a copy of the three free entertainment guides – *Time Off*, *Scene* and *Rave* – from any café, as well as the Thursday edition of Brisbane's daily newspaper, *The Courier Mail*, for an up-to-the-minute guide to what's on.

A useful website containing lots of information on events, accommodation and attractions is www.ourbrisbane.com.

Darwin

Darwin pubs are popular meeting places for the locals, with a varied nightlife ranging from rowdy live-band performances to the relative sophistication of imported casino entertainers. Although the city's hard-drinking, macho/sexist culture is on the wane, pubs are still the centre of social life. A good start is the **Tourist & Entertainment Precinct**, running the length of Mitchell Street.

Perth

A variety of publications including *Scoop* and Perth's *Cultural Guide* is

BELOW: the Edwardian-style Brisbane Arcade at Queen Street Mall, Brisbane.

available from hotels and the Western Australian Visitor Centre. Daily updates are available in the entertainment segment of the *West Australian* newspaper and every Thursday in *X-Press*, a free magazine with details of bands, exhibitions and clubs. Online Citysearch (www.citysearch. com.au) is a fast way to find out what is happening in Perth.

Hobart

Hobart nightlife is fairly quiet. Most of the action is in the Docks area and Salamanca Market.

The other area where there is a cluster of restaurants, bars and venues, as well as a vibe that suggests there might be life after 10pm, is the Elizabeth Street strip in North Hobart. **Wrest Point Hotel Casino** was Australia's first casino – it also houses a restaurant, accommodation and a nightclub. The casino opens at 1pm and operates Sun–Thur until 3am, Friday and Saturday until 4am.

For other entertainment – cinemas, pub bands and the burgeoning club scene – check the *Mercury* newspaper for what's on.

SHOPPING

Sydney

Sydney's main shopping district is bounded by Martin Place, George, Park and Elizabeth streets. Here you'll find large department stores like **David Jones** and **Myer**, the elegantly restored **Queen Victoria Building (QVB)** on George Street, the **Royal**, **Strand** and **Imperial** arcades, and the four-level **Centrepoint** shopping arcade that runs between Pitt and Castlereagh streets. Bargains include opals and sheepskin products.

Sydney's busiest area is around **Martin Place** and **Pitt Street Mall**. These pedestrian plazas provide seating for weary shoppers, and at lunch time on weekdays, office workers and shoppers gather to hear free entertainment.

A visit to **Paddington Markets** is a Saturday-afternoon ritual: they're at the corner of Oxford Street and Newcombe. **The Rocks** markets operate all weekend.

The **Westfield** shopping centre at Bondi Junction offers you all your shopping needs under one roof. With 453 stores, it also offers a state-of-the-art gym, restaurants and an 11-screen cinema.

Canberra

London Circuit is the business and civic heart of Canberra. A series of shopping complexes lies close to **Civic Square**, with department stores, boutiques, cafés and gift shops.

Each suburb has its own comprehensive shopping complex. South of the lake, **Manuka Shopping Centre** is an up-market location, including a cinema centre, several bars and stylish eateries. Canberra's city shops are open Monday–Thursday 9am–5.30pm, Friday 9am–9pm, Saturday 9am–5.30pm and Sunday 10am–4pm.

The **Old Bus Depot Markets** (tel: 02-6292 8391; www.obdm.com.au) in Kingston are the place to find everything from handcrafted jewellery to fresh produce, Sundays 10am–4pm. One Saturday a month it is home to a Regional Farmers' Market.

Melbourne

Melbourne sees itself as Australia's major fashion centre. In fact, "shopping tours" have become one of the city's biggest tourist draw cards: they include lunch and take in Melbourne's famous factory outlets and seconds shops. Try Shopping Spree Tours, tel: 03-9596 6600.

In the city centre the major department stores are **Myer** and **David Jones**. Shopping centres include the **Melbourne Central** complex, with its multi-level glass atrium, the **QV Centre** in a whole block in Swanston Street, and the refurbished post office, **GPO** on the corner of Bourke and Elizabeth streets. **Collins Place** offers over 40 stores and hosts an "Australian-Made Art & Craft Market" every Sunday. The **Sportsgirl Centre** is a well-designed modern complex, and **Australia on Collins** features over 60 stores, many with imported fashions. Suburban shopping complexes are also huge. **Chadstone** is the largest in Australia and still growing. In South Yarra and Toorak, **Chapel Street** and **Toorak Road** are for the well-heeled only. Younger, cooler designers tend to congregate along **Brunswick Street**, Fitzroy. **Richmond** has a popular strip of factory outlets and bargain clothing shops where you can also buy clothes by young designers.

Melbourne has several famous shopping arcades. The oldest, the **Royal Arcade**, dates from 1870 and, along with the intimate **Block Arcade**, is one of Melbourne's landmarks. Street markets are also very popular

Sydney Tower

For the best bird's-eye view of Sydney (and even the Blue Mountains), take a trip up Sydney Tower on top of the Centrepoint complex. Located on Market Street between Pitt and Castlereagh, the tower is 305 metres (1,000ft) high and comprises a viewing gallery, sky-lounge café and revolving restaurant. Open 9am–10.30pm daily; until 11.30pm on Saturdays.

here: there's the lively **Queen Victoria Market**, while the comprehensive **Prahran Market** attracts to Melbourne gourmands.

Adelaide

Adelaide's main shopping area is **Rundle Mall**. Adelaide's **Central Market** between Gorger and Grote streets offers a wide array of gourmet goodies and fresh produce. Wines can be bought from the cellar doors of many wineries in the Barossa Valley, Clare Valley, McLaren Vale, Adelaide Hills and the Coonawarra. The Retail Art and Craft shop at the **Tandanya National Aboriginal Cultural Institute** sells a wide range of quality indigenous art, craft, books, music and clothing, as well as the essential didgeridoos and boomerangs (tel: 08-8224 3200; www.tandanya.com.au). At the **JamFactory** on Morphett Street you can tour craft and design studios and buy locally made contemporary ceramics, glass and jewellery.

Brisbane

Every Sunday, 8am–4pm, the vast **Riverside (Eagle Street) Market** is held at the Riverside Centre in Brisbane, with 150 craft stalls and many cafés. The **South Bank Markets** also offer craft and clothing on Friday evenings and weekends. The **Brisbane Powerhouse** in New Farm is the scene for a rapidly growing farmers' market on the second and fourth Saturdays of the month.

The main shopping centres in Brisbane are located around the Queen Street Mall, with the **Myer Centre** being the most comprehensive. Large arcades include **Wintergarden on the Mall**, **T&G**, **Rowes** and **Post Office Square**.

Darwin and Alice Springs

Darwin and Alice Springs are two of the best places to buy Aboriginal arts and crafts. Darwin is known for art from Arnhem Land and the Tiwi Islands, while Alice offers some of the best desert art (traditional dot painting style).

In Darwin, try the up-market **Karen Brown Gallery** near Parliament House, **Mason's** at 21 Cavenagh Street, **Maningrida Arts and Culture**, 32 Mitchell Street or **Framed**, 55 Stuart Highway, north of the city centre.

In Alice, head for the **Todd Street Mall** for a plethora of desert art galleries, such as Papunya Tula and Gondwana. Nearby is the marvellous, comprehensive **Mbantua Gallery** at Lot 71 in Gregory Street with its diversity of styles and reasonable prices.

Perth

Out-of-town shopping centres have multiplied around Perth. **Centro Galleria** (Old Collier Road, Morley; tel: 08-9375 3228) in the city's north and **Westfield Carousel** (1382 Albany Highway, Cannington; tel: 08-9458 6344) to the south stand out as typical, American-style mega-centres.

Still large, but compact and more "select" locations like **Karrinyup** (Karrinyup Road; tel: 08-9446 8454) also include food and furnishing outlets but major in clothes, shoes and more luxurious consumables.

The new suburban malls are booming, but none matches Perth city centre for its huge range – both "regular" shops and the many specialising in good-value, genuine Australian produce. Central Perth also benefits from extra trading on Friday nights and Sundays (for retail hours, see page 380).

Other areas have their own specialities – **Fremantle** for arts and crafts, **Subiaco** and **Claremont** for style and fashion, **Guildford** for antiques.

Hobart

Elizabeth Street Mall and the adjoining **Cat and Fiddle Arcade** and **Centrepoint Hobart Shopping Centre** form the retail hub of Hobart, with all the major department stores and retail chains.

Go to **Salamanca Place** for arts and crafts and handmade goods, especially on a Saturday when the market is held.

If you are in search of antiques, **Bathurst Street** and **Battery Point** are good places to look.

SPORT

Participant

Sydney

Yachting In Sydney, the yachting season runs September–March. Races and regattas are held nearly every weekend between the 18-footers. A spectator ferry leaves Circular Quay at 1.30pm every Saturday and occasionally on other days. Spectators also turn out in full force each year for the Sydney-to-Hobart Yacht Race, on 26 December.

Surfing Surfing carnivals are held at one of Sydney's ocean beaches on most Saturdays between October and March. These consist of swimming races, surf-boat races and board-paddling events. There are also professional and amateur surfboard-riding competitions in the summer and autumn months, but the location is often not selected until the day of the contest to locate the best surf.

Golf and Tennis There are more than 80 golf courses within Sydney, nearly all of them open to the public. And for the tennis player, Sydney has public courts and private tennis clubs.

Canberra

Water Sports Lake Burley Griffin is the scene of the action during the summer months, with rowing, sailing, and kayaking all popular. Swimmers can do laps at one of the city's aquatic centres, or cool off in one of the natural swimming holes, such as Pine Island, Point Hutt Crossing and Kambah Pool.

Horse riding and Golf Canberra has 22km (13 miles) of equestrian trail winding through the surrounding bushland. It also has a number of quality golf courses including the Federal Golf Club at Red Hill and Yowani Golf Club at Lyneham.

Melbourne

Water Sports Port Phillip offers excellent sailing conditions, and yacht clubs are plentiful; the Melbourne Sailing School (www.melbsailing.com.au) offers a range of courses. Swimmers should head to the Melbourne Sports and Aquatic Centre (MSAC), the largest integrated sports complex of its type in Australia, on the edge of Albert Park Lake on Aughtie Drive. Melbourne's Yarra River is great for canoeing and kayaking.

Tennis Melbourne Park, home of the Australian Open, has four indoor courts and 22 outdoor courts

available for public hire seven days a week, except in January.

Golf Melbourne harbours some of Australia's top courses in the famed sandbelt region in the southeastern suburbs. All sandbelt clubs are private, though golf tour operators such as Gimme Golf (www.gimmegolf.com.au) can organise access to exclusive courses. Failing that, Melbourne has some of the nation's best public links.

Adelaide

Cycling An excellent cycling and walking trail, Linear Park follows the length of the River Torrens. Adelaide is very flat so cycling is an easy way to get around. Thousands of spectators line the streets each January for the Tour Downunder that features some of the world's best cyclists.

Golf There are plenty of golf courses in Adelaide and most are open to the public. The Royal Adelaide Golf Club in Seaton is South Australia's oldest and among the best (bookings essential). Closer to the city centre, the City of Adelaide Golf Links caters for all levels. The course winds its way through North Adelaide and offers great city views.

Water-skiing The River Murray is an easy day trip from Adelaide and its glassy waters in the mornings and evenings make it excellent for water-skiing and other water sports.

Brisbane

Running and Jogging Brisbane's river banks offer many kilometres of flat running tracks, and the bay provides plenty of opportunities both to the north and south of the city.

Golf and Tennis Brisbane has several lovely courses including the Brookwater Golf Club, the North Lakes Resort Golf Club and the Royal Queensland. For tennis, head to the University of Queensland's Tennis Centre at Blair Drive, St Lucia, which has 21 floodlit courts and equipment for hire, and is open to all.

Water Sports Just outside Brisbane, the Moreton Bay Islands (www.moretonbayislands.com.au) are the place for surfing and kiteboarding. Bribie Island's Woorim Beach is a popular spot for swimmers and board riders, with its own surf school. Jet-skiing, water-skiing, and para-sailing are also possible here.

Darwin

Cycling Darwin City Council has produced a map, titled Making Tracks, which shows cycle paths in and around the city.

Golf There are numerous golf courses in the Northern Territory but most public courses are located outside Darwin.

Tennis Public tennis courts are located in Ross Smith Avenue, Aralia Street in Nightcliff and Chrisp Street in Rapid Creek.

Perth

Surfing Reliable conditions mean you can catch a wave year-round in Perth; check in first with the experts at Surfing WA (tel: 08-9448 0004; www.surfingaustralia.com). Courses are held at Trigg Beach, which with Scarborough has Perth's best surf.

Kayaking Wildlife sea kayaking among seals, sea lions and penguins around Seal Island just south of Perth is a one-day excursion offered by Rivergods Paddle Adventures (tel: 08-9259 0749; www.rivergods.com.au). No experience is necessary on this supervised trip, including transport, lunch, equipment, etc.

Running and Jogging Running is popular in Perth, and the 10km (6-mile) circuit around the bridges is well used. WA Masters Athletics Club (tel: 08-9330 3803; www.mastersathleticswa.org) welcomes visitors of all ages and abilities to events on Sunday mornings at locations around the city.

Hobart

Golf and Tennis The Tasmania Golf Council (tel: 03-6244 3600) is a good starting point for golfers from abroad looking to play a round. The local club in Hobart is the Royal Hobart Golf Club, tel: 03-6248 6161. A good stop for tennis information is Tennis Tasmania (tel: 03-6334 4237; www.

tennistasmania.com.au). The Domain Tennis Centre in Hobart (tel: 03-6234 4805) has courts for hire.

Water Sports There are several scuba-diving operators based in Hobart. To make contact with a local diver, try the Tasmanian Scuba Diving Club (tel: 0418 138 293). Sea kayaking options range from day paddles in sheltered waters to exposed crossings to the offshore islands. Try Blackaby's Sea Kayaks, tel: 0418 124 072. Based in Hobart, Rafting Tasmania (tel: 03-6239 1080) offers half-day, full-day or extended tours of the Derwent, Huon, Picton, North Esk and Franklin rivers.

Sailing Getting out on the water is an integral part of Tasmanian culture. To find out about the Tasmanian yachting scene have a look at the Tasmanian Yachting Association website (www.tas.yacting.org.au).

Fishing Tasmania offers the ultimate in fishing, in idyllic surroundings. For more information see www.fishonline.tas.gov.au. Hobart-based Fish Wild Tasmania (tel: 0418 348 223) offers one- to five-day tours, principally in trout waters.

Spectator

Sydney

Football Four types of football are played in Sydney, the most popular being rugby league. Games are played in winter months at the Sydney Football Stadium at Moore Park and at other ovals in Sydney.

Cricket One of Sydney's main summer sports is cricket. The season runs October–March with international and interstate matches.

You can watch cricket at the Sydney Cricket Ground at Moore Park.

Horse Racing The city has six tracks. Randwick is the closest and principal track, but races are held throughout the year at Canterbury, Rosehill and Warwick Farm. Trotting (harness) races are held Friday nights at Harold Park Paceway, and greyhound races on Monday and Saturday nights at Wentworth Park.

Canberra

Rugby Canberra's local rugby league teams are still young, but they have a loyal following. The Canberra Raiders, launched in the 1980s, quickly became one of the strongest teams in the national league, but have fared less well in recent years. The Brumbies, the city's Rugby Union team, is even younger but has also put in a strong showing.

Women's Basketball Catch a Canberra Capitals game, and you may get to see a genuine champion in action. Local girl Lauren Jackson, one of the top players in the WNBA in the United States, plays for her hometown team during the WNBA off-season, lending her star power to an already strong team.

Motor Sports Forget the roar of the crowd – it's the roar of the rally cars that really penetrates, as they race through the forests around Canberra every March during the Rally of Canberra.

Horse Racing A more genteel atmosphere is found at Canberra's Thoroughbred Park, where race meets are held throughout the year.

Melbourne

To see the locals cast away their Victorian reserve, any major sporting event will do – but football and horse racing are the surest bets. **Australian Rules Football** – a mixture of rugby, soccer and Gaelic football – is at its best in Melbourne. Matches are held every Saturday, Friday nights and Sundays during the April–September season. The finals pit the two top teams at the Melbourne Cricket Ground before more than 100,000 fanatical supporters.

Horse Racing Held year-round on the metropolitan courses at Flemington, Caulfield, Moonee Valley and Sandown. Flemington is the home of the **Melbourne Cup**, an internationally famous racing event held on the first Tuesday in November. On this day, the entire nation stops to follow the race. Meanwhile, all Melbourne is at the track where huge amounts of champagne and betting

BELOW: rumba at the Fremantle Festival in Western Australia.

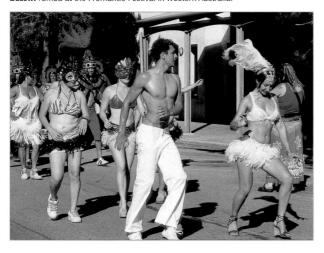

money flow. It's also the fashion event of the season.

Cricket December to February is the season for international Test cricket matches played at the Melbourne Cricket Ground, where the Boxing Day Test forms the year's highlight.

Tennis In January the Australian Open grand-slam tournament is held on the banks of the Yarra.

Motor Racing March is the time for the Australian Formula 1 Grand Prix in Albert Park, and in October bikers flock to Phillip Island for the Moto GP.

Soccer has blossomed since the natonal team's success at the 2006 World Cup. Melbourne Victory had its first 50,000+ attendance in 2006.

Adelaide

Football During winter, AFL is the sport of choice for most locals. Adelaide is home to two AFL teams who you can see play during the winter months at the AAMI Stadium in West Lakes.

Cricket In the summer months locals flock to the historic Adelaide Oval to watch Australia clash with international teams in Test matches and the faster-paced one-day internationals.

Cycling The Tour Downunder is a cycling event held each January. It attracts competitors from around the world as well as thousands of road-side spectators.

Motor Racing The city's streets play host to the Clipsal 500 each March, one of Australia's leading motorsport events featuring V8 cars. In November the Classic Adelaide Rally winds its way through 34 stages that take drivers through the Adelaide Hills and nearby wine regions.

Rugby Melbourne Storm was hugely successful in the national rugby league competition until it was found to have broken the salary cap and was stripped of its championships in 2010. The Melbourne Rebels rugby union team joined that code's national league in 2011.

Brisbane

Rugby Rugby League is the most popular spectator sport in Brisbane. There are two state teams, the North Queensland Cowboys, based in Townsville, and the Brisbane Broncos. Home games are played at Suncorp Stadium.

Cricket The Queensland Bulls are the state's top cricket team. Their home ground is the infamous Gabba at Woolloongabba.

Football AFL (Australian Football

League) is hugely popular in Brisbane, thanks to the Brisbane Lions who won a string of national titles in the early 2000s. Home games are played at the Gabba.

Darwin

Football Australian Rules Football is played in the wet season (incredibly sweaty conditions for the players). Soccer, rugby, cricket and hockey are all popular.

Horse Racing Popular all year round at the Darwin Turf Club at Fannie Bay. The locals celebrate the running of the Darwin Cup on the first Monday in August with a public holiday.

Motor Racing Held at the Hidden Valley raceway off Tiger Brennan Drive.

Perth

Cricket The WACA ground (Western Australian Cricket Association; Nelson Crescent, East Perth; tel: 08-9265 7222) is HQ of state cricket and venue for all important matches.

Horse Racing Perth has two racetracks, each a short ride from the centre. Ascot (tel: 08-9277 0777) is used for summer meetings, while Belmont Park (tel: 08-9470 8222), on the river with enclosed facilities, is popular in the winter months. Entry is generally free mid-week, unless there is a special meeting, and cheap (around A\$10) at weekends.

Hobart

The main action in Tasmania occurs on water; otherwise you can watch international and national **cricket** matches. Bellerive Oval (tel: 03-6211 4000) hosts all the major cricket tournaments.

Sydney to Hobart and **Melbourne to Hobart Yacht Races** begin on 26 December and finish at Constitution Dock.

Launceston hosts a handful of **Aussie Rules (AFL)** games each season – technically home matches for Melbourne side, Hawthorn – and draws large crowds to the Aurora Stadium.

Its other crowd-pleaser is **motor racing**, with a round of the V8 Supercars championship held at the Symmons Plains circuit, just south of the city, each November.

CHILDREN'S ACTIVITIES

There are many ways to keep even the most demanding children happy while holidaying in Australia. Below are some highlights from each major city

guaranteed to keep kids amused (at least momentarily). Alternatively, Australia's beaches and national parks provide a diverse playground.

Sydney

Conveniently, two of Sydney's leading attractions are located in Darling Harbour: the **Monorail** and **Tumbalong Park**, with a free playground and a stage for concerts.

The Search and Discover section of the **Australian Museum** lets children get their hands on all sorts of exciting exhibits. **The Powerhouse Museum** has stimulating Kids Interactive Discovery Spaces (KIDS), designed to involve younger children in hands-on activities related to the themes in the museum's exhibitions. They explore subjects such as music, machines, life in the home, film and television.

The **Opera House** runs children's events such as the Babies Proms, which allows toddlers to get close to the musical instruments (tel: 02-9250 7111). **The Art Gallery of New South Wales** holds special family events on Sundays, such as renditions of Aboriginal Dreamtime stories (tel: 02-9225 1700).

Canberra

Two major attractions with appeal to kids are the **National Zoo and Aquarium** (tel: 02-6287 8400) and the **National Museum of Australia** (tel: 02-6208 5000), with its KSpace FutureWorld gallery. Kids also love the **Questacon (National Science and Technology Centre**; daily 9am–5pm; tel: 02-6270 2800; www.questacon.edu. au). This distinctive drum-shaped structure on the lake shore specialises in hands-on science and technology exhibitions. Allow at least three hours for a fascinating visit.

Melbourne

The **Royal Melbourne Zoo** is a famously well-designed zoo, and one of the oldest in the world. It lies just north of the city centre in Parkville and provides creative walk-through environments, a butterfly enclosure, an excellent gorilla forest and a revamped elephant section. During January/February weekends the zoo is open until 9.30pm for Zoo Twilights concerts. Open daily 9am–5pm; www. zoo.org.au.

The **Melbourne Museum** has an excellent children's section and the complex now also features an Imax cinema.

Alternatively, the **Scienceworks Museum** (see page 175) has tactile displays that aim to make science and technology fun, and includes a Planetarium and Pumping Station.

Adelaide

Adelaide Zoo (see page 205). Located next to the Botanic Gardens, Adelaide Zoo is noted for its Australian birds, including pelicans, penguins, lorikeets, and blue and gold macaws. There are also sea lions, big cats and a reptile house.

For high-octane fun, head to **The Beachouse** in Glenelg. This new entertainment complex has waterslides, dodgems, mini golf, a bouncy castle and Ferris wheel. For more information tel: 08-8295 1511; www.thebeachouse.com.au.

Brisbane

There are plenty of exciting attractions aimed at children in Queensland. Theme parks on the Gold Coast have everything from water slides at **Wet'n' Wild Water World** and **Whitewaterworld** to movie sets at **Warner Brothers Movie World**. Dolphins and polar bears can keep smaller kids amused at **Sea World**, while the rides at **Dreamworld** cater to older children.

Australia Zoo on the Sunshine Coast was set up by the late Steve Irwin, otherwise known as the Crocodile Hunter. There are 14 shows daily, and, although crocodiles may be the main attraction, the zoo allows visitors to feed the Asian elephants and cuddle koalas. Cuddly koalas can also be found at the **Lone Pine Sanctuary** (tel: 07-3378 1366) near Brisbane, the first and largest koala sanctuary in the world.

The **Queensland Museum** on Brisbane's South Bank is full of inspiring interactive exhibitions for inquisitive children and young people. They can learn how to measure an earthquake, play a thongophone and piece together a human jigsaw. At the **Cobb & Co. Museum** at Toowoomba are examples of transport from the horse-drawn era. The excitement of huge cattle sales can be seen on Wednesdays at **Dalrymple Sales Yards** (tel: 07-4761 5300) on the Flinders Highway at Charters Towers. At **Tjapukai Aboriginal Cultural Park** in Cairns (tel: 07-4042 9999) the daily shows include an evening of corroboree around a fire.

Darwin

Kids will enjoy exploring the Northern Territory's diverse wildlife at the **Territory Wildlife Park**, which has a walk-through aquarium, as well as numerous kangaroos and wallabies roaming free.

A much-needed rest can be had while the children splash around at the **Howard Springs Nature Park**, which has a children's pool fed by freshwater springs (just outside Darwin; tel: 08-8983 1001).

Perth

Extra events and projects are put on at venues during school holidays: details from the Perth Visitor Centre, tel: 08-9483 1133.

Some of the best activities to keep kids occupied in Perth include the **Perth Zoo** (20 Labouchere Road, South Perth; tel: 08-9474 0444), which has great collections of native and exotic animals in natural enclosures; children's activities include an overnight stay in the summer months, when you can sleep near the animal enclosures. Open 9am–5pm daily.

Apart from being a genuinely interesting visit any time of the year, the **Western Australian Museum** (Perth Cultural Centre, James Street, tel: 08-99212 3700) organises special children's activities during school holidays.

At **Adventure World** (179 Progress Drive, Bibra Lake; tel: 08-9417 9666; Oct–Apr 10am–5pm, daily during school holidays, closed Tue and Wed out of holiday times) there's unlimited

Ticket Through Time

A number of Sydney's most interesting historical museums are managed by the Historic Houses Trust of New South Wales. If you intend to visit more than three of these 12 attractions, it would be worth purchasing a Ticket Through Time, which entitles you to admission to all the properties and is valid for three months. Go to: www.hht.net.au/visit.

use of all the rides and attractions once you have paid the rather steep entry fee. "The Rampage" is the scariest ride of all, not for the faint-hearted.

Hobart

The Discovery Space at the **Tasmanian Museum and Art Gallery** (40 Macquarie Street; tel: 03-6211 4177) has hands-on action, and its summer holiday programmes can include anything from a sneak preview of the taxidermist's latest work to putting butterflies under the microscope.

The **Terrapin Puppet Theatre** (77 Salamanca Place; tel: 03-6223 6834) introduces under-12s to the magic of performance via Hans Christian Andersen stories with an Aussie twist and other contemporary tales.

The **Imaginarium Science Centre** (Wenvoe Street, Devonport; tel: 03-6423 1466) has interactive exhibits that are changed every school term.

BELOW: admiring a wombat at Lone Pine Sanctuary in Queensland.

TRANSPORT

ACCOMMODATION

ACTIVITIES

A – Z

LANGUAGE

A – Z

A HANDY SUMMARY OF PRACTICAL INFORMATION, ARRANGED ALPHABETICALLY

Admission Charges

Compared with the UK and USA, admission charges to sights and attractions are fairly low, and often free for museums, though you may find that they charge for entry to temporary exhibitions. The "worlds" – including Dreamworld and Sea World in Queensland, for example – have some of the highest admission charges, but usually offer discounted family tickets, which can help keep a lid on costs if travelling with children. Concession prices are often available on production of a student or senior card.

For more information contact the relevant tourist office (tourist offices are listed on page 382, while contact information for Australia's National Parks and National Trust offices are listed under Useful Addresses on pages 382–383).

Budgeting for Your Trip

The cost of living in Australia has traditionally been lower than Europe and the USA (although manufactured goods tend to be more expensive in

Australia). However, since the Gobal Financial Crisis, Australia's economy has outperformed most others and the Australian dollar has become much stronger. These days Australia feels relatively expensive to visitors from the US and Europe. Mind you, Sydney has always had property prices up there with cities like London and New York, and day-to-day expenses such as public transport and dining out tend to be noticeably higher than in other Australian cities. As you move away from the east coast, where most of Australia's population lives, to cities like Adelaide, Hobart, Darwin and Perth, the cost of living is lower again. However, there is an exception once more which is the isolated towns and settlements of the Outback where the cost of transporting supplies long distances drives petrol and food prices upwards.

In general accommodation can cost as little as A$50–60 for a double room in a country pub, A$100 for self-contained cabin-style accommodation in the country, A$120 for a basic hotel room and A$200 upwards per night for five-star hotels.

The variety of climates means Australia grows lots of fresh produce that is of a high quality, although the standard in supermarkets is generally lower than what you will find in markets and fruiterers. A takeaway or dine-in café meal costs anywhere from A$10–20, a main in a restaurant ranges from $20–35 and a main in a fine dining restaurant ranges from A$25–50. In major cities, some of the most affordable and best-quality food can be found in and around Chinatown.

Travel tends to be expensive because of the distances involved and high fuel prices. Car hire can start from around A$60 per day including insurance, although significant discounted rates apply for longer rental periods. Budget airlines Virgin Blue, Jetstar and Tiger continue to have price wars and you can pick up flights from Sydney to Cairns, some 2,500km (1,550 miles), for A$149 one way. An airfare between Sydney and Melbourne can cost as little as A$60 if you book a few weeks ahead. The train between Sydney and Melbourne can cost around A$100, but when you take into account the 12 hours' travel time versus only 1½ hours on a plane, its easy to see why most people prefer to fly.

C limate

The seasons in Australia are the reverse of the northern hemisphere's. September to November is spring, December to February summer, March to May autumn, and June to August winter. Since fine, mild weather occurs during all seasons, any time can be recommended for a visit to Australia – although some months are warmer and drier than others.

About 40 percent of the country lies in the tropical zone north of the Tropic of Capricorn. In the Top End around Darwin (the monsoon belt) and near Cairns, there are only two seasons: the dry (April–November) and the wet (December–March). In the dry, there are warm days, clear blue skies and cool nights. The wet, however, is usually characterised by heavy rain alternating with sunny hot weather. On the Great Barrier Reef most rain falls in January and February.

In the southern temperate zone seasons are more distinct. Winter days in Sydney are usually sunny with a maximum of 15°C (60°F) – chilly enough to require an overcoat – while humid summer temperatures can regularly hit 30°C (90°F) and higher. Snow falls on the southern mountain ranges, but not in the cities (except Hobart). Melbourne is pleasant in spring, summer and autumn, but winter can be grey and miserable, especially in July and August. Tasmania, the island state off the southern tip of the continent, is the coolest: summers are by far the best time to visit here, as winters can be damp and depressing.

South Australia has a Mediterranean climate: summers are hot and dry with temperatures regularly above 30°C (85°F), and highs of 40°C (105°F) and above are not uncommon.

Western Australia also has a Mediterranean climate. There are four distinctive seasons and moderate temperatures in its southern parts, while the north is in the tropical zone, so Top End conditions prevail.

In central Australia, summer temperatures are generally too high for comfort. In winter, the nights may be cool, with clear warm days.

Visitors should also bear in mind the various Australian school holidays; Christmas coincides with the long summer school break, which lasts throughout January. Easter is another big break. If you are travelling during these seasons, book well in advance.

Crime and Safety

When it comes to crime, Australia is a relatively safe country. That being said, you should use the same common sense and precautions as you would elsewhere regarding your possessions and personal security. Issues surrounding prostitution, drugs and drunken behaviour occur in all cities. However, these are unlikely to affect travellers. If an incident occurs, report it to the police or, for urgent attention, call the emergency services by dialling **000**.

When it comes to safety, non-human elements can pose more of a risk in Australia. Bushfires occur regularly each year and it is important to be aware of fire bans or restrictions. If you are out in the bush and notice smoke, it is important to take it seriously and head for the nearest open space.

It is also important you thoroughly prepare if you are bushwalking or exploring the Outback. Take plenty of water and supplies, a good map and let a friend or the local ranger know of your plans in case you get stranded. Daily temperatures can reach the extremes, with searing heat during the day and freezing nights.

In northern Australia saltwater crocodiles are a real danger and have been known to take humans. They can be found in rivers, creeks, waterholes and around the coast. In popular tourist areas, croc-inhabited waterholes are regularly signposted. However, if you are unsure whether a place is croc-free, it is best not to risk swimming at all.

Box jellyfish are another danger in the far north during the wet season (November to May). Their venomous sting is extremely painful and can be fatal. During these months make sure you only swim in the special "stinger" enclosures.

Unsuspecting tourists can easily find themselves in trouble when swimming at Australian surf beaches. Lifesavers patrol popular beaches and put up red and yellow flags that swimmers should stay between. If an undertow or "rip" drags you out, raise an arm if you need help and a surf lifesaver will come to your aid.

Customs Regulations

There are no customs charges on personal belongings intended for use during your stay. Non-dutiable allowances are 250 grams (8oz) of tobacco goods and 2.25 litres (2.4 quarts) of alcohol. You may also import dutiable goods to the value of A$900 in personal baggage. Visit www.customs.gov.au.

Australian produce is of a very high standard because it is free from many insect pests and diseases common to other countries. This is due in part to the strict control on the importation of insects, animal and plant products, fruit, vegetables and seeds.

Laws strictly prohibit the export of protected Australian wildlife and products made from the skins, feathers, bones, shells, corals, or any part of protected species.

Quarantine

Australia is free of rabies, anthrax and foot-and-mouth disease, so all incoming animals are placed in quarantine. Cats and dogs (including guide dogs) are quarantined for up to 6 months, depending on the animal's country of origin – from the UK the period is 30 days. See www.affa.gov.au.

D isabled Travellers

Most new buildings, public transport and tourist attractions have wheelchair access and other facilities for the disabled. The major rental car companies have a small number of cars with hand controls (reserve at least seven days in advance). Advance notice with relevant details of your disability will facilitate the best possible assistance from airlines, hotels or railway offices. Taxi fleets in state capitals all have cars that can carry wheelchairs. Tourism Australia has further information on its website (www.australia.com). Also, the National Information Communications Network (NICAN) provides a directory of accessible accommodation, recreation and other facilities. Contact NICAN at: Unit 5, 48 Brookes Street, Mitchell, ACT 1220, tel: 02-6241 1220; freecall: 1800-806 769; www.nican.com.au.

The state automobile associations publish accommodation directories which include information on disabled access.

E lectricity

The power supply is 220–240 volts AC. Sockets are three-pin flat plugs. You may be able to find adaptors in hardware stores or at some hotels.

Embassies and Consulates

If you need help with matters such as legal advice or a stolen passport while in Australia, most countries have diplomatic representations, with embassies in major cities.

Melbourne

Canada
Level 50, 101 Collins Street, tel: 03-

9653 9674.
Japan
Level 45, Melbourne Central Tower, 360 Elizabeth Street, tel: 03-9639 3244.
UK
17th Floor, 90 Collins Street, tel: 03-9652 1600.
USA
553 St Kilda Road, Melbourne, tel: 03-9526 5900.

Sydney

A comprehensive list of every country represented in Australia is available on the Australia Department of Foreign Affairs and Trade website www.info.dfat.gov.au. A small selection of the consulates in Sydney follows:
Canada
Consulate-General of Canada Level 5, Quay West, 111 Harrington Sreet, tel: 02-9364 3050; http://geo.international.gc.ca/asia/australia.
China/Hong Kong
Consulate General of the P.R. of China/Hong Kong, 39 Dunblane St, St Camperdown Pvt Boxes, NSW 4450, Surry Hills, tel: 02-8595 8002 (9am–12.30pm); www.australia.org.hk.
France
Consulate-General of France, Level 26, 31 Market Street, St Martin's Tower, tel: 02-9261 5238; www.consulfrance-sydney.org.
Japan
Consulate-General of Japan, Level 34, 52 Martin Place, Colonial Centre, tel: 02-9231 3455; www.japan.org.au.
USA
Consulate-General of the United States of America, Level 5, 19–29 Martin Place, MLC Centre, tel: 02-9373 9200; http://usembassy-australia.state.gov/sydney.

Brisbane

China

Canberra Embassies

Over 60 countries have diplomatic representation in Canberra, and their buildings form a tourist attraction in their own right.

The embassies are mostly south and west of Capital Hill, scattered through the suburbs of Red Hill, Forrest and Yarralumla. Many of the buildings have been designed in the architectural style of the country the mission represents, such as the US Embassy in a red-brick Williamsburg Mission style and the Thai Embassy with its upswept roof corners and gold-coloured roof tiles.

Level 9, 79 Adelaide Street, tel: 07-3210 6509-206.
Italy
Level 14, AMP Place, 10 Eagle Street, tel: 07-3229 8944.
UK
Level 26, Waterfront Place, 1 Eagle Street, tel: 07-3236 2575.

Perth

Canada
Third Floor, 267 St George's Terrace, tel: 08-9322 7930.
UK
Level 26, Allendale Square, 77 St George's Terrace, tel: 08-9224 4700.
USA
13th Floor, 16 St George's Terrace, tel: 08-9231 9400.

Adelaide

Germany
23 Peel Street, tel: 08-8231 6320.
Italy
398 Payneham Road, Glynde, tel: 08-8337 0777.
UK
Level 22, 25 Grenfell Street, tel: 08-8212 7280.

Darwin

British Consulate (emergencies only) 02 44 22 22 80.

Canberra

Canada
Commonwealth Avenue, Yarralumla, tel: 02-364 3050.
Ireland
20 Arkana Street, Yarralumla, tel: 02-6273 3022.
Japan
112–114 Empire Circuit, Yarralumla, tel: 02-6273 3244.
Malaysia
7 Perth Avenue, Yarralumla, tel: 02-6273 1543.
New Zealand
Commonwealth Avenue, Yarralumla, tel: 02-6270 4211.
Singapore
17 Forster Cresent, Yarralumla, tel: 02-6273 3944.
UK
Commonwealth Avenue, Yarralumla, tel: 02-6270 6666; www.uk.emb.gov.au.
USA
21 Moonah Place, Yarralumla, tel: 02-6214 5600.

Overseas Missions

Canada – Ottawa
Australian High Commission, Suite 710, 50 O'Conner Street, Ottawa, Ontario, K1P 6L2, tel: 1 613-236 0841.
Toronto
Australian Consulate-General, Suite

1100 South Tower, 175 Bloor Street East, Toronto, Ontario, M4W 3R8, tel: 1 416-323 1155.

Vancouver
Australian Consulate, Suite 1225, 888 Dunsmuir Street, Vancouver, BC V6C 3K4, tel: 1 604-684 1177.

China (Hong Kong)
Australian Consulate-General, 23/F Harbour Centre, 25 Harbour Road, Wan Chai, tel: 852 2827 8881.

Ireland
Australian Embassy, 7th floor, Fitzwilton House, Wilton Terrace, Dublin 2, tel: 353 1-664 5300.

Japan
Australian Embassy, 2-1-14 Mita, Minato-Ku, Tokyo 108-8361, tel: 81 35232 4111.

New Zealand – Wellington
Australian High Commission, 72–76 Hobson Street, Thorndon, Wellington, tel: 64 4473 6411.

Auckland
Australian Consulate-General, Level 7 PricewaterhouseCoopers Tower, 186–194 Quay Street, Auckland, tel: 64 9921 8800.

Singapore
Australian High Commission, 25 Napier Road, Singapore 258507, tel: 65 6836 4100.

UK
Australian High Commission, Australia House, The Strand, London WC2B 4LA, tel: 44 20-7379 4334.

USA – Washington DC
Australian Embassy, 1601 Massachusetts Avenue, Washington DC NW 20036-2273, tel: 1 202-797 3000.

New York
Australian Mission to the UN, 150 East 42nd Street, 33rd floor, New York, NY 10017-5612, tel: 1 212-351 6600.

San Francisco
Australian Consulate-General, 575 Market Street, Suite 1800, San Francisco, CA 94105-2185, tel: 1 415-536 1970.

Atlanta
Australian Consulate-General, Atlanta Financial Center, 3353 Peachtree Road, NE, Suite 1140, Atlanta GA 30326, tel: 1 404-760 3408.

Emergencies

Call **000** for police, fire and ambulance assistance. This number is toll-free from any phone in Australia and can be made from public phones without a phonecard or coins. **112** is the international standard emergency number that can be dialled from any mobile phone.

G ay and Lesbian Travellers

Australia is popular with gay and lesbian travellers, although homophobic attitudes do exist, mostly in areas away from inner cities and popular tourist spots.

One of the main attractions is Sydney's annual gay and lesbian **Mardi Gras** each March, one of the greatest celebrations of its kind in the world. Sydney's Oxford Street is where all the action takes place, and outside Mardi Gras it remains a popular gay and lesbian hub, along with Newtown. **Midsumma** (www.midsumma.org.au), held each January/February, is the major gay and lesbian festival in Melbourne.

Major cities have gay and lesbian newspapers and magazines, available from many inner-city cafés, bars and pubs. Gay and Lesbian Tourism Australia (GALTA) is a network of gay-friendly tourism operators (www.galta.com.au).

H ealth and Medical Care

Australian doctors, dentists and hospitals all have modern equipment, high-level training and extensive facilities. They are also expensive.

New Zealand, Finland, Italy, Malta, the Netherlands, Norway, Sweden, the UK and Ireland have reciprocal health-care agreements with Australia, so visitors are entitled to free hospital treatment and Medicare (the Australian national health plan) benefits for GP treatment. Taking out a travel insurance policy that covers your health, before travelling to Australia, is recommended however.

Vaccinations are not required if you are flying directly to Australia and have not passed through an epidemic

zone or a yellow fever, cholera or typhoid-infected area in the 6 days prior to your arrival.

The sun in Australia has extremely strong ultraviolet rays, so extended exposure is not recommended, especially when the sun is at its fiercest between 11am and 4pm. A wide-brimmed hat and adequate-strength sunscreen are essential.

I nternet

Internet cafés are easily found all over Australia, particularly in the larger towns and cities. However, their numbers have probably peaked as smart-phone use accelerates.

M aps

Tourist information centres usually have free, quality local maps that also include useful tourism information. If you are travelling by car most car-hire companies supply road atlases. You can also pick up Australian road atlases from any good bookshop. Australia is a vast country and it is easy to get lost once you head to the Outback so it is recommended you purchase maps that detail geography as well as road and track types for Outback travel and long-distance bushwalking.

The Tourism Australia website (www.australia.com) has a wide range of state, city and localised maps which can be useful for planning your itinerary.

Media

Each major city has one daily newspaper and in some cases two. The *Sydney Morning Herald* (www.smh.com.au) and the *Melbourne Age* (www.

BELOW: Australia's distinctive coat of arms.

theage.com.au) are the two most important capital-city dailies, and can usually be found around Australia. The only national daily newspapers are *The Australian* and *The Financial Review*. Numerous weekly magazines are sold alongside local editions of international publications, such as *Newsweek* and *Time*.

The largest-selling papers are the tabloids in Sydney (the *Daily Telegraph*) and Melbourne (the *Herald-Sun*, online at www.heraldsun. com). There are about 120 newspapers catering to Australia's ethnic minorities, which are published in either English or one of 40 other languages.

Australia has a high readership of magazines: in addition to 1,200 magazine titles, airmail copies of overseas newspapers and journals are readily available at specialist newsagents and numerous bookstores in major cities.

The number of free-to-air television stations varies around the country. In some remote areas, the ABC (Australian Broadcasting Corporation) may be the only station. This is the national, advertisment-free, television and radio network – the equivalent of Britain's BBC. The capital cities also offer three commercial stations and the excellent SBS (Special Broadcasting Service) multicultural station, with shows in many languages with subtitles. With the introduction of digital television, there are now 15 free-to-air stations available to suitably equipped households.

On radio, there is always ABC (FM and AM), plus a full spectrum of commercial and public broadcast stations, offering everything from rock to classical music.

BELOW: painkillers Aussie-style.

Money

Australia's currency is in dollars and cents. The coins come in 5-, 10-, 20- and 50-cent silver pieces and 1- and 2-dollar gold coins. Notes are A$5, 10, 20, 50 and 100. Amounts of over A$10,000 must be declared on entering and leaving Australia.

The larger hotels will usually exchange cash and well-known traveller's cheques. Nearly all places accept major credit cards such as American Express, Visa, Diners Club and MasterCard.

Banks The four big banks in Australia are the National (NAB), the Commonwealth, Westpac and ANZ. Trading hours are generally Mon–Thur 9.30am–4pm, until 5pm on Friday. A few of the smaller banks and credit unions open on Saturday mornings.

Traveller's cheques in any currency can be readily cashed at international airports and banks. Bureaux de change offices are open seven days a week and are located throughout major cities – but usually charge a significant fee, so try to change money at banks when you can, despite limited opening hours.

Credit/Debit Cards and ATMs
Carrying a recognised credit or debit card such as Visa, MasterCard, American Express or Diners Club is always a good idea when travelling. A credit card should provide access to EFTPOS (electronic funds transfer at point of sale), which is the easiest and often the cheapest way to exchange money – amounts are automatically debited from the selected account. Many Australian businesses are connected to EFTPOS.

Australian currency cash withdrawals can be made from automatic banking machines (ATMs) that are linked to overseas banks. Since credit card companies generally start charging interest on cash withdrawals immediately, and charge a fee on top, it is usually cheaper to withdraw cash using a debit card rather than a credit card. Some UK banks charge a fee for using debit cards overseas, so check this out before travelling to avoid any nasty surprises on your bank statement when you return home.

Some of the islands and the Outback towns have limited banking facilities, so make sure you have plenty of cash before heading into these less populated areas.

Tipping

Tipping is not the general custom in Australia – waiters are given a decent hourly wage. Most Australians round up the amount in restaurants, or leave the change. In the more formal places, it is becoming customary to give a little more than that – about 10 percent of the total.

Porters at luxury hotels once never received tips, but since many overseas visitors give them a dollar or two, there is an increasing look of expectancy. Porters at airports and taxi drivers do not expect to be tipped, but will hardly throw the money back if you do. "It's up to you" has become the common advice from Australians. In other words: nobody really expects a tip, but it's always appreciated.

O pening Hours

General retail trading hours for stores are Mon–Sat 9am–5pm. Most shops open 10am–4pm on Sunday too. Late-night shopping (until 9pm) takes place at least one night a week in the capital cities – usually a Thursday or Friday.

Restaurants and snack bars, bookshops and local corner stores are open until late in the evening; at times all weekend. Australians still enjoy the tradition of the weekend holiday and most offices are closed on Saturday and Sunday.

Banks open Mon–Thur 9.30am–4pm and until 5pm on Friday. Some selected branches are open on Saturday morning as well. All banks, post offices, government and private offices, and most shops close on public holidays (*see Public Holidays, below*).

P ostal Services

Post offices open Mon–Fri 9am–5pm. The service is reasonably efficient but not cheap.

Post offices provide fax services at urgent or ordinary rates, the cost depending on the rate selected and the destination.

The front pages of the telephone directory give further information on all postal services, including telephone interpreter service, community service and recorded information service.

Post Restante: post offices will receive and hold mail for visitors. American Express offices will also hold mail for members.

Public Holidays

Public and school holidays affect availability of transport and hotel reservations, which often results in higher prices. The public holidays observed Australia-wide are as follows:

1 January **New Year's Day**
26 January **Australia Day**
mid-March or early October (varies in different states) **Labour Day**
late March/early April **Good Friday, Easter Saturday and Monday**
25 April **Anzac Day**
2nd Monday in June **Queen's Birthday**
25 December **Christmas Day**
26 December **Boxing Day**
In addition, the states have their own public holidays, such as Victoria's Melbourne Cup Day (first Tuesday in November).

ABOVE: sometimes the tourist route takes you off the beaten path.

Religion

Australia is a secular multicultural society and numerous religions are practised. The major cities are where you will find all types of places of worship. Christianity has the most adherents and you won't be hard pushed to find church services for major denominations in cities and towns. The major cities have some magnificent cathedrals.

Buddhism, Islam, Judaism and Hinduism also have large followings in Australia. Muslim communities can be found in the western suburbs of Sydney, concentrating around Lakemba, and the northern suburbs of Melbourne around Broadmeadows. A strong Jewish community exists in Melbourne around St Kilda East.

Student Travellers

Australia is popular with international students and backpackers so there is an abundance of budget tourism operators and accommodation providers. STA Travel has offices in every state and offers a range of products and services aimed at students. Look out for free copies of TNT Magazine for budget travel tips and information (www.tntmagazine.com.au). Universities also offer a range of services and local advice for international students, including affordable accommodation on campus.

Telephones

Emergency numbers: **police, ambulance, fire, tel: 000, or 112 from mobile telephones.**

Australia has several telecommunication operators including Telstra, Optus and AAPT. Rates vary between companies for long distance, but local calls on all networks are untimed.

Making Calls

Public telephones are located throughout cities and towns. Most public telephones take phonecards, which can be bought at newsagents and stores in various denominations. Dialling from hotel rooms is much more expensive than from a public or private phone.

Subscriber Trunk Dialling (STD) for calling long distance is available on all private and most public telephones. Dial the regional code (say 02 for NSW, 03 for Victoria, etc) followed by the local number. STD calls are cheapest after 7pm and before 8am.

International Calls

Direct-dialled international calls may be made from any ISD-connected private or public phone. International public phones are located at city GPOs, rail termini and airports. There are off-peak rates to most countries which generally apply all day Saturday and 11pm–6am Sunday to Friday. Dial 0011 followed by the relevant country code.

Time Zones

Australia has three time zones: Eastern Standard Time for the east-

Toll-free Phone Calls

Toll-free or freecall numbers are common in Australian business. Numbers beginning with 13 (ie Qantas domestic 131-313) can be called from any phone in Australia at local-call rates; numbers starting with 800, 1300 or 1800 are freecall numbers (toll-free) when dialled from within Australia.

coast states (Tasmania, Victoria, New South Wales, Queensland), 10 hours ahead of GMT; Central Standard Time (covering Northern Territory and South Australia) 30 minutes behind the east coast, 9½ hours ahead of GMT; and Western Standard Time (Western Australia), 2 hours behind the east coast, 8 hours ahead of GMT.

During the summer most states introduce Daylight Saving Time, moving the clock forward by 1 hour. New South Wales and Australian Capital Territory run daylight saving November–February; South Australia and Victoria November–March; and Tasmania October–March. Neither Queensland nor Western Australia uses Daylight Saving Time.

Toilets

In their typical no-nonsense fashion, Australians manage without euphemisms for "toilet". "Dunny" or "thunder box" is the Outback slang, but "washroom", "restroom", "Ladies" and "Gents" are all understood. Public toilets are often locked after certain hours, but you can generally use the facilities in any pub or cinema without making a purchase. Toilets are generally clean, even in the Outback.

For those who like to plan their rest stops, the government has produced the Toilet Map, available at www.toiletmap.gov.au, with details of the various public toilets in each of Australia's states.

Tourist Information

Tourist information within Australia is handled principally by state tourist offices. These offices are generally open seven days a week, and will provide brochures, maps, price lists and other information. They can often book accommodation, tours and transport on your behalf. Most towns also have a local tourist information office.

ACT – Australian Capital Territory
Canberra and Region Visitors Centre, 330 Northbourne Avenue, Dickson, ACT 2602
Tel: 1300-554 114 or 02-6205 0044
Fax: 02-6205 0776
www.visitcanberra.com.au

New South Wales
Sydney Visitor Centre, George Street, The Rocks, Sydney NSW 2000
Tel: 132-077 or 02-9240 8788
Also at 33 Wheat Road, Darling Harbour.
Tel: 1800-067 676 or 02-9240 8788
Fax: 02-9252 8738
www.sydneyvisitorcentre.com
www.visitnsw.com.au

Northern Territory
Tourism NT, 43 Mitchell Street, Darwin, NT 0800
Tel: 08-8999 3900
Fax: 08-8999 3888
www.travelnt.com

Queensland
Queensland Travel Centre, 30 Makerston Street, Brisbane 4000
Tel: 1300-872 835
Fax: 07-3535 4044
www.tq.com.au

South Australia
South Australian Visitor and Travel Centre, 18 King William Street, Adelaide, SA 5000
Tel: 1300 655 276 or 08-8303 2220
www.southaustralia.com

Tasmania
Tasmanian Travel and Information Centre, 22 Davey Street, Hobart, Tas 7000
Tel: 1300-655 145 or 03-6230 8233 (for international enquiries)
www.discovertasmania.com.au
www.tastravel.com.au

Victoria
Melbourne Visitors Centre, Federation Square (corner of Flinders/Swanson streets), Melbourne
Tel: 03-9658 9658
www.visitvictoria.com

Western Australia
Western Australian Visitor Centre, Albert Facey House, Forrest Place (corner of Wellington Street), Perth
Tel: 1300-361 351 or 08-9483 1111
Fax: 08-9481 0190
www.westernaustralia.net

U seful Addresses

Tourist Information Abroad

Tourism Australia supplies excellent information for travellers wishing to plan their trip:

London
Australia Centre, Australia House, 6th Floor, The Strand, London, WC2B 4LG
Tel: 020-7438 4601
Fax: 020-7240 6690

Los Angeles
6100 Center Drive, Suite 1150, Los Angeles, CA 90045
Tel: 310-695 3200
Fax: 310-695 3201

Hong Kong
Suite 6706, Central Plaza, 18 Harbour Road, Wanchai
Tel: 852-2802 7700

Fax: 852-2802 8211
Singapore
101 Thompson Road, United Square 08-03, Singapore 307591
Tel: 65-6255 4555
Fax: 65-6253 8431
Local Office of Tourism Australia
Tel: 1300-361 650 or
02-9360 1111
Fax: 612-9361 1388

National Trust Offices

The National Trust in Australia owns and preserves more than 180 historic properties. All of them are open to the public and Trust members are entitled to free entry. If you intend to visit a number of Australia's historic buildings it may be worth joining. Annual membership costs A$89 for an individual, A$113 for households. Non-members can pay to see particular properties. To join call toll-free in Australia 1800-246 766 or contact one of the state offices. A reciprocal arrangement exists with similar organisations in other countries, so bring their cards with you to Australia.

National
The Australian Council of National Trusts, 14/71 Constitution Avenue, Campbell, ACT 2612
Tel: 02-6247 6766
www.nationaltrust.org.au
Australian Capital Territory
1st Floor, North Building, Civic Offices, Civic Square, Canberra, ACT 2608
Tel: 02-6230 0533
www.nationaltrust.org.au

BELOW: the tourist information centre at the Outback town of Cunnamulla, Queensland.

TRANSPORT

New South Wales
Observatory Hill, The Rocks, Sydney, NSW 2001
Tel: 02-9258 0123
www.nsw.nationaltrust.org.au

Queensland
Ground Floor, 91–95 William Street, Brisbane, Qld 4001
Tel: 07-3229 1788
www.nationaltrustqld.org

South Australia
Level 2, 27 Leigh Street, Adelaide 5000
Tel: 08-8212 1133
www.nationaltrustsa.org.au

Tasmania
Franklin House, 413 Hobart Road, Launceston, Tas 7250
Tel: 03-6344 6233.
www.nationaltrusttas.org.au

Victoria
4 Parliament Place, East Melbourne, Vic 3002
Tel: 03-9656 9800
www.nattrust.com.au

Western Australia
The Old Observatory, 4 Havelock Street, West Perth, WA 6005
Tel: 08-9321 6088
www.ntwa.com.au

National Parks

Some national parks require you to purchase permits before entry. Visitor centres and regional offices where you can obtain information and permits are located throughout Australia and are often in or close to popular parks. National parks information can also be obtained from these regional offices:

ACT: National Parks and Wildlife Service
Tel: 02-6229 3201
www.npaact.gov.au

NSW: National Parks and Wildlife Service
Level 14, 59 Goulburn Street, The Rocks, Sydney, NSW 2000
Tel: 1300-361 967 or 02-9995 5000
www.nationalparks.nsw.gov.au

NT: Parks & Wildlife, Northern Territory
Goyder Centre, 25 Chung Wah Terrace, Palmerston, NT 0830
Tel: 08-8999 5511
www.nt.gov.au/nreta/parks

Qld: Parks & Wildlife Service
160 Ann Street, Brisbane, Qld 4000
Tel: 07-3227 8185
www.epa.qld.gov.au

SA: Environment & Heritage
Tel: 08-8204 1910 (info line)
www.parks.sa.gov.au

Tas: Parks and Wildlife Service
134 Macquarie Street, Hobart 7000
Tel: 1300-135 513
www.parks.tas.gov.au

Vic: Parks Victoria
Level 10/535 Bourke Street
Melbourne, Victoria 3000
Tel: 03-8627 4699; or 131-963 (within Australia) for information centre and 24-hour emergency hotline
www.parkweb.vic.gov.au

Visas and Passports

Visitors to Australia must have a passport valid for the entire period of their stay. All non-Australian citizens also require a visa – except for New Zealand citizens, who are issued with a visa on arrival in Australia.

ETA visas The Electronic Transfer Authority (ETA) enables visitors to obtain a visa on the spot from their travel agent or airline office. The system is in place in over 30 countries, including the US and the UK. ETA visas are generally valid over a 12-month period; single stays must not exceed three months, but return visits within the 12-month period are allowed. ETA visas are issued free, or you can purchase one online for A$20 from www.eta.immi.gov.au.

Tourist visas These are available for continuous stays longer than three months, but must be obtained from an Australian visa office, such as an Embassy or Consulate. A A$20 fee applies. Those travelling on tourist and ETA visas are not permitted to work while in Australia. Travellers are asked on their applications to prove they have an adequate source of funding while in Australia (around A$1,000 a month).

Temporary residence Those seeking temporary residence must apply to an Australian visa office, and in many cases must be sponsored by an appropriate organisation or employer. Study visas are available for people who want to undertake registered courses on a full-time basis.

Working holiday visas Under a reciprocal arrangement, visitors from a list of 19 countries including the UK, Canada and Japan, who are between the ages of 18 and 30, are eligible for a Working Holiday visa. This entitles them to a stay of up to 12 months and some casual employment during that time. Such visas can only be applied for in the traveller's country of origin.

Entry requirements for Australia are continually updated. Information and applications for visas should be made to the nearest Australian Government representative in your home country well before travelling (*see Overseas Missions, page 378–9*),

or visit www.immi.gov.au, which gives information on all the different types of visas, and allows online applications.

Weights and Measures

Australia uses the metric system of weights and measures. Despite the change from the imperial to the metric system in the 1970s, a 183cm person is still frequently referred to as being "6 feet tall" and many people still give their weight in stones (14lb to the stone).

The main conversions are as follows:

1 metre	3.28 feet
1 kilometre	0.62 mile
1 kilogram	2.2 pounds
1 litre	2.1 pints (US)
1 litre	1.8 pints (UK)
0°C	32°F
(Centigrade)	(Fahrenheit)

What to Wear

Generally, Australians are informal dressers, especially when the weather is warm: comfort comes before tradition. However, for special occasions or dining in fine restaurants, formal attire or neat casual dress is required. While a jacket and tie are rarely required for men, the more elegant establishments would not welcome gym shoes or shorts. In other words, dress more or less as you would in other cosmopolitan cities.

If you visit Australia during summer, include at least one warm garment for the occasional cold snap. If travelling to the southeastern states during winter, include warm clothing, a raincoat and an umbrella – temperatures in Melbourne can reach freezing at night. The weather in northern Queensland and the Top End of the Northern Territory is rarely chilly, even in August.

At any time of the year, waterproof, solid walking shoes are essential if you intend to go bushwalking. If exploring the Great Barrier Reef, bring along an old pair of trainers for reef walks. And always pack a hat.

Women Travellers

Women are generally safe in Australia, though the same degree of caution should be used as you would elsewhere. Some backpacker hostels such as Base Backpackers (www.base backpackers.com) offer women-only dorms and floors designed for use by female travellers only.

ACCOMMODATION

ACTIVITIES

A – Z

LANGUAGE

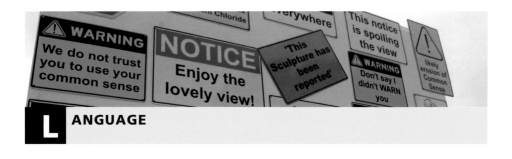

LANGUAGE

UNDERSTANDING THE LANGUAGE

Aussie Slanguage

Despite the stereotype, Australians don't actually wander around yacking at each other like cockney parodies. However, there are some definite peculiarities in the vernacular, often called "Strine". The term derives from saying the word "Australian" through both closed teeth and the nose – a local accent that some scholars claim arose out of a need to keep the trap (mouth) shut against blowies (blow flies).

The lingo has a laconic, poetic originality ("he was flash as a rat with a gold tooth…") and can be colourfully coarse ("…and as thin as a streak of pelican shit").

Following are a few oddities and words that are used in Australia and are worth knowing:

A

ABC Australian Broadcasting Corporation
ACT Australian Capital Territory (Canberra)
ACTU Australian Council of Trade Unions
ALP Australian Labor Party
ASIO Australian Security Intelligence Organisation
Across the ditch Across the Tasman Sea: ie New Zealand
Alf Stupid Australian
Alice, The Alice Springs
Amber fluid Beer
Ankle-biter Young child
ANZAC Australian & New Zealand Army Corps (World War I)
Arvo Afternoon
Avago Have a go (popular at sporting events: as in "avagoyamug!" if you think the sportsperson could try harder)
Avo Avocado

B

BHP Broken Hill Proprietary, a mining corporation
B&S Bachelors' and Spinsters' Ball (usually held in the country)
Back of Bourke Far Outback
Back of beyond Further Outback
Bag of Fruit Suit
Bail up To rob, hold up
Banana bender Queenslander
Barbie Barbecue
Barrack To cheer for, encourage
Bastard Term of endearment (when it's not a term of dislike)
Bathers Swimming costume (men and women)
Battler One who struggles for a living
Beaut Short for "beautiful" (very good, great, fantastic, as in "you beaut!")
Bible basher Religious preacher
Biker Non-gang motorbike rider
Bikey Biker gang member
Billabong Waterhole in semi-dry river. Features in many Outback songs and stories
Billy Tin container used for boiling water to make tea
Bitser Mongrel dog ("bits a this and bits a that")
Black Stump, The Where the back of Bourke begins (as in the phrase "beyond the black stump")
Blind Freddie could have seen it Something obvious
Bloody Universal expletive, as in "shootin' kanga-bloody-roos"; also "very"
Bloody Oath! True
Blowie Blowfly
Blow in Stranger
Bludger Slacker
Blue A fight
Bluey A redhead
Bogan Unsophisticated and uncultured

Bogin Start eating
Bomb A bad car
Bonzer Terrific
Boomer Huge kangaroo
Boomerang Aboriginal hunting instrument and now found in tourist shops as a souvenir
Booze bus Police breathaliser
Boozer Pub
Bottler Terrific (esp Beauty Bottler!)
Bottle-o Liquor Shop
Brissie Brisbane
Bris Vegas Brisbane
Buckley's Chance One chance in a million
Bug Small edible crustacean, as in Balmain Bug/Moreton Bay Bug
Bullamakanka Mythical, far distant place
Bull Dust Bullshit
Bunyip Australia's Yeti, Big Foot or Loch Ness monster. Lives in a billabong
Burl A try (give it a burl)
Bush The countryside
Bushie Person who lives in the Bush
Bushranger Highwayman, outlaw
Bushweek Traditionally a period of licence when rural folk hit the towns. Now used when you think someone is putting something over on you (in the expression, "What do you think this is…bushweek?")
BYO Bring Your Own (liquor to a restaurant)

C

Cadbury A cheap drunk (as in "a glass and a half")
Cark it Die
Cask Boxed bag of cheap wine
Chips Crisps (unless hot and fried)
Chockers Full
Chook Chicken
Chuck a U-ey Do a U-turn
Chunder Vomit. (Other quaint expressions include – chuck,

pavement pizza, kerbside quiche, technicolour yawn)
Cobber Antique version of "mate"
Cockie Farmer or a cockatoo
Coldie A beer
Come a gutser Make a bad mistake
Compo Workers' Compensation
Coolabah Box eucalyptus tree
Cop it sweet To take the blame or the loss agreeably
Corroboree Aboriginal ceremonial gathering
Cossie Swimming costume
Cow Cockie Cattle grazier
Counter Lunch A pub lunch
Crikey! An exclamation
Crissie Christmas
Crook Broken, sick or no good
Cut lunch A lunch mainly consisting of sandwiches

D

Dag Mild term for fool or unfashionable person; the popular adjective is daggy
Daks Trousers
Damper Unrisen bread, usually cooked in a campfire (a staple of bush tucker)
Dero Derelict person
Didgeridoo Aboriginal droning instrument
Digger Australian soldier, or any old male character
Dill Idiot
Dingo Australian native dog
Dinkie die The truth
Dinkum Genuine or honest
Do yer block Lose your temper
Dob To report on someone. ("To dob in")
Don't come the raw prawn Don't try and fool me
Doona Quilted eiderdown (duvet)

BELOW: subtle Aussie humour.

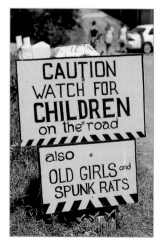

Drongo Idiot
Dumper A roundly crashing wave, unsuitable for bodysurfing
Dunny Toilet ("Useless as a glass door on a dunny")
Dunny budgie Blowfly
Dynamo A cheaper drunk than a "cadbury"

E–F

Ear-bashing Nagging
Esky Portable cooler for drinks, food
Fair dinkum Same as "Dinkie die" and "dinkum," above
Fair go A chance
Figjam F*** I'm good, just ask me (used derogatively as in "He's figjam")
Flake Shark meat
Flat out Busy/fast
Flash as a rat with a gold tooth Showing off
Flog Sell
Footpath Pavement or sidewalk
Footy Aussie Rules football
Fossicking To search for gold in abandoned works, rummage

G–H

G'day Good day/hello
Galah Fool or idiot (after the parrot of same name)
Garbo Garbageman
Give it the flick Get rid of it
Gong, The Wollongong
Good on ya Well done
Greenie A conservationist
Grog Alcoholic drink
Grundies Underwear
Gurgler, down the Down the toilet, wasted
Heart starter First drink of the day
Hoon Loudmouth young motorised hooligan
Hotel Some hotels are pubs, some hotels are hotels, some are both (simple eh?)
Humpy Aboriginal shack

I–J

Icey-pole ice lolly
Jackaroo Male managment trainee on an Outback station
Jillaroo Female same
Job To punch
Jocks Men's underpants
Joe Blake Snake
Joey Baby kangaroo
Journo Journalist
Jumbuck Lamb/sheep

K

Kangaroos loose in the top paddock Intellectually inadequate
Karked it Died
Kelpie Australian sheep dog
Kip To sleep. Also an instrument used to toss pennies in the gambling game "two-up"

Knuckle To punch

L

Lair A show-off
Lamington Aussie dessert: cubes of sponge cake, covered in chocolate and desiccated coconut
Larrikin Previously a street hoodlum. Now a cheeky or mischievous youth
Loaf To do nothing ("just loafing about"). Also means a head ("use yer loaf")
Lob Arrive ("To lob in")
Lolly Candy or sweet
Lurk A racket, a "dodge" or illegal scheme

M

Mad as a cut snake Particularly crazy
Mate's rate A cheap deal
Mick A Roman Catholic
Middy 285ml/10oz glass of beer (in NSW)
Mob A group of persons or things (not necessarily unruly)
Mozzie Mosquito
Mug A gullible fool

N

Neck oil Beer
Nervy A nervous attack (To "chuck a nervy")
Never-never Far off in the Outback, middle of nowhere
Nick Steal
Nipper Young surf lifesaver
Nit Fool, idiot
No-hoper Same as above, but worse
Nong Fool
Nuddy, in the Nude

O

O.S. Overseas
Ocker Quintessential Aussie bumpkin-loudmouth, a favourite target of comedians
Outback The bush; uncivilised, uninhabited country
Oz Australia

P

Panic merchant Chronic anxiety case
Pashing Kissing
Perve To ogle at an attractive person
Pie Floater A meat pie in a bowl of pea soup
Piece of piss Easy
Pie-eyed Drunk
Pinch Arrest, or steal
Pissed Off Angry
Plonk Cheap wine
Poker machine Slot machine (aka "pokie")
Pom English person
Postie Mail person
Prezzy Present
Private school For fee-paying pupils
Public school State school

Q–R

Quarts Pints, but only as served in Queensland
RSL Returned Servicemen's League, known for their entertainment clubs
Rack off Get lost/go away
Ratbag Trouble-maker (also a friendly term of abuse)
Rat shit Lousy, ruined. Abbreviation "RS" also used
Rego Registration (car)
Rid Insect repellent
Ridgi-didge Genuine, true
Ringer Stockman or woman on an Outback station
Ripper Good
Road train Outback truck with up to three trailers
Roo Kangaroo
Roof rabbits Possums or rats in the attic
Root Sexual intercourse
Rooted Exhausted
Ropable Very angry
Running round like a chook with its head cut off Any useless, frenetic activity

S

Saltie Salt-water crocodile
Salvo Member of the Salvation Army
Sanger Sandwich
Scab Technically a strike-breaker; often used to describe someone who's cheap and/or underhand; can also be used to mean borrow ("Can I scab a dollar off you?")
Schooner Large beer glass (particular to NSW)
Scrub Bushland
Scunge A dirty, untidy person
Semi-trailer Articulated truck
Servo Petrol/gas station
She'll be apples It'll be right
She's sweet Everything is all right
Sheila Female (derogatory)
Shoot through Leave unexpectedly, escape
Shonky Unreliable
Slats Ribs
Smoke-o Work break (archaic)
Snags Sausages
Speedos Nylon swimming trunks
Spit the dummy Get upset
Sprog Baby
Spunk Good-looking person
Squatter Large landholder in early colonial times
Station Large farm or ranch
Stickybeak Busybody
Stinger Box jellyfish
Stirrer Trouble maker
Stockman Cowboy, station hand
Stonkered Exhausted
Strain the potatoes (or spuds) Urinate
Strewth! An exclamation
Strides Trousers
Strine Vernacular Australian
Stubby Small bottle of beer, kept cold in a "stubby holder"
Stuffed Tired
Stunned Mullet Someone who looks shocked
Sunbake Suntan/bathe
Swag Canvas bed for camping
Swagman Vagabond, rural tramp
Sydney or the Bush All or nothing

T

TAB Totalisator Agency Board, legal offtrack betting shop
Tall poppies High achievers (as in the expression "tall poppy syndrome", to describe Australians' habit of attacking anyone who has achieved something)
Tassie Tasmania
Taswegian resident of Tasmania
Telly Television, also the *Sydney Telegraph Mirror*
Thongs Flip-flop sandals and, increasingly, string undergarments
Tinnie Can of beer, also a small aluminium boat
Togs Swimsuit (sometimes called "bathers", or "cossie")
Top End Northern Territory/far north Australia
Too Right! Absolutely!
Troppo Unhinged by tropical weather
True blue Patriotic
Tube Can of beer or innermost section of breaking surf wave
Tucker Food
Turps Any form of alcohol ("On the turps" – to be drinking)
Two-pot screamer Person unable to hold their drink
Two up Popular gambling game involving two pennies thrown in the air

U

Uni University
Unit Apartment, flat
Urchin Baby or small child
Useless as tits on a bull Incompetent
Ute "Utility" truck – a pick-up truck

V–W

Vegemite Brown yeast sandwich spread which Australians grow up on but is regarded by most foreigners as semi-toxic (the British equivalent is Marmite)
Walkabout Travelling on foot for long distances – an Aboriginal tradition – usually involves disappearing entirely for long periods at a time
Wheeties Weetabix or most other breakfast cereals
Whinge Complain (often used in relation to "whingeing Poms")
Wharfie Dockworker
Wog Non-Anglo Australian. Mostly used for Greek and Italian migrants
Wowser Killjoy, prude

X–Y

XXXX Beer
Yabber Chatter
Yabbie Small freshwater crayfish
Yack To talk
Yahoo An unruly type
Yakka Work
Yobbo Hoon, loudmouth – Pacific redneck
Your blood's good enough to bottle I like you

The Unofficial National Anthem – *Waltzing Matilda*

Once a jolly swagman camped by a
  billabong
Under the shade of a coolibah tree
And he sang as he watched and
  waited 'til his billy boiled
You'll come a-waltzing matilda with
  me

Waltzing matilda, waltzing matilda
You'll come a waltzing matilda with
  me
And he sang as he watched and
  waited 'til his billy boiled
You'll come a-waltzing matilda with
  me

Down came a jumbuck to drink at
  that billabong
Up jumped the swagman and
  grabbed him with glee
And he sang as he stuffed that
  jumbuck in his tucker-bag
You'll come a-waltzing matilda with
  me

(repeat chorus)

Up rode the squatter, mounted on
  his thoroughbred
Up rode the troopers, one, two,
  three
"Where's that jolly jumbuck you've
  got in your tucker-bag?"
You'll come a-waltzing matilda with
  me
(repeat chorus)

Up jumped the swagman and sprang
  into that billabong
"You'll never take me alive!", said
  he
And his ghost may be heard as you
  pass by that billabong
You'll come a-waltzing matilda with
  me
(repeat chorus)

[words attributed to "Banjo"
Paterson, c.1890]

Further Reading

General

The Australian Wine Annual by Jeremy Oliver. Rigorous guide to everything good in a bottle.

The Age/Sydney Morning Herald Good Australian Wine Guide by Nick Stock. Formerly branded as the Penguin guide.

Unreliable Memoirs by Clive James. Aussie expat and wit looks back at his formative years in Sydney and possibly finds rationale for being an expat.

The Sydney Morning Herald and **The Age Good Food Guides.** Definitive guides to eating out in, respectively, Sydney and Melbourne.

History

Australia: A Biography of a Nation by Phillip Knightley. Wide-ranging history, particularly good in its snapshots of key individuals.

Australia: A New History of the Great Southern Land by Frank Welsh. Dependable assessment of the growth of a country.

Australians: Origins to Eureka by Thomas Keneally. The first of three volumes aimed at anatomising the people of the continent.

At Home in Australia by Peter Conrad. The pictures are the draw in this analysis of a nation.

A Concise History of Australia by Stuart Macintyre. Reliable and thoroughly up-to-date account, including the Gillard ascent.

The Explorers edited by Tim Flannery. A compendium of accounts from the early days of European settlement.

The Fatal Shore by Robert Hughes. Landmark laying bare of convict transportation and its impact.

Gallipoli by Les Carlyon. Detailed account of the formative ANZAC engagement of World War I.

A Secret Country by John Pilger. Provocative analysis of the political and commercial foundations of modern Australia.

Kokoda Spirit: In The Footsteps Of Australia's World War Two Heroes by Patrick Lindsay. Analysis of searing experiences in Papua New Guinea.

Natural History

Country: A Continent, a Scientist and a Kangaroo by Tim Flannery. Palaeontology, natural history and memoir nicely combined.

Green Guide: Mammals of Australia by T Lindsey. Handbook to the country's weird and wonderful wildlife.

Green Guide: Snakes and Other Reptiles of Australia by G Swan. As above but with more venom.

The Slater Field Guide to Australian Birds by Peter, Pat & Raoul Slater. Fully illustrated spotter's tool.

Wild Australia: A Guide to the Places, Plants and Animals by Graham Edgar, Robert Edgar and Allan Edgar. Extends to insects and aquatic life as well.

Travel

Down Under by Bill Bryson. The urbane, breezy style is deceptive – some serious research has gone into this entertaining travelogue.

Explore Australia by 4WD by Craig Lewis and Cathy Savage. How to source the right equipment and find the right tracks.

Into the Blue: Boldly Going Where Captain Cook Has Gone Before by Tony Horwitz. Penetrative retracing of Cook's Pacific voyages.

One for the Road: An Outback Adventure by Tony Horwitz. One man's breezy journey and the people he encounters.

The Songlines by Bruce Chatwin. Remarkable outback journey into Aboriginal tradition and lore.

Tracks by Robyn Davidson. The adventures of a woman crossing the continent by camel.

Aboriginal Australia

Aboriginal Art of Australia by Carol Finley. Concise guide to art in all media, which includes a walk through some of the symbolism employed.

Aboriginal Australians by Richard Broome. An analysis of the impact of white settlement from 1788.

Aboriginal Myths, Legends and Fables by A.W. Reed. Straightforward retelling of some of the key stories.

The Artist is a Thief by Stephen Gray. Prize-winning detective story that delves into cultural clashes in modern Australia.

Balanda: My Year in Arnhem Land by Mary Ellen Jordan. A move from Melbourne to unfamiliar Arnhem Land with the predictable and unpredictable cultural collisions implicit in that.

My Place by Sally Morgan. Morgan's investigation of her family history reveals some wider truths of Aboriginal repression.

Wings of the Kite-Hawk: A journey into the heart of Australia by Nicholas Rothwell. Starting with the routes of early explorers and expanding to take in current issues.

Australian Language

The Dinkum Dictionary by Susan Butler. Bonzer stickybeak into Aussie lingo.

My Life As Me by Barry Humphries. Reminiscence of growing up in 1950s Melbourne, the genesis of his various characters and the path to a level of worldwide acclaim that saw Dame Edna Everage given the city keys.

Unpolished Gem by Alice Pung. Leaving the Cambodia of Pol Pot as a child, Pung's assimilation into life in Footscray along with her family is the core of this revealing memoir.

Fiction

The Art of the Engine Driver by Steven Carroll. Suburban Melbourne post-World War II is the setting for this measured look at how progress distorts the lives of ordinary people.

Breath by Tim Winton. The surf is as much the focus as the relationships in this accomplished novel.

The Broken Shore by Peter Temple. A sophisticated crime novel that reaches to the very heart of Australian society.

Capricornia by Xavier Herbert. Sweeping narrative from the 1930s that partly inspired Baz Luhrmann's film, *Australia*.

Carpentaria by Alexis Wright. Hefty and densely lyrical account of an Aboriginal community in the far north.

TRANSPORT ACCOMMODATION ACTIVITIES A – Z LANGUAGE

Cloudstreet by Tim Winton. A family saga in the West mirroring the growth of the nation in the 20th century.
Cocaine Blues by Kerry Greenwood. The first in a series of detective novels set in 1920s Melbourne.
Death of a River Guide by Richard Flanagan. A man drowning in Tasmania's Franklin River spools back through his family's history and struggle in this unforgiving land.
English Passengers by Matthew Kneale. Prize-winning novel about an 1857 voyage to Tasmania, by turns stark and hilarious.
Eucalyptus by Murray Bail. From its fairy-tale conceit, *Eucalyptus* evolves into a magical love story.
Fly Away Peter by David Malouf. Life on Queensland's bucolic coastal region plays counterpoint to the Great War.
For the Term of His Natural Life by Marcus Clarke. The great convict pot-boiler published in 1874.
A Fortunate Life by A.B. Facey. Rough-hewn yet classic autobiography of an outback farmer.
Gould's Book of Fish by Richard Flanagan. Tasmania's Sarah Island in the 1830s is the setting for this wildly ambitious freewheeling novel.
The Harp in The South by Ruth Park. Part of a trilogy of loved, if soapy, novels set in the slums of Sydney in the first half of the 20th century.
The Idea of Perfection by Kate Grenville. Beautifully honed romance in small-town New South Wales.
Illywhacker by Peter Carey. An expansive narrative by the 139-year-old self-confessed liar of the title takes us on a journey through history and the forging of the larrikin spirit.
It's Raining in Mango by Thea Astley. Saga stretching over a century and takes in gold-digging in Queensland and Aboriginal dispossession.
Last Drinks by Andrew McGahan. Multi-award-winning crime thriller.
Loaded by Christos Tsiolkas. *Loaded* unflinchingly sifts the problems of a gay Greek teenager coming to terms with both himself and a hostile city.
The Man from Snowy River by Banjo Paterson. Derring do in the southern mountains has taken on mythical status in Australian literature.
Monkey Grip by Helen Garner. Captures the tedium of life with self-obsessed hippies and junkies in 1970s Melbourne.
Morgan's Run by Colleen McCullough. The tale of a man convicted and sentenced to prison on Norfolk Island.
My Brilliant Career by Miles Franklin. Feisty teenager grapples with the stifling constraints of early

20th-century Australia.
Of A Boy by Sonya Hartnett. The story of 9-year-old Adrian, adrift in 1977 without family anchors and when three other children have just disappeared.
On the Beach by Nevil Shute. Melbourne is the last redoubt of humanity as the fallout from nuclear annihilation in the northern hemisphere heads southward.
Oscar and Lucinda by Peter Carey. Booker winner, film and calling card for the precociously talented Carey.
Oyster by Janette Turner Hospital. The arrival of a cult-like community in a remote desert settlement is the catalyst for upheaval.
Picnic at Hanging Rock by Joan Lindsay. An eerie story of schoolgirls disappearing in the picturesque Macedon Ranges.
Remembering Babylon by David Malouf. Moving story of a white youth taken in by a Queensland Aboriginal community in the 1840s.
The Secret River by Kate Grenville. Deftly explores the ramifications of Aboriginal and white communities interacting with each other, this time in early 19th-century NSW.
The Slap by Christos Tsiolkas. Skewers suburban Melbourne values in this bestselling, Man Booker prize-nominated novel.
The Sound of One Hand Clapping by

Richard Flanagan. A woman walks out into a snowstorm, leaving her family in the Tasmanian wilderness.
The Thorn Birds by Colleen McCullough. The romantic blockbuster of life on the station.
Tree of Man by Patrick White. Dissecting an Outback marriage.
The True History of the Kelly Gang by Peter Carey. The Kelly story in Ned's own words from "newly discovered" letters.
The Vivisector by Patrick White. Sydney Nolan was the model for this dissection of an Australian artist.

Children's Books

Blinky Bill by Dorothy Wall.
The Magic Pudding by Norman Lindsay.
Possum Magic by Julie Vivas and Mem Fox.
Snugglepot & Cuddlepie by May Gibbs.
Wombat Divine by Mem Fox and Kerry Argent.

Other Insight Guides

Insight Guides

Insight Guide: Australia is a top-selling title in the series, with superb photography and in-depth background reading on the history and culture of the Land Down Under. In addition, Insight's regional series includes **Insight Guide: Queensland & Great Barrier Reef** and **Insight Guide: Tasmania** to show you the larger picture of Australia's great states. **Insight City Guide: Perth** and **Insight City Guide: Melbourne** are both written by locally based writers, who show you how to make the most of these world-class cities.

Insight Smart Guides

Insight Smart Guides pack a huge amount of information into an easy-to-access A–Z format, with stylish photography and an atlas section. Titles in the Smart Guide series include **Smart Guide: Perth** and **Smart Guide: Melbourne.**

Send Us Your Thoughts

We do our best to ensure the information in our books is as accurate and up to date as possible. The books are updated on a regular basis using local contacts, who painstakingly add, amend and correct as required. However, some details (such as telephone numbers and opening times) are liable to change, and we are ultimately reliant on our readers to put us in the picture.

We welcome your feedback, especially your experience of using the book "on the road". Maybe we recommended a hotel that you liked (or another that you didn't), or you came across a great bar or new attraction we missed.

We will acknowledge all contributions, and we'll offer an Insight Guide to the best letters received.

Please write to us at:
**Insight Guides
PO Box 7910
London SE1 1WE**
Or email us at:
insight@apaguide.co.uk

Art and Photo Credits

Alamy 138, 190, 191
Alexander Turnbull Library 39
Marc Asnin/Corbis Saba 71
Australian Reptile Park 127, 127T
Australian Tourist Commission 52, 179
Australia Tourism 35, 106, 107, 134, 136, 137L, 182L, 183T, 185, 215, 215T, 235, 244, 293R, 306, 308L
Axiom 211
Ryan Bailey 159
Eleanor Bentall/Corbis 46
The Belvoir 73
Blue Hotel 6ML
Brisbane City Council Archives 48
C Bar café 249
Claver Carroll/Pictures Colour Library 129T
Claver Carroll/Superstock 208–209
Heeb Christian/Superstock 196–197
Neale Clark/Photolibrary 201T
Coo-ee Picture Library 24, 44R
Jerry Dennis/APA: 7ML, 8T, 9BR, 22, 49L, 72, 85, 110T, 111, 111T, 112T, 121L, R&T, 131, 131T, 132, 135&T, 139, 141&T, 142, 144&T, 145, 148, 149&T, 150, 151&T, 154, 155, 156T, 157&T, 158, 165R, 177, 180T, 180L, 180R, 181T, 186, 187T, 189, 212, 228T, 230T, 231, 235T, 240T, 237, 243, 246&T, 247&T, 254, 255R, 257T, 258T, 316, 317, 318T, 319&T, 320L, R&T, 321, 322T, 323, 324, 325&T, 326&T, 327&T, 328, 329&T, 330&T, 331&T, 332&T, 334&T, 335
Dubbo Tourism 147T
Naomi Everton 165L
John Fairfax Features 47
Jürgen Freund/NaturePL 220–221
Glyn Genin/APA: 2–3, 3B, 6BR, 7BL, 7MR, 7TR, 14–15, 16–17, 19, 20, 27, 54, 56R, 60, 63L, 64, 66, 76, 77R, 78, 80, 81, 82, 102–103, 109, 110, 112, 113T, 113, 114, 115, 116, 117, 118, 153, 194, 195, 199, 201, 203, 204, 205, 207L, 207R, 207T, 208, 218, 219, 262–263, 264, 265, 267, 268R, 268L, 268T, 269T, 270, 271, 271T, 272, 272T, 274, 275, 276, 276T, 278, 278T, 279L, 279R, 279T, 282–283, 282BL, 282BR, 283BR, 283T, 283BL, 284/285, 286, 287, 288T,

289, 290&T, 291L, 291R, 293T, 293L, 294&T, 295&T, 296&T, 297&T, 298, 299&T, 300, 301, 302&T, 303T, 304, 305R, 305L, 306T, 307, 308R, 310
Getty 55, 67, 70, 84, 202
Getty Images/Robert Harding 216
Great Southern Railway 269L
David Greaves/Rex Features 45
The Green papaya 248
D. & J. Heaton 5BR
Holli Hollitzer/AFP/Getty Images 57
iStockphoto 6BL, 23, 58, 59, 126, 133L, 133T, 137R, 143, 160–161, 184T, 190T, 213T, 244T, 309
Kobal Collection 75
Mary Evans Picture Library 32, 34
David Messent/Photolibrary 119
Anna Mockford & Nick Bonetti/APA 208T
National galleries of Australia 9BL
New South Wales Tourism 118T, 120, 122, 129, 139T, 145T, 146
Nick Laham/Getty Images 245
Lansdowne Picture Library 40
Lodestone Press 44L
Pete Oxford/NaturePL 193
Daniele Pellegrini/Getty Images 198
Martin Philbey 74
Photolibrary 9M, 83, 87, 133R, 147, 210, 252, 303
Pro Dive Cairns 93L, 239
Greg Probst/Corbis 214
Queensland Tourism 8M, 233T, 234, 255L, 256, 257L, 257R
Peter James Quinn/APA 130
Nick Rains/Sylvia Cordaiy 217
Rex Features 236
Reef Magic Cuises 253, 258
San Rostro/Superstock 273
Virginia Star/APA: 7BR, 7M, 9T, 10–11, 42, 56L, 62, 63R, 77L, 86, 98–99, 162, 163, 166, 167, 168, 169, 170, 171L, 171R, 172, 173, 173T, 174, 175, 179T, 192L, 192R, 192T, 340
Paul Steel 176
Peter Stuckings/APA: 8B, 12–13, 21, 53, 61, 90, 91, 92, 96–97, 100–101, 223, 224T, 225L, 225R, 226L, 226R, 227, 228, 229, 230, 232L, 232R, 233, 238, 238T, 240, 241, 242, 281
Sourdough Bakery 152
Tony Stone 18, 65

Hans Strand/Corbis 188
The Summit 123
Superstock 181, 182R, 183, 280
Andrew Tauber/APA 164T, 167T, 169T
Tetsuya 124
Thredbo 140
Ann & Steve Toon/Robert Harding 203T
Topfoto 25, 33R
Topham Picturepoint 43
Steve Vidler/Photolibrary 184, 187
Patrick Ward/Corbis 269R

Photo Features

68–69: Ricardo Idagi/NGA 68BL; Glyn Genin/APA 69BL; National Gallery Of Australia 68–69, 69BR, 69BM; Viscopy Australia 69TR.

88–89: All pictures Peter Stuckings/APA except 89BR Virginia Star/APA.

94–95: iStockphoto 94–95, 94BL, 95TR; Photolibrary 94BR, 95BL, 95BR.

250–251: Australian Tourism 250BL, 250BR, 251T; iStockphoto 250–251; NPL 251BR; Peter Stuckings/APA 251ML, 251MR.

260–261: iStockphoto 260–261, 260R, 261BR, 261ML; Nature Picture Library 261BL, 261TR.

282–283: All pictures Glyn Genin/APA.

312–313: All pictures Glyn Genin/APA.

338/339: All images Jerry Dennis/APA except 338–339 Superstock.

Map Production: original cartography Polyglott Kartographie, updated by Apa Cartography department

© 2011 Apa Publications (UK) Ltd.

Production: Tynan Dean, Linton Donaldson and Rebeka Ellam

INDEX